MODERN GROUP BOOK V

New Models
for Group Therapy

BOOKS BY DRS. KAPLAN AND SADOCK

Comprehensive Textbook of Psychiatry
Alfred M. Freedman and Harold I. Kaplan, Editors

Studies in Human Behavior
Alfred M. Freedman and Harold I. Kaplan, General Editors

Modern Synopsis of Comprehensive Textbook of Psychiatry
Harold I. Kaplan, Benjamin J. Sadock, and Alfred M. Freedman

Comprehensive Group Psychotherapy
Harold I. Kaplan and Benjamin J. Sadock, Editors

Modern Group Books
Harold I. Kaplan and Benjamin J. Sadock, Editors

HAROLD I. KAPLAN

Harold I. Kaplan received an undergraduate degree from Columbia University and an M.D. from the New York Medical College. He trained in psychiatry at the Kingsbridge Veterans Hospital and Mount Sinai Hospital in New York and became a Diplomate of the American Board of Psychiatry and Neurology in 1957; presently he is an Associate Examiner of the American Board. He began the practice and teaching of psychiatry and was certified in psychoanalytic medicine at the New York Medical College in 1954 where he became Professor of Psychiatry and Director of Psychiatric Training and Education in 1961. He is Attending Psychiatrist at Metropolitan Hospital Center, Flower and Fifth Avenue Hospitals and Bird S. Coler Hospital. He is the Principal Investigator of ten National Institute of Mental Health training programs, specializing in the areas of undergraduate and graduate psychiatric education as well as the training of women in medicine. He is the author of over seventy scientific papers and co-author and co-editor of the books listed on this page.

BENJAMIN J. SADOCK

Benjamin J. Sadock received his A.B. from Union College and his M.D. from New York Medical College. He trained at Bellevue Psychiatric Hospital. During his military service as an Air Force psychiatrist he was also on the faculty of Southwestern Medical School. Dr. Sadock became a Diplomate of the American Board of Psychiatry and Neurology in 1966 and is an Assistant Examiner for the American Board. Currently Associate Professor of Psychiatry and Director of the Division of Group Process at New York Medical College, Dr. Sadock directs the training program for group therapists and is Chief of Continuing Education in Psychiatry, Chief Psychiatric Consultant to the student health service and co-director of the Sexual Therapy Center. He is on staff of Flower and Fifth Avenue Hospitals, Metropolitan Hospital, and the New York State Psychiatric Institute. Dr. Sadock is active in numerous psychiatric organizations, an officer of the New York County District Branch of the American Psychiatric Association, a Fellow of the New York Academy of Medicine, and has written and lectured extensively in general psychiatry and group psychotherapy. He is co-editor with Dr. Harold I. Kaplan of *Comprehensive Group Psychotherapy* (1971) and co-author with Drs. Alfred M. Freedman and Harold I. Kaplan of *Modern Synopsis of Comprehensive Textbook of Psychiatry* (1972).

New Models
for Group Therapy

Edited by

HAROLD I. KAPLAN, M.D.

Professor of Psychiatry and Director of Psychiatric Education,
New York Medical College, New York, New York

and

BENJAMIN J. SADOCK, M.D.

Associate Professor of Psychiatry and Director,
Division of Group Process, New York Medical College,
New York, New York

Jason Aronson, Inc.
New York, New York

Library of Congress Catalog Card Number: 72-96937
Standard Book Number: 0-87668-081-3

The editors express their appreciation to the following persons, publishers and publications for permission to reprint portions of the works cited.

Aldine-Atherton, Inc. for ''The Marathon Group,'' by G. R. Bach, reprinted from Hendrik M. Ruitenbeek, editor, *Group Therapy Today* (New York: Atherton Press, 1969); copyright © 1969 by Atherton Press. Reprinted by permission of the author and Aldine-Atherton, Inc.

Bruner/Mazel, Inc. for ''The Use of Videotape in the Integrated Treatment of Individuals, Couples, Families, and Groups in Private Practice,'' by Milton M. Berger, M.D., reprinted from *Videotape Techniques in Psychiatric Training and Treatment*, Milton M. Berger, M.D., editor. Bruner/Mazel, Inc., New York, 1970.

Dr. Herbert Holt for the unpublished essay, ''Existential Group Therapy: A Phenomenological Methodology for Psychiatry.''

International Journal of Group Psychotherapy for ''Sexual Acting Out in Groups,'' by the members of the Workshop in Group Psychoanalysis of New York: A. Wolf, R. Bross, S. Flowerman, J. Greene, A. Kadis, H. Leopold, N. Locke, I. Milburg, H. Mullan, S. Obers, and H. Rosenbaum. *International Journal of Group Psychotherapy*, Vol. 4, pp. 369-380, 1954.

for ''Accelerated Interaction: A Time Limited Approach on the Brief Intensive Approach,'' by Frederick H. Stoller. *International Journal of Group Psychotherapy*, Vol. 18, pp. 220-235, 1968.

for ''Group Therapy and the Small Group Field: An Encounter,'' by Morris Parloff. *International Journal of Group Psychotherapy*, Vol. 20, pp. 267-304, 1970.

International Universities Press for ''Group Therapy with Alcoholics,'' by A. Stein, M.D. and Eugene Friedman, Ph.D., Chapter III of *Fields of Group Psychotherapy*, S. R. Slavson, editor. International Universities Press, 1956.

American Psychiatric Association for ''Phoenix House: Therapeutic Communities for Drug Addicts,'' by M. S. Rosenthal and D. V. Biase, *Hospital and Community Psychiatry*, Vol. 20, p. 27, 1969.

W. W. Norton & Co., Inc., and the Hogarth Press Ltd. for an excerpt from *An Outline of Psycho-Analysis*, Volume XXIII of Standard Edition of Sigmund Freud, revised and edited by James Strachey. Copyright 1949 by W. W. Norton & Co., Inc., and copyright © 1969 by the Institute of Psychoanalysis and Alix Strachey.

The Williams & Wilkins Co. for an excerpt from ''Group Therapy in Married Couples,'' by Helen Papanek, M.D., reprinted from *Comprehensive Group Psychotherapy*, Harold I. Kaplan and Benjamin J. Sadock, editors. Copyright © 1971 by The Williams & Wilkins Co.

for an excerpt from ''Videotape Feedback in Group Setting,'' by F. Stoller. *Journal of Nervous and Mental Disorders*, Vol. 148, No. 4, pp. 457-466.

Seymour Lawrence/Delacorte Press for an excerpt from *Cat's Cradle* by Kurt Vonnegut, Jr. Copyright © 1963 by Kurt Vonnegut, Jr. A Seymour Lawrence Book/Delacorte Press. Reprinted by permission of the publisher.

Contents

Preface

The emergence of group psychotherapy within the past two decades constitutes one of the most significant and extraordinary developments in the field of psychiatry. Gradually during this period, but particularly within the past five years, group therapy has come to be chosen for the treatment of a widening range of patients with highly diverse problems. Concurrently, professionals and laymen alike see a growing interest in the relationship of group therapy to sociocultural and educational concepts, processes, and systems. Predictably, these theoretical developments are accompanied by the development of myriad therapeutic approaches which vary with respect not only to their underlying philosophy but also to the planning and conduct of treatment.

Psychotherapy is an art as well as a science. What is taught via the lecture hall or seminar room constitutes just one aspect of the teaching curriculum. Training in psychotherapy must also include clinical exercises performed under the supervision of an experienced clinician who acts as a model for the student. The editors' commitment to this project, and its concomitant goals, evolved from their extensive experience as both educators and clinicians. The editors' special interest in group psychotherapy as a treatment technique, and an awareness of the need for more intensive training in this discipline to ensure its continued growth and development, led to the establishment, at the New York Medical College, of the first medical-school-affiliated postgraduate certification program in group psychotherapy. In addition, they have participated in the organization of training programs in group therapy for workers in other mental health disciplines —psychology, psychiatric social work, and psychiatric nursing.

The stated goal of this series—to provide a survey of current theoretical and therapeutic trends in this field—carries with it the obligation to pursue an eclectic orientation and to present as comprehensive an account of events at every level of its development as is possible. The organization and orientation of this series attempts to provide a comprehensive survey of the theories, hypotheses, and therapeutic techniques which dominate contemporary group practice. There are no final answers, as yet, to the problems and issues which currently face group psychotherapy. But we may help to identify these problems and issues and place them in proper perspective.

This book is one of a series of paperback volumes based on *Comprehensive Group Psychotherapy,* which we previously edited. New articles have been written for each of these volumes and certain subjects have been updated or eliminated in an effort to reach a wider audience. Invitations to participate were extended to those workers who have made major and original contributions to the field of group psychotherapy and who are acknowledged experts in a particular area of theory and/or practice. Thus the preparation of this series afforded the editors a unique opportunity to engage in a stimulating interchange of ideas and to form many rewarding personal relationships. As a result, what would appear to have been an ardous undertaking has in fact been a most gratifying experience.

The editors have received dedicated and valuable help from many people to whom they wish to express their appreciation. For their secretarial and editorial help, we would like to thank Robert Gelfand, Sylvia Houzell, Mercedes Paul, Paulene Demarco, Louise Marshall, and in particular Lois Baken, who coordinated these efforts. Spe-

cial thanks are extended to our publishers, E. P. Dutton, and to our outstanding editor, Robert Zenowich.

Finally, the editors wish to express their appreciation to Virginia Sadock, M.D., who acted in the capacity of assistant to the editors and assumed the multitudinous tasks of that office with grace and charm.

HAROLD I. KAPLAN, M.D.

BENJAMIN J. SADOCK, M.D.

Introduction

New Methods

Since 1905, when Joseph Henry Pratt first used inspirational talks to treat groups of tuberculosis patients, the number of specialized group therapy techniques has steadily increased. This increase reflects, in part, the proliferation of therapeutic techniques in psychiatry in general. As new theoretical constructs about mental illness developed, new approaches to the treatment of the individual psychiatric patient evolved. The initiation of these new methods has been paralleled by developments in the field of group psychotherapy.

This book delineates the most recent additions to specialized group therapy techniques. Among these are transactional group psychotherapy, described by Dusay and Steiner, and behavioral group psychotherapy, described by Goldstein and Wolpe. Both are relatively new to the field.

Other sensitivity training, marathon groups, and encounter groups are in their infancy and do not, strictly speaking, fall within the purview of group psychotherapy. Nevertheless, they have been included in this volume because of their growing popularity. Moreover, despite fundamental conceptual differences, there are important similarities between these new methods and traditional group psychotherapy. The worker in this field, whatever his philosophy, should have a broad knowledge of these techniques, which are described by Gottschalk and Davidson.

Other methods, such as the existential approach to group treatment, combine a philosophic approach to man's existence with specific constructs and techniques that attempt to improve maladaptive behavior. Holt, in a previously unpublished paper, describes the existential approach clearly and comprehensively.

Combined Therapy

Not every treatment modality is restricted solely to group psychotherapy. In "Combined Individual and Group Psychotherapy," Bieber discusses a technique in which the patient may see his therapist on an individual basis once or several times a week and also attend group sessions once a week, an interlocking of both techniques. As might be expected, this combined approach is often regarded with disfavor both by those therapists who feel strongly that the group method is the treatment of choice and by those who hold equally the firm conviction that the only effective treatment is to see the patient individually. Consequently, concurrent individual and group treatment has been represented as controversial by some therapists. Just how many of them are using this particular form of therapy at any given time is difficult to determine with any degree of accuracy. However, there is substantial evidence that many patients and therapists regard the combined approach as one of the more effective treatment methods.

Nature, Nurture, and Operant Conditioning

One focal area of dispute in the field of group therapy that has crucial theoretical as well as therapeutic implications is the importance of genetic and dynamic factors in psychiatric illness. Proponents of various treatment techniques disagree as to whether an understanding by the therapist or the patient of the causes and development of the patient's illness is essential to the success of treatment.

The transactional therapists, for example, maintain that insight into the historical origins of behavioral disorders is not a prerequisite for behavioral change. In keeping with this theoretical position, they focus on the here-and-now, the current interactions of group members. They make few attempts to explain the patient's present behavior within the framework of his past experiences.

Behavioral group therapists use a similar approach; that is, they categorically deny the need for historical material. Advocates of behavioral therapy postulate that symptom removal, personality change, and a higher level of emotional functioning can be effected by certain specific techniques that derive from learning theory. Within this theoretical framework, symptoms are viewed as maladaptive learned responses which in many cases can be unlearned. One does not need to focus on how these responses were learned, nor does the patient have to relive early traumatic experiences in order to unlearn them. Drawing on the contributions of such outstanding theoreticians as Skinner, Watson, and Pavlov, behavioral therapists use techniques in which the group, or more precisely, the effects of the group on individual members, serves as the medium for change.

The approach adopted by the transactionalists and the behavioral therapists is in sharp contrast with the techniques advocated by proponents of classical psychoanalysis. Those therapists who apply psychoanalytic principles to group treatment believe that the group, like the dyadic relationship, is primarily a vehicle for the examination and analysis of transference phenomena and resistances, and for uncovering thereby, the historical origins of conflict.

The editors of this volume received their early training in psychoanalytic theory, but through the years we have adopted an eclectic approach to treatment problems. Within that framework we have come to believe that a fusion of these two contrasting views is possible. In the course of our clinical work, we have learned that the group therapist can focus on both levels of the patient's experience—past and present—and that this approach may, in fact, be the most effective. The therapist can learn to separate transference distortions from the responses of individual group members who are reality-oriented toward current life experiences within and without the group.

Structured Interactional Group Therapy

In Chapter 3 the editors describe the technique of structured interactional group psychotherapy. In keeping with their eclecticism, this technique serves as a bridge between the more traditional psychoanalysis in groups and the new behavioral group psychotherapy approaches. As used by the authors, operant conditioning is adjunctive to the cognitive insights and the corrective emotional experiences that psychoanalytic practice affords. Accordingly, the reader should attempt to differentiate authoritarianism from that therapist direction which is necessary to effect reinforcement.

The wide array of group therapy approaches currently available vary not only in the planning and conduct of treatment but also with respect to the theoretical model on which they are based. Today, every school of personality theory and psychopathology—Freudian, Sullivanian, Horneyan, and others—is represented in group practice, although in certain approaches, the relationship between treatment technique and a specific theoretical model is a tenuous one.

Comparing Groups

To more fully understand the differences that exist between the new approaches, Spotnitz has written a comparison of different types of group therapy. The fact that so many techniques are available suggests that no one approach is superior to the others. Yet, in determining that a particular treatment method is suitable for a given patient, the therapist should base his judgment on a comparative evaluation of the diverse approaches available. He must consider the goals he hopes to achieve for the patient, that is, his optimal level of functioning consonant with his level of ego strength; his motivations for treatment; and such practical considerations as the patient's financial resources and current life situation, and most significant, the depth of personality exploration desired. The goal of certain psychoanalytic groups is to produce significant personality changes in much the same way that individual psychoanalysis does.

Other methods such as the behavioral and transactional group therapies, place emphasis on symptom removal and do not stress the relationship of these symptoms to past events in the patient's life.

Sexual Problems

Even when sexual problems are not primary, and regardless of diagnosis, few patients who seek psychotherapy are entirely free of sexual malfunctioning. Frequently sexual problems stem not only from psychological conflicts but also from lack of education. The interrelationship between the two is exceedingly complex, and the group setting provides a unique opportunity for the patients and the therapist to learn whether a problem is the result of faulty education, psychological problems, or both.

Masturbation is an example: in spite of the fact that many people have an intellectual awareness that it is a normal activity, typically it causes the patient to suffer some degree of guilt. This guilt is often culturally induced; it may also result from traumata associated with masturbatory activity or pathological fantasies. Whatever the causes, verbalizing masturbatory experiences can have an almost immediate guilt-reducing effect. This is also true of a variety of sexual experiences, normal and abnormal. It is common for a group member to feel that a particular sexual act is pathological, only to discover that others are acquainted with the act and view it with equanimity.

Furthermore, there is a great difference between being reassured by the therapist in the dyadic situation that a particular sexual experience is no cause for alarm and hearing that others in one's group hold a similar view. In the dyadic situation, the patient may perceive the offered reassurance as a therapeutic maneuver. In the group, members who openly share similar accounts of their sexual activities offer more effective support. The sharing of experience has an educational purpose. When a patient is unable to assimilate accurate information about sexual functioning, his block to learning can usually be traced clearly to psychological inhibition.

The reader will find various references to the management of sexual problems throughout the new models described in this volume.

Training and Standards

The expansion of group practice has underscored the need to develop responsible leadership. Only thus will the group movement remain vital and dynamic.

In the course of our participation in an eclectic training program for residents in general psychiatry, the editors have observed interesting phenomena related to training in both group and individual psychotherapy.

In clinical exercises, each trainee combines the theoretical material and technical instruction he has received in the formal training program; he adds to this amalgam certain unique aspects of his own personality. This interaction of personality traits and didactic knowledge produces a therapeutic approach that stands by itself, that is unique to the therapist and that cannot under any circumstances be replicated.

Most therapists, regardless of their theoretical orientation, treat their patient's similarities, albeit within different theoretical frameworks. Certain hallmarks of sound psychotherapy—warmth, empathy, ethics, responsibility, care, concern, and integrity—transcend the body of knowledge adhered to by a particular therapist. These qualities are brought to the program by the therapist in training; unfortunately, they cannot be taught. Intellectually brilliant young psychiatrists all too often fail in their therapeutic efforts with treatable patients. They may excel in theoretical knowledge, but they are deficient in the intuitive qualities essential for the success of treatment.

Qualities of a Group Therapist

Group psychotherapy is no panacea. Not all patients can benefit from a group experience. Nor are all clinicians in the mental health field suited to group practice. The therapist must be able to distinguish those qualities in his patients that indicate or contraindicate group therapy as the treatment of choice. But he must also be able to recognize those qualities within himself that indicate or contraindicate his pursuit of group therapy as his career goal. The section by Grotjahn, dealing with the personality of the group psychotherapist, addresses itself to the group method, and seeks to clarify the issues involved. If, in the process, this book helps a practitioner to decide that he is ill-suited to the role of group leader, that is also an important service to the group movement.

New Models
for Group Therapy

1

Comparison of Different Types of Group Psychotherapy

Hyman Spotnitz, M.D., Med.Sc.D.

INTRODUCTION

The practice of group psychotherapy is based on the finding that mental illness and mental dysfunctioning can be ameliorated through the psychological effects of several persons upon one another. The fact that improvement in mental functioning tends to alleviate and may eventually cure mental illness has inspired countless efforts to exploit the healing force of the group to meet the therapeutic needs of a widening range of patients—people with highly diverse problems seeking treatment at all phases of the life cycle. Concurrently, the commitment of virtually all schools of psychotherapy to group practice and its elaboration in their respective conceptual frameworks have encouraged the parallel development of a wide array of group psychotherapeutic approaches. These approaches have developed so rapidly and have been described so idiosyncratically by some of their proponents that the literature gives the impression that there are as many different ways of treating groups as there are group psychotherapists.

That impression is also generated by the therapist's use of himself as a professional instrument. In psychological treatment, personal influence cannot be discounted. Each practitioner is a unique personality. His style of conducting a group cannot be duplicated by another therapist, however similar their professional qualifications, treatment philosophies, and clinical skills may be.

Nevertheless, group psychotherapy as a scientific discipline owes its development to the systematic application of validated discoveries about the therapeutic needs of people with psychological problems and to carefully formulated specifics about the planning and conducting of their treatment, the selection and grouping of patients, and related considerations. These specifics are indices to the built-in limitations and potential values of group psychotherapy and thus offer a means of comparing its different forms.

This chapter serves two purposes: (1) It helps the student penetrate barriers of theory and language that separate the different systems of group psychotherapy and distinguish their actual differences from their common factors. (2) It suggests general guidelines for determining the specific effectiveness of one or another approach for a given patient. No attempt is made to discuss or even mention all the group methods that have been reported, but this comparison does encompass those methods that dominate contemporary practice.

DEFINITION OF GROUP PSYCHOTHERAPY

The presence of three or more persons in the same place at the same time is essential to qualify a procedure as group psychotherapy. The triadic formations covered by the term include one patient working with

3

two therapists as well as a pair of patients, often a married couple, working with one therapist. Another essential factor in group psychotherapy is that they meet for the express purpose of influencing one another, directly or indirectly, by psychological means. Still another requirement is that this reciprocal influence be therapeutic to the participants—in no wise harmful to any of them—and help them improve their functioning as human beings.

Defined loosely in terms of those core requirements, group psychotherapy is a procedure in which three or more persons assemble at an appointed time and place for a definite period to beneficially influence their mental health and functioning by psychological means.

The main value of that broad designation is that it serves the purpose of this chapter, specifying only the factors that distinguish all forms of group psychotherapy and accommodating the innumerable diverse factors associated with its practice—factors related to the participants and their joint activities. Among the major differences are the subjects of the treatment, the composition of the group, the therapist's general orientation and specific strategies, the goals of the treatment, and the nature of the results achieved. Experimentation with these variables, which has recently increased, accounts for the kaleidoscopic character of contemporary group psychotherapy.

Descriptive terms frequently used in the literature convey some of the most obvious differences. Groups are dichotomized as large and small, inpatient and outpatient, long-term and short-term, continuous and time-limited, open and closed. Groups based on specific criteria for membership are referred to as structured; those whose composition follows no plan are blanket groups. The dichotomy of heterogeneous and homogeneous also relates to composition.

The labeling of the established procedures is haphazard. The name may be derived from any one of the group's properties or dimensions, such as its size, membership, field of application, duration, or operational principles. The theroretical framework in which the group is conducted may or may not be indicated. For example, "family therapy" is a label attached to groups whose only shared characteristic is that they are composed of members of the same family. More adequately identified are groups whose names derive from two or more variables, such as "psychodramatic family therapy" and "activity group therapy for latency-age boys." In striking contrast are the catchy names attached to tangential variants referred to as personal growth groups, the human potential movement, etc. A strong element of salesmanship pervades such christenings as "nude marathons," "basic encounters," and "group grope."

VARIATIONS IN PRACTICE
Size

The number of participants ranges from one patient with two or more therapists, as already indicated, to one hundred or more group members. There is no fixed boundary between large and small groups, but those referred to as small or face-to-face usually contain no fewer than four patients and no more than ten. Some practitioners regard six, seven, or eight patients as the ideal number. Small groups prevail today. Even though depth of treatment is primarily a function of the therapist's technique, it is not possible to work effectively for characterological change in groups that are too large for member-to-member interaction.

Groups larger than 12 and with an upper limit of 20 or 30 patients are sometimes designated as intermediate groups. They provide a suitable format for lectures and the discussion of common problems. In larger formations, therapy necessarily merges into educational, morale-building, or social activity. Large therapy groups, usually conducted in institutional or community settings, are more or less limited to the repressive-inspirational approach. Such groups are often organized to work on a specific problem—for example, alcoholism or obesity. Some are known as self-help groups because they operate without a professional leader. In many cities, Recovery, a self-directed group of psychiatric patients discharged from institutions, conducts a supportive program known as will training.

Composition

Although groups composed of patients of the same age or sex are sometimes referred to as homogeneous, that term is more strictly applied to those in the same diagnostic category or presenting the same problem. Persons suffering from different forms of psychoneurosis or from the same psychoneurotic condition, such as hysteria or phobia, may constitute a group. Similarly, the group identified as homogeneous may be made up of homosexuals, drug addicts, or patients with the same psychosomatic condition. In medical group therapy, those with a particular organic illness, such as cardiac disease, are treated together.

The majority of groups treated in private practice are heterogeneous, selection being based on the principle of mixing rather than matching personality types. This practice, begun as a matter of expediency, has been reinforced by the finding that the balancing of persons with diversely structured personalities facilitates the development of therapeutic interchanges, provided their socioeconomic backgrounds are reasonably compatible. Thus, different diagnostic categories are represented in heterogeneous groups, among them psychoneuroses, personality disorders, the milder psychosomatic complaints, borderline conditions, and some prepsychotic and postpsychotic states.

Therapists who conduct heterogeneous groups try to exclude persons who would not benefit from the shared treatment experience or who might be a disruptive influence on others, but there are no generally accepted criteria for exclusion on the basis of psychiatric classification. Whereas some authorities, notably Slavson, exercise extreme care in selection and advocate the exclusion of patients in specific diagnostic categories from group treatment, others pay scant attention to diagnosis. For example, Berne stated that almost any patient, if properly prepared, can be assigned to a group. He advocated the policy of picking candidates at random or in order of application, on the assumption that such selection favors heterogeneity.

Some practitioners, the author among them, rather than ignoring the diagnostic factor, regard it as an inadequate source of information on how patients will behave in the group setting. Therefore, these therapists try to ascertain the types of defenses that each candidate activates in interpersonal situations. The assessment of current impulses and defenses is one aspect of achieving a balancing of personality types, which facilitates the functioning of the group as a unit. The blending of placid and excitable persons with some who tend to arouse excitement and others who check it is sought by therapists who conduct group treatment as a primarily emotional experience.

Some differences in individual modes of conducting groups are dictated by the personal characteristics of their members. Their age, sex, and one or another particular about their life status are often reflected in the labels attached to their groups.

Age. Therapy groups are conducted for people in all age categories. Groups for adults often include the middle-aged as well as young adults, but the age span is narrower in those groups conducted for children, adolescents, and elderly people. Children treated together are generally at the same developmental level.

Sex. Private practitioners customarily treat men and women together. However, participation in some groups is limited to members of the same sex.

Kinship. Some therapy groups are composed of strangers, others of persons in real-life relationships. Outstanding among the natural groups are those consisting of members of one family. Some practitioners of family therapy treat several families together; the creation of an artificial group through the fusion of natural groups has also been reported in the treatment of married couples. Relatives of patients with similar conditions—for example, parents of severely disturbed children or the spouses of alcoholics—participate in groups organized to deal with the management of these patients. Friends and neighbors as well as family members are assembled in social network therapy, a brief series of meetings organized to deal with a crisis situation in the life of a schizophrenic person; the tribal support of his natural group is solicited as a possible alternative to his hospitalization.

Socioeconomic Affiliations. People who work together may be assembled for a specific therapeutic purpose, such as sensitivity training. Although these groups are usually characterized as group work for normals, some are so conducted as to be relatively indistinguishable from conventional therapy groups. Sensitivity training is also carried on under the auspices of social organizations and churches.

Professional Status. A prime example of groups constituted on the basis of professional identity are those conducted under the aegis of training in psychotherapy. To an increasing extent, group training in the behavioral sciences is oriented to therapeutic goals.

General Orientation and Approach

Most group therapists adhere to a theoretically grounded approach, the labeling of which reflects, implicitly or explicitly, their *modus operandi* and treatment philosophy. To identify a practitioner as an analytic group therapist, as a psychodramatist, or as a behavior therapist, for example, is to give important clues to how he views and addresses himself to his patients' problems. However, some therapists rather consistently apply the procedures consonant with their own school of therapy while others operate more empirically—a difference conveyed by the terms "strict methodology" and "fluid methodology."

The majority of therapists who conduct outpatient groups practice analytic group psychotherapy. The therapist who operates according to psychoanalytic principles, as adapted for the shared treatment experience, and applies the working concepts of transference and resistance remains a relatively unobtrusive figure in the group, intervening primarily to interpret behavior. Within that frame, three somewhat different approaches have developed: Some therapists

treat the individual *in* the group; others treat him *through* or *by* the group; and still others take an intermediate position, treating the individual as much as possible through the group as an entity and focusing on him separately to the extent necessary to resolve specific problems. Parloff has referred to these positions, overlapping in some respects, as intrapersonalist, integralist, and transactionalist or interpersonalist. The intrapersonalists place the least emphasis, and the integralists the most emphasis, on the role of group processes. The interpersonalists or transactionalists try to extract maximal therapeutic leverage from group processes in order to facilitate concurrent characterological change.

The theoretical divergences are reflected in the labeling of the analytic approaches. Therapists referred to as intrapersonalists have established such designations as "group psychoanalysis" and "psychoanalysis in groups" for their procedures; "psychoanalysis" has been abjured by other therapists. For example, Whitaker and Lieberman identify their system as "psychotherapy through the group process," and Foulkes introduced the terms "group-analytic psychotherapy" and "therapeutic group analysis."

Specific Strategies

Among therapists operating in the same general frame of reference as well as among those of different persuasions, much variability in therapeutic strategies and personal functioning in the treatment sessions is reported.

Probably the most obvious difference is the way therapists relate to patient-members of the group. Personal styles of conducting treatment range from authoritarian through didactic, blank screen (where the predominant attitude is passivity), and permissive to leaderless. The term "leaderless" may denote the therapist's physical absence from some or all treatment sessions or his attitude of scientific detachment, an attitude maintained by some research-oriented practitioners. But in the present context, "leaderless" refers to the disclaimer of more responsibility for the operation of the group than that assumed by the patients—an attitude characterized by Mullan in 1955 as status denial. Leaderlessness in that sense usually implies a high degree of personal involvement, the communication of information about the therapist's real-life identity, values, and immediate emotional reactions— all expressed in behavior as well as in words in some of the new approaches.

Diversity in professional backgrounds among practitioners of group psychotherapy helps to account for the wide spectrum of strategies and attitudes reported. Rather than adhering to the traditional view of their role as one of healing sick people, some therapists implement other assumptions about the problems of their group members. Practitioners, physicians among them, who depart from the medical model to an appreciable extent find it more congenial to view the therapy group as a social system and relate to its members in terms of sociological, philosophical, or theological systems of thought. The specific problems presented by patients are often regarded as social tensions, dynamic pressures, and the like. Surveying this variegated picture, Lieberman, Lakin, and Whitaker stated:

Therapeutic strategies range from those in which the therapist possesses a total encompassing charisma and, much like a guru, acts as the interpreter of reality and the center of emotional cathexis, to those in which the therapist acts as conductor or a social engineer.

Little is known about the therapeutic implications of these departures from the more or less established role of parent surrogate.

Sessions without the Therapist. The majority of practitioners maintain the policy of conducting all sessions of a group. Others incorporate meetings without the therapist in the treatment process. This practice was introduced by Wolf and Schwartz, who refer to these regularly scheduled gatherings as alternate sessions.

Use of Co-Therapists. Most groups are conducted by a single therapist, but current reports suggest an appreciable increase in the number treated by two or more. The practice of dual therapy was probably introduced for training purposes, with the second therapist serving primarily as a recorder and observer while his more experienced colleague actually conducted the group. However, many co-therapy teams today are composed of a male and a female therapist who share this responsibility.

Co-therapy is a controversial practice. Authors who question its value argue that it compounds countertransference phenomena, that it tends to contaminate the transference reactions of patients, and that their treatment is also interfered with because competitive strivings and even serious differences between the team members develop more or less inevitably. Exponents of co-therapy claim that the family constellation is replicated with the presence of mother and father transference objects, thus facilitating the progress of specific categories of patients. Exponents also point out practical considerations, such as the fact that one therapist can conduct the group in the absence of the other.

Since 1957, when Spitz and Kopp investigated the wide range of methods employed in co-therapy, including the treatment of one patient by as many as ten therapists, many additional variations have been reported.

Group Stimulus Situations

In any type of group psychotherapy, the stimulus situation is fundamentally different from that in the one-to-one treatment relationship. In individual analytic therapy, for example, the patient is stimulated mostly through verbal communication and auditory feedback, from his own words and the interventions of the analyst. The group setting adds to these the important factor of visual stimulation and visual feedback.

In the verbal group therapies, the therapist may limit himself to intellectual communication, which is generally effective in dealing with emotional problems that originated in the oedipal stage of development. Patients whose problems are associated with pre-oedipal (preverbal) stages are usually more responsive to emotional and symbolic communications.

Group therapists have traditionally limited themselves to auditory and visual modes of influence. The major exceptions are found in psychodrama and in the play and activity group therapies for children, in which feedback from action is a significant source of stimulation. The plethora of group methods recently introduced, some under the aegis of therapy and others characterized as growth experiences, relegate auditory and visual stimulation to a less important role. These new methods operate primarily through bodily sensations, including tactile and kinesthetic. Participants are encouraged to touch one another and to engage in other forms of physical contact—sexual or aggressive or both. Even taste and smell sensations may be stimulated.

Much experimentation is going on at the present time to determine whether such stimulation is necessary or desirable in psychotherapy. In the author's experience, physical contact and tactile stimulation do not contribute to significant personality change. In some instances, they preclude successful treatment.

HISTORY OF CLASSIFICATION

Various sorting racks have been devised to accommodate the multitude of practices designated as group psychotherapy and to elucidate their significant similarities and differences. But few schemata in this field have escaped the fate of rapid obsolescence. No generally accepted classification exists today.

Early attempts to classify the group methods reflected the initial need to know the different ways psychotherapy can be conducted in the group setting. Descriptive classifications are characteristic in an early developmental period, but, after one knows how to do it, answers are needed to the questions "For whom?" and "What does it accomplish?" Successive classifications have moved somewhat closer to supplying answers to those questions, although these classifications are still hampered by the clinical-impressionistic nature of the reports on treatment and the consequent difficulties of conducting evaluative research. The classifications discussed below in chronological sequence were made over a period of 25 years, and they illustrate how different investigators have attempted to rise above the level of descriptiveness in an immature field of practice.

1943

Giles Thomas, following Merrill Moore's simple differentiation of the individual psychotherapies, discerned two major categories of group psychotherapy—the repressive-inspirational and the analytic—"with various degrees of combination of the two." Accordingly, he arrayed the methods reported by the early 1940's along an axis, with Schilder at one end and Alcoholics Anonymous at the other end (see Figure 1). In the accompanying review, Thomas stated

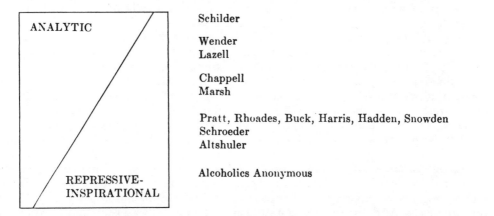

Figure 1. The first and best-known descriptive classification of the methods of group psychotherapy, by Giles W. Thomas. (From *Psychosomatic Medicine.*)

that good results had been claimed in a "large proportion of the patients treated (more than half)" but that it was not possible to compare them.

Thomas's survey, published in the journal *Psychosomatic Medicine*, was introduced by the following editorial note:

This is a new field, and the review covers extremely heterogeneous material: therapeutic procedures based completely on rough empiricisms like Alcoholics Anonymous, together with therapeutic efforts like Schilder's carefully analyzed and planned experiments and the experimentation of psychodrama based on definition of psychodynamic observations and concepts.

The critical reader may receive the impression that this field is not yet ripe for this type of descriptive reviewing and needs above all a critical evaluation of the methods employed and the results reported. However, the Editors feel that this review gives, if not a complete, a rather broad descriptive view of the various attempts of group therapy and might stimulate interest in the obvious possibilities of this type of treatment.

That statement, expressive of the customary reaction of practitioners trained in the principles of scientific reporting on treatment, is of more than historical interest. The classification that provoked this reservation has attracted much attention over the years; Thomas's schema is still used and is regarded as one of the most helpful descriptions of the group approaches. Moreover, the above-quoted comment, published in 1943, has not, regrettably, lost its pertinence. Similar views have been expressed, particularly by those engaged in evaluative research in the field. For example, Goldstein, Heller, and Sechrest observed in 1966 that

group psychotherapy literature as a whole has remained at the earliest and most primitive level of observation and inquiry. . . . The plateau of descriptiveness which the current group psychotherapy literature represents must be built on, developed, and elaborated.

1945

J. L. Moreno formulated a table of eight polar categories and three points of reference to accommodate all the group approaches. He suggested that the methods be categorized as follows:

Subject of Therapy

(1) Constitution of the group (amorphous or structured on the basis of diagnosis); (2) Locus of treatment (natural life setting or special clinical situation); (3) Aim of treatment (causal or symptomatic);

Agent of Therapy

(4) Source or transfer of influence (therapist-centered or group-centered); (5) Form of influence (spontaneous and freely experienced or rehearsed and prepared);

Medium of Therapy

(6) Mode of influence (lecture or verbal, dramatic, or other actional mode); (7) Type of medium (conserved, mechanical, unspontaneous, or creative); (8) Origin of medium (face-to-face or presented from a distance, as from radio or television).

Actual distribution of the group methods under this comprehensive plan was not reported.

1957

Raymond J. Corsini, making a distinction between methods per se and the different ways each is applied, identified more than 25 methods by name. He distributed them under the headings of directive and nondirective to indicate the degree of control exercised by the therapist. The directive therapist was described as setting limits on the group members, the nondirective as setting limits on himself; the crucial factor was considered to be the

latitude permitted for decision making, especially in regard to interpretations.

Under his main headings, Corsini arranged the group methods under four subheadings: verbal-deep, verbal-superficial, actional-deep, and actional-superficial:

Directive

Verbal-Deep: (1) *Multiple therapy* (Dreikurs, Adlerian school)—one patient meeting with two therapists; (2) *Analytic therapy* (the circular-discussional approach common to the analytic schools, the main difference in its use being in the nature of the interpretations provided); (3) *Co-therapist methods: Behind-the-back technique;* (4) *Projective methods* (circular discussion of the spontaneously produced drawings of members);

Verbal-Superficial: (5) *Will training* (A. A. Low) in large and self-directed groups; (6) *Adlerian group counseling;* (7) *Lecture methods* (Pratt's class method, the repressive-inspirational procedures employing music or other attention-getting devices, repetition lectures, and procedures utilizing visual aids); (8) *Case histories* with discussion initiated by the therapist (Wender); (9) *Anonymous participation* (answering of questions written on unsigned slips of paper); (10) *Group bibliotherapy* (including J. W. Klapman's textbook-mediated therapy); (11) *Mechanical group therapy* (short recorded messages over a loudspeaker system);

Actional-Deep: (12) *Psychodrama* and related procedures introduced by Moreno;

Actional-Superficial: (13) *Dramatics* (theatrical productions by hospitalized patients); (14) *Puppets* (used for psychotherapeutic purposes in mental hospitals); (15) *Acting-out techniques* (as introduced by Ernst Simmel for release of repressed hostilities); (16) *ABC* (alphabet writing and other simple tasks performed cooperatively by patients using a blackboard);

Nondirective

Verbal-Deep: (17) *Client-centered method* (Carl Rogers); (18) *Leaderless therapy* (Bion-Rickman's research-oriented method, in which the therapist may engage himself verbally but assumes no special responsibility); (19) *Round-table psychotherapy* (introduced by McCann and Almada, in which the therapist is inactive while a small panel of patients sits around a table and many more constitute an audience);

Verbal-Superficial: (20) *Social-club therapy* (Joshua Bierer); (21) *Alcoholics Anonymous;*

Actional-Deep: (22) *Psychodramatic group therapy* (an adaptation of psychodrama with the group meeting in a circle);

Actional-Superficial: (23) *Activity group therapy* (Slavson); (24) *Music therapy;* and (25) *Auroratone* (abstract color films synchronized with music).

Corsini's classification, which affords a panoramic view of the practice of group therapy in the 1950's, illustrates the rapid rate of attrition in group methods. Many of the methods he listed have virtually disappeared from the current literature. The schema, moreover, does not distinguish

between small and large groups. But the chief drawback of Corsini's classification lies in its failure to indicate the specific values and limitations of each method listed, the types of patients for which it is effective, and what it can accomplish.

1959

Although the classification proposed by J. W. Klapman in the second edition of his textbook on group psychotherapy has similarly outlived its usefulness, it represents the first attempt to categorize methods of group therapy on the basis of their suitability for patients. Decrying a preponderance of emphasis on any one approach as well as the waning status of approaches that he regarded as most appropriate for severely regressed patients, Klapman formulated a gradient classification presenting criteria and indices for

any given patient at any given time at any given level of aberrant psychic functioning.

He suggested that patients entering treatment in groups structured for the most disturbed patient population should be "upped" in due time to groups permitting a greater degree of autonomy. Consonant with those views, he described three degrees of disorganization observed in adult patients and matched these personality states with the optimally applicable group methods.

Patients in minimally disorganized states, encompassing most of the patients who qualify for treatment on an outpatient basis, were designated as patients of choice for analytic group therapy, psychodrama, and client-centered group therapy. Klapman listed about a dozen approaches as optimally applicable in moderately disturbed states. Among these approaches were a hierarchy of didactic procedures oriented to an improvement in intellectual functioning in groups small enough to permit two-way communication. For his third category—severely and relatively severely disorganized personality states—he recommended a score of methods oriented to different levels of ego functioning, from calisthenics and other physical activity to textbook-mediated therapy. The majority of the approaches described by

Klapman have fallen into disfavor, and his idea that the therapist is perforce limited to the lecture methods when treating psychotic patients has not been sustained. Nevertheless, the schema itself is notable in a period dominated by method-oriented classifications.

The classification by Frank and Powdermaker, also presented in 1959, has been more widely used. It suggests that the group treatment procedures, though marked by a considerable degree of overlap, fall into five general categories:

Didactic Groups, with guided discussions based on lectures by the therapist directed toward the promotion of intellectual insight and also allowing emotional interaction, used primarily with hospitalized psychotic patients;

Therapeutic Social Clubs, conducted especially for promoting skills in social participation among patients discharged from hospitals, and organized along parliamentary lines with the therapist intentionally maintaining an unobtrusive role;

Repressive-Inspirational Groups, designed chiefly to arouse positive group emotions and build morale through strong group identifications, in which the therapist gives inspirational talks and conducts relaxation exercises or group singing, and the patients may present testimonials or recitations;

Psychodrama;

Free-Interaction Groups, encompassing the various forms of group psychotherapy conducted by psychoanalytically oriented therapists and also group-centered psychotherapy, which promote an atmosphere conducive to the free verbalization of feelings and to the exposure and correction of immature attitudes.

1964

In a schema elucidating differences in depth of small-group approaches, S. R. Slavson distinguished group psychotherapy from group counseling and guidance, reserving the first term for procedures aiming at significant intrapsychic change in subjects with real pathology. By contrast, counseling and guidance, identified as different levels of psychonursing, are concerned with ego functioning and offer assistance with immediate and specific reality problems. Counseling is viewed as the most superficial and time-limited method, designed to clarify a course of action; guidance deals with emotional impediments to carrying through action by providing support and clarification without, however, tracing the blockages back to their source. Four major types of group therapy are discerned: activity group therapy for children, analytic for adults, para-analytic—a therapy of less depth for adolescents, the elderly, and specific diagnostic categories of adults, among them schizophrenic and borderline patients—and directive.

Slavson's classification illustrates one of the terminological confusions in the field, that generated by different conceptions of group counseling. Nonmedical therapists, in particular, tend to use the term group counseling interchangeably with group psychotherapy or regard it as a more intensive procedure than group guidance.

1965

Instead of compartmentalizing the systems of group treatment, some classifiers have represented them as constituting a continuum. Max Rosenbaum, for example, discerns a succession of interrelated methods, ranging from repressive-inspirational to regressive-reconstructive, which reflect the two extremes in the extent of personality change worked for. Between them he places the supportive and reparative therapies, the latter being oriented to the building up of weak defenses. A directive-didactic category, including behavior therapy in groups, is differentiated from nondirective methods, such as the group version of client-centered psychotherapy, psychodrama, therapeutic social clubs, and analytic group therapy.

1968

Howard A. Blatner's chart (see Figure 2) shows further progress toward specificity. It has a dual significance. Proposed as an aid in the selection of the type of group experience that will meet the patient's therapeutic

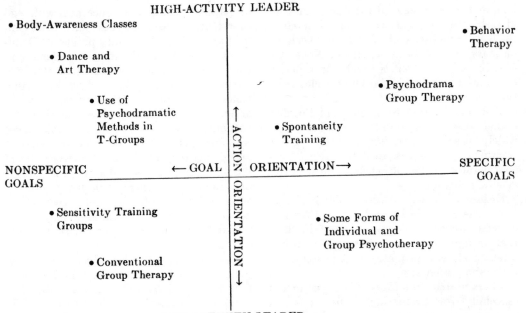

HIGH-ACTIVITY LEADER

• Body-Awareness Classes

• Behavior
Therapy

• Dance and
Art Therapy

• Psychodrama
Group Therapy

• Use of
Psychodramatic
Methods in
T-Groups

↑ ACTION
• Spontaneity
Training

NONSPECIFIC
GOALS   ← GOAL ORIENTATION →   SPECIFIC
GOALS

ORIENTATION ↓

• Sensitivity Training
Groups

• Some Forms of
Individual and
Group Psychotherapy

• Conventional
Group Therapy

LOW-ACTIVITY LEADER

Figure 2. Classification of group procedures in relation to goal orientation and action orientation, by Howard A. Blatner. (From *Voices.*)

needs most efficiently, this schema appears to be the first to focus on the group approaches that were introduced during the 1960's. Moreover, methods are differentiated in terms of factors that were not mentioned in earlier classifications—the amount of structured activity imposed on group members by the therapist and the degree of specificity of the goals on which they agree. Of interest in this context is Eric Berne's suggestion in 1966 that therapies in which the practitioner's goals are limited or diffuse be identified as "soft," while those geared to more far-reaching, clearly defined goals and to achieving these goals expeditiously be identified as "hard" therapies.

A comparison of Figures 1 and 2, reproduced from clinical reports that span a period of 25 years, highlights the on-going shift from method-oriented to goal-oriented classifications. The comparison also suggests that group psychotherapy has been developing from an assortment of more or less similar instruments for doing psychotherapy in a general sense into an armamentarium of different instruments fashioned to achieve highly specific objectives.

SIGNIFICANCE OF GOALS

In the absence of scientific findings on the comparative values and limitations of the different types of group therapy, recommendations for treatment are usually based on clinical judgment and experience. By and large, the personal predilection, theoretical allegiance, training, and expertise of the practitioner whom the patient happens to consult determine the type of group experience he undergoes. Happenstance in selection, understandable as it is in this still primitive stage of development of group psychotherapy, is undesirable. It may deprive the patient of the type of treatment experience that would be most efficacious for him; it may also expose him to a distinctly harmful treatment experience. Rapid expansion of the group psychotherapeutic armamentarium increases the responsibility of the practitioner for discriminative selection of the instrument to be applied in each case.

Specificity in treatment will eventually be facilitated by objective evaluations of the results achieved through the different approaches. Without such evidence, however, the most reliable guide to specificity is a comparison of the stated treatment goals and results reported by the proponents of each procedure. The theories applied are of some significance because they indicate how the therapist attempts to influence the group through his behavior. But primary consideration needs to be given to what is sought, anticipated, and achieved through the use of the procedure. In short, the preferred method for a patient can best be determined by investigating the respective goals and results achieved through the alternatives available.

With increasing effectiveness in the matching of methods to patients, such data will probably be included in classifications of the group treatment approaches. At the present time, the facts have to be extracted from the professional literature—a laborious and not very rewarding task, owing to the unscientific nature of much of the reporting. Differentiations are vague; the range of applicability of some methods may not be defined; follow-ups are exceptional, claims in some instances being based exclusively on behavioral change in the treatment sessions.

Like individual psychotherapy, group psychotherapy has only one *raison d'être*—to benefit the individual. Although that justification may seem too elementary to mention, the prolonged preoccupation with methodology has tended to obscure it. *How* the patient is treated in the group setting has received much more attention than the precise benefits the therapist was striving to accomplish through his procedure. Nevertheless, distinct differences in the goals reported are readily discernible.

Distinctions are made in psychotherapy between *attainable* goals and *ideal* goals. An attainable or practical goal is commonly viewed as one that helps the patient achieve the optimal level of functioning consonant with his financial resources and material circumstances, his motivations when he enters treatment, and his ego capacities. It is generally recognized that such goals represent a modification of what theoretically constitutes the ideal objective of psychotherapy—personality maturation. What this

notion implies offers a desirable criterion for a comparative evaluation of the goals reported.

Personality Maturation

Undoubtedly, the most ambitious goal that is pursued in psychotherapy is that of arresting an illness, repairing its ravages, and helping the patient outgrow his emotional immaturities so that he may realize his potential in life performance and happiness. Such an outcome, although more far-reaching than symptomatic relief or social recovery, does not necessarily mean that he has been relieved of all his problems or that he will not encounter new ones in the future. That outcome does signify, however, that he has the ability to feel, think, and behave appropriately in all normal situations and to meet the impact of extraordinarily traumatic experiences with considerable resiliency. Emotional versatility is an important measure of recovery because the seriously disturbed patient entering treatment tends to be bogged down in the essentially gross feelings of the young child. In the process of refining them and acquiring more discriminatory feelings, the patient eventually commands the hierarchy of feelings that characterize emotional evolution. The author therefore conceptualizes such curative change as the emergence of the emotionally mature personality.

Personality maturation is considered to be the natural outcome of biological and psychological growth in a succession of reasonably favorable internal and external environments. Highly specific reactions to disruptions of these growth processes at different developmental levels constitute the spectrum of functional disorders to which the psychotherapist addresses himself. The earlier the processes were thrown out of gear, the more damaging the impact on the organism. Disruptions of the maturational sequences that unfold during the first year of life are associated with psychosis. Other disruptions during the pre-oedipal period (the first two years) are associated with the impulse disorders, character disorders, severe obsessive-compulsive illness, and some psychosomatic disturbances. Vicissitudes encountered at later maturational levels are linked with psychoneurosis and the relatively minor disturbances experienced by the normal person in emotionally stressful circumstances.

In a person suffering from a deep-seated disorder, the psychotherapist usually recognizes two types of interferences with further personality growth: fixations and maladaptations. Both types are associated with the failure to meet maturational needs. Fixations result from exposure to situations of undue frustration or gratification or both. Maladaptations are perceived as the persistence of certain repetitive behaviors, patterned in these deficiency states, that drain off psychic energy into circuitous processes. These defensive maneuvers may interfere with the meeting of needs that are subsequently experienced. The psychological ingredients that would satisfy the later needs are usually available but cannot be assimilated because of the deviant patterns formed to compensate for the original deficiencies.

Patients succeed in liberating themselves from the compulsive operation of the maladaptive patterns when they are helped to engage in defense-freeing exercises and to re-experience the original fixations. They also require, concomitantly and subsequently, experiences that contribute to further growth.

Treatment oriented to the goal of personality maturation entails three essentially different dynamic operations. In this discussion, these dynamic operations are referred to as discrete steps and are focused on in the order in which each operation dominates the psychotherapeutic process, but they are overlapping concerns.

Step 1. In the treatment situation, reactivate and deal with the forces that prevent the patient from meeting his maturational needs. This step is what the psychoanalytically trained therapist refers to as controlling the development of transference. The interfering forces are aroused, analyzed, and influenced in terms of dealing with transference resistance.

Step 2. Help the patient meet his own maturational needs. This step is, in a sense, a tactical operation, engaged in to help the patient give up the maladaptive behavior. During the treatment, he experiences many psychological needs, such as a need for some immediate gratification, but in principle these needs are not met. The therapist extends aid only for meeting those needs that hamper emotional growth.

Step 3. Help the patient give up the maladaptive behavior without endangering the degree of personality maturation that he has achieved. In technical terms, this step is referred to as the working through of transference resistance.

Case History

John, 35 years old, was frequently referred to by the co-members of his group as "the great protector." He talked repeatedly in the sessions about disagreements with his wife concerning her disciplining of their 10-year-old son. John's tendency to rush to the little boy's defense whenever he was reproved for misbehaving and his refusal to associate himself with his wife's disciplinary measures gave rise to much friction in the family.

In the treatment sessions, John characteristically came to the defense of a young man whenever he was criticized by another member, a middle-aged woman. John made no effort to investigate the merits of the criticism. Objections to this behavior were voiced by several members of the group.

In the process of dealing with this maladaptation, the group came to recognize it as a component of John's infantile personality. His early years had been marked by emotional deprivation. After his parents' divorce, when John was two, he never saw his father. John eventually disclosed that he felt like a little boy. The pattern of "the great protector" appeared to represent an indirect attempt to call attention to his own need to be taken care of. The other group members responded to this understanding by helping him with his current problems with his wife. A progress report on his home life was often demanded of him in sessions when he did not volunteer such information.

As a group member, John functioned more and more appropriately as his need for help was satisfied. He tried to understand the communications of the other patients and to be helpful to all of them.

The resolution of the pattern of automatically jumping to the defense of the young man in the group was followed by a gradual but observable change in John's behavior with his family. He began cooperating with his wife in the upbringing of their son. John informed the group that he felt like a husband as well as a father.

In this case, the group therapist worked primarily on Steps 1 and 3. He conducted the treatment in such a way as to maintain a transference climate, addressed himself to the obstacles to cooperative functioning in the treatment sessions—illustrated by John's little-boy feelings—and helped the patient work through these interfering forces in the context of innumerable treatment situations. Step 2, on the other hand, was performed mostly by the group members themselves. His feelings of being understood and cared for by his co-patients, for example, helped him significantly in outgrowing the "great protector" pattern.

Emotional Feeding

As a matter of principle, the majority of analytic therapists who conduct individual treatment to produce significant personality change do not help the patient meet his maturational needs. They assume that the understanding they provide through their interpretations will suffice to free him to meet them himself through the emotional nourishment inherent in ordinary social situations. In the shared treatment experience, on the other hand, patients spontaneously "feed" one another, session after session, with feelings that satisfy different kinds of psychological needs.

Much of this emotional feeding is of little or no significance for personality growth; it provides momentary gratification without influencing the obstacles to change. But in addition to nutriments that create spells of excitement and dilute feelings of depression and alienation without helping to induce corrective change and the more conventional verbal communications of support or reassurance—all viewed by the author as meeting gratification needs—patients also pick up from one another specific feelings that stimulate growth processes. One of the special values of group psychotherapy lies in the contribution of patient interaction to the reciprocal meeting of maturational needs.

TYPES OF GROUP THERAPY

A classification of the various group procedures in terms of the type of problems they deal with and their relative effectiveness in clearing up these problems is not yet possible for reasons that have already been mentioned, notably the lack of specificity in the practice of group psychotherapy and discrepancies in the standards of reporting in the field. At the present juncture, however, these procedures can be differentiated roughly on the basis of the operational principles applied. The extent to which the practitioners employing each procedure deliberately address themselves to the three operations entailed in resolving the forces that have blocked personality maturation serves as the principal criterion in the assessment of each type of group therapy discussed.

Taking a phenomenological stance, the author has attempted to picture the field of contemporary practice and has, therefore, included in his sampling, along with the major established approaches, some that are innovative and unvalidated and whose status as psychotherapy is moot. Clinical concepts and techniques are delineated when deemed necessary to clarify their relation to the manifest goals of the treatment or the composition of the group or to facilitate the evaluation of the claims made.

Goals, it should be borne in mind, do not necessarily convey the therapeutic power residing in a method. In the course of the method's development, the results achieved most consistently come to be identified as its objectives. Goals are thus an expression of therapeutic outcome most efficaciously secured through past applications rather than a final pronouncement on therapeutic action. Hitherto untapped values may emerge in the future with somewhat different applications. As already mentioned, however, the goals currently enunciated and information on the extent to which these goals are attained provide the most reliable evidence available on the suitability of a procedure for a given patient and the predictable outcome of the case, assuming that the therapist is reasonably proficient.

The procedures surveyed below cover the spectrum of contemporary practice. The sequence in which they are discussed does not accurately reflect the order in which they were introduced; psychodrama, for example, antedates the cluster of analytic approaches that are reviewed first. Procedures with relatively similar goals are viewed in succession. The progression is from long-term to short-term, with approaches of the most recent vintage completing the series.

The author's impressions are based primarily on information provided by practitioners adhering to the procedure under review. Their assumptions, clinical practices, observations, and claims have been gathered from the literature. Personal communications from patients were another source of information. The claims advanced for each procedure were assessed on the basis of the data available.

Analytic Group Psychotherapy (Freudian)

It was pointed out earlier that therapists whose procedures are derived from individual psychoanalytic therapy differ substantially in the extent to which they integrate group processes into their conceptual framework as well as in their modifications of the parent techniques. In general, however, they conduct treatment on a long-term basis to produce significant characterological change in persons who are highly motivated to achieve such change. The treatment is conducted in a transference climate; transference and resistance phenomena are analyzed and, in some cases, worked through; the group equivalent of free association is employed; dreams are interpreted. Great reliance is placed on the acquisition of insight. Rapid change is not looked for, and the therapist does not necessarily apply himself to help the patient improve his interpersonal functioning.

Careful attention is given to the selection and grouping of patients, but criteria for admission vary. Patients with psychoneurotic conditions, character disorders, and other disturbances of the oedipal type are widely regarded as the most likely candidates. Practitioners who conduct analytic groups on an ambulatory basis usually exclude patients with more severe disorders or limit the number of such patients in composing a group. For instance, Wolf reported in 1968 that for psychoanalysis in groups he accepts persons with borderline and mild psychotic conditions and specifically excludes paranoid and hypermanic patients, those who hallucinate, severe stutterers, the seriously psychopathic, alcoholics, mental retardates, and patients with some types of cardiac disorder.

Some analytic group therapists structure treatment to include regular sessions without the therapist. Wolf claims that these alternate sessions promote

more spontaneous interactivity as well as more inappropriate responses and impulsivity.

This practice is predicated on the assumption that the group members will not seriously misbehave in the therapist's absence. Other therapists, including the author, challenge the assumption and believe that alternate sessions are undesirable for groups with acting-out or potentially psychotic patients. But such meetings may conceivably be recommended for the promotion of spontaneity in rigid and overcontrolled patients.

The goals of this method are defined in terms of psychosexual maturation. The therapist addresses himself to resolving the emotional forces that thwart maturation and focuses on the working through of maladaptive behavior (Steps 1 and 3).

Cautious assessment of ego strength and tolerance for regression is important before exposing a person with a severe disturbance to this regressive-reconstructive approach. The more deep-seated his problems, the more retrograde movement he has to engage in, and the more difficult it becomes to influence him effectively by interpretive interventions. Problems rooted in the preverbal period are more responsive to emotional and symbolic communications. Moreover, it is difficult to work on these problems without stimulating regressive tendencies that threaten the degree of adjustment to reality that the patient has achieved.

Consistent and confirmed techniques for the individual treatment of pre-oedipal patients have been reported, but the development of such approaches for group treatment oriented to meaningful change has not been claimed. Analytic therapists who accept severely disturbed persons in their groups do so within the framework of combined treatment.

Analytic Group Psychotherapy (Neo-Freudian)

Therapists who adhere to the theoretical constructs of the cultural and interpersonal schools of psychoanalysis differ notably from those who implement Freudian principles in their interpretations and formulation of goals.

Adler School (Individual Psychology). Adlerian therapists, notes Dreikurs, view their group members as social beings whose behavior is purposive and directed to social survival and self-realization. Although the group members have not learned to live together as equals, their life styles are based on self-set goals, and they do only what they intend to do. Frequently, they are unaware of these goals and intentions. Another principle of Adlerian psychology is the unity of the personality, which is viewed as an intertwining of dynamic, somatic, psychological, and social processes. Interpreting the phenomena observed in the group sessions, particularly the social aspects of the patients' problems, the therapist strives to bring them into awareness.

Psychotherapy is conducted primarily as an educational process in which emotional experience reinforces intellectual learning. Insight is not viewed as a prerequisite for change. Patients are encouraged to improve, recognize, and correct value systems that militate against desirable social functioning. An atmosphere of social equality and mutual helpfulness is created to counteract fears, anxieties, and emotional isolation. Intrapsychic dynamics are explored, and understanding is communicated, but more emphasis is placed on social reorientation and the counteracting of fears.

Changes in attitudes toward life are reported to express themselves in the alleviation of symptoms, improved functioning, and a sense of general well-being. Changes in the patient's early recollections are characteristic.

The goals are to increase the patient's self-respect and self-confidence—to remove feelings of inferiority—and to enhance his faith in his own worth and ability to grow.

Character traits and ego functioning of the mature personality are described, but precisely how these improvements are brought about is not clear from the data available. The therapist concentrates on correcting maladaptive behavior (Step 3). The goals as conceptualized do not encompass the identification and meeting of the maturational needs that preserve the illness. Unless feelings of inferiority are permitted full expression in the process of removing them, the risk of producing fresh repressions is courted. In that case, improvement may be temporary, and psychosomatic problems may ensue.

Horneyan School. The therapist, notes Rose, assumes that a unifying process goes on in the group that can be turned in a healthy direction and used to work through neurotic blocks to growth. Sensitive to group atmosphere, the therapist distinguishes between cohesiveness that serves merely to relieve basic anxiety (feelings of weakness and isolation from the real self and the feeling that others are hostile) and cohesiveness that develops when the patients get to feel that belonging to the group is a healthful experience. Conflict and the emergence of anxiety are encouraged, but the anxiety is not permitted to become so intense that patients withdraw from the group.

The democratic values of the group help to liberate strivings toward cooperative mutuality, but, when corrective processes fail to operate, the therapist may intervene on any one of three levels, focusing on the group atmosphere, on interpersonal behavior, or on intrapsychic mechanisms. Through their interpersonal reactions, the group members repeatedly demonstrate the multidimensional and self-perpetuating nature of their individual neurotic patterns. The therapist permits these patterns and their consequences to be experienced for the purpose of encouraging new modes of behavior (Step 1).

Emphasis is placed on the here-and-now. Childhood memories are used as a vehicle for the expression of immediate feelings, and neurotic reactions are seen in terms of present character structure. The idiosyncratic defensive patterns of the patient are identified not in terms of repetition-compulsion or transference reactions but in terms of abnormal character structure, originating in childhood disturbances that led to a distorted concept of the self and the world (Step 3). Interpretations elucidate discrepancies between the idealized image of the self (the ideal self) and the real self.

The goal of the treatment, in Horney's term, is self-realization. The therapist works for significant and enduring character change, a restructuring of the personality. Self-realization is correlated with the capacity to feel free and independent and possession of a unified personality, a sense of inner-directedness, and a recognition of one's responsibilities and limitations.

The group therapeutic process is aimed at producing the mature personality. The therapist arouses and deals with transference resistance (identified as patient-patient and patient-therapist relationships) and works to remove maladaptations. The meeting of maturational needs is not described.

Sullivanian School (Interpersonal Psychiatry). The therapist who operates in the framework of Harry Stack Sullivan's interpersonal theory, notes Goldman, conducts himself in the group as a representative of constructive culture. He engages in interpersonal transactions with the patients to correct their distorted perceptions and socially ineffectual behavior, and he communicates attitudes of acceptance and respect. He focuses on feelings, particularly anxiety and loneliness, rather than on unconscious memories. Maladaptive behavior, the motivation for which is explained in terms of avoidance of anxiety and the search for security, is explored in historical perspective. Much attention is given to nonverbal behavior. Transference phenomena are regarded as one among various types of personalized childhood fantasies that are carried over into the immediate situation (parataxes); these fantasies are elucidated as an aid in correcting misperceptions and modifying present behavior. Acceptance of the therapist's interpretation

of a patient's defense maneuver is facilitated by identical reactions of other group members (consensual validation), which helps each member to become aware of his behavior and to analyze it.

The therapist, as an expert in human relations, attends primarily to problems raised by the patients. In the final phase of treatment, he summarizes what has gone on in the therapy and suggests ways of improving future functioning.

The goal of treatment is to help the patient become a well-integrated and socially effective person who tends to see things as others in his culture see them and who behaves in ways they approve of.

This operational approach focuses strongly on the elimination of maladaptations (Step 3). The development of transference is not controlled because the therapist presents himself as a real person. The degree of personality maturation achieved through understanding of the patient's history and interpersonal relations and through correction of his misperceptions is not made clear.

Since the full expression of feelings and the meeting of maturational needs do not appear to figure in the therapeutic process, the improvement achieved may be superficial in nature. Later somatic illness is a possibility.

Psychotherapy through the Group Process

The model of treatment developed by Whitaker and Lieberman is illustrative of systems of group therapy that supplement concepts of individual therapy with the findings of group dynamicists. The therapist views the movements of the group as successive attempts at the resolution of unconscious conflict. The immediate behavior of the members represents a compromise between conflicting motives—disturbing and reactive—and the quality of the group climate is determined by whether the solutions worked out are restrictive or enabling.

The group members are described as homogeneous in terms of vulnerability of defensive structure and heterogeneous in their areas of conflict and ways of dealing with conflict. Candidates evaluated as highly vulnerable, including the acutely psychotic and some neurotics, are not accepted. The consistently silent patient is thought to obtain only limited benefit from the therapeutic process. The group is regarded as the major vehicle of treatment, and patients are not seen routinely on an individual basis.

As the successive group conflicts elicit habitual maladaptive behavior and attitudes originating in the patient's interpersonal relationships, the therapist focuses on modifying those maladaptations and facilitating new learning. Individual patterns that are irrelevant to the focal conflict are not investigated. The contribution to changes in behavior made by reality-testing in a climate of safety is emphasized.

The therapeutic experience itself is regarded as the core factor. Insight and catharsis may occur, but they are not regarded as significant mechanisms. The promotion of permanent change is not claimed; it is pointed out that behavioral change in the group sessions does not automatically carry over into life.

The goal of the therapist is to promote the growth of the patient. He tries to achieve growth by working on maladaptation patterns (Step 3).

Referring to the maladaptive behavior patterns that the patient brings into the group, Whitaker and Lieberman state that "some may yield, others may not." A corrective emotional experience is offered, but the therapist disclaims responsibility for resolving the patient's fundamental problems as they become manifest in the group conflict. The observation that changes in behavior may not carry over into the life situation suggests that the transference is not deep enough or that the maladaptations are not worked through sufficiently.

The inactivity of the therapist may largely be accounted for by the primacy of his interest in studying group dynamics. Whitaker and Lieberman, like Bion and others, have made important contributions to the study of group processes by withholding their influence and permitting the group to go where it wants to go. As research-oriented therapists shift their attention from group processes per se to the investigation of how these processes can be exploited to facilitate personality growth, they will probably function as more active therapeutic agents.

Existential-Experiential Approaches

These unstandardized and vaguely differentiated procedures, reported by psychoanalytically trained therapists, appear to represent a multifaceted protest against the traditional concern with childhood experience and ego psychology. Existentialists commit themselves to here-and-now interaction with their patients. Experientialists stress the primacy of experience and relatedness over understanding. Some practitioners identify themselves as both existentialists and experientialists.

Among those whose theoretical framework reflects the teachings of existential philosophy, Hora describes existential psychotherapy as a process of cognitive unfoldment and as one in which the practitioner "lives" psychotherapy instead of trying to "do" it. Rather than interpreting, evaluating, and judging, he opens himself up to existential encounter and clarifies what he understands.

The existential groups, designed for study as well as treatment, are composed of from eight to ten persons in diverse diagnostic categories. They are viewed as suffering from disturbed modes - of - being - in - the - world. Their emotional and somatic problems are attributed to preoccupations with the need to confirm one's being. Since their capacity to communicate meaningfully is restricted, they experience frequently recurring conflicts and a sense of isolation.

Revealing themselves at the start as inauthentic people who are concerned with releasing tensions, existential group members move through phases of self-discovery and growing understanding, of being burdened by their defensive strivings and of giving them up, of learning to accept their own anxiousness, and of ultimately discovering themselves as being authentically in the world. On the road to authenticity, they achieve truthfulness in expression, develop mutual regard and respect for the integrity and freedom of one another, and become more perceptive and creative in their thinking.

Group communications focus on the immediate experience. The past may be revealed through proper elucidation of the present, but this revelation is not regarded as significant. Unconscious motivation is not explored. Emphasis is placed on helping the patient achieve harmony with life.

Some existential group therapists apply the working concepts and techniques of analytic psychotherapy, despite their philosophic divergences. Others reject the operational concepts of transference, countertransference, and resistance.

Experimental therapists stress the feeling experiences of the patient. They view sickness as dynamic pressure rather than as disease, and they view health as continuous personal growth, which expands the capacity to choose. The therapist works actively to augment this capacity, using his total person and striving through his preconscious and unconscious responses to stimulate reparative forces working within the patient. The transference relationship, the function of which is to permit the development of responsiveness and counterresponsiveness, is eventually replaced by a nontransference or existential relationship. As Malone et al. state:

> The intrapersonal experiences of both therapist and patient function as reciprocals primarily through nonverbal communication.

Goals are formulated by existential therapists in terms of liberating cognitive and creative potentialities, self-discovery, and deepening understanding. They appear to be working for personality maturation and, in the results claimed, come close to describing it. Experientialists aim for characterological and other growth changes, the breaking up of repetition-compulsions, and the release of the patient from impassed living. Other goals of the experiential therapist are to promote congruence between the patient's intrapsychic realities and his manifest attitudes and behavior and to help him expand his feeling repertoire. Little attention is directed to alleviating symptoms or to improving the patient's social adjustment.

When diagnostic inquiry is bypassed and treatment is based on the therapist's advance assumptions of what his patients need, some patients may be exposed to a group experience that will not meet their specific therapeutic needs and that may, indeed, be harmful. This problem, though by no means limited to practitioners of existential psychotherapy, is well illustrated in their reports. The nature, origin, and history of each patient's disturbance are not investigated; instead, it is assumed that he will benefit from communing, interpreting, valuing, being spoken to truthfully, and the like. But, truthfulness in expression, for instance, is not likely to improve the interpersonal functioning of the person who is insensitive to the feelings of others. It is necessary at times to withhold information of a sensitive nature from group members who tend to be destructively truthful with one another. Suicidal reactions have been reported in patients who were informed by co-patients that they were latent schizophrenics or latent homosexuals. Full and conscious participation in the process of existence is not desirable for those persons in whom it arouses intolerable impulses and anxieties.

These are a few illustrations of the neglect or damage that a patient may sustain when his problem is viewed through the prism of the therapist's blanket assumptions rather than being studied. Such assumptions, whether or not they are derived from a philosophical system of thought, are not applicable to all patients and may interfere with the meeting of their particular therapeutic needs.

An exclusive focus on immediate experiencing (here-and-now) prevents the full mobilization of regressive states and makes it impossible to deal with the patient's primitive maturational needs. Controlled regression is essential for the resolution of patterns of maladaptation that originated in early-life situations.

Transactional Group Psychotherapy

Eric Berne, who introduced this approach, has referred to it as (1) a "happy remedy" for the unsuitability of psychoanalysis for conditions other than the transference neuroses, (2) an effective procedure in a transference neurosis when psychoanalysis, the treatment of choice, is not available, and (3) an appropriate forerunner of other procedures, being more general than any of them and overlapping with analytic and existential therapies at late stages.

Initially the transactional therapist focuses on loosening up resistances—the troublesome games the patient plays in the group sessions. After the patient becomes symptom-free, resistances may be analyzed, but the uncovering of the cause of his problems and of unconscious material is not stressed. It is hypothesized that the patient, by learning to control his free energy, becomes capable of shifting his authentic self from one ego state to another by an act of will. External stimuli are first relied on to accomplish such shifts, but, as treatment progresses, they are made more and more autonomously. Authenticity in social behavior is stressed.

The transactional group therapist accepts patients in many diagnostic categories. They are picked at random, with a view to forming as heterogeneous a group as possible. Rapid improvement and results as stable as those achieved through other approaches are claimed—especially in borderline cases, for which the treatment seems to be designed. Patients are reported to express confidence in the method. It is also claimed that the transactional approach is easily learned.

The goal of the treatment is to cure the patient—for example, as Berne states, to "transform schizophrenics into nonschizophrenics"—and all techniques at the therapist's disposal are used to effect a cure as expeditiously as possible.

The transactional group therapist appears to work for personality maturation, primarily by addressing himself to Step 3. The significance of Steps 1 and 2 is impossible to determine, but the use of techniques for facilitating deep transference is not described. The gratification needs of the patient are identified but not distinguished from maturational needs.

The playful character of the presentations reported may obscure the development of serious relationships. The crucial question is whether, in the course of the clever games they engage in, the patients and the therapist come to develop real feelings for one another. These feelings are indispensable for the maturation of the pre-oedipal personality.

Adaptational Approach

Broadly representative of much group treatment conducted on a supportive level in outpatient as well as institutional settings is the practical approach detailed by Johnson. Patients are helped to overcome uncomfortable and distressing manifestations of emotional illness through understanding of the anxieties they develop in group situations as a defense and protection against the dangers of close relationships. They are also helped to "practice new methods of adaptation," initially in the group sessions and later in their regular social relationships. The therapist does not attempt to remove deep-seated conflicts or to change the basic personality.

Neurotic and psychotic adults are treated in separate groups; a major criterion in the selection of the members of a group is the patient's ability to tolerate anxiety. Children, adolescents, juvenile delinquents, and geriatric patients are among the other subjects with whom this group-oriented model is employed.

The group therapist is an authority figure. He maintains control in the sessions, by active measures when necessary. He refrains from doing individual therapy in the group. He stimulates mutual analysis of the maladaptive behavior observed and encourages the ventilation and recognition of hostility. In the process of clearing away hostility, he serves as the group's scapegoat but does not attempt to work through the hostility completely. The precipitation of psychotic behavior in the group sessions is carefully avoided.

Goals, concretely formulated in advance, vary with the type of patients treated but are in all cases moderate: to improve reality-testing, promote socialization, foster awareness of how feelings are related to anxiety and behavior, and motivate patients for additional psychotherapy on a group or individual basis. The therapist strives to provide a learning-relearning experience that enables the group members to perceive the similarities between their maladaptive behavior in the treatment sessions and their habitual behavior with their life associates.

These general goals are applied in a restrictive manner in groups of psychotic patients. In long-term therapy, psychotics are permitted to become more dependent on one another and on the therapist. Specific goals for a group of psychotically ill patients are the strengthening of defenses, provision of support and dependency, and increase in repression.

This supportive approach is illustrative of the traditional group therapy programs at many mental hospitals, although the practitioners do not invariably lead their groups in an authoritarian and directive manner. Reports indicate that many of these groups are too large to permit much patient-to-patient interplay.

Undeniably, such groups perform a practical function, enabling the patient to achieve more comfortable control of his feelings and behavior. His adjustment to his present environment is improved, and his symptoms may be temporarily alleviated.

An attempt may be made to control transference and deal with common transference resistances. Maladaptive defenses are recognized, and some maturational needs are inadvertently met. Common bonds of interest develop, and feelings of isolation are reduced by the socializing effects of the group sessions.

But the results achieved are not usually self-sustaining. There is no assurance that the postpsychotic patient will not fall apart again after the group experience ends. Since the working through—emotional *un*learning —of his deep-seated patterns of maladaptation is not attempted, he is likely to revert to them in stressful circumstances. By and large, therefore, the changes effected cannot be equated with personality growth to maturation.

Psychodrama

This multifaceted procedure, introduced in 1925, has been employed in a variety of settings with children, adolescents, and adults. The use of this approach in marital counseling is also reported.

As formulated by J. L. Moreno in the context of his theories of role behavior and group structure, psychodrama requires a large staff and an elaborate format for the directed acting out of problems, but modified versions are employed by practitioners applying other theories, including psychoanalytic concepts. Some elements or techniques of psychodrama, such as role-playing, enter into the contemporary crop of procedures, which also borrow from Moreno's terminology. Moreno and Kipper characterize psychodrama as an elaborate form of encounter, the scientific exploration of the truth by dramatic methods, and the depth therapy of the group.

The acting out of immediately pressing problems or past situations is based on the principles of therapeutic interaction, spontaneity, catharsis, and reality-testing. Five instruments are described: the group (as audience and participants), the patient-protagonist, the stage, auxiliary egos (other group or staff members playing assigned roles), and the director (the therapist). Numerous techniques are employed, some of them to stimulate spontaneity of body and in action.

Psychodrama is reported to benefit persons with psychological and social problems and related somatic disturbances. Among the problems specified are psychomotor disturbances, such as tics, stuttering, and bedwetting; marital maladjustments; and inhibitions in self-expression. Psychodrama is employed with hospitalized schizophrenic patients.

The goals of the psychodramatist are to help people express themselves with greater ease, to structure internal and external experiences, and to bring forth their thoughts and feelings in structured form. An unstated goal appears to be the stimulation of spontaneity and creativity.

Some reports on this procedure suggest that emotional growth does occur, but the goals to which it is addressed do not encompass the notion of producing the mature personality. No distinction is made between gratifying a patient and helping him to mature. Dramatic experience and encounter are therapeutic only in the sense of providing some needed gratification. The psychological needs of the patient in a regressed condition are not met.

In describing the structuring of a psychodrama, Moreno and Kipper point out that

by forcing the protagonists to stick to actualities, he [the director] warms them up to present the facts directly and to express their actual experiences.

The failure to permit random behavior in the treatment setting may serve to foreclose the full development and integration of the personality. The capacity to use one's own initiative freely is an important attribute of the emotionally mature individual. Procedures that force the patient to comply with specific instructions and that do not provide him with opportunities to express himself freely or to develop awareness of the pressure of self-demand are essentially driving rather than growth therapies.

Group-Centered Psychotherapy

This short-term procedure, introduced by followers of Carl Rogers, corresponds to the client-centered method of individual counseling and is widely applied in a variety of educational, social, and industrial settings. Initially, this nondirective and nonclinical approach was employed with maladjusted and neurotic children, adolescents, and adults, but its use with more disturbed patients, including chronic schizophrenics, has recently been reported.

Little attention is paid to diagnosis. It is hypothesized that the same psychotherapeutic principles apply to normal, neurotic, and psychotic persons. However, hostile or aggressive persons are excluded from these groups on the grounds that they might threaten the climate of safety and acceptance that the therapist strives to maintain.

The group members are not viewed as objects of treatment but as potentially adequate and responsible persons who became maladjusted by excluding significant experiences from awareness and by failing to value and integrate all aspects of the self. The therapist assumes that unconditional positive regard, communicated to the members

genuinely and sensitively, will enable them to deal constructively with their problems.

Reconstruction of the perceptual field of the group member or client is regarded as the therapeutic task. His mind is not directed into particular channels, nor is he provided with interpretations. Assuming the client's own frame of reference and paraphrasing the content of his communications, the therapist clarifies the feelings expressed and consistently conveys acceptance, empathic understanding, and respect (Step 2). Transference attitudes are not distinguished from other affect-laden expressions. No attempt is made to uncover or explain the conflicts that underlie problematic behavior.

The goals sought through this procedure are to help the group member achieve a more realistic perception of himself and to enhance his self-esteem, capacity for self-direction, openness to experience, and ability to cope with stressful situations. Significant changes in personality, in attitudes about the self and others, and in behavior are claimed.

Rogerian postulates on personality organization resemble those of the Sullivanian school of psychiatry, notes Glad. The practitioner of group-centered psychotherapy—in his nonjudgmental concern with the phenomenological world of the client, his commitment to direct person-to-person encounter, and his open reflection of the feelings and attitudes he is experiencing and may verbalize when they persist—functions in a manner similar to that of the existential therapist.

People who are exposed to this approach secure a great deal of emotional release. The climate maintained in the group is particularly appealing to persons who were subjected to discipline and domination early in life and who greatly resented it. It also appeals to those who crave freedom from certain immediate personalities. The authoritarian personality is not likely to benefit from the experience, but it has been recommended for persons who have democratic attitudes and some ability to maintain understanding relationships with others.

Some degree of personality change can be achieved through this approach. The communication of understanding and acceptance serves to meet maturational and other psychological needs and leads to functional improvements. However, the treatment is directed to relatively limited goals. It does not provide the long-term psychological ingredients that are essential for emotional maturation of the individual with deep-seated problems.

Since patients are not diagnosed and are accepted on the assumption that their problems are psychological, there is some risk of mistreatment.

Behavioral Group Psychotherapy

Behavior therapy in groups encompasses a broad range of short-term procedures that are grounded in the premise that acts are more potent than thoughts and words for influencing human responses. The desensitization and assertive-training procedures focused on here were reported by Lazarus.

Group desensitization treatment, first applied to phobic patients, is now employed in a wide range of disorders, such as sexual impotence, frigidity, and, in a modified form, chronic anxiety. Psychotic patients are specifically excluded.

Various conditioning and anxiety-eliminating techniques based on modern learning theories are applied in homogeneous groups. These techniques are flexibly combined with didactic discussions and with techniques borrowed from other schools of psychotherapy, whose explanations are, however, rejected. Therapy is mainly in, not by, the group, primarily through patient-to-therapist communication. Results are evaluated in terms of the number of maladaptive habits that have been eliminated.

The therapist's attitudes in the desensitization group are didactic, sympathetic, and nonjudgmental. But in the assertive-training group he functions by and large as a participant-observer. Training in self-assertiveness implements the hypothesis that failure to assert oneself is in most cases a manifestation of anxiety. It is assumed that frankness in verbalization and the spontaneous expression of basic feelings will improve the patient's interpersonal functioning.

The group conducted for this purpose is small, carefully composed, and homogeneous, and the course of treatment usually covers from 15 to 20 sessions. The therapist opens the first meeting with an address on the art of relaxation, and preliminary training in relaxation follows. In later sessions, when productive interchanges are not going on among the group members, the therapist usually lectures. The techniques he employs may include open discussion, role-playing, modeling, behavior rehearsals, and psychodrama. A whole session is occasionally devoted to the needs of one member.

The goal of the desensitization procedure is primarily symptomatic improvement. By changing habits deemed to be undesirable, the therapist also endeavors to eliminate suffering and to increase the patient's capacity for productive work and pleasurable interpersonal relationships. It is claimed that the rate and extent of improvement achieved are superior to those produced through other procedures. Secondary benefits reported include changes in personality and self-concept, increased self-esteem, and the development of friendships among the group members.

The goals of assertive training are the acquisition of adaptive responses and the extinction of maladaptive responses. Quantitative measurement of the results achieved is more difficult in assertive training than in the desensitization procedure, but behavioral improvement in nearly all the participants is claimed. The majority of patients report that the improved modes of behavior are transferred to life situations and that they are able to develop more satisfying and enduring relationships with their associates.

The behavioral therapist exerts pressure on patients to change specific patterns of behavior. He secures improvements in functioning by extirpating maladaptations. The psychopathological forces in which these overt patterns are rooted are not investigated or dealt with.

Verbalization is permitted, but the therapist does not work for the expression of all impulses. The question thus arises: What is done with impulses that are not put into words? A person who is put under pressure to behave in ways not consistent with his impulses to action may find self-damaging ways of expressing those impulses. In patients who are not properly selected for these procedures, psychosomatic problems may develop, notably in those who have strong tendencies to repress and suppress their impulses. Patients with impulse disorders are more likely to respond favorably to this punitive approach, but they may later require treatment for a neurotic condition.

Some investigators report that personality *is* dealt with in behavior therapy. The crucial issue is whether the therapist does so sufficiently to prevent some part of the personality from becoming inhibited and repressed.

The value of this approach is that it is short-term and rapidly achieves demonstrable results. Reports do not delineate the possible long-term costs of the short-term improvement.

Gestalt Therapy

The experiential group approach developed from Gestalt psychology by Frederick Perls and his associates revolves around a flexible set of rules and games. These techniques are designed, according to Levitsky and Perls, to help the members of the group assimilate emotional and other psychological experiences with the active coping attitudes that characterize healthful feelings. They are influenced to stay with feelings they have a strong urge to dispel. Much attention is paid to physiological manifestations.

Rules are introduced as a way to unify thoughts with feelings, to heighten awareness, and to facilitate maturation. Communication in the present tense is encouraged; the past is not dealt with, other than to delineate present personality structure. The games, proposed by the therapist to meet individual or group needs, represent a commentary on social behavior and stress the polarity of vital functioning. For example, a need for withdrawal from contact is respected, but the patient may be asked to withdraw in fantasy to a place or situation where he feels secure, to describe it with feelings, and then to return to the group. The use of an awareness continuum is designed to guide the participants away from explanations and speculations to the bedrock of their experiences. Some games have a definite interpretive element, but their primary function is to move patients from the "why" to the "what" and "how" of experience.

The goals of the Gestalt therapist are to promote feelings, to prevent their avoidance, and to help the participants function in a more integrated way. It is claimed that group members become more self-confident and that the group experience increases their capacity for autonomous functioning.

The Gestalt procedure is focused exclusively on maladaptive behavior, and the therapist deals with it primarily by trying to knock out inappropriate patterns. No attempt is made to work them through or to meet the maturational needs that uphold them. The practitioner deliberately refrains from arousing old personality problems. Temporary improvements in feelings are effected by meeting present functional needs. Constructive modification of the current personality structure is sacrificed for short-term benefits.

This form of group therapy may benefit a patient who suffers from low drive. The stimulus of the situation will increase his drive intensity. But exposure of a high-drive patient to this procedure is contraindicated. The experience may traumatize him and provoke suicidal behavior.

Bio-Energetic Group Therapy

Alexander Lowen's procedure involves the body in the psychotherapeutic process and apparently does so more directly and more fully than other approaches that entail body activity and physical contact between participants. Lowen refers to the procedure as a double-barreled approach that provides insight more convincingly than the use of words alone. Personality change is not regarded as valid until it is paralleled by improvements in the form, motility, and functioning of the body.

The variety of techniques employed include simple breathing exercises to facilitate the expression of feelings, manual manipulation to soften chronically spastic areas of the body, embracing, and other types of physical contact expressive of acceptance, reassurance, and support. The participants are taught simple ways of easing tensions. Bodily expression is analyzed and interpreted as a reflection of mental functioning. Verbal interchange goes on primarily in the context of these activities. Therapeutic strategies include encouragement of the venting of negative feelings before expressions of affection.

It is reported that the participants develop a feeling of unity and a respect for the body and the uniqueness of others and are directed to new sources of health and pleasure. Hysterical episodes, precipitated by intense emotional experiences, have been brought under control through bodily contact and physical expressions of reassurance.

The goal of bio-energetic group therapy is to facilitate personality change and unification through activation of healing forces on the deepest and most powerful level.

This method is oriented to personality integration, which is certainly an aspect of emotional maturity. The therapist deals primarily with maladaptations. Maturational needs may be met indirectly.

The chief beneficiary would appear to be the person whose mental and physical functioning are not harmoniously coordinated. Another value is the rapidity of the improvements achieved, which is encouraging to patients. Discouragement may follow later if they have serious problems.

The procedure runs the risk of being a repressive form of treatment. The encouragement given to one form of activity may lead to the suppression or repression of other forms. The mobilization of more psychological energy than a patient can discharge appropriately, leading to impulse acting out or even psychotic behavior, is another possibility.

Marathon Group Therapy

George Bach, who was associated with Frederick Stoller in the development of this procedure during the 1960's, refers to it as a psychological pressure cooker in which genuine emotions emerge as phony steam boils away. He also calls it a

practicum in authentic communication, based on freedom from social fears conventionally associated with transparency.

Group pressure is exploited to generate psychological intimacy as quickly as possible. Stoller refers to the approach as accelerated interaction.

Concentrating therapy into a single experience of a day or two, often over a weekend, the marathon is an outstanding example of the continuous, time-extended format. Both clinical and nonclinical settings are used. Some practitioners conduct marathons in their homes and press their wives into service as co-therapists. Follow-up sessions may be held. Some psychotherapists report the use of the marathon as a supplementary rather than a basic procedure.

Patients are selected on the basis of interest in self-actualization and in undergoing an intensive experience. Usually strangers are assembled, but specialized marathons for marital couples and other natural groups are reported. The participants may or may not be undergoing conventional psychotherapy.

The therapist actively sets the tone and pace for intimate encounter by any means at his disposal, including rejection of professional status and assumption of the patient role to engage in the mutual exploration of feelings. The orientation is ahistorical; the participants are encouraged to own up to and share their immediate feelings and to try out new ways of being in the group.

The goals, as stated by Bach, are to produce a change in orientation and to find new and more creative ways of dealing with old problems. Rapid changes in behavior are reported. It is claimed that the participants become more interested and involved with others, more honest, and less defensive. Behavioral breakthroughs have occurred, but their permanence is admittedly unknown.

The marathon is structured to arouse emotions quickly, thus generating instant intimacy among the participants. The therapist addresses himself primarily to patterns of maladaptive behavior. The procedure is calculated to overpower such patterns by exposing the assemblage to a new experience that has an intense emotional impact. The assumption that the overpowering of defenses can be therapeutic in the long run has yet to be confirmed, notes Yalom. Pending such confirmation, the procedure should be identified as an experiment in group process rather than as a psychotherapeutic method.

Lengthy and fatiguing experiences of this nature are contraindicated for patients with psychosomatic conditions, for those who are in a prepsychotic or postpsychotic state, for people with a strong suicidal disposition, and for those whose marriages are unstable.

Disclosures made to the author by participants in weekend marathons reveal their variable effects. First, some of the values reported: Commitment to the treatment offers the hope of an immediately helpful experience, and some who have undergone it have referred to it as both enjoyable and educational—enjoyable because it dispelled feelings of loneliness and because they derived some gratification from the instant intimacy with strangers; educational because the experience helped them become aware very quickly of their own interpersonal problems. The stimulus of the situation and the exposure to a battery of emotions aroused intense emotions in them. One consequence was that innate tendencies that are usually held in check were uncovered in a matter of hours. The participants were thus able to discover what attracted or disgusted them and whether they had suicidal tendencies, harbored murderous wishes, were easily seducible, etc. One woman characterized the marathon as a dramatic introduction to individual and group psychology.

Other informants have supplemented published reports of social and psychological damage sustained in one-shot marathons or encounters. The uninhibited communications that the marathons encourage often lead to impulsive behavior. To be sexually seductive or to permit oneself to be seduced without regard for the consequences is all too often regarded as operating in the spirit of the occasion.

On returning home after a marathon, a man who had committed himself in treatment to preserving a shaky marriage told his wife that he had felt pressure from several female participants to engage in sexual intercourse during the weekend. He was puzzled to observe how enraged his wife became. Another crisis in their relationship had to be dealt with in his long-term psychotherapy.

A woman whose promiscuous behavior in the past had caused her much unhappiness participated in a marathon, where she met a married man who complained that he had never enjoyed sexual intercourse. She responded forthwith to the challenge. Because their intimacy during the weekend proved to be mutually gratifying, they ended up by having an affair. The man obtained a divorce but refused to marry his new sexual partner on the grounds that they were socially incompatible. Thus, her impulsive behavior, besides causing her fresh unhappiness, led to the dissolution of the marriage of two other persons. In other cases, guilt over the sexual stimulation of the situation has precipitated psychotic episodes.

Self-destructive tendencies of which a person has no awareness can be unleashed in an emotional experience that is highly concentrated in time and pervaded by a built-in sense of intimacy. A man, after discussing his business affairs during a marathon, was stimulated to act on the advice of other participants and commit himself to a foolhardy investment. A few days later, given the opportunity to explore his motives and weigh the risks involved, he changed his mind. In the process of marshaling the pros and cons of the new venture, he recognized that his mounting emotional involvement in the weekend events had significantly dulled his judgment. A state of manic excitement had propelled him into a decision that a person of his astuteness would not otherwise have made.

Sensitivity Training (T-Groups)

A product of the laboratory training movement associated with the National Training Laboratory at Bethel, Maine, programs for sensitivity training in groups have burgeoned in recent years, thrusting themselves into a variety of community, educational, and industrial settings for many different purposes. The members of these relatively unstructured groups participate as learners and use their on-going interpersonal transactions as data in the learning process. As the use of the group setting for experiential learning has expanded and as group leaders or trainers have tended increasingly to concentrate on affective blocks to learning, the boundaries between training and therapy have become more and more diffuse. Gottschalk and Pattison have delineated many overlapping areas. Moreover, sensitivity training itself is a far from standardized procedure. Garwood has pointed out that what occurs in the T-groups

varies with their composition and *most especially with the trainer* [her emphasis].

T-groups are generally short-term, time-limited experiences, concentrated into a week or two, with the participants meeting several hours a day in a special setting. Sometimes the group begins during a weekend in a special setting and then continues in a series of meetings conducted in the participants' own community. Originally the group format was used for the first-hand study of group processes, but the early focus has broadened to encompass the study of the participants' conscious and preconscious behavior and their interpersonal functioning. Some T-group leaders encourage the reporting of dreams and fantasies. The number of techniques employed has increased; some T-group leaders employ nonverbal techniques, including body-contact activities. Role-playing may be engaged in for the purpose of increasing self-awareness.

By and large, the leaders of T-groups state that they are not conducting psychotherapy but are trying to promote personal growth or provide positive and creative emotional experiences for the participants in order to make them more effective in their work and other life activities.

The goals of sensitivity training programs, as formulated by Gottschalk and Pattison, are the heightening of interpersonal coping skills, the sharpening of interpersonal perceptions, and the imbuing of life experience with authenticity and greater self-awareness.

Sensitivity training in groups is of value for developing leadership skills and helping people become more perceptive of their own feelings and the feelings of others, provided they are well-defended and not unduly suggestible personalities. But such training is not universally beneficial, and a substantial number of cases of serious psychological damage caused by these experiences have been described in the literature. Reports call attention to two limitations in these programs: **(1)** No criteria for evaluating personality strengths are applied in the selection of the trainees. **(2)** Sensitivity training is mandatory in many organizations.

Kuehn and Crinella recommend the systematic exclusion of four types of persons: psychotics, characterological neurotics, persons with hysterical personality traits, and those who are in a crisis situation. These authors suggest that the usefulness of the procedure depends on the maturity, experience, and expertise of the T-group leader, his knowledge of diagnosis and treatment, and the availability of professional consultation, particularly when psychiatric first aid is required.

Encounter Groups

Thirteen years after J. L. Moreno referred to encounter as a meeting on the most intensive level of communication, his wife and associate, Zereka T. Moreno, remarked in 1969, "Everybody under many flags, is doing what we started." In the interim, a philosophical concept that had permeated relatively few systems of psychotherapy became an umbrella term sheltering a variety of innovative methods, which some mental health professionals refer to as the encounter movement. Firm differentiations among these methods, some of which have already been discussed, are not yet possible. Hence, some labels are used synonymously—for example, T-group and encounter group. As a rudimentary distinction, Yalom points out:

Generally encounter groups have no institutional backing, are far more unstructured, are more often led by untrained leaders, may rely more on physical contact and nonverbal exercises, and generally emphasize an experience, or getting "turned on," rather than change per se.

Encounter as a psychotherapeutic procedure encompasses the investigation of immediate emotions in a dramatically direct manner. In contrast to the long-established approach of establishing a relationship before beginning to work on a problem, encounter therapy relies on the efficacy of blunt honesty. Total reciprocity in the revelation of feelings is worked for through a variety of verbal and action techniques. Many diverse constructs are applied. Candidates for the experience are accepted without screening.

Development of the ability to be honest and open and to express warmth freely is among the values reported. It is also claimed that buried feelings are worked through. The limitations of the procedure are the lack of appropriate safeguards for people with serious disturbances and the stigma placed on emotional unresponsiveness.

The goals of encounter therapy are formulated in terms of personal growth—to promote physical and mental awareness of self and others and of social realities.

Various explanations have been advanced for the proliferation of encounter groups. It has been attributed to the overpopularization of group psychotherapy and to widespread cravings for self-discovery and intimacy among the psychologically sophisticated. Encounter groups also serve to counteract a pervasive sense of estrangement, alienation, and loss of personal identity, produced by the accelerating tempo of technological and sociological change.

In the phenomenal development of the encounter movement, the author also discerns evidence of public dissatisfaction with the practical dictates of the established psychotherapeutic approaches and their doubtful results in severe psychiatric conditions. The length and cost of traditional treatment have stimulated a search for short cuts and guaranteed results—preferably through a less rigorous treatment experience than that oriented to personality maturation.

More specifically, encounter groups may evince a reaction to the limitations of the classical psychoanalytic method. Modifications of the orthodox psychoanalytic situation reach their extreme in the encounter groups. Instead of the dyad, for example, the groups engage as many as 20 persons. There are many variations in the number of group leaders and participants and in their modes of functioning. However, the initially directive and nonrevealing posture of the analyst and the cooperative, self-revealing attitude of the analysand are definitely renounced for mutuality in interchange. The careful control of regression, to permit the arousal and gradual working through of emotional blockages, is abdicated for more

dramatic breakthroughs and occasional peak experiences through direct onslaughts on the defense system. Instead of being limited to verbal communication, the encounter groups sanction nonverbal communication, including physical contact. Diverse activities and modes of communication are studied for their possible therapeutic effects.

Whether such experiences are harmful or helpful depends on the immediate emotional state of the participant. He is exposed to a great deal of stimulation. If he needs it and can assimilate it, the encounter will have a positive impact. If he does not need such excitement or cannot tolerate it in the heady dosages offered, the encounter is, from a therapeutic standpoint, a waste of time and the participant runs the risk of incurring damaging effects.

In general, these experiences appear to be more gratifying than therapeutic or educational. In the participant who is undergoing conventional psychotherapy, they may increase his resistance to working consistently to resolve his problems. Desires to take the easy way out are stimulated.

CURRENT STRENGTHS AND WEAKNESSES

The scientific importance of a psychotherapeutic procedure is determined by the type of problem it is addressed to and its effectiveness in clearing up that problem. As already indicated, there is a pressing need for a serious evaluation of group procedures in these terms, but outcome research has not yielded this information and is not likely to do so for some time.

One of the major shortcomings highlighted by a study of the professional literature is the lack of distinction between the group approaches that are designed to provide the patient with the type of experience he needs to become healthy and mature and those group approaches that are addressed to needs that have an immediate gratification value. Every procedure needs to be evaluated from this standpoint: Does it primarily offer a gratifying experience or one that will help the patient mature?

When this elementary distinction is made,

it becomes evident that what is really new about the procedural innovations that have become the object of controversy are the forms of gratification they provide. Feeling better in the present is often equated with characterological growth. But the success or failure of these experiences depends on their ability to produce long-range results.

Reports on the majority of the procedures reviewed suggest that contemporary practice is more involved in shoring up the personality at the premorbid level of adjustment and in teaching adaptive patterns of behavior than in working for self-sustaining change at a higher level. The procedures that are addressed to significant gains require an undue expenditure of time and effort to clear up the more serious of the oedipal-type conditions, and they fail rather consistently to clear up pre-oedipal problems. In fact, some of the approaches addressed to ambitious goals are not generally applied to patients with severe forms of mental illness. No procedure has demonstrated superiority in cases of this nature.

A moot issue among analytic group therapists is whether to adhere to the operational principles of individual psychoanalytic therapy or to extract as much therapeutic leverage as possible from group process. Many of these practitioners express their personal preference for one theoretical approach or the other, but their clinical reports do not demonstrate that better results can be secured from the approach they prefer.

The large majority of group therapists address themselves primarily to maladaptive interpersonal behavior. In one way or another, they help the patient to recognize it and to master better patterns of behavior. The acquisition of new action patterns, however, does not liberate the patient from the compulsive grip of the old patterns. Unless these patterns are freed of their emotional charge—unless they are emotionally unlearned through the solution of the underlying problem—the patient will continue to revert to them.

Each group procedure is based on a different assumption of the patient's therapeutic needs. To cite a few examples: The analytic group psychotherapist assumes that the way to help the patient is to reawaken the fundamental problem or conflict in the treatment situation and to focus on early as well as present growth needs. Practitioners who reject the historical approach assume that all the patient requires is to learn to express himself more honestly, or to coordinate his present psychic and physical functioning, to develop more awareness of his feelings, to learn to stay with what he feels, to relate authentically to others, or to have powerful and concentrated emotional experience that will unmask his defenses, etc. The behavioral therapist assumes that change entails desensitization of the patient. The T-group leader assumes that the members of his group need to increase their sensitivity to feelings.

The assumptions on which the present approaches are based often diverge to the point of contradiction, but what each strives to accomplish is a potential contribution to emotional maturity. When the treatment achieves its objective, the patient has acquired some attributes of the mature personality.

APPROACHES TO SPECIFICITY

Group psychotherapy has definitely emerged from the period when its acceptance as an effective mode of treatment was in doubt. The question, "Can it help a patient improve?" has been answered in the affirmative. However, the results obtained through its indiscriminate use have aroused much dissatisfaction. Clinical experience has amply demonstrated that the efficiency of the group psychotherapeutic process hinges on the degree of specificity achieved in relating the procedure applied to the patient's condition. Little is accomplished through haphazard use of the group setting; patients do not secure appreciable benefits simply because they are treated together. Desirable change is a function of helping each group member deal with his particular problems. Consequently, there has been a concerted effort in recent years to secure more specific results. In the process of transforming what was all too often regarded as a panacea into a precise instrument, clinicians discovered that it could be refined to produce different results.

Group psychotherapy thus appears to be thrusting toward the development of a larger number of dissimilar procedures that will influence patients in different ways. This trend is very desirable. If the group psychotherapist is committed to help people become effectively functioning individuals, whatever their problems and stage of life, many different procedures are required. But the crucial issue is not the number of approaches at his disposal, but which approach is the best to use in each situation and for each purpose.

Clinical Experimentation

The 1960's ushered in a period of great therapeutic creativity. Along with efforts to increase the effectiveness of the established approaches and to make them less interminable, there was much experimental activity, which is continuing into the present decade. The fact that some of this activity has been misrepresented to the public as psychotherapy has stimulated negative attitudes toward experimentation per se.

Psychotherapy by its very nature requires experimentation, which was vital to the development of psychological treatment and is the key to further progress. However, the practice of psychotherapy does not readily lend itself to objective evaluation. The treatment process entails confidential relationships, subjective and objective assessment by the same person, and freedom to experiment as and when necessary to achieve an immediate objective. This state of affairs makes it difficult to determine at times whether one is engaging in responsible psychotherapy or in irresponsible experimentation. Evidence of the latter occasionally comes to the fore, and efforts are being made to lay a foundation for responsible experimentation.

General Guidelines. Two basic principles of clinical experimentation that the author recommends relate to mutuality and the selection of appropriate subjects.

1. In responsible experimentation, the patient is diagnosed, and his specific problem is carefully studied. On the basis of the diagnosis and with the goals in mind, a plan is formulated for working with him. The patient is then informed what the therapist is striving to accomplish and what results can be expected. The patient is not exposed to an experimental procedure unless he consents to it; his wishes in the matter are respected. It is also made clear to the patient that, if the attempt to help him does not yield the desired results, the therapist will at least explain to him why the failure occurred. This principle is applicable in group as well as in individual treatment.

2. The patients with whom it is most appropriate to experiment are those who do not respond to the established approaches. These approaches are effective in dealing with most of the conditions associated with oedipal development and with run-of-the-mill problems for which people solicit professional help; hence, little is gained from experimenting in such cases. The subjects with whom experimentation is justifiable and most likely to be scientifically rewarding are those with more severe disturbances.

Experimentation with Schizophrenia. The main challenge in the field of psychotherapy lies in the development of more effective approaches to the pre-oedipal disorders, especially schizophrenia. Despite the fact that many cases of schizophrenia appear to have more than one cause, the disorder invariably testifies to basic defects in the maturation of the personality. The author regards this condition as psychologically reversible in principle. In his experience, the schizophrenic patient does not respond on a long-range basis to individual or group psychotherapeutic experiences that are primarily gratifying. Quite the contrary. Such experiences tend to produce psychotic episodes —which is one reason why many therapists conducting treatment on an outpatient basis are reluctant to treat the schizophrenic patient. If the procedure employed does not contribute to the reversal of the illness, it is likely to have more gratification than maturational value. The response of the schizophrenic patient is, in a sense, the ultimate test of the procedure's effectiveness in dealing with fundamental personality problems. Since relatively few group therapists work with schizophrenic patients on other than a supportive level, the scientific importance of experimentation of the nature just suggested is obvious.

Schizophrenic patients do not respond to a purely neutral approach. They need an emotionally responsive therapist, one who can tolerate the patient's emotions and feed them back to him in a controlled, goal-oriented manner.

The schizophrenic patient's individual treatment was once thought to call for two or more analysts. If the first analyst was a man, the patient was usually transferred at some stage of their relationship to a woman, and vice versa. But even with a change in analysts, emotionally responsive though they might be, they could not, in the dyad, meet the schizophrenic's special need to experience different feelings simultaneously. The multiple charge of member-to-member verbal interchanges in the group setting makes an important contribution to the meeting of this maturational need. More difficult to meet in the shared treatment experience is the schizophrenic's high-urgency need for the adequate release of aggressive energy; his co-patients are not happy to hear how much he hates them.

Combined Treatment

Present evidence suggests that what will be most effective in the treatment of pre-oedipal disorders is a highly specific combination of individual and group treatment based on psychoanalytic principles, understanding of personality development, and incorporation of meritorious techniques of various schools of practice. To resolve pre-oedipal conditions through the exclusive instrumentality of group psychotherapy would be exceedingly difficult; in the group setting the therapist does not have as exquisite control of all stimuli, including his own responses, as he has in the one-to-one relationship. The patient's group therapeutic experience usually follows a period of individual treatment, during which he works on his bipersonal problems; but in some instances, generally when there are special transference difficulties, the patient begins treatment in a group. Properly timed, the shared treatment experience is particularly valuable for the

severely disturbed person who is totally unable to benefit from group association, such as the postpsychotic college student who told the author:

I've never known how to tolerate, feel close to, feel comfortable with, find myself accepted by, feel non-self-conscious in groups and group activity with my peers.

Supplementary Treatment

Although the new short-term procedures are not corrective per se, their specific values can be exploited when they coincide with maturational needs that are uncovered in patients undergoing long-term psychotherapy. For instance, a person who suddenly experiences a great hunger for human companionship may benefit from an encounter-group experience. For one who is totally divorced from his feelings, the T-group or marathon may serve as a springboard for their arousal and expression.

The use of these supplementary measures is likely to increase, but the practitioner who recommends them to patients needs to recognize the possibly psychonoxious effects of the experience on a person who demonstrates a strong need to withdraw from people. The advance safeguard, of course, is study of the patient's current functioning and understanding of why he says he needs additional stimulation to feel more deeply or to make his life more interesting and exciting. The patient's reaction to his initial venture in instant intimacy also needs to be investigated. If the experience does not lead to emotional withdrawal, loss of identity, sense of alienation, or similar signs of severe regression, and if the patient wishes to repeat the venture in accelerated emotional education, it will probably stimulate further improvement.

CONCLUSION

The introduction of community psychiatry is greatly enhancing the reliance on group psychotherapy as the most available approach for producing the socially effective individual. To meet this additional responsibility, the present armamentarium of emotional-impact instruments needs to be substantially refined and scanned closely for their specific therapeutic and antitherapeutic effects. Dissatisfaction with all psychotherapeutic procedures will continue until they achieve significant results more rapidly. New ideas for group formation will probably emerge in this era of therapeutic creativity, and they need to be studied, not rejected out of hand. No one knows all the answers today. A demonstrably superior approach may emerge for dealing with the enormous range of psychologically reversible disease states and states of dis-ease to which human beings are prone throughout the life cycle. This superior method is conceivable, but it is not on the horizon today. At present, the key to fulfilling the promise that group psychotherapy has held out to the public is more precise wielding of the instruments it has forged.

REFERENCES

Bach, G. The marathon group: intensive practice of intimate interaction. In *Group Therapy Today*, p. 301, H. M. Ruitenbeek, editor. Atherton Press, New York, 1969.

Berne, E. *Principles of Group Treatment*. Oxford University Press, New York, 1966.

Blatner, H..A. Patient selection in group therapy. *Voices*, *4:* No. 3, 90, 1968.

Corsini, R. J. *Methods of Group Psychotherapy*. McGraw-Hill, New York, 1957.

Dreikurs, R. Group psychotherapy from the point of view of Adlerian psychology. In *Group Therapy Today*, p. 37, H. M. Ruitenbeek, editor, Atherton Press, New York, 1969.

Foulkes, S. H. *Therapeutic Group Analysis*. International Universities Press, New York, 1965.

Foulkes, S. H., and Anthony, E. J. *Group Psychotherapy: The Psychoanalytic Approach*, ed. 2. Penguin Books, Baltimore, 1965.

Frank, J. D., and Powdermaker, F. B. Group psychotherapy. In *American Handbook of Psychiatry*, vol. 2, p. 1362, S. Arieti, editor, Basic Books, New York, 1959.

Garwood, D. S. The significance and dynamics of sensitivity training programs. Int. J. Group Psychother., *17:* 457, 1967.

Glad, D. D. *Operational Values in Psychotherapy*. Oxford University Press, New York, 1959.

Goldman, G. D. Some applications of Harry Stack Sullivan's theories to group psychotherapy. In *Group Therapy Today*. p. 58, H. M. Ruitenbeek, editor. Atherton Press, New York, 1969.

Goldstein, A. P., Heller, K., and Sechrest, L. B. *Psychotherapy and the Psychology of Behavior Change*. John Wiley, New York, 1966.

Gottschalk, L. A., and Pattison, E. M. Psychiatric perspectives on T-groups and the laboratory movement: an overview. Amer. J. Psychiat., *126:* 823, 1969.

Hobbs, N. Group-centered psychotherapy. In *Client-Centered Therapy*, p. 278, C. R. Rogers, editor. Houghton-Mifflin, Boston, 1951.

Hora, T. Existential therapy and group psychotherapy. In *Basic Approaches to Group Psychotherapy and Group Counseling*, p. 109, G. M. Gazda, editor. Charles C Thomas, Springfield, Ill., 1968.

Johnson, J. A. *Group Therapy: A Practical Approach*. McGraw-Hill, New York, 1963.

Klapman, J. W. *Group Psychotherapy: Theory and Practice*, ed. 2. Grune & Stratton, New York, 1959.

Kuehn, J. L., and Crinella, F. M. Sensitivity training: interpersonal "overkill" and other problems. Amer. J. Psychiat., *126:* 840, 1969.

Lazarus, A. A. Behavior therapy in groups. In *Basic Approaches to Group Psychotherapy and Group Counseling*, p. 149, G. M. Gazda, editor. Charles C Thomas, Springfield, Ill., 1968.

Levitsky, A., and Perls, F. The rules and games of Gestalt therapy. In *Group Therapy Today*, p. 221, H. M. Ruitenbeek, editor. Atherton Press, New York, 1969.

Lieberman, M. A., Lakin, M., and Whitaker, D. S. Problems and potential of psychoanalytic and group-dynamic theories for group psychotherapy. Int. J. Group Psychother., *19:* 131, 1969.

Lowen, A. Bio-energetic group therapy. In *Group Therapy Today*, p. 279, H. M. Ruitenbeek, editor. Atherton Press, New York, 1969.

Malone, T. P., Whitaker, W. C., Warentkin, J., and Feder, R. Rational and nonrational psychotherapy. Amer. J. Psychother., *15:* 212, 1961.

Moreno, J. L. Scientific foundations of group psychotherapy. In *Group Psychotherapy and Group Function*. p. 242, M. Rosenbaum and M. Berger, editors. Basic Books, New York, 1963.

Moreno, J. L., and Kipper, D. A. Group psychodrama and community-centered counseling. In *Basic Approaches to Group Psychotherapy and Group Counseling*, p. 27, G. M. Gazda, editor. Charles C Thomas, Springfield, Ill., 1968.

Moreno, Z. T. Moreneans, the heretics of yesterday are the orthodoxy of today. Group Psychother., *22:* 1, 1969.

Mullan, H. Status denial in group psychoanalysis. In *Group Psychotherapy and Group Function*, p. 591, M. Rosenbaum and M. Berger, editors. Basic Books, New York, 1963.

Parloff, M. B. Analytic group psychotherapy. In *Modern Psychoanalysis*, p. 492, J. Marmor, editor. Basic Books, New York, 1968.

Rose, S. Horney concepts in group psychotherapy.

In *Group Therapy Today*, p. 49, H. M. Ruitenbeek, editor. Atherton Press, New York, 1969.

Rosenbaum, M. Group psychotherapy and psychodrama. In *Handbook of Clinical Psychology*,
p. 1254, B. B. Wolman, editor. McGraw-Hill,
New York, 1965.

Rueveni, U., and Speck, R. V. Using encounter
group techniques in the treatment of the social
network of the schizophrenic. Int. J. Group
Psychother., *19:* 495, 1969.

Slavson, S. R. *A Textbook in Analytic Group Psychotherapy*. International Universities Press,
New York, 1964.

Spitz, H. H., and Kopp, S. B. Multiple psychotherapy. In *Group Psychotherapy and Group
Function*, p. 391, M. Rosenbaum and M. Berger, editors. Basic Books, New York, 1963.

Spotnitz, H. The borderline schizophrenic in
group psychotherapy. Int. J. Group Psychother., *7:* 155, 1957.

Spotnitz, H. *The Couch and the Circle: A Story of
Group Psychotherapy*. Alfred A. Knopf, New
York, 1961.

Spotnitz, H. *Modern Psychoanalysis of the Schizophrenic Patient*. Grune & Stratton, New York,
1969.

Stoller, F. H. Accelerated interaction: a time-
limited approach based on the brief, intensive
group. Int. J. Group Psychother., *18:* 220,
1968.

Thomas, G. W. Group psychotherapy: review of
the present literature. Psychosom. Med., *5:*
166, 1943.

Whitaker, D. S., and Lieberman, M. A. *Psychotherapy through the Group Process*. Atherton
Press, New York, 1964.

Wolf, A. Psychoanalysis in groups. In *Basic Ap-
proaches to Group Psychotherapy and Group
Counseling*, p. 80, G. M. Gazda, editor.
Charles C Thomas, Springfield, Ill., 1968.

Yalom, I. *The Theory and Practice of Group Psychotherapy*. Basic Books, New York, 1970.

2

Combined Individual and Group Psychotherapy

Toby B. Bieber, Ph.D.

INTRODUCTION

Group therapy is now an established way of treating various psychiatric conditions; it is used by professionals with different backgrounds, points of view, and methods. The diversity is not surprising. Group therapy has a family tree branched with the intellectual heritage and innovations of many distinguished ancestors—philosophy, social psychology, medicine, psychiatry, psychoanalysis, sociology, cultural anthropology, education, and more.

Combined individual and group psychotherapy has no special history of its own. It emerged as a form of treatment when the newly evolving group methods began to engage the interest of receptive psychoanalysts and clinicians who had been well-grounded in individual psychodynamics. They started to experiment with groups and soon found that, for many patients, the combination of group and individual sessions offered important therapeutic advantages. With few exceptions, psychoanalytic principles were followed. The management of group sessions varied with the clinical decisions and personal style of the therapist, but individual treatment was conducted in accordance with the classical psychoanalytic model, or it was modified to what has come to be known as psychoanalytically oriented psychotherapy. The modifications have been more technical than conceptual. The frequency of individual sessions may now vary

from one to five sessions a week, according to individual or situational requirements. The use of the analytic couch may be eliminated with patients who require vis-à-vis communication and contact. Increasingly, more active analytic participation has displaced impassivity and remoteness.

In the 1940's there was an upsurge of interest in small-group behavior by social scientists, who began to contribute systematic work on group dynamics. They quickly caught the attention of therapists who were treating patients in groups and who were looking for theoretical explications. As the field of group therapy developed, the individual patient was sometimes seemingly lost in the group, and the emphasis on group dynamics has often occupied too central a position.

It is a sociological commonplace that the group is more than an aggregation of individuals; intermember reactions and communication, verbal and nonverbal, contribute to the group dimension. But unlike any other kind of artificially constructed small group, the therapy group aims primarily to reveal and examine, in a public situation, usually private thoughts and reactions, especially those linked to individually and heterogeneously experienced psychopathology. The group atmosphere, group cohesion, pressures toward conformity, group resistance, and other parameters of small-group organization are surely important problems in group theory and in techniques of leading

35

therapy groups, but reconstructive therapy, is concerned with the vicissitudes of individual patients, not with groups per se.

In stressing the role of the individual, the author, in 1957, wrote:

> The fallacy of "group mind" is well recognized; the fallacy of "group" therapy is less recognized. To ascribe to a group the psychological laws of the individual is a kind of anthropomorphism which is misleading.

As a way of maintaining the precedence of individual treatment goals, group therapy may be usefully thought of as therapy in a group. If one follows the principle that the therapeutic aim is to facilitate the treatment of psychiatric disorders in each individual patient, efforts at improving group techniques will not then be side-tracked into a sociological emphasis on group phenomenology.

THEORETICAL ASPECTS

Combined therapy is a unitary process consisting of dyadic and group sessions conducted by the same therapist. The occasional use of an individual session is not considered here to be combined therapy. In combined therapy the reconstructive processes in each setting do not operate as closed systems. Rather, the on-going transactions in group and individual treatment interpenetrate with each other, forming an integrated, articulated, therapeutic experience for each member of the group.

By and large, combined therapists have been oriented to the complementarity of individual and group modalities. Group sessions are not simply tacked onto the patient's schedule in a hit-or-miss attempt to provide a social experience that may yield a serendipitous therapeutic return. Instead, attention is focused on the ways in which intragroup processes influence such psychoanalytic variables as transference, resistance, insight, acting out, reality-testing, and the fate of character defenses—each a parameter of traditional, individual treatment.

Transference

Transference is a central motif in all reconstructive therapies. It is variously dealt with, according to the therapist's theoretical orientation, diagnosis, and clinical evaluation of the patient's psychiatric status.

The American Psychiatric Association glossary defines transference as:

> the unconscious attachment to others of feelings and attitudes which were originally associated with important figures (parents, siblings, etc.) in one's early life.

In clinical terms, transference can be said to be made up of content and process. The content of transference comprises a repertoire of beliefs, attitudes, and behaviors that derive from antecedent experiences with significant others but that are no longer rational, appropriate, or adaptive in current reality. When any aspect of this repertoire is activated in interpersonal relations, a transference process is set into motion. A person unconsciously perceived by a patient as a significant figure in his past is said to have assumed a transference role. Therapists refer to the assigning of roles by patients as their having made a brother transference, a father transference, and so forth. Invariably, the psychotherapist becomes the focus of the patient's transference formations.

Emphasis on the analysis of transference has varied from the extreme position of almost exclusive concentration on the projective transactions ensuing between patient and therapist to the analysis of transference as but one of many dynamics in the therapeutic experience. Some classical analysts direct the transference almost exclusively to themselves. They become the focus and repository of all transference responses and purportedly represent at various times the influential *dramatis personae* in the patient's life history.

Accordingly, the analyst must be neutral, nonreactive, noncommittal. In this way, he provides a blank screen on which the patient can depict a range of transferential objects. The projection of the irrational attitudinal aggregate onto the analyst is known as the infantile transference neurosis or simply the transference neurosis, a psychic state accompanied by regression to various antecedent phases of development. By experiencing and rethinking cause-and-effect constellations of earlier and infantile phases, the patient develops insight into inappropriate, erroneous beliefs, neurotic techniques, and unrealistic demands for gratification. Corrective emotional experience and insight then pave the way for resolving the psychopathology.

In Freud's final statement on transference in 1938, he said the analyst could represent either parent or some important figure in the past. The analyst was not proposed as a magnet for all transferential filings. Freud summarized his views as follows:

the patient sees in him [the analyst] the return, the reincarnation of some important figure out of his childhood or past and consequently transfers onto him feelings and reactions which undoubtedly applied to his prototype. This fact of transference soon proves to be a factor of undreamt of importance, on the one hand an instrument of irreplaceable value and on the other hand a source of serious danger. Thus, transference is *ambivalent*; it comprises positive (affectionate) as well as negative (hostile) attitudes toward the analyst, who as a rule is put in the place of one or the other of the patient's parents, his father or mother.*

Transference in a Group. If the analytic image is self-limiting and cannot represent a broad sweep of transferential objects, is it not more useful to provide a controlled environment, such as a therapy group, where extra-analytic transference behavior may be elicited, where the analyst can observe it, and where the patient himself has the opportunity to avail himself of the observations and reactions of others? Most authors who have reported on group and combined

* From *An Outline of Psychoanalysis*, by Sigmund Freud. Acknowledgment is made to Sigmund Freud Copyrights, Ltd., The Hogarth Press, Ltd. (© 1964), W. W. Norton & Company, Inc. (© 1949), The Institute of Psychoanalysis (© 1969), and Alix Strachey (© 1969), for permission to quote here and elsewhere in this section from *Standard Edition of the Complete Psychological Works of Sigmund Freud*, vols. 12, 17, and 23, translated and edited by James Strachey.

therapy have directed themselves to this question.

The 1950's produced key papers on combined therapy. Several authors described their observations of transference operations in a group, and they emphasized the advantages the group offered in forming and resolving analytic and extra-analytic transferences.

Lipschutz, a combined therapy pioneer, selected for his first group those among his patients whose personality and character structure suggested that each candidate might assume a specific role in the group—parent, older sibling, younger sibling, and so on. The purpose of such selections was to facilitate the formation of multiple intragroup transferences. The patients had already become acquainted with their transference role with him in individual treatment. He reported in 1952 that combined therapy did not fundamentally alter the type of parental transference the patient had developed; however, the group sessions facilitated the activation, exploration, and resolution of many different types of transferences among the members to each other.

Fried noted in 1954 that the group expanded the range of a patient's reactions and interactions and that it promoted a division of transference instead of the concentration on the analyst that she found in exclusive dyadic treatment. In a group, patients could more clearly see multiple facets of their own personalities and problems as the different members evoked various attitudes in one another.

Papanek, an Adlerian analyst, found in 1954 and 1956 that many of her private patients who had reached a plateau in individual treatment derived notable benefits from group sessions, which gave them opportunities for reality-testing in a setting more lifelike than the dyadic meetings. Cooperative relations were fostered in the group, yet the patients felt freer about expressing hostility to the analyst because they felt more assertive in this setting, where they also formed and worked through multiple intermember transferences.

Durkin describes the complex, on-going interactions among patients in a group and between each patient and the therapist as a situation that, in itself, stimulated transference. The highly charged atmosphere of the group provided the optimal conditions for transference interpretations, which were most effective when introduced at the point where the patient's emotions were alive.

Greenbaum emphasized the broad choice of transference objects and reactions in a group, a situation found especially useful for some borderline schizophrenic patients. Through the mechanism of splitting transferences, the patient could ascribe to certain members the qualities of good siblings and good parents and ascribe the opposite qualities to other members. Establishing rapport with the "good relatives" allowed the patient to feel less isolated and to begin to deal with his hostile feelings.

Sager observed in 1959 that analytic transference was neither attenuated nor basically altered by the group. Defenses that may have concealed transferences were often revealed. The group situation provided opportunities for working out highly sensitive feelings toward the analyst that might not ordinarily be expressed for fear of antagonizing him and thus interfering with personal security and realistic expectations of being helped. Before entering a group, noted Sager, the patient should be familiarized with the nature of his analytic transference; he should be able to cope with this knowledge, able to withstand exposure of transference reactions and defenses against them in the group, and able to withstand attacks against the analyst by other group members.

Schechter, an adherent of Sullivanian theory, identified therapy in groups with the preadolescent period of peer-group affiliation. Patients whose preadolescence had been disturbed by defective or traumatic peer relationships were found to be the most suitable patients for combined therapy. Schechter described the infantile transference neurosis as "dependency yearnings and unrealistic expectations" and theorized that the infantile transference should be worked through in individual treatment as a first phase of the analysis. Otherwise, premature group therapy only solidified defenses against exposing and resolving unconscious infantile dynamics. Therefore, Schechter introduced group therapy only after the infantile transference neurosis had been worked through.

Berger noted the frequent references to the multidimensional aspects of transference in groups and the unique effect of groups on transference. To further illuminate this effect, he suggested that the need for group preservation stimulated individual behavior that was protective of the group. In the case of two women, each began to act out with the other a hostile transference to her own mother, which had such destructive effects that the survival of the group was threatened. The pressures of the other members coalesced into a compelling force that steered the two women into breaking through resistances against the analyst's interpretations and resolving their transferences toward each other.

Dyadic vs. Group Transference. In comparing the two treatment modalities, Aronson found that, although the group provided a greater number of situations and personality configurations that stimulated transference reactions and the expression of a wider range of such reactions, the individual sessions provided more therapeutic control and permitted a more detailed examination of transference. The group, in fact, stimulated such a surge of multiple transferences that flooding was often precipitated. Individual sessions were needed to remove patients from a situation of overexcitation and to allow exploration of transference in depth. Patients who were under severe analytic transference pressures found that the group offered a wider variety of alternatives. They could modify resistances and deal with parental transferences in a more graded fashion. Negative analytic transferences could be concealed temporarily, released nonverbally, or expressed indirectly through identification with other group members, or the transference could be split between the good parent-analyst and the bad parent-group members. Aronson suggested that therapists concentrate on parent and sibling transferences, since these relationships seemed to be most central to the patient's personality. Should a patient feel secure enough to work out parental transference to the therapist, he had the choice of doing so in individual sessions or in the group. Otherwise, the patient could continue to work on important subsidiary transferences before coming to grips with the parental transference.

Stein compared the intense focusing of transference upon the therapist in dyadic analysis to its altered manifestation in the group, where intensity is purportedly lessened, diluted, diminished, split, diverted, and fragmented because transference is directed toward the other patients as well as toward the therapist. Accordingly, patients who cannot tolerate intense analytic transference are thought to be better off in exclusive group therapy. In the tradition of group analysis, Stein also conceptualized the group members as siblings or parents to one another. The patients may develop intense intermember transference, in part because of the deflection of transference from the therapist.

The need to work out the analytic transference, particularly before a patient enters a group, has been repeatedly emphasized in the literature. The group stimulates a multiplicity of psychodynamic mechanisms. Transference is but one parameter, albeit a major one, in a complex network of interactive processes. Therefore, prior to joining a group, the patient should have developed some familiarity with the analytic method and should be acquainted with key aspects of certain of his problems, such as achievement anxieties and competitiveness stemming from the Oedipus complex and sibling rivalry. The patient should have at least a beginning understanding of how his basic fears integrate with defenses, such as pathological dependency and masochism. Some patients are so resistive that they cannot achieve any meaningful insight and often are introduced into a group as a way of getting through to them. If the analyst in these cases has had an opportunity to work individually with the patient and has formed a clear diagnostic impression, he will be prepared to deal with the patient therapeutically when difficult, anxiety-producing encounters take place.

Transference responses, it is generally agreed, increase in a group. As to qualitative effects, some therapists share the view that analytic transference alters when patients join a group, while others, the author included, hold that it essentially does not. During the period of exclusive individual treatment, patients become acquainted with transferential nodal points and become well familiarized with the therapist's style. If the therapist is undefensive in a group setting, he will not be perceived in a dramatically different light. But when, as a consequence of group processes, new transferences do appear, they are more amenable to analytic examination because the members can build upon established experience in working out analytic transferences (T. Bieber, 1964).

Alterations in behavior, however, are observed by virtue of the demands of the new situation itself. The lessening of transference intensity and its splitting and deflection to the other members is a theoretical interpretation that, in an operational sense, may be viewed differently. In the group, the members' concentration and intensity of attention on the analyst may be drawn away and directed toward each other without necessarily altering the basic character of transference. Among certain individual patients, the group may be used as a needed defense against fears about dyadic transference, but this need does not apply to all members. Some patients lose themselves in each other as a defense against transference to the analyst or because they are wary of each other; others become very watchful of the analyst and observe his every move. When patients work through their fears, the defensive use of the group against the analyst disappears. The analytic situation is not static. As the combined therapy evolves, analytic and intermember transferences continue to change. Transference behavior diminishes, and, if all goes well, the distortions gradually fall away.

Resistance

In 1905, Freud first described resistance as consisting of conscious or unconscious behavior that blocks or impedes therapeutic progress. Soon after this discovery, he noted the importance of delineating the psychodynamics that promote resistance. Cautioning against attempts to clear away such psychological impediments by command, exhortation, or seductiveness, he stated that at least part of the underlying psychopathology is revealed by tracking down the motivational components leading to the patient's resistance. The importance Freud assigned to the analysis of resistance is exemplified by the following statement:

The overcoming of resistances is the part of our work that requires the most time and the greatest trouble. It is worthwhile, however, for it brings about an advantageous attitude of the ego which will be maintained independently of the outcome of the transference and will hold good in life.

A frequently observed dynamic in combined treatment is the block against expressing impulses that the patient fears may be unacceptable to the analyst. When other members in a group are seen to express hostility without dire consequences, the more timid identify with the aggressors and break through their own resistances against exposing negative feelings to the analyst.

The use of head-on pressures against resistance, which Freud rightly warned against in individual analysis, frequently encourages recalcitrant patients to open up when the pressures are applied by group members. But such transactions are not an unmixed blessing. In some instances, resistance may provide therapeutic leverage; in others, it presents grave pitfalls that may retard or terminate treatment.

Among the advantages of combined therapy, the lowering and resolution of analytic resistance has often been cited. Lipschutz reported in 1952 that transference resistance that had become static and sometimes threatened to halt individual analysis tended not to appear in combined therapy. He concluded that analytic resistance was short-circuited by the activity of the other members and that the group experience helped to shorten the period of resistance in the individual sessions.

Group members sometimes attack one another's defenses in maneuvers that can be compared in their effect to the technique of character analysis developed by Reich, who attempted to denude the patient of his defenses as a way of exposing the anxieties underlying the neurotic character armor. The therapist must protect one group member from another if the premature assault against defenses threatens to precipitate massive anxiety, resistance, or decompensation. The skill of the therapist and the sensitivity of the members to one another's tolerance limits usually provide the needed safeguards.

Shay described two groups of cases in 1954. In the first, intractable resistances that were interfering with individual therapy were resolved in a group. In the second, the type of resistances developed required that patients be removed from a group.

The analysis of a 35-year-old woman had foundered on resistances growing out of her pathological dependency. She was inactive in the analysis and insisted that she be given unbounded affection and solutions for all her problems in life. When the members criticized her inactive role and protested against her thrusts at being the center of the analyst's attention, she began to work in the group.

Another patient, who had previously undermined his analysis by repeatedly creating reality crises, became caught up in the tide of analytic work in his encounters with a group.

A timid, inhibited, constricted 30-year-old woman, who suffered from ulcerative colitis, responded to the group with a stimulated sense of sociability. Her interactions with the other members promoted her awareness of a need to participate in group life, and she became convinced of the importance of constructively introspecting about her problems, especially her fears of women and her competitiveness with them.

A woman who had been quite silent during a year of individual analysis, was aloof, disdainful, and condescending when first introduced into a group. Her wordless resistance was finally pierced when she was chosen as the object of a male patient's insatiable need to give love.

Among the patients who did not fare as well was one woman who, after four months in a group, developed a florid schizophrenic reaction with hallucinations, delusions, and ideas of reference. The next year, in exclusive individual treatment, she began to trust the analyst and depend on his sense of reality when she could not maintain her own.

A schizoid young man who was pressured by the group to socialize and go out with girls became so sullen and defiantly resistive that he had to be taken out of the group.

A male alcoholic and a male homosexual had to leave because they felt isolated and could not identify or form a bond with the other members.

One man was habitually arrogant and contemptuous. The other members could not tolerate his behavior, and he could not change. The resulting stalemate led to his removal from the group. In individual treatment he worked through the defensive aim of his facade, and he became aware of how he used it to disguise and conceal his inner fears and misgivings about himself.

Resistance is a behavioral mode that may be mobilized by a broad spectrum of fears of greater or less intensity. It is a psychological set and must be differentiated from legitimate differences in viewpoint with the analyst or group members. Patients balk or become recalcitrant, silent, obsessive, negativistic, or hostile. Or they may leave the analysis in obvious displays of refusal to proceed with therapy. Or they may indulge in chit-chat, attempt to please the analyst in subtle or overt ways, take flight into health, find ways of taking temporary leave through vacations, or take permanent leave by finding a new job in another area. The analysis of resistance is a central aspect of the analytic method, and all patients experience resistance during reconstructive psychotherapy.

An outstanding advantage of the group is that it permits alternate ways of interpreting and working through various blocks and impediments that sometimes defy resolution in exclusive individual analysis.

Insight

Perhaps because Freud himself never defined insight in his writings on the nature of consciousness and resistance, few analytic concepts are used more broadly and with less consensus as to significance in treatment. Without using the term, Freud nevertheless alluded to insight in the following statement:

The therapeutic effect depends on making conscious what is repressed, in the widest sense of the word, in the id.

As Cappon stated in 1964:

Part of our difficulty in this field is that we give words like insight various theoretical definitions that are often mutually exclusive or partly contradictory or, at least, inexact. . . . we have the uneasy feeling that no one definition quite captures the concept. But then we assume that each time . . . it conveys the same notion.

The various definitions of insight by English and English underscore the different shades of meaning:

(1) Reasonable understanding and evaluation of one's own mental processes, reactions, abilities, and self-knowledge. (2) The greater or less understanding of one's true condition when mentally ill; e.g., the ability to recognize the irrationality of someone's impulses. (3) The process by which the meaning, significance, pattern, or use of an object or situation becomes clear. (4) A mystical revelation.

Therapeutic insight connotes the recognition and correction of irrational beliefs. Any corrective changes in the perception of reality, however achieved, may in a broad sense be termed insight. In stricter terms, such alterations consist of cognitive and verbal awareness that one's erroneous ideas or thought sequences actually are erroneous, comprehension of why the ideas are erroneous, confidence approaching certainty that the ideas are false, and receptivity to appropriate conceptualizations.

The importance assigned to the role of insight depends on one's view about psychopathological processes, whether in individual, combined, group, or other therapies. The conceptualization of psychopathology by I. Bieber (1960) has contributed substantially to the formulations on neurotic process in this chapter. Simply stated, his adaptational theory is that psychopathology in an adult comes about and is maintained by clusters of beliefs linked to unrealistic expectations of threats and fears of injury. Constellations of defensive, adaptive, and maladaptive reparative mechanisms then become integrated with the unrealistic beliefs.

One of the major functions of resistance is to prevent insight. Resistance guards against many types of perceived threats, especially the danger of insight when the patient senses it may expose him to realizations, actions, or consequences he fears or feels helpless about. The game pattern of psychoanalysis is the patient's maneuvers against the threat of insight and the analyst's efforts at mitigating the patient's fears about achieving insight.

. In recent times, action and interaction have been increasingly emphasized as the dominant group modalities that promote therapeutic change; insight has tended to be de-emphasized, especially in dyadic treatment. Some consider insight therapy to be, at best, part of the Establishment, old-fashioned, and even antisocial; at worst, it is argued, insight does not help.

The differences between group and individual methods that relate to reconstructive changes have been much overdrawn. The distinction between dyadic therapy as the setting for insight and the various group therapies as settings for interaction is a spurious one. As is implicit in the concept of corrective emotional experience, interaction is a central characteristic of dyadic therapy, although it may be subtly expressed. Transference, too, may be subsumed under interactive processes, as indeed may all interpersonal transactions in therapy as in life. This writer cannot share the enthusiasm of those who hold that a reconstructive, therapeutic experience can unfold and proceed with optimal results without insight. To be sure, the activities and engagements in therapy groups are more concrete, visible, and kinetic than in a one-to-one encounter; for this very reason, groups that stress encounter, contact, and interaction may be more helpful to patients whose mode of personal problem-solving is *acting through* rather than *thinking through*. Some patients are compelled to assimilate self-knowledge intuitively through unstructured, unsystematic, freewheeling, interpersonal engagements. For those who are not so constricted, insight, as defined in its strictest sense, remains the royal road to consciousness.

As a first phase of insight, a male homosexual may learn that his sexual avoidance of women is based on a belief of attack by other men. But unless he is *convinced* that he will not be attacked, insight is only partial; he is not likely to alter his sexual adaptation. The next problem is how to convince him. Through repetitive dreams, transference reactions, and life situations, patients learn to reappraise irrational beliefs again and again. Old beliefs are reexamined in new ways and from different angles until a conviction about the falsity and unreality of a neurotic idea is established. The group experience furthers the working-through process because the members provide consensual validation by promoting the reality-testing needed to strengthen the growing belief that a feared attack will not, in fact, occur.

Partial insight, sometimes erroneously thought of as intellectual insight, is a superficial knowledge of one's psychodynamics without the confidence that old beliefs are irrational and that new, corrected beliefs have reliable, personal application. The polarization of insight into intellectual and emotional spheres is misleading. All insight is intellectual. Insight is cognitive at some level of consciousness, but it is most effective at the verbal level because the greater mastery involved provides greater safeguards against slipping back into old ways.

In the case of a 27-year-old woman who was reared in a female-dominated, sexually restrictive home, the group experience convinced her that it was safe to enter into a sexual relationship with a man for the first time in her life. When she was three years old, her father had abandoned the family, consisting of a maternal grandmother, mother, younger sister, and older sister. After a year in individual treatment, the patient was aware of the main historical roots and highlights of her neurosis. In the group she could test and reinforce her new discoveries. Masochistic attempts to deny that she was a pretty woman were consistently and constructively assailed. She had been taught that men were cruel, aggressive, and somehow different as humans from women. The group provided the confidence for her to have intimate experiences with men, which increasingly gave her self-confidence in their presence, and she learned that her affection was valuable to them. A crucial element in her improvement was the reinforcing influence of the women members, who consistently reassured her that she was not betraying them by having a sexual life.

Acting Out

As early as 1905 in *Three Essays on the Theory of Sexuality*, Freud suggested the idea of acting out as it is understood presently without his naming it as such. He viewed perversions as psychopathology in action; neuroses, seen as the negative of the perversions, were thought to be expressed within the self, as in somatic or obsessive symptoms. In a series of 1914 papers on technique, he described acting out and restricted it to the transference situation:

The patient does not *remember* anything of what he has forgotten and repressed, but *acts* it out. He reproduces it not as a memory, but as an action; he repeats it without, of course, knowing that he is repeating it.

Freud had already stated this idea in a postscript to the analysis of Dora, where he had discussed transference.

Freud's two versions of acting out are represented in current thought by those who limit the interpretation of acting out to transference transactions and by those who have expanded the meaning and apply it to any behavior set off by neurotic, irrational impulses. One must keep in mind, however, that not all neurotic behavior is an expression of neurotic impulses. When some inhibited, submissive patients begin to express assertiveness or anger, they sometimes break through in an exaggerated, inappropriate way. The impulse to defend oneself and to be assertive is not neurotic, but the exaggerated behavior has to be regarded as such.

Whatever one's point of view, there is agreement that the reality basis for acting out in a group is greater than in individual sessions because the group stimulates multiple, shifting, and complex interactions that promote acting out. Therapists who conduct groups are especially concerned with this phenomenon. Insight is a desired goal of reconstructive therapy. As such, it has achieved an elitist halo of health, progress, and intellectuality. But acting out has a somewhat pejorative cast, perhaps because of its association with the perversions and sociopathic behavior. Transference, resistance, and insight are intrinsic elements of analytic therapy; so, too, is acting out. Whether in individual sessions or in a group, however, acting out is useful only if it delineates a neurotic process. It is self-evident that the transgression of appropriate, rational lines of behavior among group members or between therapist and patient disrupts the therapeutic situation and defeats its aims.

Bry, representing the action hypothesis, pointed out that in individual therapy no sexual acting out and very little acting out of aggression can be permitted. In contrast, acting out in a group is inevitable, and, if it does not threaten the welfare or survival of the group, it can have therapeutic as well as diagnostic value.

Durkin, representing the view that acting out is limited to the transference situation, stated:

There is no categorical difference between acting out and transference. Rather, acting out is a particular *form* of transference.

This view was illustrated by a sequence of subtle sexual acting out by two members in a group of four:

A young woman, who habitually took her shoes off and rested her legs on the analytic couch, permitted her stockinged foot to come into contact with the arm of a young male patient sitting at the other end of the couch. She was conscious of her purpose and said so; it was a sexually motivated act. Later, in several individual and group sessions, the transferential meaning of her behavior was analyzed. Her seductive act symbolized incestuous wishes toward her brother; the young man's participation represented acting out of his incestuous feelings toward his sister; to a third patient, who had had a traumatic primal-scene experience, the act represented a voyeuristic encounter. In the past, these three patients had brought similar material to their individual sessions, where it was not developed and was soon repressed. These problems reappeared as acting-out behavior in the group, where it had great therapeutic value.

Stein has made a similar point.

The availability of the group members as multiple transference objects who are realistically present in the group and who will actually respond to transference manifestations results in ' group member interaction which can be designated as a therapeutic type of acting out in the group session.... Patients utilize roles in the group based upon unconscious fantasies to act out and to try to get the other patients to act out transference roles and conflicts. For this reason, pathological character traits and attitudes are more quickly apparent in group psychotherapy and are more readily available for therapeutic scrutiny.

Berger observed that the group supports certain types of acting out, including hostile expressions to the analyst. Hostility to the analyst is not usually as readily expressed in the individual sessions, where it can become a tangled situation serving as a basis for resistance.

The more commonly expressed type of acting out consists of hostile acting out among the members themselves. The following sequence illustrates the triggering of hostility when a member feels rejected and sexually competitive:

A pretty 23-year-old patient, Sally, a group favorite, was discussing her relationship with a close friend. A male patient, John, interjected, "Was that the girl I met you with the other day?" Sally answered, "Yes, that's the one." The discussion contiued for several minutes, and then another male patient, Peter, burst out in anger, "I am feeling very hostile to John. He is butting in with a remark that doesn't mean a thing." Peter's resentment about a brief, apparently inconsequential interruption suggested that his reaction was a promising one to pursue.

Turning to the new theme, the group soon discovered that John had somehow felt rejected by Sally and her friend when he ran into them. The interpolation of his question was an attempt to repair hurt feelings by automatically replaying the traumatic situation in encapsulated form, hoping to find acceptance this time around. Peter, who had similar problems about rejection by women, responded with competitive rage to John's defensive demonstration to the other men in the group that he had superior personal knowledge and contact with Sally. In the analysis in the group, the anxiety about rejection by women that both men were experiencing was interpreted, as were the

differences in their defensive reactions. The individuated and complex determinants for their feelings of rejection then remained to be worked out in the individual sessions. The uninterrupted analytic explorations yielded conceptual enrichments that enabled them to return to the group and insightfully pursue the meaning of competitive behavior.

The Process of Combined Therapy

As already noted, participation in a group stimulates in a patient many more response combinations and crosscurrents than occur in individual treatment, but the interruptions in a group, the tempo of responses, and the time available do not favor detailed probing. There is also an opposite effect. As Fried (1954) has pointed out, although the group elicits an accelerated and variegated production of raw material, the hostile attacks that members sometimes direct toward one another may also inhibit productions.

In combined therapy, the reconstructive processes that transpire in each setting do not freeze within rigidly held boundaries; there is reciprocal feedback. In general, the productions and themes of individual sessions are predominantly concerned with detailed explorations of historical background and belief systems that support underlying neurotic patterns and unrealistic defenses. In the group, attention focuses more centrally on the exposure and analysis of defenses. The on-going transactions of each situation interpenetrate with the other, forming an integrated, articulated experience. Further, self-directed, intrapsychic behavior is more characteristic of the individual sessions; in the group the behavior is more social and outer-directed. The individual setting provides fertile ground for tracking personal history, analyzing dreams, and involving the patient with the many nuances and interpretations usually referred to as analysis in depth.

Selection of Patients

Certain types who would generally be categorized as borderline patients have often been reported as especially suited for combined therapy. The generalization may indeed be valid; however, this writer has been unable to correlate diagnostic typologies with treatability in a group in attempts to prognosticate how any particular patient will fare in combined therapy.

There are as many exceptions as there are rules in selecting patients for a group. Total personality and the indicators of therapeutic movement are more decisive than diagnostic categories in choosing participants. The criterion for selecting patients for combined treatment that seems most productive is to bring together patients who are reasonably similar in outlook and level of sophistication and who appear to be potentially compatible. By and large, when a group is comparatively homogeneous, it has a greater chance of surviving because the sessions interest the members more, the group atmosphere is congenial, communication is easily facilitated, and so therapeutic work prospers. Naive, uneducated people tend to feel uncomfortable with those who are capable of complex, high-order thinking. When such a mix-match occurs, it tends to inhibit strong group cohesion. Sometimes the members of poorly matched groups accept, tolerate, and even like one another, but a feeling of solidarity, sustained mutual interest, and participative relatedness does not evolve.

In one group that failed, an inherently intelligent but poorly educated cabinetmaker found himself included with several professionals, and he obviously felt out of his depth. A cleavage occurred when he immediately sought out a young woman, a stenographer, who was having the same reaction. They felt inadequate in relation to the others, who were perceived as power people. In the weeks that followed, their problems with authority were analyzed, and the possible snobbish counterreactions of the others were probed, although these probes for counterreactions turned up nothing of importance. The sense of unease that the two members had generated gradually subsided, and an agreeable atmosphere developed, but, as a working unit, the group failed, largely because it did not have a good fit.

Yet these same two patients might have jelled in another group of intellectuals. No two therapy groups are alike. Individual differences and defensive reactions are immeasurably varied. In one population, group unity may be easily threatened; in another, cohesion develops quickly and maintains its stability. Some older groups can tolerate a young person in their midst; others cannot. A borderline schizophrenic may benefit from association with neurotics, or he may not, depending on a myriad of variables. The questions at bottom are always, *which* young person, *which* schizophrenic, *which* cabinetmaker? And what are the rest of the members like? One depends not a little on clinical hunches in organizing a group. Some hunches pay off; others do not.

CLINICAL EXAMPLE

Transference, resistance, acting out, reality-testing, and so on—each constitutes a major parameter in the interactional processes of a therapy group. Like a symphony, the group may create a cacophony of sound, or one or another theme may be salient. As noted in the following account of a group of six, different psychoanalytic variables interweave or become easily identifiable as central group themes.

The Patients

The group members were organized from a roster of patients who had been treated individually for periods ranging from ten months to ten years. They came from heterogeneous religious and class backgrounds. As intelligent young adults living in New York and, on the whole, working successfully, they seemed to have enough in common to form a cohesive therapy group.

James. James had been married the previous year; severe reactive anxiety brought him into treatment. He had recently become the father of a son, an event that only worsened his marital situation, and he was in the midst of an unpleasant divorce. In his social life he was gregarious and well-liked and had many friends. Yet he felt painfully ill-at-ease at the first and only group meeting he attended. He was so inhibited and frightened that he could scarcely respond to the simplest question. In individual sessions he was able to deal freely with the dynamics of his postmarital and postpartum reactions, but the group precipitated a flood of anxiety and overwhelming feelings of worthlessness and depression. He refused to return to the group, a decision that was accepted without any attempt to change the patient's mind. Clearly, he was unsuitable for therapy in a group, at least at that time. The group of two women and three men continued without him.

Beth. Beth, 24, had been in treatment since her disturbed adolescence, with time away for college, a year in Europe, and other interruptions that sometimes lasted for several months. She had made remarkable progress through the years and continued to do so. Beth had a complicated, ambivalent relationship with her mother—dependent, fearful, hostile, envious, yet closely identified. Her father was a blunt, noisy, but affectionate man whom the mother held in slight contempt. Beth was competitive but submissive toward a younger, aggressive sister and an older, even more aggressive brother. He was the mother's favorite and was treated by both parents as the family princeling. Beth sought his affection but received only occasional acceptance. A beautiful young woman, she was also a talented dancer and choreographer. In her late teens, she had decided to follow the dance profession.

Carl. Carl, an attorney, was a personable, much-sought-after man-about-town who had entered treatment because he was aware of his resistance to marriage. Love affair followed upon love affair, each absorbing him until he had to face the possibility of marriage, whereupon he would abruptly break the relationship. Despite his active life, he felt lonely, restless, and dissatisfied. His deeply entrenched separation anxiety was traced to a traumatic childhood. At the age of six he was sent away for almost a year to a place he recalled as an orphanage. His father had taken ill, the mother could not support their two young sons, and so she found work as a housekeeper, keeping only Carl's younger brother during that critical year. Later in life, the mother's childhood sweetheart reappeared. He became attached to the family to such an extent that Carl addressed him as "Uncle."

Sean. Sean, a commercial artist, began analysis as an exclusive homosexual, became exclusively heterosexual, and at the time he joined the group was romantically involved with another artist, whom he ultimately married. Sean was the youngest of four sons. The father had been detached and cold and the brothers sadistic and rough, but the mother favored Sean. Even as a child, he had been outstandingly handsome. His brothers would tease him about having rosy cheeks and long eyelashes "like a girl." He feared his castrating brothers and found refuge in drawing and painting, an occupation his family demeaned until it turned out to be lucrative.

Mary. Mary was a 30-year-old housewife who had married a businessman immediately after she graduated from college. She had been trying to become pregnant for several years with no success. A language major in college, she now idled away her time in meaningless pursuits. Her parents had been divorced when she was a small girl. She dearly loved her father but seldom saw him. She was closely attached to her mother, a nervous, hypochondriacal, handsome woman who fancied herself to be a shrewd investor but who was constantly involved in one financial scrape after another until her recent remarriage to a man of considerable wealth.

Mary sought treatment because of her drinking problem. After about a year of marriage she began to drink, at first small amounts. When she entered treatment, she was up to anywhere from a half to a full bottle of gin or vodka a day, and she lived in dread that her husband would discover it. She was intensely ashamed and hated herself for her addiction. Her husband thought she wanted psychoanalysis because of psychological sterility, which was largely true, although she was unaware of it through the first months of analysis. Her interest in sexual activities was sporadic. During erotic periods she would want sexual intercourse several times a day; then periods of inhibition would set in, and she would be sexually disinterested, but she always had relations during her fertile period.

Henry. Henry was a biologist. He was married and had three children. Severely obsessive, he sought help when he began to have potency difficulties. He was very loquacious but charming in the individual sessions and used an interesting flow of talk as resistance against probing into any sensitive areas, and there were many. He lived largely by a code of denial. His wife, children, and members of his immediate family were described as quite perfect people, or, if not perfect, they had such redeeming qualities as to make the flaws seem attractive. The only one who was credibly described was his mother, whom he criticized, but he did not admit to feeling hostility toward her. When a group was suggested, he began to indicate some reservations about joining but then caught himself: He could not reveal that he had trepidations about facing a group. With a show of bravado and enthusiasm, he had said, "Sure, I'll be able to tell everybody what's wrong with them."

Transferences

The transference to the analyst, a woman, was for each patient essentially that of mother. Since family experiences were idiosyncratic and no two mothers or patients were alike, transferences varied. As an example, Beth, who had been dependent on a somewhat rejecting mother, would, through the years of individual treatment, become unexpectedly hostile on occasion. She would pout, hang her head, become silent, or express anger and dissatisfaction, as though she were being injured and oppressed. When she joined a women's group, she had already made notable inroads into the bad-mother transference fed by a paranoid undercurrent. Still, her hostility sometimes exploded in full force, but never in the group. Contrary to the often-described pattern of exposing hostile analytic transference in the group, this patient's negative transference was openly expressed only in the dyadic situation. For some time before she entered the present group, no sudden emotional storms had occurred.

Mary was not so much concerned with the analyst's affection as with her approval and respect. She tried to establish a pathologically dependent relationship by putting herself in a helpless position in various ways, such as asking advice about very simple matters that she could well handle by herself. As a consequence, she had a lowered sense of self-esteem. In reparative attempts, she sought approval for her intelligence, discernment, taste, and so on.

Sean had been in individual analysis for three years before joining the group. The analytic transference was well on its way toward resolution, despite evidences of over-attachment. His fiancee tended to view the analyst as a mother-in-law, and Sean, on his part, indicated to both analyst and fiancee his filial analytic transference.

Carl's need to have all women fall in love with him extended to the analyst, whom he perceived essentially as the oedipal mother. He attempted to do small favors, impart useful information, show interest in her clothes and office furnishings, and be humorous and agreeable.

Henry's curtain of words and denial patterns suggested self-deception and negative transference elements. On the one hand, he had to maintain face; on the other hand, he was too distrustful to admit he was often depressed, claiming instead that he never felt depressed.

The Group in Action

The first session was somewhat beclouded by James's extreme tenseness. The members made attempts to include him into the self-introductions and, in general, to integrate him into the opening gambits, but they soon realized that he felt more comfortable when left alone. At the next meeting they noted his absence and expressed satisfaction that he had dropped out.

As many new facets of behavior come into view when a patient goes from one group to another as when he goes from individual to group therapy. For example, a homosexual patient who has been consistently agreeable in a mixed group may express aggression when transferred to an all-homosexual group. Beth had previously been a member of an all-female, nonhomosexual group, where she had behaved quite like a middle-child com-, promiser. She would be hostile and difficult in individual sessions, but in the women's group she was almost always girlishly friendly, rarely hostile, rarely openly competitive, and usually given to underrating her popularity with men. Two years transpired between termination of the women's group and her joining the present group, and Beth had made significant strides in the interim. She now presented herself in a very different light. She was gay and vivacious, flashed her legs, and tossed her hair. She presented herself as a sexual woman. Individual analysis revealed that she felt protected by the men and could reveal her sexuality in their presence. At the same time, she had resolved her fears of women to the extent that their presence did not inhibit her.

Mary felt envy and competitiveness. She brought this problem to her individual session after the first group meeting when she reported a dream:

I was standing in front of a mirror, brushing my hair. It was breaking at the ends, and I was upset about it. My husband was leaning on the dresser, watching me. I turned around and saw a young woman standing in the doorway.

Mary and Beth each wore her hair fashionably long. Beth was identified as the woman in the dream. Mary's feeling was that she was being seen at a disadvantage, since her hair was in poor condition. In essence, the dream depicted Mary's perception of her weak position in a triangular situation.

Resistance in the Group. In the phase of getting acquainted, one or another patient usually takes the lead in exposing his history and current life situation. Beth was the first, partly because she had had experience as a group member, partly because she warmed under the attention she was receiving, partly because the others were more resistive.

Carl tried to be an authority figure and preferred to play the role of listening analyst. The others were each consciously guarding a secret and had stated so in their individual sessions prior to joining the group. Henry would not reveal his impotence; Sean did not feel ready to reveal his previous homosexuality; Mary could not bring herself to talk about her alcoholism; Beth held back for some weeks before bringing up her involvement with a married man.

The secret-keepers were testing analytic loyalty and power, among other dynamics. Would they be betrayed? Did they have to tell? The idea that group sessions were not offshoots of confessional revival meetings, and that the decision to share information was a personal one, strengthened the conviction that each had independent choices. The secrecy was needed as a defense for the time being because each member required a feeling of assurance against rejection by the others.

These and other dynamics were worked out in individual sessions, and it remained a question of time before the withheld material emerged. Sean was the first to break through. He talked about his homosexuality, setting off a chain reaction of loosening resistance. As the group process developed, Carl brought up his fear of marriage, Beth talked of her love relationship, and Mary began to discuss her conflicts about pregnancy. But Mary did not reveal her drinking problem, and Henry did not refer to his potency difficulties.

Interaction. From the first, Carl was attentive to both Mary and Beth, but he showed sexual interest in only Beth. Once he called attention to her miniskirt; another time he commented, "You look good tonight," as he looked at her approvingly. Mary's response was to try to break the Beth-Carl dyad by compelling Carl's attention in a show of great interest in his problems. She picked up his comments with alacrity and gave them serious attention. Through all the talk, however, the message to him was, "Pay attention to *me* and only to me."

Sean made no attempt to enter into these maneuvers. More often than not, he sat quietly on the sidelines, but the group soon learned to respect his occasional but always trenchant comments.

In the first several group meetings, Henry's behavior was discordant with that manifested in individual sessions. In the group he was relatively quiet, without being silent. He would ask questions of the others and closely follow all that was transpiring.

By the fifth meeting, the group had become cohesive; the blush of the getting-acquainted phase had faded; they were anchored. At the fifth meeting, Carl started rationalizing a psychosomatic symptom. He was supposed to join his girlfriend at her parents' home in the country, but at the last minute he decided not to go because he felt a cold coming on; besides, he would have to take some work along, and he would not feel like doing it there if he had a cold. The group responded by pointing out his escapism. Carl resisted by minimizing their comments and cracking jokes about amateur shrinks. Then, twinkling at Beth in an apparent change of subject, he asked, "And how are you doing with your boyfriend?" Now Henry wheeled into action. Pale and angry, he excoriated Carl for bragging, being a wise guy, pretending he was above it all, and substituting rationalizations for the truth. At first the group was taken aback, not so much by the substance of his remarks as by his rush of emotion; however, they quickly recovered and then spent the rest of the session in heated discussion. In this encounter Sean became a central figure, for his air of sobriety, fairness, and good sense was valuable to the group.

Henry's acted-out rage was a turning point in his analysis. It helped him recognize his competitive hostility on the one hand and his identification with Carl on the other. Carl's resistance had become for Henry a mirror image of his own resistance, and he began to recognize clearly a wish to have Beth to himself. In his individual sessions he began to work out the basis for his jealousy; it opened up a broad avenue involving father-son dynamics. Henry's jealousy was a transference reaction to his own father, who let his son know about his extramarital affairs from time to time. Henry could now admit that he was bugged by Carl's style and by the way women members responded to him. Derivative of Henry's oedipal problems was his fear that he would somehow lose out with his analyst with Carl in the

picture. Sean was not seen as a threat because he did not come on with the women.

Carl's reaction to the encounter was one of anxiety and inhibition, which lasted for several weeks. He complained about Henry in his individual sessions, and in the next few group sessions he retreated into the background while Henry came forward. Carl did not recover fully until Henry brought up his jealousy in the group, together with the admission that Carl represented, in part, a father figure. This knowledge had a supportive effect; the idea that he could be perceived as a father figure gave Carl a feeling of importance. He had never envisioned himself in that role. This sequence enabled him to begin to explore, particularly in his individual sessions, the part he played in his own complex family drama. Furthermore, his transferences to the analyst and to the other members became clearer to him. The analyst and Beth represented two aspects of a maternal image, a nurturing mother and a sexually hedonistic mother who ignored rules that normally regulated sex and family life. Henry was perceived as a younger brother demanding attention. Sean represented order, justice, and victory over adversity; he provided concrete evidence that a former homosexual could reverse his sexual adaptation and marry and, therefore, that a man with less serious difficulties could solve his problems.

Sean's improvement was a test of reality that was also extremely helpful to Henry. Mary was seen by the entire group as the helpless loser, and each member identified her with the loser in himself, a personification of his own masochism. The group fought for her recovery as one struggles for victory by the underdog.

The Fate of the Group

At this writing, the group is still on-going, but Sean married and terminated treatment shortly thereafter. He was replaced by two new members, a woman and a man. The man had also been homosexual and had reversed his sexual adaptation in individual and group treatment with an all-homosexual group.

Beth is now living with her lover, who is in the process of being divorced; marriage is planned for the future. Mary's drinking has abated but not impressively; however, she has returned to school and is working on a master's degree. Henry has never discussed in the group his symptoms of impotence. He is fully potent at present and is well-motivated to work constructively in his combined analysis. Carl's creativity has expanded, and he works more effortlessly and with greater enjoyment. He still has not been able to develop a lasting relationship with a woman. As in the past, he has fallen in love, but the thought of marriage stirs anxiety. Since he is now familiar with the dynamics of his problems, he does not panic and run when pressed for marriage. Rather, he has been able to state his position and let the decision about continuing the relationship rest with the woman.

CRITICISMS OF COMBINED THERAPY

In a paper written in 1918, Freud warned that the application of psychoanalytic therapy to numbers would inevitably alloy the pure gold of analysis plentifully with the copper of direct suggestion. When group therapy methods first began to attract psychoanalysts, many of the more traditionally minded raised objections but not so much about the antianalytic effects of suggestion. In his 1952 report, Lipschutz wrote:

I have discussed transference in the group with many outstanding psychoanalysts. Their immediate reaction was a negative one. All, as one, observed that as soon as more than one person is introduced into the analytic situation, the factor of transference in the original sense is completely destroyed.

In the present era, criticisms of combined therapy come from three sources: first, psychoanalysts who oppose group therapy as a significant instrument for therapeutic change and who are skeptical about the reconstructive achievements of combined treatment for the reason that it includes the group; second, group therapists who are opposed to individual therapy and who oppose combined therapy because it includes regular, individual sessions; third, analysts who support and practice both exclusive group therapy and exclusive individual therapy but who believe that the pure gold of either cannot tolerate the alloy of the other.

Increasingly, conceptualizations about psychodynamics and psychopathology seem to dim and all but fade away in the plethora of new procedural forms and variations. Such preoccupation with form often masks a poverty of content. The many problems about the management of patients—whether in groups, individual sessions, or both—would approach solutions more readily if attention were turned more toward appraising psychoanalytic and psychodynamic assumptions about psychopathological processes. Treatment forms would then become less a matter of subjective opinion and more a matter of practice following clearly defined postulates.

REFERENCES

Aronson, M. L. Technical problems in combined psychotherapy. Int. J. Group Psychother., *14:* 425, 1964.

Berger, I. L. Modifications of the transference as observed in combined individual and group psychotherapy. Int. J. Group Psychother., *10:* 456, 1960.

Bieber, I. The meaning of masochism. Amer. J. Psychother., *7:* 433, 1953.

Bieber, I. A concept of psychopathology. In *Current Approaches to Psychoanalysis*, p. 22, P. Hoch and J. Zubin, editors. Grune & Stratton, New York, 1960.

Bieber, I. Sadism and masochism. In *Handbook of Psychiatry*, vol. 3, p. 256, S. Arieti, editor. Basic Books, New York, 1966.

Bieber, T. B. The emphasis on the individual in psychoanalytic group therapy. Int. J. Soc. Psychiat., *2:* 275, 1957.

Bieber, T. B. The individual and the group. Amer. J. Psychother., *13:* 635, 1959.

Bieber, T. B. Discussion. Symposium on combined individual and group psychotherapy. Int. J. Group Psychother., *14:* 433, 1964.

Bieber, T. B. Acting out in homosexuality. In *Acting-Out—Theoretical and Clinical Aspects*, p. 142, L. E. Abt and S. L. Weissman, editors. Grune & Stratton, New York, 1965.

Bry, T. Acting out in group psychotherapy. Int. J. Group Psychother., *2:* 42, 1953.

Cappon, D. Discussion. Symposium on combined individual and group psychotherapy. Int. J. Group Psychother., *14:* 438, 1964.

Durkin, H. Relationship of transference to acting out. Amer. J. Orthopsychiat., *25:* 644, 1955.

English, H. B., and English, A. C. *A Comprehensive Dictionary of Psychological and Psychoanalytic Terms.* Longmans, Green, New York, 1958.

Freud, S. Advances in psychoanalytic therapy. In *Standard Edition of the Complete Psychological Works of Sigmund Freud,* vol. 17, p. 167, J. Strachey, editor. Hogarth Press, London, 1955.

Freud, S. Papers on technique. In *Standard Edition of the Complete Psychological Works of Sigmund Freud,* vol. 12, p. 150, J. Strachey, editor. Hogarth Press, London, 1958.

Freud, S. An outline of psychoanalysis. In *Standard Edition of the Complete Psychological Works of Sigmund Freud,* vol. 23, p. 174, J. Strachey, editor. Hogarth Press, London, 1964.

Freud, S. Analysis terminable and interminable. In *Standard Edition of the Complete Psychological Works of Sigmund Freud,* vol. 23, p. 238, J. Strachey, editor. Hogarth Press, London, 1964.

Fried, E. The effect of combined therapy on the productivity of patients. Int. J. Group Psychother., *4:* 42, 1954.

Fried, E. Combined group and individual therapy with passive narcissistic patients. Int. J. Group Psychother., *5:* 194, 1955.

Graham, F. W. A case treated by psychoanalysis and analytic group therapy. Int. J. Group Psychother., *14:* 267, 1964.

Greenbaum, H. Combined psychoanalytic therapy with negative therapeutic reactions. In *Schizophrenia in Psychoanalytic Office Practice,* p. 56, A. Rivkin, editor. Grune & Stratton, New York, 1957.

Hulse, W. C. Transference, catharsis, insight and reality testing during concomitant individual and group psychotherapy. Int. J. Group Psychother., *5:* 45, 1955.

Lipschutz, D. Psychoanalytic group therapy. Amer. J. Orthopsychiat., *22:* 718, 1952.

Lipschutz, D. Combined group and individual psychotherapy. Amer. J. Psychother., *11:* 336, 1957.

Papanek, H. Combined group and individual therapy in private practice. Amer. J. Psychother., *8:* 674, 1954.

Papanek, H. Combined group and individual therapy in the light of Adlerian psychology. Int. J. Group Psychother., *6:* 136, 1956.

Reich, W. *Character Analysis.* Orgone Press, New York, 1945.

Sager, C. The effects of group psychotherapy on individual psychoanalysis. Int. J. Group Psychother., *9:* 403, 1959.

Sager, C. Concurrent individual and group analytic psychotherapy. Amer. J. Orthopsychiat., *30:* 255, 1960.

Schechter, D. E. The integration of group therapy with individual psychoanalysis. Psychiatry, *22:* 267, 1959.

Shay, J. Differentials in resistance reactions in individual and group psychotherapy. Int. J. Group Psychother., *4:* 253, 1954.

Stein, A. The nature of transference in combined therapy. Int. J. Group Psychother., *14:* 413, 1964.

3

Structured Interactional Group Psychotherapy

Harold I. Kaplan, M.D. and Benjamin J. Sadock, M.D.

"Everything secret degenerates; nothing is safe that does not show it can bear discussion and publicity."

LORD ACTON

"All personal secrets have the effect of sin or guilt."

CARL JUNG

INTRODUCTION

The authors were trained as individual psychotherapists and have continued to subscribe to the theoretical and therapeutic principles which govern psychoanalytic psychotherapy. Over the years, however, we had experienced a growing dissatisfaction with the results of our efforts to treat individual patients. And, more significantly, we had grown increasingly sensitive to those aspects of the dyadic relationship which, in our opinion, characteristically impede the implementation of the essential goals of psychotherapy.

The Evolution of Structured Interactional Group Psychotherapy

Our interest in group psychotherapy as a clinical technique developed gradually, as an outgrowth of this heightened awareness of the limitations of individual treatment. More precisely, our criticisms centered on the fact that individual psychotherapy creates a special situation which, in itself, would be considered an unnatural medium for emotional change and growth.

It is generally conceded that the human personality does not evolve solely from biological determinants. Nor is the texture of the child's earliest relationship with his mother the sole determinant, however crucial it may be for his later development. Personality can best be understood as the combined product of the child's biological endowment and his psychological experience, which derives in large measure from his interaction with all the key individuals in his social environment—not only with his parents, but also with his siblings, aunts and uncles, friends and teachers, etc. Implicit in this formulation is the etiological proposition that all emotional and mental difficulties that cannot be attributed to constitutional or organic factors must be considered to arise from disturbances in the individual's interpersonal relationships. It follows, then, that if it is to be effective, psychotherapy must provide the patient with a corrective emotional experience, or, more accurately, with a series of corrective interpersonal experiences, which, in turn, will enable him to modify the learned emotional responses which underlie his neurotic behavior patterns. We had come to recognize that the kind of corrective emotional experience we consider a prerequisite for the success of treatment could not be provided within the framework of the one-to-one doctor-patient relationship.

Individual psychotherapy seeks to illuminate the relationship between the patient's current problems with other people and within himself, on the one hand, and his conflictual feelings toward crucial figures and events in his past, on the other, by exploring his transference responses to the therapist, who is traditionally cast in the parental role. Concomitantly, the therapist, by assuming attitudes toward the patient which differ significantly from those held by his parents, may produce what Alexander called the corrective emotional experience. Apart from the fact that the efficacy of this particular technique is open to question, individual psychotherapy can be criticized on the grounds that it emphasizes one sector of the patient's psychological experience. This is not to say that individual psychotherapy does not permit the patient to act out a variety of roles in his relationship with the therapist. However, by virtue of the fact that the therapist is the sole focus of cathexis, such manifestations are limited to a level of fantasy when they involve a variety of people in the patient's life.

It seemed to us that the multiple transference components of the patient's behavior might emerge more clearly in a group situation, where he is given an opportunity to engage in dynamic interaction with a number of individuals. In contrast to individual psychotherapy, group therapy represents reality; and in this setting the corrective emotional experience acquires new depth and meaning: The patient faces a variety of people who are possible targets for his transferential reactions and responds to them to the extent of his "abilities." In the process, he is forced, under pressure from the group, to recognize the distortions in his responses to selected members of the group. At the same time, he comes to understand that these inappropriate responses derive from repressed feelings and attitudes which were originally directed toward figures and situations in his past. Finally, the patient is motivated to explore and, ultimately, to modify these inappropriate impulses and attitudes, by his compelling need to be accepted by the group.

We concluded from these considerations that an individual approach to psychotherapy was not sufficient in itself, and, in 1953, one of us (H. I. K.) began to treat groups of patients for the first time, using a new directive approach called "Structured Interactional Group Psychotherapy." At the same time, however, we realized that group therapy could not supplant individual therapy entirely, particularly when treatment is based on psychoanalytic concepts.

The over-riding goal of group therapy is to effect permanent changes in the behavior of the individual patients who comprise the group. But there is not sufficient opportunity in this setting to elicit from each group member the genetic and dynamic data which, according to psychoanalytic theory, are essential to the understanding of human behavior. In fact, the lack of detailed data regarding individual patients constitutes a major source of the criticism which has been leveled at group therapy. Presumably, these data would not be required for experiential-existential group approaches which focus on the here-and-now, i.e., on the patient's immediate emotional response, and attach little importance to the origins, meaning, and implications of that response. It is our contention, however, that behavior (and symptoms) cannot be modified without reference to their pathogenesis and content. A detailed anamnesis of each group member would, therefore, be considered a paramount requisite for the success of treatment. Inasmuch as these data can be obtained only in individual session, it was stipulated that all our group patients must also see the therapist for individual treatment. From the outset, we assumed that the combined use of group and individual treatment would enhance the possibility of a successful therapeutic outcome, and the results of our efforts in the years since attest to the validity of this assumption.

THE THERAPEUTIC PHILOSOPHY

Structured Interactional Group Psychotherapy evolved, within this theoretical framework, from two interdependent premises: First, as noted above, we are proponents of what is generally referred to as the directive approach to group therapy. That is, we believe that the success of treatment can best be assured if the therapist assumes an active role as leader of the group. Second, if the therapist is to function effectively in this capacity, we consider combined individual and group therapy a mandatory condition of group therapy. Obviously, this is an oversimplified delineation of the components of Structured Interactional Group Psychotherapy. The content of the premises on which this treatment approach is based, their underlying rationale, and the nature of their inter-relationship merit further elaboration.

The Design of Structured Interactional Group Psychotherapy

The various methods of group therapy are frequently viewed as a continuum: Those methods which entail a high degree of structuring on the part of the therapist (and have limited therapeutic goals) are placed at one end of the continuum; unstructured methods which entail minimal activity on the part of the therapist (and attempt to fulfill the traditional goals of psychotherapy) are placed at the other end.

Structured Interactional Group Psychotherapy belongs in the middle of this continuum: The therapist structures much of the group's activity; however, his efforts to control and direct group interaction are specifically designed to implement the traditional goals of psychotherapy. Thus such structuring consists in the application of specialized techniques which enhance the traditional techniques of group therapy and serve, thereby, to facilitate treatment. More precisely, the therapist structures the group's activities by actively intervening to circumvent the methodological problems which are inherent to this treatment modality. We do not share the optimistic view held by some of our colleagues that these problems can best be resolved, ultimately, through spontaneous group interaction. Rather, we feel that undirected interaction

exerts a malignant influence on the treatment process which may, in fact, impede the possible eventual solution of the problems.

A brief discussion of some of the characteristics of traditional forms of group therapy, as compared to Structured Interactional Group Psychotherapy, may serve to clarify the role and function of the therapist in this setting. In traditional groups, each patient achieves catharsis and varying degrees of insight into his difficulties through his own efforts. Concomitantly, the patient's progress depends in large measure, on the degree to which intrapsychic and/or interpersonal factors restrict—or foster—his participation in the group process. In theory, each patient comes to the fore at various times during a group session—either of his own volition, or at the insistence of other group members. In actual fact, however, one or more patients in a traditional group may remain withdrawn and uncommunicative for long periods of time. In Structured Interactional Group Psychotherapy, the therapist takes specific steps to correct this imbalance. For example, at each session group activity focuses on a particular member of the group who has been selected beforehand by the therapist. Through this and other techniques, which are discussed in detail below, the therapist is able to ensure the participation of each patient in the group. Moreover, since participation in group treatment must be properly channeled if it is to yield therapeutic gains, the therapist may intervene, within the framework of Structured Interactional Group Psychotherapy, to further enhance the patient's efforts to achieve catharsis and insight into his difficulties. Those activities on the part of the therapist are the cornerstone of Structured Interactional Group Psychotherapy.

Admittedly, traditional group therapy permits greater spontaneity among group members. On the other hand, the spontaneous emotional interaction which is a paramount feature of traditional group therapy may block or retard therapeutic progress. Emotions such as rage, anger, and distress are infectious. When the intensity of such emotions exceeds the limits of the patient's tolerance, the group situation becomes chaotic. Accordingly, Structured Interactional Group Psychotherapy attempts to avoid the perils of the "affect-laden" group. In his role as group leader, the therapist provides the guidance which is essential if cognitive processes leading to insight are to occur.

The Integration of Psychoanalysis and Operant Conditioning

Liberman has described operant conditioning in the therapeutic setting as the use of the therapist's overt and covert responses to reinforce the patient's adaptive patterns of behavior and to inhibit his maladaptive patterns. When a group therapist directs attention toward a withdrawn member who has just contributed to group interaction for the first time and when he approves of and accepts the contribution, then he is selectively strengthening and reinforcing that mature behavior. Such reinforcement may also take place between members of the group.

When a particular group member is the focus of attention and interest, the therapist has many opportunities to apply verbal operant conditioning methods. By reinforcing selected behavior of the group members, either collectively or individually, he is able to effect behavioral change.

A passive man who was unable to assert himself was asked by the therapist to make a critical comment about each member of the group—including the therapist—in a go-around. Reluctant to do so at first, he eventually acceded to the request. After completing the task, during which he was able to tell one member that she was obese and another that he was an opportunist, the passive patient received the approval of all the members. Assertiveness was thus reinforced.

As used by the authors, operant conditioning in Structured Interactional Group Psychotherapy is adjunctive to the cognitive insights and the corrective emotional experience that psychoanalytic practice affords. The two frames of reference are not mutually exclusive in this treatment method. The working through of a tranference dis-

tortion—such as seeing the therapist as a stern, punitive father figure—can be effected not only by the leaders and the other members' interpretations within the psychoanalytic frame of reference but also by operant techniques. These techniques reinforce the patient's ventilation of angry feelings consonant with that tranferential reaction—but do not reinforce the fantasied retribution he had come to expect as a result of past experiences. Thus, Structured Interactional Group Psychotherapy serves as a bridge between psychoanalysis in groups and behavioral group psychotherapy.

The Integration of Individual and Group Therapy

There is some agreement that group therapy is more effective and less troublesome when it is carried out in conjunction with individual treatment. As noted above, the multiple transference components of the patient's behavior emerge with greater clarity in the group setting. However, for obvious reasons, the origins and implications of the patient's transference to the therapist, and to other group members, can be explored in greater depth in individual sessions. Concomitantly, individual sessions provide the patient with an opportunity to express feelings he is not yet ready to discuss in the group. They may also serve to reassure those in whom the group experience has aroused excessive anxiety, to give overly shy members an opportunity to communicate with the therapist, and, generally, to solidify gains made in the group.

These considerations apply, to varying degrees, to all methods of group therapy. However, the integration of individual and group therapy has a particular significance for Structured Interactional Group Psychotherapy: The therapist's detailed knowledge of each member of the group, which can be acquired only in the intimacy of the one-to-one treatment setting, and his continued awareness of the emotional status and needs of each patient are crucial to the success of his efforts to direct and control group interaction and group inter-relationships. At the same time, the therapist's individual rela-

tionship with each patient in the group reinforces his role as leader and removes the
taint of authoritarianism from his efforts to
structure the treatment process. For, in a
sense, the therapist's activities in the group
setting are perceived as an extension of his
traditional role in individual treatment.

THE FORMATION OF THE GROUP

Eligibility for Structured Interactional Group Psychotherapy

As a general rule, those patients who are
seen individually by other therapists are not
considered suitable for Structured Interactional Group Psychotherapy. Structured
Interactional Group Psychotherapy can be
truly effective only if the group therapist
has sufficient genetic and dynamic understanding of each patient in the group and,
as noted earlier, this knowledge can be acquired only in individual treatment. If his
eligibility for Structured Interactional Group
Psychotherapy is not contraindicated on
these grounds, the prospective patient is
seen by the therapist for diagnostic evaluation in one or more initial interviews before
he is accepted for psychotherapy.

Formal diagnosis is based on the criteria
set forth in the *Diagnostic and Statistical
Manual*, second edition, issued by the
American Psychiatric Association. But we
believe that clinical diagnosis must include
more than the standard phrase used for the
diagnostic category which the patient
exemplifies. In the course of these initial
interviews, the therapist also formulates a
comprehensive statement of the fundamental aspects of the patient's life, i.e.,
somatic, intrapsychic, interpersonal, and
cultural. On the basis of these data, the
therapist is able to assess the patient's
eligibility for psychological treatment in
general and for combined individual and
group therapy in particular.

Obviously, not all patients who are accepted for individual treatment would, from
the outset, be considered suitable candidates
for Structured Interactional Group Psychotherapy. Individual treatment can help, in

such instances, to prepare the patient for the
group experience. In fact, however, such
patients are relatively few in number. Because of its unique features, eligibility for
Structured Interactional Group Psychotherapy is not subject to the restrictions
which necessarily limit participation in more
traditional methods of group therapy.

Accordingly, the choice of patients for
Structured Interactional Group Psychotherapy follows the same lines as for individual psychotherapy: Patients who are inaccessible to individual treatment because of
organic or constitutional defects or extreme
regressive states must also be excluded from
group therapy. With these exceptions, Structured Interactional Group Psychotherapy
can generally be used successfully to treat
patients who suffer from every type of neurosis and personality disorder, including
those syndromes which are not generally
thought to be amenable to group therapy:
By virtue of the fact that it incorporates
specific techniques to ensure participation
by every member of the group, depressed
and withdrawn patients can benefit greatly
from this type of treatment. Patients who
suffer from mild psychoses, variously described as latent, borderline, or prepsychotic
states, are also considered eligible for Structured Interactional Group Psychotherapy.
And, once again, this can be attributed in
large measure to the unique features of
Structured Interactional Group Psychotherapy: In his role as group leader, the
therapist uses his skills to control the
amount of stimulation to which these patients are exposed, to diminish anxiety, and,
in general, to assuage the emotional tensions
which lead to disorganized behavior.

The Composition of the Group

As a rule, groups tend to function best
when they are heterogeneous, not only with
respect to clinical entity, but also with respect to such factors as sex, age, social status,
and cultural background. Ideally, then, the
group will include individuals who demonstrate enough variety in personality and
emotional problems to prevent reinforcement and overintensification of their diffi-

culties. To the extent that this is feasible, the group should be comprised of an equal number of male and female patients. And, finally, we have found that heterogeneity with regard to age, social status, and cultural background facilitates communication and interstimulation among group members. It should be noted, however, that some similarity in these areas may be desirable. To illustrate, although patients from ages 16 to 60 may benefit from Structured Interactional Group Psychotherapy, one middle-aged patient in a group of young individuals might feel isolated and out of touch:

A fifty-year-old woman who was assigned to a group of young adults was perceived as a castrating mother figure by her co-patients and was the target of considerable hostility. Furthermore, despite his persistent efforts to interpret this collective transference response, the therapist was unable to resolve this therapeutic crisis. This problem did not arise, however, when the patient was subsequently assigned to another group which was similar in composition, except that it included another individual in the same age range. For one thing, there was a dilution of the transference. Second, these older patients tended to support each other, so that they were better able to deal with the hostility of younger group members.

On the other hand, groups which are heterogeneous with respect to clinical entity are not suitable for all patients. When all the patients in a group have similar difficulties, they share a certain commonality of suffering which may facilitate their participation in treatment. Two types of patients seem to do best in a homogeneous group: acting-out adolescent patients, particularly those with drug-abuse problems, and regressed patients. In any event, heterogeneous groups should not include more than one or two patients in these categories. Because they are so demanding of the time and attention of the therapist and of the other group members, these patients generate a great deal of resentment which can have no therapeutic value and may block the treatment process.

Decisions with regard to grouping may stem from other considerations: The therapist who undertakes the treatment of both husband and wife may develop a bias toward one or the other marital partner. As long as he is aware of this bias, it need not interfere with treatment, provided these patients are seen separately in individual session. On the other hand, the therapist may find it more difficult to conceal his lack of objectivity when he must confront both patients in a group setting. Even if the patients themselves remain unaware of his prejudices, he runs the considerable risk that they might be detected by other group members who identify and empathize with the "victim." In light of these considerations, we believe that it is advisable to place marital partners in different groups.

Assignment of husband and wife to the same group is contraindicated on other grounds as well: Some inhibition of sexual data is almost inevitable under such circumstances, especially if one partner has withheld certain information about his past or present activities from the other. But even if the husband and wife have been perfectly honest with each other, so that there are no secrets between them, joint group therapy may generate feelings of competition and resentment which may lead to destructive acting out.

A husband was admitted to his wife's group after she had been a member for a period of time because the therapist felt that this couple could benefit from such structured interaction. In addition, he felt confident of his ability to maintain his objectivity toward both patients. And, finally, he knew, from the data obtained in the course of their individual treatment, that these partners knew everything there was to know about each other. On the surface, then, his decision was a valid one. However, one week after her husband entered the group, the wife took steps to establish herself as the center of the group's interest and concern (and divert attention from her husband). Apparently, she felt sufficiently threatened by his presence to initiate her first extramarital affair, thus obviating the less complicated marital relationship which had existed previously.

Patient Orientation

The sooner the patient joins a group, the better his prognosis. Whereas, in the past, the authors saw patients individually over a long period before they entered the group, we have come to recognize that resistance to both group and individual therapy is greatly diminished if patients are moved into group therapy early in treatment—ideally, after one or two individual sessions. This is not always feasible, of course. As noted earlier, some patients must be seen in individual session for a period of time in preparation for the group experience. In the normal course of events, however, the patient is told about group psychotherapy as an adjunct to individual psychotherapy during his first consultation. More specifically, the therapist explains to the patient that the cornerstone of his treatment will be individual psychotherapy; group therapy is presented as an additional modality which is available to the patient to supplement individual treatment in much the same way that a laboratory session serves to supplement a chemistry lecture. Nevertheless, most patients express initial anxiety about the prospect of group therapy which cannot be entirely alleviated by this explanation.

Obviously, patients can be expected to vary considerably in this respect. To cite one example, those patients for whom peer relationships constitute a major source of anxiety, such as might be seen in an only child, for example, will usually be more resistant to group therapy than those patients whose problems center on their relationship to authority. The latter welcome the support of their peers in dealing with the therapist, who is perceived as a threatening authority figure; the former prefer the one-to-one situation which enables them to recapture infantile feelings of omnipotence. The patient's immediate response to the suggestion of group therapy can help to elucidate his unconscious needs and motives:

After group therapy had been suggested, a patient reported the following dream in individual session: "I enter a room with lots of people. I see you sitting in your chair and become furious and run away. You follow me out and put your arms around me and console me." The extreme dependency needs of this patient and her need to be the center of the therapist's attention thus became apparent at the outset of treatment.

At other times, the patient's initial re-sistance to group therapy may be based on realistic considerations: If the patient's anxiety is excessive to the degree that the therapist feels he may be traumatized if he is exposed to the group prematurely, the subject of group therapy should be dropped temporarily. In that event, the patient is told that group therapy will be discussed again at a later date, if it seems desirable to do so, and that he will not be compelled to participate.

Finally, the therapist seeks to further diminish the patient's anxieties with respect to group therapy by assuring him that if he goes into a group and does not like it, he can leave at any time and still remain with the therapist in individual therapy. When this problem arises, however, the patient is encouraged to explore his reasons for "disliking" the group, and in most cases his resistance to continuing is overcome.

The New Group

Introducing different group members to each other upon the formation of a new group or introducing a new member to the members of a pre-existing group involves essentially the same process. Invariably, patients are uncomfortable and anxious at their first group therapy session; therefore, it is the task of the therapist to make this experience as untraumatic as possible.

At the first meeting of a new group, the group leader discusses the procedures and rules of Structured Interactional Group Psychotherapy. He then asks each member to talk about himself briefly, i.e., to give his name, age, and marital status and to summarize his educational background, his work status, and the major emotional problems that brought him into therapy. Each member is allocated from five to ten minutes for this purpose. However, within this time period, the therapist may supplement the patient's introductory statements with significant details that he feels the group should be aware of—provided, of course, that he has not been placed under any restrictions in this regard by the patient. If a patient does not want to disclose a particular aspect of his life at the first group session, the therapist must not bring it up until the patient's resistance has been worked through. We believe, however, that ultimately the patient should be prepared to talk as candidly in group as he does in individual sessions.

The therapist's intervention may take other forms during these introductory self-summaries. When patients are too verbose, he may have to limit discussion, even though at this point in treatment the patient may experience the therapist's intervention as a rejection, which will have to be worked through in individual session. Conversely, withdrawn and schizoid members may have to be drawn out and given support. Above all, all the members of the group must have an opportunity to talk during this first session. The patient who is unable to participate for one reason or another may feel neglected; and while some patients may feel an immediate sense of relief because they have escaped exposure, this can only delay their integration into the group. In other instances, the patient may perceive this neglect as indifference to his problems on the part of both the therapist and the group, and he may withdraw from treatment altogether.

Once a new group has been formed, it has a life of its own, independent of the admission of new patients from to time and the discharge of others. And this, in turn, is a reflection of the stability and continuity of treatment, as epitomized by the therapist.

The New Member in Group

In time, each group develops a culture of its own, and the older members transmit the particular standards which have been adopted by the group to new patients when they enter therapy. This is a gradual process, however, and the new member must feel comfortable in the group before it can occur.

During his first group session, the patient is introduced by name and provides a capsule summary of his background. Each of the regular members then introduces himself in turn; he gives his name, age, and occupation, and briefly discusses the problems that brought him to therapy for the edification of the new member. Ten or fifteen minutes may be devoted to these introductions. During the remainder of the group session, the new

patient is up for discussion, a technique which is discussed in further detail below. The new patient is not told beforehand that he will be the center of the group's attention, lest this prospect evoke excessive anxiety. But this is rarely perceived as a betrayal by the therapist. Once the group is in session, the procedure is explained, and its traumatic aspects are minimized; and, of course, the patient is further reassured by the protective presence of the therapist. In theory, the procedure is a relatively simple one: The group members ask the new patient questions about himself. In fact, when the group is more sophisticated and experienced, such questioning is reminiscent of a skilled psychiatric examination. Although it may cause some temporary discomfort, there is no question that this procedure helps to integrate the newcomer into group psychotherapy more rapidly, inasmuch as both the older members and the new member acquire some knowledge of one another's background and emotional difficulties at the outset.

THE TREATMENT PLAN

Practical Considerations

The Physical Setting. The setting in which group therapy is conducted has received minimal attention in the literature. It has been our experience, however, that specific aspects of that setting may help or hinder group interaction; as such, these routine details merit brief consideration. Obviously, the room used for group psychotherapy should be large enough to comfortably accommodate all the members of the group; physical discomfort due to overcrowding, etc., however minor, will in most cases reinforce the patient's resistance to therapy. Within the consultation room, we have found it useful to have the members of the group sit in an unbroken circle; that is, individual patients are not separated from each other, or from the group as a whole, by physical barriers, e.g., conference tables. The advantages of this circular seating arrangement as a symbol of group unity are self-evident.

Apart from the fact that male and female, patients are encouraged to occupy alternate seats (to avoid polarization), group members may, of course, sit wherever they choose (as long as they remain within the circle). And the seat chosen by the patient at the start of the group session may provide the therapist with valuable clues as to his emotional status: The patient who is particularly anxious or feels threatened by the group may want to sit close to the therapist. And, conversely, physical separation from the therapist may be indicative of hostile or aggressive feelings. The type of chair the patient sits on is important in itself. Wooden chairs, for example, are warmer than metal chairs, and, therefore, are more desirable. On the other hand, easy chairs are too comfortable; patients are more apt to withdraw when they are too relaxed. Finally, since it is important to maintain a certain level of tension in the group, patients are not permitted to smoke in the consultation room. Smoking reduces anxiety, of course, but it also limits spontaneous emotional expression: The patient uses the time it takes to light or puff on a cigarette to censor his thoughts and responses, or to modify them, so that they can be presented in more acceptable form.

The Size of the Group. The number of patients in the group will, of course, depend on the size of the consultation room. Provided adequate space is available, a group may include as many as 15 members. Ideally, however, the size of the group will be limited to ten or 12 patients. It can be speculated that one or two of the members of any typical group will be withdrawn schizoid patients whose participation will be minimal, and another one or two members will be absent from any given group therapy session, which means that from six to eight patients will actually participate in each session. Efforts to have every patient participate in every session, at least to some extent, are most likely to be successful in groups of this size. If the group is too small, it may succumb to long periods of impenetrable silence. And, of course, if the group is too large, not everyone who wishes to participate can do so within a fixed time period. Under such circumstances, it becomes more difficult to prevent the secondary discussions between two or three members which lead to group fragmentation.

The Length of Group Therapy Sessions. Group therapy sessions may vary in length from one to two hours. The group requires at least one hour to get really involved in the problem under discussion. But no discussion, or series of discussions, can hold the attention and interest of either the group or the therapist if the session continues for more than two hours. (For this reason, the group therapy marathon has seemed to the authors to be of value only if the therapist has carefully screened each participant beforehand and considers him capable of such sustained interaction and has further established that the patient can tolerate the continued stress which is a concomitant of this innovation.) We have concluded from our own experience that, after a certain period of time, patients can no longer assimilate the intense stimulation of group therapy, and we believe that the length of the group therapy session must be determined by such psychodynamic variables.

Apart from such considerations, the therapy session should not extend beyond the limits of the therapist's ability to function effectively, and, of course, this has particular relevance for Structured Interactional Group Psychotherapy. Furthermore, the therapist must assess his clinical capacity at the outset. Due to the misconception (which, unfortunately, is nonetheless prevalent) that psychiatrists sell time (they sell their unique professional skills, not their time), it is important that all the groups treated by the therapist be allocated the same amount of time, and that the same amount of time be allocated to the same group each week. This must be clearly established by the therapist at the first meeting of each new group, and he must insist on strict adherence to this schedule. Varying the time arbitrarily causes patients to feel cheated. But, more important, many patients are reassured by the therapist's ability to control the length of the session, for this is perceived as a manifestation of his ability to control the group.

The Frequency of Group Therapy Sessions. Typically, one group session is held each week, so that four or five group sessions are held per month. The authors have found that it is useful to increase the frequency of sessions, so that an extra group session may be held on a regular basis. For example, a group which meets regularly every Tuesday may also have an extra session on the first Thursday of the month. In any event, it is essential to establish regular meeting times which should only be changed if the therapy session falls on a holiday, or if the therapist is ill or cannot be present for other reasons. Because regularly scheduled group sessions are important to the success of treatment, it is essential that missed group sessions should be made up by scheduling an extra meeting for the preceding or following week; proximity in time to the missed session helps to reinforce the concept of regular meetings. Although the concept of regularity is stressed, it may be necessary to increase the frequency of group meetings temporarily if the resistance encountered in a group has, in the therapist's opinion, reached critical proportions. This should not be done arbitrarily but only to overcome certain unique resistances of the group as a whole, or of a particular member.

Finally, Structured Interactional Group Psychotherapy differs significantly from traditional methods of group therapy in respect to the frequency of group sessions in that the group meets regularly during the summer month while the therapist is away on vacation. Briefly, during this period, the members meet without the therapist and report to him weekly on the content and procedure of each session. There is no charge for group sessions scheduled while the therapist is on holiday; but the attendance of the patients at these group meetings is mandatory (unless, of course, they are away on vacation themselves); indeed, it is considered as important as attendance at the regular sessions during the year. There is no guarantee that the patient's symptoms will remain in remission or that he will use this period to consolidate his gains; on the contrary, he may lose valuable ground. Consequently, we believe that Structured Interactional Group Psychotherapy can be most effective if it is provided throughout the year.

Financial Considerations. The fees for psychotherapeutic services vary from one area of the United States to another and differ according to the background, skill, and reputation of the psychotherapist: in addition, within any given area, they will be determined by the supply and demand for psychiatric specialties. Thus, in the New York area, for example, charges for group therapy range from $10 to $30 per session, per patient. This charge is considerably less than the fee for individual psychotherapy, which ranges between $25 and $75 per session. However, beyond such considerations, the financial arrangements for Structured Interactional Group Psychotherapy pose important and unique problems which differ significantly from those encountered in individual psychotherapy.

To begin with, patients in group therapy must feel confident of their equality in the eyes of the therapist. Therefore, as evidence of the therapist's lack of bias, all patients are charged the same fee for each group session, regardless of their financial resources, which group they have been assigned to, or the length of time they have been in treatment. The authors have found that this approach diminishes rivalry between group members and serves to preclude crises in the doctor-patient relationship which might otherwise arise on this account. In contrast to the uniformity which characterizes fees for group therapy, fees for individual psychotherapy are determined by a variety of factors: the patient's income, the therapist's customary fee at the time the patient begins treatment, frequency of therapy sessions, etc. Consequently, patients in Structured Interactional Group Psychotherapy may be paying different fees for individual therapy. In fact, patients within any one group know they are being charged different fees for individual treatment, and this discrepancy is a frequent topic of discussion. On the other hand, they also know they are being charged a uniform and standard fee for group therapy, to the extent that if the fee is changed in one group, it is changed simultaneously for all patients in all groups. If the therapist is to function as the group leader, such equality is *sine qua non* of treatment.

Billing Procedures. As is customary, monthly bills are submitted to patients for services rendered in both individual and group therapy. Once again, however, insofar as it emphasizes uniformity, which implies equality in treatment, Structured Interactional Group Psychotherapy differs significantly from individual psychotherapy in respect to billing procedures.

In individual psychotherapy, previously scheduled sessions may be canceled upon 24 hours' notice, and the patient will not be charged for the session he has missed, provided he can justify his action to the therapist's satisfaction. Initially, the authors attempted to apply the same rules to group psychotherapy. But the system proved unworkable in this setting. For one thing, we could not take the time to explore with various patients their conscious and unconscious reasons for missing group sessions and to determine whether their absence had been justified. In addition, these discussions frequently incorporated competitive elements which further impeded the resolution of this question: If Patient A was charged for a missed session, he could not understand why Patient B had not been and felt he was being treated unfairly. Accordingly, it was decided that all patients would be charged for all group sessions which were conducted by the therapist. Furthermore, although the patient's absence from a group therapy session might be justified on grounds of illness, hospitalization, an important business trip, etc., no excuse would be accepted as good and sufficient cause for not charging him for the therapy session he had missed. Essentially, then, all patients are billed on a monthly basis for the number of group sessions scheduled that month. And, since all patients are treated the same in this respect, this procedure has been accepted with equanimity. Most important, patients take the issue of missing group sessions quite seriously, and attendance at group sessions is generally excellent.

Financial Crises in Therapy. As noted above, the fee for group therapy is usually approximately 50 per cent less than the fee for individual sessions. Obviously, then, patients are better able to afford the fee for group therapy than the fee for individual treatment. In fact, patients who suffer financial reverses in the course of individual therapy may be forced to terminate treatment because the cost of such treatment, however essential, may well be prohibitive.

On the other hand, the psychiatrist who conducts combined individual-group therapy may exercise a certain flexibility on behalf of patients who are in financial straits, in that he may diminish the frequency of individual sessions temporarily, or even suspend individual treatment entirely. The fact that the patient is charged only for group therapy will, of course, significantly reduce the cost of treatment. In most instances, these patients can manage the lesser expense involved in group therapy. But even if the patient must run into debt to continue therapy, he will incur less of a debt by continuing in group therapy than by continuing in both group and individual therapy.

As noted above, the authors consider combined individual and group therapy a mandatory condition of Structured Interactional Group Psychotherapy. Accordingly, we are understandably reluctant to permit a patient to continue in group therapy without the accompanying individual sessions. Nevertheless, at times of financial crises, such an arrangement does provide a valuable "holding" operation, until the patient has achieved sufficient economic stability so that he is able to resume individual therapy. Certainly, it is sounder therapeutically to restrict the patient's participation in treatment than to permit him to continue in both individual and group therapy, with the understanding that payment for treatment can be deferred.

A patient who had suffered a serious financial setback was permitted to continue in both individual and group treatment with the understanding that he would pay the therapist when he was able to. In fact, his financial situation did improve eventually and he was able to pay the considerable debt he had incurred. At this point, however, it became apparent that the therapist might not have acted in the patient's best interests after all: The patient admitted—with some relief—that while he was in debt, he had felt that he could not express his anger toward the therapist and had even censored his "unacceptable" thoughts because he did not want to offend the therapist who had been so kind to him during this period.

Rules and Procedures

Confidentiality. Structured Interactional Group Psychotherapy is based upon a fundamental positive relationship between the patient and therapist and between the patient and other group members. And one cornerstone of this dual relationship is the patient's firm conviction that his communications in both the individual and group treatment settings will be regarded as confidential and privileged information. Catharsis can take place only if the patient is secure in this knowledge. Consequently, the abrogation of confidentiality—whether inadvertently, by the therapist, or deliberately, by a member of the group or by a member of another group—may seriously impair treatment and, in extreme cases, precipitate its termination.

The Doctor-Patient Relationship. Before he enters group therapy, the patient is encouraged to be as open with his group members as he is with the therapist in individual session. At the same time, however, he is assured that he will not be compelled to discuss any detail of his life with the group until he is ready to do so. And, of course, patients frequently do explore sensitive areas with the therapist in individual session which they cannot bring themselves to raise in group therapy sessions.

There are exceptions: In one group a patient reported that he had an atrophied testicle, the result of a trauma, a fact he had made known to the therapist previously in individual session. At that point, another member of the group reported that he, too, had only one testicle, the result of a congenital anomaly, a fact which the therapist had not been aware of. The patient then explained that he had been too embarrassed to mention this in individual session. Once he found out that someone else had the same affliction, he no longer felt this overwhelming sense of shame, and he was able to talk about this problem.

Such situations occur rarely, however. As noted earlier, in the normal course of events, the patient discusses such sensitive areas with his individual therapist first. If he does not want a specific matter brought up in the group, the patient must inform his therapist accordingly, prior to the group session, so that the therapist will not raise the issue himself when he feels it is in the patient's interests to do so. Unless the patient has imposed a specific prohibition, the group leader will automatically assume that any material discussed in individual session may also be discussed before the group. When the patient imposes such a restriction, the therapist should, of course, attempt to explore with the patient the various factors which underlie his resistance. Although the therapist may agree that a particular subject should not be covered in group, at least for the time being, more often the therapist will attempt to dissuade the patient from avoiding the subject.

Whatever the source of his resistance, if the patient does not wish to discuss a subject, it is incumbent upon the therapist to honor his decision. To be treated in such a manner, that is, to have his wishes respected and honored, is most reassuring to the patient. Conversely, any violation of the patient's confidence would seriously impair the doctor-patient relationship, which, in turn, would have an adverse effect on treatment.

The Ethics of Group Relationships. Similarly, the positive relationship between the patient and other group members, which is essential if group therapy is to be effective, is based in large measure on adherence to these ethical principles. When he enters group therapy, each patient is informed that the contents of all therapeutic sessions are confidential and must not be discussed with anyone outside the group. When a patient breaks this rule, he is immediately advised by the therapist that he will not be permitted to continue in therapy if he violates it a second time. Perhaps because patients realize that the therapist would be justified in taking such action, in thousands of group sessions conducted over a period of almost 20 years, the authors have found that confidentiality is rarely breached.

The Chain-Reaction Phenomenon. Information may also be spread between groups. It is particularly important, for example, that the confidentiality be emphasized when husbands and wives who see the same ther-apist in individual session have been assigned to different groups. Under such circumstances, one can understand that marital partners will be strongly tempted to gossip about discussions that take place in the respective group sessions, but such gossip is no less dangerous and potentially destructive to therapy.

A female patient, aged 36, told her husband, who was also in therapy, that the husband of one of the members of his group had been having an affair. She had learned of this in the course of a secondary discussion with a member of her own group. The patient understood that such information was no less confidential; in this instance her violation of this cardinal rule could be attributed to her transient hostility to the therapist.

In fact, her information was incorrect, but its transmission had serious repercussions for therapy nevertheless. Once these misunderstandings had been clarified, the destructive impulses which had led to her breach of confidentiality were interpreted, and the patient was warned that a recurrence of such behavior would result in the termination of treatment. Confidentiality was never broken again.

Friends and other members of a family who are in individual treatment with the same therapist but in different groups are subject to the same temptations. For example, let us say that Patient A in Group 1, Patient B in Group 2, and Patient C in Group 3 are close friends socially. Patient A may then be tempted to discuss some particularly interesting item he has learned from a patient in his own group (1) with his friends, who may then pass this information on to their co-patients in Groups 2 and 3. While such a chain-reaction dissemination of information is usually harmless, it does represent a violation of confidentiality, and, as such, it can present serious problems. Accordingly, while the therapist must expect chain reactions, he must exert every effort to reduce them to a minimum. And, when they do occur, it is his responsibility to confront the patients and to make the necessary interpretations.

Extratherapeutic Contact. As the group as a whole, and his fellow group members as individuals, become an emotional focal point for the patient, there is an in-creased tendency to socialize, i.e., to establish contact with the group outside the treatment setting. Initially, the authors were quite permissive in this respect, and in fact found it useful therapeutically, in that it fostered identification and empathy among group members. In time, however, we realized that contact outside the group may be undesirable on several counts: For one, socializing threatens confidentiality. Second, socializing conduces to sexual acting out which may constitute a therapeutic crisis. And, finally, excessive extratherapeutic contact may impede the patient's growth and development as a social being.

After they had been in therapy for two years, the members of one group who had been permitted to socialize had developed few outside relationships. Since their social life revolved around the group, these patients simply had not had an opportunity to test new modes of behavior with others. Only after socializing was prohibited and group members were forced to form relationships in the outside world was there evidence of progress in this area.

In light of these considerations, and on the basis of our experience, it is the opinion of the authors that socializing outside of group therapy sessions is therapeutically undesirable and should be discouraged.

The Termination of Treatment. The patient who terminates therapy by mutual agreement with the therapist is discharged "with medical advice"; the drop-out is discharged "against medical advice" (AMA). After the patient and the therapist have agreed that the patient is ready to terminate treatment, the patient remains in group therapy for a three-month trial period before this decision is "finalized." This permits the patient to withdraw from treatment gradually; and it gives the therapist additional time to carefully evaluate the patient's psychological status. If all goes well, the patient is discharged from treatment with the understanding that he can return to the group whenever he feels the need to do so for any number of follow-up sessions. The authors have found that most patients avail themselves of this privilege only sparingly. More frequently, their relationship with the group tapers off gradually, although they may remain in contact with one or two group members. And, of course, this is a measure of the success of treatment.

In contrast, the patient who leaves the group AMA is ostracized by the group, and his attempts to maintain contact with individual group members are frowned upon. In brief, the AMA status is depicted in the most negative light possible. As a result, most patients are highly motivated to resolve their emotional problems, so that they can be discharged with medical advice.

"Wild" Group Psychotherapy of Drop-Outs. Patients who have dropped out of group psychotherapy against medical advice often form their own groups, meeting and conducting a type of wild group psychotherapy without the benefit of direction or supervision by a qualified group leader. Such groups represent a form of rebellion without a cause that must fail ultimately. More specifically, attempts by group dropouts to meet on their own are manifestations of a unique type of resistance that cannot be worked through without professional help.

SPECIALIZED TECHNIQUES IN STRUCTURED INTERAC-TIONAL GROUP PSYCHO-THERAPY

Structured Interactional Group Psychotherapy is based upon the dynamics common to all psychotherapy: relationship, catharsis, insight, ego-strengthening, reality-testing, and sublimation. And the techniques employed are based on the fundamental principles of psychoanalytic theory. Thus they include exploration of the patient's personal history to facilitate the expression of repressed material and ward off tendencies to act out, the use of free association and the interpretation of dreams, and the analysis of transference phenomena and of resistance.

Structured Interactional Group Psychotherapy is unique, however, in that it also employs specialized therapeutic techniques, geared to this particular treatment modality, which are specifically designed to enhance the traditional procedures delineated above via operant conditioning methods.

"The Patient is Up"

The cornerstone of Structured Interactional Group Psychotherapy, theoretically and technically, is the procedure whereby a specific patient is "up" for discussion by the group. The rationale underlying this procedure was discussed in some detail earlier in this chapter. In brief, its purpose is to foster participation in treatment. In contrast to those therapists who seem to view personality change as a mystical, osmotic process, we consider such participation essential if the patient is to achieve creative change within himself and in his relationship with others; furthermore, it is our considered opinion that there is a close correlation between the extent to which the patient participates in treatment and the degree of change he is able to achieve. On the whole, the articulate patient rarely presents a problem in this respect. However, the participation of the withdrawn or schizoid patient—who is encountered just as frequently in psychotherapy—becomes an over-riding therapeutic goal. This technique ensures fulfillment of this goal.

In essence, each week, the therapist selects the patient he feels will benefit most from group interaction to be the focus of the therapy session. In a sense, the session belongs to that patient. Typically, he will talk about himself for 15 or 20 minutes; at the conclusion of this monologue, the group will begin a general discussion, which, however, will continue to revolve around the patient who is up. The therapist may interject his comments, either in the course of the patient's initial presentation or during the subsequent group discussion, if he feels that certain relevant aspects of the patient's behavior have not been covered, or have not received sufficient emphasis. Thus, to a significant extent, the therapist provides the structure of the group session.

As the center of attention, the patient who is up occupies an enviable position in the group and patients frequently vie for this opportunity. In fact, many patients keep a rather careful record of which patient is discussed each week in order to make sure that all the members of the group are up for discussion the same number of times each year. Moreover, since the therapist makes the final decision as to who is up for discussion each week, these records serve to ensure equality of treatment. Nevertheless, such equality in frequency of discussion is not always feasible. A patient who is going through a period of crisis may have to be the focus of group attention in two or three sessions out of cycle. Group members tend to accept this without protest; they understand that occasionally a patient may need extra time when he is faced with an emergency. Conversely, they will object if a dominating, grasping patient tries to get more than his fair share of the group's attention; such a patient usually evokes considerable hostility on the part of his co-patients.

As noted above, the therapist's decision with regard to the selection of the patient who is up is based on his evaluation of the needs of the individual members of the group. Thus the withdrawn schizoid patient, who finds it difficult to relate to others and will not participate in group discussions voluntarily, will have to be "forced" to participate in treatment. Group members rarely make an effort on their own to draw these patients out. As a rule, the members of a newly formed group, in particular, will tend to overlook such patients, and to direct their attention, instead, to the verbal, articulate, and insightful patient. The fact remains, however, that even if the therapist must set the stage for this response, it is extremely beneficial for the withdrawn patient to feel that the group is interested in him and wants to know more about him.

The Go-Around

Intimately related to the preceding technique, which is designed to ensure participation in treatment, is a procedure referred to as the go-around, which seeks to involve the patient more deeply in therapy by encouraging him to explore and verbalize his emotional problems. When he is the focus of a group session, the patient makes himself available for psychological exploration. Such exploration is facilitated by the go-around, whereby each member of the group is given

an opportunity to discuss his personal response to the patient who is up.

In broad outline, after the group members are seated in a circle, as is customary, the therapist decides on the starting point of the go-around. Each patient then proceeds in orderly sequence to evaluate the focal group member and to explore his transferential feelings toward him, until all the members of the group have participated in the discussion. Spontaneity is encouraged, and patients may enter the discussion out of turn. But the therapist must see to it that such spontaneity is kept within certain bounds. When affective reactions reach chaotic proportions, the group takes on the characteristics of a mob. Our therapeutic philosophy in this respect, as outlined earlier in this chapter, can be underscored in this context. Specifically, we feel strongly that psychotherapy cannot proceed unless rational cognitive processes are brought to bear upon affective responses. Contrary to the view held by certain proponents of the encounter method, the ventilation of affect, in itself, has little psychotherapeutic value. Since the group situation is conducive to this form of expression, group therapy can be effective only if patient interaction is directed and controlled by the therapist, who can then make orderly, constructive interpretations. Finally, at the end of the go-around, the therapist may summarize its content and suggest particular areas of further exploration during the after-session.

The After-Session

After the formal group session has been terminated, the group members continue their discussion of the patient who is up at an after-session, which is held outside the therapist's office and without his presence. Attendance at the after-session is mandatory.

Since the after-session may continue for several hours, it is most practical to schedule it in the evening so that patients who work or have other commitments during the day can attend, although patients can usually manage to attend formal group therapy sessions during the day, since these are less time-consuming. As a rule, groups meet with the therapist from 5 to 6:30 P.M. and proceed from there to the after-session which may last until 11 or 12 o'clock, depending on the patient being discussed, the content of the session, etc.

Practical arrangements for the after-session are made by the members of the group, although they may—and frequently do—consult with the therapist before specific plans are finalized. Most often, the after-session is held at the apartment of a group member who lives in the general vicinity of the therapist's office. If several group members live in the area, their apartments are used in rotation. Obviously, the availability of a member's home for therapy sessions, no matter how ideally located, may be outruled on several grounds. The presence of the patient's mate and/or children would, for example, constitute a limiting factor.

Whether or not the patient's mate is in therapy himself, he will have definite opinions and feelings about his mate being in treatment. Depending on his personality structure, he may support the therapeutic efforts of his spouse or represent a potentially destructive influence. These attitudes and prejudices will be transmitted to group members if the mate "happens to be around" during an after-session held at his apartment and may require subsequent interpretation by the therapist. But, apart from such considerations, complete privacy is a mandatory condition for the after-session because of the highly personal—and confidential—nature of group therapy. This means that a patient may have to persuade her mate to visit a friend on the evening the group meets, which may not be easy. When children are involved as well, it becomes even more difficult to ensure the group's privacy. Nevertheless, patients do seem to manage somehow, so that arranging for after-sessions does not usually present an insurmountable problem, when two or three apartments are potentially available to the group for this purpose. But, when it does arise, this problem must be dealt with. The use of a private meeting place is essential for effective group therapy; a restaurant, for example, will not suffice.

There is an added advantage in having the group meet in a patient's home: The group has an opportunity to learn something about the patient's environment. In one instance the group was particularly appalled by the shabby home of a patient who had been perceived as a "natty dresser," a "man-about-town." Indeed, this was the facade he presented to the world. In fact, however, this patient was extremely despondent, and his shabby, depressing surroundings accurately reflected his inner sense of despair.

Finally, after-sessions should be distinguished from the alternate sessions which are a frequent component of traditional group therapy approaches. Both are held without the therapist. However, in contrast to the after-session, which represents an extension of the formal group therapy session, the alternate session is held on another night of the week. But the most important difference between them lies in the fact that in contrast to the after-session, attendance at alternate sessions is usually poor, and they may tend to be disjointed and nonproductive.

The Pre-Session

Sometimes a group will meet at a restaurant during the dinner hour for a "warm-up" session before the formal group session. The pre-session was born out of necessity. In view of the need to conduct group sessions in the evening, and the limited number of evening hours available, certain groups which meet at 8 or 9 P.M. were not able to allot sufficient time to their after-sessions.

In order to introduce some elements of structure into the pre-session, the group may delegate a member or phone the therapist, who will recommend that the group focus on a specific member during the pre-session. The discussion of the patient who is up then continues during the group session in the therapist's office.

Despite such innovations, the pre-session is essentially a compromise. Although it is of some value, it cannot be as effective as the more structured after-session.

Summer Sessions

As mentioned earlier, the group continues to meet on a weekly basis during the summer month that the therapist is on vacation. Usually, a schedule is prepared the week before the therapist's departure, indicating in which patient's home the sessions will be held. Because patients have more time to travel, these vacation sessions are frequently held at the homes of group members who live in the suburbs. And, as is the case during the rest of the year, the therapist encourages the group to meet at a different home each week, so that they can see how their co-patients live and observe their behavior in a natural setting.

Two types of report form are distributed to the group prior to the summer vacation period, with the understanding that they are to be filled out and mailed to the therapist's summer address within 24 hours after each group session. These reports serve to keep the therapist informed of the content of these sessions. Both forms are appended. Form A is filled out by a predesignated reporter who not only reports on the content of the group session, but also follows up on all absent members to learn why they missed the group session and how they are getting along, and informs the therapist of his findings. Form B is designated to permit a more personal type of communication; sufficient space is provided to enable each group member to comment in detail on his progress. The therapist regards the contents of these reports as confidential.

These summer sessions, together with the required reports to the therapist, serve to prevent breakdowns in communication, which are probably the greatest source of anxiety for patients in therapy. As a further precaution, patients are also permitted to phone the therapist if they feel the group was unable to help them to resolve a critical problem. Actually, few patients find it necessary to take advantage of this privilege, but all patients are reassured by the knowledge that the services of the therapist are available to them.

Ancillary Treatment Techniques

The patient is up and the subsequent go-around are standard procedures in Structured Interactional Group Psychotherapy. However, several ancillary techniques have also been utilized from time to time.

The Subject Session. When appropriate, the group therapist may suggest that a group session be modified, so that another method of patient exploration be used in lieu of the go-around. During the subject session, which constitutes one such modification, the group leader suggests that the group discuss topics which have particular relevance for the patient who is up. Thus, the subject session is still another manifestation of structured interaction, and, as such, it facilitates communication, discussion, and psychic exploration.

At any given session, the therapist may suggest that the group discuss the following subjects, among others: (1) sexuality, infidelity, masturbation, coitus; (2) manifestations of aggression, and the warding off of aggressive impulses; (3) significant temporal events, such as the assassination of President Kennedy.

The following clinical excerpt may help to illustrate the potential therapeutic value of the subject session:

A young woman who had severe guilt feelings about masturbation, and was too embarrassed to discuss this either with the therapist in individual session or with the group, experienced a strong sense of relief when the therapist introduced this subject at a group session. After she heard several other group members freely admit that they masturbated and describe a variety of masturbatory techniques, the patient was able to discuss masturbation openly for the first time.

Categories. At other times, the therapist may deliberately use provocative words or phrases in an effort to elicit an emotional reaction from the patient who is up. And, once again, this technique is designed to encourage verbal expression—and participation in treatment. Although most patients find the category method traumatic and anxiety-provoking, they are willing to concede that it forces one to express feelings which would never be verbalized under normal circumstances.

An endless variety of categories can be used for this purpose. The patient who is up is asked to classify other members of the group on the basis of appearance, intelligence, sexuality, etc. And, in so doing, he is given an opportunity to verbalize his major affective reactions to specific group members. The therapist then encourages the focal member to rate himself in each of these categories. At this point, the patient reveals feelings he has about himself, i.e., his self-image, which he would not touch on normally.

The patient who is up is instructed to discuss his various categories and the criteria he used in making his selections in the after-session. In addition, group members are asked to discuss those listings and categories they found particularly upsetting, or pleasant, or meaningful, and to explore their responses and associations. Those classifications which refer to appearance, intelligence, sexuality, and aggression seem to be the most provocative. At any rate, we recommend that the category method be used sparingly; its frequent use may be too traumatic—and may diminish the effectiveness of this technique.

Review Sessions. The therapist conducts a review session at his first meeting with the group after he returns from vacation, at his last meeting with the group before he leaves on vacation, and whenever he feels there is a need for such a session during the therapeutic year.

During the review session, all the patients present are discussed. Each patient is requested, in turn, to summarize his present psychological status briefly. Comments and interpretations may then be made by both the therapist and the other group members. It is important, however, to limit the length of the patient's summary, as well as the subsequent comments and interpretations, so that every patient will have an opportunity to participate. If a session is one and a half hours long, for example, and there are ten members present, each patient should be discussed for approximately ten minutes during the formal session in the therapist's office. Patients are instructed to conduct the after-session along similar lines. If the after-session is scheduled to last for four hours, each patient will be the focus of discussion for approximately 25 minutes.

Carefully structuring the review session in this manner helps to prevent disorder and makes it possible to cover many patients within a limited period of time. When the therapist has returned to the group after a lengthy absence, these conditions must prevail if he is to become acquainted with the current status of each patient and resume his role as the leader of the group.

Psychodrama. Psychodrama may also be used as an ancillary technique in Structured Interactional Group Psychotherapy. When he feels that this method may lead to a breakthrough, the therapist asks the patient who is up to step outside the consultation room while he and the other group members devise an appropriate psychodramatic situation for the patient, based on their knowledge of his psychological conflicts. Roles and content are predesignated: one patient may play the role of a mother (or father), another may portray a child, a third may be a friend or a lover. Once it has been conceptualized, the patient returns to the session, and the psychodrama is enacted. When it has been concluded, the group members and the patient who is up discuss their reactions to the episode.

Obviously, this technique is most valuable when it is used for patients whose feelings are so deeply repressed they cannot be elicited through traditional treatment techniques:

A 50-year old depressed patient had not been able to discharge her affective response to her mother's death ten years previously. Accordingly, the therapist suggested psychodrama as a possible means of facilitating the discharge of repressed material. It was decided that one group member would play the "deceased mother returned to visit her daughter," and the patient was instructed to speak to her in any way she chose. Within a few minutes, the patient-daughter had expressed the despair, grief, and anger which were associated with her mother's death via this role-playing technique.

We realize, of course, that no true and permanent solution can be achieved through abreaction. Nevertheless, it is of value in that it demonstrates to the patient the existence and intensity of his emotions and serves as an introduction to the ensuing working through of what has come to light in the patient's acting out.

Personal Movies and Photographs.
While verbalizing one's past and present life
experiences is valuable in itself, seeing movies and photographs of the person involved
and the situations described adds a very
meaningful dimension to these accounts.
This holds true for the patient concerned,
for his fellow group members, and for the
therapist. Frequently, the members of the
group have an intense personal reaction to
the photograph of a person they had only
heard about, because they have identified
with that person or because he has become
the target of their strong feelings of hostility
and aggression.

Audiotape Recordings. A patient's verbal contribution to a group session may be
tape-recorded and the recording played back
at a later date with remarkable effects. Obviously, patients should never be tape-recorded without their knowledge and permission, for to do so would threaten the
privacy and trust which are so important to
the doctor-patient relationship. This rarely
presents a problem, however. Patients do not
object to being taped as a rule, as long as
they are aware of it beforehand and are assured of the confidentiality of their communications.

Videotape Recordings. Videotape
equipment may also be used to enable patients to see themselves first-hand on a television monitor while they talk, and this device can have equally dramatic effects. In
addition, videotape, like audiotape recordings, can be stored and played back at a
later date when it seems appropriate to do so.

DYNAMIC FACTORS IN STRUC-
TURED INTERACTIONAL GROUP
PSYCHOTHERAPY

The Transference in Combined
Individual and Group Therapy

It is commonly conceded that the foundation of all psychotherapy is the transference.
In individual treatment the transference is
concentrated on the therapist; identification
of the transferential components inherent in
the doctor-patient relationship is a pre-

requisite for the success of treatment. Constructive analysis of the transference is
equally crucial to the efficacy of group therapy. In group therapy, however, the cathexis which is directed only toward the therapist in individual treatment is displaced upon
other persons in the group (which further
dilutes the transference). Concomitantly,
transference phenomena become more complicated.

The patient's basic transference—to the
therapist—is positive, but temporary periods
of hostility or fear of the therapist are inevitable. In group therapy, these negative
feelings toward the therapist may be held in
check because of the patient's fear of retaliation. The patient's hostility may then
be displaced and redirected toward his fellow
group members. On the other hand, the
support that group members receive from
one another may facilitate the expression of
hostility toward the therapist.

In any event, it behooves the group leader
to keep these complex transferential situations clear and unchaotic. Because transferential reactions, whether positive or negative, are subject to contagion, by which they
become greater than the sum of the group's
parts, there is a risk attached to their expression in group. This is particularly true
when strong negative feelings are directed
toward the therapist. It is essential, of
course, that the patient eventually express
his hostile feelings toward the therapist,
who may be the parent surrogate. However,
the authors have always maintained that the
expression of major transferential reactions
—especially negative ones—should be reserved for individual treatment sessions,
where they can be analyzed more objectively.
The unbridled expression of transference responses in group can produce chaos and the
"wolf-pack" phenomenon, whereby the
group gangs up on the therapist—or another
patient. Whereas such behavior can be extremely destructive in the group setting, it
can be dealt with in individual sessions in a
most constructive manner.

Interpretation in Group Psychotherapy

Interpretation is an index of the skill of the
therapist, particularly when it involves elu-

cidation of the transference and other unconscious processes. In group therapy, however, interpretation is not the sole prerogative of the therapist; it may also be made by other patients in the group. Concomitantly, a patient's behavior may be interpreted in the group session per se or in the after-session or pre-session (or in sessions which are held while the therapist is on vacation).

When giving interpretations, the therapist needs to beware of unmasking a patient before the group beyond a point the patient can accept. From this point of view, it is preferable that interpretation come from other members, and this occurs constantly as patients respond to the unconscious needs of one another through identification and empathy. Nevertheless, the therapist must evaluate the accuracy of such interpretations. When the interpretations of group members are cogent, the therapist must point out their cogency. When interpretations are insensitive or inaccurate, the therapist must correct them as promptly as possible. If such an interpretation is made during the formal group session, it can, of course, be corrected immediately. If the interpretation is made during an after-session, it may have to be corrected when the therapist sees the "misunderstood" patient in individual session.

In general, group members look to the therapist for validation of the interpretations made by their peers, but when a patient speaks with authority (which is especially true of patients who have had some professional training), it may be necessary for the therapist to confront the authoritarian patient with the fact that he is subject to the same misperceptions as other members in the group. Above all, the therapist must never abdicate his role as leader of the group, and his evaluation of the validity of interpretations made by group members must reflect his capacity for leadership.

The Dynamics of Group Interaction and Group Inter-relationships

The Nuclear Group Member: The Therapist Surrogate. Every therapeutic group includes several self-appointed group leaders. These patients, who are usually healthier than their peers, tend to function with particular effectiveness as catalysts in group interaction. And when the therapist is not present, e.g., in the after-session and the pre-session or during summer meetings, these nuclear or focal members play a meaningful and active role in the group as surrogate therapists. It is the collaboration of these patients that makes structured interactional techniques meaningful in group therapy.

Accordingly, it is important to utilize the skills and participation of the nuclear patient in group therapy, to the extent that it is possible to do so: During those periods when the nuclear patient's relationship with the therapist is a positive one, he can be a potent ally. On the other hand, when he develops a negative transference toward the therapist, he may play a particularly destructive role in therapy. In short, the therapist must be constantly aware of the nuclear patient's psychological status if his skills are to be utilized effectively.

Other factors must be taken into consideration as well: As a rule, patients who assume this nuclear role gain certain unique benefits from group therapy: They achieve a marked increase in self-esteem, and their ego is strengthened considerably. At times, however, the nuclear group member may use his preoccupation with co-patients as a means of evading his own problems and of exposing himself to the group.

The patient, a 28-year-old psychiatric resident, identified closely with the therapist. Because of her innate sensitivity and her psychiatric training, she readily assumed the role of therapist surrogate. And her interpretations of the behavior of other patients were usually accurate. It soon became apparent, however, that these activities, which, on one hand, helped her to grow and develop both personally and professionally, often served to justify her resistance to examining her own problems and resolving her conflicts. Furthermore, her sexual transference, which was directed toward the therapist, was acted out with other group members without any attempt to gain insight into her behavior.

At one session, when the patient made an interpretation that was questioned by the therapist, she reacted with violent rage instead of trying to validate the accuracy of her interpretation. Using her leadership position in the group, she then attempted to mobilize group support for her resistance. And she was stunned when the group refused to cooperate. Finally, her competitiveness with the therapist, as well as her striving for power, were interpreted in a go-around. After this confrontation, the patient's behavior, both in and out of group, began to change rather dramatically. But it is safe to assume that if this conflict had not been exposed, and resolved, this patient would have left therapy—feeling justified in her resistance.

Dominant Behavior by One Group Member. Occasionally, a group will include a member whose neurotic need for power causes him to be extremely controlling and dominating. Typically, his co-patients will react to this type of behavior with anxiety and hostility. Only a strong and reasonably secure group member can be expected to challenge such a dominating patient, and at times the group will simply be unable to restrict this destructive behavior. The group will then look to the therapist to control the patient, and the therapist must provide such controls to preserve the group. Not infrequently, the therapist will then become the object of the dominant member's hostility, which, in turn, may elicit a strong countertransference. Nevertheless, the therapist must persist in his efforts to encourage the patient to examine the origins of his aggression. For unless he gains some insight into his behavior, such a patient will continue to represent a threat to the survival of the group.

Cooperation among Group Members. Because of the empathy that exists among group members, they welcome an opportunity to provide practical assistance to one another. From time to time, such opportunities do arise, and, if it seems necessary to do so, the group leader must place restrictions and limitations upon such assistance. For example, when a patient finds himself in economic straits, another group member will usually offer to lend him money. It is the responsibility of the group leader to see that any transactions of this type are kept within the bounds of good judgment, that the amounts involved are not too great,

and that the loans are repaid. Whether or not such feelings are verbalized, in the eyes of the group, the therapist bears a good deal of the responsibility for such transactions.

Sexual Acting Out. Depending on the make-up of the group, and the rules set forth by the group leader, there may be a great deal of sexual activity in a group, or almost none at all. Most patients are very serious about their group commitment and do not view therapy as a Roman holiday, as an opportunity to engage in unrestricted sexual activity. Since he cannot prevent it, it is usually better for the therapist to be accepting in his approach to sexual acting out in group, but it should certainly not be encouraged. His best position would seem to be, "I do not recommend sexual activity among group members and would like to discourage it on all levels." If such behavior becomes a serious problem for certain patients, the therapist may forbid sexual acting out in group; if it persists, he may then ask those involved to leave the group. When he does take a firm stand, in this respect, the restrictions he imposes generally serve to curb destructive behavior.

A married patient who was angry at her husband informed the therapist in individual session that she had decided to seduce a passive male member of her group who was obviously attracted to her. The patient planned to tell her husband about the affair after it had been consummated. The therapist pointed out that such acting out would pose a real threat to her marriage; moreover, it was forbidden on therapeutic grounds. As a result, the patient was forced to deal with her anger toward her husband in a more constructive way.

"Pairing" is another possible consequence of group therapy. While such behavior is based on a mutual sexual attraction, it would not necessarily be classified as sexual acting out. Nevertheless, it is directly opposed to the philosophy inherent to group therapy. In his volume on group psychology, Freud commented on the effects of pairing on the stability of the group:

"... Two people coming together for the purpose of sexual satisfaction ... insofar as they seek solitude, are making a demonstration against the group feeling. The more they are in love, the more completely they suffice for each other. . . . Even in a person who has in other respects become absorbed in a group, when sexual impulsions become too strong, they disintegrate every group formation."

On these grounds, and in the light of the fact that such pairing may, in fact, reflect a transitory transference on the part of one partner or another, we believe that such behavior should be discouraged.

"CRISES" IN STRUCTURED INTERACTIONAL GROUP PSYCHOTHERAPY

Some Aspects of the Therapist's Role as Group Leader

While the personality of the psychotherapist has been investigated to some extent, little is available in the literature with respect to the correlation between personality and the type of therapy he practices. The principles of Structured Interactional Group Psychotherapy can be taught to most therapists, but it cannot be administered effectively by all therapists. This type of therapy requires the expenditure of a tremendous amount of energy on the part of the therapist. He must be outgoing and must enjoy working actively with a group. (And, of course, he must also possess the requisite skills of the individual psychotherapist.)

With specific reference to group therapy, as we have emphasized throughout this chapter, in Structured Interactional Group Psychotherapy, the therapist, who often serves as an ego-ideal with whom his patients identify, must function as the strong leader of the group. One might speculate that the psychiatrist can best function in this role if he maintains a certain degree of anonymity. In fact, however, this is not always feasible. Inevitably, group patients get to know a great deal more about their therapist than do patients in individual psychotherapy. Because of the chain reaction phenomenon, described earlier, if the therapist tells one group something about his personal life, however unimportant, he

has told it to all his groups, in a manner of speaking. And, with the pooling of information that takes place among group members, an enormous amount of data may be learned about the therapist. This does not impair the group's perception of the therapist under normal circumstances. However, when a crisis arises in the life of the therapist it may raise certain predictable problems.

When the therapist is suffering from a temporary physical illness, the nuclear group members usually step into the breach and facilitate group functioning (as they do during the summer months). However, when the therapist's crisis is emotional, and his ability to function is limited as a result, more fragile members who are particularly prone to anxiety, may be forced to withdraw from the group. In fact, even some of the healthier patients may withdraw from treatment because of the discomfort that is generated. More frequently, however, the great majority of patients will try to support their fellow group members until the situation is stabilized. Thus, while any crisis in the therapist's life will interfere with group functioning to some degree, it may also serve as a growth experience for the group. While this is not always true of traditional group methods, Structured Interactional Group Psychotherapy produces groups of exceptional cohesiveness which helps the patient withstand the vicissitudes of treatment—and, ultimately, the vicissitudes of life.

Resistance to Group and Individual Therapy

As noted earlier, patients are billed for all group sessions they fail to attend, whatever the reason for their absence. And we have found that this rule serves as a powerful incentive for regular attendance. In addition, however, a good deal of psychological pressure is placed upon all members to attend every group session. Particular emphasis is placed on the fact that the patient is an important part of the group and that other group members count on his participation; he is made to understand that if he misses sessions frequently, the group will not be able to function properly —to the detriment of all patients. If a patient misses an excessive number of group sessions, this problem is discussed in individual session. If these sessions are unproductive, that is, if the patient does not gain sufficient insight into his resistance to modify his behavior, it may be necessary to remove him from the group.

The patient may attribute his erratic attendance at group sessions to any one of a variety of factors: One patient may protest that although he considers group therapy a valuable experience he finds it too anxiety-provoking. Another may say that he gets nothing from the group; and a third may be convinced that his group is not as good as other groups. Obviously, in such instances, it would be a mistake for the therapist to transfer the patient to another group, unless he is convinced that the patient's dissatisfaction is well-founded. There is still another variation: Patients who prefer individual sessions to group therapy may try to make a deal with the therapist by offering to continue in one form of treatment, but not the other. The therapist must then establish that the patient is, in fact, attempting to avoid the anxieties attached to the group situation and try to help the patient understand his true motives. Above all, the therapist must not allow himself to be manipulated in this situation. Whatever its source, every effort should be made to resolve the patient's resistance; clearly, his removal from the group would be considered a negative sign in terms of his general prognosis.

In fact, such situations occur only rarely. As noted earlier, most patients become emotionally involved with their group, and this, of course, tends to reduce their resistance to treatment. But it may give rise to another problem: Not infrequently, patients become less involved with individual therapy as their interest in group increases, to the degree that group therapy may actually cause resistance to individual therapy. Since it is an integral part of Structured Interactional Group Psychotherapy, it is equally important that the patient's resistance to individual treatment be resolved.

EVALUATION OF STRUCTURED INTERACTIONAL GROUP PSYCHOTHERAPY

For obvious reasons, reliable statistics on the efficacy of any one type of psychotherapy are unavailable. Most therapists report empirically on the usefulness of a particular technique, and so it must be with the authors of this chapter. In our work we have found that most patients share our feeling that Structured Interactional Group Psychotherapy constitutes an unusually satisfactory technique. And, since many of our patients are repeaters and have been in treatment with other therapists who subscribe to a variety of techniques, presumably their judgment would have considerable validity. The goals of psychotherapy, whether individual or group, and whatever the specific treatment technique employed, are the same: anxiety reduction, personality change, and emotional growth and development. Feedback from patients who have been discharged from Structured Interactional Group Psychotherapy indicates that they feel these goals have been attained.

In addition, clinical data are available which clearly attest to the efficacy of Structured Interactional Group Psychotherapy. The fact that, over a period of 18 years, none of our patients has committed or attempted suicide, is evidence of the value of this form of treatment in the management of the depressed patient. The extremely low drop-out rate (under 5 per cent) is clearly indicative of the acceptance of this treatment modality by an overwhelming majority of patients, regardless of diagnosis. Finally, while we lack conclusive evidence that Structured Interactional Group Psychotherapy influences the duration of treatment, there is no question that the unique techniques employed seem to facilitate the expression of repressed problems and conflicts and serve thereby to expedite their resolution.

SUMMARY

An attempt was made in this section to describe the theoretical framework and methodology of a new method of group psychotherapy—not previously reported on in the literature—called Structured Interactional Group Psychotherapy. As practiced and taught by the authors over a period of 18 years, it has evolved as a technique used primarily in combination with individual psychoanalytic psychotherapy.

The core techniques of Structured Interactional Group Psychotherapy, i.e., the patient is up and the go-around, are designed to ensure patient participation in treatment and to structure group interaction so that it can best fulfill each patient's therapeutic needs. Ancillary techniques, such as the after-session, the subject session, the category method, and summer sessions (and report forms), are designed to further enhance the treatment process.

In the opinion of the authors, and of their patients, the results achieved through the use of Structured Interactional Group Psychotherapy—in combination with individual psychotherapy—have been most satisfactory.

REFERENCES

Alexander, F. Analysis of the therapeutic factors in psychoanalytic treatment. Psychoanal. Quart., *19:* 482, 1950.

Freud, S. Group psychology and the analysis of the ego. In *Standard Edition of the Complete Psychological Works of Sigmund Freud*, vol. 18, J. Strachey, editor. Hogarth Press, London, 1955.

Liberman, R. A behavorial approach to group dynamics. Behav. Ther., *1:* 141, 1970.

Rosenbaum, N., and Berger, M., editors. *Group Psychotherapy and Group Function.* Basic Books, New York, 1963.

Slavson, S. N. *A Textbook on Analytic Group Psychotherapy.* International Universities Press, New York, 1964.

Wolf, A. Group psychotherapy. In *Comprehensive Textbook of Psychiatry*, A. M. Freedman and H. I. Kaplan, editors. Williams & Wilkins, Baltimore, 1967.

Wolf, A., and Schwartz, E. *Psychoanalysis in Groups.* Grune & Stratton, New York, 1962.

FORM A   GROUP _____   DATE _____
                 (Identify by meeting time)

REPORTER _____

Members Attending _____

_____

_____

Members Absent _____

_____

NAME   Participation in group -- a short summary by
                                            reporter
                    Note members who are absent and reason
_____

_____

_____

FORM B
Personal Report Form
to be presented
around group

GROUP _____

DATE _____

REPORTER _____

NAME
(Signature)

Personal comments from each group member.
How are you feeling?
Highlight of week?   Major Problem?   Mood?

_____

_____

_____

4

Transactional Analysis in Groups

John M. Dusay, M.D. and Claude Steiner, Ph.D.

HISTORY

Transactional analysis is a technique of psychotherapy that has been in use since about 1954. Developed by Eric Berne, it is an original theory of personality and a distinct departure from currently held views of psychotherapy.

Berne's first insight into his theory was provided by one of his patients, who told him the following story: While vacationing at a ranch, an eight-year-old boy in his cowboy suit helped the hired man unsaddle his horse. "Thanks, cowpoke," said the hired man. "I'm not really a cowpoke, I'm just a little boy," answered the assistant. The patient then remarked:

That's just the way I feel. I'm not really a lawyer. I'm just a little boy.

This patient was a successful professional, but he often acted, in treatment and in his everyday life, like a little boy. In treatment, when addressed, he sometimes would ask, "Are you talking to the lawyer or the little boy?"

It was this observation that caused Berne to consider the value of dividing the behavior of persons into distinct ego states, which he defined as "coherent systems of feelings and behavior patterns." The initial division of the ego into Child and Adult was soon followed by an additional ego state— the Parent. These became the basic concepts of structural analysis.

In a relatively short period thereafter, Berne developed transactional analysis and made some germinal statements about script analysis. The bulk of the complete system of transactional analysis was developed in a period of about three years. Script analysis was developed a decade later by Steiner and such others as Crossman and Karpman.

Early in 1958 Berne began to meet with a group of professionals who had shown interest in his theory. This group called itself the San Francisco Social Psychiatry Seminars and later changed its name to the San Francisco Transactional Analysis Seminar. The group met without interruption, except for occasional holidays, at Berne's home every Tuesday night until he died suddenly on July 15, 1970. Since its inception, transactional analysis has acquired an international organization with more than 700 members with seminars and institutes in 50 cities of the United States, and wth a quarterly publication, *The Transactional Analysis Bulletin.*

Berne's training was that of a psychiatrist and psychoanalyst. His psychoanalytic studies spanned 13 years at the New York and San Francisco Psychoanalytic Institutes. The precursors, in Berne's thinking, of transactional analysis can be found in a series of articles on the subject of intuition published by the *Psychiatric Quarterly* between 1949 and 1962. In these articles Berne focused his interest on the capacities of the ego (later to be termed the Professor or Adult in the Child), which seemed to be not strictly rational or conscious. The theme of ego states also has precursors in Berne's association and work with Federn and Penfield.

Berne's interest in the Child was many-faceted. He always emphasized that the Child ego state was the most worthwhile part of the personality, and he insisted on having a party for the Child after the scientific sessions on Tuesday nights.

THEORY OF PERSONALITY

The building blocks of the theory of transactional analysis are three observable forms of ego function: the Parent, the Adult, and the Child. They may seem to resemble three basic psychoanalytic concepts—the supergo, the ego, and the id—but they are, in fact, quite different.

The Parent, Adult, and Child differ from the superego, ego, and id in that the former three are ego functions. They represent visible ego behavior rather than hypothetical constructs. When a person is in one of the three ego states—for instance, the Child—the observer is able to see and hear the Child, but no one has ever seen the id or superego. Transactional analysis focuses on the ego and on consciousness because these concepts explain and predict behavior more effectively than do psychoanalytic concepts.

Structural Analysis

A person operates in one of three distinct ego states at any one time (see Figure 1). These ego states are distinguishable by skeletal-muscular variables and by the content of verbal utterances. Certain gestures, postures, mannerisms, facial expressions, intonations, and words are typically associated with one of the three ego states. In examining his own behavior, an observer also has information about his emotional state and thoughts, which are part of the ego state being observed. Diagnosis of ego states is made by observing the visible and audible characteristics of a person's appearance or ego

The Child. The Child ego state is preserved in its entirety from childhood. When in this ego state, a person behaves as he did when he was a little boy or a little girl. The Child is usually not more than about seven years old and may be as young as one hour or one day. When a person is in the Child ego state, he sits, stands, walks, and speaks as he did when he was, say, three years old. This childlike behavior is accompanied by the corresponding perceptions, thoughts, and feelings of a three-year-old, as described by Werner.

The Child ego state tends to be fleeting in grown-ups because of a general societal injunction against childish behavior. However, Child ego states can be observed in situations that are structured to permit childlike behavior, such as sports events, parties, and church revivals. A good place to view the Child ego state in grown-ups is at a football game. Here, childlike expressions of joy, anger, rage, and delight can be observed, and it is easy to see how, aside from bone size and secondary sexual characteristics, a man jumping for joy when his team scores is indistinguishable from a young boy. The similarity goes further than the observable behavior, since the man is not only acting but feeling, seeing, and thinking like a boy.

In the Child ego state, a person tends to use short words and expletives like "golly," "gee," and "nice," delivered in a high-pitched voice. He adopts stances characteristic of children: a downward tilt of the head, upturned eyes, feet apart or pigeon-toed. When sitting, the person may balance on the edge of the chair—fidgeting, rocking, or slouching. Jumping, clapping, laughing expansively, and crying are all part of the repertoire of the Child ego state.

Aside from situations that permit childlike behavior, the Child can be observed in a fixated form in schizophrenics, in infantilized female symbols like Marilyn Monroe, and in comedians, whose profession requires them to appear habitually in a Child ego state. Of course, the Child ego state is readily observable in children.

A Child ego state much younger than a year is rarely observed, since most persons who express this ego state habitually are severely disturbed. However, this type of a very young Child appears in normal persons under circumstances of severe stress and when great pain or joy is felt.

The value of the Child should not be

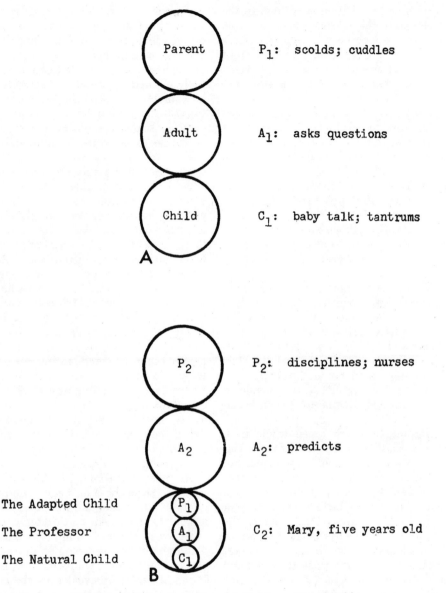

Figure 1. A, Mary, five years old; B, Mary, 35 years old.

underestimated. It is said to be the best part of a person and the only part that can really enjoy itself. It is the source of spontaneity, creative change, and joy.

The Adult. The Adult ego state is essentially a computer, an impassionate organ of the personality that gathers and processes data for the purpose of making predictions. The Adult gathers data about the world through the senses, processes them accord-

ing to a logical program, and makes predictions when necessary. Its perception is diagrammatic. The Child perceives in color, in space, and from one point of view at a time, but the Adult may perceive in black and white, often in two dimensions, and from several points of view at the same time. In the Adult ego state, a person is isolated from his own affective and other internal processes, a condition indispensable for the proper observation and prediction of reality. In the Adult ego state the person has no feelings, even though he may be able to appraise his Child or Parent feelings. A rational Parent ego state is often confused with the Adult ego state. However, the Adult is not only rational but also without emotion.

According to Piaget, the Adult grows gradually through childhood. This development proceeds as a consequence of the interaction between the person and the external world.

The Parent. The Parent is essentially made up of behavior copied from parents or authority figures. It is taken whole, as perceived at an early age, without modification. A person in the Parent ego state will behave like his parent or whoever was or is *in loco parentis*.

The Parent ego state is essentially non-perceptive and noncognitive. It is simply a constant and sometimes arbitrary basis for decisions. It is the repository of traditions and values and is, therefore, vital to the survival of civilization. It operates validly when adequate information for an Adult decision is not available, but in certain people it operates in spite of adequate Adult information.

The Parent, although taken whole from others, is not a fixated ego state, since it can change over time. A person's experiences can add to or subtract from the Parent's repertoire of behavior. For instance, rearing a first-born child greatly increases the range of responses of the Parent. In general, the Parent ego state seems to change throughout life, from adolescence to old age, as the person encounters new situations that demand parental behavior and as the person finds authority figures from whom examples for such behavior are adopted.

Operation of Ego States. Structural analysis, then, is organized around the fundamental concepts of the ego states. These ego states operate one at a time—that is, a person is always in one and only one of the three ego states. This ego state is called the executive or is said to have executive power. However, while one ego state has the executive power, the person may be aware of literally being beside himself, observing his own behavior. The feeling that the self is not

the ego state in the executive usually occurs when the Child or Parent has executive power while the real self, perhaps the Adult, observes without being able to behave. While one ego state is cathected—that is, imbued with the energy necessary to activate muscular complexes involved in behavior—another ego state may be sufficiently cathected to become conscious to the person, even though it is unable to activate the musculature.

The fact that a person can operate in one ego state while another observes makes possible internal dialogues between two ego states. For example, after a few drinks at a party, a man may be swept by the music into an expansive, childlike dance. His Child is in the executive while the Parent observes his gyrations and mutters something like, "You're making a fool of yourself, Charlie," or, "This is all very well, but what about your slipped disk?" This comment by the nonexecutive ego state may decathect the Child and transfer the executive to the Parent, in which case Charlie stops dancing, perhaps blushes, and retires to his seat, where the situation may be reversed, with Charlie, now in the Parent ego state, looking disapprovingly at other dancers. Becoming aware of the conversations that occur between the executive and the observing state is an important step in therapy, as has been pointed out by Ellis.

At times it is somewhat difficult to diagnose ego states because people tend to masquerade their Child and Parent as Adult ego states. Opinionated and judgmental attitudes are often couched in rational language. The Parent, masquerading as an Adult, may express very logical points of view, but their Parental nature is revealed by the emphasis or the unspoken but clear attempt to impose the points of view on others. From his Adult ego state, a husband may ask his wife, "Why isn't dinner ready?" From his Parent masquerading as an Adult, he may ask the identical question. The difference, however, is that in the former case the husband is simply asking a question, but in the latter case he is attempting to pressure and blame his wife for her being lazy and disorganized.

Sometimes, two sets of muscles seem to be powered by two separate ego states at the same time. For instance, a lecturer's voice and facial muscles may indicate an Adult ego state while an impatient toss of the hand reveals a Parent ego state. In such cases, it is likely that the behavior is Parent in Adult disguise or that Parent and Adult are alternating rapidly.

Alternation between ego states depends on the permeability of the ego state boundaries. Permeability is an important variable in psychotherapy. Low permeability leads to exclusion of appropriate ego states. Exclusions of the Parent, Adult, and Child ego states are all pathological, since they preclude the use of ego states that in a given situation may be more adaptive than the excluding ego state.

For example, at a party the excluding Adult is less adaptive than the Child. The purpose of the party is to have fun, which the Child can do. The Adult, analyzing and computing data dispassionately, would deter the party's purpose. A father with an excluding Adult prevents the more adaptive Parent from properly raising his children. For example, when Johnny asks his father, "Daddy, why do I have to go to bed?" the Adult response would be a lecture about the physiology, psychology, and sociology of sleep. The more adaptive Parent would simply say, "The reason you have to go to sleep is because I said so," or, "Because it's bedtime," an answer that is much more appropriate to the situation.

On the other hand, extreme permeability is another form of pathology, often manifested by inability to remain in the Adult ego state for a sufficient time.

Every ego state, being a substructure of the ego, is in its own way an adaptive organ, having as its function adaptation to the demands of reality. All three ego states share in this function, each one specially suited for specific situations. The Parent is ideally suited where control is necessary—control of children, of unknown situations, of fears, of unwanted expressions by people, and of the Child. The Adult is suited to situations in which accurate prediction is necessary. The Child is ideally suited where creation is desired—procreation and creation of new experiences.

One more concept of importance is contamination. This phenomenon is character-ized by an Adult ego states' holding as fact certain ideas stemming from the Parent or the Child. For instance, a Parent idea such as, "Excessive masturbation leads to insanity" could be part of a person's Adult ego state. Decontamination of the Adult is an early therapeutic requirement in treatment. A successful technique to decontaminate ego states is having the person alternately speak first for one and then the other of his ego states. This technique, originated in psychodrama and later adapted by Gestalt therapy, is a convincing demonstration of the reality of ego states. A person who feels guilty because of excessive masturbation could be asked to speak from his Child ego state about the guilt and fears of insanity due to his masturbation and from his Adult about the well-known fact that masturbation is harmless and normal. Verbalizing these different points of view tends to separate the two ego states, a process that facilitates decontamination of the Adult.

Thus, transactional analysis is a theory based on variables, observable and verifiable by patients as well as by therapists and theorists. The wish to include the patient in the understanding, observation, and verification of behavior theories generates the extensive use of colloquialisms and the insistence that most of the relevant variables in treatment are conscious and, therefore, available to the patient's awareness by simple attention to certain areas of his behavior.

Second-Order Structural Analysis

Script analysis requires an understanding of second-order structural analysis, the analysis of the structure of the Child.

Consider a five-year-old child, Mary (see Figure 1A). Mary is capable of operating in three ego states. In her Parent ego state (P_1), she scolds and cuddles her little brother as she sees her mother do; in her Adult ego state (A_1), the Professor, she asks difficult questions ("What is sex, Daddy?" "What is blood for?"). In her Child ego state (C_1), she behaves as she did when she was two years old—she talks baby talk, throws a tantrum, or rolls around on the floor.

Thirty years later, Mary (see Figure 1B) is again capable of behaving in three separate ego states. The Parent (P_2) disciplines her five-year-old daughter and nurses her newborn baby; her Adult (A_2) knows how to cook and how to extract an appendix and makes accurate predictions about events and people; and her Child (C_2) is identical with the five-year-old Mary described above. Of the three modes of the Child in the 35-year-old Mary, one is most likely to be apparent. Mary's personality, as it is known to others, depends on which of the three possible Child ego states is usually cathected.

If her Child is primarily P_1, she is likely to have a script that is the result of her parents' behavior when she was, say, five years old. She behaves in ways exemplified and forced on her by her parents. This Child ego state, P in C_2, has also been called the Adapted Child because, although still a Child ego state, it is molded to parental demands. In the case of persons with self-destructive scripts, it is also called the electrode because of the electrifying manner in which it seems to control the person's mental life and behavior. In these cases, P in C_1 is also called the witch-mother or ogre because it seems to have supernatural qualities similar to the witches and ogres in fairy tales.

If Mary's Child behaves mostly as A_1, the Professor, she tends to be inquisitive and lively—bright-eyed and bushy-tailed—as contrasted with the more emotive, powerful, perhaps overwhelming behavior of C_2, which is called the Natural Child or the prince or princess.

When in the Natural Child (C_1) ego state, the person is turned on or in a peak experience. Some people's Child is exclusively the Natural Child, but societal strictures against this form of behavior are strong; as a consequence, the Child of very few people operates at this level. The acute psychotic state in which a confused Natural Child takes over completely is in essence the breakthrough of the Child after a period of Parent domination.

It is important to distinguish, in 35-year-old Mary, the Parent (P_2) from the Parent in the Child (P_1). Both ego states are superficially similar in that they both involve certain behavior that is Parental, such as finger-wagging and certain words, such as "ought" and "should." On close examination, how-

ever, the differences become clear. P in the C_2 is a little girl acting like mother, but P_2 *is* the mother. P in the C_2 wants to be like mother and imitates her ("Johnny, you better be good"), all the while checking for reassurance from the parents ("How am I doing, Mommy?").

The Parent in the Child is a fixated ego state not amenable to change. Unlike the Parent (P_2), which changes over time, P in C_2 can only be affected by decommissioning it. In treatment, this technique is referred to as "showing mother (or father) to the door" and implies that the P in the C_2 is decathected and not allowed to exert its influence on the rest of the personality.

The Adult in the Child (A_1) is called the Professor because this part of the personality is thought to have an extremely accurate grasp and understanding of the major variables that enter into interpersonal relationships. This grasp is manifested in the capacity to detect the psychological, covert aspect of relationships. The Professor or the Adult in the youngster is tuned in to and is able to detect the real meaning of transactions and is, therefore, able to understand that which the first-order Adult misses. However, in matters other than psychological transactions, the Professor operates with limited information. A good analogy to clarify this point can be found in a very shrewd peasant who is able to hold his own in any interpersonal situation in his home town but who, when he goes to the big city, is not able to cope with the more complex situation, which requires a great deal of information not available to him.

Transactional Analysis

Just as the ego state is the unit of structural analysis, so the transaction is the unit of transactional analysis. The theory holds that, for purposes of group treatment, a person's behavior is best understood if examined in terms of ego states and that the behavior between two or more persons is best understood if examined in terms of transactions. A transaction consists of a stimulus and a response between two specific ego states. In a simple transaction, only two ego states operate. One example is a transaction between two Adult ego states: "How much is five times seven?" "Thirty-five." All other combinations of ego states may occur in a transaction. Transactions follow one another smoothly as long as the stimulus and response are parallel or complementary (see Figure 2).

In any series of transactions, communication proceeds if the response to a previous stimulus is addressed to the ego state that was the source of the stimulus and is emitted from the ego state to which that source addressed itself. Any other response creates a crossed transaction and interrupts communication. In Figure 2, Transaction A is complementary and leads to further communication while Transaction B is crossed and will break off communication. Crossed transac-

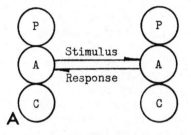

S: How much is five times seven?
R: Thirty-five.

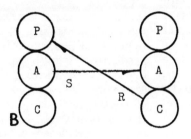

S: How much is five times seven?
R: I hate math!

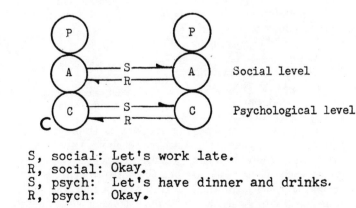

S, social: Let's work late.
R, social: Okay.
S, psych: Let's have dinner and drinks.
R, psych: Okay.

Figure 2. A, A complementary transaction; B, a crossed transaction; C, a complex, ulterior transaction.

tions not only account for the interruption of communication but are an essential part of games.

In addition to simple transactions, there are complex, ulterior transactions. Such a transaction operates on two levels—social and psychological. In Figure 2, transaction C is between A and A:

Let's work late on these accounts, Miss Smith; we'll catch dinner on the way to the office.

And between C and C:

Let's have dinner and drinks together, Sally, and maybe we'll get some work done later.

In an ulterior transaction, the social level usually covers the real, psychological meaning of the transaction. Interpersonal behavior is not understandable until the ulterior level and ego states involved are understood, when they are present.

Interpersonal behavior or what occurs between two or more people is divided into withdrawal, activity, rituals, pastimes, intimacy, and games. Withdrawal is lack of communication or transactions. Activity or work is a project designed to deal with the material of external reality. A ritual is a series of simple, complementary transactions, the elements of which have a very high order of predictability. A pastime is a similar series, not quite as predictable and relating to a single subject matter. Intimacy is defined as what will occur between people in the absence of the other forms of time structure. A game is a behavioral sequence that (1) is an orderly series of transactions with a beginning and an end; (2) contains an ulterior motive—that is, a psychological level different from the social level; and (3) results in a payoff for both players.

Motivation. The motivation for playing games comes from their payoff. Structural analysis describes the relevant parts of the personality, just as a parts list describes the parts of an engine. Transactional analysis describes the way in which the parts interact, just as a cutaway engine shows how the engine parts relate to each other. But to understand why people transact with each other at all, one must postulate some driving force, and this explanation is found in the motivational concepts of stimulus hunger, structure hunger, and position hunger. Games provide satisfaction for all three of these hungers, and this satisfaction is referred to as the advantage or payoff of the game.

Stimulus Hunger. Considerable research indicates that stimulation is one of the primary needs of higher organisms. On the basis of these findings and on clinical evidence, Berne evolved the concepts of stimulus hunger and stroking.

A stroke is a special form of stimulation one person gives to another. Because strokes are essential to a person's survival, the exchange of strokes is one of the most important activities people engage in. Strokes can vary from actual physical stroking, to praise, to just recognition. To be effective, a stroke must be suited to its recipient. For example, Spitz has shown that a very young child needs actual physical stroking; without it, he will die. On the other hand, adults may require only symbolic strokes like praise or expressions of appreciation.

Stimulus hunger is satisfied by stroking or recognition. Stroking is a more basic need than recognition, and it is said that a person needs stroking lest his spinal cord shrivel up, like the babies who died of marasmus, microscopically seen as dehydration and shrinking of central nervous system tissue. Usually, the needs for actual physical stroking are eventually replaced by symbolic stroking or recognition. The average adult can satisfy his hunger for stroking through, among other things, a ritual that is essentially an exchange of recognition strokes. For example, the following is a six-stroke ritual:

A: Hi.
B: Hi.
A: How are you?
B: Fine, and you?
A: Fine. Well, see you.
B: Yeah, see you around.

A game is transactionally more complex than the above ritual, but it is still an exchange of strokes. It might be noted in passing that "Go to hell!" is as much a stroke as "Hi," and people will settle for the former form of stroking when they cannot obtain the latter.

Certain persons are unable to accept overt

or direct recognition, requiring more disguised forms. Such an example is the woman who rejects all admiration of her looks, interpreting them as sexual advances, but accepts compliments about her sewing ability. People who cannot obtain or accept direct recognition for one reason or another tend to obtain it by playing games, which are a rich source of strokes.

At the same time that a game provides strokes for the player, it also provides protection from intimacy. Intimacy is a situation in which strokes are given directly and, therefore, most powerfully. Intimacy can be a threat to the person—essentially a threat of excessively intense stroking. A game is a carefully balanced procedure, designed to obtain an optimal amount of stroking.

Strokes can be obtained without resorting to games, which are basically subterfuges. Games are learned in childhood from parents as a preferred method of obtaining stimulation. A person giving up a game has to develop an alternate way of obtaining strokes. Until he does, he is subject to despair resembling marasmus in children who do not receive enough stroking.

Structure Hunger. The satisfaction of structure hunger is the social advantage of the game. Structure hunger is the need to establish a social matrix within which the person can transact with others. To satisfy structure hunger, the person seeks social situations within which time is structured or organized for the purpose of obtaining strokes. This need for time structure is an elaboration of stimulus hunger and, therefore, just a more complex form of that basic need. A game structures time in many ways. For instance, a game of "If It Weren't for You" provides for considerable time structure with its endless face-to-face recriminations. It provides for additional time structure in that it makes possible the pastime of "If It Weren't for Him (Her)," played with neighbors and relatives, and sometimes "If It Weren't for Them," played at bars and bridge clubs.

Position Hunger. The satisfaction of position hunger is the existential advantage of the game. Position hunger is the need to vindicate certain basic, life long, existential positions. These existential positions, colloquially known as the patient's racket, can be illustrated with a sentence such as, "I am no good," "They are no good," or "Nobody is any good." These positions are continually reaffirmed by internal conversations that take place, in the mind of the person, between himself and the Parent. Position hunger is satisfied by recognition received internally, from the Parent.

After a game of "Rapo," the players go home, and White may say to himself, "That proves women are bitches; are you happy, Mom?" And his Parent will answer, "That's my good little boy." This transaction reinforces the existential position of the player. Every game also has the effect of advancing the script or life plan of the person.

Sample Games. Two games are described here in detail. The first is a soft game called "Why Don't You—Yes But," and the second is a medium-hard version (second-degree) of "Rapo." The softness or hardness of a game refers to the intensity with which it is played and the morbidity of its effects. First-degree is the soft version, and the third-degree is the hard version of a game.

"Why Don't You—Yes But." This is a common soft game, played wherever people gather in groups. It generally proceeds as follows:

Black and White are mothers of grade school children.

White: I sure would like to come to the P.T.A. meeting, but I can't get a babysitter. What should I do?

Black: Why don't you call Mary? She'd be glad to sit for you.

White: She is a darling girl, but she's too young.

Black: Why don't you call the baby-sitting service? They have experienced ladies.

White: Yes, but some of those old ladies look like they might be too strict.

Black: Why don't you bring the kids along to the meeting?

White: Yes, but I would be embarrassed to be the only one to come with her children.

Finally, after several such transactions, there is silence, perhaps followed by a statement by Green, such as, "It sure is hard to get around when you have kids."

"Why Don't You—Yes But," the first game analyzed by Berne, fulfills the three parts of the definition of a game. It is a series of transactions beginning with a question and ending with an irritated silence. It contains an ulterior motive because, at the social level, it is a series of Adult questions and Adult answers while, at the psychological level, it is a series of questions by a demanding, reluctant Child, unable to solve a problem, and a series of answers by an increasingly irritated Parent, anxious to help, in a quandary.

The payoff of the game is as follows: It is a rich source of strokes, it provides a readily usable form of time structure wherever people congregate, and it reinforces an existential position. The position in this case is exemplified by Green's statement, "It sure is hard to get around when you have kids." For White, the game proves that parents are no good and always want to dominate you and, at the same time, proves that children are no good and prevent you from doing things. For Black, the game proves that children or grown-ups who behave like children are ungrateful and unwilling to cooperate. For both Black and White, the existential advantage fits into their script. A script can be provisionally defined as a predetermined life plan. Both White and Black come away from the game feeling angry or depressed according to what their favorite feeling racket is. After a long enough succession of such games, both White and Black may feel justified if they get a divorce, attempt suicide, or quit trying.

"*Rapo.*" This game is played by a special type of personality. "Why Don't You—Yes But" can be played by almost anyone, but Rapo's psychological content attracts only a few persons. It is a sexual game, so it requires a man and a woman, although it may be played between homosexuals as well. It proceeds, typically, as follows:

At a party, after considerable flirtation, White and Black find themselves alone, reading aloud from the *Kama Sutra*. Aroused by the inviting situation, Black makes a sexual advance toward White. White abruptly leaves the room, and Black is left feeling ashamed and humiliated.

Again there is a series of transactions, beginning with a sexual invitation and ending with a sexual rebuff. On the social level, the game looks like a straightforward flirtation ended by Black's breach of etiquette, right-fully rebuffed by White. On the psychological level between Child and Child, White has first enticed and then humiliated Black.

The payoff, again, consists of strokes, a way to structure time, and, existentially, a ratification of the position that "Men (women) are no good," followed by feelings of anger or depression, according to preference. Again the script is advanced, since enough episodes of this game may justify murder, rape, suicide, or depression for the players.

Game Aspects. It takes at least two persons to play any game. One person cannot play a game by himself. The frequent accusation of therapists, marital partners, and other persons in disrupted relationships—"You are playing a game with me!"—is essentially incorrect and is usually just one move in a game of "Psychiatry—Transactional Type" or "Uproar."

Games can be two-handed or many-handed. The game of "Rapo" is two-handed; "Why Don't You—Yes But" is many-handed. There are, however, three major, interconnected roles—Victim or Patsy, Rescuer, and Persecutor or Oppressor. These three roles tend to recur in most games and are an integral part of several major games, such as "Alcoholic," "Cops and Robbers," "High and Proud," and the various psychiatric rescue games.

Roles in a game are interchangeable—that is, a person can play all the roles of the game at one time or another. Karpman gives the example of the therapist who starts the game of "Rescue" as a Rescuer, with his patient as Victim; then switches to Victim, as his patient works up a large debt and makes early morning emergency calls; and finally switches to Persecutor, as he disregards, discounts, discharges, hospitalizes, or in some other way insults the patient, who now is again in the role of Victim.

Related to the payoff in games is the concept colloquially called trading stamps. Trading stamps—enduring, nongenuine feelings like depression, low self-esteem, and sadness—are collected and saved up by persons who play games so that, when enough are accumulated, they can be traded in for a blow-up, drunken binge, suicide attempt, or some other script milestone. The only enduring feelings that are considered genuine are joy and despair due to a loss. Anger may be genuine—but not if it endures beyond the events that cause the anger.

A racket, defined as the person's existential position, finds expression through the activity of collecting trading stamps. The person, for instance, whose existential position is, "I'm no good," can continually promote this position by the collection of low self-esteem stamps (gray stamps), while the person whose position is, "You're no good," can do the same through the collection of anger stamps (red stamps).

Script Analysis

The lives of some people can be very clearly seen as an endless repetition of certain games. Just as the concepts of Parent, Adult, and Child are often discounted as a mere renaming of the Freudian structures of superego, ego, and id, so is the concept of games often seen as a mere renaming of the phenomenon that Freud called the repetition-compulsion. Freud's concept of the repetition-compulsion certainly refers to the same phenomenon as that referred to by the concept of games. When closely examined, however, the concept of games transcends the meaning of that of the repetition-compulsion. The repetition-compulsion is an explanation that, in effect, suggests a backward-looking person who compulsively repeats an act in an attempt to bring about the resolution of an experience of the past. The concept of games, however, is both backward-looking and forward-looking.

It is the forward-looking aspect of games that is relevant in the concept of scripts. Seen in this context, the essential meaning of games comes into relief. For instance, to the "Rapo" player whose script involves eventual suicide, the game is a necessary aspect for the unfolding of the script. The same game of "Rapo" is played by a person throughout the years from early childhood to eventual tragic ending.

Every game has a childhood antecedent that is the basis of the game as played in adult life. The game of "Rapo," for instance, may have as a childhood example the situation in which a little girl, standing in a mud puddle, invites a little boy to play. The boy enthusiastically plunges in, and, as soon as he covers himself with mud, she daintily steps aside and walks off, saying, "John Brown, you are a mess."

One patient recalled how, as a 13-year-old, she played a soft game of "Rapo" while being walked home or at school dances. Later, she allowed boys to become sexually aroused while parked in a car and enjoyed their confusion and vulnerability under such circumstances. At college, she played the better-known form of "Rapo". And later in life, after an unsuccessful marriage, she began to walk into bars unescorted and became more and more depressed at every nauseating, filthy drunk who approached her. The game is the same throughout her life, but it becomes increasingly hard until, in the end, thoughts of suicide seem reasonable.

In this "Rapo" player, the backward-looking, repetition-compulsion aspects of the game are related to the patient's childhood relationship with her father. In its forward-looking aspects, however, the game is the indispensable element without which the script would never come to its final, tragic outcome. This person's life can be seen as a chain of games, one after another. Yet it is not enough to postulate a chain of games in which every stimulus leads to a response and in which the termination of every game leads to the initiation of the next one. The sequence of her games, all leading to tragic suicide, is not simply an endless, repeated effort at solving a childhood dilemma but a purposeful life plan. Every game is part of a chain leading to a preconceived goal. The "Rapo" player in question thought of herself in her teens as a tragic heroine and realized at an early age that her end would be dramatic and tragic.

Speaking of scripts, Berne stated in 1966 that, when the script comes to light,

it will then be found that the patient is actually spending his whole life in a predetermined way, based on decisions he made in early childhood, when he was much too young to make such serious commitments.

In other words, human beings often make early childhood decisions that become essentially a blueprint for their life course and, just like a stage script, control and make fated every major move in the rest of that person's life. The decisions made by the young child are based on all the information at his disposal at that time. With that information in mind, the child decides that a certain set of assumptions, a certain position, a certain life course are reasonable solutions to the predicament in which he finds himself as a child. Script analysis is the analysis of the childhood decisions, their consequences in adult life, and the process whereby these decisions are reversed so that the person may again make autonomous choices.

Berne briefly outlined his concepts of script and script analysis in his early writings but never pursued them to any extent, probably because his understanding of scripts was that they were unconscious and relatively inaccessible except through intense psychoanalysis, preferably in an individual psychotherapy context. In his understanding of scripts, Berne remained attached to psychoanalytic concepts, since he thought of them, essentially, as transference phenomena. Steiner, working with alcoholics, came to the conclusion that scripts are neither unconscious nor especially understandable as transference phenomena, and he developed a theory based on the notion that scripts are the result of consciously made and remembered childhood decisions and that they are accessible for understanding and change in the group treatment context.

The Script Matrix. Erikson postulated that decisions made by human beings about their identity occur ordinarily in adolescence and that, in order for these decisions to be valid and healthy, they have to be built on the effective resolution of a number of previous psychosocial crises over the issues of trust, autonomy, initiative, and industry. When the young person has not appropriately settled these crises, his choice of identity is disrupted. Script theory postulates that people often make decisions about their identity in different periods of childhood, perhaps as early as the first year of life, and that these decisions are adaptations to the pressures of the context in which the child lives. This context is seen to be essentially and primarily the person's parent or parents and is represented in script analysis by the script matrix (see Figure 3).

According to Crossman, the child in a normal household is nurtured, protected, and raised by the Parent ego states of his parents,

with their Adult and Child ego states playing lesser roles. In a script-genic household, however, it is not the Parent of the mother or father that is in charge of bringing up the offspring but a pseudo-Parent, which is in reality a Child ego state. The Child ego state is incapable of performing the necessary functions of a father or mother. The youngster's predicament in such a household is the need to obey or go along with the crazy Child in the parent, who is primarily concerned not with the well-being of the offspring but with carrying out its own script injunctions derived from its own parents, the youngster's grandparents. Thus, in the formation of scripts, the most important influence or pressure impinging on the youngster originates from the parental Child. That is, the Child ego states in the parent of the person are the determining factors in the formation of scripts.

Every person has three ego states, and the three ego states of both his mother and his father have to be understood as well if the person is to be understood. Self-destructive scripts are called hamartic, from the Greek word *hamartia*, tragic flaw. For persons with self-destructive scripts, the Child ego state in his mother or father has all the features of a witch or ogre. This witch or ogre, generally known as the parent's crazy Child, has the most profound influence on the offspring. In these cases the three- or four-year-old is under the unquestioned and unquestionable rule of a confused, scared, often wanton, and always irrational child.

The Injunction. The injunction is always a prohibition or an inhibition of the free behavior of the offspring. It is always a negation of an activity. The injunction reflects the fears, wishes, angers, and desires of the Child of the parent. Some injunctions affect a very small range of behavior, such as "Don't sing," "Don't laugh loudly," or "Don't eat too many sweets." Others are extremely comprehensive in range, such as "Don't be happy," "Don't think," or "Don't do anything." In every case the injunctions are statements by the crazy Child in the parent of what he or she wants the offspring to do. The malignancy of these injunctions and their potential for creating scripts depend on how severely the crazy Child is willing to punish or threaten the offspring to obtain compliance.

Learning or the modification of behavior occurs through reinforcement or punishment. When severe punishment is used to enforce injunctions, the wished-for inhibitions are accomplished most effectively. In household situations where the Child ego state of a parent over-rides the protective function of the Parent and operates as a pseudo-Parent and when this pseudo-Parent is willing to use punishment to achieve its desires, the situation can be compared in severe cases with a concentration camp in which a pair of 150-pound children beat a 40-pound three-year-old. The severity of some of the injunctions found in hamartic scripts cannot be minimized. Children in such situations have to either follow the parental injunctions or die.

When the witch-mother, ogre, or crazy Child is not willing or able to use punishment to accomplish his means, he is restricted to achieving them through the reward of desired behavior. This process is less confining to the offspring and produces scripts that are much less dramatic in impact but tend to be melodramatic. These scripts involve life patterns and styles that are narrow and repetitive but not obviously or impressively so. The lives in such melodramatic, banal scripts—rather than having the usual dramatic prologue, climax, and catastrophe of hamartic scripts—tend to simply ebb away silently. Banal scripts are the rule, hamartic scripts are in the minority, and script-free lives are the exception.

Decisions. Children are born into a biologically assured mutuality, described by Erikson. This mutuality ensures, in most cases, an initial position of basic trust, in which the infant feels that he is at one with the world and the world is at one with him. Transactional analysts describe this position as one of the four possible basic existential positions a person can assume. Starting with the basic trust position, the four positions are: "I'm okay, you're okay," "I'm okay, you're not okay," "I'm not okay, you're okay," and "I'm not okay, you're not okay."

The theory of transactional analysis has, as one of its metaassumptions, the belief that human beings are born with a positive potential that only needs to be empowered

to manifest itself. This view is in sharp contrast with the Judeo-Christian view, shared by Freudian theory, which sees man under the influence of internal sinfulness, original sin, or a death instinct that needs to be curbed in order for him to survive as a human being. The colloquial expression of this basic transactional analysis belief is:

Children are born princesses and princes and are turned into frogs by their parents.

Children, if given permission, are seen as driven to the highest expression of humanity. It is their birthright to be protected in the expression of their full capacities, but these capacities are often enjoined against and interfered with. Adoption of a script occurs when the youngster's inborn expectations and tendencies are not met. Instead, supernatural (parental) sources seem to apply considerable pressure in overwhelming ways that, unless yielded to, make life extremely difficult. The child is forced to abdicate his birthright, and he does this by readjusting his expectations and wishes to fit the situation. This process is a crucial point in the development of scripts and is called the decision.

The decision is the point in time when the youngster, applying all the adaptive resources of his ego, modifies his expectations and tries to align them with the realities of the home situation. A script results from a decision that is premature and forced. It is premature because it is made under pressure and long before a decision can be properly made. The decision is as good and as viable as the skills of the Adult ego state of the youngster making the decision.

Making the decision eases pressure and increases satisfaction, and that is why it is said that the youngster's choice is the one of a prince who, under the influence of the witch's or ogre's curse, has to choose between remaining an uncomfortable prince and becoming a comfortable frog. Becoming a frog not only requires a transition from "I'm okay" to "I'm not okay" or "You're not okay" but also requires the adaptation of a conscious fantasy about the kind of a frog the youngster sees himself as being and the kind of a life he will lead thenceforth.

From the point of the decision on, the

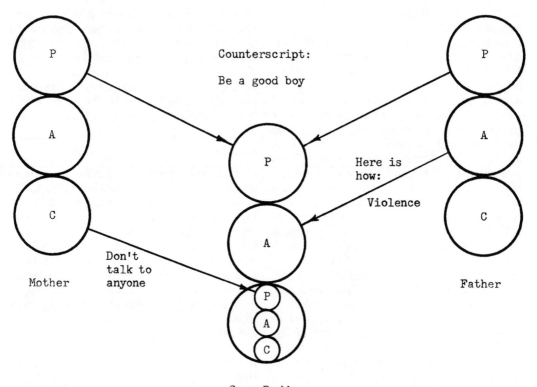

Son: Buddy

Figure 3. A script matrix.

person behaves as if he were someone other than himself. This behavior is much more than mere dissimulation or surface-masking. The youngster who finds himself unable to make sense of the pressures under which he lives needs to synthesize his decision in terms of a consciously understood model. This model is usually based on a person in fiction, mythology, comic books, movies, television, or possibly real life. When the youngster decides to live in a manner exemplified by such a person, he proceeds to live a stereotyped, preordained blueprint or presciption for life that, unless consciously changed, remains until the person's death. The choice of life style and mythical hero is always accompanied by a somatic concomitant or component that is the physical manifestation of the decision, a phenomenon observed by Reich in his work with bodily correlates of character.

The early decisions of children are the results of the pressures and wishes of their parents and are adaptive maneuvers made by the youngster to ease the pressure on him and to make life bearable in his family context. Scripts are always the results of parental wishes, but, when the logical conclusions or ramifications of the youngster's decision begin to manifest themselves, the parents complain loudly, with injured pride and indignation. A classic example of an injunction, a decision, and the ensuing parental cry of indignation follows:

Buddy, an 18-year-old boy of exceptional intelligence, had spent the previous six years in one form of detention or another. He was charming and pleasant all the time except for occasional outbursts of explosive anger, always preceded by a period of morose and ominous unwillingness to communicate. These outbursts, which always resulted in tissue damage for him or those he attacked, were justified later by saying, "All I know is I'm not taking nothin' from nobody."

He recalled that his mother raised him and a number of younger siblings while his father was in prison for manslaughter. He did not remember his father, but he knew of him as a violent man. Buddy recalled how, as he tore through the house, his mother would screw her index finger into her temple and smilingly say, "That boy is craaazy." She used to punish him severely for blabbing to neighbors about personal or family affairs, especially if his blabbing reflected badly on her. At the time of his first severe outburst of rage, when he attacked his sister with a kitchen knife, he recalls his mother's outraged cry:

Buddy you are *too young* to be chasing your sister with a knife.

Analysis of Buddy's script (see Figure 3) indicates that his mother enjoined him against speaking at times of stress and gave him permission to emulate his father's violent example or program. When he combined these two elements into a decision to settle matters through violence rather than through discussion, she, like most parents when their children follow their instructions, was outraged and hurt.

The Counterscript. Tragic life scripts have a total, preordained trend, but this trend is reversed at least once in the person's lifetime for a period of time. This lapse in the script is called the counterscript and has its source in the Parent ego states of the person's father and mother. In the case of Buddy, whose mother's Child said, "Don't talk to anyone (be violent)," her Parent said, "Be a good boy." As a consequence, Buddy characteristically spent one to two years in some form of detention, was released for being "a good boy," and then, in a manner described as "fatal" by one of his psychiatrists, again exploded into his script.

The counterscript needs to be clearly distinguished from a change of script. The importance of this distinction is exemplified in the therapy of, say, alcoholics. Every binge is followed by a period of sobriety, which is easily interpreted as being a cure. Whether it is a cure depends on whether the person has overcome the parental injunctions, and the trained script analyst can distinguish between a script change and a counterscript, which is simply another scene in the scenario.

A Script Check-List. When diagnosing the various aspects of the script, the therapist will find it useful to keep in mind a list of items that make up a script, colloquially called a script check-list. Because various meanings are given to the word script, the word, as used here, refers to this check-list.

Ideally, when talking about a patient's script, the observer is referring to the whole check-list rather than to an item or so. On this basis, "White's injunction is 'Don't think.'" is more accurate than "White's script is, 'Don't think.'"

The check-list is presented here in the order in which the items are usually most easily diagnosed. Colloquialisms are included in quotation marks.

Life Course. This is what the patient has planned to do; it is the outline of the patient's life. It should be possible to state the life course in a succinct phrase, such as "drinking myself to death," "almost always succeeding," "killing myself," "going crazy," or "never having fun." The life course is best stated in the first person singular and in language understandable by an eight-year-old to emphasize that it represents the patient's early formulation of what his life course would be. The life course is usually easy to surmise and is almost always revealed in the patient's presenting problem.

Four subitems of the life course are the decision, the position, the mythical hero, and a somatic component. The decision is the moment when the position (okay, not okay) was embraced. The mythical hero is the character in real life, history, or fiction that the person's life course is intended to emulate (Jesus Christ, Cinderella, Superman, Oscar Wilde). The life course is the reaction to a negative injunction, and this reaction usually has a somatic component. Any effector organ may be involved (tear glands, neck muscles, heart, sphincters).

Counterscript. When the person seems to be escaping the script's life course, he engages in activities that look like departures from the script. These activities form the counterscript and represent acquiescence to a cultural or parental demand, such as "being on the wagon" or "drinking socially."

Parental Injunction. This is composed of two parts: (1) the enjoiner, the witch-mother or ogre or more generally father's or mother's crazy Child; and (2) the injunction. The injunction is thought always to be an inhibiting statement: "Don't think!" "Don't move!" "Don't be assertive!" "Don't look!" If the injunction is not preceded by "Don't" or if it is too complicated, it has not been distilled to its most basic meaning. Therefore, the injunction "Consume excessive quantities of alcohol!" is probably not the last word, but "Don't think!" may be.

The Program. This is how the youngster has been taught by his parents to comply with their injunctions. Thus, if the injunction is "Don't think!" the program may be "Drink," "Fog out," or "Have tantrums."

The Game. This is the transactional event that produces the payoff that advances the script. For every script there is one basic game, and all the person's other games are variants. For a "Kill myself" life course, the game may be "Alcoholic" with such variants as "Debtor," "Kick Me," and "Cops and Robbers"—all of which produce the same payoff—namely, stamps that can be traded for a free drunk.

The Pastime. This is the social device whereby patients with similar scripts structure time. With alcoholics the pastime is "Alcoholic" and its various subforms, such as "D.T.'s," "Cirrhosis," "Disease vs. Habit," and "Hangover."

When a person is playing the pastime, the gallows transaction is likely to take place. In the case of the alcoholic, White tells the audience about last week's bender while the audience—including, perhaps, the therapist—beams with delight. The smiles of the Children in the audience parallel and reinforce the smile of the witch-mother or ogre, who is pleased when White obeys the injunction and, in effect, tightens the noose around White's neck.

The Tragic Ending. This is important to therapists treating self-destructive scripts. The tragic ending is usually specific as to time, place, and method. It is a sort of *modus operandi* that characterizes each individual. Suicidal persons stick to a certain form of suicide, thus affording the therapist a script antithesis, a transactional stimulus intended to disarm the self-destructive injunction. The script antithesis does not dispose of the script, but it buys time during which treatment can lead to script abandonment. The most impressive result of a script antithesis is found when the patient hears, as he is about to leap off the bridge, the voice of the therapist saying, "Don't jump!"

The Therapist's Role. This is the role that the patient expects the therapist to play. For example, alcoholics commonly expect the therapist to play the role of Patsy, Rescuer, or Persecutor.

Permission, Protection, and Potency

Transactional analysis is a theory of personality designed for contractual group treatment, and permission, protection, and potency are the fundamental treatment concepts of this therapeutic approach. Because the person in psychiatric difficulties is following parental orders that are the cause of his difficulty, the basic task of the therapist is to give the person permission to behave otherwise—that is, in a manner that is autonomous rather than adapted to parental demands. Disobeying parental orders is frightening because no alternative ways of life are known to the person and because parental retaliation is feared. Therefore, temporary protection has to be provided by the therapist until the person is able to validate his new way of life. Both permission and protection, to be effective, require potency. Potency or therapeutic power is a combination of Adult competence, Parent advocacy and commitment to the patient, and Child zest and optimism, which are the therapist's contributions to the therapeutic process.

CLINICAL APPLICATION

Patients tend to get better in psychotherapy; but the reasons they get better may differ from the reasons the therapist gives, as Frank notes, the therapist's theoretical orientation may be of secondary importance or of no importance at all. Any patient or therapist in the treatment room brings his entire anatomy, physiology, and cultural and developmental history to bear when he offers a stimulus to another person, who, in turn, responds with all these influences affecting him. The final common path between the therapist and the patient is the transaction. But the therapist who looks for certain clues from a patient and tries to fit these clues into the most closely corresponding description of a game is not doing transactional analysis. The therapist who begins with observations of transactions and then makes inferences as to what has gone on in the past, discovers characteristic games of the patient, and is able to work out his script—which may be unique from all others described in the past—*is* doing transactional analysis. This method is analogous to the drawing of a road map on an uncharted region being explored and is the opposite of reading a road map and applying it to the terrain.

A limited and easily defined vocabulary that patients can learn and use is employed in transactional analysis, and the technical words can be held to a bare minimum of six: Parent, Adult, Child, transaction, game, and script. Every treatment group and individual course of psychotherapy develops its own colloquial terms to describe and classify the behavior observed. Two advantages of using this simplified vocabulary are, first, it has the general advantage of better mutual understanding, and, second, the Child ego state often determines, in a hidden sort of way, the behavior of the person in different situations, and this ego state responds to words that are readily understood by small children up to the age of adolescence. Most conversations in a transactional analysis group would be understood by a young child.

Although some clinicians cling tenaciously to polysyllabic vocabulary in working with patients, its influence in curing patients has yet to be demonstrated. That patients say, "Doctors use such big words," does not need to be further demonstrated. The use of technical jargon in discussions with colleagues may still have some time-saving advantages, but even that is open to question. However, it is well-known that the clinician who uses polysyllabic words may impress his colleagues and enhance his professional esteem.

Useful words and phrases are those that can be defined and used by all members of a group. "Coming on" is defined as a stimulus emerging from a particular ego state, such as "He is coming on Parent." Another useful working term is "hook." This means the switching of attention from one ego state to another, such as, "We hooked his Adult when he went to the blackboard and drew a diagram." Words that imply understanding but that, on closer analysis, confuse and compound misunderstanding are specifically avoided.

"Communication" is one of these words. When uttered in a group, it is usually met with affirmative head-nodding, implying understanding; but simple questioning reveals that most patients in therapy groups do not have a working definition of this word. When it is used by a boss in a company, it has the meaning of, "listen carefully to what I'm saying, and do it my way." But a subordinate may understand communication as meaning, "Now here's my chance to tell my brilliant idea." In a therapy group, when the leader says, "Communication is important," it may have different implications to various members. The therapist may be saying covertly, "Damn it, stop resisting and listen to my theory." But a patient may be saying, "Oh yes, give me some more reassurance."

Another pair of words in vogue at the present time are "mature" and "immature." Although most people nod their heads affirmatively and smile when maturity is mentioned or frown and shake their heads negatively when immaturity is mentioned, closer examination may reveal the meaning of "Grow up and do it my way" for maturity and "You childish imbecile" for immaturity.

"Making progress" is implied to be something good, but it has been found to mean playing games better or getting more sophisticated in a hidden manner, secretly ensuring that nothing will happen. An "interesting evening," "working toward," and many other vaguely defined cliches are exposed and avoided by the transactional analyst, who is especially cautious with those expressions that are suffering from popularity or up-to-dateness.

At first, learning the elements of clinical practice may appear complicated, but the transactional analyst may be viewed as similar to the master surgeon, who spends years preparing himself for surgery by studying anatomy, physiology, diagnosis, history-taking, pathology, and the technicalities of using instruments, handling live tissue, and suturing. His Adult has a fundamental reservoir of data that were quite complex initially. The master surgeon during an operation looks like an artist playing a violin.

When the surgeon makes an incision, expecting to find a diseased appendix, and confronts a cancer instead, he does not panic or immediately run back to his surgical textbook. He is in a position to make quick and clean decisions, shifting to meet the demands of the situation. His movements appear instinctual and intuitive to observers, which they may be at the moment, but later in the locker room he can describe his actions and procedures in a logical Adult fashion. His attention to details and to the foundations on which his procedures rest did not enslave him but actually freed him and made him a more autonomous surgeon. Similarly, the clinical application of transactional analysis rests on a foundation of described and classified procedures, operations, and group theory.

Selection of Patients

"No selection" is the dictum to be applied in selecting patients for transactional analysis groups. A group that is heterogeneous as to age, sex, diagnosis, or severity of illness has been found to be preferable to homogeneous groups, in which games, pastimes, and life scripts are similar and tend to reinforce one another. There are certain exceptions to this no-selection dictum. For instance, some illnesses are best treated by other means. Research has indicated that manic psychotics in the manic phase respond better to limited stimuli and lithium therapy, and they should be treated by those methods. Phobias, hysterias, and obsessional neuroses with their accompanying character abnormalities are probably best treated by Freudian psychoanalysis. Freud himself said that psychoanalysis is more or less unsuitable for other types of psychological illness, which seems to have been confirmed by later developments. Behavioral therapists have found that certain specific types of monosymptomatic phobias may be treated better by their techniques, and this type of treatment should be chosen, rather than transactional analysis, when available. And medical problems that are masking themselves as psychological problems—such as thyroid disease, adrenal tumors, and frontal lobe brain tumors—should be treated by the appropriate medical or surgical methods.

Patients should also be excluded from treatment groups when it can be predicted that their game patterns would counterindicate their being in a group, as in the case of an extortionist who plays "Now I've Got You, You S.O.B." Certain types of patterns that may be open to litigation, such as "Courtroom," should be temporarily excluded from groups, as should patients who are playing such hard games as "Do Me Something," in which they clearly indicate that, if placed in a group now, they will not talk and will not get better. They should be listened to and should not be included in groups until they are better prepared.

Goal of Treatment

The only goal of treatment is to cure patients. The word treatment has been specifically chosen to emphasize that people are not coming to the therapist to have therapy for a specific period of time or to engage in a process that will somehow make them better. Transactional analysis is a contractual treatment of individuals in a group setting. Although group process and dynamics are thought to be important, the primary attention is given to how an individual gets along with or does not get along with other people in the group. Statements like, "George smiled when you said oops—did you notice that?" are characteristic of transactional analysis groups. Statements like, "What does the group think or feel about that?" are not characteristic of transactional analysis groups.

Contract

Simply stated, a treatment contract is an acceptable answer to the question:

How will *you* know and how will *we* know when you get what you are coming to the group for?

The answer to this question is worked over in the presence of all group members which allows each member of the group to sort out the vast number of transactions that take place during a group session and to focus on the stimuli and responses that they consider relevant. All material is not important or relevant, and patients appreciate the opportunity to avoid wasting time on interesting sidelights. They know what each member is aiming for; they then decide their course of action.

Transactional analysis is a contractual type of treatment, and Steiner found that the elements of a patient-therapist contract are similar to a legal contract. Because the four requirements of a legal contract have evolved over hundreds of years of litigation, it is thought that they are necessary and desirable for social intercourse. Retrospective analysis of workable contracts in transactional analysis groups has found these four requirements to be valid for treatment contracts.

Mutual Consent. Mutual consent implies that both the patient and the therapist know and agree on what they are working. In transactional analysis, the contract is arrived at by complementary Adult-to-Adult transactions and ends with an agreement. The therapist does not accept just any goal the patient presents, and he does not quietly sit back and allow the patient to think that they are working toward the same goal if they are not.

An important distinction is to be made between a contract to do psychotherapy and the function of caring for a patient or offering a patient protection. When a psychotic patient, a contaminated Adult who is unable to cathect his Adult ego state, is brought into the hospital with or without his consent, the therapist acts from a Parent ego state, deciding what he thinks is best for the patient at that particular time. The therapist uses his Adult, relying on the scientific literature and his past experience as to what will be most helpful to the patient. He will not be doing psychotherapy and should state this to the patient and the patient's relatives and other interested parties, such as the judge who has sent him to the hospital.

If the therapist in this case is interested in doing psychotherapy, he waits until he has an Adult discussion with the patient. If the therapist says to the patient, "What do you want to get out of your hospitalization?" and the patient responds, "Screw you, Doc,"

the therapist does not pretend to be doing psychotherapy. If the patient on the other hand says, "I don't want this to happen again," then the optimal time has arrived to discuss treatment goals. If the timing is poor, the patient may justifiably be angered by the therapist's intrusion, which has humiliated and angered many young schizophrenic patients, who then decide never to give therapy a trial again, excluding from consideration therapists who may be able to do them some good.

Care and protection are offered to confused geriatric patients brought into psychiatric receiving centers. Medical attention or social work benefits them more than any pretense of psychotherapy. And an increasingly common problem is the adolescent coming down from a bad trip after ingesting psychedelic drugs. He is given protection but not contractual psychotherapy.

Consideration. Consideration means that each of the two parties gives the other something for his efforts. The therapist gives his time, skill, and professional knowledge to the best of his ability to the patient. The patient pays the therapist, usually with money. Without the payment of a substantial fee, readjusted and different for individual patients with varying economic backgrounds, there is a covert Child-Parent situation.

One patient, whose treatment was paid for by a welfare agency, was an ideal and compliant group member ("good patient") who got nothing from the group for several sessions, until the therapist reviewed the treatment contract and noticed that she was giving no consideration. After they agreed that she would pay a small sum of money out of her own personal funds for each visit, weeks went by without payment on her part. When confronted, she broke into tears of rage and protested that the therapist was exploiting her, like all other men in her life.

Her stated reason for seeking treatment was that she wanted to establish a relationship with a man, an experience she had not had before in her life. Attention to the second requirement of a contract exposed a basic decision, made early in her childhood, that was lodged in her Child ego state. This life decision and the life style she lived after it was made, during her toilet-training period, persisted for more than 50 years and was brought out early in treatment only because of attention to the contract.

Situations in no-pay clinics demand special attention to the consideration given by patients to therapists, and in many clinics it is easy to arrange for a small but significant monetary payment. If money is not given, then such things as art work, poems, or essays—objects of meaningful value to the patient—may be considered valid. The therapist who neither demands nor expects his patient to give him anything would be well-advised to examine his Parent ego state, which may be in control and trying to save or rescue people in distress, or his Child ego state, which may be feeling worthless or ineffective.

Competency. The therapist must be competent by way of training and experience to perform what he claims he will be doing. If he offers or accepts with mutual consent a schizophrenic's request to work toward not having a relapse and not being rehospitalized, he must have had the training to work with people who have these types of disorders. It is also the therapist's responsibility to judge whether or not there is a probability of attaining the desired goal.

The patient must be competent to enter into a valid contract. If for psychological, chemical, or medical reasons he is unable to cathect Adult at that moment in time, he is not competent and cannot authentically decide on psychotherapy. It is important to discuss the aims and goals of treatment with the parents of minor children or—in the case of people who have had their civil rights taken away from them—the judge, probation officer, or guardian at that time.

A parent or guardian frequently wishes to take a minor out of treatment just when it appears the child is experiencing some change in his life style. This reaction is understandable in script terms because the minor is living the type of life that he was forced to live by his parents' negative injunctions. The therapist can avoid such premature termination of therapy by having the parents in treatment or at least in occasional consultations simultaneous with the treatment of their son or daughter.

Game patterns, when diagnosed, allow for a high degree of predictability of future behavior and allow the therapist to offer the patient or the parents educated guesses as to what will happen in the course of treatment. These interpretations, described by Allen and Houston, are called anticipatory interpretations.

Mr. and Mrs. Firth were told by the therapist that they would feel anxious and probably attempt to withdraw their son, Fred, from treatment when he wanted to leave home by claiming that they could no longer pay the therapist's bill. They had a history of playing "Debtor," although they enjoyed a high income, and the therapist's specific prediction was based on this game diagnosis. When, indeed, they embarked on the predicted course, their Adult ego states were so intrigued that they decided to experiment some more with the therapist by letting Fred move into an apartment and still continue treatment.

Legal Object. The therapist is unable to form a valid treatment contract if he agrees to work with a patient toward something that is not legal. If the therapist, by error or by being seduced into some game, does agree to work toward some illegal goal, he runs the risk of losing the respect of his patient. The patient can usually congratulate himself on having found another patsy to watch his maneuvering.

Nature of Contracts. Contracts are stated simply in commonly understood language and are specific. For instance, rather than say that he is working toward the "alleviation of sexual inhibitions," a man will say:

I want to be able to get an erection with my wife at least once a week.

Rather than say that he is working toward "fulfilling my true potential as a responsible head of my household," a patient will say:

I wish to make $100 or more a week in take-home pay.

Other examples of typical contracts stated specifically in transactional analysis groups are:

I want to graduate from the University of California with a bachelor's degree in English at the end of the semester.
I will not get fired from my job for at least two years.

The specificity and simplicity of contracts

avoid several clinical games, particularly the game of "Now He Tells Me," in which, after two years of therapy, working toward some vague and ill-defined goal, the patient says:

Well, I really didn't care about that anyway; what I was actually coming here for was . . . .

With these types of contracts the therapist also has a baseline from which he can judge the effectiveness of his treatment. Either a person achieves his contract, or he does not. Long discussions in group sessions about how hard a patient is trying and case conferences where the clinical staff sit around a conference table, drinking hot coffee and discussing significant progress, are viewed as useless pastimes or, worse, as games, both of which ensure that the treatment will be a failure. If the patient is successful in achieving his goal, even if it is in a short period of time, both he and the therapist can authentically congratulate themselves. If the patient fails to achieve his goal, then three possibilities exist. The first is the therapist's responsibility: He agreed to a contract containing a goal that was unattainable, meaning that he did not have a straight Adult-to-Adult treatment contract to begin with. The second possibility is also the therapist's responsibility: Treatment was not conducted properly by the therapist; transfer to another therapist or consultation is indicated at this point. The third possibility is fully the responsibility of the patient: He knows why he did not get what he came into treatment for and chooses to remain with his *status quo.* An example of this is the patient who plays "Poor Me." After game analysis and thorough understanding, he decides that to knock off his game would be too great a financial hardship, as he is receiving substantial amounts of welfare aid. Of course, patients have the right to not get better if they so choose. The therapist has the obligation to place the patient in a position of choice.

The attainment of a specific, well-chosen goal, such as those mentioned above, implies deep personality change.

Harry, a patient who wished to make $100 or more a week in take-home pay, was a middle-aged bachelor with a high intellectual quotient and a college background, but he had never been able to hold a job prior to entering treatment. He depended on his mother, who had instituted this state of dependency with a negative injunction of, "Don't leave me (or you will die). He had found over the years that, by playing games of "Stupid" and "Kick Me," he was successfully unsuccessful at holding a job. In order to attain his treatment goal, he had to knock off his two games and be in a position of financial independence, thereby coming into direct conflict with his mother's negative injunction.

The fulfillment of the specific contract is viewed as being similar to the melting of an iceberg. Although only a small and well-defined piece of ice can be seen above the surface, below there is a huge mass capable of sinking large ships. The ice on top cannot be dissolved without a complete dissolution of the below-the-surface mass. When Harry achieved his contract, he also achieved a state of independence.

Sometimes people choose to play different games from the self-destructive games that have kept them from obtaining their stated goals. This is not symptom-substitution or antithetical to treatment. It is a physiological concept in that people have to do something to get strokes and human recognition. The concept of symptom-substitution presupposes that one accepts the validity of the psychoanalytic view of emotional disorder. In fact, symptom-substitution and relapses after the successful termination of treatment have been very seldom reported in transactional analysis patients. Behavioral therapists, notes Wolpe, have fairly well established that the psychoanalytic view in these regards is mythological, and distinct behavioral changes, when they occur, are valid and lasting.

Not all patients are striving for a reorientation of their life style or goals. Some are satisfied to have a cure at the structural level so that they are able to experience their ego states without contamination or exclusion, as in the case of a psychotic boy who was satisfied in treatment to be able to "not return to the hospital" and "not do what the voices tell me." Another psychotic patient completed treatment after fulfilling a contract to finish college, which was gratifying to him upon its attainment. He still played many games that were disconcerting to his social contacts and that kept him from developing close friends; but, after discussing this problem with his therapist, he stated that he preferred not to be well-socialized. He left treatment feeling that it was successful.

Cures at the game level afford a patient a certain social control over repetitive patterns of behavior, such as getting fired, rejected, or drunk all the time. The attainment of such a goal as not getting fired does not ensure a person of a happy and successful life, but it may help him to feed his children and put them through school, and it has other worthwhile advantages. Patients have left groups after attaining social control of their games and deciding that further treatment would not be worth the trouble involved for them.

Script cures imply reorientation of the patient and distinct life changes. They usually take more time but not always. Those patients who are interested will continue with treatment after structural analysis—involving ego states, decontamination, and recathexis—and game analysis. An example of a script-level cure would be a successful cure of an alcoholic who has become a happy, infrequent, social drinker rather than remaining in the game "Alcoholic" by just not drinking, waiting sometimes for years to fall off the wagon.

The treatment contract is the baseline of treatment in transactional analysis and is referred to in critical situations. The attainment of the contract is well-suited to scientific investigation because a specific and observable end point is more precise than hypothetical explanations of success or failure. Both the therapist and the patient have to put it on the line.

Protection

Protection is supplied by the transactional analyst in two areas. First, the therapist protects the patient by being qualified to do what he implies he will be doing in contractual therapy—handling unexpected as well as expected situations that arise in treatment and being in a position to decide what to do, whether in a therapy group session or on the telephone at 3 o'clock in the morning. The therapist's professional qualifications, background, knowledge and experience of group dynamics and of individual dynamics and pathology are critically important.

Second, the therapist gives Parent protection, a transaction that is necessary for patients who are in a state of despair, particularly at critical points in treatment when a patient has decided to give up a game that has been with him for years, like a life-long friend. The therapist finds a similar type of despair combined with anxiety when a person is deciding to go against his script injunction, which may mean not listening to his mother for the first time in his life. This protection is from the therapist's Parent ego state, and denying this protection to the patient in despair is as much an error in treatment as is giving a patient too much protection. A foundation, therefore, must be laid down by the therapist before the first patient ever sets foot in his consultation room.

Professional Qualifications. The consideration of a person's educational and professional background raises several important questions that may impinge on what the therapist says to the patient at any moment in treatment. Do years of medical school and psychiatric training improve a therapist's chances of curing his patients in a treatment group, or would the experience of sailing around the world in a small boat better qualify a therapist for curing patients? One is reminded of the earlier days of psychoanalysis, when an artist with no clinical degrees was chosen for training in the Vienna Psychoanalytic Institute. Since then, Erik Erikson has risen to hold a place of esteem in the scientific world.

Transactional analysis at its onset was practiced chiefly by psychiatrists, psychologists, and social workers who had a place in developing its theoretical tenets. Other mental health workers, such as psychiatric nurses and pastoral counselors, have also received training. The definition of qualified has never been satisfactorily established, and at this point professional snobbishness and prejudice have as much to do with determining who can practice as do controlled scientific studies. Indeed, a recent study indicated that medical students had treatment results at least as good as more experienced psychiatrists in working with certain types of patients. The training of people outside the traditional mental health fields has been undertaken on a limited basis and is viewed as experimental. Richness and diversity of backgrounds may add as much to the ability to cure patients as long years of formal clinical study. The Schiff Rehabilitation Project in Fredricksburg, Virginia, trained ex-schizophrenic patients to be excellent transactional analysts with good results.

This experimentation with different educational and personal backgrounds is not to be misconstrued as a lessening of qualifications. Transactional analysts must have an adequate knowledge of gross anatomy, biology, physiology, pharmacology, somatic treatment, child development theory, psychology, psychopathology, psychoanalysis, somatic illness, the natural history of psychiatric disorders, and community resources, including referral and consultation possibilities. In addition, learning the specific theory and observing the principles of transactional analysis in action entail a minimum of two years of rigorous study and constitute a major life commitment by the therapist.

Individual Dynamics and Pathology. Individual psychodynamics and psychopathology are taught at transactional analysis seminars, which stress actual case presentations, on-going clinical experience with individual supervision, and observation of experienced clinicians in action. Berne used a particularly useful method of teaching psychodynamic and transactional analysis theory. He treated patients who were seated in a circle surrounded by an outer circle of observing trainees. At the end of an hour and half, the two groups switched seats, and Berne carried on a teaching conference, with the patients observing.

A minimum of two years is necessary to learn the clinical application of transactional analysis under the supervision and observation of a qualified transactional analyst. A personal transactional analysis is thought to be necessary only if the trainee requests treatment. If it is best for any group therapist to have had many varied experiences in groups himself; but it is usually not necessary to stress this, since most people wishing

to do group treatment have a natural predilection in that direction.

Continual reassessment of a therapist's skills is necessary. The idea that the competent therapist can be trained at one period in his career and then depart and do treatment without reassessment or re-evaluation deprives him of two distinct advantages. First, he is not able to share his experiences with others and compare them with newer approaches and techniques; and second, he may develop blind spots because of his own changing life circumstances. Failure to see the effects of such changes can have deleterious effects on his patients. To prevent blind spots, transactional analysts have instituted on-going weekly or biweekly seminars in most urban areas of the United States and in several foreign countries. Indeed, the San Francisco Transactional Analysis Seminar is the longest continually on-going seminar in group therapy known to the authors.

Group Dynamics. A knowledge of the anatomy and physiology of small groups is as important to the therapist as is a minute analysis of what he says at any one point in time to an individual patient. A ship's cook may be able, with extraordinary luck, to extract a diseased appendix from a sailor at sea; but the prepared surgeon, with his knowledge of anatomy and physiology, has a much better chance of treating his patient without complication. The application of individual psychodynamics to the psychodynamics of groups is thought to be haphazard and, at best, experimental. Two classical concepts currently stressed do not seem to be sufficient equipment for a scientific therapist. The first is the principle of identification with the leader, outlined by Freud, and the second is the principle of the re-creation of a family type of constellation in a therapy group. These basic theories of group process have been joined by varied observations on what has happened in groups, but this diversity lacks a succinct and usable matrix.

Berne (1963) has presented a comprehensive, consistent, and pragmatic approach to the functioning and dynamics of groups. What follows is a brief summary of two of the most important aspects of group dynamics—group process and the authority principle. There seems to be no principal' theory available to deal with larger groups, such as therapeutic communities, so these comments are directed at small treatment groups of no more than ten members. Without attention to these principles, the therapist is much like the ship's cook—who may be well-meaning, intelligent, and sober but who does not have the armamentarium necessary to perform his surgical task.

Group Process. A treatment group has a simple structure. An external boundary separates the members of the treatment group from the outside world. This boundary is symbolized by a closed door in a room at a specific address at a particular time. Also, at least one major internal boundary separates the leader from the members of the group (see Figure 4).

The treatment group is distinguished from a crowd by having a distinct external boundary. The application of therapeutic techniques to a crowd is unfeasible, and the

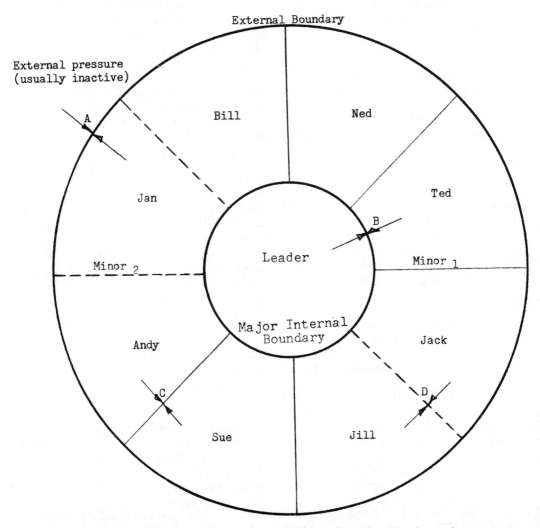

Figure 4. A, external group process across the external boundary; B, major internal group process across the major internal boundary between the leader and members; C, minor₁ process across the minor₁ boundary as between nonrelated members; D, minor₂ process across the minor₂ boundary as between spouses or clique members.

clever mob psychologist first establishes himself as the leader and then sets up certain boundaries in order to gain control.

A party has an external boundary that separates the participants from the rest of the world, but it is distinguished from a treatment group in that there is no major internal border signifying leadership at a party. Therapy groups in which the leaders attempt to give up their leadership role and be one of the boys are viewed by transactional analysts as parties and not treatment groups. In one such group, observed over a period of two years, the members spent most of the group time struggling to place the abdicated leader back in his role. While their attention was focused on this goal, little time or energy was left for the exploration of individual problems. This group was like a party in which members got to know each other better while learning about the dynamics of a party.

The treatment group also has minor internal boundaries between the patients, the boundaries represented in the room by their own chairs. And a few groups have different classes of minor internal boundaries, represented in Figure 4 by the broken line between Jack and Jill, who in the group happen to be husband and wife. Also, there are different types of boundaries between Bill, Jan, and Andy and the others as Bill, Jan, and Andy happen to form a teen-age clique. This diagram represents the structure of a simple transactional analysis group, as there are no further subdivisions here. Inside this leadership circle is one therapist, but the circle can be subdivided by having co-therapists or assistant therapists. Large organizations, such as the Army and corporations, would have many subdivisions in both the leadership role, which is inside the major internal boundary, and the membership slots, which exist between the external and major internal boundaries.

In the simple structure shown here, the single leader must function both as a therapist and as his executive arm, known as the group apparatus. When doing psychotherapy, the leader is functioning as an active therapist; when performing other functions—such as announcing the schedule for the next meeting, arranging furniture,

and emptying ashtrays—he is functioning as his own group apparatus. In larger organizations the group apparatus is usually carried out by persons subservient to the leader, such as the police or the bailiff in a court.

In some groups these two functions are confused; for example, the therapist empties an ashtray, turns to the group, and says, "What did you think of my emptying the ashtray?" This question starts an irrelevant discussion, for which the therapist is responsible, and may waste hours of time. If the therapist does not keep these distinctions clearly in mind, he may further mix up already confused patients. An example would be the social worker who, as an active therapist, encourages her clients to discuss their personal lives frankly in a treatment group; however, she may also be working as a delegate of the group apparatus of her entire social work organization, which necessitates her deciding on the funds allotted to the patients in her group. In this case, the worker is inviting her patients to play some sort of clinical game with her as they pretend to be frank but actually withhold information that could cut back some of their funds. Military psychiatry has been plagued with similar problems, since the psychiatrist must function as both a doctor (therapist to his patient) and an officer (responsible for the fulfillment of the military operation). The game possibilities become clear when a soldier in the doctor's office hints that he may be homosexual. As a therapist, the Army doctor may treat the sexual problem, but, as an officer, he is obligated to report this infraction of the rules. In some situations the confusion between the active treatment leader and the group apparatus have been made clear by a parole officer's wearing a badge to a group treatment session in which he is supposed to be functioning as an active psychotherapist.

Certain inpatient wards in hospitals have tried to resolve this difficulty by having one resident do psychotherapy and another resident decide on such administrative problems as discharge, medication, and action to be taken at times of rebellion. Within some treatment settings these problems are unavoidable; when they are, a terse and clear-cut Adult presentation of the differing roles of the leader, including the presentation of a visual diagram, may elucidate an otherwise haphazard situation.

Group process is defined as the transactions across any boundary of the group structure. Group process can be sorted into a useful and rigorous framework for deciding when the therapist talks, to what area he directs his comments, and who should sit next to whom. The four areas of group process are represented by arrows in Figure 4.

The external group process occurs between the group as a whole and the rest of the world, Arrow A. In a simple transactional analysis group in private practice, this process is usually inactive. In large organizations it can, at times, acquire major importance. If the executive of a social organization decides there are not enough funds to continue the group treatment program, the group may need to band together to fight off this threat of dissolution. This banding together is known as group cohesion and may unite leader and members, who temporarily abandon their differences to fight off a common, external enemy. Similarly, nations at war, when their borders are threatened, may set aside their internal struggles to ward off the external pressure. The writer has seen welfare recipients and social workers on the same picket line, fighting to continue desired treatment programs. Another instance of external pressure is when a supervisor decides that a particular type of treatment in the group is to be discontinued. Then, external group process is the most important factor in that group.

The major internal group process occurs at Arrow B, where most of the significant action takes place. This process occurs between the therapist and each individual patient. In transactional analysis terms, it usually takes place between the Child in the patient and the Parent of the therapist, and most major games, including transference and countertransference maneuvers, are played at this boundary. In the group shown in Figure 4, only eight areas of major internal process are possible. With the addition of a co-therapist in the leadership circle, the number of possible vectors doubles, which

can add to the source of confusion. This is a major argument against having a co-therapist. Also, with a co-therapist, another area of group process is introduced: that between the two co-therapists, which would be diagrammed by a line drawn through the middle of the leadership section. This process is exploited by patients adept at playing the game of "Let's You And Him Fight." Transactions pitting one patient against another are represented by the minor internal process (Arrow C), which may be subdivided in the case of marital couples and cliques (Arrow D).

The time and energy employed in any one aspect of group process may take away from the full reservoir of time and energy available. This theory can be stated in the equation: External Group Process + Major Group Process + Minor Group Process + Group Activity = Group Cohesion. Practically speaking, if the therapist decides to spend the group's time and energy in interplay between Jack and Jill, little time will be spent on other minor internal processes or at the level of major internal process.

A gauge of a group's cohesion is its attendance rate. Berne (1955) has documented remarkably consistent rates in different voluntary groups of about 85 per cent, and attendance at this level is indicative of a healthy group with adequate cohesion. If the attendance drops below 70 per cent, transactional analysts label the group "ailing," and attention to group dynamics, a review of the patients' contracts, and individual dynamics are indicated. If cohesion cannot be improved, consultation is desirable. Of all the measurements that can be made of group activity, the average attendance rate is the simplest and can be expressed in direct numerical terms. For this reason, transactional analysts tabulate the attendance rates and periodically compare their cohesion rates within their own groups and with other therapists.

Authority Principle. The authority principle means that any member of a hierarchy is compelled to comply with the wishes of those above him, and those below him are compelled to comply with his wishes. Seen in this aspect, the authority diagram, with the patients drawn in, implies that those higher than the leader in the diagram may have an influence on what happens at any given moment in a treatment setting. They seldom do, but such an influence is possible at critical moments.

When a veteran perches himself on a window ledge after a treatment session, any member in his organization—even the President—may have something to say to either him or the therapist. A Vice President of the United States has been known to call a governmentally funded institute and inquire into certain proceedings.

Any member within the organization—whether the therapist, his supervisor, or a patient—has three choices in facing the authority principle. One, he can comply, usually by playing the organizational game. Two, he can rebel—either openly, by attempting to change the organization, or covertly, by playing other games. Three, he can leave the organization.

If the organizational game is one of "I'm Only Trying to Help You," the worker in the organization is expected to discharge only a small number of clients. If by some new approach he discovers a way of discharging large numbers of clients, he may have to account for this discharge rate in the next staff conference. Condemnation of the worker by the organization members is usually secret and, if pointed out by an outside consultant, is usually met with an indignant repudiation. A distinction between two different types of staff conferences can, therefore, be made. One is a morale conference, reinforcing the organization games; the other is an authentic review of curative techniques, which may upset games.

In certain labor forces, a certain quota of work to be done is either overt and written into the contract or hidden. When a worker exceeds this this quota, he may be tapped on the shoulder by the union boss, who says, "Slow down, son." In certain governmental agencies specializing in mental health, good work by an eager staff, which shows up in frequent and early discharge rates, is rewarded by a diminution of funds and the discharge of some therapists and administrative leaders.

The formal authority diagram has four different aspects—all of which conform to the authority principle (see Figure 5). The formal organizational diagram, including the patients, describes the slots and responsibilities in the organization, including a job description for each slot. The personal authority diagram fills in these slots with each person's name and a comment on his personality. The cultural authority diagram lists the canonical works that guide the activities of the organization and of the therapists. The historical diagram is filled in with those leaders of the past whose biographies and personal attributes are known to the organizational members.

Two types of therapists may be distinguished according to which aspects of the authority diagram they follow. The political therapist pays attention at critical moments to the historical authority diagram and the personal authority diagram. In times of stress, he is apt to call on Joe, his immediate supervisor; Harry, the section chief; and Dr. Frimp, the chief of the department. In his head he also wonders, "What would Freud have done in a situation like this?" The political therapist turns to these aspects of the authority diagram as his primary guide; he uses the formal organization chart and resorts to the formal literature only as a secondary measure.

The procedural therapist, on the other hand, is interested in the formal job description and the cultural diagram as evidenced by the written literature, which is his primary concern. At a critical moment, he is more apt to run to the library to read the literature than to run to his supervisor's office. He uses his supervisor and inspiration from historical authorities only as backup support.

Both types of therapists have advantages and disadvantages, and it is of benefit to the patients in treatment groups if the therapist knows on what aspects of the authority diagram he relies at critical moments. It is less perplexing to patients if they know who their therapist idolizes from past history, and it is less confusing to the therapist to know which articles and canons he has read in the past may contribute to what he says to a patient at a given moment. Such questions as,

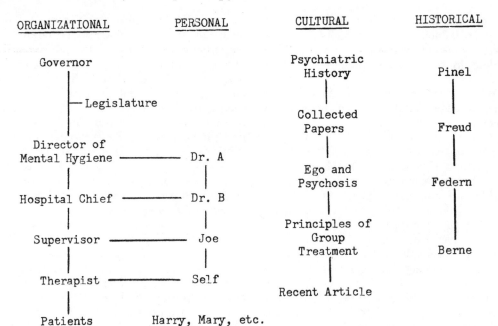

Figure 5. Complete authority diagram in a typical state hospital.

What are the three most important articles or monographs that you have read in your professional career? What three people have influenced you most in your career?

are explored in a formal way in the training of a transactional analyst.

This type of attention to all aspects of the authority diagram is necessary for the therapist to know the foundation of his own professional background, so that he can offer protection to his patients. The therapist, after this form of rigorous attention and preparation, is well-prepared to invite patients into his consultation room. In this position, he will be stimulated in treatment groups by the challenging situations that are offered and will not be shackled by the anxiety of "Am I well-prepared?"

Protection as a Transaction. Protection is also used in a more specific way in treatment. Protection, as Crossman notes, is nurturing statements from the Parent of the therapist to the Child of the patient at critical moments when such protection is desired and needed.

When a patient gives up a life-long game, protection is authentically desired and po-

tently applied. When a person who has learned to structure his time by playing the game of "Now I've Got You, You S.O.B." is cured of that game, he is in the same position as a child whose best friend has moved away. Consistent clinical findings of despair are noted at this point in treatment.

When a patient is given permission to not listen to his mother's or father's negative injunction, an existential vacuum is created, and it is met by anxiety and, again, despair. At these times, the patient, for a short period, needs the Parent of the therapist to fill the vacuum.

Timing is an important consideration. The therapist should not undertake certain operations immediately before going on vacation. Nor should he make himself unavailable to patients who may need him, since it is considered poor technique for an active psychotherapist to be out of telephone contact with his patients.

Occasionally, patients exploit protection transactions, making a game of them. For instance, a patient may cry, "Help," but when the therapist responds by giving him help, the patient turns the situation and says, "That wasn't good enough." The therapist then knows that he has been engaged in a game. An authentic help transaction is initiated by the patient who says, "Help"; the therapist says, "Here": and the patient says, "Thank you."

Support of this type is not supportive therapy, in which change is not expected in in the patient. Rather, this is support and help offered to a patient immediately after change occurs, change that the therapist has expected to occur in treatment. This specific aspect of protection is found in conjunction with permission.

Permission

The transactional analyst gives the patient permission to get better. This is a position antithetical to the negative injunction that the Child of the parent presented to the patient in early childhood (see Figure 3). Four specific areas of permission are given attention: permission to get the most out of treatment by using it effectively, permission to experience different ego states, permission to go straight (not play games), and, finally, permission to overcome the witch-mother or ogre-father and to live life differently.

Patients have not been trained in principles and techniques of group treatment; therefore, it is the therapist's responsibility to structure the group effectively and to use the time to best advantage. When a patient enters a group and asks a common question, "What are we supposed to do here?" the therapist tells him if he perceives the question to be an Adult stimulus. He ends by stating something like:

Tell us why you are here and how you will know and how we will know when you get what you came for.

The therapist has already prepared the patient for group treatment by introducing him to the concepts of transactional analysis and by letting him know what he is in for. The therapist may also elect to spend a few minutes in a didactic review of group structure and dynamics, which will also serve as a review for other members of the group, who usually appreciate this opportunity to think.

The therapist may also suggest to the patient that he read certain outside literature. No harm is done by patients' thinking and using logic in approaching their problems, and they are given permission to do just that. The distinction in this case is between using intellect and intellectualizing. Some groups in vogue at the present time have excluded the thinking aspect of treatment in favor of the feeling aspect. The term affectualizing may have to be considered. Transactional analysts have found from experience that talking straight to patients and giving permission to think does not exclude their ability to have authentic feelings.

Permission to Use Time Effectively. The assumption that individual psychopathology will show up in treatment groups has to be questioned, since individuals tend to masquerade or hide their problems from one another and from the therapist. Patients reporting on prior group experience have said things like:

I was different in the therapy group from the way I was on the outside.

Other patients have reported sitting silently in groups for months, and others have mentioned that they passed the time in their therapy groups on things that they considered to be irrelevant but interesting. Such interesting evenings are avoided in transactional analysis groups. One patient kept count and reported that he made more than 300 interpretations of his problem—all to no avail. The therapist must allow patients to experience their actual problems in the group. He does this by giving them permission to structure their time usefully, but he specifically avoids giving them permission to engage in irrelevancies.

The problem of the therapist in giving patients permission to structure their time most effectively deals with blocking withdrawal and pastimes and in not covertly giving the patients permission to either withdraw or engage in pastimes.

A therapist had decided to tape-record his session for playback to his supervisor, and he began the meeting by saying, "I am going to tape-record this session. Do any of you have any feelings about that?" The next 90 minutes were taken up with various and sundry feelings about tape recorders. Not one of the patients in the group came to treatment because he was having ill feelings about tape recorders. The therapist could have avoided this waste of time by not secretly giving the group permission to pass the time. Instead, he could have said, "I am going to record the group meeting, and I will handle the tape as I do any other confidential material. If you wish to say anything that you do not want on the tape, kindly pull the cord out from the socket." The meeting could then have proceeded. If, after this type of straightforward presentation, a patient revealed by his gestures or appearance that he was uncomfortable, he may have had authentic feelings about the presence of a tape recorder, and the therapist would then question him about his withdrawal. This type of suspicious behavior would be directly dealt with, since it would be relevant for that particular individual.

If the therapist anticipates using a tape recorder, videotape, or another such device in a treatment group, he should inform prospective patients when they are deciding whether or not to undertake group treatment. Doing so is not a matter of psychotherapeutic strategy but of basic human decency.

All people need strokes, and patients in groups are no exception. People may structure time and obtain strokes in a social situation in six fundamental ways:

Withdrawal. Withdrawal is one way of structuring time in a social setting. There are two types of withdrawal: One, engaging in extraneous fantasies, like Huckleberry Finn's thinking about fishing when the teacher was talking about arithmetic; and two, engaging in elaborate autistic fantasies.

Withdrawal has very little effectiveness in gaining strokes from other people, and the transactional analyst specifically tells patients to talk if they are experiencing difficulty in this area. Withdrawal is sometimes encouraged, as in the case of an extroverted salesman who was given permission to reflect silently and think things over. But the therapist, as a rule, avoids giving patients overt permission to withdraw, and he refrains from focusing on silence as a meaningful and relevant topic. If the therapist says, "My, you seem silent tonight," then silence is seen as a significant way to get strokes from the therapist and unfortunately is defined as a pertinent treatment topic.

Rituals. Rituals are a series of highly predictable complementary transactions and are an elementary way of receiving strokes from other people. A good way to warm up a session is with informal greeting rituals, whereby the therapist says "Hi" to everyone and elicits a response. The therapist pays close attention when he enters the treatment group to see who is talking, who has said something to him, and who has not. To one who is silent, he may offer a ritualistic comment like, "Hello, George," and George's response will immediately pull him out of a state of withdrawal. But if the therapist does not use this simplest of manuevers, George may remain withdrawn the entire session.

Other than for a pathologically silent patient, rituals have little benefit and should be out of the way by the first or second minute of the meeting. Some consider it good etiquette to say good-by to patients at the end of each session by mentioning their names. This is one stroke for the road.

Pastimes. Pastimes are a similar series of transactions but are less stereotyped than rituals. They are what the name implies.

Two landladies over a back fence may carry on a Parent-to-Parent pastime of "Ain't It Awful?" for years:

Gladys: Isn't it awful how juvenile delinquency is on the rise?
Mabel: Yes, it is; parents don't raise their children like we used to.
Gladys: And our property taxes are going up again.
Mabel: And isn't it awful, etc., etc., ...

Pastimes such as "General Motors" and "Baseball" are common among working men on their coffee breaks when they are faced with one of the serious philosophical problems of life—sitting across the cafeteria table from one another for 15 minutes with the necessity of saying something. It would be especially serious if they didn't have anything to say. There is a multiple-choice, sentence-completion quality to pastimes:

I like a (Ford, Chevrolet, Plymouth) better

than a (Ford, Chevrolet, Plymouth) because [fill in with 25 words or less].

The response is:

Well, I like a (Ford, Chevrolet, Plymouth) better than a (Ford, Chevrolet, Plymouth) because [25 words or less].

Housewives commonly play "P.T.A.," and young urbanites at cocktail parties delight in passing time with "Psychiatry."

Pastimes may be allowed to proceed for a short period of time in a transactional analysis group for a further warm-up, but they have little value beyond that. One notable exception is when the therapist decides that a patient is in a difficult position, such as after an unresolved game of "Uproar." At such a time, the therapist may allow a pastime to proceed in order to think over the situation and consider further operations. In this respect, a pastime is analogous to a punt on the fourth down, which is occasionally a victorious strategy for a football team, although it must temporarily give up possession of the ball. Letting the pastime continue gives the patient and the therapist temporary escape while they wait for another opportunity to transact the business of psychotherapy. Transactional analysis groups, especially, must avoid the pastime of "Psychiatry— Transactional Type."

Activity. Activity is synonymous with work and is usually composed of Adult-to-Adult transactions, such as two people getting together to build a boat. Adult-to-Adult activity is difficult to maintain for any length of time, as may be seen in the example of the surgical operating team. The chief surgeon, assistant surgeons, nurses, and technicians engage in Adult-to-Adult transactions for several minutes, and always at critical moments in the operation, but the activity is broken by operating room levity or a temper tantrum on the part of the surgeon. The nurse who is a witness to the surgeon's tantrum takes it in stride, since she intuitively knows that the momentary break in the Adult-to-Adult activity is necessary and will probably lead to better results in the long run. Play, humor, and physical exercise have also been introduced into the routine of astronauts traveling through space.

When it is productive, activity is used in groups, such as during the discussion of the treatment contract, the gathering of certain historical material, and the discussion of transactions or games that were perceived by group members. Because transactional analysis is a logical and rational form of treatment, the therapist is usually Adult-programmed, and much of his time is spent doing work in the group—which does not detract from the desirability and necessity of the therapist's using his Parent and Child qualities.

Games. If withdrawal, rituals, pastimes, and activity are not occurring in the treatment group, then, because of the basic necessity to receive strokes, patients resort to games. Most people have only a small repertoire of games, and these are almost always antithetical to the patient's getting what he came to treatment for. The often-fired patient who wants to keep a job for at least two years will usually initiate the game of "Kick Me" if other ways of structuring time are blocked. The game level of time-structuring is where most of the action focuses in transactional analysis groups.

Intimacy. Intimacy does not usually occur within the confines of a treatment group; however, it has been reported. Moments of potent script cure may be intimate moments between the therapist and the patient. Intimacy defies specific definition, but it is game-free behavior, and it is not withdrawal, rituals, activities, or pastimes between two individuals. When it happens, there is no question about it. Poets have been writing about intimacy for more than 3,000 years, and their descriptions come as close as any to putting it into words.

Intimacy is to be distinguished from pseudointimacy, in which thoughts, feelings, and actions are dramatic pledges of warmth and closeness between two persons but which usually has a game payoff, as in the case of a man and a woman who pledge their deepest and most-longing devotion to each other, have a night of bliss, but by the next day or month depart with an empty feeling. Innumerable examples of pseudointimacy in drug experiences and in therapy groups have been reported. Some of these are likely to be examples of such pastimes as "Greenhouse," "Ever Been," and "Higher-Than-Thou."

Permission to Experience Ego States. Structural analysis is that part of transactional analysis that enables a person to recognize and experience his own Parent, Adult, and Child—including, in certain instances, the second-order parts of his structure.

Permission to think is the same as permission to use one's Adult. A blackboard, chalk, and eraser are present in the transactional analysis treatment room. They are placed in a prominent place so that the therapist and any of the patients may outline and diagram what they think has been transacted at any particular time in the group. The presence of the blackboard signifies that every type of action that takes place with the group, whether it be a Child outburst or a statement of Parent prejudice, is at any time subject to Adult appraisal. Being subject to appraisal does not mean that there is a constant Adult censor present but, rather, that it is permissible to describe and discuss events when desired. The blackboard is used in learning situations from kindergarten through postdoctorate studies and has most likely been a significant part of each patient's life, regardless of where he was born and educated.

The use of the blackboard has three distinct advantages: First, it is an instant permission for a patient to cathect Adult, and it works even when a patient is exhibiting gross overt delusions, panic, or a temper tantrum in a group. The direction "Would you please write that on the blackboard" makes it necessary for the patient to stand up, take the chalk in his hand, and draw arrows, which in itself takes a certain amount of Adult control. The second advantage of using the blackboard is that, whenever a patient decides to draw his own structure or that of others, he commits himself in the existential sense. He is saying, in essence:

This is the way I see my [their] thoughts, feelings, actions, or behavior now.

The third advantage of using the black-

board is the general advantage that all visual aids have in learning situations; it helps to imprint and crystallize data.

A patient infrequently rebels against the blackboard, saying something like:

That's just what I had in the third grade, and I didn't learn anything then.

This rebellion can be handled by saying, "What do you remember from the third grade?" The patient can easily catch on as he recalls that some of the most memorable situations were times in which he remembers the teacher working out mathematical problems on the blackboard.

The use of the blackboard by experienced transactional analysts is, therefore, seen as further permission to think and experience the Adult ego state, and it has not inhibited patients. Of course, the therapist does not take a Parent attitude and make patients go to the blackboard for punishment. The blackboard is used sparingly, but it can be turned to when needed.

Permission is also provided for patients to experience their Child ego state. Many times this permission is not necessary, but experiencing the fear and more natural aspects of the Child is often difficult.

A shy and inhibited girl would speak only when spoken to. Her contract was to be able to talk with her dates. She was asked to join the other group members and the therapist, who were sitting on the floor with their shoes off, talking Child language. She balked at this, but, when she finally let go and let her Child out, she screamed, "I won't do this, I won't! I'm not supposed to make an ass out of myself." Even she laughed at this outburst.

Although the therapist gives a blanket permission at the beginning of the group and continually reinforces it—"You can say anything you want to here"—there are times in which specific attention is needed to bring out a person's Natural Child so that he can experience it himself. At this point, the transactional analyst uses techniques similar to those used by Gestalt therapists and psychodramatists. There have been other times when on-going patients in transactional analysis groups have been referred to weekend marathons and encounter groups, sometimes conducted by auxiliary therapists and sometimes conducted by the patient's own therapist. Some of these experimental groups have been conducted in a transactional analysis framework, particularly those known as permission classes, described by Steiner and Steiner, and script rehearsals using psychodrama techniques, described by Dusay (1970). At the present time these uses are considered experimental.

Permission for a patient to experience his Parent ego state is less necessary, since most patients seem to have enough of that already, particularly in hidden ways. However, this type of Parent is usually a punitive or inhibiting type, as is seen in a simple experiment performed in groups in which the therapist says:

Let's all let out our true feelings about each other now.

A general tendency is for groups to tell each other how much they disapprove of or dislike each other and what annoys them. It is much harder for people to say what they like in other people when they are presented with this spontaneous challenge. In one experimental group the members were requested to say only positive things to each other. After ten minutes, hurt Child and critical Parent interventions broke in.

People who have been orphaned or have lost one of their biological parents in childhood sometimes have lacunae in which they find it difficult to be Parents in certain circumstances. In such a case, they usually borrow a Parent from another member of the group or from the therapist. Preliminary observations have indicated that patients who come from families where the parents were divorced have been able to raise their own offspring easily up until the point at which one of their parents left home, signifying that the Parent in their head has only limited development.

Permission to Be Straight (Not to Play Games). Permission not to play games is best exemplified by a hard player of "Kick Me" who had been fired from some 30 jobs, which was considered a remarkable feat, since she was only 32 years old. Her treatment contract was to maintain her present job for two years without getting fired. When other ways of structuring time were blocked, it became necessary for her to structure her time by playing her favorite game in the group setting. She used the most common method of playing "Kick Me" in groups by telling one aspect of her life in one meeting and then retelling the story at the next week's meeting with completely different details, making it sound like a common lie. This behavior produced surefire results because, with six to eight other people in the group, the Child in her head could count on someone's having a punitive Parent ego state that specialized in catching children when they did things wrong, kicking her, and pointing out her gross inconsistencies with a triumphant sneer.

After seeing this pattern occur three times in the group, the therapist, after an Adult-to-Adult discussion of the game dynamics involved, gave the other patients permission not to kick her. Frustrated by this lack of response, she tried harder and harder to get kicked in the group. At this point, the therapist gave her permission to stop playing "Kick Me" by saying:

We'll be glad to give you strokes even if you don't play "Kick Me."

Then the therapist produced an example by commenting on her good appearance. After several months, she was able to accept the permission, and she has successfully maintained her job outside of the group for more than four years, which is a record for her. The other patients, who played such complementary games as "Now I've Got You, You S.O.B." were also frustrated and were given permission not to attack and jump on her.

Permission to Overcome the Script Injunction. The script transaction · that causes life-long pathology is demonstrated by the vector from the Child in the parent to the Child of the patient; this part is known as the Adapted Child. If a patient in treatment desires a major life change, it is this area that must be rectified. The Child is adapted to the desires and wishes of the witch-mother or ogre-father who has told the patient to be a failure of some sort or another. In the case of an alcoholic patient, transactional analysis takes the view that an alcoholic needs permission not to drink because he is already under orders to drink. Permission is a transaction by which the therapist aligns the patient with his original Natural Child ego state, which is self-preservative and growth-oriented.

The permission transaction has two parts: first, a Parent-to-Child command, exemplified by the statement, "Stop drinking"; and second, a rational, logical, and easily understood Adult-to-Adult explanation, such as:

You will not be able to keep your job if your drinking persists.

If the patient's Adult is not involved and does not understand the logic, the permission simply becomes a command that may be resisted or ignored by the patient.

Many alcoholic patients have seen a variety of therapists, including some who assume the Rescuer or Patsy role in the game of "Alcoholic" and who somehow neglect to use the basic permission transaction. On close inspection, many alcoholics report that, in their travels through treatment, they have never been specifically told, "Don't drink." This type of literal and specific transaction can be understood and responded to by the Child. Scientific statements alone, such as,

This particular medication will make you better and help you to stop drinking.

are true but meaningless to a biologically young child and to the Child in the patient. The converse situation—in which the therapist is Parental only, usually from a position of prejudice against alcoholics—produces a Child who rebels, since he has no cooperation from his Adult.

Ruth was a young woman who had seriously attempted suicide several times in the past, had had frequent psychiatric hospitalizations, and had seen many psychotherapists. She had been unwanted by her father, who had said to her, "Get lost," several times in her childhood as he shooed her out of the room in which he was trying to relax. At one time, when her father was intoxicated, she definitely remembers that he said to her, "I wish you were dead." Since her early childhood, she had been living a constant struggle between getting lost, which she did often, and killing herself, which she had tried seriously several times.

The therapist was somewhat surprised when she unequivocally stated that none of her prior psychotherapists had taken a direct antithetical position to her ogre-father and had never said to her in dramatic and straightforward terms, "Do not kill yourself." She did recall, however, hearing several statements of concern, as one therapist said, "You must be terribly unhappy to do what you did. Tell me about it. Another therapist took the position that it was her right to kill herself, and he spent time philosophizing about her right to be or not to be. This approach was seen as an Adult-to-Adult philosophical discussion, which was stimulating to the patient, but it did not relieve her of the burden of a life pattern of struggling against suicide.

When it was established by way of a treatment contract that she did not wish to die but preferred to live, the therapist in no uncertain terms gave her permission to live by saying, "Do not kill yourself—live." The patient responded by saying, "Thank you." This permission was the direct opposite of and was antithetical to the negative injunction with which the patient had been structuring her life. If she ever finds herself standing on a bridge, deciding whether or not to die, she has at least one strong and well-stated permission to live in her head—one that is not couched in vague, sympathetic, or psychological terms.

After receiving permission either to go straight, not play a game, or go against the negative injunction of the script, the patient is in a frightening and sometimes desperate position. At this point, protection transactions may be necessary.

Potency

Potency is the timely decision to apply certain operations used by transactional analysts to cure patients. It is distinguished from omnipotence, which is the patient's fantasy of what wonderful, superhuman feats the therapist may perform. Omnipotence fits nicely into the game of "Gee, You're Wonderful, Doctor," and implies certain script characteristics of the patient, such as "Waiting for Santa Claus" or waiting for the doctor to open his desk and give him the golden apple. Occasionally, the therapist shares this fantasy with the patient from the position of

With all these degrees, or wonderful feelings, or empathy, I must be able to cure patients.

Retrospective analyses of the final common path between therapist and patients who have been cured, as well as critical analyses of patients who have not benefitted by treatment and have not realized their treatment contracts, have revealed that certain distinct transactions, applied at the right time, are beneficial and others are not. Protection refers to a therapist's ability to come through when the patient needs him from any ego state. Permission deals with conveying the idea that change is okay. Potency is the quality of doing the right things at the right time. The ultimate in therapeutic potency is when the analyst succeeds in bringing about the overthrow of the negative injunction of the patient's parent. Overthrowing this injunction sometimes happens early in treatment; one transactional analyst claims that once in a long career he did it in one session. But this accomplishment has little to do with the length of treatment. The most important part of treatment is the preparation of the patient to be receptive and the therapist's willingness and ability to apply the correct operation.

Four curative forces are in effect in any treatment group. First is the natural drive that human beings have toward health. This force is found in all patients at birth in their drive toward growth, and it can be thwarted only by adverse transactions later in life, sometimes starting with a tense nipple in the first few days of life. The second curative force is that, within the confines of a therapy group, the patients are recognized as human beings and obtain strokes. The third curative force comes from the corrective emotional experience of confrontations and encounters with other people. All three of these forces are operative in all groups to different degrees, and any group leader can organize a group and allow these first curative forces to occur, which explains why patients tend to get somewhat better in any therapy group, regardless of the sophistica-tion or background of the therapist, provided he is an understanding and fair human being. The fourth curative force is the specific behavior of the therapist. If the therapist is able to do certain things beyond those that a good scout master would do, his chances of curing patients should be increased, and he is justified in collecting a fee.

Berne (1966) detailed four categories of operations that are carried out by the therapist:

Decontamination means rectifying the situation when the patient's thoughts, feelings or behavior are disguised or adulterated. The therapist analyzes and diagnoses the structure of individual personality by paying attention to ego-state pathology.

Recathexis occurs when a patient is able to experience different ego states, and it is particularly useful in the case of ego-state exclusion. A patient who has a fixed Parent ego state will let his Child out. This operation, like decontamination, deals with the analysis of the patient's personality structure and is primarily concerned with exclusion and contamination.

Clarification is the attainment of Adult control by a patient. It is experienced by his understanding what he is doing, what parts of his personality are involved in it, and how to control and decide whether or not to continue games. Clarification contributes to stability by assuring that hidden Parent and Child game behavior can be monitored by the patient's Adult. It prevents him sliding into Parent or Child.

Reorientation implies that a patient is in a position to change his script and experience his life differently. From an existential standpoint, the patient views himself as okay, and he does okay things. He does not view himself in a life position as being not okay and as struggling, trying hard, or working toward doing okay things. The operations that bring about this orientation, colloquially put, change a patient from a frog to a prince or princess. The operations are script changes.

Potency in Structural Analysis. To effect the processes of decontamination and recathexis of ego states, the therapist and the patients become adept at diagnosing ego states. Particularly intuitive therapists or patients can usually see hidden Child, hidden Parent, or hidden Adult in other people, as Berne (1970) notes, but they find it more difficult to see within themselves. Attention to six different areas allows for a clear-cut diagnosis. If this procedure seems cumbersome, the therapist can rest assured that 90 per cent of the time he will intuitively be correct. If he wishes to try for 100 per cent, then he must focus attention on these six areas:

Behavioral. Ego states show up in gestures, attitudes, and specific mannerisms. The pointed finger of a lecturing Parent, when superficially the Adult ego state seems to be in control, gives a clue to interference from the Parent ego state. The squirming Child, the impatient tapping of a foot, and other elements of body language give away various parts of the Child ego state and are useful in transactional analysis. These are signs of nonverbal communication.

Vocal. A person has at least three voices, as is evidenced by the busy executive who speaks in one manner early in the morning to his young son who spills prune juice on his freshly pressed suit, in another voice to business associates with whom he is conducting business, and in still another voice to his wife while making love. Quick switches are sometimes humorous and are used in the professional theatre and entertainment world. The most easily recognized switch is when the executive in his Adult manner answers the telephone and says, "This is Mr. Jones," and, discovering that it is his wife calling him, immediately changes his voice to a softer, sweeter, and more child-like quality.

Do you want me to pick up some milk on the way home?

Vocabulary. Certain words belong to certain ego states. The words "should," "ought," "must," "good," "bad," etc., are recognized as coming from the Parent ego state. "Theoretically," "it seems as if," and "probabilities are" are representative of the Adult. Child ego state words are usually short and terse, such as "Wow" and "Ouch."

A study by Poindexter and Dusay pointed out that a patient fulfilled his contract in a transactional analysis group only after the words "should" and "supposed to" dropped out of his vocabulary in the therapy hour.

Historical. Less dramatic but of a confirming nature is a patient's recollection of the very first time he saw the pointed finger, which is diagnosed as Parent ego state. He may historically identify it as coming from one or the other of his parents at a particular point in his life. A grimace on the face of the girl who delighted in playing "Kick Me" and getting fired from jobs was traced to her earliest memory, knocking an ashtray off her mother's coffee table and onto the floor when she was three years old. She remembers tightening her face just before her mother slapped her. This tightening of her face was noticed in her expectant Child immediately before she was taken to task for telling a lie in the group some 30 years later.

Social. Group treatment has one distinct advantage over individual psychotherapy. When a person is coming on (the vector of a transactional stimulus) in a Childlike way, he is able to elicit a Parent response from one of the more parental members of the group. This is known colloquially as hooking the Parent. It is, of course, possible to hook any particular ego state. The converse is also true as an observable phenomenon: When a patient comes on in a Parent manner, one or two of the members of the group usually rebel dramatically.

Subjective. This is the reliving of an ego state. If the first five methods of diagnosing and recathecting ego states are incomplete, subjective re-experiencing is usually accomplished. Gestalt techniques and techniques of psychodrama are particularly useful here. A patient who is characteristically in his Adult ego state and complaining that he has little fun in life may be seated on the floor while all others transact with him only on a Child level, using such words as they used when they were three, four, and five years old. Although the Adult protests, with encouragement and confrontation he is eventually able to experience his own Child.

When a person is transacting on two levels at the same time, one level with words and the other level with a bodily gesture such as the Parental finger, the therapist may request him to stop talking and to use only his finger to transact his business. Then the therapist has him place his hands in his lap, with the finger down, and talk without the embellishment of the finger. Different feelings are elicited from the two different ego states, and at that moment the patient, with help from other group members, experiences the two ego states. The next time he transacts on two levels, it will be more difficult for him to say, "Oh, it was my unconscious," since he will have become distinctly aware of the two different ego states operating within him.

Potency in Game Analysis. Much of the action in a transactional analysis group focuses on game behavior. The recognition of game behavior by the therapist or other patients is aided by attention to the diagnostic procedures described above. When the therapist recognizes that the transactional stimulus from a patient is an invitation to a game or when he observes a game in progress among group members, he is in a position of deciding what response will be of most benefit to the patient. When the therapist does not recognize that he is being invited to play a game or does not know when one is in progress because of his insufficient experience, inadequate training, inattention, or preoccupation with trivia or profundities, then his response is likely to be naive, and whether or not his response is of benefit to the patient will be left to chance. When the therapist is aware of a patient's invitation to play a game, he has four types of response available to him:

Expose the Game. David entered the group and his first question was, "What are we supposed to do here?" A series of helpful suggestions from other group members were swiftly provided, all of which were successively rejected by David. When the therapist clearly recognized the "Why Don't You— Yes But" game, he explored the relationship of this behavior to the patient's contract, which was to be able to make more money. When the therapist ascertained that the patient was also playing the game with his current employer, the therapist decided that

exposure was necessary, and he waited for the next opportunity. When asked, "What should I do now?" the therapist used an antithesis by saying, "We can't suggest anything you haven't already thought of." With subsequent exposure of the same game, David would catch himself and laugh knowingly when he was beginning to play. Then, as his Adult took control and said, "There I go again," this knowing laugh signified that he was aware of what he was doing at the time he was doing it, which placed him in a position of choice.

Play the Game. Fanny for years had been a backward patient at a remote state hospital after committing an act of infanticide. Currently functioning as a middle-class housewife, she maintained herself by following the doctor's advice that she take her medicines and by essentially saying, "Gee, aren't you a wonderful doctor," and "Gee, isn't this a wonderful clinic." Her stated Adult-to-Adult contract with the therapist was to be able to remain at home and not be rehospitalized. The therapist, therefore, chose to play her game of "Gee, Aren't You Wonderful" and modestly agreed with her endorsement of his talent. Although other group members occasionally took issue with Fanny as to her opinions of the therapist's qualities, she persisted and has to date, seven years later, fulfilled her contract. Unfortunately, with this treatment decision, she must remain in therapy indefinitely. However, her visits to the doctor are now for one 30-minute appointment every six months, which is satisfactory to her and satisfies the therapist.

Ignore the Game. Richard presented historical data about how his parents would unfairly beat him when he was a child. In the group setting he was inconsistent, which was easily detected by the therapist because of differences in the details of a story that he had told to the therapist in prior private sessions. The temptation for the therapist to publicly expose the inconsistency was nearly irresistible; however, at this point the therapist chose to ignore the invitation to play "Kick Me" with the patient, feeling that Richard could succeed in getting kicked almost anywhere, which was confirmed by his social history. Had the therapist exposed the game at that point, the patient would probably have left the group because he would have considered it an unfair kick, and he could receive those anywhere. He remained to explore his behavioral patterns and later related that he sought negative attention in preference to no attention at all.

Offer an Alternative. Under different circumstances the therapist decided to play "Kick Me" with Rose, a patient who over a period of ten years had undergone various modalities of treatment, including long-term and short-term hospitalization, drugs, electric shock, individual therapy, and group therapy. Through all this treatment, she persisted in periodically playing an especially archaic game of "Uproar," whereby she would respond to stimuli almost indiscriminately and usually end up hospitalized.

During a group session, the therapist admitted that he was considering going along with her psychotic game of "Uproar," which was complicated by a Child-Adult ego-state contamination, and he was trying to decide whether or not to call the police and remove her to a receiving ward. Before going along with the "Uproar," the therapist offered her the alternative of playing "Kick Me" by describing her behavior judiciously and stating, "Rose, you are making an ass of yourself." With a surprised and incredulous look on her face, Rose halted the archaic "Uproar" and directed what was previously free-floating criticism specifically to the therapist's Parent. During the session she berated the therapist for treating her that way and accused him of being like the therapists in the past—only worse. But finally she pouted her way into a position of "Why Does This Always Happen to Me?" Although she was angry and pouting when she left the session, she did leave at the regularly scheduled time, through the front door, without a police escort, and she was able to resume her daily functioning without a needless trip to the inpatient ward.

Choice of Response. None of the four types of response is invariably good or bad, but the therapist makes his choice relative to the treatment contract; however, in most circumstances the therapist decides not to play

the game and does not take a role in the game. It is less meaningful to ask whether or not the therapist plays a game with a patient and more meaningful to ask, "Under what circumstance should he play a particular game?"

Game antithesis may be Adult in nature. The therapist diagnosing a game may, at the right time, when he is talking to the well-cathected Adult of the patient, draw the game on the blackboard and have a scientific discussion of the transactions, gimmicks, and payoffs involved in the game. The two may engage in a discussion of how this particular game is deleterious to the patient's receiving what he came to treatment for.

The most potent antithesis is not that of an Adult-to-Adult transaction between therapist and patient but that of a quick, incisive, intuitive response—when the Child of the therapist is in a natural and free state and is not shackled by such Parent inhibitions as "Don't look at certain parts of the body" or "Make sure you maintain your professional appearance." It is not damaging to the patient for the therapist to say what is on his mind quickly if the therapist's Adult has ascertained that this is a safe and correct point for letting the Child out.

A patient who played "Now I've Got You, You S.O.B." waited patiently until she found the therapist doing something wrong and said, in essence, "Now I've Got You!" The therapist glanced at her and quickly said, "You've got me." Even the resentful and angry Parent of the patient was decommissioned by this intuitive antithesis, and she laughed.

Potency and Scripts. Potency means that the therapist must at a certain point in treatment transact with the patient, using as much force as the biological parent used in presenting the negative injunction in the formation of the script. All the theories and techniques of transactional analysis come to bear in a potent transaction. The time at which a potent statement is applied is also critical and is left to intuition.

From an operational definition, intuition is the free, uninhibited, and Natural Child of the therapist looking at what is happening.

Intuition is seen by the transactional analyst as mainly heightened and superior perception, and it is accomplished by that ego state in the therapist that is unencumbered by such parental ethical considerations as, "Don't look at things like that," "Be polite," and "Be an adult and think." Little children somehow know the good guys from the bad guys, and they know who to run to in the room and who to avoid. This childlike quality gives rise to the intuitive process. It may not be too comforting a concept to say that, when the right time to say something comes, you will know it. But, at this point, it remains the best statement.

Certain observable and necessary conditions preceding specific potency transactions have been curative on a script level. The retrospective analysis of five patients who had script cures has revealed that both the therapist and the patient knew at what moment the important transaction took place, and it was so specific that it is doubtful that the therapist and patients will forget that moment. In all five cases analyzed, there had been a Parent-to-Parent transaction at some time in the course of treatment that indicated some sort of agreement on basic values. There had also been an Adult-to-Adult transaction at some point in the treatment, usually around the formation of the contract. And there had been a Child-to-Child transaction. In these cases, the patient experienced all three of the therapist's ego states, and the therapist experienced all three of the patient's ego states. Moments of specific treatment with potency have not been at the level of withdrawal, ritual, activity, pastime, or game behavior. It is assumed that these situations were as close to intimacy as possible between the therapist and the patient.

Operations. Therapeutic operations used by the transactional analyst fall into eight categories. These have been elicited from numerous case presentations and several years of clinical experience with patients. But in the treatment group, the therapist is not encumbered by sets of rules or lists of operations and procedures that are effective in any given situation. Like the skillful surgeon, he has filed in his mind a repository of experience, necessary data, and procedural operations. Not all procedures are applied in any one transactional analysis, but Berne (1964) found all of the following tactics useful at certain times.

Interrogation. The therapist questions the patient about certain points so that he may be confident of getting an Adult response. Questioning provokes the patient's Adult and helps the therapist and the patient to document certain points that may have future usefulness, for instance:

What did you actually say to her before she slapped your face?

Excessive interrogation is specifically avoided, since patients are most happy to play "Psychiatric History."

Specification. The therapist categorizes certain information in order to fix it in the patient's mind as well as in his own. Specification is useful for later reference in more decisive therapeutic operations. It is a declaration on the part of the therapist, for example: "That's your father in your head again." It is not used hypothetically but only when the therapist has observed something definite that can be agreed on in an Adult-Adult transaction between the patient and the therapist. If used hypothetically, the patient may agree and start a good game of "Psychiatry."

Confrontation. This is used to shake up the contaminated Adult, Parent, or Child by pointing out an inconsistency. The object of this operation is to redistribute cathexis. It is not used to criticize or scare the patient. A simple example is when Mr. Fitz, with a red face and a loud voice, exclaims, "I am not angry!" and the therapist says, "You're shouting."

Explanation. Many times the patient's Parent, Child, or contaminated Adult rules his behavior in a treatment group. Explanation is the exchange of data that strengthens the Adult ego state. For example:

When Gladys smiled at you, it frightened the little boy in your head, and, because your Adult was not functioning well, your Parent came out and made that remark to her. That's why you have trouble with seductive women.

When the Adult explanation is correct, and the response is Adult, such as, "I thought that was it all the time," the explanation has been successful. When, however, the response is Childlike—"Yes, and furthermore. . ."—the therapist has been hooked into a game of "Psychiatry—Transactional Type."

Explanation—like interrogation, specification, and confrontation—is an intervention to be used for future reference in treatment or as specific information that may be useful to the patient in figuring out problems outside of the consultation room. Interpositions are operations by which the therapist wedges something between the patient's Adult and other ego states, which allows a more stable Adult and makes it more difficult for the patient to slide into Child or Parent behavior.

Illustration. Illustration follows successful confrontation and usually reinforces its effect. Illustration appeals to the Child as well as the Adult and may soften some of the effects of an unsuccessful confrontation. For example, in confronting the seductive skirt-raising by a "Rapo" player, the therapist may offer an illustration something like:

When you walked into that cocktail lounge the other night, it sounded just like Little Red Riding Hood walking through the forest and not seeing the big, bad wolf behind the tree.

Illustrations, at best, are humorous, and they should be intelligible to the Child of the patient as well as to the Adult, and so they are couched in vocabulary that a five-year-old child could understand. They have relevance to the Adult because they are appropriate and make sense. The little boy or little girl in the patient also likes them and usually smiles because he can form a visual image. Occasionally, the Parent resents the use of illustrations and may angrily say something like, "That's silly." Then an illustration to separate the Parent and Adult ego states is provided:

While we were talking your father popped up from behind the chair and said, "That's silly." Did you notice that?

If the patient laughs (Child) or responds from the Adult—"Let's keep him behind the chair"—the illustration has been successful.

Confirmation. This is the gathering of further useful data that add evidence to prior confrontations. The confirmation is necessary to firm up positions taken with confrontation and illustrations. When a patient's Child is thwarted from playing a game, it usually does not give up the first time. It comes on stronger and harder. At this point, the therapist confirms his original confrontation of the game at the time of recurrence. For example:

When your Child decided to knock off "Kick Me," you told us you weren't going to be pushed around any more. So then you went out and told your boss to drop dead, and he fired you. Although you were jumping on him, you ended up getting kicked in the long run. So that must mean that your basic game is "Kick Me."

One should use confirmation when he is certain that the Parent of the patient will not turn on the Child of the patient and say, "I told you so, stupid," and he is certain that the Child of the patient will not turn on the therapist and say, "You are always criticizing me." If the therapist is feeling especially bright or smug immediately prior to offering some confirmation, he would do better to leave it out.

Interpretation. Interpretation is dealing with the Child who distorts and masquerades and attempts to confuse. These operations correspond to the strategies of orthodox psychoanalysis. Structurally, the therapist decodes, detoxifies, regroups ideas, and rectifies the distortions of the Child's presentation of past experiences. The Adult, after the preceding six operations, is uncontaminated and acts as a computer in estimating the probabilities of the Child's presentations. The Parent attempts to thwart interpretation by disapproval. For example: "You make everything sound sexual," which is seen as a moralistic standpoint, or "I don't have to listen to that, young man (or old man)," which is haughtiness or snobbery. The Child is receiving gratification and, therefore, increases its efforts to hide and confuse.

Probability estimates are Adult-to-Adult transactions, such as,

That recurrent monster in your dreams, most likely, is the evil part of your mother.

Other clues leading to successful interpretation originate with intuitive guesses. This means that the Child of the therapist senses the Child presentations of the patient, colloquially expressed in some groups as catching the vibrations, and the Adult of the therapist then presents the message in a logical, decoded manner to the Adult of the patient. The therapist also gets clues of coded messages by observing Child-to-Child transactions among other group members.

The preceding six operations of interrogation, specification, confrontation, explanation, illustration, and confirmation focus on decontaminating and cathecting the Adult. They make treatment easier and afford the patient social control. This is why transactional analysts take the position: Get better first, and find out why later. Waiting sometimes for years for a successful interpretation to produce change is uneconomical and may be especially hard on the patient's family.

Crystallization. This is a presentation, from the therapist's Adult to the patient's Adult, of the patient's position, and it represents the technical end point of the transactional analysis. It may be expressed as:

So you are now in a position to knock off that game, if you so choose.

In an existential sense the therapist is indifferent as to what choice the patient makes, his job being over when the patient is in a position of choice. This is the therapist's Adult position. Of course, the Parent of the therapist may be concerned about the patient's getting better and doing things that he thinks are best, and he may so state if asked. The therapist's Child has more fun with the healthy, smiling, and laughing Child in the patient.

Results

As the concepts of transactional analysis were widely applied over the last ten years, reports of its effectiveness have been forthcoming. Clinicians in the private practice of psychiatry and psychotherapy report that more than 80 per cent of the patients fulfill their treatment contracts. The advantage of gauging effectiveness in this manner is that it is specific and can be discussed openly, and reliance on the therapist's judgment is not necessary.

An improvement scale has been devised by Breen whereby patients in groups and therapists may qualitatively and quantitatively specify the patient's position from minus three to plus three. Zero means that the patient is playing his games at their usual intensity. Plus one is the level of social control where games are suspended, but anxiety and restlessness prevail, and continued treatment is necessary. Plus two is when the patient experiments with new possibilities and is offered protection by the therapist in the group. Plus three is when the patient attains a position of autonomy, can solve his own problems as they arise, and no longer needs the aid of treatment. In the other direction, minus one means playing the game harder. Minus two implies apathy and only half-hearted playing. Minus three means withdrawal, suicide, homicide, or other script conclusions. These classifications lend themselves to research techniques more easily than do other criteria for improvement.

Schiff has reported dramatic results in the treatment of adolescent and young adult schizophrenics in a residential treatment center, using the concepts of transactional analysis. During the past five years more than 30 patients have been brought into the "family" and have undergone regression and reparenting. All these patients met the diagnostic criteria as having verified schizophrenic reactions by clinical observation and psychological testing. On leaving the residential treatment center, 70 per cent were free of observable manifestations of schizophrenia, and extensive psychological testing revealed no evidence of schizophrenia in the present or by past inference. To date, not a single relapse has resulted in hospitalization in the cured schizophrenics. At the termination of treatment, 20 per cent had clear problems. Most of them were patients who had had long episodes of prior hospitalization and a history of heavy medication in past treatment. Another 10 per cent were thought to be treatment failures. The Schiff Rehabilitation Project has now branched into outpatient follow-up work, and several of the cured schizophrenics are doing reparenting in other treatment projects. Active research projects are going on within the confines of this project on the subjects of passivity and thinking.

Transactional analysis has been applied widely within the confines of the California state penal system, and Ernst and Keating have reported the results in the scientific literature. Social control by prisoners within the penal system has been markedly improved, which is of critical importance for these types of disorders. Poindexter reports that business and industry have turned to the concepts of transactional analysis for consultation. The re-employment of mental patients has been gratifying, using this approach, and industry has been particularly impressed by the ease and rapidity with which psychological thinking can be translated into practical effectiveness. Browne and Freeling have reported this same advantage in the use of transactional analysis by over-burdened general practitioners in England.

REFERENCES

Allen, D., and Houston, M. The management of hysterical acting-out patients in a training clinic. Psychiatry, *22:* 41, 1959.

Berne, E. The nature of intuition. Psychiat. Quart., *23:* 203, 1949.

Berne, E. Concerning the nature of diagnosis. Int. Rec. Med., *165:* 283, 1952.

Berne, E. Concerning the nature of communication. Psychiat. Quart., *27:* 185, 1953.

Berne, E. Group attendance: clinical and theoretical considerations. Int. J. Group Psychother., *5:* 392, 1955.

Berne, E. Intuition. IV. Primal images and primal judgment. Psychiat. Quart., *29:* 634, 1955.

Berne, E. Intuition. V. The ego image. Psychiat. Quart., *31:* 611, 1957.

Berne, E. *Transactional Analysis in Psychotherapy.* Grove Press, New York, 1961.

Berne, E. Intuition. VI. The psychodynamics of intuition. Psychiat. Quart., *36:* 294, 1962.

Berne, E. *The Structure and Dynamics of Organizations and Groups.* J. B. Lippincott, New York, 1963.

Berne, E. *Games People Play.* Grove Press, New York, 1964.

Berne, E. *Principles of Group Treatment.* Oxford University Press, New York, 1966.

Berne, E. Staff-patient staff conferences. Amer. J. Psychiat., *125:* 286, 1968.

Breen, M. An improvement scale. Trans. Anal. Bull., *9:* 1, 1970.

Browne, K., and Freeling, P. *The Doctor-Patient Relationship.* E. & S. Livingstone, Edinburgh and London, 1967.

Crossman, P. Permission and protection. Trans. Anal. Bull., *5:* 152, 1966.

Dusay, J. Response. Trans. Anal. Bull., *5:* 36, 1966.

Dusay, J. Proceedings of the eighth annual meeting of the International Transactional Analysis Association. Trans. Anal. Bull., *9:* 36, 1970.

Ellis, A. *Reason and Emotion in Psychotherapy.* Lyle Stuart, New York, 1962.

Erikson, E. H. *Identity and the Life Cycle.* International Universities Press, New York, 1959.

Ernst, F. The use of transactional analysis in prison therapy groups. J. Soc. Therap., *8:* 3, 1962.

Ernst, F., and Keating, W. Psychiatric treatment of the California felon. Amer. J. Psychiat., *120:* 974, 1964.

Fast, J. *Body Language.* M. Evans, New York, 1970.

Frank, J. *Persuasion and Healing.* Johns Hopkins Press, Baltimore, 1961.

Freud, S. Group psychology and the analysis of the ego. In *Standard Edition of the Complete Psychological Works of Sigmund Freud.* vol. 18, p. 67, J. Strachey, editor. Hogarth Press, London, 1955.

Hartman, H. Ego psychology and the problem of adaptation. In *Organization and Pathology of Thought*, p. 304, D. Rapaport, editor. Columbia University Press, New York, 1951.

Karpman, S. Script drama analysis. Trans. Anal. Bull., *7:* 26, 1968.

Perls, F. *Gestalt Therapy Verbatim.* Real People Press, Lafayette, Calif., 1969.

Piaget, J. *Logic and Psychology*, Basic Books, New York, 1957.

Poindexter, R. Employment of former mental patients. In *Current Psychiatric Therapies*, vol. 4, p. 267. Grune & Stratton, New York, 1964.

Poindexter, R., and Dusay, J. How much better are your patients? Trans. Anal. Bull., *4:* 5, 1965.

Reich, W. *Character Analysis.* Noonday Press, New York, 1968.

Ruesch, J., and Kees, W. *Nonverbal Communication.* University of California Press, Berkeley, 1956.

Schiff, J. Reparenting schizophrenics. Trans. Anal. Bull., *8:* 47, 1969.

Schiff, J. *All My Children.* M. Evans, New York, 1971.

Spitz, R. Hospitalism, genesis of psychiatric conditions in early childhood. Psychoanal. Stud. Child, *1:* 53, 1945.

Steiner, C. *Games Alcoholics Play: The Analysis of Life Scripts.* Grove Press, New York, 1971.

Steiner, C., and Cassidy, W. Therapeutic contracts in group treatment. Trans. Anal. Bull., *8:* 29, 1969.

Steiner, C., and Steiner, U. Permission classes. Trans. Anal. Bull., *7:* 87, 1968.

Werner, H. *Comparative Psychology of Mental Development.* International Universities Press, New York, 1948.

Wolpe, J. *The Practice of Behavior Therapy.* Pergamon Press, New York, 1969.

5

Behavior Therapy in Groups

Alan Goldstein, Ph.D. and Joseph Wolpe, M.D.

INTRODUCTION

When successful new ways of attacking old problems come along, responses to them seem to follow a certain sequence. First:

It can't work; it defies all the accumulated knowledge about the problem.

Second, after the initial demonstrated successes:

All new things work for a while; this is just another fad destined to die out.

Third, after hard evidence of effectiveness and refusal to die out:

Why that's what we've been doing all along. We've just been calling it by different names.

Applied learning theories relative to the community of psychotherapists have reached the third stage. Many who are aware of the effectiveness of behavioral therapies look for the similarities with their own *modus operandi* in order to diminish as much as possible that uncomfortable state of cognitive dissonance inevitable when ingrained attitudes are challenged. Indeed, there are similarities. Well-controlled scientific studies give underpinnings to only a portion of what transpires in the successful therapist-patient interaction. Where there is as yet no science, therapists must make use of art. Even where there is science, many therapists have, by trial and error, arrived at therapeutic strategies approximating those deliberately constructed by others from laboratory data.

A constructive approach is to set out to discover what is different about behavioral approaches to group therapy. The differences appear on two levels, the theoretical and the practical. Those who adhere to set, nonbehavioral theoretical systems may find some technical interventions useful.

The behavioral approach is the first approach directly based on well-established laws of human behavior. With the exception of Rogerian therapy, it is the only approach that has been subjected to well-controlled studies designed to test validity and effectiveness. Attempts have been made to integrate established behavioral interventions into the matrix of group therapy processes. Unfortunately, there is little in the way of scientifically evolved principles that bears on group processes as opposed to individual behavior. Obviously, the most significant human behavior of concern to psychotherapists occurs in the social context—that is, within the group activities that lie in the sphere of life of each person. But the study of the individual personality—individual responses—has historically been the focus in clinical psychology and psychiatry. Other sciences, such as sociology and social psychology, have focused more on group variables, but few attempts have been made to incorporate this knowledge into psychotherapy. The most salient information available is from the accounts of therapists practicing group therapy, and these are usually nothing more than observations and speculations.

HISTORY

The history of conditioning begins with Ivan Sechenov (1829–1905), the father of

Russian physiology. His hypothetical structure, which was later adopted by Pavlov, considered the function of the brain in terms of a physical reflex, consisting of three components: sensory input, essential process, and efferent outflow. All behavior consisted of responses to stimulation, with interaction of excitation and inhibition operating at the central link of the reflex arc. Following this model, Pavlov embarked on a series of experiments, using primarily the salivary response in dogs to various stimuli. In these experiments, he demonstrated many of the phenomena later extended to all types of learning.

In American psychology, the impetus for adoption of the behavioristic approach was furnished by the translation into English of the works of Bekhterev and Pavlov. Watson's 1919 book established him as the father of American behaviorism and exerted an important influence on theory and experiment in American psychology.

An experiment by Watson and Rayner stands out as one of the most notable single studies in the conditioning literature, although its immediate impact on clinical applications of conditioning was nil. Because of the predictive significance of Watson's work, excerpts from their article, published in 1920, are presented here:

In recent literature various speculations have been entered into concerning the possibility of conditioning various types of emotional response, but direct experimental evidence in support of such a view has been lacking. If the theory advanced by Watson and Morgan to the effect that in infancy the original emotional reaction patterns are few, consisting so far as observed of fear, rage and love, then there must be some simple method by means of which the range of stimuli which can call out these emotions and their compounds is greatly increased. Otherwise, complexity in adult response could not be accounted for. These authors without adequate experimental evidence advanced the view that this range was increased by means of conditioned reflex factors. It was suggested there that the early home life of the child furnishes a laboratory situation for establishing conditioned emotional responses. The present authors have recently put the whole matter to an experimental test.

Experimental work has been done so far on only one child, Albert B. . . . At approximately

9 months of age we ran him through the emotional tests. . . . In brief, the infant was confronted suddenly and for the first time successively with a white rat, a rabbit, a dog, a monkey, with masks with and without hair, cotton wool, burning newspapers, etc. . . . At no time did this infant ever show fear in any situation. . . . The test to determine whether a fear reaction could be called out by a loud sound was made when he was 8 months, 26 days of age. . . .

One of the 2 experimenters caused the child to turn its head and fixate her moving hand; the other, stationed back of the child, struck the steel bar a sharp blow. The child started violently, his breathing was checked and the arms were raised in a characteristic manner. On the second stimulation the same thing occurred, and in addition the lips began to pucker and tremble. On the third stimulation the child broke into a sudden crying fit. This is the first time an emotional situation in the laboratory has produced any fear or even crying in Albert.

Before attempting to set up a conditioned response, we, as before, put him through all of the regular emotional tests. Not the slightest sign of fear response was obtained in any situation.

The steps taken to condition emotional responses are shown in our laboratory notes.

11 months, 3 days— (1) White rat suddenly taken from the basket and presented to Albert. He began to reach for the rat with left hand. Just as his hand touched the animal the bar was struck immediately behind his head. The infant jumped violently and fell forward, burying his face in the mattress. He did not cry, however.

(2) Just as the right hand touched the rat, the bar was again struck. Again the infant jumped violently, fell forward and began to whimper.

In order not to disturb the child too seriously, no further tests were given for 1 week.

11 months, 10 days— (1) Rat presented suddenly without sound. There was steady fixation but no tendency at first to reach for it. The rat was then placed nearer, whereupon tentative reaching movements began with the right hand. When the rat nosed the infant's left hand, the hand was immediately withdrawn. He started to reach for the head of the animal with the forefinger of the left hand, but withdrew it suddenly before contact. It is thus seen that the two joint stimulations given the previous week were not without effect. He was tested with his blocks immediately afterwards to see if they shared in the process of conditioning. He began immediately to pick them up, dropping them, pounding them, etc. In the remainder of the tests the blocks were given frequently to quiet him and to test his general emotional state. They were always re-

moved from sight when the process of conditioning was under way.

(2) Joint stimulation with rat and sound. Started, then fell over immediately to right side. No crying.

(3) Joint stimulation. Fell to right side and rested upon hands, with head turned away from rat. No crying.

(4) Joint stimulation. Same reaction.

(5) Rat suddenly presented alone. Puckered face, whimpered and withdrew body sharply to the left.

(6) Joint stimulation. Fell over immediately to right side and began to whimper.

(7) Joint stimulation. Started violently and cried, but did not fall over.

(8) Rat alone. The instant the rat was shown the baby began to cry. Almost instantly he turned sharply to the left, fell over on left side, raised himself on all fours and began to crawl away so rapidly that he was caught with difficulty before reaching the edge of the table. . . .

(II) When a Conditioned Emotional Response has been Established for one Object, is there a Transfer?

Five days later Albert was again brought back into the laboratory and tested as follows:

11 months, 15 days— (1) Tested first with blocks. He reached readily for them, playing with them as usual. . . .

(2) Rat alone. Whimpered immediately, withdrew right hand and turned head and trunk away.

(3) Blocks again offered. Played readily with them, smiling and gurgling.

(4) Rat alone. Leaned over to the left side as far away from the rat as possible, then fell over, getting up on all fours and scurrying away as rapidly as possible.

(5) Blocks again offered. Reached immediately for them, smiling and laughing as before.

The above preliminary test shows that the conditioned response to the rat had carried over completely for the 5 days in which no tests were given. The question as to whether or not there is a transfer was next taken up.

(6) Rabbit alone. The rabbit was suddenly placed on the mattress in front of him. The reaction was pronounced. Negative responses began at once. He leaned as far away from the animal as possible, whimpered, then burst into tears. When the rabbit was placed in contact with him he buried his face in the mattress, then got up on all fours and crawled away, crying as he went. . . .

(7) The blocks were next given to him, after an interval. He played with them as before. . . .

(8) Dog alone. The dog did not produce as violent a reaction as the rabbit. The moment fixation occurred the child shrank back and as the animal came nearer he attempted to get on all fours but did not cry at first. As soon as the dog passed out of his range of vision he became quiet. The dog was then made to approach the infant's head (he was lying down at the moment). Albert straightened up immediately, fell over to the opposite side and turned his head away. He then began to cry. . . .

(10) Fur coat (seal). Withdrew immediately to the left side and began to fret. Coat put close to him on the left side, he turned immediately, began to cry and tried to crawl away on all fours. . . .

To test for persistence of the conditioned reactions, the experimenters allowed 31 days to pass with no further contact with the above-mentioned stimuli. On resumption of the tests after 31 days, Albert showed essentially the same responses. Immediately after the tests, Albert was taken from the hospital, and there was no further contact.

Our own view . . . is that these responses in the home environment are likely to persist indefinitely, unless an accidental method for removing them is hit upon. The importance of establishing some method must be apparent to all. Had the opportunity been at hand we should have tried out several methods, some of which we may mention. (1) Constantly confronting the child with those stimuli which called out the responses in the hopes that habituation would come in corresponding to "fatigue" of reflex when differential reactions are to be set up. (2) By trying to "recondition" by showing objects calling out fear responses (visual) and simultaneously stimulating the erogenous zones (tactual). We should try first the lips, then the nipples and as a final resort the sex organs. (3) By trying to "recondition" by feeding the subject candy or other food just as the animal is shown. This method calls for the food control of the subject. (4) By building up "constructive" activities around the object by imitation and by putting the hand through the motions of manipulation. . . .

The Freudians 20 years from now, unless their hypotheses change, when they come to analyze Albert's fear of a seal skin coat—assuming that he comes to analysis at that age—will probably tease from him the recital of a dream which upon their analysis will show that Albert at 3 years of age attempted to play with the pubic hair of the mother and was scolded violently for it. (We are by no means denying that this might in some other case condition it.) If the analyst has sufficiently prepared Albert to accept such a dream when found as an explanation of his avoiding tendencies, and if the analyst has the authority and personality to put it over, Albert may be fully convinced that the dream was true revealer of the factors which brought about the fear. . . .

Our argument is meant to be constructive. Emotional disturbances in adults cannot be traced back to sex alone. They must be retraced along at least three collateral—to conditioned and transferred responses set up in infancy and early youth in all three of the fundamental emotions.

Watson's suggestions have become core concepts in most behavior therapy techniques. Around 1930, the conditioned reflex experiment assumed a new role when it provided the concepts for the development of learning theories that included more complex behavior. The different theories expounded by Hull, Guthrie, Tolman, and Skinner led to feverish experimentation to test hypotheses deduced from theory. The result is a comprehensive body of literature based directly on well-controlled laboratory data. Theorists still differ, but there are many laws of learning on which all would agree. This offers a high degree of predictability when a change in behavior is the goal. These phenomena have been identified by certain technical terms which are operationally defined.

LAWS OF LEARNING

Conditioning

In classical conditioning, learning is demonstrated by the acquisition of a conditioned response. The paradigm for the development of a conditioned response is that presented above in Watson and Rayner's discussion of Albert. A stimulus that already has the capacity to elicit a response, an unconditioned stimulus, is presented in close temporal contiguity with a conditioned stimulus, which elicits no response or, in some cases, a different response. With repetitive pairings of the conditioned stimulus and the unconditioned stimulus, the conditioned stimulus develops the capacity to elicit a response similar to the one elicited by the unconditioned stimulus. When such a response appears, it is

called the conditioned response. In the case case of Albert, the unconditioned stimulus is the loud noise; the unconditioned response is the complex of observable components of fear. The conditioned stimulus is the rat, and the newly elicited components of fear to presentation of the rat is the conditioned response.

In a procedure generally known as operant conditioning, learning occurs through a different sequence of events. The essential element distinguishing operant conditioning from classical conditioning is that in operant conditioning the unconditioned stimulus follows some predetermined behavior when it occurs spontaneously. In such a procedure, the unconditioned stimulus is designated the reinforcing stimulus or reinforcement. Learning is measured by the change in probability of occurrence of the response as a result of the pairing of the response and the reinforcement. A simple example is the increasing rate of bar-pressing by a rat when food (reinforcement) constantly and immediately follows the bar-presses.

Extinction

After a conditioned response is established, it is, except under special circumstances, subject to elimination through repetitive presentations of the conditioned stimulus without the unconditioned stimulus or through repetitive performances of the response without reinforcement. Continually exposing Albert to the rat without the loud noise or no longer delivering food to the rat contingent on bar-pressing would lead to extinction of the conditioned response.

Generalization

When a response has been conditioned to a particular conditioned stimulus, stimuli similar to the conditioned stimulus also have the power to evoke the conditioned response. This phenomenon is referred to as stimulus generalization. The response varies in strength, depending upon the similarities of the generalized stimulus to the conditioned stimulus. As the stimulus becomes less similar, the strength of the response becomes weaker. The phenomenon of generalization, like the others discussed here, has been demonstrated in all modalities of learning, including conditioned emotional responses, motor learning, and verbal learning.

An example of semantic generalization is furnished by Lacey and Smith's 1954 experiment in which only the word "cow" was followed by electric shock when presented in a list of words. Heart rate monitoring showed that, after conditioning, other rural words in the list—such as plow, corn, and tractor—also elicited the conditioned response, while nonrural words did not.

An experiment by Noble demonstrated that the visual presentation of a nonsense syllable followed by shock resulted in generalization to the subvocal thought of the word. Thoughts conditioned to an unpleasant or painful unconditioned stimulus are avoided. Experiments such as Noble's give an operational definition of the concept of repression and allow for the study of its parameters.

When an extinction procedure is applied to a generalized stimulus, extinction occurs more rapidly than extinction to the conditioned stimulus would. The farther out the stimulus is on the generalization gradient—that is, the more dissimilar it is to the conditioned stimulus—the more rapidly extinction occurs. If, after extinguishing the response to a generalized stimulus, the experimenter again presents the original conditioned stimulus, he finds that the conditioned response has been weakened. This phenomenon, called generalization of extinction, is of considerable importance in understanding clinical techniques used in the extinction of pathological behavior.

Counterconditioning

Extinction occurs in classical conditioning when the unconditioned stimulus is withheld. The elimination of the conditioned response can be greatly facilitated if, in addition to withholding the unconditioned stimulus, the experimenter presents another unconditioned stimulus in its place. When that elicits an unconditioned stimulus response incompatible with the conditioned response, then counterconditioning is said to occur.

Again using the example of Albert's conditioned fear of rabbits, when the rabbit, the conditioned stimulus, was presented in contiguity with feeding, the new conditioned stimulus, then counterconditioning would occur because food elicits a response antagonistic to fear.

Not only does counterconditioning speed the elimination of conditioned responses, but it can be effective in eliminating the conditioned response under special circumstances in which extinction would not do so. Again, this phenomenon has particular relevance to clinical contexts.

Partial Reinforcement Effect

In most life situations, behavior is not constantly followed by reinforcement. When the reinforcement is withheld during some laboratory trials of operant conditioning, the learned response is far more resistant to extinction. By gradually reducing the ratio of reinforced to nonreinforced trials, the experimenter can teach the subject to emit the conditioned response sometimes thousands of times without reinforcement.

An example of the different effects of persistence of behavior between learning under 100 per cent reinforcement schedules and partial reinforcement schedules may be seen in everyday behavior. Candy vending machines have a history of very nearly 100 per cent reinforcement—that is, every time one puts a coin into the machine, candy (reinforcement) is delivered. If someone finds that a machine fails to deliver, his response of putting in coins quickly extinguishes. On the other hand, since gambling slot machines are programmed on a partial reinforcement schedule, the behavior of putting in coins persists, even after long periods of no reinforcement, attesting to the power of partial reinforcement in retarding extinction.

Conditioned Emotional Response

When a subject is presented with pairings of a conditioned stimulus and a painful unconditioned stimulus, the conditioned stimulus soon elicits the emotional responses previously associated with the unconditioned stimulus (fear responses).

Escape Responses and Avoidance Responses

When the situation is changed so that some behavior on the subject's part results in terminating the painful unconditioned stimulus (escape response) or allows him to avoid the onset of the unconditioned stimulus in the interval between the conditioned stimulus onset and the unconditioned stimulus onset (avoidance response), then all components of fear tend to drop out after a few trials. At the same time, the avoidance behavior becomes very strong. Note that a new and strong behavior, the avoidance response, has been learned without following it with the usually required external reinforcement. An explanation lies in the fact that termination of a conditioned stimulus previously paired with pain is in itself reinforcing. This conditioned stimulus now has the power to motivate by its onset and reinforce by its offset new behavior not present in the original conditioning situation.

Every clinician knows that people can and do consistently (compulsively) engage in behavior that in the long run reaps unpleasant results. Ought not the unpleasant results serve to eliminate such behavior? Studies by Solomon and Wynne may give some clues to help solve the paradox.

Dogs were placed in a large box with two compartments. One compartment had an electrifiable grid, and the other compartment had no grid. The compartments were separated by a barrier. When the barrier was up, it confined the dog to one side of the box; when it was down, it allowed him to move from one side to the other with a vigorous jump.

The dog was placed in the grid compartment. A tone was sounded and the barrier was lowered (conditioned stimulus), followed in ten seconds by an electric shock through the grid (unconditioned stimulus). At the onset of shock, the dog showed typical fear behavior and sooner or later jumped the barrier, terminating the shock and the tone. After a few trials, the dogs developed a stable avoidance behavior, jumping the barrier a few seconds after the onset of the conditioned stimulus. At this point, signs

of fear decreased, and the animals were soon performing the avoidance response in a calm way.

Subjects conditioned in this way continue to perform indefinitely without ever again experiencing the shock. The habit is remarkably stable. The experimenter may alter the situation so that, in the above experiment, when the dogs jump into the "safe" compartment, they land on an electrified grid that delivers a short-duration shock. The dogs not only continue to jump at each presentation of the conditioned stimulus but do so with more vigor and persistence.

Extinction of Avoidance Responses

Setting up an extinction procedure, such as disconnecting the grid, does not lead to extinction of the avoidance response. The dogs are continually reinforced for jumping by reduction of fear and, therefore, continue to make the avoidance response. If extinction is to work at all, the subject must be confined in the situation by blocking the avoidance response.

Avoidance behavior, learned in the context of mildly painful stimuli, does tend to extinguish by blocking. But when severely painful stimuli have been used, there is resistance to extinction. The subject exposed to the conditioned stimulus, with his learned avoidance response blocked, often learns superstitious behavior.

On the first trial in confinement the dogs typically begin to show signs of fear in the ten-second period after conditioned stimulus onset. Whatever behavior is being engaged in at the end of the ten seconds, the point at which shock was presented in the conditioning trials, becomes reinforced, and the superstitious avoidance response begins to evolve. It is superstitious from the experimenter's point of view, since the behavior bears no relationship to avoiding the shock; nonetheless, the dogs persist on subsequent trials. If the barrier to the original avoidance response is removed, the dogs may again engage in the original avoidance behavior. If they persist in the second avoidance behavior, reinstatement of the original behavior may be arranged by merely blocking the second learned behavior.

Just as other conditioned responses are elicited by stimuli somewhat similar to the conditioned stimulus, so avoidance responses are evoked by generalized stimuli.

LEARNING THEORY IN INDIVIDUAL THERAPY

Wolpe (1958) described a series of therapeutic interventions, designed for treatment of human neurosis, that were based indirectly on laboratory-produced data. He reasoned that only three kinds of process are known to bring about lasting changes in behavior: growth, lesions, and learning. Since neurotic behavior is demonstrably the result of unfortunate learning or a lack of appropriate learning, its elimination must require relearning or additional learning experiences. In accordance with this hypothesis, empirically established principles of learning were applied to the special problem, neurosis.

To overcome learned fear responses, Wolpe proposed the following principle:

If a response antagonistic to anxiety can be made to occur in the presence of anxiety-evoking stimuli so that it is accompanied by a complete or partial suppression of the anxiety responses, the bond between these stimuli and the anxiety responses will be weakened.

The animal research establishing the usefulness of counterconditioning was uniformly dependent on feeding as the counterconditioning response. The question arose as to whether other responses more suitable to clinical practice might also serve as counterconditioning agents. A series of experiments using neurotic human subjects was undertaken, employing relaxation, sexual responses, and assertive responses as counterconditioning stimuli.

The method using relaxation as a counterconditioning agent to anxiety most closely parallels the animal experiments. It is mainly applicable to phobias and related fear habits. Through interviews and questionnaires, an anxiety hierarchy on the phobic theme is established. This hierarchy consists of stimulus situations to which the patient reacts with graded amounts of anxiety—the most disturbing item placed at the bottom of the list and the least disturbing at the top. This hierarchy represents the generalization gradient described above. When the response to a generalized stimulus is counterconditioned, the responses to stimuli all along the hierarchy are also reduced in strength. When relaxation is counterposed with a weak anxiety response-linked stimulus and relaxation is able to predominate, the response is weakened and, with repetition of the procedure, eliminated. The next most potent stimulus, having been weakened by generalization of extinction, then may be subjected to the same procedure. The patient is then exposed to each of the hierarchical steps in turn until he is desensitized to the entire hierarchy. The real stimuli in the hierarchy are sometimes presented, but imagined stimuli are much more frequently used. Anxiety response decrement to imagined situations transfers to the real situation. Wolpe labels this procedure *systematic desensitization*

Sexual responses as counterconditioning stimuli are used mainly in cases where anxiety is conditioned to various aspects of sexual situations. When anxiety conditioning has resulted in complete inhibition of sexual responses, systematic desensitization is employed. More often, however, the sexual inhibition is only partial and sexual responses can be elicited without impediment in circumstances far out on the generalization gradient. The patient must be able to bring a willing partner into the regime. Then exposures to sexual situations can be arranged in a hierarchical way. It is necessary to begin at a point where sexual arousal predominates over anxiety. Repeated exposures are carried out until very strong sexual feelings are present and anxiety is eliminated. Each step up the hierarchy is then handled in the same manner until all anxiety is removed and the related sexual inhibitions overcome.

Assertive responses are used against anxieties conditioned to interpersonal situations. The word assertive has a rather wide meaning; it includes not only aggressive behavior but also overt expression of affectionate, friendly, and other nonanxious feelings. Wolpe gives this rationale for the procedures:

Assertive responses are mainly employed in situations that occur spontaneously in the normal course of the patient's life. . . . I have found them of value only for overcoming unadaptive anxieties aroused in the patient by other people during direct interchanges with them. In these circumstances assertive responses are extremely effective. To take a common example, a patient feels hurt when members of his family criticize him and responds by trying to defend himself, by sulking, or by an outburst of petulant rage. Such responses are expressive of anxiety and helplessness. But some measure of resentment is, understandably, almost invariably present at the same time. The patient is unable to express this resentment because, for example, through previous training, the idea of talking back to his elders produces anxiety.

Now just because this anxiety inhibits the expression of the resentment, it might be expected that an augmentation of resentment motivation sufficient to procure its outward expression would reciprocally inhibit the anxiety and thus suppress it, to some extent at least. The therapist increases the motivation by pointing out the emptiness of the patient's fears, emphasizing how his fearful patterns of behavior have incapacitated him and placed him at the mercy of others, and informing him that, though expression of resentment may be difficult at first, it becomes progressively easier with practice. It usually does not take long for the patient to begin to perform the required behavior, although some need much initial exhortation and repeated promptings. Gradually the patient becomes able to behave assertively in progressively more exacting circumstances and reports a growing feeling of ease in all relevant situations. A conditioned inhibition of the anxiety responses is clearly developing, presumably on the basis of their repeated reciprocal inhibition—a process in all respects parallel to that involved in the overcoming of animal neuroses.

A kind of play-acting is often employed to prepare patients for difficult situations. The most frequently used form is called role-playing, in which the therapist assumes the role of the antagonist while the patient plays himself. The situation is acted out, with feedback given by the therapist between scenes. On occasion, the therapist may take the role of the patient while the patient plays the antagonist so that the therapist

may model the appropriate responses for the patient. With several repetitions, the patient grows less anxious and finds an appropriate way of dealing with the situation. He is then instructed to carry it out outside the consulting room and to report the results. By dealing with his personal difficulties in a hierarchical way, the patient gradually arrives at a level of appropriate assertiveness in step with the reduction of anxiety in his interactions with other people. For those patients who have already learned appropriate responses but are conditioned to inhibit them, the therapist need only work toward these responses being applied in everyday life.

Since Wolpe's 1958 book, a considerable number of experimental tests have indicated the effectiveness of his procedures. In addition to the uncontrolled studies, which are common to all therapy approaches and are in the long run of little value, there have been well-controlled studies that demonstrate the effectiveness of behavior therapy over and above other approaches—for example, studies by Paul, Lang and Lazovik, and DiLoreto. Additional well-designed studies have established that the procedures produce improvement over and above that attributable to factors, such as relationship, that are responsible for improvement—for example, work by Rachman and by Lomont and Edwards. Other empirically based developments include clinical applications of operant conditioning and vicarious learning or modeling by Bandura.

In operant conditioning, behavior is changed by arranging for reinforcement to follow the selected responses to be modified. For example, bar-pressing increases when food (reinforcement) follows it. From this simple case, experimenters like Holland and Skinner have made extensions to more complicated situations, which may involve control of schedules of reinforcement and discrimination training. The extension of this control to human behavior was first reported by Lindsley in a study of psychotic behavior. The technique has since been adapted to many clinical cases, including mental defectives (Orlando et al.), autistic children (Ferster and DeMyer), and anorexia nervosa patients (Bachrach et al.). Because the therapist needs to maintain control over reinforcement, these techniques have been confined mainly to hospitalized patients and to children whose parents and teachers have been taught the procedures of operant control. Operant reinforcement is a powerful factor also in one-to-one psychotherapy, as Truax reports, even when it is being inadvertently applied by therapists who attribute results to other theoretical models.

Bandura and his followers have shown that new behavior and existing patterns can be modified by vicarious experiences, such as those offered by modeling.

Thus, for example, one can acquire good response patterns merely by observing the performance of appropriate models; emotional responses can be conditioned observationally by witnessing the affective reactions of others undergoing painful or pleasurable experiences; fearful and avoidant behavior can be extinguished vicariously through observations of modeled approach behavior toward feared objects without any adverse consequences accruing to the performers; inhibitions can be induced by witnessing the behavior of others punished; and finally the expression of well-learned responses can be enhanced and socially regulated through the actions of influential models.

Some reports—by Creer and Miklich, for example—describe the use of modeling to promote change in a clinical setting.

BEHAVIOR THERAPY IN GROUPS

The majority of reported behavior group therapies consist of the direct transfer of individual-oriented procedures, such as systematic desensitization to a group of people with homogeneous problems. Lazarus reported the use of systematic desensitization in groups of patients presenting phobic complaints, frigidity, and impotence. Lazarus also described assertive training groups, in which the primary treatment used is assertive training as previously discussed in relation to one-to-one therapy. Experimentally designed comparisons of such group procedures have supported the proposition that they are superior to other group approaches.

Particularly well-controlled studies include those by Paul, wherein therapists treated public speaking anxiety by means of systematic desensitization and insight-oriented therapy with appropriate control groups. DiLoreto compared systematic desensitization, client-centered therapy, and rational-emotive therapy in the treatment of interpersonal anxiety. Both the Paul and the DiLoreto studies demonstrated the superior effect of systematic desensitization to the other approaches.

In a well-controlled study, McFall and Marston demonstrated the superior effectiveness of assertive training, relying heavily on behavior rehearsal (role-playing) in groups, over placebo and no-treatment conditions. Behavior rehearsal subjects were divided into two groups, one receiving feedback and the other, no feedback. Behavior rehearsal coupled with performance feedback showed the strongest treatment effect.

Group Process Approaches

Features of nondirective group experiences can be incorporated into a behaviorally oriented approach to group therapy. From the developments in humanistic psychology, a wave of enthusiasm has emanated from groups with a relative lack of structure and with a focus on what Rogers calls the process and the dynamics of the immediate personal interaction.

These groups have been variously referred to as T-groups, encounter groups, and marathons. Many therapists operating in this mode have incorporated techniques from Moreno's psychodrama, which is often credited as the first system in group psychotherapy. Gestalt therapy concepts have also been incorporated, particularly the concept of the here-and-now which directs the focus of group activities to the feelings of group members about events occurring within the group. This emphasis shares with behavior therapy the hypothesis that the response patterns presently extant within a person are a more productive focus for bringing about change than is insight into historical determining events. As will be seen, significant observations from this field may be productively incorporated into a basically behavioral approach to groups.

Many observers have noted that, when a group is loosely structured, the pattern of development tends to follow a roughly sequential course. Rogers has described the course as:

1. Milling around. This phase is exemplified in part by a period of initial confusion, awkward silence, and polite surface interaction, which Rogers refers to as cocktail party talk.

2. Resistance to personal expression or exploration. When one of the members risks revealing some rather personal attitudes, other members display ambivalent responses, tending to cut off the exchange of personal feelings.

3. Description of past feeling. Even though some members express ambivalence about personal communication, the expression of feelings begins to assume a larger role in the discussion as members recount past experiences.

4. Expression of negative feelings. The first expression of feeling relevant to other group members tends to be negative in content. Rogers hypothesized that negative expression is the safest way of testing trustworthiness: The expression of deeply positive feelings is much more inhibition-bound than is the expression of negative feeling.

5. Expression and exploration of personally meaningful material. Rogers hypothesized that, when negative feelings have been expressed and accepted, a climate of trust begins to develop, which allows for the discussion of topics that are associated with unpleasant feelings and that are avoided in interpersonal relationships outside the group.

6. Expression of immediate interpersonal feelings in the group. Sooner or later, the group members bring into the open the feelings they experience at the moment toward one another. These feelings are sometimes positive, sometimes negative.

7. Development of a healing capacity in the group. At this stage of development, the group members become supportive in a way that facilitates therapeutic movement by each of them. This stage is marked by helpful suggestions and empathic acceptance.

8. Self-acceptance in the beginning of change. This phase is seen as the beginning of change, as members begin to accept their modes of behavior.

Rogers goes on to list additional stages, including feedback, in which the individual member acquires a great deal of data as to how he appears to others.

Thorpe and Smith discuss the phases of group development as: (1) test the therapist, (2) begin group-centered operations, and (3) group acceptance. Taylor identifies as the phases: (1) candid self-revelation, (2) transforming personal problems into group problems, and (3) group interpretation. For Abrahams, the phases are relationships in terms of the past interaction, lessening of resistance, and development of a therapeutic attitude of mutuality. Although the terminology used by various people making observations is different, they describe essentially the same process of development, resulting in a cohesive and empathic group in which free expression and considerable feedback between members are present.

In contrast, when a group is presented with a great deal of structure from the onset, the members tend to get stuck in the first or second of the phases described by Rogers. Although some progress may be made, the full force of group processes may not be brought to bear on behavior change.

Schutz explores the relationship between the body and the emotions. He cites such examples as people who sit in a group with their arms or legs crossed very tightly. Communication with these people is difficult. Their closed-off emotional state is expressed through their body posture. He describes methods by which body activity leads to a breakdown of conditioned emotional responses and verbal inhibitions. An example is taken from the area of inhibitions to the expression of hostility.

The expression of hostility is inhibited at an early age. After several years of punishment for hostile expression, a person may find it difficult even to experience these feelings, and he is unable to deal appropriately with situations in life that require such expression. Schutz suggests several physical activities as a starting point toward breaking down these excessive inhibitions. The most effective is pounding on a couch or pillows. He notes that, after such an exercise, a person may then be able to express hostility verbally and may feel less anxiety as a result of this sort of expression. The process fits the avoidance learning paradigm in its formation, and the physical expression is on a counterconditioning model, wherein the anger developed in the exercise inhibits the anxiety previously conditioned to hostile expression. Of course, no punishment follows the hostile expression in the group. Indeed, the hostile expression will likely be positively reinforced by the approval of the therapist and the group members, thus fulfilling the requirements of operant conditioning.

Method

Each person in the group is first seen in individual therapy. As usual, the therapist takes a history and does behavioral analysis to establish the goals of therapy. He then proposes a treatment plan based on the patient's individual needs. Some interventions are most appropriately carried out in individual therapy. But group therapy is recommended when the patient has particular problems in personal interactions. The goals of group therapy are integrated into the total treatment plan for the individual.

The interaction of the group is begun in an unstructured manner so that the individual patients may begin to relate to one another in ways that are not typical of their close relationships outside of therapy. Then a maximally productive atmosphere evolves for exertion of the group feedback, reinforcement, motivations, and other therapeutic interventions.

Five to seven patient participants and two therapists take part in a group. Where possible, the group members are also the individual cases of the two therapists, so that maximal continuity of treatment is maintained. The groups are heterogeneous in sex and age but homogeneous in degree of psychological sophistication and intelligence.

The first session lasts about two hours, but no time limit is set beforehand. The structure given in the first session is minimal; one of the therapists states that all the patients have similar problems and that the first few sessions will probably be spent in getting acquainted. He then suggests that each person introduce himself and that he briefly state what he hopes to derive from group therapy. The therapists then assume the role of facilitators, to initiate the development of an atmosphere in which positive group variables are present.

By the fifth meeting, the sessions last between three and four hours. No session is terminated until each member has been involved in some way and closure is achieved on the issues raised. By this time the therapists are involved in interventions appropriate to the individual needs of the patients. This usually requires, on the average, 45 minutes to an hour for each member present, but time is not allotted in any set way. The therapists periodically clarify the goals for each member and evaluate progress by discussion with each member in turn.

During emotionally charged episodes, a patient may report sudden awareness and say that the event has been tremendously important, which seems to promise that a drastic change will occur. Such an episode parallels what has been called a peak experience, which some have claimed is capable of changing the course of a person's life. Unfortunately, observations over a long-term period indicate that many repetitions on the same theme are required before any long-lasting change in the person's life occurs.

Behavioral Analysis. The group setting offers an opportunity for a far more thorough behavioral analysis than does individual therapy. When dealing with the patient in an individual session, the therapist is able to observe his behavior in relation to only one person—the therapist—which gives little knowledge of the patient's possible responses to other people. The patient is often able to report a great deal about his interactions, but there are certain behavior patterns of which he is hardly aware—either of the behavior itself or of the relationship between this behavior and the feelings, attitudes, and behavior of others in response to it.

A patient reported that some people told her she was a very critical person. She felt that this might in some ways be true but did not know what she did that made others see her as critical. The therapist could not fill in the information gap because she was never critical toward him. When she became a group member, however, two men in the group evoked responses from her that were very hostile and controlling. The therapist was then able to identify specific behavior that elicited specific replies from these other people. The group then gave the patient feedback in specific concrete terms and encouraged expression of her feelings in appropriate ways.

Therapeutic Interventions. The group therapist has powerful therapeutic interventions available to him that are not available to the therapist performing only individual therapy. Since personality is here defined as the sum total of the patterns of learned responses—feelings and attitudes as well as motor responses—it is useful to delineate the operations that facilitate relearning when personality changes are sought. Within the group setting, five operations have been specified: feedback, modeling, behavior rehearsal, desensitization, and motivational stimulation and social reinforcement.

Feedback. Every effort is made to encourage members to respond as honestly and openly as possible to one another. As the members become able to do so to a greater degree than customary social interchanges permit, everyone in the group is subjected to an unprecedented and valuable experience through the emotional, attitudinal, and verbally expressed action tendencies. Some furnish immediate feedback, allowing a member to form connections between his behavior and the responses of others. In the beginning, the feedback tends to be expressed in general terms—such as, "You strike me as the typical salesman type" and "You really don't like women, do you?" The therapist then works toward restatement in more concrete terms so that the recipient may more easily discriminate the particular behavior that elicits such responses.

Alice: I hate to say this, but you strike me as a pretty unpleasant fellow.
(Pause.)
Bob: What do you mean?
Alice: I don't know, it's just how I feel you.
Bob: Well, that's just too bad!
Therapist: Well, Alice, I'm glad that you're so able to be open about your feelings about Bob because being open here often leads to something useful. I wonder if you could think back to when you first felt that way.
(Therapist reinforces Alice's openness in order to encourage the feedback process, then attempts to guide the comments toward more concrete and specific behavior.)
Alice: It was right from the beginning. It's just the way he, like, sits there. (To Bob) And you never approve of anything anyone says.
Charles: Yeah, I got that feeling, too.
Bob (to group): Well, I . . . I mean, I don't feel that way. (To Alice) I haven't even said anything to you. The only time we talked was about how you were having some trouble with your husband. I don't think I said anything much, just a few questions.
Therapist: Does anyone else have any feelings about what's going on here?
Doris: Yeah, I don't think it's what he says. I noticed, when Alice was talking about how she was feeling kind of uneasy last week, that Bob was kind of looking down his nose at her.
Alice: Yes, that's it. (To Bob) You really do look down your nose at people.
Therapist: You mean, literally, that is the way Bob holds his head sometimes when listening to you? I've noticed that, too. (To Bob) Does that correspond to your feelings about Alice? That is, it's generally interpreted, when someone has that pose, that they are looking down on the other person and seeing them as less worthy.
Bob: On, no! It's just not so. I really took a liking to Alice and kind of admired her way of saying things straight out. I got angry when she attacked me like that and said to myself, "Well, if that's the way you feel, okay. I just won't have anything to do with you." But I never felt superior or anything.
Therapist (to Bob): Well, sometimes we pick up little habits that we're not even aware of, and usually people don't say anything out of politeness. Has anyone ever objected to that before?
(The therapist's statement is an attempt to reduce the threat of the feedback and to bring out a possible benefit in Alice's life for her recognizing and changing a behavior.)

Bob: Well, there is this guy. (Pause.) I had been told that at first, when you first meet me, I seem snobbish, but, after getting to know me, it's not so.

Therapist: Well, it seems that several people have noticed that you look at times as though you are looking down on the persons you are listening to, even though it seems as though there is no particular attitude on your part which motivates it. I'll tell you what. If you allow us, when you are posturing in that way, we'll let you know, okay?

Bob: Yeah, that's okay. I certainly don't want to give that impression. If the way I'm looking at people when listening is giving that impression, that's something I want to change.

The goal is to make these connections as explicit as possible. Very often, being able to discriminate in this way about behavior is the first step toward change. Once a person becomes aware of the effect of his behavior, he may choose the behavior he would like to begin to change. Of course, it is not always a simple matter of presenting data. More often, people are threatened by feedback, and avoid it. In such cases, the intended recipient must be allowed sufficient time in the group to feel reasonably comfortable. Even when he is able to take the feedback, many repetitions may be required before the feedback is accepted.

Greg is a 39-year-old single man, presenting complaints of multiple phobias of long duration. In addition to individual treatment, group therapy was recommended. In the group, it soon became apparent that Greg was completely unable to take from others. He attempted to set up a giving relationship with each member and with the therapists. This stance was appreciated by many of the members and was well-accepted by others from his first session.

The group soon noticed that any time a member attempted to give Greg advice, support, or warm feelings, Greg responded with immediate rejection and sometimes anger. Shortly after such an interchange, Greg would make an attempt to re-establish his helping role with the person he had rejected. He was quite skillful and usually succeeded at once. If the helper relationship was not re-established by the end of the group session, Greg would make contact with that person outside the group before the next session.

The therapist attempted to give Greg feedback about his pattern at his second session, but

Greg harshly rebuffed him. One by one, the members became recipients of Greg's rebuffs as they, in turn, attempted to make their relationship reciprocal by giving to Greg in return. By the sixth session, Greg had been given the same information by at least four people, including the therapist. Generally stated, he had been told that he was not able to accept help from others, which impeded the deepening of the relationship.

At the 15th session, Greg reported to the group that an ex-girlfriend had said something to him that seemed to be connected with what he had been hearing in group. She had told him that it was because he had not allowed her to grow that she had terminated the relationship. (This had been the course of each of his relationships with women.) He was always doing things for her, so that she felt stifled. Greg allowed that maybe there was something to what the group had been saying, after all.

The account below is from Greg's 16th session.

Greg: I can't be everybody's master, priest, rabbi, doctor, psychologist, father. I just can't keep that role—kind of on the humorous side . . . .

Therapist: It's kind of a burden.

Greg: Well, for me, it is. I'm sure other people can handle it, and it doesn't mean anything, you know, but for me, it's a sort of being-controlled process. I don't know how other people have been playing that role for years. I don't know how to use people very well.

Therapist: Would that be "using" in a derogatory sense?

Greg: Oh, you mean use as opposed to abuse. I think maybe I abuse. But I think maybe I got myself into this spot, so I've really got no right to gripe.

Therapist: What I mean is, when you lean on someone else, that has a kind of derogatory implication.

Greg: Well, no. I lean on Jane. I think we lean on each other. I think there's difficulty in that relationship for the obvious reason that I've discussed before. Number 1 and number 2, I kept getting to feel a little crowded by her, and—I hate to say this—well, bored because, again, it's the same singular point of view . . . same thing. Sure, she's bright; sure, she's witty; sure, she's read, you know, but you can almost hear what she's going to say and just wind up in a little crowded. On the humorous side of this, I have. . . . You'd think we were important, and we're not. When this thing about the head of the family —I have a couple of cousins in New York. . . . I saw one of them I think about 32 years ago. . . . There's this Paul Miles—that's not important, but Paul's the one I saw—when the word got out within three weeks that I had a call from my mother . . . now, these guys are—one's pushing 60. . . .

Pat: What?

Greg: This thing about my mother that I'm supposed to. . . . Now let's see. I don't even know you—what the hell do you want from me? Making long distance calls from New York . . . and I thought, what the hell does this all mean? What is the family structure all about?

Pat: I don't understand what you're talking about.

Greg: Didn't I grumble one day I was being stuck. My mother said she wanted me to be the head of the family when she broke her shoulder, and I said I didn't want the role. When these guys called me, I really thought, "Well this is the real bottom." You know, when you get caught this way. I just had to have out and had to have. . . . (Pause.) Then I, too, have my economic problems at the moment, but then everybody is—all marginal people are in a squeeze now; we're in a bad economy.

Jack: I told Phyllis we should all open a store. . . .

Greg: It's a question of priority with me and keeping with them and plodding. Journey of a thousand miles . . . takes one step to start and then that's it. Better to put one foot in front of the other and stick to the issues, break up all the patterns and substitute your own. . . .

Therapist: You get so little from other people except problems, huh?

Greg: I think what I used to get was some feeling of being useful. It's kind of like Eric Fromm now that he's—what, 70?—finally wrote— the only important thing is if you're doing useful works—after all those years of being productive. In a sense, that's exactly the way I was built and formed. It *is* useful work to advise, to do research, to do the writing for somebody. It *is* useful work to help my brother. It *is* useful work to help my sister and my brother-in-law. It *is* useful work to take care of my mother. It is useful, you know, and this was not only compensation. In the meantime, I was thinking. . . .

Therapist: There is one person you left out.

Greg: Who? Let's see, brother, mother, sister. . . .

Pat: You!

Greg: I'm sorry, I lost you. I don't know how to do that except by plodding toward freedom.

Therapist: It's useful to people to feel needed? Is that on your list?

Greg: Well, to help them, I studied engineering,

and I redesigned my brother's home—house. It was dog work—and it was expected of me—so I did the drawings, and I did all the revision drawings.

Therapist: Do you ever feel that he can be useful to you?

Greg: Well, he has. He's been useful. I don't want to grumble. I don't like giving the impression that this is their fault or that they're wrong and that I've been the great wronged innocent because that's not accurate.

Therapist: I'm talking about something quite different.

Greg: Well, I have lost you.

Therapist: Do you see it as being useful if you make people feel as though they're needed?

Greg: How do you make people feel that they're needed? I don't know. You ask them to do things—involve them in things—you ask them to help you with something—you get them involved. What's the implication?

Pat: Do you do that?

Greg: I think . . . yeah. . . .

Therapist: How about Phyllis? You have been helping her. Is she able to do anything for you?

Greg: Sure she's helped me. I think we've helped each other, at least I hope so.

Phyllis: You've done so much more for me than I think you would let me d) for you.

Greg: Well, we must *distinguish two things*, Phyllis. I have two roles.

Phyllis: Yes, I know. I'm just counting your professional role because I think that, in the conversations that we've had, the real business takes about five minutes, and the other hour and a half are just therapy for me, really.

(Phyllis had asked Greg to represent her in **a** legal matter, and he is doing so.)

Jack: Oh, that's great.

Greg (to Jack): You tend to underestimate the value of that young lady.

Phyllis: How many mornings I've called you lately and gotten you out of bed, or how many times I called you late at night when I knew—when I knew—that you had nothing to tell me, you know, I just called because · I wanted to hear somebody who sounded reassuring.

Greg: You know that may not sound right. Don't take this the wrong way. Technically, that's a lawyer's function in the first part of these problems. . . .

Phyllis: But no lawyer. . . .

Greg: But primarily you're calling me as a friend, and I'm treating it that way, that's all.

Phyllis: Yeah, but. . . .

Greg: Shall we chew the rag about what happened?

Pat: Do you ever call Phyllis because you want to say something?

Greg: No, I don't think I ever have. I see there's another thing. There is a thing here. We've really gotta get over the humps in this legal thing before, you know, 'cause see I oughta know, and I'm not cutting you off to the point that I can't fool with or question. . . .

Therapist: Has anyone here had the feeling that they could be needed by Greg?

Joan: No, like, I never really felt—I've always felt that I could reach out and touch you but that you would never fall back on me, that you could never, like, you know, that you could—it's funny, looking at you, I said, "Jesus Christ, if I keep on, I'm going to be just like that!" You built such a shell! It's seems like—it really scared me and, like, I thought that really helped me a lot. I really think it helped me a lot, but I never thought. . . .

Greg: As the bad example. (Laughs.)

Joan: No, no, but not only that. You've always like, you know, you seem so considerate of my feelings, and if I've ever shown any concern for you, like, I always get the feeling that you either don't see it or you want to ignore it. You make me feel embarrassed to show consideration for you.

Phyllis: I think it's that you don't expect other people to have feelings toward you. You don't accept that concern and interest. Like, if you would call me up at three o'clock in the morning and *ask me to go out and buy a candy bar* for you and bring it to your house, I would do it for you because I feel that you've helped me so much! Not professionally, but just as a person, you've really made me feel good on nights when I've been really down, and you've talked to me and tried to cheer me up. You call to see how I'm doing! You know.

Greg: Yeah, but that's only human.

Phyllis: No, it isn't! There's a hell of a lot of people who never—but what I'm saying is I have a feeling that, ah, that I would like to do things for you or, you know, make you feel better sometimes. And yet, I have the feeling that if. . . .

Greg: After what you've said and what she's said, I feel shy. I don't like. . . .

Phyllis: But I just have the feeling that if you ever wanted me. . . . (Aside to group) He's not even listening.

Joan: He has turned red. (To Greg) I've never seen you blush.

Phyllis: Well, I just have the feeling that, even if you had something that you wanted me to do, you would never ask.

Greg: I was raised to take care of myself. In that isolation, I mean, you have to be able to do everything yourself.

Therapist: You can always explain things, but the point is, what can you do to make your life most enjoyable for yourself?

Greg: Well, I don't think it's right to call people through the night.

Phyllis: Yes, it is.

Greg: Well, I don't mind when people call me if they're really upset, you know.

Phyllis: You see, that's like sometimes when I talk to you, I feel guilty for taking your time because I know that if you're. . . .

Greg: Anytime that that happens. . . .

Phyllis: I'm not talking about when you're busy. (Greg tries to cut Phyllis off.) I'm talking about when you've got time, and you sit there, and your work is sometimes slowed for two hours, and sometimes it's late at night, and you've been eating dinner, and I'm sure your dinner sits there and gets cold. Yet I have the feeling that if you really felt bad at eleven o'clock at night or twelve o'clock, you wouldn't call me and say, "Gee, I just feel like talking for a little while, and you do it for me, so I naturally. . . ."

Greg: I don't want you to feel guilty.

Joan: It's not a question of feeling guilt, it's a question of wanting to do it and feel good about doing it.

Phyllis: That's it!

Therapist: Everybody has a need to be needed, and it's very hard in relation to you to get that fulfilled.

Phyllis: When people are nice to me, I want to. . . .

Greg: I'd better straighten this out. Phyllis has gotten an earful from me, more than once in those conversations about—I don't know what about, my rotten mood or the lousy job that I do. . . .

Phyllis: Yeah. Yeah, but you've never called me and said, "Hey, I'm in a really rotten mood. Well, I just feel like talking." You know.

Therapist (to Greg): Let me guess the context in which that was said. You were saying that you *too* feel bad, so it's okay for Phyllis to lift *her spirits*, you can also feel bad.

Jack: Always the doctor!

Greg: Well, I felt lousy that night. Okay, I was in it with her is all I was saying.

Pat: Well, what Phyllis was saying was could you ever be in that mud pack first? And leave it to somebody else to get you out?

Phyllis: Yeah, but. . . .

Greg: The stunt is to enjoy the mud pack, but I'm not avoiding the issue.

Phyllis: Look, what I'm saying is, sometimes when you're down and, just if you feel like talking, that you would come to me and that I could do in part for you what you're doing for me. So that I can feel that I'm giving you something instead of feeling that I'm always taking, that's all. I just—I want to do nice things for you because you do nice things for me.

Jack: You're . . . you're turning him inside out.

Therapist: But there's something about that, isn't there?

Greg: Yeah, that I feel shy, and I was a very shy child.

Phyllis: And I'm not saying to be dependent. I'm not saying for you to lean on me. I know that you can take care of yourself, you know, you're a big boy, and you can take care of yourself.

Greg: I'm not a big boy. I'm a weak person.

Phyllis: But what I'm saying is, you know, occasionally, when you feel like talking or if it's something I can do for you, you shouldn't try to do everything yourself or keep it to yourself. I want to do things for you because you do things for me. I'm just saying that I'm the type of person who has to feel that I'm giving something, too. I want you to know it's there. I don't always feel, like, I feel if you were really. . . .

Therapist: Everybody needs that.

Greg: Well, there is some inhibition in this relationship for the simple reason that I *really* have to try to get us over this hump. I want to get through this damn hump. I don't want to get into it.

Phyllis.: Yeah, but I'm not talking about professionally.

Therapist: You see you set yourself up in this way with as many people as you can. It's never reciprocal.

Greg: Well, you see, I don't know anything about being a psychologist, but I do know that, being in legal areas, you got to have really pretty—I've stretched, you know, because of Phyllis and who she is. I am the way I am, but I don't—you can't deal like this.

Phyllis: But I don't mean talking to you about. . . .

Greg: The first couple of months in these cases there is—and you do get calls and, you know, they seem to be toughest around the holidays, Christmas, New Year's, et cetera.

Phyllis: You know, if I had a big attorney from

_____, for example, and I called him up at eleven o'clock at night and said. . . .

Greg: That depends on how rich you were. (Laughs.)

Phyllis: And I said. . . .

Greg: Seventy-five bucks an hour is what they get.

Therapist: I think you're getting engaged now in discussion which is off the point.

Greg: Yeah, I'm jumping aside.

(Everybody talking and laughing at once. The therapist moves to a chair closer to Greg.)

Greg: Uh oh! Here he comes. (Moves his chair back.)

Therapist: No, I'm not really after you.

Greg: Like hell you're not.

Therapist: I'll tell you about an experience I had about a while ago. It was really very meaningful. I was in a group with all therapists, and the same thing kept coming up. As a group, these people can't take from other people. I think that's one of the reasons.

Greg: One of the reasons they are what they are.

Therapist: Yeah, and I became very aware of that in myself. Very threatening, when people were giving to me. And I was as anxious during that couple of days as I've ever been in my life. We were just falling apart over this very issue. When I kind of broke through it, and I let someone really give me something, it was satisfying, and I felt as though I couldn't get enough of it. In fact, when I think about it now, I still get upset. It was a terribly meaningful kind of thing.

Greg: Yes, but, you know, one thing I have to say here, and I'm not getting intellectual— you know, I think it is a hairy world, as Pat would call it. Either you set your terms and make sure to take care of yourself—you know, that's the way it is. People are self-centered, selfish. . . .

Therapist: I don't find that to be true.

(Long pause.)

Phyllis: I think the worst thing that my husband did to me was that he took away the feeling that I was an individual, you know. When he stopped letting me do things for him, that is really when everything started falling apart.

Greg: Is it the worst feeling?

Phyllis: Yes, and he wasn't letting me do things for him. And when I felt that I was just sort of sitting around, keeping house and keeping busy and that I wasn't helping him in his work or just helping him through his day, you know, or making him feel better, that I wasn't giving him anything, that he wasn't letting me give him anything, you know, that is such a rotten feeling, I used to sit around and cry over it. It wasn't only the fact that he wasn't coming home for dinner, and I was lonely, My God, he wouldn't even let me make him dinner and talk about his day and see what he's doing and, you know, and I just felt that I wasn't needed. And that's what started the whole thing.

Greg: Well, maybe I fear myself, too, that I would become totally dependent.

Therapist: That's because your need is so great, and that's because it never gets met.

Pat: You mean you feel all bewildered by it because you've never had it met at all, and it will overwhelm you.

Therapist: But it doesn't. That's the point. You can start taking from everybody around, a little from each, and not load it all on one person.

Pat: I'm saying that, as long as you keep it under cover, you are terrified of it. It controls you.

Greg: Well, I don't know. There's been a lot of things happening in my life.

Pat: I guess the point is whether you can be realistic about it now. I mean, like, if you really say to Phyllis that she would not control you by helping you.

Greg: She'd control me?

Pat: She would not.

Greg: I don't know.

Pat: Well, then maybe you can let her give a little. I mean, how much can the other give? You have to get the feel of it and know that she won't pull you down.

Therapist: Would you like to get in touch with some of that?

Greg: It depends on what it involves. I've enjoyed this, I'd just as soon let it go at this. I'm sure you're getting ready to do some physical thing, banging around. I think I can forgo that.

Jack: Ah, you pussy cat, you.

Therapist: We can stick to something you have already seen done. Nothing unfamiliar to you. I'd like for Joan to lead you around with your eyes closed.

(The therapist feels that Greg is accepting somewhat the feedback he has been getting and may, for the first time in the group, allow himself to take something. He has always in the past vigorously rejected any suggestions of this sort by the therapist.)

Greg: With my eyes closed?

Therapist: Yeah, would you mind that?

Greg: Where do you want us to go? In there?

Therapist: That's up to Joan.

Greg: I could tell you where I'd like to go. I'd like to go to the bathroom and come back.

Greg allows himself to be led by Joan and then by Phyllis but is unable to stick to the suggestion that he not talk. As he is being led, he repeats several times to each of them, "You all right?" After being led around, Greg is placed in the center of the circle and begins to talk about himself in a more open way then ever before, confiding things about himself that he has felt. He is able to accept to some degree the interest and support of those around him.

Modeling. The term modeling, used by Bandura, refers to the process of learning that takes place through observing others performing the to-be-learned task. In groups, modeling may occur spontaneously when the member has observed the appropriate behavior of others and of the therapists. It may also be deliberately aroused. The therapist enacts a part or asks another member to enact it within the context of behavior rehearsal (see below).

The group is usually heterogeneous in terms of problem areas. For example, Member A may have difficulty in dealing with a motherly woman, but Member B is quite adequate in that area; so A can observe B dealing with a motherly group member in an appropriate way. Members often observe interactions, apply the observed behavior outside the group, and report back that it was helpful. The learning may occur while the learner sits quietly, with all appearances of being uninvolved in the interaction taking place.

The therapist may intentionally set up modeling situations in a variety of ways. The one most frequently employed involves the therapist's taking the place of a group member engaged in an interaction. Another technique is adopted from psychodrama. The therapist or a member (A) moves behind another member (B), who is actively engaged in an interchange. The group understands that, when A takes this position behind B, A is then speaking as if he himself were involved on the same level as the person he stands behind. A's responses are taken and replied to as if they came from B.

Behavior Rehearsal. When a situation arises in the group relating to a patient's difficulties with people outside the group or within the group, some form of behavior rehearsal is very often helpful. The format used most often is one in which role-playing is employed. The patient is asked to pick another member or members to play the part of the antagonist. The situation is re-enacted as it actually happened. Feedback about the performance is given, along with suggestions for more appropriate responses. The revised behavior is then enacted over and over again until the patient is satisfied with the way he has handled the situation.

Variations include role reversal, in which the patient plays the part of the antagonist while the selected member plays the role of the patient. This variation is useful in making clear the role of the antagonist for subsequent role-playing. In addition, the selected member models for the patient another way of dealing with the problem. As the selected person enacts the role of the patient, the patient receives feedback about himself. This sort of feedback sometimes results in such comments as:

Is that the way I come across? Well, I can see why I had trouble there.

These comments are followed by a change in behavior when a similar situation arises.

When role-playing is in progress, an obvious decrement in anxiety is usually observed as the situation is repeated. For repetition of the procedure functions as a form of desensitization to the expression of feelings that have been inhibited.

A group member became anxious whenever she was required to make demands of authority figures. She was having difficulties with the plumbing in her apartment, which was obviously the responsibility of the landlord, but she was made anxious by the mere thought of calling him to make the repairs. The group role-played the situation by way of preparing her to make the call. With repetitions of the situation, she progressed from anxiety with stammering and perspiring, to the ability to state her case calmly, insisting that the plumber come in at her convenience. She was then able to carry out the call to the landlord to her complete satisfaction. This she found to be quite rewarding, and it raised her self-esteem considerably. Efforts were made to have her extend this sort of assertiveness to more and more situations, which she came to be able to do.

Another example from a group session follows:

Kate: I understand exactly what you mean, but something like—you said something, you know, that you're afraid the person will back away from these. Do you think that's what sort of the motivating factor behind these types of feelings? 'Cause, like, when I had this conversation with the girl today, she said, you know, I knew how she felt, like she had just spilled out her guts to me, and it was sort of, like I was on the spot, I had to say something to make her feel like, "It's all right, really, I won't betray you or go out telling everybody. You can trust me, you know, you did the right thing to tell me. But I didn't know how to say it. So I . . . she was, like, nervous. She said, "Thanks."

Therapist: You didn't know really how to handle it—that kind of feeling she was letting out?

Kate: Well, I did, but I should have said, like, "I'm glad. I'm glad you told me," or something, 'cause that's how I felt. But instead I said, "Well, I was curious anyway because we really didn't get a chance to talk the last time I saw you, and I've been meaning to ask you about it." But it ended on a sour note. I'm thinking, "Gee, now she's . . . now I've killed the whole thing, and we had it really going good, but now I killed it." But then, I figure I'll see her tomorrow night, so things will be all right.

Therapist: What will you say when you see her?

Kate: "You know, I was really glad you told me that." Well, I don't know. If the two of us are alone, maybe I'll say something like that, "I was really glad you told me."

Rita: You could call me for something. You could call me and talk to me.

Kate: Well, maybe those words . . . . I don't see how it fits in, but something to that effect. I'm not going to just leave it.

Pat: Because if you say, "I'm really glad you told me," it's like, "I'm glad you have problems."

Kate: I know.

Pat: But I think what you mean is you're glad that she felt that she could take you into her confidence, that she could turn to you, that you're somebody someone can turn to when they're in trouble.

Therapist: Why don't you pick somebody out of here to practice that on?

Kate: Pick somebody out? Rita, would you like to do it?

Rita: I'm the girl?

Kate: Yeah.

Rita: Okay.

Kate: We're driving along in the car or something. I'm driving, and, like, she gets in, and she'll probably feel a little, you know, I don't know what she feels like . . . .

Rita: Okay

Kate: You get in and say, "Hi, how are you"?

Rita (playing the role of Rhoda): Hi, Kate.

Kate: Oh, hi, Rhoda. Uhmm . . . (Aside to group) You know, like, I don't know whether to ask her if everything's all right with her sister now. Maybe I will. I think I will. Did you get things worked out with your sister? Did anything happen with your sister?

Rita: Uhmm, it's okay, just forget about it. I'm sorry I called you up and bothered you so much on the phone yesterday.

Kate: Oh, Rhoda, that really shocks me because, like, I was really glad, you know, that you felt you could tell me.

Rita: I know I don't see you too often, and I could tell from what you said at the end that you were really busy, and I shouldn't have bothered you.

Kate (aside to group): That's just what she'll say, too. (Back in role) I'm really sorry you feel that way. That's ridiculous, I mean . . . .

Rita: Don't worry about it. Let's just forget about it.

Kate: Rhoda, I don't really want to forget about it because, like, I think maybe it's the first time we every really—you really ever opened up to me, and I was ever—and, you know, I don't want to lose it because it made me feel good, and, if I seemed like I was busy, I just had to get ready to go . . . .

Rita: You told me you weren't busy.

Kate: No, if it seemed like I was busy. . . .

Therapist: What were you really feeling at that important time when you made her feel you were busy?

(Therapist leads Kate to use an open expression of feeling that is appropriate.)

Kate: I guess I just didn't know what to say at the end of our conversation, but I guess, uh, you know, so I just sort of cut it off, and, you know, I felt bad right after I hung up, and I was going to call you back and say, wow, sort of make it nice again, but I had to run out, so that's why I brought it up now.

Rita: Well, I don't understand what you're trying to say now.

Kate: I don't know what to say.

Pat: How about if you say that I'm really glad

you told me that because now I can tell you stuff that's on my mind, too. I mean, let her know it's going to be reciprocal. You're not just going to be the one to confess to.

Kate (still in role): I'm really glad you told me that 'cause I've had a lot of things—I remember the time that I was thinking of dropping out of school, and you said you should have called me, but now, Rhoda, I feel like I could call you because, you know, just to talk things over.

Rita: Well, I just felt a little funny last night because it was, like, you know, you just kind of cut it off at the end, and here I was saying all those personal things to you. It was like I was talking to a stranger.

Kate: It's funny how just some little thing at the end can ruin the whole thing that was going so good 'cause I felt—I don't know—for the first time I felt close, and then I guess I sort of blew it at the end, but I hope it can be better in the future—or now. I hope it can be better now.

Rita: Okay, it will just take me a little while to get over that, but I think I understand. I am glad that you listened to me last night.

Kate (laughs): I'm glad you're glad.

Therapist: Very nice. Now let's try it again, straight through, okay?

The situation is repeated, with Kate performing smoothly and with no sign of the hesitancy that marked the first try. Kate reported at a later session that she had a similar conversation with Rhoda that resulted in a renewed closeness. Practice of this kind usually leads to a generalization of more appropriate responses in a variety of situations.

Desensitization. Desensitization refers to a variety of procedures for gradually reducing or eliminating the capacity of given stimuli to elicit negative emotional responses, such as anxiety, fear, and guilt. When the person no longer responds with the inappropriate emotional response, desensitization is said to have occurred. When the goal is removal of unadaptive emotional responses, the techniques of desensitization form a basic armamentarium. The experimentally validated principles relied on are counterconditioning and extinction.

Gerald was a 20-year-old single man. His presenting complaint was unwanted homosexuality and various existentially described discomforts. A careful behavioral analysis indicated strong negatively conditioned emotional responses to

women, with sexual interaction the most threatening behavior, resulting in elaborate avoidance
habits. Gerald and his individual therapist agreed
that, if Gerald was to become heterosexual, the
elimination of anxiety in the presence of women
must receive first priority in therapy so that an
alternative avenue would be available. Group
therapy was recommended for the treatment of
interpersonal behavioral deficits. The individual
therapist was having difficulty with systematic
desensitization because desensitization using
imagery had not sufficiently reduced Gerald's
anxiety to allow for follow-up in the real-life
situation. They agreed to use the group setting
to extend the range of stimuli for desensitization.

Gerald has brought up a problem. He feels
uncomfortable when talking to a girl he knows
outside the group. The therapist has suggested
that he try to carry on a conversation with one
of the girls in the group and has moved Gerald
and his choice of partners, Kate, so that they are
sitting close together.

Gerald: See, now, right now, I feel pressured
for conversation, and that's exactly what I
feel any time I'm at school. I feel pressured
for conversation, yet I want it, you know,
so I'm. . . .

Kate: I feel pressured a lot, like, ah, especially
when somebody's talking to me and I, you
know, I'm really interested in what they're
saying, and they're talking a whole lot. I
feel like I should be able to do the same.

Gerald: Well, what it actually is is that I understand what you're saying, and I have that
same problem, so there's nothing I can say
about it.

Kate: Yeah, I feel like I'm just talking now. I
don't know how to communicate to you
either.

Gerald: See, right now, see, there's this girl—her
name is Nancy—at school, and everything
that I say so far as problems go, she'll understand and sympathize with me, and it's
dead because there's nothing there, and
she'll do the same thing for me, and there is
no uplift, you know. I don't feel, like, ex-
hilarated. It's always down. Then, because
there's silence, "Well, what have you been
doing all day?" And that's what I'll do—
I'll make a joke to start a conversation.

Therapist (to Gerald): What are you really feeling?

(Although the content of Gerald's statements
indicates that he is looking for meaning in
his relations, the therapist is operating under
the assumption that Gerald's loss for words,
his feeling down, and his feeling pressured
for conversation are indications of the

amount of anxiety aroused by social contact
with women.)

Gerald: Nervous. Because the conversation is
dead, and I feel hopeless and lonely. I feel,
like, we're not getting anywhere because
we're both sympathizing with the other—
each other's problems. And . . . and, like, so
what? I mean, we're still down. And what
can you do?

Kate: Make jokes. (Laughs.)

(Kate is also uneasy in the company of the opposite sex. Therapist has moved behind Kate
so it is understood that he is modeling for
her. He restates Kate's last comment with
a more direct communication.)

Therapist (modeling Kate): I must admit that I
am feeling very uncomfortable right now.

Gerald: Yeah. Well, I know because, see, you
just made a joke, and well there was—I feel
like I have to say something, and I don't
know what to say because I'm identifying
so much with the problem 'cause I'm having
it right now, too. Well, let's not go through
this. . . .

Therapist: And it made you very uncomfortable,
too?

Gerald: What are we going to do? There's a girl,
Nancy, just like Kate, right now just like it,
just like it.

Co-therapist: There must not be silence? Absolutely no silence?

Gerald: Yeah, there mustn't be silence, and, if
there is silence, it should be relaxed.

Kate: Well, I'm relaxed, I think. (Laughs.) I
don't understand why you get so worked up
about this whole thing.

Gerald: Because I always feel down. Somebody
to sympathize with my problems or. . . .

Co-therapist: You have all the responsibility?

Gerald: Yeah.

Kate: I won't tell you what I feel like doing because it's real, you know. . . .

Pat: Do it!

Rita: Go ahead.

Gerald: What do you feel like doing?

Kate: I don't know if I can do it.

(Everybody is telling her to do it.)

Gerald: Or at least tell me what it is.

Co-therapist: I'm really interested.

Lynn: You'll be doing something you really want
to do. Both of you.

Kate: I feel like just sitting on your lap and relaxing and just playing around. I don't feel
like talking about anything.

(The spontaneous interaction triggered by moving Gerald and Kate close together and
having them talk is moving in a productive
direction. Gerald is being exposed to the

feared situation of physical contact with a girl under circumstances that are safe, in that the degree of contact is controlled by the setting. He is dealing with a circumstance low in the hierarchy of his fear of sexual contact. There is maximal group pressure on Gerald to deal directly with the fear.)

Gerald: Well, ah, it just seems. . . .

Kate: 'Cause it's really not. . . .

Gerald: Well, with that, see, I don't know how to take what you just said because that could be joking. You were just messing around, or you could have been serious, and, if you were serious, I couldn't handle that. Because then I'd have to make a pun of the whole situation, and I wouldn't want to because I'm nervous that you'd sit on my lap.

Therapist (modeling Gerald): I'm nervous that you want to sit on my lap.

Gerald: I wouldn't know what to do. So I'd hold you. So what? We'd start to talk somehow.

Kate: Well, I . . . yeah.

Pat: Doesn't that sound like such a challenge? Don't you feel that you have to go over and sit on his lap?

Kate: I couldn't do it in front of all these people, that's all. You know, I couldn't. . . . I'd be embarrassed to do it in front of everybody else.

Gerald: I feel hopeless. I just want things to be bright and cheery and warm in feeling.

Therapist (modeling Gerald): Do you mean to tell me you really would want to sit on my lap?

Kate: Yeah.

Gerald: You really would?

Pat: She's only one of four.

(Everybody laughs.)

Gerald: What brought that on?

Kate: I don't know.

Gerald: Maybe that's what I should have asked.

Kate: Why try to analyze, you know.

Pat: You're backing off. He asked you a straight question: Why do you want to sit on his lap?

Rita: Look at him and tell him why.

Kate: You look cuddly.

Co-therapist (modeling Gerald): I really don't know how to take such positive things. They really make me embarrassed.

Kate: I am afraid that you would feel that you had to do something.

Gerald: You're right. I'm aware that you feel that, and that's what makes me more afraid.

Pat: Why do you think you have to do something?

Gerald: Because I don't want to be uncomfortable, and, at the same time, I know that

people respond to my nervousness, and they get uncomfortable so, therefore, I don't want to do it because then I'll have two problems —mine and theirs. I would like to be left alone with plenty of time to—when I feel that way and feel that I'm pushing the other people away, I don't want them to go away.

Kate: Yeah, but by trying to mask it so that you don't feel nervous, you make yourself more nervous.

Therapist: Where are you now?

Kate: I'm kind of scared. I'm kind of scared because everybody wants me to do something, and I want to do something, but I'm still kind of scared.

Co-therapist: Okay, let us try.

(Co-therapist sanctions the flow of events and further exposure.)

Kate: All right.

(Kate sits on Gerald's lap.)

Therapist: Gerald, how do you feel?

Gerald: I feel silly.

Rita: I would tell him what I would like to do, but in such a way as to make him comfortable.

Therapist: Suppose you just got up and did it? I mean, that's about as comfortable as you can get.

Gerald: I don't understand. Or maybe I really didn't hear it, that's why.

Rita: I mean like reaching you and telling you what she wanted to do but in such a way that it didn't frighten you.

Gerald: How would that be done?

Rita: I mean I could just walk over and stroke your brow. (She does so as she talks.)

(Rita's attention increases the threat, and the therapist is contemplating bringing in more structure to the hierarchical presentation of threatening stimuli but decides to hold back at this time.)

Gerald: Oh, wow, uh-huh!

Co-therapist: Not too much, not too much.

Gerald: No, because then I think that she has other intentions and I. . . .

Rita: That could be, like, just really nice, like. . . .

Kate: I wasn't thinking that. . . .

Gerald: Because you see, I don't. . . .

Rita: That alone could just give you. . . .

Gerald: Even though I understand Kate, I don't feel with her. Like this girl, Nancy, she has the heaviest crush on me, and I don't know how to handle it. She'll lean her head against my shoulder just for a second while she's laughing. . . .

Co-therapist: Okay, let us talk away this little incident.

(Co-therapist again cuts off Gerald's avoidance response.)

Therapist: Are you uncomfortable, Rita?

Rita (to Gerald): No, I hope I'm not making you uncomfortable. I mean, like, just like the ugliest person in the world could come up to you and just, like, you know, and just do that and, like. . . .

(Rita strokes Gerald's forehead.)

Gerald: Uh-huh. That makes me shake and tremble.

Rita: It really makes you shake and tremble? I mean, you just couldn't almost just close them out and just feel their touch?

Gerald: If I closed them out, I'd be aware that I'm closing them out.

Rita: You could shut your eyes.

Gerald: You want me to shut my eyes now?

Rita: I'm just saying for you to imagine it. Just sitting there with your eyes shut and feel the nice soft fingers running across your forehead and then down and under. . . . It's just like one finger, and it's really, really light, and it's kind of cool, and your face is warm, and so that feels good because it cools and maybe, like, right across your eyelids . . . and kind of tracing your eyebrows, too, and coming down here and moving back a little bit and in there and all the way up, and that brings us up to maybe around here and, you know, really light and cool. . . .

(Rita strokes Gerald's forehead as she talks.)

Gerald: Yeah, but, see, you're having intentions.

(Gerald again expresses anxiety about what will be expected of him in a sexual context.)

Rita: Uh-uh.

Co-therapist: You really must be honest.

Rita: I really don't.

Gerald: I can't believe that, or else you wouldn't be touching me.

Rita: No.

Gerald: But now, you see, you're doing that. . . .

Rita: I guess it's kind of hard to believe. . . .

Co-therapist: Just take it in, Gerald.

(Co-therapist attempts to limit the stimuli on Gerald by removing the need for action on his part. It is essential to limit the stimuli conditioned to fear so that each step is small enough to be counteracted by positive feelings.)

Gerald: I don't know what to do with it.

Co-therapist: Just take it in. You have nothing to do. Just take it, take it.

Gerald: But, see, well, because I can't believe that—I guess you have intentions, whether it's sexual or just a strong feeling for me and, if you did, I haven't established it with you, so I feel very uncomfortable. 'Cause you're

coming toward me, and I'm standing here. And I have to reject you for trying to work into something that would be forced because you did it first.

(Long pause. Gerald looks as though he is relaxing now.)

Therapist: I'll tell you what: Gerald, Kate, stand up for a minute, will you? Will you stand, Gerald? Gerald, could you tolerate lying on the floor?

(It appears that Gerald has become reasonably comfortable with the degree of stimulation being offered. The next step is to increase the amount of stimulation by an increment small enough to again be counterconditioned by the positive stimulation in this situation.)

Gerald: Yeah. (Gerald sits on the floor.) Lean back?

Therapist: Yeah, and just close your eyes, and you don't have to do anything or say anything, okay? Just be aware of what's happening, okay?

Kate: Would you like something for under your head?

(Long pause, and suddenly Gerald flinches and sits upright.)

Gerald: I don't know. See, these things happen, and I get really frightened. I get dizzy, and I don't feel like I'm in anything. I feel like I'm real far away.

Therapist: Lying down is too much for you?

Gerald: Well, yeah, I get this in school, too. (Heavy sighs.)

Therapist: How are you feeling now?

Gerald: A little shaky.

Therapist: Well, just sit there and try to relax for a few minutes.

(Long pause, and Gerald lies down again. The three girls present begin to stroke his hand and forehead.)

Co-therapist: You don't have to respond to anything, Gerald.

Gerald: Yeah, but I feel it. I feel all wretched.

Therapist: Relax. You don't have to do anything. There's no obligation on you. See if you can just relax. (Very long silence.) It's all right, it's all right. Just pay attention to the sensations.

Gerald: It's scary.

Therapist: That's all right.

(Again a long silence broken by heavy sobbing and crying. The girls move back away from Gerald.)

Therapist: Just keep your eyes closed for a few minutes, Gerald. And, if you can, describe what you just went through.

Gerald: At first, it was kind of absurd because I felt like I was laying here, and there was, like, these bosomy girls all around—nude. And, ah, they were just rubbing my chest and my hair and giving me all the sensuous pleasure I could possibly want—that a man could possibly want. And then, and then I felt I had to respond or something, you know, give the feeling back or something, playing the game, and I couldn't. And then the touching got heavier and heavier, and I felt like, like, these bosomy girls grabbing me and then, like, Pat—at first, it was warm, but then it was so warm, it was almost mothering, and . . . and . . . and I was being mothered, and I didn't want to be mothered, and and then, and then I went back to the girls and then, then, then the warmth went back to the mothering again, and and I, and I just—there was no way out. There was no way out. And then, and then I didn't know what to do.

(At this point, the choice of direction taken by the therapist illustrates a clear difference between a behavioral approach and a dynamically oriented one. It seems clear that Gerald's inhibitions about sex have generalized to all women from threatening erotic feelings toward his mother. Rather than pushing for insight at this juncture, the therapist pursues a course of setting up additional situations that will lead to further counterconditioning of inappropriate fear responses to women. The procedure is not intended to disparage the value of Gerald's having an understanding of his responses. Indeed, later in the session an explanation is given in terms of learning processes. But to interject such a discussion at this time would interrupt the important process of doing something that will lead to desensitization.)

Therapist: At first it was pleasant, but then, when it reminded you of mother, it wasn't pleasant at all.
Gerald: No.
Therapist: About touching? Is there. . . .
Gerald: Pat, Pat, dear, you know, I felt someone rustling my hair, and, and, like, it kind of bothered me 'cause there was, like, I don't know—the only word I can think of is chaos, you know, scramble, scramble, scramble, which is exactly how I feel. I didn't want that, and then I was touching somebody's hands, and they were cold, and that was, like, you know, but that was like a symbol for, like, the way I feel about girls, and then there was Pat and was warm. Boy, she's my friend, she's my friend, but all of a sudden, she turned into my mother. And, and, and,

then I didn't know what to do. I didn't know what to do.
Therapist: Was there any of that contact which was pleasant?
Gerald: Yes, with Pat for a while, for a few minutes. But there was nothing sexual about it. It was very warm, and I . . . I felt the warmth, really felt it, but it, like, it got so strong that it was smothering, and then it was my mother.
Pat: That's the last time I give you a back rub.
Gerald (laughs): Oh. (Sigh.) Well, then she, I guess she was on my chest, and, when she did, it was like Phyllis—like "I understand, Gerald, I understand, I'm your friend." And she was rubbing my chest to make me feel better, and I . . . I know she understands, and I'm glad, but I still don't know what to do. See, that's why I always feel—even with closest friends—'cause I don't know what to do, you know, it doesn't matter how much I like them.
Therapist: Even though you don't know what to do, what would you like to do right now at this moment?
Gerald: What would I like to do? (Sighs.) See, there's something—one thing I like to do with somebody, I like to feel.
Therapist: What?
Gerald: The right to feel. I like to feel okay. So when I talk to somebody, there's quick, quick, back and forth feeling and ideas going right—no jittery thinking. And then, then to meet a girl, you know, to just meet her and start liking her, start dating her, and start kissing her, that's what I like to feel, but I don't—never felt it.
Therapist: Well, if she turns into mother, that's pretty hard to do.
Gerald: But see, the girls I dated never turned into mothers, they just—well, they have in a way, but I always felt them cold.
Pat: Know what? It's kind of nice just to touch you. When I touched your chest, it wasn't really to make you feel better, Gerald, sorry to say, it's just kind of, like, to touch your chest, and it was nice to know that there were artificially set limits which I couldn't step over in good taste and which in my mind I can't step over, anyway, but then I could just enjoy touching you. It was nice, you know? But I didn't have to worry. Like, those are good feelings. As long as I didn't have to worry that I'd have to put out or that I have—I'm gonna get some uncontrollable urge, and I'm going to go act on it—that's what terrifies me. You know, I could

go there and play with you and that—that
... that really scares me. I can never know
how close to get to you because I'd be afraid
of turning you on because I wouldn't go
through with it because, you know, I'm
going with Jimmy. Sooner or later, I'd have
to talk to you about it just like that because
I really like you, and I would like to hug
you with the impression that I'm going to
end up trying to screw you. 'Cause I won't.

Gerald: Yeah, and maybe that's why I feel
warmth with you because you're safe. You've
got no intentions, and I know it.

Pat: Well, so what?

Gerald: Well, that way, I can touch all I want
and feel secure. I can touch without feeling,
"Where's this leading to?" Well, I was in a
way thinking that.

Pat: Yeah, but that's a good thing to have, to
have somebody you can do that with.

Gerald: Yeah, but, see, that's different. 'Cause
you don't do that with girls—I mean, you
don't, like, on friends.

Therapist: Okay, Gerald, let's try something
else, shall we?

Gerald: All right.

Therapist: Are you up to it?

Gerald: Huh?

Therapist: Um, one of the girls. Ah, who would
you like to touch your hand?

Gerald: I guess Pat.

Therapist: Pat. Are you still thinking of it as safe?
Who's the least safe? Lynn?

(The therapist suggests the girl in the group who
apparently is least likely to remind Gerald
of his mother. The assumption dictating this
course is that Pat is closer on the generalization gradient to mother—therefore, eliciting
more anxiety than Lynn, who is more distant
on the gradient. In terms of desensitizing in
a hierarchical fashion, the least disturbing
stimuli should be presented first.)

Pat: I would be a mother.

Therapist: Okay, now, Gerald, if you start to feel
uncomfortable, let us know.

Gerald: Yeah, I guess so.

Therapist: Now?

(Lynn puts her hand on Gerald's hand.)

Gerald: Much worse.

Therapist: Worse?

Gerald: Because she's being more gentle and, ah,
the whole thing is feeling softly now.

Therapist: I want you just to think about her
touch on your hand, okay? And not all the
ideas that go with it, okay? The touch on
your hand. You feel a hand on yours. Concentrate on that.

Gerald: I. . . .

Therapist: No thinking. Just pay attention to the
feeling.

(The therapist attempts to cut off the avoidance
behavior of intellectualizing the experience
and insists that Gerald stay focused on the
physical sensations.)

(Long silence.)

Therapist: Just pay attention to what she's doing.
How do you feel?

Gerald: That's pleasant.

Therapist: Don't you feel better now? Suppose
she takes both your hands in hers?

Gerald: I . . . I can't. . . .

Therapist: Just pay attention to the sensation.

Gerald: I . . . I can't separate them . . . they're
hard to separate.

Therapist: Stop thinking. Just pay attention to
what you're feeling.

(Long silence.)

Gerald: Uh. . . .

Therapist: It's all right. That's all we're going to
do is this, okay? Just pay attention to the
sensation. Stop thinking about it.

(Long silence.)

Therapist: If it feels uncomfortable, you tell her,
and she'll take her hands away. No thinking,
just feeling, all right? Sensation and how it
feels.

Gerald: I have to explain something first.

Therapist: No, you can't do that. You absolutely
can't do that. What do your hands feel like?

Gerald: What do they feel like?

Therapist: Are they feeling warm?

Gerald: They're warm.

Therapist: Pay attention to that warmness.

Gerald: That's the thing—I do. . . .

Therapist: Tell me about it afterward. How do
you feel?

Gerald: Okay.

Therapist: Good. Does come to be nice after all?

Gerald: Um, yeah, yeah.

Therapist: Okay. That's all I wanted to ask you.
How do you feel?

Gerald: Um, okay, I guess.

Therapist: Is there anything you need to tell
me now?

(Having accomplished the goal at hand, in having
Gerald become comfortable with the physical
contact, the therapist opens the way to
discussion of whatever Gerald would like.)

Gerald: Yeah, in a way. 'Cause when I was really
enjoying her hands is because I was seeing
a picture . . . I was liking that picture. And
to the touch, it was like . . . I don't know
whether the picture was getting me away
from the touch or what.

Therapist: A picture of what?

Gerald: Well, I was lying here, and Lynn was sitting here, and she was looking at me, and for some reason we were on a beach, and I was looking at the sun, and she was looking at me and telling me something that's funny. And she really likes me, you know. We just like each other, and she's putting her hands on mine, and she's telling me something funny, and I was getting hysterical, but I could relax and lay back, and I'm smiling because she's touching me and saying, "Isn't that funny?" And I was saying, "yeah," and I'm smiling, and she's still touching and the whole big thing, you know. But it wasn't, like, exactly Lynn. It was like, it was like a little painted image.

Another form of desensitization is through physical activity. As mentioned by Schutz, a physical exercise often leads to an increased capacity in the area of verbal expression.

Pat presented the problem of never being able to express anger. As a result, she would often go to great lengths in placating others, even though it left her resentful. Within the group she could always be counted on to patch up things when any hostile emotions were beginning to be expressed. Any anger that she herself felt led to her responding with anxiety.

The following verbatim account was preceded by an exercise in which Bill was to break into a tight circle formed by the other group members. The original object was to have Bill, who was extremely passive and devoid of affect, begin to express some assertiveness at the physical level.

Pat: Man, I couldn't stand you. Oh, God, I fought like I seldom fight. I never have an opportunity to fight. It's nice to really come out and out and *fight*! Yeah, even one that you don't actually punch. But the time before, you had your hand on my waist, and I thought I would retch.

Therapist: Who are you talking to?

Pat: Him. (Indicating Bill.)

Therapist: You're talking to Bill?

Pat: Sorry. I mean it was, like, too much. I was really glad to have this way. I had a tight hold and didn't have to let anyone in. It's personal.

Bill: It's better or it's worse.

Pat: I said it's *personal*. I mean I was going to preface it with, "Don't take it personally," because it's meant personally. I just like. . . .

Rita: She tolerates you.

Pat: This is very bad for somebody who likes. . . . I would like to feel tolerant and permit

other life styles to go on. But, man, you're living your own life.

Co-therapist (to Bill): How do you like what she is saying?

(Effort is made to have Bill respond rather than sit immobile in his chair—his typical response to anger.)

Rita: Boy, oh, boy. I could never say anything better.

Bill: I'm saying to myself, "Well, I guess that will be too bad because I am what I am." But the other—but that's the way I am. I'm sorry.

Pat: What did you say that for? It's because of that I can't stand you. The first one I have respect for. It's that little addition.

Bill: That's funny; that's strange.

Pat: It's not funny, and it's not strange. The thing, "Accept me for what I am," and then you can't say, "I'm sorry." If I say something . . . that's why I hate it worse when I see it in other people. Which meant I really didn't deal straight with you, but this has been sitting on my mind for about five minutes now. Just making this statement.

(Pat's comments are quite uncharacteristic, as she has reported never confronting anyone before.)

Gerald: I felt the same way. I want to be close to Pat, and I felt very comforted and warm just being beside her.

Pat: Yeah, I can trust you.

Gerald: And I felt, like, you know, kind of like we were really close and, like, one, almost. I could have my arm around you, and, for the first time, I actually felt warmth from a girl's body, just warmth, you know. Usually, I guess because I'm so nervous, I don't even feel it.

Pat: I was wondering because I didn't—you're very tall, and you have a lot of weight to you, and, when you leaned over like that, I thought, "Oh God." It must be a nice feeling, though.

Gerald: Yeah, it was.

Therapist: How did it make you feel?

Pat: I'd like to get his weight off me, so I pushed him back. Just lightly, I didn't shove him.

Therapist: No strong feeling. . . .

Pat: No, no.

Kate: I wanted Bill; I wanted you to get in, but I said, if you're going to get in, you'd better be strong about it, and then I would feel glad that you're in. But if you come in and not. . . .

Lynn: I was pissed off.

Kate: And force your way in, then I said I wouldn't want you in. I really do—I didn't feel I didn't want you in. I wanted you so hard, and, when you gave up, like, you almost—you had my arm apart, you could have gotten in. And I said, "What did he give up for?" You shouldn't have given up, you know, like, I was really disappointed that you gave up.

Lynn: I figured you didn't really want to come in. But that's a little ludicrous. It took you six times longer than it took Kate, which is ludicrous. You know, Kate just can't be any stronger than you are, and you could have gotten in. Besides, like Kate said, you could have gotten in between us. I was very pissed off. We went to a lot of trouble, and he managed to get through. Like my arm was out; Kate was already out. It would have taken nothing to get in between Kate and me. And instead he backed off. You know, after all that struggling, he took three times longer than he should have. Then you went around to the other side. I was just as glad. Gerald, you turned out to be such a nice person.

Co-therapist (giving feedback to Bill about how and what his expression is communicating): I really don't understand why this has always happened to me. People just put me down and jump on me, and I'm very confused about, and it really hurts. I don't know what to do about it.

Rita: A very funny thing happened. I got very angry when he got my arm, and I thought, "Damn it." And we were standing there and all, and all of a sudden I felt like he was Jack, and yet you're not anything like him, but I just couldn't stand it.

Bill: Well, I hear the rejection or the putting down, and it hurts, but it confuses me as to why everybody does it.

Co-therapist: Okay, tell everybody why it is hurting you right now—to their faces that you are hurt by what they have said.

Pat: I can't help it. This is supposed to be for honesty, and I'm sitting here trying hard not to hurt you, and that's ridiculous. I'm getting no place, and you're getting no place. I dislike you for a reason, and I feel like I have to hold you up. And I can't stand it. It's what I did for years—all my life—I can't stand it.

Therapist: Bill. (Pause.) Didn't you have something you wanted to say to Pat?

Bill: Well, no, Carl said something. . . .

Co-therapist: Did you have something?

Bill: I'm confused about it. It's just. . . . Well, I would say, "Please accept me."

Pat: You completely put me out for saying that.

It would take me a long, long time to accept you 'cause I'd have to get myself straight first. 'Cause I have to get myself to the point where it's not up to me to hold up other people. So, maybe in time.

Bill: That makes me feel good that you said that.

Lynn: How could it possibly make you feel good?

Bill: I don't even know what I'm looking for, though.

Gerald: You're weak, Bill. You're weak.

Pat: You bring out all the mother in me, which I cannot abide when it's a male with pants on.

Co-therapist (giving feedback to Bill): I do the best I can. When people jump on me, I don't understand it. It's really unfair.

Kate: You seem like a little boy now.

Co-therapist (giving feedback to Bill): People are telling me always what I am and what I do is wrong, and I try, and they still think I am wrong.

Pat: Don't you have any straight reaction? I just told you I can't stand you because you seem like a kid to me. Don't you at least feel like hitting? No, that would be like. . . .

Co-therapist: Bill, do you like what people are telling you?

Bill: No.

Co-therapist: Okay, stand up and tell them in a loud voice that you don't like what they are telling you.

Bill: I feel bad, though.

Pat: How can you feel bad when I just threw all this stuff at you? You at least have a reason to say something.

Co-therapist: Tell her what you don't like about what she is telling you or what you want.

Therapist (modeling for Bill): Get off my back.

Pat: It's where I belong unless you're just going to tell me to get off.

Bill: Be quiet, Pat.

Pat: Be quiet. You sound like you're a school teacher.

Bill: *Be quiet!*

Pat: Now I'm supposed to stomp my feet.

Kate: Come on, Bill, tell her off. I can't stand it.

Co-therapist: Come on.

Bill: Stop it.

Pat: Stop what?

Bill: You don't have to do that.

Pat: I do have to do it. Because you drive me right up a wall.

Bill: That's too bad.

Therapist (modeling for Bill): If I get mad at you, you won't know what to do.

Pat: I'm getting mad at you. I'll have some kind of respect for you.

Therapist (modeling for Bill): But if I get mad, Pat, I'm sure you will not be able to take it.

Pat: Anger at least is straight. You can deal with anger.

Therapist (modeling for Bill): You scare me. You really scare me.

Pat: If I could, I'd kill you because you make me feel male, which is what I can't stand.

Therapist (modeling for Bill): Yeah, I think you would kill me. That's what scares me. How can I fight that?

Pat: Can't you try something?

Therapist (giving feedback to Bill): I just want to say my apologies. . . .

Pat: *Holy Jesus!* You want to make me retch?

Bill: I'd like . . . I'd like to be strong.

Pat: Don't ask me for favors. The strength doesn't come from me if I'm. . . .

Co-therapist: Do you like what she is saying?

Pat: Can't you even call me a name, at least something?

Co-therapist: Say this: "I don't like you." In a loud voice, time after time. Do that!

Bill: I don't like that.

Pat: What?

Bill: I don't like that!

Co-therapist: More!

Pat: What don't you like?

Bill: *The way you're running me down.*

Pat: Running you down?

Co-therapist: *More!*

Bill: Yes. I don't like the way you're running me down.

Co-therapist: *Louder!*

Bill: *I don't like the way you're running me down!*

Co-therapist: *Louder!*

Pat: You deserve every minute of it.

Co-therapist: *Don't pay attention. Louder! Louder!*

Bill: I don't like the way you're running me down. *I don't like the way you're running me down.* I DON'T LIKE THE WAY YOU'RE RUNNING ME DOWN.

Pat: I don't like the way you run around expecting other people to pick you up and wipe your nose.

Bill: I'm not expecting that.

Pat: Well, you just sit there like a lump and make them feel like they have to.

Bill: But they don't.

Pat: What?

Bill: Have to pick me up. I can take care of myself.

Pat: Is that why you sit there like a puppet without strings?

Bill: That's not what I'm doing.

Therapist: Tell her what you feel.

Bill: I feel angry with what you're saying.

Co-therapist: *Okay, go on.* Don't listen to her,

go on. Don't listen to her, go on. Don't listen to her arguments.

Bill: I am angry.

Co-therapist: *Louder. Louder.*

Bill: *Angry.* ANGRY. ANGRY.

Co-therapist: *Go on, go on.*

Pat: Why do you hold your hands like that then?

Co-therapist: *Go on. Go on.*

Pat: Don't answer to me. I don't want you to answer. . . .

Co-therapist: *Go on.* Don't react to her. *Go on.*

Bill: Just. . . .

Pat: Have you any idea how I felt? The idea of this was not so that I would end up, and you wouldn't be angry. For Christ's sake, be angry.

Bill: I am.

Pat: THEN SHOW IT!

Bill: I don't know how.

Co-therapist: It takes time, but go on, try.

Pat: Go ahead, at least do something. At least pretend.

Bill: But I am angry. I AM ANGRY. ANGRY. ANGRY. ANGRY.

Co-therapist: Go on.

All: ANGRY! ANGRY! ANGRY! ANGRY! ANGRY! ANGRY! ANGRY! ANGRY! ANGRY!

Pat: You look it!

Bill: I am. *I am angry.*

Co-therapist: *Angry! Angry!*

Bill: I am angry.

Rita: You're shuttin' up fast enough, that's for sure.

Bill: *Stop it!*

Co-therapist: All your anger!

Bill: STOP IT!

Therapist: Okay. Here, Bill, here. (Therapist puts pillow in front of Bill.)

Gerald: Okay, let's see, hit it.

(Therapist hits pillow with great force.)

Therapist: *Hit it. Hit it. Hit it.* HIT IT. HIT IT.

Co-therapist: *Voice!*

Bill (pounds pillow): *Stop it! Stop it!! Stop it!!* STOP IT!! STOP IT!!! (Louder still.) STOP IT!!! STOP IT!!!

(Bill stops, and long pause ensues.)

Bill: I am relieved.

Pat: It's relieving.

Therapist: How do you feel?

Bill: Relieved.

Therapist: Pat? You?

(Pat sighs.)

(Long pause.)

Bill: The . . . the . . . the strength in being able to do it.

Therapist: You didn't know you were so strong, huh?

Pat: I didn't know you could get that angry.

Rita: The first time is wasn't real anger. It was told anger. But you got really angry. You got plenty angry. Straight from the inside. Straight from the inside.

Pat: I'm not fighting with you for a long time.

The result of the above interchange was that Pat and Bill became much more comfortable with each other, and each was able to be more directly expressive within the group. Both reported that they found it less of a problem being appropriately expressive outside the group after this session; however, further interchanges on the same theme were required.

Though this method is borrowed from encounter group procedures, it is used in a way that facilitates desensitization. It is followed up systematically across group sessions with definite goals in mind for each member.

Group Motivational Factors and Social Reinforcement. Group pressure is a powerful motivating factor in changing attitudes and actions. The group therapist's role in actuating this potential is one of solidifying and channeling this pressure on each member in a therapeutic direction. He identifies the inappropriate and specifies the more appropriate behavior. The direction of change is kept constantly overt by references to the goals to be achieved by each member, making them clear to all present the appropriate direction for each one. The therapist does not hesitate to interrupt or correct any member's advice that tends to be irrelevant or potentially distracting or oppositional to movement toward determined goals. The therapist has the particular advantage that he is identified as the expert, that he has little difficulty in applying solidified group pressure when he so desires.

In some groups there is always at least one protagonist present, providing an additional motivating force. The co-therapists cooperate in the process of confrontation when necessary. One therapist deliberately assaults and overruns a particularly difficult avoidance behavior, and the other therapist supplies the patient with needed support during the process. Confrontation is a particularly undesirable activity from an individual therapist, but it is quite safe in a group as long as a co-therapist or other group members give the needed support.

Gerald related a story in which he and a friend had made arrangements to meet two girls. The friend backed out, and Gerald sat down to decide whether or not he would keep the appointment alone. He found himself torn between doing so and seeking out a male sexual partner. He chose the latter course and ultimately was left depressed by this action.

The verbatim interaction recorded below takes up just after Gerald's narration of this story, laced with many statements of his existential suffering at the hands of a cruel world.

Therapist: Why didn't you go to see those girls? (Therapist chooses to concentrate on avoidance behavior.)

Gerald: Because I had only met them once and ... um ... I wasn't really that particularly interested. The kid, the homosexual kid played a guitar, and this girl plays a guitar, and I could sing, but I just ... um, you know, two guitars, it would be fun. For me, with me with two girls there ... um, I think that would be a little too much pressure, not exactly sexual pressure because I felt that, if I thought it was a threat, I could easily handle that. I was no longer taken back by it, the fact that there was sex involved. In fact, I was even imagining that I would be sitting there and even kissing her and touching her, but ... um ... with two there, I just found that kind of tough to handle, two girls. So I didn't go, and I sat there, and I thought, "Well I should go call Phyllis," and I just sat there because I knew the attraction was still for Rittenhouse Square and finding somebody there, you know, this always lingered in the back of my mind. And I can't make it with girls. That's the whole thing that's blocked off completely. I mean, it's just not there.

Therapist: Have you made any progress with girls?

Gerald: Progress in the sense that I'm not afraid of them.

Therapist: That's progress.

Gerald: Yeah, but that's it. As close as you can get to it. Like Phyllis is the one person .... If I could make it with anyone, it would be her, but there's no sexual feelings there at all. It's simply when she's happy, I'm happy; when she's sad, I'm sad. I try to make her happy, you know, we do everything that a normal couple would do, except there's no sexual feelings involved. There's nothing, just nothing.

Pat: If you can keep her clean, you can keep her.

Gerald: Huh?

Pat: I said, if you keep her clean, you can keep

her. That might be the reasoning you had in your head.

Gerald: Keep her clean of what?

Pat: Any kind of sexual feeling.

Gerald: No, I'm not trying to keep her clean.

Pat: No, but I'm saying your head might be.

Gerald: I don't understand.

Pat: Girls that you feel attracted to or even slightly attracted to bisexually, you're scared of them, and, like, you really like her, and you feel if you ever let loose any kind of sexual feelings toward her, you might feel—the rest of you might feel that that's too threatening.

(Pat joins the therapist in pressuring Gerald to deal with his fear.)

Gerald: If it's true, I don't know about it. I just don't feel anything. I can hug her and kiss her on the cheek, but I don't know what it means, I don't know. I don't have any feelings, I just don't have any feelings. I don't have any feeling practically except that thing with that kid. That was something that I kind of watched and watched and tried to test in suspicion, et cetera, to find out whether it would be true or not. That's the only time I had asserted any kind of feeling of hope. It was the first time in years, in years, I mean that. I haven't felt anything like that since I was about eight or nine. (Gerald steers the discussion back to the area of his needs in relation to another person, which, although important, is a characteristic avoidance behavior.) And now this feeling, to me that was feeling, that was pure emotion, so overwhelming that I felt like crying. But it just proved to me that that person, even though he said he was sensitive, and he said that—not that he said it, but I found, well, through his talk, he was saying in a roundabout way that he was sensitive, that he needed love, that he needed one person, not one of these one-night-stand-type things, yet that kind of underground-type life just restricts the feelings at all. I mean, it's still animalistic, it still molds. . . .

Therapist: Why don't you set up some kind of step-by-step procedure with someone—a girl? Can you set up a step-by-step procedure?

(Therapist again brings the discussion back to dealing with fear of heterosexual behavior.)

Gerald: Louise.

Therapist: What happened there? Did you follow it through?

Gerald: I just didn't have the feeling. I got stoned the first time with her, and I felt sensual

feelings, but there were no sexual ones. First, we tried it without being stoned, and I sat there, and I lay beside her. I slept with her, but not sexually, just slept with her, you know, when I used to go over to her apartment, so there was no fear of that, you know. They just aren't there.

Therapist: They just aren't there because they're blocked. Fear interferes with them.

Gerald: They're so blocked that I don't even know that they're there.

Pat: In the situation that you set up for yourself, did you have any definite limits that you put on yourself—like there would be no more than lying next to her, I mean, absolutely no more, no matter what kind of feelings might come up? Did you put limits on yourself? Or were you. . . .

Gerald: No, I wanted to think that I could—I wanted to think that what was inside me, that thing that is blocked off, was really there. You know, that sexual feelings were really there, and I wanted to believe it so much that I put no limitations on my sexual inspirations.

Pat: Sometimes that can have a very bad effect on you.

Gerald: Yeah.

Pat: You mean, if you would feel so much as her left earlobe looked attractive, you can bet that would have been stopped. Because of the way you had it set up, it would be a snowball thing. I mean, you must have known all along that, once you started feeling it, the whole thing would come. Do you know what I mean at all?

Gerald: Not that last part.

Therapist: It's only going to work if the ultimate threat is removed.

Gerald: What's the ultimate threat?

Therapist: To perform sexually.

Pat: Like, do it. Like, when I had that thing going with Ralph, I had to know that I could get comfortable with hugging him because I knew that was all I would do, no matter what I felt and, like, supposing I had felt like kissing him, I wasn't. Just do one thing at a time, and it took a lot of the pressure off. I could feel that because I knew in the back of my head nothing more was going to be.

Gerald: Did you love him?

Pat: No, I didn't. I didn't know it then, but I mean, like, that's a hairy thing, I mean that whole thing isn't what I mean. What I meant was, if you have a very small box all chewed out with what you're permitted to do, then you'd be more likely to be able to do that than if it is open-ended and once you set foot in it, for all you know, you might take the next step and maybe the next step and maybe the next step and, if you knew you were only allowed to do one, and then you had to stop because that's how you set it up. You often felt a lot freer being able to do that one.

Therapist: You've got to stop searching for the feeling, you know, trying to make it come out, because you're killing part of it. The idea is to take the first step, whatever it is, maybe just lying in bed, and do nothing more than that.

(Therapist attempts to clarify Pat's statement by use of more concrete terms.)

Pat: And know that you aren't supposed to any more because it will kill it. And you're confused about what happened about that guy, aren't you? I sounded more like you knew you didn't want to have sex, partly because you badly wanted a person.

Therapist: To be close to somebody.

Pat: Yes. That comes out so clear.

Gerald: Yeah, I know, that's what I mean.

Pat: There's nothing unusual about that.

Gerald: But it's a male, it's male.

Pat: Well, that's still just learning, but, I mean, like, you're in need for a person—that's normal.

Gerald: I know. I know that's normal, but it's just directed to the male.

Pat: As a matter of fact, it seems like an improvement in what you're aiming for. That you didn't want the sex.

Gerald: It's always been that way. Really, it's always been that way. All the time that I've searched this sex thing, it's always been searching for that, anyway, you know. But since I couldn't get that, well, settle for the temporary thing. And then, that doesn't even do any good either because, as I was hugging him, and here he was on me, he was doing all these things—a body, but what I was feeling was inside, but his body, what is it? It's a lump of flesh, and I didn't know what it meant. I didn't know how to handle it. See, that thing about lying beside a girl and stuff, I don't see how that works. It's just been done, especially with Phyllis, you know. We always sleep together on a couch; we sit and hug each other; we hold hands.

Therapist: You are simply not listening. You have to be willing to follow step-by-step procedure without trying to run so far ahead of yourself, just as you have developed the capacity to sleep or sit with Phyllis by following the initial steps asked of you.

Co-therapist: Withhold all judgments. You have to take these steps.

Pat: It's like you could maybe—you've stayed with girls before and, like, stay with her with the idea in your head that it would be nothing more than your body next to her body. And know in your head that you're not gonna reach out and that you don't want and that this time you're not gonna put your arm around her and you're not gonna and you're not supposed to try to kiss her and you're not gonna. . . .

Gerald: I don't . . . see, I don't do it because I'm supposed to or I'm obligated. I don't have that feeling anymore, you know.

Pat: No, I'm not saying that; I'm saying that, to free any kind of feeling in yourself, you have to start at a place that you're not repulsed by, and you have to do it and keep doing just that, no more until not an absence of repulsion but an acceptance about it being an okay state and maybe even liking just that and no more, until maybe it comes to the point when it's no longer sufficient just to lie there, you would really like to maybe put out your hand. But you have to do the whole thing continual, that just one thing from doing something like lying next to her until you can take it, until it's nice, until you like it, until you might want more, but just with one thing at a time. It might take a week, it might take a couple of weeks with just that one thing, knowing all the time that you're not going to do more than that. Otherwise, I don't see how you can feel free. It sounds peculiar that you're gonna find freedom through restriction, but, by restricting yourself to that one thing, it's safe to feel. It's not safe to feel anything if you think, "Oh, my God, I've reached out for her hand; the next thing you know maybe I will put my arm out, and maybe I'll kiss her." That would be terrifying.

Therapist: Well, look, you've been through all these facts before. Why is it that you're not able to follow through?

(It appears that sufficient repetition of Pat's point has occurred and that another try is required.)

Gerald: Because of this plan. I guess that's the biggest reason.

Therapist: You're just not going to let anybody tell you what to do?

Gerald: No, it's not that. It's just that, here I had one thing set up—do this. I do it. To me, it needs feeling.

Therapist: Of course, it needs feeling, but the fear is still too great. The feeling will come if you can stick to the plan. You're just not giving it a chance. You now have feelings of warmth with girls—comfortable in nonsexual settings which you did not have three months ago.

Gerald: Well, the thing is that, because it's so scientifically prepared, that how could any feelings come about?

Therapist: Do you trust him? (Indicating cotherapist, who is Gerald's individual therapist as well.)

(Gerald's individual therapist has indicated to the therapist that Gerald has engaged in prolonged verbal expression centering upon his need to trust before doing what is recommended, although this trait has come up only briefly in group sessions.)

Gerald: No.

Therapist: Then, that's the problem, isn't it?

Gerald: Yes.

Pat: You tried to tell him that before?

Therapist: Can you accept the fact that it doesn't make any difference whether he's treacherous or not? The fact of the matter is that what he's telling you can be useful to you.

Co-therapist: You don't know if it works before you've tried it, whether it's planned or scientific.

Jack: What have you got to lose?

(Up to this point, the main pressures for following the outlined therapy have come from the therapist and Pat. Now Jack joins in, applying pressure. Typically, when the therapist takes a firm and persistent stand, he solidifies group pressure, adding to the motivational stimulation present.)

Gerald: Only to find out that I've been right.

Therapist: Well, you're gonna make sure you find that out, huh?

Pat: If you did find out you were absolutely right, at least you'd be on one side of the fence or the other.

Gerald: If what I'm doing now is true, then I wouldn't be on any fence whatsoever.

Therapist: There are not too many things, really, that we know a great deal about, but this is something we know something about. And all it takes is a minimum of faith on your part, enough to get you to follow the procedure, and, if you can't give that, we really can't help you. That's where it's at. It doesn't make any difference what kind of a person Carl is or I am. It's totally irrelevant. (Pause.) Do you want it?

(Therapist attempts to get a verbal commitment from Gerald, since such a commitment has proved a necessary forerunner to desired behavior from Gerald.)

Gerald: Want what?

Therapist: What we've got to offer.

Pat: Do you know if the procedure works? I mean, like. . . .

Gerald: I've been told that it works.

Pat: What kind of proof do you need before you could give your faith to it? Like, actually believe it enough to try it.

Gerald: It's the kind of proof that I guess no one could offer. It's a proof in which someone can convince me that people who have been cured through this approach, that in degree and in qualitatively, they are no different than me.

(Gerald seems to be setting up impossible conditions for his cooperation.)

Pat: But you started off saying that.

Gerald: That we were both in the same psyche, we both saw the same things.

Pat: Don't just chuck it out.

Gerald: I really have to because. . . .

Pat: What makes you think that you're so weird?

Gerald: Because you can name anything, and I'd be it.

Pat: So will anybody under the pressure. You make the promises good enough, and the punishments bad enough, and you'll change.

Therapist: Did you say you'd believe it?

Pat: He would "be it."

Therapist: That's something untrue.

Gerald: Then what is true?

Therapist: How we've been trying very hard to get you to cooperate in this matter, and you're not believing that.

Pat: You aren't cooperating.

Co-therapist: You can try, but it will be very hard to take.

(Gerald has become more and more agitated as the interchange has progressed. The cotherapist now offers needed support.)

Gerald: It certainly would.

Therapist (with slight irritation): Well, in that case, I wouldn't try.

Gerald: Huh?

Therapist: If I were you, I wouldn't try. Or anything else.

Joan: It sounds like The Iceman Cometh.

Pat: What could be worse than what you've gone through in the past two days. Gerald?

Gerald: See, what happened in the past two days was just like a kind of topping on my entire life, you know. Like, I'm going through the whole circle, you know, round and round and round and round and finally, you know, I know it's complete—I read all about it.

Therapist: You keep looking in the wrong place, Gerald. You've looked in that place before.

Pat: And you've come up not liking it again.

Gerald: But, seriously, it was different. The feeling that I had, the person was different.

Therapist: How can you give your total faith to that? How can you really give your total faith, you know, just like that, total trust to that situation? No threat at all of the sort you were experiencing then in terms of what we're trying to set up for you, huh? I suggest to you the difference is that you knew damn well it wasn't going to work; you really didn't invest anything in it.

Lynn: Did you really believe that it was going to be complete and tremendous?

Gerald: I was hoping for it.

Pat: That seems that you were leaving stuff out again; you were leaving yourself out.

Bill: Way out. Wasn't he setting up a failure?

Gerald: I don't understand. I don't understand what you mean.

Pat: You didn't throw your whole self into it. You wouldn't prove that you were what you feared you were.

Gerald: He was a person with the same things that I've been feeling, so that was—well, I'm not even—it happened, but it was wrong.

Jack: You said what he wanted to hear, didn't you?

Gerald: I didn't ask him. He said it. It crossed my mind, and that's why I kept on questioning him in this way.

Pat: You're still running away from it. What can possibly be done?

Jack: You know, you got very mad last week when Greg was on the grill, and I think you were extremely annoyed about him not—him faking it and everything else not getting into it.

(In the last session Gerald had become very annoyed with Greg because of his intellectual mode of avoiding information being offered by the group. Jack picks up the similarity in the present interaction and furnishes feedback to Gerald about his immediate behavior.)

Therapist: It's always easier to sit around and rationalize.

Joan: That's seems to be his thing. He gets really wrapped up.

Therapist: All it is is that he is avoiding the major issues.

Jack: You do the same thing you talked about last week.

Lynn: Like, it's important to reflect what you know about a conversation.

Jack: He's hitting everything with a bull's eye.

Therapist: In fact, I don't think he sees progress he has made. I think you totally deny that.

Pat: Can't you see? Here you had a supposedly perfect setup yesterday, you really did, and that wasn't enough, and it would have been enough when you started here. It would have been enough, but it's not good enough for you anymore. Like, you know that there's something missing now, and you're repulsed by it. You don't like it, but that's, like, about as big a step as you can possibly make. It's like going off and getting married tomorrow. I mean, like, why expect the height of the Empire State. That's an enormous step.

(Pat now swings to support of Gerald. Throughout the interchange she offers both pressure and support. She, along with the co-therapist and later Greg, give the support needed to balance the therapist's consistent blocking of avoidance behavior.)

Joan: You're like you're coming from here, you're down here, and now you've got to get up there.

(Joan, who has been quietly observing, now joins the therapist, Pat, and Jack in applying pressure.)

Therapist: Gerald doesn't have to work his own way out; Gerald has to have some faith at this point.

Pat: Technique is the important thing. I know it works.

Gerald: I'd like to compare my feelings. . . .

Pat: You want out. You want to have little catchalls where you don't have to put your whole thing in it. You want it structured so much that you don't have to do it.

Greg: No, he's afraid to make the next move.

Therapist: This will not solve all your problems. You're not going to immediately find the person to fill the void in your life. You've got to open the door to that. It's not sealed. We're not saying to you that, once you're able to have a heterosexual relationship, that all the world is going to turn into rose-colored garden. Don't worry about that. You don't even have to set yourself up for that.

Bill: You're really fighting that. I really don't grasp this whole thing. Is he fighting himself?

Therapist: He's fighting about doing what's very, very threatening.

Bill: Why would he be threatened?

Pat: Because it's sink or swim. And he's afraid he'll sink at the end. This is the only thing that will enable him to swim. (Pause.) Like, you know what ticks me off? When you said you were with Louise, and you felt sensual feelings, but not sexual, so they didn't count. That's turd.

Jack: It sounds like an English class.

Pat: It's not that at all. That isn't the point. It's just that you have such high expectations for yourself, you couldn't see that that was part of the same thing, like you start with the sensuous, and you get to like it, and it just gradually evolves, but it is part of the same thing that you want it all at once.

Gerald: I was stoned, and I had to.

Pat: I don't care what you were.

Gerald: I made her more beautiful than she was. . . .

Pat: This is plain fuck! You felt this.

Gerald: All right, so I accept it, so I go through. . . .

Pat: So then acknowledge it.

Therapist: Sit around and cry, Gerald. Sit around and cry.

Gerald: I don't cry.

Jack: You know you sound very, very immature. Extremely immature. It sounds that way. I know it's difficult.

Greg: It's a very deep basic fear. If it were me, I'd be scared to death.

Joan: Yeah, exactly, which is what he is.

Jack: Yes, but I keep thinking about last week, and you weren't here. He got on Greg, and it's like the same thing, almost.

Therapist: That's right, it is the same thing.

Jack: Is it the same thing? That's what burns me most of all. You jumped on him because he wasn't giving out. He was just taking, and he wasn't getting into it, and he was rejecting all kinds of help and everything else.

Pat: Well, this is help.

Jack: And it just seems to me you're doing the exact same thing you got on him for.

Pat: And you set yourself up for failure by expecting so much.

Greg: But isn't the point that you came back here? Haven't you shown courage already?

Gerald: No.

Lynn: Yeah, but Gerald, if you felt the security you wanted in a relationship with him, you wouldn't have needed us.

Gerald: That's right, I know. But it wasn't a courageous act. It had nothing to do with that. I was scared shitless.

Greg: If it was a courageous act, would you have admitted it? Have you ever admitted that you have any courage? I think coming back here and knowing you were going to be asked to move on was a courageous act.

Gerald: I didn't know I was going to be asked to move on.

Jack: I think you learned one hell of a valuable lesson.

Gerald: See, I can't make a decision if I'm confused or if I don't know what feelings are about. I can't take a step if I know that I don't know what I'm doing.

Pat: What don't you know in a planned program like that? What is there to know? You know that you're to do one thing which is to bring you absolutely no fear.

Bill: He's obviously scared to death of the work. You must be petrified. "I'm going to change completely." Is that what you feel like, be an entirely different person?

Gerald: No. I can envision myself being married and having kids, and I find it very warming, you know, imagining that situation. But, from here to there, I can't find any connection. I don't know where it is.

Joan: Well, that' a goal, I think, maybe. A goal, and you're right here now, and it looks kind of bleak, but, for Christ's sake, you don't know what's in between. Because you haven't taken any steps. At least you've taken steps. You're here, but, along with what we're talking about, you haven't done anything.

Therapist: You can't have all the solutions to all of the problems that may arise before you take the first step. You have to take the step.

Co-therapist: You have found homosexuality unsatisfactory and sought alternatives. You have made that decision.

Gerald: I don't have any guts; I don't have any. . . .

Therapist: Okay, let's all cry for Gerald, now.

Gerald: No, I'm not. . . .

Therapist: Well, how do you want us to feel about that, Gerald?

Gerald: I'm telling you factually; I have no guts.

Therapist: How do you want us to feel about that?

Jack: Or don't you want to have any guts? That's a great excuse.

Gerald: No, not at all. I feel as if I'm about three or four years old, and I can't do anything. The only thing I can do is lie in a crib and cry or smile. That's it, that's all I can do.

Therapist: Well, how do you want us to feel about that?

Pat: You can learn to tie your shoes, and they're telling you how.

Gerald: Huh?

Therapist: How do you want us to feel about that?

Gerald: I'm telling you; I'm not asking you to feel anything for me.

Therapist: I feel as though I'm being asked to see how pitiful you are.

Gerald: Well, what I'm trying to say is. . . .

Lynn: I think you sort of felt that, in being yourself, that you really can't look around to see how we're reacting and what we want you to do, kind of what we want for you. You're just so wrapped up, like, I keep on getting that impression from you that you just, like, you're wrapped up to the extent that you just have no perspective, like, no focus, no nothing. You have to be able to get together and, like, it's good to get the fluid around and search, but you have to have a foothold to be able to walk in, and you're just so wrapped up that you're lost.

Jack: How are you honestly going to feel if you don't do anything and you remain the way you are? Are you happy the way you are? Do you think you're going to get any happier the way you are? So, obviously, the situation you are in demands a change, and you're the only one who can change it. God ain't gonna come down and pat you on the nose.

Lynn: That's like literature that you read in the English that everything is just so perfect and feelings are so close.

Therapist: So you have to learn to take whatever anybody can give you who is around you and not expect everything in the world from each.

Lynn: If you can get, like, 2 per cent from this person and 3 per cent from that person, it doesn't always have to be from the same person.

Gerald: I know, I know, but, see, from all that you said, I've thought about this, and I guess that's kind of the reason why I can't enter into a sexual relationship with a girl because it's too adult a thing. It's something like, "Here I am, only four years old, and I'm supposed to have sexual intercourse with a girl." There is a whole series of things. I have to start building things, you know, I have to start building.

Therapist: That's bull shit. You'll spend the rest of your life being overwhelmed by all that. Take one step at a time, and the step you have chosen is becoming heterosexual, and let's stick to that first.

Pat: The step-by-step isn't bull shit. Just what are you building?

Therapist: Well, he's got to start at four years old.

Pat: Oh, no. Forget about the child. What courage does it take to lie down? Who cares whether you've got courage?

Gerald: It's fear that, if it happens, I'll be out.

Pat: Of what?

Gerald: I'll be—these feelings that I have or these ideas, whatever they are, and then have sexual intercourse, and it works and

everything, I'm there, now I'm there, I have the sexual feelings, but where's the rest of me, you know?

Therapist: How about crossing that bridge when you get there?

Joan: Yeah, struggle along and don't feel as though you have to fall head in. Just go along step by step.

Pat: See, you can't do anything but the day-by-day with this thing.

Jack: It's not a golden city at the end of this thing; it's just part of it. There's more disadvantages here than there are advantages.

Gerald: I don't want to hear that shit. I know what Pat said and Joan said.

Greg (to Jack): That was semicruel, but you're saying it with a smile.

Pat: We're just trying to be realistic. That's what I've been saying. Be a little realistic so you can really find the feeling.

Jack: It just doesn't happen that way. But it doesn't happen that way. Everything is a beautiful thing and happens wrong.

Pat: No, it doesn't. Where you've got problems, you've got to get rid of them.

Lynn: It just, like, happens. I mean, like, I can remember, like, getting together, and it just happens.

Jack: Gradually?

Lynn: Yeah.

Jack: You don't even know what's happening sometimes.

Lynn: Like, I kind of knew it was happening, and I didn't resist it. It was enjoyable, and I guess I just never pictured myself falling, like you do.

Jack: You mean to tell me that you didn't have any bells ringing?

Lynn: No.

Jack: Oh, that destroys the whole bit because I think you're supposed hear bells.

Pat: You're being nasty.

Greg: Your humor is a little cruel, Jack.

Pat: Let's cut the shit, huh? Just one thing, can you do the behavior modification?

Gerald: What's that?

Pat: Can you take one step and know that it's only that? And you're to do it until you're not only comfortable, but you like it.

(Pat elicits a commitment from Gerald.)

Gerald: Yes.

Co-therapist: Gerald, would you take that you don't trust me as excuse for not doing it?

Gerald: It's part that, not exactly the sexual thing, but other things that we've talked about. I don't trust you.

Therapist: I have a solution to that. Don't talk about it, okay? Just stay on this one issue.

Jack: One step at a time.

Therapist: Do you know what the first step is that Carl set up for you—the first step specifically?

(The therapist attempts to capitalize on Gerald's commitment by working out a specific assignment.)

Gerald: Sitting beside a girl.

Pat: Which one?

Therapist: You can do that comfortably now.

Gerald: I can hold a girl's hand.

Pat: Phyllis?

Gerald: Hum ... Louise's—any girl's hand comfortably.

Pat: For any period of time?

Gerald: I get a little nervous when I want to get up and, like, switch a channel of the television or something. She might think that I'm rejecting her.

Pat: You're thinking too much.

Gerald: Yeah, but it's only in that kind of situation where I have to get up and move. But if I'm just sitting there, it's fine.

Therapist: Where are you ready to start? At what point do you feel uncomfortable?

Gerald: It's really the sexual—I mean, things that are considered sexual. I can put my arm around a girl and put heads together and just sit there and talk whatever, but I can't kiss—I can kiss on the cheek, but that's all.

Therapist: Okay, that's a good point to take up from Phyllis understands and is cooperative, so tell her what the plan is. You are to sit with her—fully clothed—and to kiss mouth to mouth. If at anytime you begin to feel uncomfortable, stop and relax yourself. Then, when you are feeling relaxed, start again. Spend 20 minutes to half an hour at this at a time. Remember, you are to do nothing more—just kissing, even if you begin to feel aroused. Also, Gerald, when you begin to think about how useless it is or something else of the sort, take that as a sign that you are anxious, and stop and relax. Don't try for positive feeling or become discouraged if it doesn't come. Just pay attention to the sensations of the moment. Okay?

Gerald: Yes.

Therapist: Good. When can you set up this arrangement with Phyllis?

Gerald: Tuesday it could be done 'cause. . . .

Therapist: How many times between now and our next session? That's one week.

Gerald: Well, I guess two or three.

Therapist: Okay, let's try for three.

At this point the focus of the discussion shifted to another member. Within five minutes, Gerald began to sob. Pat and the co-therapist moved close to him and comforted him, while the rest of the group continued with the new subject at hand.

The next week Gerald began the session by saying:

I'm really glad I went through all that last week. I really have been feeling good, and I can see that I won't get into all that crap with Carl [his individual therapist] again. I went through the steps, and at first it was scary. I started thinking about how useless it is and everything. Then I relaxed and kept on until it was comfortable. I really feel good about it now.

Confrontation is not confined to the armamentarium of the therapist. Very often group members confront one another, and often with beneficial effects.

Just as group pressure motivates the initiation of new behavior, group approval of action completed serves as a powerful reinforcer of that action, further increasing the probability that the new behavior will be repeated and broadened. Once a person begins to conform to group pressure, he receives reinforcement through direct statements of approval. More importantly, he is reinforced by being accepted as having tried and by added acceptance of his pain and sharing of his joys. He comes to feel part of the group. The feeling of belonging that develops further increases the motivational and reinforcing power of the group.

REFERENCES

Abrahams, J. Group psychotherapy: implications for direction and supervision of mentally ill patients. In *Mental Health in Nursing*, p. 77, T. Muller, editor. Catholic University Press, Washington, D. C., 1950.

Bachrach, A. J., Erwin, W. J., and Mohr, J. P. The control of eating behavior in an anorexic by operant conditioning techniques. In *Case Studies in Behavior Modification*, p. 153, L. P. Ullman and L. Krasner, editors. Holt, Rinehart & Winston, New York, 1965.

Bandura, A. *Principles of Behavior Modification*. Holt, Rinehart & Winston, New York, 1969.

Creer, T. L., and Miklich, D. R. The application of self-modeling procedure to modify inappropriate behavior. Behav. Res. Ther., *8:* 91, 1970.

DiLoreto., A. O. *Cognitive Psychotherapy*. Aldine Publishing, Chicago, 1970.

Eysenck, H. J., editor. *Behavior Therapy and the Neurosis*. Pergamon Press, New York, 1960.

Ferster, C., and DeMyer, M. The development of performances in autistic children in an automatically controlled environment. J. Chronic Dis., *13:* 312, 1961.

Guthrie, E. R. *The Psychology of Learning.* Harper & Brothers, New York, 1935.

Holland, J. G., and Skinner, B. F. *The Analysis of Behavior.* McGraw-Hill, New York, 1961.

Hull, C. L. *Principles of Behavior.* Appleton-Century-Crofts, New York, 1943.

Kimble, G. A. *Hilgard and Marquis' Conditioning and Learning.* Appleton-Century-Crofts, New York, 1961.

Lacey, J. I., and Smith, R. L. Conditioning and generalization of unconscious anxiety. Science, *120:* 1045, 1954.

Lang, P. J., and Lazovik, A. D. Experimental desensitization of a phobia. J. Abnorm. Soc. Psychol., *66:* 519, 1963.

Lazarus, A. A. Behavior therapy in groups. In *Basic Approaches to Group Psychotherapy and Group Counseling,* p. 149, G. M. Grazda, editor. Charles C Thomas, Springfield, Ill., 1968.

Lindsley, O. R. Operant conditioning methods applied to research in chronic schizophrenia. Psychiat. Res. Rep. Amer. Psychiat. Assoc., *5:* 118, 1956.

Lomont, J. F., and Edwards, J. E. The role of relaxation in systematic desensitization. Behav. Res. Ther., *5:* 11, 1967.

Maher, B. A. *Principles of Psychopathology.* McGraw-Hill, New York, 1966.

McFall, R. M., and Marston, A. R. An experimental investigation of behavior rehearsal in assertive training. J. Abnorm. Psychol., in press.

Moreno, J. L. Philosophy of the third psychiatric revolution, with special emphasis on group psychotherapy and psychodrama. In *Progress in Psychotherapy,* F. Fromm-Reichmann and J. L. Moreno, editors. Grune & Stratton, New York, 1956.

Noble, C. E. Conditioned generalization of the galvanic skin response to a subvocal stimulus. J. Exp. Psychol., *40:* 15, 1950.

Orlando R., Bijou, S. W., Tyler, R. M., and Marshall, D. A. A laboratory for the experimental analysis of developmentally retarded children. Psychol. Rep., *7:* 261, 1960.

Paul, G. L. *Insight vs. Desensitization in Psychotherapy: An Experiment in Anxiety Reduction.* Stanford University Press, Stanford, Calif., 1966.

Perls, F. S., Hefferline, R. F., and Goodman, P. *Gestalt Therapy (Excitement and Growth in the Human Personality).* Julian Press, New York, 1951.

Rachman, S. Studies in desensitization. I. The separate effect of relaxation and desensitization. Behav. Res. Ther., *3:* 245, 1965.

Rogers, C. R. *The Process of the Basic Encounter Group.* Western Behavioral Sciences Institute, La Jolla, Calif., 1968.

Schutz, W. C. *Joy.* Grove Press, New York, 1967.

Skinner, B. F. *The Behavior of Organisms: An Experimental Analysis.* Appleton-Century-Crofts, New York, 1938.

Solomon, R. L., and Wynne, L. C. Traumatic avoidance learning: acquisition in normal dogs. Psychol. Monogr., *67:* 19, 1953.

Taylor, F. K. The therapeutic factors of group analytic treatment. J. Ment. Sci., *96:* 976, 1950.

Thorpe, J. J., and Smith, B. Phases in group development in the treatment of drug addiction. Int. J. Group Psychother., *3:* 66, 1953.

Tolman, E. C. *Purposive Behavior in Animals and Men.* Appleton-Century-Crofts, New York, 1932.

Truax, C. B. Reinforcement and nonreinforcement in Rogerian psychotherapy. J. Abnorm. Psychol., *71:* 1, 1966.

Ullman, L. P., and Krasner, L., editors. *Case Studies in Behavior Modification.* Holt, Rinehart & Winston, New York, 1965.

Watson, J. B. *Psychology from the Standpoint of a Behaviorist.* J. B. Lippincott, Philadelphia, 1919.

Watson, J. B., and Rayner, R. Conditioned emotional reaction. *J. Exp. Psychol., 3:* 1, 1920.

Wolpe, J. *Psychotherapy by Reciprocal Inhibition.* Stanford University Press, Stanford, Calif., 1958.

Wolpe, J. *The Practice of Psychotherapy.* Pergamon Press, New York, 1969.

6

Sensitivity Groups, Encounter Groups, Training Groups, Marathon Groups, and the Laboratory Movement

Louis A. Gottschalk, M.D. and Robert S. Davidson, Ph.D.

INTRODUCTION

Some of the most pervasive problems experienced by members of our society are boredom, fear of intimacy, fear of self-disclosure, lack of commitment, loneliness, and alienation. Students complain of a wide gap separating them emotionally and intellectually from their parents, their teachers, other adults, and each other. Some people are puzzled about the apparent meaninglessness of existence. If they are unable to find ready answers in organized religion, they struggle to find earthly reasons besides earning a livelihood, existing, reproducing, achieving. Many of those who try to comfort themselves by allegiance to traditional religious explanations of the meaning or purpose of existence are dissatisfied and are working toward having their religious organization more involved in secular matters and more helpful in guiding their lives. In a society that has distinguished itself by the invention of new psychoactive drugs that can influence man's emotions and thought, many persons are seeking to control the neurochemical environment of their brain and, hence, the oppressive anxiety and depression of their subjective experience by overusing tranquilizers, sedatives, antidepressants, and even psychotomimetic pharmacological agents. Those who cannot afford to purchase these chemicals or who are uninformed about their effects and availability fall back on that age-old pacifier, alcohol, and hide periodically from themselves, their memories, or their impulses by escape-drinking. People in great industrial organizations worry about fragmentation of goals and expend their efforts on how to improve management decision-making, labor-management relationships, and mutual collaboration.

In this contemporary scene, there has come to fruition the growing conviction that many of these discontents of civilization can be favorably influenced through various techniques involving small groups.

HISTORY

During the 1920's, social scientists began to study natural groups in society, with the conviction that the solution to social problems could be facilitated by the study of social interaction and normal social groupings. This conviction was translated into social work practice with groups and social welfare projects. Likewise, within the mental health framework a variety of group approaches were developed, including the group discussion method of the 1920's, culminating in the 1930's with the formation of the group psychotherapy movement.

In the 1930's a spurt in the development of an intellectual climate was conducive to the widespread application of principles of social psychology. The fervor of the decade was reflected in the progressive era in the classroom, the church, and psychoanalysis. The goal of society was no less than the uplifting of the entire society. The "war of democracy" and its aftermath of economic depression created a universal need for help and stirred the cultural consciousness of many professions. It was the era of the social gospel dedicated to the reformation and salvation of not just the individual but society. It was the era of psychoanalytic optimism that the soft voice of reason might free man from the tyranny of his emotions and consequent problems of society.

In this sociocultural arena, Kurt Lewin developed his now famous field theory and began to implement action research as an approach to social change. Lewin, his early collaborators, and his students constituted an academic and community test force that, on the one hand, led to the development of small-group sociology as an academic discipline and, on the other hand, laid the groundwork for the laboratory movement as a community enterprise.

The direct development of the training laboratory came from the collaboration of three men: Leland Bradford, Ronald Lippitt, and Kenneth Benne. All three had an educational background in psychology, experience in working with community educational projects, and involvement in numerous national projects dealing with major social problems related to human relations. They had been exposed to and influenced by J. L. Moreno's methods of psychodrama and had experimented with various role-playing procedures in community educational projects directed toward effecting social change.

The seminal ideas of the laboratory movement were developed in Bethel, Maine, during a conference at the Gould Academy. There, a procedure was developed for training people from communities in the process of democratic group formation. The new method was to be a laboratory for self-examination of group process. Between 1949 and 1955, each summer at Bethel, a variety of experiments were tried with different methods of refining the laboratory group method. Two rather different methods began to emerge. In those early years, the mornings at Bethel were spent in training groups (T-groups), which were relatively unstructured, small, heterogeneous groups of people who focused on an analysis of their immediate interactions. The afternoons were spent in action groups (A-groups) composed of persons from the same organization, who focused on structured group-task exercises, including planning for action back home. However, the action groups rapidly changed into training groups unless strenuous effort was made to keep the action groups task-oriented. The basic dichotomy between a personal, subjective orientation and an external-task, group-work orientation has remained the crucial issue in the training laboratory movement.

Since 1955 the training laboratory movement has developed in such diverse directions that it is difficult to trace a single pattern. Training laboratories, often with great autonomy, were established in other parts of the United States. This development has resulted in submovements that often have disparate goals and methods. In the past 15 years, the movement has become multipurpose and multimethod. The major branches of this diversification can be noted briefly.

The laboratory movement in education has been one of the major institutional bases for the method, even though only a minority of schools of education participate widely in group training laboratories for their students. This movement aims at enhancing the educational enterprise beyond cognitive learning to include socioemotional learning. Human relations training in the classroom exemplifies this tradition.

The laboratory movement in business and industry has been the most firmly established institutional base. The concern here is for the improved function of administrative leadership and the more humane and effective function of work groups. This training movement has focused both on the sensitization of leaders to their impact on their work team and on task-oriented learning experiences for teams of persons who work together (Argyris, 1962).

The training movement in social action was the initial concern of the founders of the movement, but community social action groups seem to have been uneven in their development. Only in the late 1960's was this concern again receiving attention in the laboratory literature. However, instead of the early interest in helping natural community groups to function in a more democratic fashion, the current concern focuses on laboratory consultation to community agencies.

The training movement as a therapeutic method for normal persons found expression in the early T-groups and has steadily gained in popularity and prestige. This part of the movement was totally influenced by the upsurge of interest in humanistic and existential psychology. It has also been the source of origin of many variants, such as marathon groups, sensitivity groups, encounter groups, and personal growth laboratories.

Finally, the training movement has continued to provide impetus for the scientific study of group dynamics, group process, leadership functions, decision-making, and conflict resolutions. However, the early pioneers in the laboratory movement with research orientations from the fields of psychology and sociology have, for the most part, departed from the scene and have transferred their research to the more scientific arena of their respective disciplines, leaving the laboratory movement as a predominantly clinical and applied discipline.

As one surveys the literature of the laboratory movement, especially the small monographs published by the National Training Laboratories (NTL), a definite trend is discernible. In the 1940's the movement expressed a concern for a method of teaching American communities techniques for participatory democracy. Group process and task-oriented group function dominated the scene. In the 1950's, the concern shifted to individual growth, self-knowledge, actualization, and maturation. Indeed, the movement shifted in emphasis from an educative to a therapeutic goal. Subse-

quently, the rather distinctive differences between training and therapy became more and more blurred.

DEFINITIONS

In 1962, Weschler et al. stated:

> Today it is difficult to talk about what sensitivity training or psychotherapy is and should be. Nor is it necessary to draw a clear-cut distinction between them.

Nevertheless, some definitions may serve as guideposts.

Training Laboratory

A training laboratory is an educational procedure that aims to create a situation in which the participants, through their own initiative and control but with access to new knowledge and skilled professional leadership, can appraise their old behavior patterns and attitudes and look at new ones. A laboratory recommends a temporary removal of the participants from their usual living and working environment, where attempts to re-evaluate attitudes or to experiment with new behavior patterns might involve risks and possible punishment. It provides a temporary artificial supportive culture (hence the designation "laboratory") in which the participants may safely confront the possible inadequacy of their old attitudes and behavior patterns and experiment with and practice new ones until they are confident in their ability to use them.

The assumption of the laboratory method is that skills in human interactions are best learned through events in which the learners themselves are involved. The training activities, therefore, are social experiences in which the trainees take part and then reflect on their patterns of participation. Essentially, the laboratory scene provides an occasion for experimental learning.

Sensitivity Training

Sensitivity training is any of a set of experiences, including but not restricted to the training group, attempting to help each participant recognize and face, in himself and in others, many levels of functioning (including emotions, attitudes, values, and intellect), evaluate his behavior in light of the responses it elicits from himself and others at these various levels, and integrate these levels into a more effective and perceptive self.

Training Group

T-group, the most common format for sensitivity training, is a relatively unstructured group in which individuals participate as learners. The basic data for learning come from the participants themselves and from their immediate experiences within the group as they interact with each other in the effort to create from their own resources a productive and meaningful group. The experience is designed to provide a maximal opportunity for the participants to expose and analyze personal behavior and group performance, to learn how others respond to their behavior, and to learn effective personal and group functioning.

Marathon Group

This term is used to describe a sensitivity training group that meets continuously for periods of time ranging from 12 to 36 hours. The purpose of this technique is to heighten the impact of sensitivity training by not interrupting the interactions being generated within the group. Members leave the room only for absolutely necessary reasons. Marathons have been used in weekend laboratories, where the total amount of time available is short, and in longer-term laboratories as a device to move the group to a greater depth of involvement and group interaction. Proponents of such groups report heightened emotionality, a greater expression of negative feelings, and a decrease in defensive role-playing because of fatigue and nearly constant pressure to be more open.

A variation on the marathon is the weekend encounter group, whose sessions are three or four hours in length but occur several times during each day and evening of the weekend, with time out for eating, exercise, and sleep. In such a group there are usually many opportunities for formal and informal pairings, triads, and quartets. These small groups plus the varied activities allow for normal social relationships. Many trainers believe that, rather than detracting from the pressure-cooker formula of the marathon, these more informal groups allow less-threatening relationships to develop. These relationships are then deepened during the formal sessions. The theory is that the participants develop more trust during their informal encounters and therefore relax their guard because of lessened fear rather than heightened external pressure.

Trainer

The trainer is the experienced educator within a sensitivity training group who serves as a resource to the group. Since the primary social learning data for the participants come from their own involvement with each other and with the group, the role of the sensitivity training group trainer is different from that of the usual role of an educator. He cannot assume the role of the expert, controlling and directing the group, without making the group dependent on him, thereby undercutting the experience of group responsibility and participation that is supposed to be the primary source of learning data. The trainer, therefore, is supposed to serve as a facilitator, helping the group to make its own decisions and to use its own resources. He does this by calling the attention of the group from time to time to the behavior being exhibited and the relationships emerging in the group and by helping the group to clarify its own goals and procedures. The trainer focuses primarily on here-and-now events and relationships that have been experienced within the life of the group.

LABORATORY TRAINING

Three different group activities are subsumed under laboratory training: (1) the sensitivity, personal encounter, or training group; (2) the task-oriented group involving structured group exercises aimed at teaching group function skills; and (3) intervention laboratories that are established for functional work groups in the community or industry. All three types of group activities may overlap or may be conducted separately.

T-Groups vs. Traditional Group Therapy

The sensitivity or T-group has received the most publicity, yet in itself it is the least innovative and may prove to be the least significant of the three group activities. The overlap between T-groups and group therapy is considerable, and at times they are indistinguishable. The problem is compounded by the fact that T-group leaders vary so much among themselves that one cannot really describe a model or typical T-group. One can only describe typical differences between T-groups and group therapy. In the early days, the distinctions between the two kinds of groups seemed fairly clear. But both the T-group and group psychotherapy have been changing over the past 20 years. Now one can cite examples of therapy groups that follow the T-group pattern and vice versa.

Participants. Traditionally, the T-group is designed for normal people with good ego defenses and good ego-coping skills who can readily learn from experience. The group therapy participant, on the other hand, is selected because he has deficient ego skills and an inability to learn from immediate experience.

Although T-groups may be made up of nonrelated persons, much of the T-group method has been concerned with groups of people who work together. Group therapy, in contrast, has traditionally been conducted with persons who have no extragroup relations.

Although T-groups and their variants are used as therapy groups for normals, therapy groups are also used for nonpatients, such as wives of alcoholics and parents of neurotic children. The distinction between education, training, and therapy becomes blurred, as does the distinction between patients and nonpatients.

T-group literature has long debated the merits of working with related vs. unrelated members. The issue seems to be resolving itself in terms of goals. T-groups aimed at personal growth are likely to be composed of unrelated members; T-groups aimed at work-group intervention are likely to be carefully composed of persons with interlocking work or community relationships. The same can be said of therapy groups. The traditional advantages of working in therapy with persons who have no relationship with each other are well-known. However, the recent development of family therapy has stressed the importance of working with people who are intimately related to each other. Similar emphasis has been made in therapeutic work with groups of married couples, in extended family therapy, and in social network therapy.

Goals. The T-group seeks to heighten interpersonal coping skills, sharpen interpersonal perception, and increase self-awareness and the authenticity of life experience. In group therapy, these goals may be seen as prerequisite learning that will enable the patient to work out his emotional problems.

But some T-group trainers disdain group process or group growth, for they see their goal as solely personal change. On the other hand, many group therapists see individual change as accomplished only through effective group process. Hence their therapeutic effort is directed at maximizing group process. In this instance, the T-group and the therapy group have reversed the traditional stances of both fields.

Leadership. In the T-group, the trainer or leader is seen as an expediter or catalyst who may become fairly assimilated into the group—at least in theory. In group therapy the leader is traditionally a therapist who not only catalyzes group process but also has a responsibility for making the group experience a therapeutic experience for each patient. The therapist can never fully shed his role, even if he attempts to do so.

But some T-group trainers see the leadership function as indispensable for effective T-group function—some of them acting in very authoritarian or autocratic roles that give little control to the T-group participants. Other trainers work toward total assimilation and actually give up leadership role and function. Likewise, in group therapy, therapists maintain various degrees of leadership, ranging from those who do individual therapy with a patient while the group watches to those therapists who deal only with group process and never with individual patients. Yet other therapists of existential persuasion move toward assimilation into their therapy groups, with virtually total abnegation of the therapeutic role. In addition, there have been a number of recent experiments with alternate sessions of therapy groups where the therapist is not present and even experiments with leaderless therapeutic groups.

Duration of the Group Activity. The T-group experience is short-term. Typically, T-groups meet for several hours daily for two weeks. On occasion, the experience has been lengthened to a month or more; in the other direction, there has been experimentation with one or two continuous group sessions—marathon-type experiences. The therapy group typically meets for one to two hours over a long period of time, even four or five years in extreme instances.

There has been increasing emphasis in the laboratory movement on follow-up work. Recent articles have suggested that the first T-group experience is only 20 per cent of the task, to be followed by many months of subsequent meetings with the group membership. On the other hand, some therapy groups are now being conducted on a short-time basis, such as crisis intervention groups, diagnostic intake groups, and marathon therapy groups.

Content of Discussion. The T-group has been seen primarily as an arena for the elaboration, analysis, and discussion of conscious thought and feeling, interpersonal interaction, and here-and-now issues. The therapy group has been concerned with the genetic there-and-then, the intrapersonal, the preconscious, fantasy, and dreams. The T-group focuses on "how we function in this group"; the therapy group focuses on "using that group to see how I function."

T-group emphasis on the conscious here-and-now has remained a major focus, but many trainers have expanded the repertoire of the T-group to the exploration of dreams, fantasy, and primary intrapersonal experiences as relevant to the major focus of the T-group. On the other hand, much of family therapy and group therapy has moved to a here-and-now focus and to an exploration of the interpersonal, with a de-emphasis of the genetic there-and-then and purely intrapersonal experience.

Other Facets of the Laboratory Movement

The laboratory movement has initiated and supported research on group dynamics, group leadership, and participant function that has contributed significantly to the general body of group theory. These data and related research techniques have not yet been substantially incorporated into the body of psychiatric theory; they may prove more germane than T-groups in the areas of group therapy, family therapy, and community psychiatry.

The laboratory movement has introduced a number of innovative techniques that may have therapeutic applicability. Examples include leaderless groups, group action techniques, role-playing, and psychodramatic methods. In addition, the emphasis on group process dynamics has had a direct and continuing influence on the group dynamics approach in group psychotherapy.

The development of structured laboratory exercises for task or action groups has considerable importance for community psychiatry. Very often the community mental health worker is called on to provide consultation to work groups in the community. Since the T-group is best known, there has been a trend toward turning group consultation in the community into pure T-group sensitivity exercises. Such exercises may be neither asked for, contracted for, nor relevant to the immediate tasks that face the community group. Group consultation is just beginning to be developed as a skill in community mental health work, and here the interests of the community mental health movement not only overlap but are at times identical with the group consultation concerns of the laboratory movement.

The laboratory movement innovations in the area of organizational intervention are also of direct relevance to community psychiatry. The corollary interest in mental health has been the milieu therapy movement. In mental health, the concerns have been more diagnostic than interventional. In fact, Schiff has pointed out that mental health professionals are notoriously untrained and unskilled for administrative intervention. Yet the concern for increasing the humaneness of social systems is remarkably similar to that of the laboratory movement. Recently Klein, Peck, Scheidlinger, and others have begun to develop some preliminary models of small-group interaction as basic for community mental health work and community intervention. Already a number of community mental health centers are using consultants from the laboratory movement to plan and implement community intervention programs.

The laboratory movement techniques, especially the T-group method, have been applied or modified for the training of mental health professionals. A number of university departments of psychiatry now provide some type of training group experience for their psychiatric residents, other professionals, and staff. In addition, many community mental health centers are introducing training group experiences for in-service training of staff, including indigenous workers and nonprofessionals.

A number of derivative methods of group therapy have been generated by the laboratory movement. Such methods in some areas have been sensationalized, have become fads, or have challenged therapeutic concepts. In any case, such methods merit careful professional presentation, investigation, and evaluation. An example is the attempt to appraise seriously the marathon group movement, described by Stoller.

Since the laboratory movement encompasses many types of people involved in powerful human-change activities, clinical consultation is needed. This is not to say that untoward reactions will necessarily reflect faulty procedures. It does suggest,

however, that the mental health professions may provide a real contribution to the laboratory movement by collaboration in responsible laboratory exercises. Also, clinical consultants may assist in anticipating and preventing untoward reactions. Finally, with the present variability in the laboratory movement, clinicians will encounter problems in which clinical care follows the onset of unfortunate experiences.

GOALS AND PURPOSES

Sensitivity training may range in goals between two extremes: (1) the mainly *agency-oriented* or *task-oriented* training, so structured as to enlighten the participants concerning more effective communication, problem-solving methods, and leadership patterns, primarily for the purpose of better influencing the environment, particularly other people; (2) the *communion-oriented* training, so structured as to give participants a variety of experiences, often nonverbal, which put each participant in touch with inhibited sensory and emotional facets of his personality, not for purposes of influencing people but for purposes of improving his capacity to be closer to others.

There is a wide range of task-oriented and communion-oriented sensitivity training groups and facilitators. Paradoxically, an apparently task-oriented group may develop a great sense of communion, and an apparently communion-oriented group may be completely sacrificed to the demands of the task, depending on the agenda of the participants and the leadership styles of the group facilitators.

Theoretically, a group of sales people being trained by the laboratory method to deliver the most effective sales pitch and to develop the best closing methods might be thought of as receiving sensitivity training in that the participants are being consciously sensitized as to how they come across as persuaders. They are being taught more effective communication; they are being made aware of the nuances of both their own and their customers' lexical, vocal, and kinesic means of communication. The primary goal of this awareness training is the control and change of other human. beings, generally, of course, without intent to harm. Yet an important side effect of this training may be the development of communion and a feeling of union among the participants without any conscious planning on the part of the trainer.

At the opposite end o° the continuum is the primarily sensory-experiential group, such as one practicing Esalen massage, in which either a one-to-one or a many-to-one sensory-emotional union is intended during a thorough and loving-encounter massage given or experienced by participants in the nude. In such an encounter the less cognitive material introduced (except for how-to explanations) the better. Here the communion of feeling between the masseur and the person being massaged and the internal experience of each are the goals of the sensitivity training.

Common to both types of groups, regardless of the amount of cognitive and sensory input, is the laboratory or experiential method—learning by doing, practicing, trying different ways of relating to other human beings, getting immediate feedback. Somewhere on the continuum toward the task-oriented side of center are the East-Coast-style T-groups as practiced originally by the National Training Laboratories— more agency, less communion. Toward the communion side of the continuum are the West-Coast-style T-groups as presented, for example, by the Institute of Industrial Relations at the University of California, Los Angeles (UCLA), and as increasingly practiced by NTL. Personal growth labs, ordinary marathons, encounter groups, and nude marathons theoretically fall more toward the communion end of the continuum.

The nude marathon is an example of the communion type of group experience; it is not intended as an orgy. The spirit of such an encounter group depends somewhat on the participants and a great deal on the motivation and agenda of the facilitator. The experience of being literally uncovered before one's peers may be a constructive emotional experience, an initially embarrassing and later satisfying self-revelation leading to self-acceptance of one's body, an antidote to repression, a deeply moving sharing of fears and anxieties, a motivation to care more for the body, an esthetic delight, or a sexually stimulating event. In short, it may mean different things to different people. Since the nude marathon is not, when ethically facilitated, primarily agency-oriented, the participants are likely to perceive each other not as sexual objects but as human beings with whom to experience mutual feelings, evaluations, and sensations as uncovered, natural people. Whether being in the nude aids the process of communion is not known. Proponents assert that it increases acceptance of one's body and that this acceptance is enhanced by open discussion and by sharing nonsexual ways of observing and experiencing another unclothed person.

The earliest NTL groups (basic skills training groups) were given considerable didactic material, particularly in group dynamics. But within several years a definite separation developed between the T-groups, whose subject matter became the interpersonal relations of the participants, and the A-groups, whose subject matter included skill in leadership, understanding group process, conflict management, and other agency-oriented functions. Since 1956 a movement in the NTL has tried to reintegrate the T-groups and A-groups within the laboratory. However, the clinical influence—that is, the interest in individual transactions—has been so strong on the West Coast that T-groups in that section of the country are hardly distinguishable from encounter groups. Sensitivity training as practiced at UCLA, for instance, is intended much more for the total growth of the individual—with his search for personal indentity, his ability to be open and authentic, his manner of giving and receiving love and affection—than for his intellectual understanding of group process and human relations problems.

Even so, it is interesting to note the differences that appear in the stated goals of sensitivity training groups conducted by the Institute of Industrial Relations at UCLA and those of marathon encounter groups. Some of the UCLA goals are stated very much in agency terms, such as:

to increase the *effectiveness* of our relations with others we need to know... what we do that is *useful* ... you may get a more accurate image of yourself as an *instrument* of interpersonal relations ... learn how to help groups *function* more *effectively*.

NTL literature, as in Bradford et al., also lists five objectives for participants of T-groups that are slanted toward task or agency orientation: (1) increased sensitivity to emotional reactions in one's self and in others; (2) better ability to understand the consequences of one's reactions; (3) better understanding and development of personal values and goals that are in line with democratic relationships; (4) development of cognitive concepts that can be used to link personal values to actions; and (5) better ways of integrating intentions and actions. Other goals in NTL members' writings include learning to diagnose individual, group, and organizational behavior; gaining self-insight; understanding the actions of people in groups; and learning what conditions facilitate or inhibit group functioning.

In contrast, the communion-oriented goals of encounter groups, as Gazda describes them, provide experiences for: (1) leveling with other members as equals; (2) developing trust and intimacy; (3) taking responsibility for one's own actions—realizing that one can make choices; (4) feeling free to express honest aggression explicitly and to share affection, loneliness, fear, and joy; (5) exploring new ways of being one's self and of discovering one's potential; (6) developing fully by facing up to crises, taking risks, and dropping protective roles.

Thus, the goals of sensitivity training run the gamut from better-performing beings to more social beings. In actuality, the training process, so long as it encourages authentic interaction in the here-and-now, is almost bound to increase communion regardless of the stated objectives (see Figure 1).

Many organizations—whether private businesses, school systems, the government, churches, or charitable institutions—encourage their personnel to take sensitivity training in the hope that they will function more effectively in the performance of their roles, and agency function. Although better functioning may be a result of the training for some participants, follow-up studies of T-groups show more communion-type changes, such as increased openness, flexibility, and interest in people. Both the personal learning and the organizational change that come from the T-group experience may be largely the result of increased self-acceptance and of lessened defensiveness in the participants.

TECHNIQUES

Regardless of its type, an experiential group devoted primarily to the actualization of the participants uses certain fundamental attitudes and processes to help its members grow.

The Facilitator

The facilitator or trainer is probably the single most influential factor in the group. But in a well-functioning sensitivity training group, it is difficult to distinguish

Cognitive and Perceptual				*Sensory and Emotional*	
AGENCY ├──────┼──────┼──────┼──────┼──────┤ COMMUNION					
Salesmanship training	Early NTL T-groups	Conflict management labs	More recent NTL T-groups	Experiential encounter groups and marathons	Esalen massage
Supervisory training		Leadership training labs	UCLA T-groups, church, and YMCA groups		

Figure 1. Sensitivity training goals cover a wide range, from agency-oriented to communion-oriented.

the facilitator from any other member. He interacts as an actual member of the group, although he has the additional responsibilities of seeing that the other members are supported or confronted when necessary and that the group process continues to offer the members opportunities for growth. He sets the example for emotional expressiveness by his spontaneous affective and intellectual behavior toward the other participants. This means that he cannot remain in an aloof role. Nor does he behave primarily as a teacher who gives didactic inputs. It is his own openness, his daring to reveal his own feelings and to confront others about theirs, his staying in the here-and-now that sets the tone for the group and encourages the participants to drop their stereotyped social roles.

Rather than enunciating rules for the group, at least at first, he illustrates through his own actions. Later on, if he were to formulate some principle that furthers the group process, he might announce the one major rule: no physical violence. And then he might add a few suggestions such as: (1) Express your feelings and actions in the here-and-now. (2) Talk directly *to* people in the group and not *about* them to the group. (3) Try to be specific about your feelings and perceptions and do not generalize; statements such as "Most people feel this way" and "All men are like that" are out. (4) Instead of asking the question "Why?" ask for feelings. "Why" makes people rationalize. (5) Try to make "I" statements in which you express your feelings and perceptions. These are much more effective than interpretations of your feelings and keep defensiveness from developing in others by blaming them with "you" statements. Example: "I'm furious with you!" rather than "You're too dumb to fight your way out of a paper bag!"

Intervention

Interventions unfreeze the attitudes and definitions of people toward themselves and others that block and inhibit their natural growth. In general, as Tate notes, there are two main types of intervention in the group: contrasting and substituting.

Contrasting interventions are usually verbal; substituting interventions are usually nonverbal. Contrasting interventions are cognitive; substituting interventions are experiential. Contrasting interventions involve a verbal comparison by a group member or the facilitator between what is actually happening in the group and what another member perceives is happening. Substituting interventions involve introducing experiences for group members from which they may grow. Contrasting interventions help a group member to understand so that he can improve his behavior. Substituting interventions may improve his behavior but not his understanding; what are substituted are experiences he has missed, usually in his early life, or has had infrequently in his development. Substituting interventions provide the participant with new information about himself. Contrasting interventions, on the other hand, usually provide no new information but help the participant become better at discriminating the veracity of information he possesses.

An example of contrasting intervention: A facilitator points out that, although a group member has just announced that he is happy, he still looks depressed. The group and the member then explore this incongruity together.

An example of substituting intervention: A facilitator leaves his seat and sits beside a group member who needs support.

Stimulation

Development is possible for everyone in four main areas of experience: cognition or thinking, perception, affect or emotion, and sensation or physical feeling at the sensory level. In this culture, thinking and perception are highly valued, and affect and sensation gain limited value, so sensitivity training groups, particularly encounter groups, are likely to encourage the experience of physical and emotional expression. Cognition and perception are typically agency-oriented, but affect and sensation are primarily associated with communion. To an agency-dominated person, emphasis on affect and sensation seem disruptive and threatening— something outside the realm of his control.

Some people are almost completely out of touch with their gentler feelings of affection or sadness, and others are not even aware of stronger affects, such as anger or elation. Most people are shy about the expression of certain feelings.

The facilitator can use some exercises or devices to stimulate experience in each of the four areas mentioned. But the greatest influence for change is the democratic and accepting attitude of the facilitator and the group rather than any gimmick or device. The exercises are intended only as boosters to launch the group or individual into the orbit of an experience. There are literally hundreds of experiential stimulators. Only a representative few are discussed below.

Cognition Stimulation. One of the simplest of the diagrams that explain the purpose of sensitivity training is the Johari Window, so-called because it is the brain-child of Joseph Luft (Jo) and Harrington Ingham (Hari).

The diagram (see Figure 2) indicates that one's public self is that part known both to oneself and to others; that the hidden self, representing what one does not divulge, is known to oneself but not to others; that the blind self is a part known to others but not to oneself (for example, how one looks or sounds to others); and that one's undeveloped potential is unknown both to others and to oneself. In sensitivity training, the participants attempt to expand their public selves by purposely taking the risk of revealing some of their hidden selves. There is also the hope that, through honest feedback from others in the group, each participant's blind self will become smaller. The dotted lines in the diagram represent

	Known to Self	Not Known to Self
Known to Others	Public Self	Blind Self
Not Known to Others	Hidden Self	Unknown or Undeveloped Potential

Figure 2. The Johari Window is used to explain the purpose of sensitivity training in cognitive terms.

the new boundaries of the public self as a result of group interaction. In the process, a small part of the undeveloped potential, represented in the diagram at X, will become available to each group member. When group participants ask the facilitator for some intellectual structuring of the encounter process, this diagram is helpful.

Sometimes simple explanations of interpersonal exchanges can become meaningful when put in terms of the Parent, Adult, and Child of Berne's transactional analysis, as explained by Harris. By encouraging a group member to question the values and assumptions of the critical or ignoring Parent and the overly rebellious, indulged, or adjusted Child, the facilitator can often make astoundingly good sense for that group member out of an apparently complicated interpersonal or intrapersonal situation.

Other cognitive inputs by the facilitator may include requesting group members to reveal their hidden agenda and discuss various other aspects of group dynamics. The introduction of cognitive inputs is probably best reserved until such inputs can be used to clarify an immediate group experience. If presented without reference to group experiences, they have little meaning.

Perception Stimulation. One of the best devices to enlarge one's perception is role-playing, which can be done in a number of ways. One can, for example, follow Shapiro's theory of a number of subselves in the individual—reminiscent of Federn's 1943 concept of multiple ego states in every person—and encourage a member who is having an intrapersonal conflict to role-play it by himself (the facilitator acting as coach), using several chairs to represent the selves in conflict and moving from one chair to another as he speaks extemporaneously for each subself. Gestalt therapy methods also fit this category of perceptual expansion. Role-training is a psychodramatic technique in which, with the help of other group members, one can play out a conflicted relationship, ask others to play the same scene—handling it as they perceive it—and then try out some of the suggested solutions.

In recent years videotape has allowed

participants to see as well as hear themselves in social action. Wherever this device is used, it reveals its great value for self-revelation.

A favorite device for perceptual enlightenment is the group-on-group technique. This consists in having one half of the T-group observe the other half of the group in interaction. Each person in the observing group chooses a partner to watch in the interacting group. Group A, the first half of the T-group to interact, works together for 20 to 30 minutes while being observed by Group B. Then Group B feeds back information to Group A about what Group B observed about both individual and group behavior and process. After that, each member of Group A joins his observer from Group B for five minutes, and the observer feeds back to the Group A member whatever he can of his (A's) behavior, i.e., A's blind self. Then Group B, the other half of the T-group, interacts while Group A observes, and the feedback process is reversed. This technique is generally most effective early in the life of the group.

Having each member of the group draw a picture of the group with crayons on large pieces of paper is a technique for opening up a great deal of interpersonal perception. The group members may be represented symbolically or actually. The participants, working simultaneously, are given about 20 minutes to draw the group and then each speaks in turn, showing his drawing and telling how he perceives each member and why he represented each as he did.

Affect Stimulation. The general verbal techniques used by the facilitator to stimulate affect are to keep asking participants for feelings rather than thoughts and to serve as a model by showing his own feelings. An attitude of unconditional acceptance and the practice of active listening for feelings as well as for content encourage the expression of affect.

If a member starts to cry, a sympathetic participant may shut off the crying member's feelings too quickly by moving in right away with the Kleenex or a physically comforting gesture. It is often better to let the weeping person experience his sadness in depth before making the comforting gesture.

Finney has developed a verbal method of breaking through the ideational shield into affective states. In this method, which Finney calls "say it again," the facilitator sits in front of a group member, takes his hands, and asks him how he feels. As the member begins to talk, the facilitator makes him repeat emotional phrases by telling him, "Say it again," sometimes feeding him what he intuitively senses would be appropriate phrases, which the group member may feel free to repeat or reject. By having the group member talk constantly on a feeling level, the facilitator frequently breaches the barrier to affect, and much emotion pours out.

Somewhat similar is a technique derived from Janov, in which the group member is encouraged to imagine himself as a child and to call his daddy or mommy for help. Frequently, much repressed feeling comes out under such circumstances.

Both the facilitator and the group members are expected to feel free to move around in the group and to show affection and empathy either physically or verbally. They should feel free to care physically for each other by touching, taking a person's hand, putting their arms around him. All these physical methods of communicating are of the substitution type and, as such, increase access to or expression of a group member's blocked-out or limited experiential data.

A device that aids in releasing anger is pillow-beating or mattress-pounding. By encouraging a group member who is evidently repressing his rage to beat up a hated introject in the form of a pillow, much relief may accrue to him, especially when he acts with the blessings of the group.

By such nonverbal expression, a group member is often able to bypass inhibitions that have hindered his perception of his emotional self from an early age. The affect that emerges is often painful at first, but the relief is worth the effort.

Sensation Stimulation. Gestalt therapy has particularly emphasized getting in touch with the senses in order to function fully as a person. Perls has a famous dictum:

You must lose your mind to come to your senses.

The child in each person can be revived joyously if he allows himself to re-experience childlike modes of relating. Perls, Hefferline, and Goodman have developed special exercises to revive the senses of taste, touch, smell, sight, and sound. Encounter groups have taken these and similar experiential exercises into their repertoire of antirepression devices. In one exercise to help revive the sensation of taste, the group members eat a silent meal together, concentrating on the food, its taste, and its texture. Smelling various substances while blindfolded or paying attention to the smells of the earth, grass, flowers, and trees may make group members feel more alive again by re-establishing their union with nature, a union often repressed from childhood.

An artist may make a great contribution to the experience of a group by pointing out different designs, shadings, colors, and textures in the environment or by sitting in a group and drawing his impressions of members, their poses, and their interactions and then discussing his perceptions with the group. Group members often benefit from being encouraged to look at each other, to consider carefully which side of another person's face seems more dominant, to examine the texture of someone's skin.

With eyes closed, the group members may listen to music of different sorts; or they may go out into the woods in the quiet of an early morning, with each one sitting by himself for half an hour, listening to the sounds of nature, and tuning in on his own feelings. After this solitary experience, the group members come together again and share.

Touching, of course, is one of the most potent of all contacts—one of the first experienced by infants. It is rare that a touch fails to elicit a response from a group member. A simple but effective exercise in touch stimulation consists of one person's standing behind another and, at a signal from the person in front (a partly raised arm, for example), touching that person with both hands on the head. This action is repeated three times. The person doing the touching tries to imagine a flow of energy from him through his hands and into the person in front of him. When several people take turns touching another this way, great differences become apparent to the person being touched, and he usually feels that he knows each toucher much better from this contact. If this exercise is tried, (1) the person being touched must keep his eyes closed; (2) the person touching must do nothing but touch (he must not, for example, give a massage); (3) the touching must be done completely in silence; and (4) it must be done unhurriedly.

Another simple exercise in learning about another person through touch is to sit or stand in front of him, place your palms flat against his in a patty-cake gesture, and then move your hands together with his in any way that suits the mutual feeling of the partners. Sometimes this exercise results in aggressive pushing in a power play, sometimes in a delicate hand-dance, sometimes in a joking, funny, or hilarious encounter. As with other nonverbal exercises, this one is done without talking.

A great deal of the kinesthetic sense may be experienced in the pushing, wrestling, hand-wrestling, bio-energetic exercises of Lowen and by lifting and rocking group members or passing them around in the inside of a tight circle formed by the group. A well-known version of this last technique is described by Schutz as roll and rock. In this exercise, the facilitator or group having decided that a member needs a special kind of affection, the group forms a tight circle with the subject inside. Standing with eyes closed, he is rolled around in a circular motion from one person to another in the group while he relaxes against the tight circle, trusting the group to support him. After a short period of this rolling, the group members gently help the subject lie down in the center of the circle. Then they carefully pick him up and, holding him at their chest height, rock him slowly back and forth about a dozen times. They then lower him gently to the floor and either leave him there with his eyes closed for several minutes until he has completely absorbed the experience or sit beside him, all continuing to touch him until he gradually rejoins them from his reverie. The whole exercise, usually an emotionally moving experience for all participants, is completely nonverbal.

Nonverbal Techniques for Special Situations

Some nonverbal exercises are peculiarly helpful for group members who need to experience and fulfill directly, more than to talk about, some deeply personal need.

The Outsider. He seems to stay aloof from the group, he does not join in, he does not respond to encouragement by the group to participate. Particularly—but not necessarily—if he himself admits to feeling left out, the following exercise can be explained to him, and the group can then carry it out without words.

The group forms a very tight circle, with arms locked around each other. The outsider is placed physically outside of the circle and is told that he must break through to the center in any way he chooses, except that he may not physically hurt anyone. The group cohesiveness ensures his having to work hard to achieve his getting in.

The Nontruster. Like the roll-and-rock exercise described above, several simple experiences may become turning points in the nontruster's group life. In one, the subject, eyes closed, stands 18 inches or more in front of someone strong enough to support him. Facing away from this partner, at a signal or when he and his partner are ready, he falls backward into the arms of his catcher, who must, of course, not let him down. After several instances of giving himself in this vulnerable way to another person, the nontruster is much more likely to allow himself to be vulnerable in other ways with the group.

Another exercise that develops trust is the blind walk, in which one person, eyes closed, is led by his partner through a house, outside into the garden, up and down steps, and so forth. The nontruster completely relies on his partner not to let him trip or hurt himself. This exercise is particularly helpful for people who are anxious about being dependent or submissive.

The Timid Person. A humorous and noisy exercise to use when someone in the group speaks timidly or seems unable to show aggression or self-assertion is the karate-chop experience. In this exercise, the facilitator or an assertive group member stands facing the timid person, and the two pretend to be karate antagonists, making fake karate chops and kicks at each other, without touching but yelling the karate "Hai!" as loudly as possible with each chop. The group vocally encourages the timid one to yell more loudly, to be "vicious," and to let go. The usual result of such an exercise is increased acceptance by the timid person of his aggressiveness.

General Group Inhibition or Warm-up. A series of two- to four-minute non-verbal exercises help in warming up a cold group. The following are a few suggestions:

1. The group members choose partners. One rolls up in a ball on the floor, and his partner unravels him while he resists strongly. Then the partners reverse roles.

2. One partner plays dead and takes on the waxy flexibility of the catatonic. The other partner places him in different positions, finally putting him in an appropriate rest-in-peace position.

3. Partners, lying on their stomachs and facing each other, arm-wrestle while making great grunts and groans of anguish.

4. Partners sit on the floor back to back, arms engaged, and try to "talk" with their backs.

5. Partners sit facing each other, eyes closed, and explore each other's hands, arms, faces, necks. Or they "talk" with their hands.

6. Partners lie with heads on each other's shoulders, bodies at 180 degrees to each other, eyes closed, listening to music while each has a fantasy about the other. When the music stops, they share their fantasies, first with each other and then with the group.

After each of these exercises, the partners talk to each other about their experiences. During the exercise itself, however, no words are said, although appropriate sounds are permissible.

Sociometric Feedback. The following problem is posed to the group:

All of you have been together on a ship that has just sunk. You [point to one member] have just found a small life raft capable of holding three other people. Ahead is an island on which you can live fairly comfortably; but, because it is out of the shipping lanes, you will have to be there at least six months. What three other people in this group will you ask to join you on the raft, row to the island, and live there together? What do you expect of them during that six-month period? [Build in your own questions.]

Each person in the group announces his choices and talks about his decision with the group. Often someone is left out by everyone else. This can be turned into a growth experience for the person left out as he discusses his feelings and gets honest feedback from the group about why he was avoided. The difficulties and style of choosing companions with whom to live become sources of confrontation and feedback.

Group Cohesiveness and Humor. This exercise is a delightful version of the island fantasy, particularly after the group has become fairly cohesive and needs a release from tension. The group members lie on the floor in a close circle, with their heads as the axis in the center, bodies extending out, eyes closed. They are asked to have a fantasy about their life together on a lush tropical island, where food, water, and weather are no problems. Once someone starts the fantasy, each person spontaneously adds whatever occurs to him. The project usually becomes a warm, affectionate, sometimes moving, often hilarious experience of joy, humor, and closeness. The facilitator may bring the exercise to a close by some appropriate fantasy, such as the group's being picked up by a passing ship. Very often no one wants to leave the island.

TECHNICAL AND POLICY ISSUES

Are there conflicting goals in sensitivity training? In trying to conceptualize the wide range of practices subsumed under the name of sensitivity training and to evaluate the meaning of research on the T-group process one may find the terms "agency" and "communion" helpful. Bakan used these terms

to characterize two fundamental modalities in the existence of living forms, *agency* for the existence of an organism as an individual, and *communion* for the participation of the individual in some larger organism of which the individual is a part.

Agency is manifested by protecting, asserting, and expanding the self; by remaining separate and alone; by mastery, control, and affecting people and things; by repression of innovative and spontaneous thought and emotion except in the service of mastery; by the accumulation of wealth and possessions; by achievement of status and power. In our society one's place in the pecking order is determined by how successfully he functions in the realm of achievement. Western culture is a monument to the success of the agency use of human energy. The purpose of agency is to relieve one's existential anxiety by keeping busy controlling the environment.

Communion, on the other hand, is manifested by the experience of openness and nondefensiveness; by joining with others; by contact—physical, intellectual, emotional; by removal or lack of repression, especially inhibition of feelings. The purpose of communion is to experience intimacy with some other living thing.

Sensitivity training was developed originally to help people function more effectively as team members in task groups either in businesses or in institutions, to help them understand and control group processes, and to help them become aware of their impact on other people. The learning was intended to be task-oriented, to achieve a goal. However, an important by-product of the earliest T-groups was the experience of communion, an experience so satisfying that participants began to resent the introduction of agency-oriented theoretical verbal inputs. So other groups, A-groups, were set up for the purpose of teaching specific task-oriented interpersonal skills.

The need for communion evidenced by the early sensitivity training group participants was to become a *Zeitgeist*. It is still a growing spirit in this country and in the world, an antiagency movement participated in by hippies, students, and drug-users of all descriptions as well as staid and well-functioning adults. The encounter group, the experiential group, the group that is more communion-oriented than agency-oriented answers the need of the middle-class to mitigate agency with communion and sometimes to discard agency almost completely. Growth centers such as Esalen and Kairos in California and Aureon Institute in the East are mainly supported by middle-class seekers of communion. Rock festivals such as Woodstock and Newport allow the younger generation to participate in communion. It is interesting to note that the earlier sources of communion—the church, fraternal organizations, and the family—have lost some of their ascendancy as means of providing collaborative experiences. Many churches have now incorporated sensitivity training in an effort to regain their original communion function.

The main value of sensitivity training, regardless of its justification through the rationale of its task-oriented function, may quite possibly be that it allows participants to experience communion. Thus, in considering research that would support sensitivity training as worth its salt from an agency viewpoint, one should not be too surprised to find that (1) most facilitators of sensitivity training groups are not enthusiastic research people, preferring instead to participate in the experience itself, and (2) a good deal of research ends up with findings of communion-oriented functions. For example, the sensitivity-trained people show increased openness, flexibility, and ease in interpersonal relationships, although they may not show a concomitant increase in such agency functions as influencing people, interest in achieving, and completing a task. The question, "How valuable is sensitivity training?" depends on the philosophical value system of the questioner. To an agency-oriented questioner or researcher, the T-group must result in more effective functioning, in an agency sense, before he will consider it valuable. To the communion-oriented questioner—and there are fewer of these in American culture—the T-group should result in more contact, more participation, more love for one's fellow man. Except in some almost completely nonverbal encounter groups, sensitivity training groups blend agency and communion, with a steadily growing surge toward communion.

Exploitation

If the intensive group experience is essentially a leaderless group, how can the group handle skillful participants who are covertly exploitative? An ethic is often promulgated in a training group that the members can be trusted and that there need not be a leader. There is no certainty that a group-appointed leader has any way of checking and correcting deep-seated neurotic conflicts or blind spots or of refraining from forcing his own private value judgments or orientations on the other group members. If enough of the members in a group are honest, not corrupt, and altruistic, they can check the exploitative and sociopathic participant in his attempt to take over the group and have them do his bidding. But groups that invite people to join them in practicing hostile and aggressive behavior with one another may attract persons who, in everyday life, specialize and excel in these kinds of human behavior. There is no way of guaranteeing that the milder or more inhibited member who hopes to learn how to become more assertive by joining such a group will not be completely squelched or encouraged to behave in a socially destructive manner, not only in the group but outside the group.

Sociopaths

How can a training group handle sociopaths, especially if they predominate in the group? There is no evidence that intensive group experiences change the moral or ethical behavior of a person. Groups that are constituted principally of socially destructive or sociopathic people are likely to behave collectively like their participants. The mass effect of such a group on an individual participant who has a sense of group belongingness or social responsibility will be a disruptive one.

Group Attention

Does the squeaky wheel tend to get the attention in training groups? Outspoken, socially proficient people tend to fare best in intensive group experiences, for there are social rewards for articulate and persuasive verbal communication. The reticent member is generally encouraged to speak up, to assert himself, to open up. An increase in group pressure is brought to bear on silent members. This approach sometimes has a salutary effect. An alert group leader or group participants who seriously feel concern for nonsqueaky people bring out such members, often in a sympathetic and reassuring way, but this happy eventuality cannot be guaranteed.

Leadership

Do persons who win leadership roles in training and action groups really constitute the best leaders? This question opens a whole bag of questions about leadership, its functions, its goals, and its purposes. Probably people who win leadership roles in intensive group experiences and maintain such leadership roles win them by acclaim or by consensus; otherwise, they are not tolerated for a prolonged time in an on-going group process. Such persons may not necessarily be the best leaders for the group that has permitted them the experience of taking a leadership role or for groups outside the specific group experience in which they have just participated. Obviously, leadership has many different functions and goals. Strong leadership may be exerted by someone who is not actively participating in the group, as, for example, by someone who has written a drama or a novel or an essay that has major and long-continuing effects on individual and group behavior. Moreover, leadership may be manifested in many ways other than by articulate verbal interaction—for example, by public self-defeating behavior, suicide, standing on a high building and threatening to jump, walking nude down the street, robbing a bank. The roles and functions of leadership need more careful study and explication before one can authoritatively and readily answer the question raised above.

Sociopathic Leadership. What about ensuring against sociopathic leadership? This is a problem! There is no clearly identifiable professional or institutional base for the recruitment, training, and practice of laboratory practitioners. Trainers are recruited from a variety of disciplines, backgrounds, and experiences. Their training is varied. Their practice is extremely variable. Within the laboratory movement this variability is perceived both as a strength and as a weakness—but it does present problems. Without an identifiable discipline, there are no norms for performance, no explicit forms for evaluation. Instead, shifting social sanctions support or undermine the context of training laboratory practice. The lack of disciplinary identity also presents problems in terms of clinical issues. The laboratory movement has yet to acquire a professional status. The issues confronting professionalization are complex, for the movement does not have a relatively uniform ideological base, nor are its goals confined to a narrow range of clinical or organizational concerns. Consequently, the laboratory movement has continued to develop apart from more structured and institutionalized concerns of university departments, well-delineated research fields, and the clinical professions. Schools of education and schools of business administration represent the major sources of institutional and professional support.

Strong Leadership. If one is a participant in a group with a strong, professionally trained leader, how does one distinguish the group process from group therapy? As noted earlier, the boundaries between the training group and the traditional therapy group are becoming blurred. This blurring of distinctions can have some serious consequences for some group participants. In contrast to most psychotherapies in which a patient asks to be changed in some respect—to be relieved of distressing symptoms or what he regards as personality or behavioral deficiencies—the training group participant does not regularly frame his goals in such terms. Rather, he wants to learn about groups, his behavior in groups, and how to improve his functioning in groups. When the training group is under way, many training group participants find that they are being induced to change in ways they did not anticipate. They find that the trainer and various group members are calling on them to stop certain ways of behaving, talking, thinking, and feeling, and that different ways of behaving are being prescribed. The pressure of the group and trainer may not necessarily be in the same direction. Or the trainer's silence may mistakenly be taken as a sanction, endorsement, or recommendation for behavioral change made by one participant with regard to another. Some of the T-group participants may become seriously upset under such pressure to alter their identity, especially when they do not recognize this identity as a problem or difficulty and when they have not even thought of trying to modify some aspects of their identity.

Countertransference. How about clearing adverse countertransference or seriously biased value judgments from trainers or facilitators? There is at present no professionally organized way of doing so. Indeed, more and more responsible professionals agree that some program of training is needed to minimize arbitrary, narrowly judgmental, personal value orientations of the group leader. Gottschalk and Pattison have stated:

An ethic is often promulgated in a T-group that the group should be trusted and can be trusted. There is an implication, moreover, that the trainers in a T-group have not only the sanction and blessing but the stamp of approval of the National Training Laboratories [or some other sponsoring organization] as wise, experienced teachers of group dynamics, counselors, and emotionally well-adjusted individuals.

Unfortunately, just as the distortions of the group members enter into the group processes, the unresolved emotional conflicts and the private value judgments of the T-group trainers may obtrude themselves into the group process. These colorful contributions to the group activities need not in themselves be a cause for concern, for such is life. But a participant in the T-group has the idea, somehow, that the group-appointed trainer, as any other group-appointed leader, has some way of checking and correcting deep-seated neurotic conflicts or blind spots or refraining from enforcing his own private value judgments or orientations, unless invited to do so, on the other group members. But there is apparently as yet no satisfactory system for such check-outs for trainers. Few have ever had a personal psychoanalysis, so that this avenue is not available for repeatedly exploring pathological countertransference reactions or other neurotically determined attitudes or behavior.

Each trainer goes through [one or] several T-groups himself. This procedure may select

conceivably the more extroverted, self-confident, and socially proficient individuals but guarantees nothing about the trainer's emotional and intellectual acumen with respect to recognizing and preventing the development of disruptive emotional breakdowns in T-group members or his ability to examine such developments critically and discover his role in permitting or inciting them to occur.

Trainers for the most part are free to hold any theoretical orientation they choose. The influence of theoretical orientation on trainer behavior and the relative merits of different theoretical orientations are largely empirical questions that will require considerable research and time to resolve. It is therefore useless to debate such issues here.*

Authenticity

Regardless of the type or caliber of leadership and intensive group experience, what is authenticity with respect to personality? A key goal of all laboratory training has been called authenticity in interpersonal relations. This term signifies a relationship that enables each person to feel free to be himself and communicate openly with himself and others. Authentic, in this sense, refers to conscious or readily accessible emotions and thoughts and not to those that are unconscious and, hence, not easily available to awareness. Thus, a person could be encouraged to be more open and express some usually withheld hostility. This change could be labeled as becoming more authentic from the viewpoint of laboratory training, but underlying this hostility might be discovered, possibly through psychoanalytic therapy, more valid emotional love and yearning for others but anxiety over revealing it. The hostile emotion would then be a defensive emotion—the psychological mechanism of turning into the opposite. Though authentic, in the sense of being part of the individual's personality facade or character armor, the hostility would not typify the deeper, basic emotional need of the person.

Authenticity relates in part to what one is really like behind one's facade. One's facade, however, is also very much a part of oneself, and many people fail to realize that this

* From *The American Journal of Psychiatry*, volume 126, pages 823–839, 1969. © 1969, the American Psychiatric Association.

facade was socially acquired and need not, in every respect, be ready for the rubbish heap. Characteristic ways of relating to one another may be socially useful and reflect conventional ways that human beings, in Western culture, relate to and communicate with one another. Many of these traits can be so inflexible and ritualized that the more spontaneous, emotion-laden, or healthy impulsive aspects of a person are never permitted to appear. On the other hand, indiscriminate, sensual, aggressive, disorganized, and chaotic thinking or other kinds of expressive behavior are not necessarily more authentic.

Defenses

Why call one's facade necessarily defensive? One's characteristic way of relating to people does, indeed, sometimes result from previous painful experiences with other human beings and, hence, reflects guardedness, fear of closeness or intimacy, fear of being spontaneous, and so forth. The problem is that many people in everyday life may well reinforce one's guardedness and self-protective behavior. It is, in the writers' opinion, a serious error for therapists and trainers involved in intensive group experiences to blithely assume that the world, and hence all the groups in which one may be involved, is populated with friendly, loving, protective, sympathetic, altruistic people. Persons who are learning about how they function in groups need not go through the painful rediscovery that some people in groups are ready and poised to hurt them, possibly because that is the only way such hostile people know how to relate to people, possibly because they feel the best defense is a good offense. Many group leaders, extrapolating from psychoanalytic psychiatry, believe that psychological mechanisms and adaptive behavior can routinely be regarded as defensive and must be dismantled. Such was never done indiscriminately in psychoanalytic practice, and there are no advantages in proceeding in such a fashion outside the psychoanalytic process.

Intimacy

With strangers, what are the limits, if any, of intimacy? Is opening one's innermost feelings to strangers more authentic, more healthy, more characteristic of adjustment? Many of the sensitivity and encounter group and marathon group programs developing in the United States, which is relatively affluent and where most people can meet such physical needs as shelter and food, now emphasize the need to overcome what is perceived as a remaining psychosocial deficiency of existence, namely, loneliness and alienation. These programs emphasize that everyone's existence will automatically become more meaningful if stranger-anxiety is immediately and continuously dispelled and if everyone becomes completely intimate with anyone encountered. One is almost in the position of a devil's advocate if he asks whether there are limits to the notion that everyone should be equally intimate with everyone else and whether preference for limiting intimacy to a few others and for situations of privacy is necessarily deviant. These issues need to be explored during the group process.

CLINICAL ASPECTS

UCLA T-Group

The format of the UCLA T-group experience for business and professional people consists of two weekends at the university conference center on the shore of a lake. Between the weekends there are five weekly meetings consisting of dinner followed by a three-and-a-half-hour T-group session. On each of the weekends, about 100 participants arrive at the conference center before five o'clock Friday afternoon. They register and then relax at the self-service, unofficial bar. Nearly all the participants are strangers to each other.

After dinner comes the first session, a short orientation to the laboratory. Schedules are handed out, facilitators are introduced, and the goals of the laboratory are briefly stated.

After this brief introduction, the T-groups of 15 or 16 persons each go off to their meeting rooms, which are living rooms or bedrooms in motel-type cottages. Chairs and sofas are always arranged in a circle so that everyone can communicate with the whole group. The facilitator usually passes out stiff five-inch by eight-inch cards on which the participants print their first names. They set the cards in front of them on the floor or a coffee table. Facilitator styles vary, but often at this point the leader makes a short introduction, in which he states that the group will be largely unstructured, with no set agenda.

He usually states or implies that the participants will probably learn more from discussing the relationships and process within the group itself (here-and-now data) than from discussing outside activities (there-and-then data). He then defaults as leader, leaving the participants to their own devices as to how to become a group.

Each participant uses his own strategies in this process of group formation and, as time goes on, becomes aware of his own feelings and the feelings of others, partly by being encouraged to attend to his own inner processes and partly by feedback from other group members. He becomes aware of the problem of communication, of how little he and others actually listen with involvement, of how much they misinterpret. He also becomes aware of the real differences in the needs of members, their goals, and their ways of approaching problems.

Feedback and confrontation with other group members give a person an increased awareness of his own impact on others. The trainer often models feedback by giving members his own genuine reaction to their behavior, particularly in terms of his feelings.

The first session ends after two hours when the participants return to the bar, go to their rooms, relax in the village, or whatever.

During the next day, there are morning, afternoon, and evening sessions, with a two-hour break after lunch for informal walks, sports, meetings, rest, and relaxation. From time to time, as the facilitator deems it appropriate, he may introduce nonverbal exercises as interventions, but the main process is verbal interaction. As the weekend progresses, the interaction moves perceptibly from superficial role relationships—with the emphasis on cognitive, generalized, there-and-then topics—to genuine openness and the expression of emotion shared by group members with each other in here-and-now interaction. The first weekend concludes after the Sunday morning session and lunch.

During the next five weeks, each small group meets separately for dinner and a three-hour session (exclusive of dinner) with its facilitator and continues its work of learning less-defensive relationships from its own experience. The culmination of the course comes on the final weekend, which is structured like the first but has a very different feeling because of the greatly increased depth of openness and affection among the participants. The sensitivity training officially ends after the final Sunday morning sessions, although many groups continue to meet informally for some time, and some even engage their facilitator for a while.

NTL groups often meet for continuous periods of one or two full weeks rather than being spaced over a period of two weekends with an intervening five weeks of dinner meetings, as is the custom at UCLA.

Theory Sessions

Experience in the group precedes the introduction of theory. This is a basic principle of laboratory training. Yet raw experience without intellectual understanding may not produce learning that is useful and that can be taken from the laboratory to a person's outside life. In an NTL sensitivity training group, theory sessions are set up at varying intervals, and information is given on such topics as group members, problem-solving in groups, and styles of presenting oneself to others.

UCLA groups often truncate or skip theory sessions. But neither the T-group nor the theory session is complete without the other, according to NTL belief.

Focused Exercises

Exercises that highlight some specific behavior are sometimes introduced into the T-group. In standard sensitivity training, these exercises are likely to be carried out verbally and to consist of practice in various ways of communicating (one-way vs. two-way), leading groups, role-playing, role training, managing conflict, observing others, and observing group process. In the less cognitively structured encounter groups, the facilitator is likely to introduce at appropriate times many nonverbal exercises to stimulate and work through sensations and feelings of participants. In any case, after such an exercise, the group members are usually asked to share their experiences, whether they joined in actively or passively.

Informal Contacts

Some of the most valuable happenings associated with the laboratory method are the frequent informal contacts between different members and facilitators outside the scheduled sessions. During these informal meetings, much back-home information is shared, thus contributing to the data bank of shared knowledge between members through which they find more feelings and interests in common. The bonds of friendship established informally enhance the authenticity developing in the T-group. Late evening bull sessions between participants are considered of great value.

RESEARCH

Outcome Research

Evaluation of the effects of any change agent is difficult, as exemplified by the fact that many books and papers are written on how to do psychotherapy but relatively few on the evaluation of its effects. The relative paucity of good research into the outcome of psychotherapy has been occasioned by problems of research design, the setting up of adequate controls, and lack of interest of many psychotherapists in such research. On the other hand, evaluative research of the effects of psychoactive pharmacological agents is much more common and well-developed, probably because the use of such therapeutic agents involves the participation of the medical profession and the possibility of malpractice suits against either the physician who prescribes such drugs or the pharmaceutical company that manufactures and develops them. Pressure to pursue evaluative research into the effects of training groups is minimal because no profession monopolizes the administration of such procedures, because of the unresolved question of whether such techniques constitute education more than therapy, and because the majority of encounter group facilitators and trainers prefer to avoid doing such research. In fact, most of these practitioners scorn the up-tight investigator who seeks objective evidence of

change; instead, they readily accept the testimonials of growing numbers of people who have attended such groups.

Research into the effectiveness of T-groups involves all the ramifications and problems of psychotherapy research. Many factors are known to influence behavioral and attitudinal changes in psychotherapy research. First, of all, the goals of psychotherapy itself are important. These goals differ considerably with different psychotherapy programs. For example, the psychotherapeutic program that has as its major aim an increase in the emotions experienced by an obsessive-compulsive patient will, obviously, require assessment procedures or measures different from those used for the psychotherapeutic program that aims to decrease a person's emotions or his capacity for emotional arousal. A psychotherapeutic program that seeks a change in a complex character trait requires an evaluative measure different from that needed by the psychotherapeutic procedure that aims to help a person over an immediate crisis reaction. So, in considering the evaluative research with various kinds of training groups, one must attempt to enumerate the goals of such group activities.

The therapist's personality, it has been well established, may influence the outcome of treatment. The effects of the psychotherapist's personality on the outcome of treatment has been studied most thoroughly and for many years by such psychoanalysts as Orr and more recently by such nondirective or client-centered therapists as Truax and Carkhuff, Bergin, and Shlien and Zimring. These studies indicate that the attitude and personality of the therapist does influence the immediate and often subsequent course of psychotherapy and that some psychotherapists regularly achieve patient improvement and others achieve patient worsening. Even in five-minute interviews, where standardized instructions for eliciting speech from the subjects are read and where the interviewer is silent during this time and maintains an unreactive facial expression, a content analysis of the subject's verbal behavior has shown significantly greater amounts of anxiety and hostility with some interviewers than with others (Gottschalk and Gleser, 1969).

Apart from the personality of the therapist or the patient, the therapeutic agent, whether psychoactive drug or psychological procedure, can be influenced by a person's mental set about the expected effect. For example, in a double-blind study, Gottschalk et al. (1968) noted that the written statements that subjects could expect to feel more peppy and energetic after ingesting a pill resulted in significant increases in achievement strivings, as measured by a content analysis procedure, whether or not the subjects received a placebo, 100 mg. of secobarbital, or 10 mg. of dextroamphetamine. The effects of the dextroamphetamine and the induced mental set were additive and resulted in greater achievement-striving scores when the drug and mental set were given together than when introduced separately.

Furthermore, psychopharmacological research on the effects of psychoactive drugs shows solid evidence that the socioeconomic class of patients can influence the effects of any one psychoactive pharmacological agent. For instance, Rickels et al. found that placebo responses are poorer and psychoactive drug responses are better in middle-class, neurotic, general practice patients; the reverse is true for lower-class, neurotic, psychiatric clinic patients. Higher-class patients, in response to tranquilizers and sedatives, complain more about drowsiness than do lower-class patients, who complain more about stimulation and autonomic nervous system side effects. If such factors are known to influence the outcome in instances where the therapeutic agent (a drug) is standardizable, certainly these same factors may be involved in outcome research of training groups, where it is impossible to standardize the therapeutic agent.

Improved Group Functioning. Process-centered groups have as one of their major goals the training of participants to experience and to recognize group dynamics and their own contribution to group dynamics. A test of such training is its practical application in improving the work of task-oriented groups at home. Campbell and Dunnette, after reviewing the literature in this area, concluded that there is only inconclusive evidence that T-group training has positive utility for organizational functioning. Stock, in her review, suggested that people from different kinds of organizations with different kinds of motivations and with different kinds of training group experiences learn different things in such groups and, hence, carry back to their organizations different potentials for attitudinal change. Thus, the final effect on the back-home group is likely to be varied.

Better Socialization and Interpersonal Relations. A number of reports claim to show that experience in T-groups and encounter groups produces increased skills in communication, independence, flexibility, self-awareness, and sensitivity to the feelings of others. Not only are these changes observed in the group, but they are apparently maintained in the back-home setting. Comparisons of persons who have completed a group experience and those who have not tend to show that the experimental subjects show two to three times as many interpersonal changes as do the control subjects. According to Bunker, for example, about 33 per cent of the 229 group members he studied tended to show increases in openness, receptivity, tolerance of differences, operational skills in interpersonal relationships, and understanding of self and others; only 15 to 20 per cent of the 125 persons in the control group showed such changes. An even higher percentage of favorable change in group participants—64 per cent—was reported by Boyd and Elliss.

Burke and Bennis studied the impact of the human relations laboratory on changes in the perception of self and other group members. Using a group semantic differential, they found that perception of the self and the ideal self converged and that the way people saw themselves and the way they were seen by others became more similar over a period of time.

Despite the evidence in favor of positive effects from T-group training, a number of problems exist in such studies. One of the difficulties is that the amount of change reported appears to vary with the source of the judgments. The trainee's opinion of the effectiveness of his behavioral change tends to be far more optimistic than that of observers. For example, Miles reported that, of 34 high school principals who had participated in NTL programs, 82 per cent indicated improved functioning subsequent to their training. Ratings by their back-home colleagues, however, indicated that only 30 per cent had changed. Taylor also found that the participants' own responses were more enthusiastic than those of their associates. Campbell and Dunnette, in summarizing the evidence for change, state that about 30 to 40 per cent of the trained persons they surveyed were reported to exhibit some kind of perceptible change.

The interpretation of data submitted by judges is difficult because peers tend to assign less change to colleagues who complete a group training experience than to either their superiors or their subordinates. Compounding the serious problem of judge bias is the fact that these studies were based solely on opinions obtained at the conclusion of the training period. There was no pretraining baseline.

Enhanced Sense of Well-Being. A number of encounter group leaders view the major function of the group as simply providing an intense emotional experience. This view shifts the criterion for assessing success to the internal subjective state of the participant. If one assumes that reactions to the encounter group are to be treated as private events, such as civic appreciation or recreational enjoyment, then reports of success may be assumed to have face validity. The participant may take whatever he chooses or is capable of choosing from the experience provided.

That most participants retrospectively report global satisfaction with their group experience is indicated by the survey findings of three investigators. The most careful study was that conducted by Rogers, who obtained responses to his questionnaires from 82 per cent (481) of the clients who had participated in groups he had led. Three-fourths reported that the group had been a helpful, positive experience; 30 per cent stated that the experience had been "constructive," and another 45 per cent described it as a "deep, meaningful, positive experience." An additional 19 per cent checked that it had been "more helpful than unhelpful."

About the same degree of participant satisfaction, 78 per cent, is implied by Bach, whose 1968 analysis is based on reports by 612 participants. A 1967 report by Bach is more enthusiastic; there he reported that 90 per cent of 400 marathon group members evaluated their 24- to 48-hour group encounters as "one of the most significant meaningful experiences of their lives."

Mintz obtained follow-up reports from her group participants and found that, of 93 who evaluated their experiences immediately after the termination of the marathon group, 66 per cent reported they had profited greatly and 30 per cent reported they had profited moderately. In a sample of 80 who evaluated their marathon group experience after at least three months, 46 per cent said they had profited greatly and 41 per cent said they had profited moderately. A further analysis revealed that the rate of declining enthusiasm appeared to be differentially related to whether the participant was himself a psychotherapist. Although 70 per cent of the nontherapists reported immediately after group termination that they had greatly profited, only 34 per cent reported after three months or more that they were greatly helped. On the other hand, psychotherapists tended to maintain their enthusiasm or even increase it—62 per cent reported in the immediate response that they had profited greatly, and 67 per cent reported improvement in the follow-up response.

Most of the clients who choose to respond to the inquiries of their former group leaders report that they gained something from the experience. Neither Bach nor Mintz provides information regarding the number of eligible respondents who failed to reply to these questionnaires, and they do not attempt to compare the characteristics of the responders and the nonresponders.

Besides the issue of response bias, three other methodological problems limit the value of these studies: (1) No control groups aid in assessing the impact of technique, leader personality and style, level of leader training, length of meeting time, and other such obvious variables. (2) Measures were taken only after the group had disbanded, not prior to the group experience, which increased the opportunity for rater bias. (3) The measures used are global rather than specific, making it impossible to determine the specific nature of the change experience, in terms of interpersonal sensitivity, empathy, objectivity, and other such presumed goals of the encounter groups.

A person who is already quite effective in groups when he first comes to a T-group may show no change. Is he to be counted as a failure? Also, when evaluations rely on self-reports, the results are contaminated by attitudes and response sets that may have little to do with what has been learned.

When investigators attempt to identify specific rather than general changes induced by encounter-type groups—such as changes in self-concept, changes in inner or outer directedness, and changes in attitude and personality—the findings are less positive. Stock found that persons who reported the greatest degree of change in their self-percepts were also those who had become much less sure of what kinds of people they are. Kassarjian attempted to determine whether sensitivity training influenced participants to become more other-directed, as is claimed by some, or more inner-directed, as claimed by others. He failed to find any reliable directional shifts in ten groups of participants compared on measures taken before and after training. Kassarjian concluded that social character may not be one of the variables affected by such training. Other studies reveal that students who were exposed to a program of sensitivity training showed no significant change in such standard personality measures as the California Psychological Inventory, Minnesota Multiphasic Personality Inventory F-scale, and the Cattell 16-Personality-Factor Questionnaire.

The paucity of standardized scales makes it difficult to assess the attitude and personality changes that may be fostered in encounter groups. Of the attitude scales employed, only the Fundamental Interpersonal Relations Orientation-Behavior appeared to give positive results, as reported by Smith and by Schutz and Allen.

In summary, participants in encounter groups report favorable reactions and are frequently described by others as showing improved interpersonal skills. But the evidence is meager that such participants undergo significant attitude changes or personality changes, and the evidence that group training improves group or organizational efficiency is not persuasive. What is clearest is that these groups provide an intensive affective experience for many participants. In this sense, the groups may be described as potent. As is the case with all potent agents, they may be helpful when properly administered in small doses and noxious when excessive or inappropriate doses are given.

Other Kinds of Research

Besides outcome research, other kinds of research in the area of laboratory movement are being pursued by a few investigators. For example, Cooper has studied the influence of the trainer on participant change in T-groups. He reports that, when the trainer is seen as attractive, participants identify with him and become more like him in attitude and behavior. Also, when the trainer is seen as self-congruent (genuine, direct, honest, sincere), participants change in ways that foster their own congruence.

In a review and critique of the research on trainer effects, Cooper found a number of limitations: (1) The findings are based mostly on small samples. (2) Most of the studies rely for their measurements on participant perception of behavior and not on direct observation of changes in behavior by unbiased observers. (3) There is lack of agreement and clarity about what constitutes the research focus; hence, widely varying measuring instruments are used. (4) Little attempt is made to establish a causal relation between specific trainer behavior and observed group or individual changes.

Marathon therapists claim that the maintenance of psychological defense systems, which inhibit the expression of emotions unacceptable in most ordinary social contexts, are more likely to break down in the longer, uninterrupted time period of the marathon group than in the traditional therapy group. This has been referred to as the too-tired-to-be-polite phenomenon. A recent process study by Myerhoff, Jacobs, and Stoller compared emotionality in marathon and traditional psychotherapy groups. The therapist was the same for both groups.

A generally higher rate of occurrence and variability in the expression of negative feelings was found in marathon groups.

EVALUATION

Assets of the T-Group Method

The T-group provides a vehicle for teaching the importance of interpersonal relations in natural group functioning. The T-group teaches through experience rather than through didactic description. An analogy might be made with the teaching of arithmetic. The teacher can do a problem on the blackboard, but the student does not learn the arithmetical maneuver until he has actually solved a number of similar problems for himself.

The T-group provides a means of sharpening perceptual skills—of recognizing interpersonal perceptual distortions, learning how to check out interpersonal perceptions, and learning how to correct interpersonal perceptions. A corollary is the learning of one's own functioning in a group—seeing the role one plays vis-à-vis others, how one distorts the presentation of self to others, and how to obtain corrective feedback.

The T-group teaches people how they communicate with others, the variety of modes of interpersonal communication, and how to increase the effectiveness of communication while decreasing the noise in the communication system.

The T-group provides a degree of experiencing isolation, similar to the isolation of psychotherapy, that may enable participants to test out different modes of interaction and broaden their repertoire of human relations skills.

The T-group and related laboratory exercises have provided theory and method for effective intervention in organizations. This intervention· may range from natural community groups (churches) to community action groups (urban renewal), service organizations (YMCA), and business and industry (Shell, Esso, Bell Telephone).

The human relations emphasis in the T-group and laboratory method provides a technique for nurturing human growth that may be incorporated into the educational structure to counterbalance many of the dehumanizing elements of American culture, particularly the mechanistic elements in the American school system.

The laboratory movement has given impetus and support to the scientific study ·of group function, leadership, and function of different types of groups, which have received little emphasis in the clinical professions. The T-group provides a natural laboratory.

The T-group and laboratory movement, less tied to professional conventions, have introduced many innovations in group interaction that may have clinical applicability: brief therapy groups, intensive group experiences, use of nonverbal interaction methods, refined use of group process analysis, and increased effectiveness of task groups.

Liabilities of the T-Group Method

For the most part, the major problems that have arisen in the use of the laboratory method have not escaped the attention of leaders of the movement. In some exemplary instances, careful measures have been taken to deal with these problems. In other instances, such problems have been almost totally ignored.

Incompetent Leaders. Leaders have various degrees of competence, with few reliable norms for performance and with no professional peer group to whom they must answer. Thus, leaders may be incompetent—either accomplishing little or allowing unnecessary and destructive group activity.

Responsibility is not clearly defined. This lack of responsibility may range from a sense of no concern as to where a group ends up in its interaction to a failure to respond to members who are undergoing undue stress or personal decompensation.

The T-group has sometimes not been provided with appropriate leadership to teach or guide a group into optimal effective function. There is a common notion in T-group theory that the group can be trusted to provide a just guideline for appropriate interpersonal attitudes and behavior. But a group of people can be tyrannical and destructive, just as it can be beneficent and supportive. Carl Jung opposed group therapy because he felt it placed people at the mercy of others. The same objection is raised by such right-wing groups as the John Birch Society, who perceive group methods as ways to rob a person of his autonomy.

Shifting Focus. Among recent innovations in T-groups has been the introduction of various nonverbal techniques for increasing self-awareness. These techniques include various role-playing maneuvers, various types of body-contact-exploration maneuvers, and such action techniques as wrestling and lifting members. This trend raises a number of theoretical, technical, and ethical issues beyond the scope of this discussion. The one point to be made here is the shift of focus. These techniques, or some of them, may have a definite value. However, the focus has shifted from interpersonal learning and group process learning to individual learning. That shift in itself is not questionable. But if personal issues become the chief focus, then the original goal for T-group method as a democratic group process educational experience has been lost. The proponents of these new T-group techniques have reverted to the origins of group methods, when individuals were treated *in* a group, not *by* and *with* a group. The distinctiveness of group process and group method is largely discarded. Much may be learned through these innovative group techniques—but at the expense of what can be learned about how groups function. Some trainers have not recognized that they cannot have it both ways.

Time Limits. The question of time-limited experience has received inadequate attention. It is assumed that the T-group members all learn at the same rate, that the length of T-groups is a relatively minor variable in learning, and that preparation for learning and reinforcement of learning are relatively secondary to the immediate T-group experience. But the evidence from psychotherapy and education indicates that there are notable individual differences in cognitive and emotional learning. Some effort has been made to address this issue in the training literature, but generally no attempt has been made to define learning goals that can be accomplished in time-limited interaction and learning goals that require longer-term spaced reinforcement. The most careful experimental work in this regard has been done in terms of time-limited psychotherapy and brief therapy. It is surprising that this matter has not been a subject of more T-group research. Apparently, the time limits used for T-groups have been those of convenience and propitiousness rather than those proved to reach the learning goals sought.

Lack of Carry-Over. The T-group may provide a forum for more honest confrontation of self and others, but it may also be a hit-and-run game. For example, one may talk quite freely to a stranger on an airplane but be totally incapable of confiding in one's relatives. The T-group may foster a sense of pseudoauthenticity and pseudoreality—a sense that this is really living while the rest of life is phony. The reality of the situation may be that the T-group participant can afford to act in ways that ignore reality because he does not have to live with the consequences of his behavior. Some people return to national sensitivity groups year after year because they feel, "Here I can really be myself." They are, in fact, unable to be themselves. Or they may be inappropriately capable of sharing intimate details of their psychological life in a group of people but not able to do so when they should with someone close to them.

The T-group may foster a sense of new-found patterns of relationship that may be inappropriate to a participant's real-life circumstances. For example, T-group participants may return to their organization with new ways of being—only to find that the new self is not accepted by the old work group. The result may be ostracism or, more likely, a quick extinguishment of the new T-group self through involvement in everyday life and work that provides negative reinforcement of the new learning. The laboratory movement has sought to circumvent this problem by training people from an entire work group. But that solution does not adequately address the problems of differentiating a special group behavior from everyday group behavior. For example, if a patient talked to all his friends as he talks to his therapist, he would soon run out of friends.

Yet the T-group member may assume that T-group behavior should become the norm for interpersonal relations with everyone within his ken.

A premium may be placed on total participation, on experiencing, without self-analysis or reflection. The result may be an exhilarating experience but not a learning experience. A crass way of putting it is, "All id and no ego." One need not go that far, but an example will suffice. In several group process teaching laboratories, mental health professionals who had been in prior sensitivity and encounter groups participated. They reported that they had learned about themselves in their previous group experiences but that they had acquired little if any knowledge about how groups actually function. Nor had they acquired any usable knowledge about how they might effectively work with groups. The group laboratory should aim not only at acquiring understanding of the self but also at learning how to use the knowledge and experience in the group.

The T-group experience has often been conducted with a work group, disregarding the fact that this group must continue to work together after their T-group experience. The group is asked to participate as if their real-life work-role relationships did not exist. The result may be both nonlearning and disaster. For example, in one professional work team that participated in a T-group experience, the members were instructed to tell each other how they really felt about each other. The members told off their chief in the T-group. The result was total disruption of the effectiveness of that work team thereafter.

More important is the issue of goals. In this instance, the trainer ignored the goal of helping the professional team work together and share appropriate perceptions and feelings. Instead, "experiencing" and "honesty" became the catchwords for an exercise in the group denial of reality. At stake is the question of how to increase the effectiveness of a team that works together and has real, ongoing, and intimate relationships that may be influenced by revelations made in the T-group.

The above example points up another area of confusion. The professional team entered the T-group with a contract that asked for help in making the work group more effective. The trainer had his own personal contract, which dealt only with change in individual members, and he ignored the contract to help the team. A contract to help a team may not necessarily result in helpful changes for individual team members; and helping individual team members to change may not necessarily be helpful to team function.

The T-group has often been conducted with little concern for how the learning in the T-group setting is to be transferred to the on-the-job setting. Trainers may assume that the transfer of learning will occur automatically, that attention to transfer issues may interfere with the group process, or that the T-group experience is intrinsically valuable and that transfer of learning to the job or community is, in a sense, irrelevant. Pattison (1965) has reviewed research data which suggested that in-group behavior change in psychotherapy groups is often *not* accompanied by change in behavior outside the group. The same has been observed for T-groups. Until recently, much of laboratory training focused on the T-group experience alone and ignored the fact that little transfer of learning was occurring. Nor were provisions made for changing the T-group procedure to accomplish transfer of learning. More recently, structured programs for subsequent follow-up training experiences have sought to remedy this problem.

Deleterious Effects. The assessment of T-group results has failed to consider seriously the deleterious effects of group participation. The lessons learned long ago by psychoanalysts about the detrimental effects of adverse countertransference reactions and the rationale for the preparatory psychoanalysis of the student psychoanalyst before he undertakes a psychoanalysis under supervision have often been ignored by nonpsychoanalytic psychotherapists. Most outcome studies have been limited to investigating conditions of no change or degrees of improvement. In fact, there has been a subtle but pervasive notion that psychotherapy is purely a beneficial maneuver—at least in the hands of competent practitioners.

The recurring discovery of negative therapeutic effects occasioned by the therapist has, been noted by such authors as Shlien and Zimring, Truax and Carkhuff, and Orr. The detection and recognition of such effects is a thorny research problem that admits of no easy solution. An enthusiastic partisan tone within the T-group movement fosters the concept that a T-group experience would be good for anybody and always profitable. The result may be a deluding distortion of participants' responses and a deceptive oversell.

Adequate participant selection criteria may be lacking. Persons who cannot tolerate or learn from intensive interpersonal relations may be involved in such groups. At best, these persons emerge untouched and unmoved; at worst, they decompensate.

There is no reason to assume that a small group will automatically develop into a structure supportive of increased selfhood. Yet some trainers covertly assume that T-groups will always proceed in benevolent fashion. In fact, some T-groups tyrannize their members—as do some therapy groups. In their eagerness to develop autonomous, democratic groups, some trainers overlook this fact. If the goal is to develop effective democratic groups, more attention must be paid to training groups in how to achieve that goal, rather than merely letting them flounder in dubious self-discovery.

The T-group has often ignored the necessity and utility of ego defenses. Exposure and frankness, attack and vulnerability may become premium values. Often, little attention is paid to the necessity for support and nurturance. Human foibles, inadequacies, and the normal range of variation in life style may be given short shrift. Some leaders have even theorized on the value of some type of total exposure. This trend ignores individual differences in the capacity to tolerate stress and frustration. Rather than adjust its expectations to the needs, capacities, and interests of each person, the group may use, as its covert norm, the self-reliant man who can take anything the group dishes out.

The T-group may foster a concept that anything goes, regardless of consequences. Instead of creating interpersonal awareness, it may foster personal narcissism. If a person can say anything he wishes, he may come to assume that just because he feels like expressing himself is justification enough to do so. This attitude may preclude effective communication, for he then ignores the other person's receptivity and the effect of his message on the other person. Communication may be seen not as an interpersonal event but merely as the opportunity to express oneself. The principle of optimal communication is ignored, and the principle of total communication is favored.

Summary

To summarize the assets and liabilities of the T-group method, one may state that the T-group presents a powerful means of involving people in human behavioral analysis. The method provides possibilities for a highly significant contribution to the humane quality of existence in Western culture and its various work and community components. The training laboratory has potential as a powerful instrument. Its liabilities lie in the area of utilization, as with any powerful instrument. Without adequate training, supervision, and guidelines, a powerful instrument may be destructive, just as a valuable drug may have undesirable effects if used unwisely or in incorrect doses. The liabilities described are not intrinsic deficits; rather, they are deficits of training, experience, clarity, and precision of goals. They can be avoided. Leaders within the laboratory movement are addressing themselves to the task.

Of more concern are the peripheral and derivative products of the laboratory movement—groups that have picked up bits and pieces of the laboratory movement but without the democratic concerns of the originators, without the clinical experience of the early leaders, without the informal communicative guidelines that tend to keep professionals within a self-corrective framework, and without the continuous inquiring, self-critical, self-evaluative, and research perspective.

Despite the enthusiasm that the laboratory movement has fostered, its practitioners have not fully realized how powerful are the tools they have developed. Therefore, their enthusiasm may not yet be tempered by respect and concern that these tools be rightly used.

OUTSIDE CRITICISM

Sensitivity Training as Brainwashing

Certain right-wing conservatives, particularly members of the John Birch Society, have viciously attacked sensitivity training as a form of Communist brainwashing, as Dieckmann reports. But brainwashing is the use of educational procedures, including some principles of psychology and psychiatry, to interfere with normal, healthy interpersonal relationships, particularly at the individual level, for the purpose of physically and ideologically manipulating the recipients. Sensitivity training, on the other hand, is the use of educational procedures, including some principles of psychology and psychiatry, to develop open, accepting, and spontaneous interpersonal relationships, particularly at the individual level, for the purpose of helping people to understand both individual and group behavior, thereby freeing them from being manipulated or manipulating without their knowledge, and to experience warm personal relationships with other people.

The purpose of brainwashing is indoctrination, leading to the acceptance of a closed system of values. The purpose of sensitivity training is the development of awareness and acceptance of the feelings of oneself and others and the acceptance of responsibility for one's own acts, leading to clearer, independent thinking and realistic behavior. With sensitivity training, a person develops a better understanding of group dynamics and individual motivation.

Both brainwashing and sensitivity training are usually carried out in small groups of ten to 16 people.

Brainwashing Techniques.
The Communists used brainwashing during the Korean War. They divided American prisoners into small groups, each headed by a personable social scientist who announced that all the Communists wanted was the physical cooperation of the Americans—that is, they wanted the Americans to listen to the truth as the Communists saw it and to participate in discussions. For their cooperation, those being indoctrinated would be given good food, shelter, clothing, and medical care, and they would not have to work.

During the first six months, virtually no indoctrination took place. The prisoners referred to this as the dog-eat-dog period. They learned to reject any kind of authority, and each man was for himself. The individual and not the team or group became important. About half of the deaths of prisoners took place during this period from what psychiatrists later referred to as give-up-itis, a kind of individual depression-withdrawal, culminating in death.

After the first six months, the Communists began a formal education period, which they carried out seven days a week, every waking hour, for the next two years. The curriculum consisted of a discussion of the evils of capitalism, the number of American heroes who were wealthy, social injustices in the United States, and so forth—all of course, from the Communist point of view. The lectures were delivered to large groups of prisoners and lasted four to five hours. During the lectures the prisoners were compelled to stand up, so that they could not sleep, and were allowed no coffee or cigarettes. After the lectures, groups of ten to 12 men discussed the lectures in any way they wanted, with the guidance of a Communist instructor who lived with them in their barracks as a presumably friendly, cooperative, patient helper. Each prisoner had to participate in this discussion by putting into his own words what the lecture was about. He did not have to agree with the speaker. Group pressure was brought to bear on recalcitrant nondiscussant prisoners, since the group could not eat until every member had participated.

There were also more interesting activities, all centering around Communist propaganda, such as guest lectures, little theatre groups, movies, athletic programs, and arts and crafts instruction. Prisoners were rewarded for attending these activities by being allowed to participate in sports and by being given cigarettes, candy, and currency.

Two additional attitude-changing devices were brought to bear on the prisoners: informing on fellow prisoners and self-criticism.

American informers were encouraged by being publicly given material goods of some sort and by receiving extra status and approval from the Communists. What did they inform about? Simply any misdeed or anti-social acts or attitudes (in terms of Communist objectives) expressed by their fellow prisoners. The rationale was this: The anti-social prisoner needs to be helped. Therefore, do not inform out of hostility but only out of concern for your buddy. It is your social responsibility to inform the Communist leaders of disaffection in your group.

Since the person informed on was not punished but was only admonished kindly, he realized that he was not physically endangered by the informing. But he also realized that someone in his group, he knew not whom, had revealed him to the Communists. Three consequences of the informing resulted: (1) Each prisoner developed a lack of trust in his buddies. (2) Since no one was really punished, the act of informing was undertaken without guilt, and, the rewards to the selfish nature of the informer being considerable, he could thus regard informing as positive. (3) The prisoners started withdrawing psychologically from each other. Each American insulated himself in his own inner solitary-confinement cell, unable to communicate meaningfully with others. Nevertheless, a yearning for communication does not die easily. So the Communists set up a limited negative form of self-revelatory catharsis for the prisoners, which consisted of having the prisoners sit in a small group and admit their faults. They participated in this group activity because it kept their captors from nagging them and, in fact, brought their approval and also because it was virtually the only meaningful group belonging that was permitted. Since no one helped relieve the guilt and embarrassment of the prisoners as they revealed their less-acceptable impulses and acts, paranoid thinking eventually came to be a symptom of the men in these groups, even to the point of their believing that other prisoners could read their minds. It is this self-criticism aspect of brainwashing groups that the right-wing critics refer to as sensitivity training.

As a further refinement of attitude control, the Communists allowed only depressing and negativistic mail from friends and relatives to reach the American prisoners and withheld all the positive, loving, and encouraging letters. As a result, the prisoners stopped even thinking about their families and were thus cut off from their last source of emotional support.

Two main outcomes of this brainwashing were (1) the loss of the American prisoner's belief in his value as a human being worthy of dignity and respect and concomitantly his feeling that he was expendable for the good of some class survival and (2) a rampant form of the disease of give-up-itis. The general characteristics of survivors of this program were quietness, lack of exuberance, no interest in bull sessions, and lack of guilt when freely exploiting other people.

Brainwashing vs. Sensitivity Training. About the only similarities shared by sensitivity training and brainwashing are the use of small groups led by social scientists and a type of group pressure brought to bear on members. In the case of T-groups and encounter groups, however, the group pressure is to drop artificial roles and unwarranted covering-up mechanisms that interfere with collaborative group processes. Early in the sensitivity training, the group often express negative feelings, including criticisms of other members. This is a natural phenomenon of these groups. Many people believe that less is risked by someone who exposes negative feelings toward himself or others, for negative feelings are likely to draw negative feelings in return. But if warmth or affection toward others is expressed, a person who is uneasy about human warmth or love does not know what response to expect, and so he experiences more anxiety. Defensiveness and lack of trust are the most natural ways to experience interpersonal relationships in their early stages. Negative feelings, when accepted without undue rancor, usually give way to positive feelings. In the case of brainwashing, empathy and acceptance are almost totally discouraged. Instead, an attitude of each man for himself and his own best interests is systematically promoted.

The sense of group belongingness in brainwashing is experienced only in the self-criticism sessions. But group cohesiveness in sensitivity training is developed through empathy, identification, sharing of such emotions as joy and humor, life values, ethics, frustrations, longings, ideals, goals, and caring about the development of both oneself and the group. Instead of encouraging the formation of a group of self-serving, isolated, critical, informing individuals, as brainwashing does, sensitivity training attempts to weld the individual and group needs so that neither individual nor group is harmed by what each needs to develop fully. In sensitivity training, the greater the growth of the individual, the more valuable he is to the group; and the greater the growth of the group in awareness, acceptance, and caring, the more valuable the group becomes to the individual.

In sensitivity training there are no rewards for criticism in the sense of tearing down the feelings of oneself or others. Encouragement is given to people's taking risks in revealing personal feelings regarding other group members for the purpose of giving honest feedback and cutting through inappropriate covering-up defenses. For example, it is expected that people's styles of relating with others will become known to the members of the group. If a group member's style is repressive to other members of the group or to group growth, someone confronts him with this information. Such a confrontation may seem at first to be very negative, may cause feelings of anger, rejection, and hurt, and may result in a temporary strengthening of the defense mechanisms of the recipient of the feedback. But this reaction in itself is not harmful. Growth or change of any kind is often accompanied by risk and usually by pain. The child learning to walk falls down many times; learning to talk, he is often misunderstood and sometimes ridiculed; learning to master tools, he hurts himself; learning to ride a bicycle, he takes many tumbles; playing contact sports, he may be bruised or break a bone. So in interpersonal relations, learning new ways of growth entails psychological hurt. Dropping unnecessary self-protection defense mechanisms may seem to leave one vulnerable, and hostile bullies may appear to take advantage of the vulnerable person. Sensitivity training does not pretend to be an affair of sweetness and light; there can be pain along with the growth.

The main real difference between brainwashing and sensitivity training lies in their purposes. Brainwashing is an agency-oriented method to bring people into a completely dependent and selfish relationship with the ideological leaders while breaking down kinship among peers so that the individuals composing the group can be manipulated at the leader's will. Sensitivity training is a communion-oriented method that encourages responsibility for one's own actions, a spirit of inquiry among group members, a sense of empathy and identity among peers, a spirit of collaboration with each other and with the leader, a strong sense of belongingness and participation. The result of brainwashing is distrust, defensiveness, isolation, and lack of empathy. The result of sensitivity training is increased trust, openness, a sense of belonging, and empathy.

In hearing the arguments of ultraconservatives against sensitivity training, one is impressed, particularly by the Birchers, with their inability to conceive of the communion aspects—the sharing and belongingness—of the process. They perceive the process almost entirely as being agency-oriented and against the individual. Sensitivity training has become a vehicle for the right-wingers on which to project their own repressive, agency-oriented processes. The very tactics they use in attacking sensitivity training are those employed in the Communist process of brainwashing American prisoners—propagandizing, pointing out the occasional failures of sensitivity training as being typical of the results, denying the value of peer group relationships, attacking the democratic process of sensitivity training with the same smear and negative-instance tactics with which the Communists attack United States democracy and capitalism, and insisting that their concepts of God and the United States are the only true ways that one can believe, as the Communists set up their god of Communism as the only truth.

Sensitivity Training in the Schools

In some sections of the country, the ultraconservative elements have strongly attacked what they call sensitivity training in the public schools. In almost every instance, this term has referred to some informative discussion group, most often about the feelings of students concerning various aspects of the subject matter they are studying, sometimes sex. It would be a rare event, indeed, to find a real sensitivity training session for students. Nor would such training be particularly appropriate, except in special group counseling sessions. Discussions that begin at a topic level—for instance, a school group discussion of drug use and abuse—may turn into T-groups, but they would usually be appropriately handled by a counselor.

There has been a growing movement to involve teachers in sensitivity training. This is a healthy movement if teachers, by participating in T-groups, become more aware of their feelings, their roles, their impact on others. Ultraconservatives get upset when they think that teachers who have had T-group or encounter group experience will try to set up groups of their own in their classrooms and invade the privacy of the students (actually, the parents may sometimes be worried about being discussed), inflicting possible emotional trauma if any student should reveal more than was socially acceptable by community standards. The authors do not know how much of this T-grouping goes on in schools outside of group counseling or even if it would do any particular damage unless handled clumsily by a teacher.

What is of concern is the growing tendency of relatively few ultraconservatives to put great pressure on boards of education and school administrators to cut out of their curricula any innovative procedures involving dialogue within groups of students, especially if the dialogue or discussion allows freedom of expression of the students' personal feelings and fantasies. All such group discussions are now labeled sensitivity training by ultraconservatives and then, by their cloudy thinking and heavy-handed implication, become dangerous brainwashings, group criticism, self-criticism, and invasion of the privacy of the individual.

Glasser found his discussion methods so maligned by Birchers that he has publicly announced he does not do sensitivity training. A sex education course in the Anaheim,

California, public schools that was touted as a model for the country was recently reduced to a pale shadow of itself by an ultraconservative group's repeated rabble-rousing attacks on the board of education and superintendent of schools. The leader of the group, a former Marine officer, revealed to a Los Angeles newspaper the power tactics his group used in destroying the board of education; the article contained chilling overtones of Hitlerian methods. In many communities the ultraconservatives have set up this straw man: Innovative discussion group = sensitivity training = brainwashing = Pavlovian conditioning = Communist plot. Therefore, to protect our God, our country, and our children, we must drive this menace of sensitivity training out of our schools and attack it wherever it appears and in whatever guise.

In general, the public is too little informed about sensitivity training to be able to combat right-wing charges that it is being brainwashed. More important, the public does not know that most of the student discussion groups are more-effective educational aids and *not* sensitivity training. These discussion groups are more effective than former didactic teaching methods because they involve the empathy and emotions of students and, therefore, make subject matter personally meaningful to them.

Richard Jones has presented a passionate case for educating the whole child, allowing him to experience himself in a feeling and imaginative sense as well as enlarging his fund of factual knowledge and increasing his cognitive ability. Repeatedly, Jones makes the point that, in solving problems and in posing problems, children and adults need to be able to express their emotions, share them, and use them; one way to help children learn to control and therefore use emotion is to bring it into discussion in the classroom.

Jones's idea of constructing knowledge, as opposed to attaining it by absorbing cognitive material or even by solving problems posed by someone else,

presumes freedom and skill in the sharing and use of controlled emotion and imagery.

Therefore, emotional skills as well as cognitive skills need to be taught. Jones points out that, as humans, people are always imagining and that at times they are helpless and feel alone while doing this. If they are experiencing all three states—imagining while they are helpless and alone—then they are anxious. It is this anxiety that interferes with learning. Yet American culture tends to set up the conditions for the state of anxiety—children are taught embarrassment for feelings and are guarded against imagination. Since repression is part of the cultural mores, opposition of the ultraconservative type can be expected wherever these mores of repression are threatened. Yet without feelings and imagination, children cannot become personally involved in the subject matter, and it will be only superficially learned.

To summarize the main points: (1) School discussion groups that enlist the use of children's personal feelings and imagination with cognitive material are logically valid because the groups involve an integrated, meaningful learning experience. (2) The expression of feeling needs to be controlled sufficiently so that it can be used constructively to deepen the learning process. Feeling can be controlled through learning about it, experiencing it, expressing it, and then constructing new percepts with it. Such control can be gained through peer group interaction about cognitive material. (3) Such discussion groups are not actually sensitivity training. (4) Whatever these discussion methods are called, they are intended to educate the whole person intellectually and emotionally. (5) Attacks by ultraconservatives on integrated learning methods, usually group discussions, whether launched under the guise of attacking sensitivity training or for some other reason, must be met by informed adults with clear thinking and knowledge of the dynamics of learning rather than by fear, confusion, and withdrawal from the barrage of name-calling.

The agency aspect of the learning process —problem-solving, achieving status, grades, knowledge—must be tempered by the communion aspect—joining feeling and imagination with cognition, experiencing and sharing passion and emotion.

REFERENCES

Argyris, C. *Interpersonal Competence and Organizational Behavior*. Richard C. Irwin, Homewood, Ill., 1962.

Artiss, K. L., and Schiff, S. B. Education for practice in the therapeutic community. Curr. Psychiat. Ther., *8:* 233, 1968.

Astrachan, B. M., Harrow, M., Becker, R. E., Schwartz, A. H., and Miller, J. C. The unled patient group as a therapeutic tool. Int. J. Group Psychother., *17:* 178, 1967.

Bach, G. R. Marathon group dynamics. II. Dimensions of helpfulness: therapeutic aggression. Psychol. Rep., *20:* 1147, 1967.

Bach, G. R. Discussion. Int. J. Group Psychother., *18:* 244, 1968.

Bakan, D. *The Duality of Human Existence*. Rand McNally, Chicago, 1966.

Batchelder, R. L., and Hardy, J. M. *Using Sensitivity Training and the Laboratory Method*. Association Press, New York, 1968.

Beckhard, R., editor. *Conferences for Learning, Planning and Action*, National Training Laboratories Selected Reading Series, vol. 6. National Training Laboratories and National Education Association, Washington, D. C., 1962.

Benne, K. D. History of the T-group in the laboratory setting. In *T-Group Theory and Laboratory Method: Innovation in Re-education*, pp. 80–135, L. P. Bradford, J. R. Gibb, and K. D. Benne, editors. John Wiley, New York, 1964.

Bergin, A. E. An empirical analysis of therapeutic issues. In *Counseling and Psychotherapy: An Overview*, p. 175, D. Arbuckle, editor. McGraw-Hill, New York, 1967.

Berne, E. *The Structure and Dynamics of Organizations and Groups*. J. B. Lippincott, New York, 1963.

Berzon, B., and Solomon, L. N. The self-directed therapeutic group: three studies. J. Counsel. Psychol., *13:* 221, 1966.

Biderman, A. D., and Zimmer, H., editors. *The Manipulation of Human Behavior*. John Wiley, New York, 1961.

Block, H. S. An open-ended crisis-oriented group for the poor who are sick. Arch. Gen. Psychiat. (Chicago), *18:* 178, 1968.

Boyd, J. B., and Elliss, J. D. *Findings of Research into Senior Management Seminars*. Hydro-Electric Power Commission of Ontario, Toronto, 1962.

Bradford, L. P., editor. *Group Development*, National Training Laboratories Selected Reading Series, vols. 1–4. National Training Laboratories and National Education Association, Washington, D. C., 1961.

Bradford, L. P. Biography of an institution. J. Appl. Behav. Sci., *3:* 127, 1967.

Bradford, L. P., Gibb, J. R., and Benne, K. D., editors. *T-Group Theory and Laboratory Method: Innovation in Re-education*. John Wiley, New York, 1964.

Bredesen, K. N. Small group work—the need for some guidelines. Amer. J. Psychiat., *126:* 876, 1969.

Bunker, D. R. Individual application of laboratory training. J. Appl. Behav. Sci., *1:* 131, 1965.

Burke, R. L., and Bennis, W. G. Changes in perception of self and others during human relations training. Hum. Rel., *2:* 165, 1961.

Cadden, J. J., Flach, F. F., Blakeslee, S., and Charlton, R., Jr. Growth in medical students through group process. Amer. J. Psychiat., *126:* 862, 1969.

Campbell, J. P., and Dunnette, M. D. Effectiveness of T-group experiences in managerial training and development. Psychol. Bull., *70:* 73, 1968.

Cooper, C. L. The influence of the trainer on participant change in T-groups. Hum. Rel., *22:* 515, 1969.

Crenshaw, R. How sensitive is sensitivity training? Amer. J. Psychiat., *126:* 868, 1969.

Davies, J. C. *Neighborhood Groups and Urban Renewal*. Columbia University Press, New York, 1966.

Dieckmann, E., Jr. Sensitivity training: the network of patriotic letter writers, Pasadena, California. Amer. Mercury, 1967.

Durkin, H. E. *The Group in Depth*. International Universities Press, New York, 1964.

Edelson, M. *Ego Psychology, Group Dynamics and the Therapeutic Community*. Grune & Stratton, New York, 1964.

Emmons, S. Anaheim controversy: sex education—new direction emerging. Los Angeles Times, Los Angeles, March 29, 1970.

Fairweather, G. W. *Social Psychology in Treating Mental Illness: An Experimental Approach*. John Wiley, New York, 1964.

Federn, P. Psychoanalysis of psychosis, part I. Psychiat. Quart., *17:* 3, 1943.

Gazda, G. M., editor. *Innovations to Group Psychotherapy*. Charles C Thomas, Springfield, Ill., 1968.

Glasser, W. The *"Sensitivity Letter,"* Bulletin No. 15. Educational Training Center, Los Angeles, 1969.

Glasser, W. *Schools Without Failure*. Harper and Row, New York, 1969.

Gottschalk, L. A. Psychoanalytic notes on T-groups at the Human Relations Laboratory, Bethel, Maine. Compr. Psychiat., *7:* 472, 1966.

Gottschalk, L. A. Some problems in the evaluation of psychoactive drugs, with and without psychotherapy, in the treatment of non-psychotic personality disorders. In *Psychopharmacology: A Review of Progress, 1957–67*, pp. 255–269, D. N. Efron, J. O. Cole, J. Levine, and J. R. Wittenborn, editors. Public Health Service Publication No. 1836, United States Government Printing Office, Washington, D. C., 1968.

Gottschalk, L. A., and Auerbach, A. H. Goals and problems in psychotherapy research. In *Methods of Research in Psychotherapy*, pp. 3–9, L. A. Gottschalk and A. H. Auerbach, editors. Appleton-Century-Crofts, New York, 1966.

Gottschalk, L. A., and Gleser, G. C. *The Measurement of Psychological States through the Content Analysis of Verbal Behavior*. University of California Press, Berkeley, 1969.

Gottschalk, L. A., Gleser, G. C., and Stone, W. N. Studies of psychoactive drug effects on nonpsychiatric patients. In *Psychopharmacology of the Normal Human*, pp. 162–188, W. Evans and N. Kline, editors. Charles C Thomas, Springfield, Ill., 1968.

Gottschalk, L. A., and Pattison, E. M. Psychiatric perspectives on T-groups and the laboratory movement. Amer. J. Psychiat., *126:* 823, 1969.

Hare, A. P. *Handbook of Small Group Research*. Free Press of Glencoe, New York, 1962.

Harris, T. *I'm OK—You're OK: A Practical Guide to Transactional Analysis*. Harper and Row, New York, 1969.

Janov, A. *The Primal Scream. Primal Therapy: The Cure for Neurosis*. G. P. Putnam, New York, 1970.

Jones, M. *Beyond the Therapeutic Community: Social Learning and Social Psychiatry*. Yale University Press, New Haven, 1968.

Jones, R. M. *Fantasy and Feeling in Education*. New York University Press, New York, 1968.

Kaplan, S. R. Therapy groups and training groups: similarities and differences. Int. J. Group Psychother., *17:* 473, 1967.

Kassarjian, H. H. Social character and sensitivity training. J. Appl. Behav. Sci., *1:* 433, 1965.

Kernan, J. P. Laboratory human relations training: its effects on the "personality" of supervisory engineers. Dissert. Abstr., *25:* 665, 1964.

Klein, D. C. *Community Dynamics and Mental Health*. John Wiley, New York, 1968.

Klein, W. H., LeShan, E. J., and Furman, S. S. *Promoting Mental Health of Older People through Group Methods*. Mental Health Materials Center, New York, 1964.

Kuehn, J. L., and Crinella, F. M. Sensitivity training—interpersonal "overkill" and other problems. Amer. J. Psychiat., *126:* 840, 1969.

Lakin, M. Some ethical issues in sensitivity training. Amer. Psychol., *24:* 923, 1969.

Lippitt, R. L. *Training in Community Relations*. Harper and Row, New York, 1949.

Lorr, M., and McNair, D. M. Methods relating to evaluation of therapeutic outcome. In *Methods of Research in Psychotherapy*, p. 573, L. A. Gottschalk and A. H. Auerbach, editors. Appleton-Century-Crofts, New York, 1966.

Lowen, A. *The Betrayal of the Body.* Macmillan, New York, 1967.

Luft, J. *Of Human Interaction.* National Press Books, Palo Alto, Calif., 1970.

Malamud, D. I., and Machover, S. *Toward Self-Understanding: Group Techniques in Self-Confrontation.* Charles C Thomas, Springfield, Ill., 1965.

Mann, R. D. *Interpersonal Styles and Group Development: An Analysis of the Member-Leader Relationship.* John Wiley, New York, 1967.

Massarik, F. *Explorations in Human Relations Training and Research. A Sensitivity Training Impact Model: Some First (and Second) Thoughts on the Evaluation of Sensitivity Training,* No. 3. National Training Laboratories and National Education Association, Washington, D. C., 1965.

Mayer, W. E. Why did so many GI captives cave in? U. S. News World Rep., *40:* 56, 1956.

Mayo, C., and Klein, D. C. Group dynamics as a basic process of community psychiatry. In *Handbook of Community Psychiatry and Community Mental Health,* pp. 47–64, L. Bellak, editor. Grune & Stratton, New York, 1964.

McGrath, J. E., and Altman, I. *Small Group Research: A Synthesis and Critique of the Field.* Holt, Rinehart, & Winston, New York, 1966.

Miles, M. B. Changes during and following laboratory training: a clinical-experimental study. J. Appl. Behav. Sci., *1:* 215, 1965.

Mintz, E. E. Marathon groups: a preliminary evaluation. J. Contemp. Psychother., *1:* 91, 1969.

Moreno, J. L. The Viennese origins of the encounter movement, paving the way for existentialism, group psychotherapy, and psychodrama. Group Psychother., *22:* 7, 1970.

Myerhoff, H. L., Jacobs, A., and Stoller, F. Emotionality in marathon and traditional psychotherapy groups. Psychother. Theory Res. Pract., *7:* 33, 1970.

Orr, D. Transference and countertransference: a historical survey. J. Amer. Psychoanal. Assoc., *2:* 621, 1954.

Otto, H. *Guide to Developing Your Potential.* Charles Scribner, New York, 1967.

Parloff, M. B. Group therapy and the small group field: an encounter. Int. J. Group Psychother., *20:* 267, 1970.

Pattison, E. M. Evaluation studies of group psychotherapy. Int. J. Group Psychother., *15:* 382, 1965.

Pattison, E. M. *A Brief History of the American Group Psychotherapy Association: The First Twenty-Five Years: 1943-1968.* American Group Psychotherapy Association, New York, 1969.

Pattison, E. M., Courlas, P. G., Patti, R., Mann, B., and Mullen, D. Diagnostic-therapeutic intake class for wives of alcoholics. Quart. J. Stud. Alcohol, *26:* 605, 1965.

Peck, H. B. The small group: core of the community mental health center. Commun. Ment. Health J., *4:* 191, 1968.

Peck, H. B., and Kaplan, S. Crisis theory and therapeutic change in small groups: some implications for community mental health programs. Int. J. Group Psychother., *16:* 135, 1966.

Perls, F. S., Hefferline, R. E., and Goodman, P. *Gestalt Therapy.* Dell, New York, 1965.

Phillips, M. *Small Social Groups in England.* Methuen, London, 1965.

Redlich, F. C., and Astrachan, B. Group dynamics training. Amer. J. Psychiat., *125:* 1501, 1969.

Rickels, K., and Downing, R. W. Drug- and placebo-manifest anxiety, clinical improvement, and side reactions. Arch. Gen. Psychiat. (Chicago), *16:* 369, 1967.

Rickels, K., Gordon, P. E., Mecklenburg, R., Sablosky, L., Whalen, E. M., and Dion, H. Iprindole in neurotic depressed general practice patients: a controlled study. Psychosomatics, *9:* 208, 1968.

Rickels, K., Jenkins, B. W., Zamostien, B., Raab, E., and Kanther, M. Pharmacotherapy in neurotic depression: differential population, responses. J. Nerv. Ment. Dis., *145:* 475, 1967.

Rickels, K., Ward, C. H., and Schut, L. Different populations, different drug responses. Amer. J. Med. Sci., *247:* 328, 1964.

Rogers, C. R. The process of the basic encounter group. In *Challenges of Humanistic Psychology,* p. 261, J. F. G. Bugetal, editor. McGraw-Hill, New York, 1967.

Rosenbaum, M., and Berger, M., editors. *Group Psychotherapy and Group Function.* Basic Books, New York, 1963.

Scheidlinger, S. Therapeutic group approaches in community mental health. Soc. Work, *13:* 87, 1968.

Scheidlinger, S. Innovative group approaches. In *Progress in Community Mental Health,* pp. 123–136, L. Bellak and H. H. Barten, editors. Grune & Stratton, New York, 1969.

Schein, E. H., and Bennis, W. G. *Personal and Organizational Change through Group Methods: The Laboratory Approach.* John Wiley, New York, 1965.

Schiff, S. B. Continuing education for professional personnel. In *The Practice of Community Mental Health,* p. 571, G. Grunebaum, editor. Little, Brown, Boston, 1969.

Schutz, W. *Joy.* Grove Press, New York, 1967.

Schutz, W., and Allen, V. L. The effects of a T-group laboratory on interpersonal behavior. J. Appl. Behav. Sci., *2:* 265, 1966.

Shapiro, S. B. Some aspects of a theory of interpersonal contracts. Psychol. Rep., *22:* 171, 1968.

Shlien, J. M., and Zimring, F. M. Research directives and methods in client-centered therapy.

In *Methods of Research in Psychotherapy* p. 424, L. A. Gottschalk and A. H. Auerbach, editors. Appleton-Century-Crofts, New York, 1966.

Silver, A. W. Interrelating group-dynamic, therapeutic, and psychodynamic concepts. Int. J. Group Psychother., *17:* 139, 1967.

Smith, P. B. Attitude changes associated with training in human relations. Brit. J. Soc. Clin. Psychol., *3:* 104, 1964.

Sprott, W. J. H. *Human Groups.* Penguin Books, Baltimore, 1958.

Stock, D. A. Survey of research on T-groups. In *T-group Theory and Laboratory Method: Innovation in Re-education,* p. 395, L. P. Bradford, J. R. Gibb, and K. D. Benne, editors. John Wiley, New York, 1964.

Stoller, F. H. Accelerated interaction: a time-limited approach based on the brief, intensive group. Int. J. Group Psychother., *18:* 220, 1968.

Tannenbaum, R., Weschler, I. R., and Massarik, F. *Leadership and Organization: A Behavioral Science Approach.* McGraw-Hill, New York, 1961.

Tate, G. *Strategy of Therapy: Toward the Engineering of Social Growth.* Springer-Verlag, New York, 1967.

Taylor, F. C. Effects of laboratory training upon persons and their work groups. In *Research on the Impact of Using Different Laboratory Methods for Interpersonal and Organizational Change,* p. 115, S. S. Zalkind, chairman. American Psychological Association, Washington, D. C., 1967.

Truax, C. B., and Carkhuff, R. R. *Toward Effective Counseling and Psychotherapy: Training and Practice.* Aldine Publishing, Chicago, 1967.

University of California at Los Angeles. *Extension Bulletin.* Fall, 1970.

Weschler, I. R., Massarik, F., and Tannenbaum, R. The self in process: a sensitivity training emphasis. In *Issues in Human Relations Training,* National Training Laboratories Selected Reading Series, vol. 5, p. 33, I. R. Weschler, editor. National Training Laboratories and National Education Association, Washington, D. C., 1962.

West, L. J. United States Air Force prisoners of the Chinese Communists. In *Methods of Forceful Indoctrination: Observations and Interviews,* p. 270. Group for the Advancement of Psychiatry, New York, 1957.

Whitaker, D. S., and Lieberman, M. A. *Psychotherapy through the Group Process.* Atherton Press, New York, 1964.

Whitehorn, J. C., and Betz, B. J. A comparison of psychotherapeutic relationships between physicians and schizophrenic patients. Amer. J. Psychiat., *113:* 901, 1957.

7

The Qualities of the Group Therapist

Martin Grotjahn, M.D.

INTRODUCTION

The study of the group therapist as a person is not an idle, academic, or narcissistic occupation. It is of central importance because group psychotherapy, much more than standard psychoanalysis, is based on the dynamics of interaction. The person of the therapist is generally of great importance, but he is the central and decisive influence in the group process. Therapists have often speculated about the psychoanalytic atmosphere, but only recently have they begun to realize that this atmosphere depends on the therapist's personality. His personality can be an obstacle or an advantage.

The contact between therapist and patient is probably the most important vehicle of therapy. The literature on psychotherapy often discusses transference and countertransference and demands that the therapist know himself well enough to control his countertransference. It is also important to use this countertransference.

An additional important trend is becoming more and more visible: Psychoanalysis of the therapist is limited in its approach because it does not reach the conflict-free areas of the personality, which are of great importance in therapy. These conflict-free areas become obvious in the group therapist and his work, since they are therapeutically more approachable in the analytic group experience of the therapist himself. The therapist's physique, age, sex, cultural edu-

cation, sense of values, and sincerity are all parts of the therapist's personality that may never be touched in analysis but that play an outstanding role in treatment, especially in group therapy. The therapist must consider these conflict-free areas of the personality and their influence on the group. And he must use his awareness of his person to turn it into an advantage in treatment.

Personality traits include many things—whether the analyst or group therapist is active or passive; whether he is inclined to mood swings, from depressive to enthusiastic, from optimistic to pessimistic; whether he has a sense of humor, is witty or dull; whether he shows tolerance or signs of puritanism; whether he is free with tenderness or on the strict side, at ease or overcautious, even-tempered or given to fits of impatience or dogmatism; whether he is spontaneous or adheres to rules; whether he shows inner freedom or rigidity—all have a direct bearing on what is called the therapeutic atmosphere. And the therapist's conscious awareness of himself and his impact on people may decide the intensity and the speed with which a working alliance is established.

QUALITIES OF A PSYCHOTHERAPIST

A psychotherapist must be a man of all seasons. He must be reliable; he must invite trust and confidence. In order to do so, he must have trust and confidence in himself in the first place and in other people in the second place.

He does not need to be superior in his knowledge, not even in his intelligence, and any one of his patients may be superior in some respect—but none should be superior in honesty and sincerity. He must be an expert in the mastery of communication, whether it be the therapist's communication with himself or with the people he tries to understand. This honesty must extend into the unconscious. What a therapist says must be truly felt. How much he says and to whom and when and, most important, how he says it—that is a question of his style.

The therapist must be a man who has experienced life to the fullest. He may be young, or he may be old, but he must have had the courage to experience life in all its shades, and he must know how it feels to be alive. He must have known fear and anxiety, mastery and dependency, and, most of all, he must not be afraid to love, as he does not need to be a stranger to hate. He ought to be a man of reading, since the experience of having lived with the great figures of literature is part of his knowledge. The images he must learn to understand can be found among friends, lovers, patients, colleagues, enemies; but the models of true integration are still the characters documented in the great literature of mankind, starting perhaps with the Bible. And a therapist must have known one woman in love; through her he may know them all.

At the end, an analyst should look back on his life as a proud expression of a lifelong creative effort. He should consider himself as his own favorite patient, one who has to learn as long as he lives. This thirst for knowledge, for truth, and for learning belongs, together with honesty and sincerity, to his basic qualifications. They make it possible for him to rely and to relate. He does not need to develop a relationship easily and quickly. The relationships he forms must be deep and based on trust. He will experience disappointment, but he must not become paranoid because of it. He does not need to become a knower of men, since knowing men includes suspicion to meet baseness.

A wise and experienced pioneer of psychoanalysis in Berlin was in a mood of depression, disappointment, and rage. He had befriended a young man, the son of a colleague. He had helped the young man in his work, advised him in his marriage, arranged the proper management of some of his money, and stood by him in some rather threatening situations. Then a kind of estrangement developed, and the old man and his young friend discussed it on a long walk through the Swiss Alps. The old man talked with all insight and honesty and gave a full and probably correct and deeply penetrating interpretation. He was quite satisfied, but the young man remained preoccupied in glum silence. The next morning the old man found himself the target of a public scandal, spread by the young man. Perhaps it was the young man's only way to free himself from the good father, since the love of fathers is dangerous for sons.

It is not necessary for a good therapist to be at all times fully aware of human baseness. He needs a certain hopeful illusion to carry on what Freud called his impossible work.

A German proverb says:

Truly noble characters do not learn from bad experience.

In his attitude toward some of his disciples, Sigmund Freud was a good example of this proverb.

The drive to understand somebody else, which is essential for the therapist, should be a libidinous need, not a destructive, hateful one. That is why so many psychologists understand a person well but do not necessarily understand him in a way a realist may know him.

The therapist's lifelong learning and his constant creative effort for growth and maturation may single him out from the multitude of people, and there is a definite professional trend to isolation, alienation, and detachment. The affection of the people with whom he has worked may mislead the therapist into what Ernest Jones has called his God complex. The truly mature analyst knows this danger and remains skeptical of himself, since he knows that he is not quite as bad as he fears he could be and that he is probably not quite as good as he hoped he would be. At all times, the therapist should realize better than anybody else that, in the words of Ralph Greenson, "the best of us are just good beginners."

In his honesty, the therapist must have the courage for what Carl Jaspers describes as unlimited communication, both consciously and unconsciously. He must be a master in what Franz Alexander calls dynamic reasoning. He must learn how to see people not only in the here-and-now and in their relationship to him but also in their long-term psychological development, from the beginning to today, with a vague guess about tomorrow. His understanding may start with the understanding of a particular person here and now, but it must extend to understanding how people became what they are. In this sense, the psychologist is a historian.

In order to safeguard his own mental health and the health of his patients and his own family, he must be aware of himself. This awareness must include great parts of his unconscious. It is this awareness that is a tool of his trade and that Theodor Reik called the third ear.

The true psychologist must be driven by the wish to understand, and in that way he is a scientist. At the same time, he must be able to stand the tension of not understanding. As Reik says, it is better not to understand than to misunderstand. Like a good Quaker, the therapist must be able to wait for the light to shine, even if he has to suffer through a period of darkness.

Heinz Kohut postulated for the psychoanalyst "central firmness and peripheral looseness." This fortunate formulation means that the therapist must have a strong ego identity. He must know at all times who he is, who he has been, and where he is going. But he must be proud of his peripheral sense, by which he perceives people— their affectionate and living relationship to him and others and their hostility, viciousness, and ill will.

If the therapist's basic love for psychological truth is all-prevailing, it will protect him from becoming a judge or a policeman. He must be able to accept dilemmas and contradictions. He must combine his lust for discovery with the patience to listen. He must shift frequently from gaining insight to problem-solving and thinking. He must

follow his patients with a partial but reversible regression; at the same time, another part of him must remain observing, rational, and integrating. He must offer himself as a more or less blank screen in order to invite the development of the transference. And, as Zetzel and Greenson note, he must simultaneously be human and real enough to establish a working alliance. If he tries to remain a blank screen only, he will lose his patient, since nobody wants to be analyzed by a blank screen. If he offers himself too loudly as a helper or teammate in the working alliance, the patient may feel dominated, not understood. It is the bipolarity that makes the work of the therapist difficult.

The therapist does not need to deny that his living interest in people grows from instinctual sources. During the years of his training and his work, the trend to understand must become de-instinctualized and desexualized. Like a surgeon, he must want to penetrate, and, like a physician, he must want to heal. If his original infantile wishes to understand are based too much on hostile penetration, he will endanger his work. When he is too much afraid of these trends to penetrate the mother, he will not go deep enough with his understanding.

He must accept his motherliness. He must not try to be a man only, even if it is not possible for him to be man and woman at the same time. He must accept a partial identification with the mother he wanted to penetrate and to destroy. Finally, he has to restore her within himself.

The therapist does not need to be eloquent, not even erudite or outstandingly logical, but he must be able to comprehend and to relate.

One of the many contradictions he has to tolerate in himself: He has to be patient and impatient at the same time, like the ocean, which, with great power and impatience, thunders at the beach but takes centuries to grind stones to sand.

He must be able to love and to hate, to be a friend and an enemy to the same person. Only when he does not deny his ambivalence will the patient be able to trust him. It is like the trust of the mother who has made the child sick, so it seems, and who then helps, understands, and heals. The therapist must be aware of his patient's need for symbiotic fusion with the mother. This need, as Mahler and Guntrip have noted, is the basis for the wish to be understood.

QUALIFICATIONS OF THE GROUP PSYCHOTHERAPIST

It is difficult and perhaps impossible to analyze the qualifications for being a psychotherapist. It is even more difficult to specify the qualifications for work with groups.

Spontaneity

The group therapist must be a person of great spontaneity or responsiveness. As the word implies, responsiveness is connected to responsibility. The response must be spontaneous, natural, and direct, but it must be combined with an always ready sense of responsibility not to hurt the psychological atmosphere that engulfs therapist and group simultaneously.

Perhaps there are advantages for a group therapist in being schizoid—that is, in being able and willing by nature to split himself and endure contradictions. It is easier for the schizoid therapist to perform with ease and with grace the rather deep splitting of his person. He always has to remain firmly grounded in his identity; at the same time, he must be able to split off parts of his personality, which he then projects into different members of his group in order to understand them by partial projective identification. He has to perform this splitting process at all times in order to remain simultaneously a participant and an observer, an active member of the group and the central figure—perceiving, interpreting, and integrating.

The experienced analyst who starts working in a group has to learn something that can be learned only by years of experience—the use of spontaneity as a technical device. Many therapists have the impression that they are getting better in their relationship to the people they are trying to understand because they develop a certain trust in their spontaneous responses. An analyst in a one-to-one relationship may have time to wait, to think, to speculate—like a slow-moving chess player. The efficiency of a group therapist is much more dependent on the quick and correct use of his spontaneous responses, growing out of his intuition, empathy, and feeling for the situation. He learns to trust his hunches more and more, and he acts like the conductor of an orchestra.

A therapist frequently understands a move or reaction or a therapeutic intervention only after it has taken place. When a therapist works with other therapists as patients in his group, he is often challenged and may realize only afterward the reasons that prompted him in his spontaneous response.

The group therapist is nothing if he is not spontaneous. He depends on his immediate, intuitive, emotional, and honest responses. He cannot wait, think, and consult with himself, as in analysis. He cannot test and probe, correct, and finally integrate and interpret, as in psychoanalysis. He shoots from the hip and the expert will testify that he frequently hits the target with the right interpretation or interaction.

Trust

The free use of spontaneity is only possible in a therapist who trusts himself, as he also must have a certain trust and confidence in the group. This trust demands courage and the ability to withstand bad experiences.

The question of basic trust leads directly to the central problem of group therapy. A trusting therapist invites trust. Just as a trusting mother gains the confidence of her children, so does she give to her children the basis for their self-confidence. Only the well-mothered child, as Winnicott notes, develops the kind of basic trust that is necessary for mental health in later life. And, as Erikson and Guntrip note, nobody can develop this basic trust by himself. A person can develop everything else in the process of individuation, but the basic trust, says Fairbairn, has to be started with the experience of the mother-infant symbiosis. If this relationship is traumatized or even destroyed, it cannot be restored in analysis. In the specifically different mother transference of the group, such basic trust and self-reliance may possibly be invited and developed. At least it can be better-developed from tender beginnings in the group than in a one-to-one relationship. The analyst may be astounded to find that members of a group begin to trust the group more than they trust the therapist alone. It is this trust that the therapist must be able to invite, handle, and, finally, deserve. The group therapist must know how to develop and protect the trust of the group—primarily to the group and secondarily to himself, as the parental and central figure.

The therapist's spontaneity, his responsiveness, his ability to project temporary identifications are of central importance. They are the tools of his trade and determine the efficiency of the therapeutic group process—more so than in individual analysis. In the group, the therapist is like the conductor of an orchestra. In analysis, a therapist is like a critic who sits in the audience and occasionally gets up, stops the concert, makes a remark, and sits down again to listen. He does not conduct. He limits himself more or less to interpretations. But the group therapist reacts first and interprets later. That is the reason why only a therapist who has learned to trust the different aspects of his countertransference is fit to work well in groups.

Performance

The comparison with the conductor points up another qualification that is essential for the group therapist and much less important for the analyst. When the author once mentioned a certain technical maneuver to Franz Alexander in a discussion of the therapeutic process, he stated:

The success of such technique depends entirely on how good an actor you are.

The author was shocked and surprised, since he had never considered himself an actor, but he finally realized the difference between an actor and a performer. A good performer is not somebody who acts as if he were somebody else. A performer performs a task that has to be done; he does it carefully, with skill and elegance. He chooses to do it

in a way that can be observed and understood by others. A conductor communicates with the language of his body what he hopes and wants the orchestra to do. He shows what he does, but what he does is real and not pretended. He performs his duty. But an actor behaves as if he were conducting. When the author is angry in the therapeutic situation, he allows himself to feel his anger. He uses his judgment to decide how much anger to show and when and in what form. But the basic emotion must be honestly and truly felt. There is a great difference between an actor who acts the role of a general and a general who performs his duties so that his men and eventually his nation can see what he does and may judge him. The trust of the group is partly based on seeing the therapist in his performance.

The author occasionally allows the members of the group to see his true self. This is a part of the therapist's honesty—and an effective safeguard against the group's infantilization and the therapist's own megalomania.

A group of psychiatrists met one day after some of them had viewed together—unrelated to the group—four movies from a research institution on sexual information for physicians. They told the men who had not seen the movies what they were all about. One member of the group came 20 minutes late, listened to the talk awhile, and said with indignation:

"I have an emergency on my ward—that's why I was late—and I have lots to do. I did not come down here to listen to this locker-room nonsense."

With slightly overemphasized and pointedly polite superiority, the group therapist turned to him and said:

"I am well aware that this is a conversation not quite up to the high standards of our group. It was my intention to prepare the field in this way to loosen up the resistance against discussing sex in this group of men, who all know each other outside of the group and whose wives know each other. From there I planned to penetrate into the secrecy of everybody's marriage and sexual behavior."

The therapist used his responsive annoyance at the criticism to describe what he was doing. At the same time, he performed the difficult task of showing his annoyance to a group of psychiatrists who amounted almost to a board of experts. Almost immediately, somebody looked at the therapist and said: "All right, what do you want to know?" The group leader continued the performance by addressing each member of the group with a pointed question about something that was a sore point for him and that was carefully kept taboo and. so far, excluded from the group discussion. After a fruitful and rather deep-going session, the therapist turned once more to the young man and asked him whether the progress of the group justified the introduction of the locker-room atmosphere. He and the group agreed that the procedure was right—and so was his challenging of it.

Firmness

The central firmness of the group therapist allows him to be recognized as to who he is. This is of importance for the growth and maturation of the group, its cohesion and trust. The therapist is the central figure, symbolizing the parent in all the shades of various transferences. His peripheral looseness toward the different members of the group must allow him to perform his duties by being father to one, mother to all, affectionate friend to somebody who needs one, disciplinarian to somebody who may at that time be working on problems of authority. He must not get lost in the pitiful spectacle of a multiple personality. His central firmness or ego identity will protect him against that. He must remain what he is—he, himself, and nobody else.

Naturally, this firmness does not exclude his constant readiness to learn, to change, to develop, to grow and mature. The therapist is not a patient in his group, but just as a good parent allows the members of his family to recognize him in strength and in weakness, so the good therapist—more than the analyst—shows himself as a real person. Doing so invites the members of the group-family to become independent and to avoid the danger of regressive infantilization, which is prevalent in psychoanalysis. Doing so also counteracts the patient's suspicion that he is being manipulated when he sees what the conductor does. It is the basis for the group's working alliance.

Humor

Another character trait of great importance can help the group therapist keep his group from unnecessary infantilization, and that is the group therapist's sense of humor. It is needed in group therapy to a higher degree than in individual therapy because it helps the group see the therapist as a real person. It counteracts the transference that idealizes the therapist as an omniscient parental figure. A man with a sense of humor invites the group to look at him realistically and to correct transference distortions. Humor still leaves the situation open for changes as the transference demands it. The therapist's sense of humor reassures the group that he will accept the multifaceted transference trends. It allows the patients to pierce the therapist's facade or character defenses, and so it is a most important safeguard against the infantilization of the group. Just as children may as well know the strengths and weaknesses of their parents in order to become independent, so it is important for the group to see in the therapist a transference figure and a real person. Only then can they, unlike the patient in individual therapy, use him as a transference figure and simultaneously as a teammate in the group team effort. No therapist can remain a blank screen within the group forever.

The therapist has to be somewhat on guard with his always ready wit and his fondness for the wisecrack and the sharply pointed and often painfully penetrating remark. Such remarks show his incompletely resolved ambivalence and perhaps some sadistic traits, which have no place among the tools of a therapist. He employs his wit occasionally to counteract the trend to infantilization or hero worship, which is such a convenient way to hide hostility.

He hates to confess a mistake, but, if somebody thinks he can nail the therapist down in a contradiction or a mistake, he may say:

"I always considered the possibility of making a mistake. It would be the first time."

Such ironic remarks are not meant to be taken seriously, but they do imply a certain indirectness. Kidding makes the therapist alert to danger, since it does not lead to the free communication he tries to develop. He also does not join in social laughter, which is often meaningless. Therefore, his groups probably laugh less than groups of other therapists. He joins in the laughter only when he truly feels like it and when something funny has happened. It is a good sign in the development of group cohesion when all members—and the therapist—join in laughter once in a while.

A humorous attitude shows the therapist not as a sadistic, cutting wit but as an understanding and kind mother.

It was the therapist's habit to be on time or even ten minutes early, so that he could open the doors between his waiting room and his consultation room to watch the group assemble, which often gave him valuable clues to the interaction that followed. Once the therapist came shooting into the office at the last minute, and the group commented about it. One of the men looked sternly at him and said:

"I assume you had a motorboat accident while taking your morning walk?"

The therapist found this remark extremely funny and reacted to it loudly and happily.

A therapist who laughs with the group and at himself protects the group from becoming infantilized. They recognize the parental figure in his strength and weakness. It is one aspect of the basic honesty in communication.

Transferences

The proper use of the therapist's counter-transference nourishes and develops different aspects of the multiple transference situation in the group. With his central identity he is able to offer himself as a screen for different projections. He is guided by his knowledge of multileveled and multichanneled communication. He is aware that in every group three transference relationships must be differentiated: transference to him as a central figure, as in analysis; transference to other group members, as in a family; and transference to the group, as a mother symbol.

The individual analyst can slowly and deliberately interpret the transference, but the group therapist must react spontaneously—otherwise he is lost. To react spontaneously, he must feel the meaning of his position in the group at all times.

The peer transference situation in the group-family imposes a demand on the therapist that is less necessary in individual treatment. The group therapist should not fight with the members of the group for dominance by narcissistically displaying his brilliance or by showing his superiority in other ways. His only—and almost silent—superiority should be his honesty, courage, and frankness to understand the unconscious. The group therapist should use the peer relationship as an effective way to exercise therapeutic pressure. He should be able to handle this relationship not with envy and not with interference but by inviting it and protecting it. A jealous parent is not a good parent. The analyst in the analytic situation almost invites resistance: The patient feels he must defend his sickness against the father who wants to destroy it. The peer relationship in the group situation invites cooperative effort and is one of the most effective therapeutic potentials in group work.

More than the individual analyst, the group analyst must accept in himself a considerable amount of maternal identification. The group is the symbol of the mother, and a great part of the group therapeutic efficacy is based on a pre-oedipal maternal transference. The symbolic meaning of the group as a mother helps to steady the course of the group progress.

The therapist's maternal attitude facilitates the experience of weaning and individuation. The breaking of the mother-infant symbiosis may amount to an experience of rebirth in the group. In his maternal identification, the group therapist can be passive, indulgent, waiting, silent. It is a time of rest and saturation for him, awaiting the group's delivery from sickness.

A good mother has to learn that a child is a going concern, in Winnicott's words, and the good therapist, as mother, must learn how to trust the group, just as he would trust a child who is developing his own impulses for mastery and for becoming human. Trust in the well-mothered child is rewarded by the child's self-confidence—a good model for the therapist to understand the progress of a well-conducted group.

Fallibility

The group therapist may make mistakes; he is expected and allowed to do so. His honesty makes it possible for him to accept the correction of his mistake by the group, the way the head of a family listens to others in the family council. The therapist does not lose his position by admitting to a mistake. On the contrary, his central position may be confirmed. The only unforgivable mistake he can make is to pull rank, which a group of growing-up people will not tolerate.

The author does not like to confess to having made a mistake; however, he lets his patients feel that he respects them, that he listens to them, and that he most certainly takes them seriously and considers what they say meaningful. If a patient calls him an S.O.B., he considers the remark, in the first place, a sign of the patient's negative transference, but there is always a nagging thought that he may have done something that rightfully caused the patient to react that way. If an entire group unanimously stands up in censoring the therapist, he is sure that he has misjudged the situation. But even then, there are exceptions, and he has been in situations where he felt and actually was misunderstood by everybody. These are the moments when the therapist may retreat into a silently waiting attitude. A group therapist should always be ready to respond quickly but slow to retaliate.

Splitting Mechanism

Unlike an individual analyst, the group therapist must not consider himself always in the focus of all the multiple transference trends. It would be a mistake if he concentrated on the one transference trend in the group that relates to him, as in analysis. The therapist must be aware that approximately two-thirds of the interaction leaves him in the role of the observing bystander. Besides the transference to him as the central figure, the group re-enacts interfamily attitudes toward the family of peers and toward the group as a mother symbol. Therefore, the analytic group therapist has great freedom to work as an observer and participant instead of an interpreter.

Ross and Kapp suggested that the therapist use inner visualization to catch his own unconscious reaction to the free-associative material of the patient. This inner visualization while listening, this view with the third eye, helps the therapist find the understanding first in visual form and then in verbal formulation. The author has used this approach for many years without being fully aware of it. Only lately has he developed it into a useful technical tool that has grown to characterize his style of empathy.

A not-especially-depressed patient told the group about a dream: He took a walk with his daughter, crossed a river, and admired the overwhelmingly beautiful landscape. The therapist was still busy in his mind with the last interaction between some group members and was not quite willing to follow into the dream, and so it did not speak to him. When he turned into himself to perceive the visual images that appeared on his inner screen by listening, he saw hieroglyphics cast into the walls of an Egyptian tomb; then appeared the sarcophagus, from which the body of the Pharaoh had been removed to show the exquisitely painted picture of the goddess of death on the bottom—outstretched arms ready to receive in death her Pharoah, her son and brother and lover. From there it was only a question of how to formulate the insight in order to confront the patient with his preoccupation with death.

Special beauty in dreams generally signifies the beauty of the peace one hopes to find after death. Later, returning to the dream, one can show that frequently the longing for death is a hope for the final reunion with the powerful, beautiful, and eternally waiting mother. Every group at some time or other has to deal with the problems of death and dying, loss, mourning, and grief.

In a letter to Stefan Zweig in 1931, Sigmund Freud compliments the author on his book *Mental Healers* and congratulates him for recognizing correctly that Freud's achievement is less the result of intelligence than of character. Freud adds:

At the time when the microscope was a new instrument in the hands of physicians, textbooks on physiology declared that a microscopist had to possess very special and rare qualifications. Later on, the same requirements were made of surgeons; today every student learns to use the microscope, and good surgeons are trained in schools. That not everyone carries out his job equally well is something for which there is no remedy in any field.

THE GROUP THERAPIST AS A PATIENT

A man who accepts his patienthood— Erikson's word—becomes a good physician later. A good physician learns how to use the experience of being sick to become a better physician. But, as a rule, the medical man is a poor patient—and that is nothing to be proud of. The situation is the same in the development of a good group psychotherapist. Psychoanalysis teaches insight and understanding, but group psychotherapy offers therapy to the therapist.

When a physician goes to another physician because he is sick, he inevitably says to his colleague: "I want you to treat me like any other patient of yours." To which the consulted colleague is honor-bound to answer: "That was my intention anyhow." And then they both promptly relate to each other like two colleagues discussing a most interesting third person. In the case of serious illness horrible results can originate in such a situation.

It is only partially true that the physician has to become a patient. The question is how to do it. The physician actually is different from the average patient, who knows little about his body and nothing about the function of his inner organs, and different, too, from the neurotic patient, even if he has read something about his unconscious.

The physician in medical treatment and the therapist in training each have to learn how to split themselves into two parts—one part remains a therapist and joins his colleague as co-therapist; another part becomes a patient in therapy. This splitting makes the working alliance in the training and therapeutic situation different from other treatment situations. If not handled correctly, it seriously limits the therapeutic efficacy of training analysis. The therapist in training or therapy has to learn how to perform such a split, and the teacher has to be aware of it. If the teacher accepts his therapist-students only as students, they will never become patients, since they want to become what the training analyst is—an accepted member of the analytic community. To be effective, training must combine the therapeutic alliance with a learning alliance.

The Analytic Group Experience

It has been said that a psychiatrist passes through three stages: Young psychiatrists talk about their cases, established psychiatrists talk about money, and senior analysts talk about themselves. After 40 years of work in psychiatry and 30 years in psychoanalysis, the author is presumably ready for the third stage. Accordingly, he would like to mention the reasons he has turned to group psychotherapy; this turn is a result of continued introspection and examination of his work as a psychotherapist and as an instructor of psychotherapists.

A senior colleague once confessed with some embarrassment to a great teacher that he felt fed up with supervision because for many years he had taught little children how to spell cat, and they still did not know how. By contrast, the author recently had the chance to observe the development of six capable young psychiatrists while in training. He saw them through almost three years of twice-weekly group sessions, and it was his impression that they learned a great deal —perhaps more than they would have learned in the same time in individual psychoanalysis. They gained understanding of themselves and insight into each other and their interaction, both consciously and unconsciously. This learning was deepened by interpretation and by the emotional experience of honest and free response to the members of the group. They experienced their relationship to the therapist as a central figure more or less as they would have done in the one-to-one relationship of psychoanalysis. They also experienced the relationship to each other, thus including peer relationships in the learning situation. A threefold transference relation developed in the group: to the therapist, to each other, and to the group as a mother symbol.

This group of young doctors did not differ greatly from a group of experienced analysts who formed another group the therapist studied for several years. All had undergone long, repeated, therapeutic, didactic analyses before, during, and after their training was officially terminated as successful. With growing analytic sophistication, they all realized that the one-to-one relationship was not enough to give them a satisfying and lasting therapeutic experience. They all had learned to master the one-to-one relationship, frequently as a form of resistance. They had learned to handle and manage their different analysts and to block further progress effectively. The change from the one-to-one analytic isolation to the group experience and peer relationship continued and deepened the analytic process they had started in their analyses and carried on in their work.

One analyst is not enough in the terminal stage of an analysis for an analyst. Repeated analysis by different analysts has been recommended and tried by Kubie among others. But analysts learn how to deal with their analysts and how to disarm them, so another analyst is not the solution to this phenomenon. Equally unsatisfactory is an always-longer training analysis. Neither is a friend able to continue the analysis of an analyst where his training left off. In such a friendship, there is too much affection, too much relaxation, too little freely expressed hostility and not enough working through of the transference phenomena.

A new transference situation is needed, and it is provided by the one-of-us relationship in the group. The transference of peers to each other and to the group as a mother image is needed in order to analyze the analyst within the family transference. Most analysts growing older in their profession lose the trust, confidence, and faith in their colleagues that they had when they started as young men and accepted an analytic working relationship to older training analysts. As they grow older, a certain therapeutic skepticism takes hold. In the one-to-one relationship this skepticism becomes even stronger. It is easier to reactivate confidence and trust in a group relationship than in an individual setting.

A middle-aged analyst went to a therapist who, many years previously, had seen him through a part of his analytic training. The analyst was in one of those depressions significant for aging analysts: He felt isolated, alienated, bored, skeptical, disappointed, almost cynical. The older analyst spent some time with him and then invited him to join one of his groups. This one was reserved for analysts, since they close ranks in defense of psychoanalysis when outsiders are present. Also, their methods of free-associative communication are sometimes frightening or unintelligible to the uninitiated. The middle-aged analyst joined the group with the usual resistance; but at the first meeting he surprised the older analyst by telling two symbolic stories that highlighted his entire life development. After the session, the therapist did not want to confess outright that these stories were new to him, so he said diplomatically:

"You know, we never fully analyzed the meaning of those two significant stories while you were in analysis."

The younger analyst said bluntly:

"Because I never told them to you!"

An association too revealing to be told to the parental image of the analyst was easily told as an introduction and presentation to the family of peers.

Two additional observations may help to explain why the analytic group experience is of special therapeutic and learning importance for the analyst as well as for the later group therapist. These observations relate to conflict-free areas and negative transference.

Conflict-Free Personality Trends. Ernst Ticho discussed this problem in a paper, hoping to analyze these conflict-free areas in the supervision of the student therapist. The author prefers consistent and careful analysis in the group. Many areas that do not cause special conflict in the analyst may never appear in his analysis; they will show up in his relationship to his patients, but they may not become visible under supervision. They will certainly become obvious in the relationship to the peers in the group. These areas involve such things as the distribution and combination of activity and passivity, maleness and femaleness, other-directedness and inner-directedness, enthusiasm and sobriety, masochistic and sadistic trends, sensitive and insensitive social consciousness, tolerance and intolerance, loving and hostile trends, spontaneity and intellectualization, patience and impatience.

Negative Transference. The transference to the training analyst is by implication a transference to an authoritarian parental figure. Since the student therapist wants to become like his analyst, he submits to him and seems to do so willingly. But secretly and out of reach, he harbors a trend to rebellion and postpones this negative part of his attitude, which is typical in the analytic training situation. Often, this rebellion is expressed only later in the life of an analyst. But in the group situation, where the peer relationship prevails, it comes to the surface of consciousness and can be analyzed.

An ever-deepening criticism of analytic training is becoming apparent. Analysts have failed in the therapy that is a part of training. Clinical evidence is given by the majority of analysts and the pathology of analytic group behavior.

The problem of negative transference and hostility in training analysis has remained a central, controversial issue. This is not just a transference problem. It is also a realistic problem. Since the patient, in his desire to be like his analyst, postpones his rebellion and much of the negative transference until he is through with his training, it usually hits him with great force and leads to all kinds of personal problems internally and to manifest problems in interaction with his colleagues. The analyst carries his unresolved hostility into the family of analysts, and a repeated analysis helps little.

The problem of the analysis of negative transference is also a countertransference problem: Fathers want to be loved by their student-sons, who, after all, represent the future. Therefore, analysts tend to relate differently to their training candidates in action, behavior, and interpretation than to most of their other patients.

Kubie has discussed these problems and has confessed that the transference neurosis is never really dissolved in a training analysis. As a remedy, he asks for a real relationship in the form of a controlled, disciplined, low-intensity friendship after the formal analysis. He also suggests a change of analyst during the terminal stage of training. The new analyst is supposed to take a better look at the leftover transference to the first analyst.

In the author's experience, the analytic group experience offers decisive help in the final resolution of negative transference relationships because the transference in the group situation is not simply a continuation of the infantile transference neurosis. The group offers a re-enactment of the family transference neurosis. In the group there is a freer expression of hostility than in the one-to-one relationship. A young man does not wish to attack an older man who represents a professional ideal, and an older man has learned from experience to be cautious with a colleague. In a therapeutic group, however, these trends are less intense and are more easily interpreted.

The group members can freely dish out hostility, and the therapist—the central figure—can freely respond to it. The members, knowing that their peers share their feelings, are encouraged by the fact that they will not be isolated in their hostility. The central figure, on the other hand, is much freer to accept hostility, before it is interpreted, since he knows that rarely will the entire group join in hostile rebellion. And the central figure can much more freely express his counterhostility in a group, since he can trust the group to control his responses, if need be.

The intensity of the peer relationship in the group transference makes up for the diminution of the ambivalent father transference. A great and almost unmanageable burden is shifted from the one-to-one relationship to the group-family, where the burden can be felt, expressed, interpreted, and integrated.

The Family Romance. Analytic training liberates the individual analyst in training from the tyranny of his unconscious, but his family romance remains largely unanalyzed. The transference of the infantile past into the psychoanalytic situation is accomplished in the setting of individual analysis, but it is repeated and deepened in a different way through the transference of the family romance into the analytic group situation. There the infantile past can be experienced, interpreted, understood, and integrated.

Freud may have known this; the minutes of the early meetings of the Viennese Psychoanalytic Society show that these seminars were originally organized for the purpose of teaching psychoanalysis, but they soon assumed the character of modified therapeutic group sessions. Another example of an early analytic group experience was the intimate daily discussions of Freud, Jung, and Ferenczi on their ocean crossing to America.

It is true that the student body of an analytic training institute forms a kind of analytic family. But this family remains in an unconsciously motivated transference situation and, therefore, is in need of being analyzed. This analysis can best be done in the family transference setting of group psychotherapy.

The analytic group experience gives the therapist in training a chance to analyze the repressed family romance. The group process facilitates an analysis of a collective family transference neurosis. Such a group experience could be the road to academic freedom and democracy in psychoanalysis and psychotherapy. If offers an analysis of dogmatism before it is deeply entrenched.

Transferences. The transference situation within the analytic group is threefold. A transference relationship to the central figure of the group is formed approximately according to the transference situation in individual analysis. An equally strong—and sometimes even stronger—transference is toward the other members of the group—the siblings, whether they be older or younger, of the same sex or the other sex. A third and very important transference is especially visible in groups of experienced analysts—transference to the group as a mother figure.

The dynamics of the group process facilitate insight and interpretation of the complex transference phenomenon. Every member of the group is both participant and observer, therapist and patient. He can at any time change from one role to the other, offering new insight and new approaches to old defenses established in the one-to-one relationship.

Transference phenomena in the group, as compared to those in individual therapy, are not lessened or diluted or diminished or kept more realistic or quickly corrected. All these claims are partially true and partially not true—but beside the point. The transference in the group is always different from the individual analytic situation, since it is specifically, significantly, and essentially a family transference, with the emphasis on the peer relationship of the siblings. The transference may be regressive, or it may be progressive, but it is always seen in relationship to the family romance as transferred to the group. Parents tend to assume, "Once a child, always a child." And training analysts tend to assume that candidates remain candidates forever, and sometimes this is true. Group psychotherapy facilitates the process of weaning on both sides, and in many cases the group experience is essential to this individuation. The analytic group-family offers natural trends to health, growth, and maturation similar to those found in any family. These trends are stronger in the group than in the isolation of the analytic one-to-one situation.

The group situation offers more transference gratification with less danger than does the formal or standard analysis. A member may receive support and affection from other members of the group. The central figure of the therapist can show affection or hostility to a higher degree and more spontaneously, since he is always aware of the corrective influence of the group. He can express himself much more freely because the group renders the therapist less powerful than he is in individual therapy. His power is replaced by the more flexible therapeutic pressure of the peer group.

The patient in individual psychoanalysis behaves like an only child. In a group the patient behaves like a member of a family with a number of children.

Didactic Groups

Young psychotherapists are inclined to use intellectualization as a form of resistance. An often-heard phrase in a didactic group is:

We all talk like a bunch of smart professionals.

The avoidance of intellectualization, after it has been repeatedly called by that term, may lead to a new form of resistance: Insights are resolutely rejected because they may sound too intellectual to a board of experts. There are sometimes episodes of resistance in a group of therapists, where every interpretation is labeled a rationalization and only emotions are considered therapeutically valid.

Perhaps, in a group, colleagues have to learn how to replace questions by associative responses. In the first stage of group formation, professional members try to confirm their impressions and planned interpretations by fishing for more clinical evidence. They soon realize that their spontaneous response is more important and usually contains the proper interpretation. They then develop the courage for human response, overcoming the handicap of the medical person who is suspicious of spontaneity and who has been trained to filter his responses carefully.

Work in groups of psychiatrists or psychoanalysts is tough for the central figure. Whether experienced or inexperienced, in training or accomplished in years of practice, a group of colleagues will recognize the therapist's weak spots. They use their therapeutic skill to put their finger where it hurts most, and the narcissistic therapist in charge may feel in need of a hiding place. If he is open, responsive, and ready to learn, he will succeed—like a father who does not pull rank but who accepts true democracy and real freedom in his family. Only then can the group become a learning experience as well as a therapeutic one.

The conduct of a training group for therapists is excellent postgraduate training for the central figure as well as for the members of the group. The therapist has to perform in the presence of six or eight alert and specially trained critics. At times, the experience almost amounts to a board examination. Anyone who passes such a test has received a real baptism under analytic fire. Only total honesty and sincerity save the therapist. The analyst who has difficulty in allowing himself to feel his hostility or his need for tenderness benefits the most. He can learn how to be more free, spontáneous, and responsive. The same group that exposes him also protects him until he finds his way to an attitude appropriate for him. The psychoanalyst satisfies his need for intimacy in the one-to-one relationship, but in the group he satisfies his need for participation in the growth and maturation of a family.

At the beginning of the author's work with groups, he was concerned about his inadequate knowledge of the patient's history when trying to make a genetic interpretation. He now uses the time during the patient's preparation for the group to elicit this material, and he accepts new members for a group only when he knows them and they know him fairly well. He has also noticed that after a while in the group one knows much more about a patient than one realizes. The more experienced the therapist becomes, the less often does he request individual sessions for information or clarification.

The group as the analytic mother allows a therapeutic alliance between members of the group that transcends the transference to the central figure. There is a courageous and honest attempt to deal in a free and spontaneous way with each other and with the central figure.

When working in groups, the analyst's narcissism takes a severe blow. When he steps out of his professional isolation, he sees that he is not the only good therapist. But he also realizes that he is not making many more mistakes than his colleagues. He may find that people he has not especially respected are quite different in the intimate interaction of a group, and this is a worthwhile human experience. After the group experience, a new, humble, and realistic attitude replaces his narcissism and makes him a better therapist.

The Therapist's Wife

Morgan treated therapists and their wives simultaneously and concomitantly. The author once preferred to split up couples and place the partners in different groups, since he assumed it would be better for them to develop courage for free communication with others before he let them try it on each other. But he soon agreed with Morgan's idea that a great deal of a therapist's future depends on his attitude toward his marriage, his wife, and his children. The analyst should never be a therapist in his own family; there he should act and react, not analyze. But it is easier and more meaningful for a therapist to gain insight into his Mother Superior complex while working with his wife in the same group.

Group psychotherapy seems especially suited to satisfy the specific needs of therapists and their spouses because it offers them an extended analytic family. The therapist's wife has to learn that nobody can be a therapist in his own family, even if he is considered an expert and The Professor by his wife. In the extended family of the group, a learning experience is offered to him—how to be helpful and understanding without using the tools of his trade. To learn this is important for the happiness of his family, and it influences his therapeutic attitude later.

Furthermore, analytic group work with therapists and their wives brings relief from the burden of secrecy. The partner in the analyst's marriage often feels left out of an important part of her husband's life. In the group with him, she is introduced into his work, its pleasure and its pain, its frustration and its hope. Secrecy leads to a skillful and unfair way of infighting in a therapist's family and to the abuse of the therapist's gentle art for that purpose.

The therapist's cursed need to be Mother Superior can be analyzed in a couples group. This need is frequently neglected in individual analyses, since it is often conflict-free—it belongs to the medical attitude of healing. Many analysts and perhaps all physicians have an unconscious need to show their wives that women are bad mothers and that doctors are much better if given a free hand. The doctor's Mother Superior complex leads him to unfair competition at home, causing heartbreaking trouble and frequently leading to a sadomasochistic, malignant acting out, which can be aggravated by quick and unannounced role reversals. Frequently, the children pay the price for the parents' competitiveness.

The identification with the mother is probably the basis of creative work, as it can be studied so strikingly in the life and work of Sigmund Freud. Nevertheless, the therapist must be aware of how destructive competition at home with his wife may become if not analyzed and corrected. Besides endangering his relationship to his wife, the competition may have the most destruc-

tive influence on the growth of the children and their sexual identification. A mother needs support from her husband, not competition.

Any woman so foolish as to marry a physician who is, in addition, a therapist must gain insight into her husband's tendency not to project his own femininity onto her but to keep it jealously embedded in his own behavior. In this respect the therapist strays specifically from the normal course of heterosexual development. The therapist's wife has to learn how to invite her husband to trust her with his femininity and to love it not in himself but in her. The other women in the group of therapists often restore a woman's strength and belief in her own femininity, which has been endangered by a therapist-husband's competitiveness in this respect. A therapist at home can be dangerous when he treats his wife by a method that is often called by the group "gaslighting." It means to drive somebody slowly, consistently, deliberately, and occasionally successfully into madness by skillfully undermining her self-confidence and identity as a mother, wife, and woman.

A therapist's wife has many opportunities to fail. One of the many things she has to learn in the beginning of her marriage is that her husband, supposedly an expert in the art of loving understanding of people, is omnipotent neither at home nor in his office. The love of wives must stand that disappointment.

Because he works in utter isolation, the therapist loses the benefits of feedback from his colleagues, and this line of communication can be re-established in group work. With increased freedom, the therapist's dialogue in his group, in his family, and finally with his patients becomes less defensive, freer, deeper, and more spontaneous. He even learns how to overcome his isolation at home and how to be more trusting, open, and ultimately more honest.

The analytic group method permits him to see himself through the frank and open response of others to him. It is a great experience that husband and wife should share. As Morgan wrote:

For better or worse we are stuck with our profession, even more than with our families.

The Therapist's Mental Health

The therapist does not need to be a paragon of mental health. He can proceed in the face of his own anxiety, even if it sometimes borders on a slight phobia, just as he can proceed efficiently with all kinds of psychosomatic conversions, such as high blood pressure, migraine, and perhaps even a gastric ulcer. It is preferable for a therapist to overcome his symptoms, and he sometimes does. The analysis and correction of conflict-free areas in a neurotic co-worker takes time, and the therapist may work well before his own therapy is completed.

The author has his doubts about paranoid trends in a group therapist, since a suspicious therapist may communicate his suspicions in a way that does not benefit the group process. A therapist who has passed through a psychotic episode may do well to disqualify himself for his own and his patients' sake, even if he sometimes shows a remarkable understanding of the sickest patients. This is not the understanding of a therapist but the understanding of a fellow sufferer. It may lead to a kind of understanding that rests in itself and never matures into therapeutic intervention.

A slight and perhaps even chronic depressive position may actually be a qualification for a therapist. In the face of so much often-unnecessary human suffering, a sensitive person almost must become slightly depressed. It is a kind of existential despair, a way of being human, an acknowledgment of our impossible profession. It does not interfere with the therapist's functioning. It may give him that kind of maturity a child expects from his parents.

The group therapist may be a man who knows anxiety and fear as well as depression and despair. In the therapeutic alliance with his patients, he must not fear his fears.

Conclusion

The analytic group experience in the later stages of the group therapist's maturation has great therapeutic and training efficacy, since it emphasizes the experience, interpretation, and integration of a family transference. The experience of the group process gives the therapist insight and understanding into the therapeutic group process.

The benefits of individual analysis, which are essential for the training of any therapist, must be combined with analytic group experience, which offers deepened therapeutic efficacy. The group replaces the authoritarian parent, who invites rebellion and resistance, with the strong and effective peer relationship within a group family. Under the observation of a group, the conflict-free areas of the therapist's personality, which might never be reached by the training analyst in individual analysis, may be brought out into the open and approached by the group analytic process.

GROWTH AND MATURATION

Some analysts develop the belief that they are superior to all others. Some become bitter and cynical about therapeutic needs, or they become exhibitionistic and narcissistic, depressive or resigned. Their reputation by then may be affirmed, and an encounter with these great men of therapy may still be worthwhile for the patient.

Therapists are not patients among patients, even if at times they allow themselves to become members of the group-family. If they deny themselves this therapeutic alliance with their groups, they become rigid or lazy or old in the worst sense of the word—meaning of closed mind.

A therapist is mature when he has learned how to deal with the inner and outer reality of himself and his patients. He becomes wise when he has also learned how to deal with the problem of death and dying. He will have died young if he refuses to learn with his patients and from them. There is a definite difference between therapeutic benefit and learning. The therapist is not a patient among patients, but he remains a student among people who want to learn how to live. With their mistakes and with their needs, they can teach the therapist—no matter how old he is or how many years he has spent in his profession.

The author sometimes has the impression that people with a European background and upbringing develop an effective therapeutic relationship more easily. He is not talking about defensiveness against a puritanism long passed. He is talking about a specific European attitude that he had a chance to observe in the early days of the Berlin Institute of Psychoanalysis. Students and analysts continued their discussions in the coffeehouses after the meetings and debated with enthusiasm, skill, joy, artistry, and intense emotion. They did not need enemies when they had friends. This open hostility toward a friend forms an essential part of any working alliance. Similarly, therapists are not lovers, not even friends, to their patients. Neither are they enemies. A working relationship is a fighting relationship; the healthy ego of the patient fights with the therapist against the bad, the evil, the sinful, and the sick. Many people think that one should not fight with a friend. The author has learned that one should fight only with his friends. In group psychotherapy this attitude is an absolute necessity, and the group knows it without being told.

In this kind of infighting, the therapist needs strength and endurance. He must not be a hit-and-run therapist—a therapist who has a good intuitive sense about the patient's sensitive areas, which he invades with speed and accuracy, but then does not stand his ground and work. Instead, he retreats with the same speed at which he advanced. He prefers an easy peace to the necessary encounter. He does not give the patient time for working through. What was intended to be a maturing experience may turn into a trauma followed by defensive measures, complicating later work.

The therapist may know fear, but he is not allowed to retreat from it. He must learn from a surfboard rider how to use the power of sickness in order to ride on top of it to health.

The therapist may also know temptation toward his patients, whether it be a feeling of intimacy or an urge to violence. Occasionally, he even may allow himself to show his feelings of affection and tenderness until he understands them and masters them.

The group situation offers the therapist much greater emotional and verbal freedom than does the atmosphere of intimacy in individual analysis. The group is an effective supervisor.

It would be an abuse of the therapeutic situation if the therapist presented himself as a patient, as some therapists claim to do. However, it would be a severe insult to the principal rule of honesty, frankness, and sincerity if the therapist were not willing to offer his unconscious for understanding by the group. He has to learn how to function between the two opposite mistakes of becoming a burden to the group and trying to be the master and out of reach.

It is easier to grow old gracefully as a group therapist than in the isolation of the dyadic analyst. The therapist must not abuse his groups as tools of treatment for himself, but he must accept the help of the group in the continuation of his self-analysis.

Beethoven is supposed to have said, "If you understand my music, you are saved." Reformulated a little, the adage means that, when the therapist is understood by his group patients, he has learned something—and they have benefited, like a family who understands that Mother or Father has freed the way to further growth, maturation, and individuation.

REFERENCES

Erikson, E. H. *Childhood and Society.* W. W. Norton, New York, 1950.

Fairbairn, W. R. D. Synopsis of an object relation theory of the personality. Int. J. Psychoanal., *44:* 224, 1963.

Greenson, R. R. The selection of candidates for psychoanalytic training. A panel report. J. Amer. Psychoanal. Assoc., *9:* 135, 1961.

Greenson, R. R. The working alliance and the transference neurosis. Psychoanal. Quart., *34:* 134, 1965.

Grotjahn, M. The process of maturation in group psychotherapy and in the group therapist. Psychiatry, *13:* 63, 1950.

Grotjahn, M. Special problems in the supervision of group psychotherapy. Group Psychother. *3:* 308, 1951.

Grotjahn, M. *Psychoanalysis and the Family Neurosis,* W. W. Norton, New York, 1960.

Grotjahn, M. Supervision of analytic group psychotherapy. Group Psychother. *13:* 161, 1960.

Grotjahn, M. Supervision of analytic group psychotherapy. Group Psychother. *13:* 222, 1960.

Grotjahn, M. On being a sick physician. In *New Dimensions in Psychosomatic Medicine*, p. 117, C. W. Wahl, editor. Little, Brown, Boston, 1964.

Grotjahn, M. Analytic group therapy with psychotherapists. Int. J. Group Psychother., *19:* 326, 1969.

Guntrip, H. *Schizoid Phenomena, Object Relations and the Self: The Developing Synthesis of Psychodynamic Theory*. International Universities Press, New York, 1968.

Jones, E. *The Life and Work of Sigmund Freud*. Basic.Books, New York, 1955.

Kohut, H. The evaluation of applicants for psychoanalytic training. Int. J. Psychoanal., *49:* 548, 1968.

Kubie, L. Unsolved problems in the resolution of the transference. Psychoanal. Quart., *37:* 331, 1968.

Mahler, M. *On Human Symbiosis and the Vicissitudes of Individuation*. International Universities Press, New York, 1968.

Morgan, D. Psychoanalytic group psychotherapy for therapists and their wives. Int. J. Group Psychother., *21:* 107, 1971.

Nunberg, H., and Federn, E., editors. *Minutes of the Vienna Psychoanalytic Society*, vol. 2, *1908–1910*. International Universities Press, New York, 1967.

Reik, T. *Listening with the Third Ear*. Farrar, Straus, & Giroux, New York, 1948.

Ross, W., and Kapp, F. A technique for self-analysis of counter transference: use of the psychoanalyst's visual images in response to patient's dreams. J. Amer. Psychoanal. Assoc., *10:* 643, 1962.

Winnicott, D. *The Maturational Processes and the Facilitating Environment: Studies in the Theory of Emotional Development*. International Universities Press, New York, 1965.

Zetzel, E. The theory of therapy in relation to a developmental model of a psychic apparatus. Int. J. Psychoanal., *46:* 39, 1965.

8

Existential Group Therapy: A Phenomenological Methodology for Psychiatry

Herbert Holt, M.D.

INTRODUCTION

The field of group therapy has become stabilized in the United States to the extent that there have emerged three basic approaches to its practice. Moreno's psychodrama is perhaps the best known. Those who come to the sessions may choose to remain strictly spectators, but the implication of the method is that even those who do not participate in the drama carry away from the sessions some benefit in greater understanding of their own and others' personalities. Other practitioners—for example, Slavson and his associates—adopt stricter procedures with an eye to scientific methods of control, carefully matching the membership of their various groups and working deliberately toward predetermined goals. A third school of thought, represented by Wolf and his associates, tries to maintain Freudian procedures in the group setting. That is to say, the analyst tries to maintain toward the members of the group the same detached and observant attitude that he would employ in individual therapy. He therefore becomes the focus of collective projections and is able to point out to the members of the group the characteristic ways in which they interact with each other. But his own personality is not directly involved; he is always understood to be a group leader.

Existential group therapy as currently practiced offers a fourth way, one which may be said to include the insights of previous methods and transcend the differences between them. It deserves attention because its theory and methods offer help not otherwise available to many individuals. The use of the word "existential" implies a connection with the philosophy of Heidegger and Sartre and with the European psychoanalytic tradition associated with the name of Binswanger. Both Heidegger and Sartre, however, have elaborated on the method of thought of their teacher Husserl, the principal exponent of the philosophical technique called phenomenology. Thus existential analysis, as both an individual and a group method, is phenomenological in its method and existential in its assessment of the realities of the contemporary human situation.

EXISTENTIAL ANALYSIS AND PHENOMENOLOGY

In a manner suggestive of Horney's holistic approach, phenomenology takes as its starting point the need to understand each individual in terms of his unique total experience. The difference is that in phenomenology the attempt is made to suspend all theoretical preconceptions and systems in order to reach the structure of the experience in its own terms, as it "appears" to the individual. His behavior and his subjective states are regarded as part of a single living reality. Experience is not subjected to analysis into its constituent units but is described and made conscious in terms of its phenomenological unity. It is unique and individual, and it can be described adequately only from the individual's point of view in a manner that makes it comprehensible in its totality. Subjective states are understood phenomenologically as part of a life style which imposes a certain comprehensive structure on an individual's experience of the world, which even determines what he will experience and what he chooses to avoid. It adds up to something, to a mental structure that causes him to organize all his experience to serve a certain image of himself and of his phenomenological world—that is, the total world of his experience.

Requirements for a Phenomenological Approach

Spiegelberg lays down three requirements for any approach that claims to call itself phenomenological. It must start from direct exploration of what is experienced and of the manner in which it presents itself to individual consciousness. It must seek out the structure behind what is experienced and the relationships between its various elements in terms of space and time. And it must try to see how the structure develops an image of the phenomena as it is taking shape.

This is in fact a concise description in philosophical terms of the therapist experience in the group. It shares something with the natural attitude of the empirical physician who establishes a position of detachment from which he observes, diagnoses, and prescribes treatment for the condition he has decided is present in his patient. But neither the nature of his "data" nor the requirements of his role as a human

being in a group enables the therapist to remain a detached observer if he is not to distort the situation. What is more, if he does not participate as a human being he will not be able to penetrate to the decisive realities of the individual personalities of the group members.

Phenomenology suggests that the uniqueness of human experience requires a particular viewpoint if it is to be adequately comprehended. Reacting to centuries of philosophical argument about the reality or lack of reality of the world of experience, phenomenology insists that the proper direction of the investigation is the question of what it is to experience a world and how it feels to experience one's own body.

Bracketing

The primary technique of the investigation is a process that Husserl called "bracketing." It means putting mental brackets around the question of the truth of objective reality—coming to no conclusion about the reality or unreality of what is experienced—in order to redirect attention to the more productive consideration of how the individual experience "appears" or "presents itself" to consciousness. The technique of bracketing makes possible a reduction of raw experience to its phenomenological unity. In therapeutic practice there are two stages in this process: First a separation of internal from interpersonal experience, which of course is desirable because it enables an individual to begin to be able to refrain from working out unconscious processes in his various relationships and thus to avoid reifying his symptoms. The next step is the further reduction of internal experience to the images that underlie awareness of it. These underlying images, which in clinical terms are revealed most starkly by dreams, daydreams, and fantasies, are the most direct and concrete representations that we can reach of what Husserl spoke of as the transcendental ego.

Phenomenological Reduction and Therapy

When applied to the practice of therapy, the focus of interest is no longer communication of the philosophical conclusions, or an adequate written formulation of what they are, but the shared experience of living human beings. That is why, though accepting the method of phenomenological philosophy, we reject, as the existentialists also have done, many of Husserl's conclusions about the transcendental ego and the nature of pure consciousness. Phenomenological reduction can be carried to a degree of abstraction which violates clinical reality, but the process can be carried forward only to the point at which it illuminates most clearly the structure of experienced reality in individuals. At an early point, we make use of the categories of existential philosophy, which speaks of the nature of "being-in-the-world" in three basic modes —the *Eigenwelt* of consciousness, the *Mitwelt,* which is the way in which we experience others in our world, and the *Umwelt* of our experienced biological environment, which includes not only awareness of the external conditions of the individual's ecological situation but also the phenomenological experience of his own body, since it is experienced as an object of awareness to the experiencing subject, just as the world itself is. When, by bracketing, these modes of "being-there" in the world are grasped in their totality, the therapist is freed to share with patients the communication of the structure of their way of experiencing themselves in their world. The *Eigenwelt* emerges in terms of its dreams, daydreams, and fantasies, and in the process a patient becomes aware of the "self" which is the subject of experience.

ADVANTAGES OF THE GROUP SETTING

There are several reasons for thinking that the group setting is particularly appropriate for this achievement. The work of Spitz and others supports the hypothesis that the basic experience of childhood is *Mitwelt* rather than *Eigenwelt* experience, interpersonal relationship rather than strictly internal consciousness. For people whose childhood experience was defective in certain primary stimuli, for whatever reason, the therapeutic group may provide a more natural *Mitwelt* than that of individual therapy, making possible the provision of experience necessary for growth to psychological maturity. In the second place, as the existentialists claim, experience, being direct and unequivocal, is never the same to talk about as it is to share. We gain insight into the nature of individual structures of experience by sharing it with others in the same space and time, and in therapeutic groups the individuals can experience as much as each of them can at whatever level each has reached, the possibilities for new and more authentic styles of life.

Shared Experience

It is this which provides the overriding justification for group therapy, which makes understandable the considerable investment of time and emotional energy that patients make in order to maintain the group. It is not for the sake of common interests or for a superficial kind of fellowship or even for something so vaguely desirable as friendship that they do so. It is not necessary that the members know each other well or even like each other, or that they engage in sexual or hostile acting out either within or outside of group sessions. Most important is that the group be something unique to the experience of the individuals involved—a locale in which no false imagery need be maintained but a mature identity may be discovered and strengthened.

The Therapist's Role

The concept of shared experience is the basis for the therapist's participation in the group process. He is actively and personally committed. He brings to the shared experience the qualities of his humanity as well as the tools of his phenomenological method. He commits himself fully as an individual while at the same time seeking to discover how each individual in the group experiences himself. The "consention" approach to dreams, which means sharing the feeling expressed by the dreamer to his own awareness, is the model for the therapist's participation in all the experience communicated by the group members to each other and to him. He shows the others how they can learn to experience the ways in which they seat themselves, how they hold their bodies, the pace of their action and speech, their tone of voice, and particularly what use they try to make of others and what reaction they characteristically make to the others' attempts to use them for their own purposes. They can learn that identity need not be lost when experience is shared with other members of the group. They can learn to come to terms with their unique life situations, to be present in them and open to the possibilities of the future. They can become aware of the possibility of "standing out" as individuals, and, finally, of the fact that to be in the world is to be moving continually on the way toward death.

Existential Anxiety

This final awareness is called "existential anxiety," and it is the common ground that the therapist shares with all the rest in their common humanity. Only when this anxiety emerges gradually as the structure that underlies all neurotic patterns of response can the choice be made between authentic living and a continued pattern of neurosis. Regardless of how it is made— and it need not be made one way or the other, for either way is hard—it will be perceived as a choice, and people will be aware that there is a difference between demanding identity from others, whether parents, friends, or working associates, and maintaining it for themselves. The existentialist insight makes us aware that the modern breakdown of traditional institutions, which provided identity and an imagery adequate for the whole span of life, has left us with the necessity of living alone, without images. The burden of this need, which we all feel to some degree, is all too often met by forcing on others a kind of fixed imagery that violates their human freedom. Psychoanalysis made us aware of the degree to which these tendencies have overloaded the imagery connected with the nuclear family, the one institution that now has to bear much of the burden formerly borne in large part by others. Adulthood requires the breaking of this parent-child imagery, which we seek to impose in all our human relationships, but it forces us to acknowledge to ourselves every day the anxiety of death.

TECHNIQUES

To maintain oneself against the downward pull of this knowledge is no small human achievement, and there is no set procedure for accomplishing it in existential therapy, any more than there is in everyday life situations. But the focus of whatever happens is on the here-and-now, the present effects. A member of the group may react to something immediately taking place. He may bring an insight from individual therapy that is still on his mind, or he may present to the others the content of a dream or a fantasy. The therapist may initiate the flow of conversation, or he may encourage a member of the group to begin with something that is important to him at that moment. All such data becomes current and shared experience among the group members. The existential therapist feels free to react to all such communications in his own right, if he chooses to do so, as well as to encourage the others to make responses out of their own experience. The focus of the inquiry is the nature of the response in the immediate situation rather than the content of the imagery and its relation to the unconscious life of the patient. Historical, etiological factors are certainly not ignored, and in fact are encouraged in the conversation. The stress, however, is on their current function. The therapist feels free not only to respond to the content of a given act or statement but also to say how he experiences the members of the group as living entities, as individuals functioning in human relationships. He can demonstrate what it means to take responsibility for the body-image that they present to the world, what it means to fail to do so, and what the connection is between this presentation of self and the images of dreams, daydreams, and fantasies. By such means he can hope to provide the "cueing-in" experiences of childhood growth stages for those who never fully experienced them before.

PARTICIPANTS IN EXISTENTIAL GROUP THERAPY

Unsuitable Types

It is apparent that even with the new biochemical sophistication that makes many former untreatables accessible to therapy, this type of therapy makes considerable demands on both patients and therapists. Thus existential group therapy is not indicated in all cases. One may treat individually people who suffer from various forms of borderline schizophrenia, on the basis of a firm sense of identity and a refusal to be set up by the patient in a certain way. It is not so easy to maintain such a relationship in groups, and accordingly there are several phenomenological types of people whose suitability for existential group therapy needs further study. There are those who despite fantasy wishes for closeness are unable to stand it, who resist and in every way demonstrate that they do not wish to enter into the genuine give-and-take that authentic closeness implies. Another group of people, much more plausible on the surface, includes those who have invested a great deal of emotional energy in

an intellectual understanding of their problem but in practice are rigid about this understanding, identify their thoughts with their selfhood, and focus their demands on an intellectual apprehension of what they are doing, meanwhile refusing to understand or enter into a shared relationship. Still others think only in black-and-white terms, to the extent that they must construe others as either lovers or haters of them, with no gradations in between and no possibility of a genuine interest in them which does not involve some kind of total reaction. Such people insist on making themselves the center of their world and relating everything else, as in early childhood, to the satisfaction of their own needs.

Suitable Types

What kind of patients are able to profit most from existential group therapy? In general, those people whose symptoms do not fit into any of the classic diagnostic patterns from the early days of psychoanalysis but whose sense of themselves has not developed sufficiently to give them confidence in their ability to live a meaningful life. Those are the people the psychiatric profession regard as having a nonspecific "problem of ego identity," to use Erikson's phrase. They have not moved far enough over the boundary between magic thinking and mature relationship. Once they begin to learn the technique of bracketing, they can apply it to the reactions of others in the group and to their own reactions. They can begin to learn what it means to maintain themselves in relationship to others and to allow others to be themselves in relation to them.

AIM OF EXISTENTIAL GROUP THERAPY

Ultimately the aim of existential group therapy is the same as that of individual therapy. It seeks to enable individuals to experience their own identity and take responsibility for it, to accept the limitations but also the rewards of their uniqueness. It is designed to help them discover how to experience others, not in black-and-white, for-or-against terms, but as individuals in their own right, people with whom they can voluntarily enter into an authentic relationship for cooperative purposes. Although such results are possible in other therapies, they are in the forefront of what existential group therapy seeks to achieve. It is not simply a search for symptom removal or even for a new way of relatedness to others. Desirable as these results are in all cases, and in many the sum of what can reasonably be hoped for, this type of therapy sets for itself a more comprehensive purpose.

Existential group therapy, then, is a clinical methodology which has developed an inclusive theoretical position. It draws upon the descriptive techniques of phenomenology and the existential understanding of man's condition in his biological and social world and in his world of consciousness. It is an active therapy most effectve for those who have achieved enough of a sense of themselves to maintain a minimal identity in a group. With the help of others they may go on to learn how voluntarily to enter into authentic relationships with people who have made the same kind of achievement.

REFERENCES

Binswanger, L. The Case of Ellen West. In *Existence*, R. May, editor. Basic Books, New York, 1958.

Binswanger, L. *Being-in-the-World*. Basic Books, New York, 1963.

Boss, M. *Psychoanalysis and Daseinsanalysis*. Basic Books, New York, 1963.

DeRosis, L. The existential encounter in group psychoanalysis. J. Psychoanal. in Groups, *1*: 2, 38, 1964.

Holt, H. The case of Father M. Transac. N.Y. Instit. Exist. Anal., *2*: 5, 1965.

Holt, H., and Winick, C. The consention approach to dreams. J. Rel. and Health, *1*: 2, 1965.

Holt, H. Existential analysis in groups. J. Psychoanal. in Groups, *2*: 1, 1965.

Holt. H. The hidden roots of aggression in American society. J. Existentialism, *5*: 21, Winter, 1965.

Holt, H. The psychiatrist: an alienated being in our time. Transac. N.Y. Instit. Exist. Anal., *2*: 6, 1965.

Holt, H. Existential group therapy. In *International Handbook of Group Psychotherapy*, J. Moreno, editor. Grune & Stratton, New York, 1966.

Mullan, H. Existential factors in group psychotherapy. Int. J. Group Psychother. *11*: 4, 449, 1964.

Powdermaker, F. B., and Frank, J. D. *Group Psychotherapy*. Harvard University Press, Cambridge, 1953.

Rosenblum, M. Current controversies in group psychotherapy. In *International Handbook of Group Psychotherapy*, J. Moreno, editor. Grune & Stratton, New York, 1966.

Spiegelberg, H. The idea of a phenomenological anthropology and Alexander Pfander's psychology of man. Rev. Exist. Psychol. and Psychiat., *5*: 122, 1965.

Spitz, R. Hospitalism. Psychoanal. Stud. Child *1*: 53, 1945, and papers in succeeding volumes.

9

The Reduction of Interracial Prejudice and Tension Through Group Therapy

Arthur S. Samuels, M.D.

INTRODUCTION

For centuries communication between the black man and the white man in the United States, as in most parts of the world, has been severely limited in frequency and content. The rigid social and economic barriers imposed by slavery and segregation have had a truly dehumanizing effect on both races. To be white has generally meant to be privileged and superior, to be black, to be deprived and powerless. The image of the individual black man and individual white man has been obscured almost to the point of invisibility by the resulting haze of stereotypy. The quality of communication between a member of one race and a member of the other has been and to a large extent remains like that of a mechanical diplomatic exchange between two nations engaged in a long cold war. The main message exchanged for many years has been, in effect:

We don't really trust each other, but for the time being we will maintain the *status quo* because we are afraid that we will lose something or that you will hurt us if we attempt to change things.

With the upsurge of new nationalism and the enhancement of nonwhite racial identity that followed World War II, the black message has been changing with increasing acceleration. The message of modern black militancy is:

We are not inferior; we hate you for treating us as inferior. We have a right to whatever is necessary for improving our situation. If we destroy you in the process of achieving our rightful position, it is only what you have long deserved.

And the general white response is also changed:

How can you turn your backs on all we have done for you? How can you threaten the system that is beginning to acknowledge your needs? We will defend with our lives what we have; we will destroy you if you try to use force.

Thus, centuries of uncommunicated feelings are finally emerging in a crescendo of mutual distrust, fear, and hatred. Their expression has reached explosive proportions in many communities. Sincere attempts to correct basic socioeconomic injustices are being made, but their efficacy is hampered by the inability of members of each race to really feel and understand the humanness of the other. Real differences in culture between the races are exaggerated in the stereotypes that each holds of the other. One cannot successfully identify with or constructively comprehend the motives of unidimensional stereotyped images. Those who work with people know how crucial it is to an authentic relationship that there be an inner resonance to the experiences of the other human being. This level of empathy is impossible to achieve when one experiences himself as a member of a category, white race or black, confronting a member of the other category —when there is little or no communication at the personal, human level.

But behind the fear and hatred are black and white human beings capable of reason and understanding, strikingly similar in their deepest yearnings and frustrations. The urgent need now is for the development of a means of penetrating the venerable barriers to interracial communication, to make possible a relating on a truly fraternal, human-to-human basis. In Martin Buber's terms, the I-It of racism must give way to the I-Thou of meaningful encounter.

The problem posed here is the social equivalent of the problem that confronts any psychotherapist. An essential goal in the therapeutic encounter is the establishment of authenticity: the ability to perceive the other as he really is, not as earlier experiences lead one to expect him to be. In group therapy, too, particularly in those groups emphasizing existential approaches, the peak experiences of the group occur when an I is clarified by meaningful sharing with a Thou. Buber has described the healing process as one in which one person aids another to establish a better identity. If one allows the other person to be different and still accepts and confirms him, then the first will have helped him to realize himself as he could not have done alone. This is the core goal to be achieved in each interracial group. When this goal is achieved, when blacks and whites are able to accept and confirm one another in their differentness, each feels stronger, more individual, yet closer to the other because of their differences.

Most of the problems encountered in conducting an interracial group are similar to those involved in leading experiential psychotherapy groups. The major difference is that the focus is on the illumination and reduction of social pathology. The adaptation of the psychiatric model for group therapy to the treatment of social pathology offers exciting prospects from the point of view of psychiatric theory, social change, and individual commitment.

PREJUDICE

A voluminous literature deals with the individual and social determinants of prejudice, ranging from the analysis of historical determinants to the appraisal of psychological experiments designed to reveal the psychodynamics of prejudice. Some familiarity with this literature is helpful in anticipating and understanding the problems that occur in interracial groups. It is possible here to cite only the most recent and significant works.

Campbell, Allport, and Myrdal describe sociological factors that contribute to ethnocentrism and bigotry. The Group for the Advancement of Psychiatry published an excellent monograph in 1957 dealing with the psychodynamics of prejudice as related to school integration. Psychoanalytic studies by Kardiner and Ovesey, McLean, and Seward explore the complex psychodynamic origins of prejudice. Grier and Cobbs provide much-needed insight into black attitudes and feelings. Some of the most meaningful insights into the reality of the black experience, as it relates to attitudes toward whites, may be gained from the autobiographical works of Brown, Cleaver, and Malcolm X.

Psychodynamics of Prejudice

On the individual, intrapsychic level, prejudice often represents a faulty attempt to cope with intolerable feelings of self-contempt by directing the hatred away from the despised parts of the self and onto another person or group. The others, through the distortions of racial mythology, can be made to serve as substitutes for the rejected parts of the self. The individual may then enjoy an illusory feeling of superiority; he experiences only the superior aspects of himself as he looks down on the inferior others.

As Binderhughs points out, racial and ethnic characteristics define convenient targets for this mechanism because people who are seen as different are initially perceived as objects to be kept out defensively; as automatically wrong, inadequate, and sinister, they must be rejected. The projection onto them of unacceptable impulses and undesirable characteristics then makes it impossible to achieve any real perception of similarities, of common human qualities.

Relating is based on projection rather than on introjection and identification.

Segregation itself further fosters prejudice and racial paranoia. The segregated group is identified with segregated thoughts, feelings, actions—the sexual, aggressive, excretive, or destructive aspects of behavior that society sets apart as unacceptable. At the same time, segregation makes impossible the communication that might correct these distortions.

Brody describes the effects of cultural deprivation and exclusion in societies in which some members are permitted only fragmentary participation in the value system and goal-directed responses. Socialization in such a society presents the members of excluded groups with poorly perceived and conflicting standards for behavior, eventually handicapping long-range planning for the achievement of future goals. Thus, in American society, hard work in school as a means of obtaining entry into a good college and finding a good job has no real relevance to children of impoverished families, and grade symbols become meaningless to them. Since the ultimate goals are not attainable, these young people may substitute immediate pleasure-seeking as a value in itself. They may achieve status in the eyes of their peers, who share this value and its mode of realization, but they cannot escape awareness of the conflict with the goals of the larger society. Their awareness of their low prestige in terms of the larger society contributes to the development of severe identity problems.

Members of such minority groups who do manage to improve their condition may develop feelings of hatred and revulsion toward characteristics of their own group. They may attempt to adopt the standards and values of the dominant group, including its prejudices. Brody and Derbyshire's study of Negro college students in Baltimore finds that many have embraced not only the anti-Semitic and anti-Oriental prejudices of the larger white society but the anti-Negro prejudices as well.

Grier and Cobbs, black psychiatrists, cite many case histories in which the discrepancy between what a black person feels he really is and what he feels he should be in order to be of value in the larger white society predispose him toward hatred of his own group, contempt for his own self-image, neurotically self-induced low self-esteem, and severely disabling, self-defeating patterns of behavior.

A black woman in an interracial group described this process well when her inability to enjoy a compliment paid her by one of the black men in the group led her to share her feelings about herself. She had been raised in a neighborhood of Creoles, Negroes who are generally proud of their light skin color, European features, and French background, but she herself was dark, with Negroid facial features. As a child, she felt shunned because of her appearance; she thought of herself as physically inferior, undesirable. She retreated into a world of books, encouraged in this activity by an aunt who was very important to her. Although she succeeded in working her way through college and achieved further success as a teacher, her physical image of herself was that of ugliness. Her appearance was associated with dirtiness and degradation. In selecting sexual partners, she chose only men who matched this debased image—men of lower intelligence and narrower interests, who tended to use and degrade her physically. She felt chronically anxious, lonely, and depressed. After much interchange with white and black group members and much soul-searching, she finally began to reach into herself, to establish her own values, and to see herself through new eyes. She could accept and even enjoy her color and appreciate more the many things about herself that were of great value.

Sociological Theories of Prejudice

The identification and exploration of sociological factors that influence attitudes toward members of another race has been the focus of a sizable body of research. The findings of some of these studies provide a useful theoretical background for evaluating the problems involved in and the benefits that may be derived from interracial group processes. They can provide some guidelines for a therapeutic approach. Further research is necessary to determine whether social criteria may actually provide a basis for predicting optimal group conditions and to investigate the complex manner in which different factors interact to produce positive or negative changes in attitude.

The Effect of Contact on Attitudes.

Contact between members of different ethnic groups in a natural social setting does tend to produce an attitude change, but the direction of the change depends largely on the conditions under which contact takes place. Favorable conditions tend to reduce prejudice; unfavorable conditions may increase prejudice and intergroup tension. Amir has reviewed the literature describing the effects of contact between groups with different ethnic backgrounds. His findings and their clinical applicability are presented here.

Contact Situations Promoting Positive Attitudes. Positive changes in attitude seem to occur in a contact situation when members of different ethnic groups occupy similar socioeconomic status or when contact takes place between members of a majority group and high-status members of a minority group such as white and black professionals. Positive changes are also more likely to occur when some authority or the prevailing social climate supports intergroup contact, a finding that has generally been validated by experiences with school desegregation. When school desegregation is supported by local officials and prevailing values, it results in a reduction of prejudice and an increase in cooperation between the races; but under the reverse conditions there is a negative effect. In a small interracial group a positive attitude by the group leader is one of the major determinants of positive results.

Intimate relationships are more likely to produce positive changes in attitude than are more casual contacts. The very process of deep and sustained interaction involves the replacement of stereotyped perceptions by individual encounter. In such an experience with members of another race, a person tends to break down the rigid tendency toward overgeneralization that is an important mechanism in prejudice.

When interracial contact is pleasant or rewarding, positive changes in attitude are more likely to occur. When interracial meetings are held in an industrial plant, for example, feelings between the races tend to improve if desired job changes occur as a result of the interchange. It is helpful to leaven interracial group discussions with coffee, picnics, and parties in order to provide members with an opportunity to enjoy simply being together.

Prejudiced attitudes are markedly reduced when different groups come together in pursuit of a common goal that is more significant than their separate purposes. This phenomenon is seen most dramatically in times of common disaster, as in the countless acts of heroism and compassion that breached racial barriers during New Orleans' 1964 hurricane. It is helpful to direct interracial groups toward a task that will bring mutual rewards—either a maturational goal, like increased self-acceptance, or a more tangible aim, like greater safety in the streets.

Contact Situations Promoting Negative Attitudes. When the contact situation evokes competition between members of different races, antipathy between the groups increases. This tendency may be countered by emphasizing the common goal of individual fulfillment—everyone gains—and by pointing up the destructiveness inherent in intergroup competition—one group must lose.

Negative attitudes may be strengthened if interracial contact is unpleasant, involuntary, or tension-laden. Unfortunately, this is the more common situation at present. But an effective leader can convert these potentially destructive encounters into positive ones. When blacks and whites are forced to attend a meeting and neither group wants to be in the company of the other, it is usually best to begin by helping both groups to ventilate their anger at finding themselves captives in the situation. The leader's genuine empathy with the anger and the group's shared experience of expressing anger toward a common target—be it the leader or the meeting's organizer—set the stage for more productive work. The leader may also point out that the best way to deal with forced participation in an unwanted experience is to work toward making the experience rewarding for all.

Tension, particularly fear, does provide a much-needed motivating force for action. When people are afraid of being hurt, they attack first or do something to defend themselves. Leading the attack are usually those who are most angry or most frightened and who have a tendency to act on their impulses. The majority may prefer peace and safety to the risk of being hurt. This majority welcomes the opportunity to have its anger ventilated and responded to. The experience may clear the way for constructive interaction.

Intergroup contact may strengthen negative attitudes if the status or prestige of one of the groups is threatened or reduced as a result of the contact situation. To avoid this, the group leader must sincerely value the contribution of each member, regardless of the member's status outside the group. The thoughts and feelings of the most inarticulate members may often, if carefully attended to, provide greater understanding of what is really going on in a group than the carefully phrased contributions of those who are better educated and more skillful in the use of words.

In one meeting of a small interracial group designed to examine its members' prejudices, the leaders were finding it very difficult to deal with the erudite verbiage of two highly intellectual white lawyers, who had embarked on a discussion of the economic aspects of prejudice. Finally, a black woman, a domestic worker, broke in with a timid smile:

"I like working where I work now because I feel at home there. I'm accepted as part of the family, and no one tells me what to do. But you're something else! When I sat down next to you, you moved away from me. I don't believe you would stay in the same room with me, because I'm black, if we were somewhere else!"

With this perceptive comment, the group was able to become involved in a more meaningful interpersonal discussion.

If members of one group are experiencing frustration because of recent defeats or failures, economic deprivation, and chronic inequities, any contact with members of the group considered responsible for their frustration will increase their prejudice. The disadvantaged group will use the contact situation only to ventilate their resentment and to blame the others. This situation presents one of the most difficult obstacles to constructive interaction in interracial groups. The unending citation of injustices experienced outside the group encourages continued hatred. Group members feel over-whelmed by their inability to correct or ameliorate the external conditions, and this feeling of impotence destroys their enthusiasm about the group situation. They feel that, in the light of massive social injustice, the establishment of a few contacts with members of the other race is a waste of time.

Leaders may deal with these feelings of futility by pointing out that good experiences in the group are of value in themselves and that their constructive potential increases when positive reactions to members of the other race in the group are carried into relationships outside the group. In fact, some group members may decide to go on to begin new groups themselves, immeasurably broadening the social universe within which the results of their own experiences can be communicated to others. The group experience may also provide some practical help with problems of discrimination in the outside world. Group members may be able, because of their different points of view and statuses, to offer concrete solutions and fruitful suggestions or insights into attitudes that tend to trigger or exacerbate hostile reactions.

A young black secretary in the group complained bitterly that she had twice been passed over for promotion to a supervisory position. Each time, the position was given to a white girl not as well-qualified as she. A white member was so incensed by the story that he helped the secretary file a complaint with the local Office of Equal Opportunity.

In another group, a white policeman complained that he could never trust the blacks on his beat, that they always looked at him angrily. The black members of the group confronted him with the fact that he frowned at them whenever he looked at them and that this frown made them angry and uncomfortable. The policeman also learned, by listening to the blacks in the group, to understand the realistic background for the anger his frown mobilized. With time, much of his own rage toward blacks was replaced by compassion.

In a confrontation between two groups, the differences in their moral standards and values stand out sharply. Recognition of these differences may strengthen negative attitudes unless an open attempt is made to evaluate each group's standards in terms of its own unique history and culture.

A white member became angry at a black member, toward whom he had previously felt friendly, because of the black's persistent pattern of coming late to meetings. The black man responded:

"I don't go by white man's time! I learned long ago that, when I'm on a job, my white boss will get away with anything he can and give me as little money for my work as he can get away with. I get even by taking my own time as much as I can. It's my time, and I plan to keep as much of it as I can. I'm responsible to myself first!"

The white member continued to feel annoyed but he also began to wonder whether his own compulsive punctuality might not rob him of the experience of being master of his own time. He was experiencing new respect for the black man.

Reference Group Support. One of the major criticisms lodged against efforts to bring about changes in racial attitudes is that changes in attitude, even if effected, do not necessarily result in changes in behavior. This criticism is not unfounded. When one considers the quantity of complex factors that affect behavior, he must expect a certain lack of consistency between ideas and deeds.

A major determinant of a person's attitudes and behavior toward members of another race is the attitudes and behavior of persons who are close to him. Those people who are influential in his life provide what sociologists refer to as reference group support for his attitudes and behavior. Senderrich has demonstrated that, if this determinant is removed from the situation, the person will act independently—that is, in accordance with his own racial attitudes. And his racial attitudes will change if his reference groups change and, to a lesser extent, if overt behavior changes.

Interracial groups provide the person with new reference group support. As a member becomes closer to the group, its attitudes may become potent enough as determinants to offset the conflicting attitudes of his other reference groups.

A frequent occurrence in effective interracial groups is the member's growing sense of alienation from friends outside the group when racial topics are discussed because of his exposure to the examination of his own attitudes and those of other group members and to closeness with members of the other race. He finds that those outside the group lack any understanding of the other race, that their stereotypes are naive and destructive. This discovery may present a serious conflict to the group member, resulting·in the need to remove himself either from his former reference groups or from the interracial group. If members stay with the interracial group long enough, however, their new attitudes become more securely established, and they are less threatened by the attitudes of others. Thus, interracial groups may be most effective when conducted for relatively long periods of time. If they are made a permanent forum for exchange between the races within an institutional framework, such as a hospital or a school, they can provide the strong positive reference group support necessary to counterbalance negative attitudes outside the group.

The group's role in attitude change may be further enhanced if concrete actions are suggested to members in order to alter overt behavior. If, for example, members agree to make a social overture toward someone of the other race outside the group, the follow-up exchange of experiences and feelings within the group may provide valuable insights into the interplay between older attitudes and new ones.

Allport's Group Relations Theory. According to Allport's group relations theory, a person's mode of conduct is determined by his personality, the manner in which social forces impinge on him, and his need to conform. The three components of conformity are: a common disposition to prefer what is familiar, an emotional commitment to a particular way of life, and a deep-seated insecurity based on status needs.

Rosenbaum, Santowsky, and Hartley say that this theory may provide the basis for predicting the outcome of integrated therapy sessions, and the author's experience confirms this suggestion. Group techniques are aimed at changing and strengthening the participant's personality and at providing him with an increased sense of self-worth and value. When a member realizes that his presence in and contributions to the group are important, his self-esteem increases.

An integrated group whose goals include open disclosure and mutual acceptance forms a small temporary society with pressures to conform to ideals that, although they are not usually spelled out formally, do differ from those of the outside world. As the participant's self-esteem within the group increases and the group becomes important to him, the group's ideals also assume greater significance. At the same time, being with and talking to members of of another race in an environment conducive to self-expression and growth become familiar experiences, helping to offset the conformity produced by earlier confinement within his own race. An emotional commitment to maintain stereotypes about race is supported in many subtle ways outside the group, but this rigidity is challenged over and over again in the group's quest for frank, honest interchange based on the realities of the here-and-now. Status within the group is based on evidences of real openness and nonpossessive warmth. Attempts to achieve status by clinging to racial fronts, as in the outside world, are quickly exposed.

Thus, a well-functioning interracial group geared to facing interracial feelings deals directly with two of the three factors cited by Allport as determining conduct: the impingement of social forces and the need to conform. The third factor, individual personality, is influenced by these groups in an indirect manner.

The Changing Scene in Race Relations

Binderhughs has described the massive increase in black self-esteem in recent years, an increase facilitated by the growth of the black power movement in this country and by the surge of nationalism among new African states. The concept of black culture as a valuable heritage and of blackness as a positive identity instead of as just non-whiteness has provided blacks for the first time with an alternative to the values of white America, as the study of black history has for the first time offered blacks a meaningful past. The recent redefinition of blackness replaces subservience and inferiority, the consequences of an acceptance of white

values, with dimensions of independence, initiative, pride, and power.

With the emergence of this new-found self-esteem and sense of power has come the ability to be openly angry at the injustices of the past and to express hatred toward all whites as symbols of black degradation. These expressions of anger and hatred evoke great anxiety in whites, who have little understanding of their own racism. Whites feel that they are granting blacks more opportunities and benefits than ever before; they are confused and offended because the black response is one of anger rather than appreciation. They fail to understand that the very concept of giving has its roots in an infuriating sense of superiority. Blacks feel that no one may give them what was always rightfully theirs but was torn from them by life in a white world—their own self-respect.

The philosophy of black separatism is another aspect of the complex process of building a new black identity that most whites can neither understand nor accept. The problem here is similar in part to the conflicts that emerge in interaction between adolescents and adults. The adolescent must strive to achieve autonomy, but the adult fears and resists this change in their relationship. The adolescent is aware of his relative helplessness; he feels he must isolate himself from the powerful adult world in order to achieve independence and self-determination. Adolescents join together during this period, finding security in shared values and strength in numbers in confronting adults. The adolescent trusts himself to maintain his autonomy in a free, open relationship with adults only after he feels secure in his own identity. But there is a vital difference between the adolescent-adult relationship and the black-white relationship. The adolescent struggle to achieve autonomy is an aspect of the normal development of emotional and physical maturity. The manhood for which blacks struggle now was denied to them for centuries by the deprivations and humiliations of life in a white world.

The current situation demands the establishment of situations that permit open expression of black hatred, white understanding of its origins, and reduction of the destructiveness inherent in its incommunicability. These features are inherent in the black-white dialogue. The supporters of black separatism have no desire to talk to whites. Some blacks may have to become more comfortable with their blackness before they feel free to join with whites. Others will be able to participate and so learn that they can appreciate the values of their blackness more readily by interaction with whites.

The evolution of black separatism and white reaction to it is an important process that occurs frequently as an interracial group is formed. It recurs at important points in the development of the group— when black identity appears to be threatened by increased closeness with whites. This trying experience may be used to promote interracial understanding if the group leader remains aware of both its positive and its negative aspects.

THE RACE OF THE GROUP LEADER

There is greater depth of self-exploration in the initial interviews when the patient and the therapist come from the same racial and social milieu, as Carkoff and Pierce and Heckel have shown. This fact may be an important indicator of later therapeutic success, since other studies show depth of self-exploration during early clinical interviews to be highly correlated with constructive change. But when the patient and the therapist come from different races or classes, the patient responds to the introduction of personally relevant material in a mechanical manner, without evidence of its emotional impact.

In an interracial group some of these therapist-participant barriers can be broken through with time, but many such difficulties can be avoided from the beginning by using co-therapists, one black and one white. The presence of co-therapists of different races evokes other conflicts, but these conflicts in themselves provide major themes for group work, and this arrangement more readily permits the verbalization and working through of such conflicts.

Some of the points cited above are illustrated by Brayboy and Marks in their description* of what occurred when a black co-therapist was added to an on-going analytic group that was previously conducted by one white therapist.

All the group members were white except for Bob, who had been in the group for 18 months. When he entered the group, there were some superficial references to his color. A few members sincerely searched themselves for feelings of prejudice, but these feelings were generally not worked with. In dreams and fantasies, Bob revealed his image of the white therapist as a white devil with supernatural powers. The white members had similar primitive dreams about Bob. When a white male member had sexual dreams about him, Bob felt angry and demeaned.

At the black co-therapist's first meeting with the group, a new white woman was also added to the group. Several group members automatically identified the female as the new co-therapist. Bob went even further, openly refusing to accept this new black man as the co-therapist, insisting that the woman must be the new leader. He was overtly threatened by the co-therapist's presence, claimed that he didn't know blacks could be psychiatrists, and dreamed of being consumed by a wolf. To him, the black leader was a rival who destroyed his unique position in the group and who might refute some of his rationalizations concerning race. Bob became steadily more withdrawn in group sessions and finally wrote a flight-into-health note, saying that he had decided not to return to the group after its summer recess because he was doing so well.

The male members perceived the two therapists as engaged in a masculine power struggle, with the difference in color contributing to the dramatic fantasy of a fight for survival. This reaction was associated with their concern about how to handle their own aggression. In later sessions the projection of their own primitive, animal drives onto black men was a frequent theme. They expected the black co-therapist, in a position of power, to be as cruel and predatory as the white man has been in his treatment of blacks.

The female members responded to the new co-therapist quite differently. They accepted him freely, without apparent anxiety. They did complain that he failed to offer them enough support and protection, but this complaint was related more to his personality and therapeutic style

---

* Originally published in the *American Journal of Psychotherapy*, volume 22, pages 474–480, 1968.

than to his race. Their positive attitude toward him was maintained throughout the life of the group.

About two months after joining the group, the black leader conducted the group alone for six weeks. The resistance to his presence that had been expressed by superficial verbalizations or nonparticipation disappeared magically during this period. Hostility was directed, instead, to the absent co-therapist. When the white leader returned, the group became engaged in tactics that seemed to be aimed at dividing the two leaders. They continued to project their own struggles for dominance onto the therapists.

These maneuvers are common in any group led by two therapists, especially therapists of the same sex, and did not seem to be based on racial factors. The group work continued, and the members showed symptomatic and characterological improvement.

Some months later, an openly bigoted white man entered the group, followed by another new member, a black woman. The members refused to respond to the bigoted white man, but neither did they support the black woman when she angrily challenged his racism. They did, however, condemn him on other grounds, such as ignorance and stupidity.

Of particular interest in this study is the difference in reaction between male and female members to the black male leader. Of further significance is the avoidance of racial conflict, despite the prejudiced distortions obvious in both black and white members. The group avoided discussing sex, race, and aggression as they related to their own feelings about race. To approach these feelings would have required more active participation in these areas by the leaders. Leaders naturally tend to avoid those feelings within themselves that are feared or unpleasant. Such feelings are potentially more disturbing in a group setting, and, unless the leaders can experience them openly with the group, they tend to be avoided there just as they are in most other social situations.

As a single white therapist in a group of black adolescents in a ghetto service facility, Alsdort found it almost impossible to get into a meaningful discussion of black-white relationships, although progress was made in other important areas, such as impulse control and difficulties with adults and with the opposite sex. Crucial to the success of this group was the presence of a black adult

observer who served as an essential mediating link between the white therapist and the black members and between the therapist and the black staff. The leader was aware of his anxiety about being on alien turf, of his fear of being misunderstood, and of his fear of being at the group's mercy physically and emotionally.

White Leaders

The white group leader has more difficulty in relating to black members of the group than to white members for many reasons, which vary greatly from person to person according to his own personality and experiences.

The white leader has difficulty in understanding and conceptualizing what is normal, adaptive behavior in modern black culture. In evaluating black patterns of behavior that are adaptive in a socioeconomic group so different from his own, he may judge them pejoratively because of their differences from his own standards. Thus, the white male psychotherapist may automatically think of the black matriarch as castrating, although her role as family head is actually based on a network of other more positive motivations, such as the desire to be a responsible mother. Since he has generally experienced blacks as subordinate, he may have difficulty tuning in to the strong positive aspects of the black life style, such as the black man's masterful use of dramatic style in dress and speech to achieve the masculine status denied him by the white world.

In addition to the gross stereotypes and prejudices that each white leader must confront in himself before leading an interracial group, many more subtle variations of prejudice are evoked as the group develops. The leader's openness in observing these variations in himself and in sharing them with the group is a most effective catalyst for group progress.

A white leader may inhibit his own aggressiveness and assertiveness to avoid feeling or acting like a boss or overseer. Behind this reticence hides a prejudiced image of himself as superior and of blacks as inferior. He avoids revealing this image to himself and fears angry retaliation from black members if he reveals it to them.

A variation of ·this theme is denial of white capabilities, privilege, and power. The white leader may, in effect, apologize for being white. His presentation of himself may imply:

I'm miserable and helpless, like you, so you have no cause to be jealous of me or to hate me.

Group members can see through this ploy readily and are mistrustful of what they perceive as dishonesty.

One respected leader told her group at its first meeting that she was proud of being white, enjoyed it, and would not compromise herself by denying what she valued in her whiteness. Her statement evoked some anger initially, but both black and white members realized that they admired and liked her for knowing who she was and being true to herself.

White leaders may hold back negative feelings about black members for fear of hurting them. This reticence may represent an overcompensation for underlying prejudiced feelings of being all-powerful in comparison with blacks, who are seen as helpless.

Some white leaders feel more comfortable relating to blacks. They fear that whites will more readily see through them and recognize their faults, whereas blacks will be less perceptive or will withhold criticism because they are in awe of whites.

Other white leaders restrain their spontaneity because they fear that whatever they say or do may be taken as proof of their prejudice: Hostility will be attributed to racism, affectionate disregard of racial differences will be seen as a cover-up for underlying prejudice. This overcautiousness does, indeed, often represent a fear that carefully guarded prejudices will be exposed.

Ayers suggests the establishment of a training program for whites in the psychosocial aspects of the black experience. This course might include readings in black history and culture and an exposure to that portion of the scientific literature that facilitates both increased understanding of blacks and attitudinal changes. Further sensitization to black patterns of culture may be achieved by actually experiencing life in black ghetto areas, preferably as a temporary resident, by reviewing videotapes of black interaction, and by engaging in dialogues with blacks from all walks of life. This direct immersion in the sights, sounds, and rhythms of black culture will result in a more acute understanding of black language, values, and behavior. It should also encourage an appreciation of black culture as a legitimate product of a unique past, not as disintegration of white patterns.

Black Leaders

The Quality of Black Prejudice. The quality of black prejudice against whites is different from that of white prejudice against blacks. The persistent realities of discrimination and socioeconomic oppression are constant proof to the black man that the white is indeed on top and the black on the bottom. It makes little difference, from the black's point of view, whether the individual white is an active oppressor or is passively enjoying the consequences of white superordination. As long as the white occupies one of the first-class seats, a black is pushed into a second-class seat and hates him for it. At times, blacks actually prefer whites to be active in their racism; it seems more honest.

The prejudgments most blacks hold about whites cannot, in many respects, be characterized as unrealistic stereotypes. Repeated experience serves to confirm the reality of the black's expectations: Most whites are *not* to be trusted, since they are incapable of treating blacks as equals; they think they have a right to be top dog and will assume that right at the black's expense, despite protestations to the contrary. When whites profess to be different from these stereotypes, most blacks actively disbelieve them until the difference has been proved over and over again. Even then, white egalitarianism may be interpreted as self-delusion or treachery. The feeling is that, inside the many threatening and few friendly exteriors, all whites are really the same. It becomes the task of the white to prove that he is genuine in his beliefs that blacks are to be valued as human beings and are to be treated with dignity and respect.

It is difficult for blacks to become aware

of the differences between their prejudices and their realistically negative expectations. But they can, by committing themselves to reaching beyond the stereotypes, gradually encounter whites they can really trust. They can become sensitized to the differences that do exist in the white population and responsive to their modes of expression. They can replace blanket hatred with a more productive, discriminating anger against some whites and against an oppressive system, rooted in the past, that must be changed.

Overprotectiveness toward Blacks. In the case of the black group leader, often he must, first, become aware of his own prejudices against whites and, second, commit himself to helping black group members become aware of their prejudices. The second task is usually the more difficult. The black who chooses to become a group leader usually has enough faith in his own identity strength to search out prejudices within himself but, in his need to protect black members he considers weaker than himself, he may insist that they have no prejudices, only realism, or that weakening their defensive prejudice will cripple them for coping with the everyday world.

Anger toward Whites. Another serious difficulty encountered by black leaders lies in handling their own anger toward whites who speak as if they were all-knowing. The white leader may be annoyed at such a participant, but the black leader tends to overreact, particularly if the member outdoes him in verbal ability. The realistic threat posed by the white member's greater facility with words is compounded by the black leader's prejudiced expectation that this white liberal intellectual is really trying to establish his superiority as a white man. Some black leaders respond with a similar mixture of prejudice and realism toward group members, white or black, who seem to come to meetings to tell everyone else how to handle their problems and who relate on an impersonal level only. Again, the white leader may become annoyed, but the black leader tends to become incensed.

Racial Identity Problems.

Prejudice toward Black Members. As pointed out by Calnek, black therapists who work with black clients have an unusual burden, for they have to deal with both their own feelings and the feelings of their clients about being black. The black leader who has achieved middle-class status may have taken over white perceptions and evaluations of the behavior of blacks in the course of learning to compete successfully within the white system. In the process he may also have lost contact, to some extent, with the life style of blacks of lower socioeconomic status. In his efforts to keep a protective distance between his present life and his past, he may be even more prone than his white co-therapist to misjudge and be offended by certain aspects of black behavior patterns. The same may be true for the black leader who comes from a white-oriented, middle-class family background and who has had little first-hand contact with lower-class patterns. This insecurity or ambiguity about his own identity may cause such a leader to insist, in effect, that black members act white before he accepts them, rather than accepting them in the context of their own life style.

A highly educated black leader was aware of feeling superior to all the black members of his group and to most of the whites, but he seemed more comfortable with his feelings of superiority toward the whites. The blacks touched off his feelings about his "inferior" black background, and his automatic response was to tighten up and put an emotional distance between himself and the offending group members.

Overidentification. An essential feature of the black leader's role is his ability to empathize with other blacks because of their common experiences. In this process, however, black members may be used as extensions of the leader's ego. He may encourage in them the expression of conflicts he himself is unable to express—for example, he may give subtle or overt encouragement to the expression of anger about racial problems without really attempting to move past this anger toward a real dialogue with whites. In using members in this fashion, the leader is unable to achieve insight into his own behavior and cannot assist the members to understand theirs.

Intolerance of Passivity. In the current black revolution, any tendency toward docile behavior is regarded by the black activist as self-degrading and incompatible with the new black image. Although passivity may represent self-depreciation in many blacks, it may also represent other feelings, such as comfort with one's identity and way of life and disinterest in changing what is comfortable and familiar. The black leader who demands assertiveness of his black members may inhibit them from ever feeling thoroughly at ease in the group situation.

One black leader was often furious with the blacks in his group for not delivering. He knew that, for most of them, this was their first experience of closeness with whites in a situation where they could talk freely. He sensed that they felt:

We have some nice new white friends; let's not rock the boat.

His anger at the degrading aspect of their reaction prevented him from being truly accepting of the black members. He was therefore, unable to encourage in the group the permissive attitude that would have freed members to express their anger as well as their desire for acceptance.

Intolerance of Acting White. Because of his fear of his own tendencies to deny his blackness, a black leader may be particularly antagonistic toward a black member who acts white.

At one meeting, a fastidiously dressed light-skinned Negro junior executive came into the group for the first time and told the group, in effect:

I made it; the trouble with you blacks is that you don't really get out and try.

The black leader, himself a college graduate and of middle-class background, reacted with such fury to the newcomer's white mannerisms and know-it-all attitude that he was unable to begin to relate to him or to make any effort to help him become part of the group. The black executive never returned, much to the leader's relief.

Light-Skinned Black Leaders and Blacks Who Have Made It. A particular type of prejudice, based on poor racial identity, exists among some blacks who are light in color or who have earmarked themselves for

professional success. Some light-skinned blacks employ derogatory stereotypes about blackness, very much as whites do. Light skin color is a source of self-esteem; blackness in oneself or others is rejected. Similarly, as discussed by Beisser and Harris, some successful black professionals—and others who admire their success—have chosen to reject their socially imposed heritage of passive-aggressive subservience by identifying with the open aggressiveness and manipulativeness of whites. This identification is facilitated by being of lighter skin color, but the mechanism is present in many other blacks who have succeeded professionally. These blacks feel that what they have achieved is due to their success in emulating whites. They cannot feel the comfort and excitement of self-fulfillment. They are not successful blacks but successful white imitators. They are the victims of a chronic, unrelenting need to defend or improve their tenuous positions.

Some of these blacks have been very active in the civil rights movement, but their role is like that of guilty whites who, with an attitude of *noblesse oblige*, work on the periphery of the black movement rather than in the center. They see themselves as working for a group of poor unfortunates, often with the conviction that deprivation is self-imposed, that anyone who really wants to make it can do so. They do not see themselves as engaged in a common struggle to achieve self-respect.

With the advent of the black power movement, these blacks no longer need to reject their blackness. They can begin to embrace their own blackness as beautiful. As such a black tries to re-integrate the previously denied portion of his identity, he may experience ontological guilt for his previous lack of authenticity and neurotic guilt for having failed to share the burden of being black. To cope with these feelings, he may become violently antiwhite, pouring much of his energy into the cause of black power. Or he may deny his guilt by asserting that, since he had to work for what he got, others should be capable of doing the same. He may also attempt to disown his guilt by projecting it onto others, accusing them of not being interested or active enough in the black movement.

This type of prejudice on the part of blacks is particularly difficult to reach in an interracial group. In the extreme case, the black's integration of his newly found black identity is so tenuous that it is threatened by any meaningful contact with whites. His rage and the fear that the white introject inside him may take over his identity are subtly projected onto whites with whom he comes into contact. Since he often occupies a position of leadership, this problem may have serious repercussions.

At a meeting of members of important civic and civil rights groups held for the purpose of setting up interracial discussion groups to attempt to reduce tension between the races, a very light skinned black member, who had come to the meeting late, seemed to object to almost every constructive plan offered. He finally announced that he considered it necessary that blacks hate whites and that anything done to reduce this hatred would be destructive to the black-is-beautiful and black power movements.

There was, of course, some validity in his position, and the other blacks present were able to comprehend his implication that a black feels stronger when he can hate whites openly. They also knew, however, that they were able to feel strong as blacks without hating all whites. They could perceive the self-destructiveness of a philosophy that uses hatred as the cornerstone of its strength.

The light-skinned black remained adamant in his negativism. When it finally became obvious that he would be outvoted, he proposed the establishment of a discussion group for white policemen and members of a black organization composed of former delinquents. In this seductive challenge he was actually proposing, under the guise of establishing a context for constructive dialogue, a group composition that was most unlikely to succeed and that would be most liable to end as an arena for the expression of hatred.

Awareness and working through of this problem in an interracial group is a difficult and challenging task. The rewards are great if the challenge is met because it can bring a great sense of peaceful resolution to the group member or leader who is so involved. It also unlocks for contribution to the community the positive efforts of a talented person who is truly an expert on race relations because he has experienced both sides of the conflict within himself.

GROUP PROCESSES AND TECHNIQUES

The structure of groups formed primarily for the purpose of reducing interracial tension is unique, as are the processes encountered in such groups. The techniques that may be successfully employed in these groups include those familiar from therapy groups and encounter groups and other techniques that are relevant only to interracial problems. The use of originality in devising new approaches and techniques to relate to a specific group need at a particular time is of much more value than adherence to a fixed routine. Of particular importance is the awareness of countertransference. In an interracial group, countertransference is neither to be ashamed of nor avoided, and it may be used effectively to stimulate openness and honesty.

Group Structure

Selection of Members.

Voluntary Groups. It is difficult at first to enlist the voluntary participation of members in an interracial group. Optimally, such a group should be sponsored jointly by black and white community organizations or by organizations already formed for the purpose of improving race relations. Members may be actively recruited from church groups, fraternal organizations, unions, municipal government, the police force, the school system, etc. Once the group is functioning successfully, persons who have heard about it from its members often apply for membership.

Compulsory Groups. When persons are assigned to attend an interracial group by their employers or by organizational officials, many experience an initial resentment of forced participation but usually find the group a rewarding experience. In fact, the shared feeling of resentment of compulsory involvement in an uncomfortable situation may serve as the first bridge for communication between black and white members.

Such groups may prove beneficial to any professional, business, educational, governmental, or service organization in which blacks and whites must work together. These groups are especially meaningful to persons who come into contact with members of the other race in the course of their daily duties. Insights and suggestions that arise in the group may be immediately applied to daily experience. If participation in the group is made compulsory, members should be compensated for their time or relieved of certain other responsibilities so that meetings may take place during regular working hours.

When it is possible, as in the case of large organizations, members who come from the same section of the organization should be assigned to different groups to avoid the inhibiting effect of the presence of an immediate superior or a co-worker. Within a school system, for example, groups should include both teachers and principals, but, at least during early phases, teachers and principal from any one school should be assigned to different groups. This procedure also provides for a broader viewpoint of common problems. On the other hand, friends who wish to attend the same group and who may benefit from the security of an established relationship in an unknown situation should not be separated.

Group Balance and Heterogeneity. Reference group balance can be an important factor in the success of a group. In interracial groups it can be crucial. It is most important to have close to an equal number of black and white members. If more than 70 per cent of the membership is of one race, free interchange tends to diminish. It is a valuable experience, especially for whites, to be in the minority for one or two meetings. But, if this situation is prolonged, members of the minority tend to speak for their race as a whole rather than as individuals, thus reducing the personal impact that is vital to group effectiveness.

It is also helpful to balance the group with respect to personality, verbal ability, and ability to express emotions—crosscutting the racial groupings. For example, members

who can express their feelings help the more intellectual members to stop thinking long enough to feel, and intellectual members can aid those who tend to emote too much to conceptualize more. All balanced heterogeneity in the group aids in crossing racial barriers.

In one group, two young men of post-high-school age, one white and one black, found themselves allied in arguing the case for modern youth, in opposition to a group of more conservative, middle-aged members of both races.

Differences in socioeconomic backgrounds can provide a rich learning experience.

A laborer and the owner of a large factory were together in a group. It was a revelation for the laborer to learn that the factory owner was suffering acutely in his efforts to maintain his factory's position in the competitive world of business while working to bring about sincerely desired improvements in working conditions for his personnel. The industrialist's insights into the laborer's problems were similarly broadened.

It is particularly important that an interracial group contain members of both sexes. Many racial myths and fears are centered around sex and are best explored in the context of personal interaction.

It is more difficult at first to develop a sense of group cohesiveness in a group whose membership is really heterogeneous. Often both language and cultural barriers impede communication, and it is necessary to support vigorously the contributions of members who are unsure of their verbal skills. In the long run, however, the depth and breadth of the interchange fostered by such heterogeneity promotes a more thorough working through of problems and a more meaningful cohesiveness.

Duration. Groups should meet at least once a week for sessions of one and a half to two hours. Shorter sessions do not afford enough time for a warm-up. It may be helpful to start the group off with one longer session, perhaps even a 12- to 24-hour marathon, but longer sessions held regularly tend to be too fatiguing for efficiency and may interfere too much with other activities.

The optimal duration for this type of group depends largely on its goals. Members must meet together long enough to establish relationships of sufficient trust to deal intimately with their feelings of hostility and prejudice and ultimately to become free to experience positive feelings for one another. This process always involves some work with other personal problems indirectly related to problems of race. If the group has been successful, the working through of racial material actually becomes secondary, after a period of time, to the sharing of other, more personal problems and concerns, which are more appropriately dealt with in a regular psychotherapy group. Indeed, the emergence of these more personal problems is a signal that the group is succeeding: Members, as individuals, are turning to other members, again as individuals, for help, transcending racial barriers.

A group with experienced leadership may work through racially focused impediments to communication in a period of 12 weeks. Shorter or longer periods may be dictated by the depth of prejudices involved or by the ultimate goals of the group. The group may also be established on a permanent basis, meeting once a month to maintain interracial rapport and communication after an initial period of more frequent meetings has achieved these goals. With any such group, regular follow-up meetings or social events are strongly advisable, perhaps even necessary, to maintain the gains achieved, since manifold forces in the community impede interracial communication and foster regression to former prejudiced thought patterns.

Size. Groups function best when there are no more than 12 members. With a larger number, too many members are omitted or withhold themselves from the ongoing interaction When the group contains too few members, each participant's responsibility for contributing to the interaction and keeping the ball rolling may become uncomfortable.

Informal Social Contacts. Meeting for coffee after the group meeting helps members to experience one another in a social setting less stressful than that of the group meeting itself and may aid in the expansion of patterns developed in the group to include situations in daily life. If several groups are meeting at the same time, coming together over coffee broadens the social universe.

Dances, picnics, and parties may be planned after the group has been meeting for a month or two. These social functions not only provide a positive force toward group cohesiveness but also provoke the discussion of problems that may not have arisen in the formal group setting, such as stereotyped fears of the other race's sexuality and of emotional involvement with a member of another race. The increased ease with one another that informal social interaction seems to foster among group members offsets the disadvantages of socializing encountered in the usual psychotherapy group.

Obviously, however, too much socializing impedes group progress by defining the group situation as one in which members must work at acting friendly and polite, denying prejudices and hostilities. Unfortunately, some current well-meaning programs in interracial communication limit the contacts of participants to social situations only, resulting in the formation of temporary friendships but leaving basic attitudes untouched.

A white church established a program of weekly supper meetings for its members and members of black churches. Polite conversation was exchanged and some superficial friendships were established, but interest and attendance soon waned because the social situation actually discouraged an honest, vital interpersonal interchange.

The Role of Group Leader

The group leader's principal task is to keep the members involved with one another so that they can confront one another with any stereotyped distortions they may have, thus freeing them to relate on a more meaningful level. To do this effectively, the group leader not only must provide guidance and support as the leader but must also set the example for openness by his own involvement. If the leader merely moves others toward involvement and sets himself apart or above the group as some kind of uninvolved teacher or sage, he produces a new segregated situation in which he is the superior being and everyone else is on a lower, sicker level. This situation seriously retards interaction and polarizes the group on a parent-child axis. The leader must be open with his own feelings, honestly concerned with the goal of becoming closer to everyone in the group, and, most important, open to the discovery of his own prejudices and willing to share their resolution with the group.

To do all this, the leader will find it most helpful to have a co-leader of the opposite race. The presence of black and white co-leaders in the group not only permits greater self-expression on the part of the leaders but also provides a ready source of ethnic and cultural validation, which helps clarify racial problems.

A group leader uses his own involvement at a deep intrapsychic level to promote introspection, interaction, and group progress. This technique is exemplified by an incident that occurred during the eighth session of a group:

Anthony, a moderately militant young black member, invited all the group members to a christening party for his first child. At the next meeting the white group leader told Anthony how meaningful and pleasant it had been for him to be a guest in Anthony's home. Anthony ignored this expression of friendship with a nonchalant comment about how he, too, had enjoyed the drinking and music.

Then the group went on to talk about the need for a separate black nation within the country. Anthony launched into a warm interchange with Robert, another black in the group, whose personality was different from but complemented his own. They realized how much they needed each other. It looked as if they might become fast friends who could benefit from each other greatly.

The group leader acknowledged how much they had to offer each other, but he also expressed his own hurt at being left out by the twosome. With this, Anthony saw that he had, indeed, left the white man out. He expressed sorrow about it because the group leader did mean something to him as a friend. His comment brought up a new discussion of the ramifications of racial separation.

The same situation occurred at the next meeting. This time Robert expressed, with great conviction, his feeling that the blacks in the group did not need the whites. The blacks had lived in the homes of whites as servants and knew all about them, but whites knew nothing of blacks except an Uncle Tom exterior.

The white leader felt the exclusion even more strongly this time. He felt personally useless as an individual, and he experienced hopelessness about the possible value of the group in which he had invested so much of himself. Later, he began to feel angry at both Robert and Anthony and expressed this feeling, although he didn't understand it.

That night the leader dreamed that Anthony was being carried off by a group of blacks much darker than he. They were going to stab him and perhaps castrate him for something he had not done. The leader identified strongly with Anthony in the dream. As he awakened, he was calling out helplessly to the attackers that what they were doing was unjust and a horrible mistake.

When the leader related the dream to the group at the next meeting, he realized that he had, indeed, been made to feel like an impotent castrate by the perception that the blacks had no use for him. The dream dramatically illustrated both of the feelings he had had in the group—the hopeless incompetence of not being able to feel effective, which resulted from black rejection, and the retaliatory rage against Anthony. In response to his discussion of the dream, Anthony and Robert smiled in unison. Robert spoke for them both:

"Now you know how it feels to be treated as we are."

In this episode the white leader did, indeed, live through the injustice of not having his capabilities recognized and needed, as it is experienced daily by blacks. For the first time, he could really understand their frustration and rage.

Through his own personal involvement, the group leader was showing the group that it was safe to involve oneself on an open emotional level with other group members. He could later share with the group his new personal understanding of black bitterness and, even more meaningfully, show how this understanding permitted him eventually to have a deeper kind of friendship with Anthony and Robert.

Resistance to Personal Involvement

Many people come to their first meetings with an air of intellectual curiosity, either because they feel something should be done about interracial problems or because they are active workers in various racially oriented movements. It is difficult, but particularly important, to invite them in the first session or two they attend to talk about their own personal feelings about being black or white. Otherwise, they may soon drop out of the group to continue doing their work without ever recognizing the personal biases that often hamper their ability to cross racial barriers effectively. Often these people seem to be using their professions in an attempt to work out their racial problems without facing them squarely.

The most common defenses against interaction are denial and focusing on people and events outside the group. Some members may take many weeks to feel comfortable enough in the group to relate on a personal level. Although the principal effectiveness of the group lies in open emotional interaction of a personal nature among its members, conversations about topics peripheral to the group do serve as a medium for reducing initial anxieties about being together. Timing is important in the introduction of more open expressions of feelings.

New members sometimes come into the group and express rage during the first meeting they attend, before they establish relationships with any of the other members. They are merely using the group as a sounding board. The leader's task in this case is to let the newcomer learn that the group really wants to get to know him and is not going to permit itself to be used in such an impersonal way. An appropriate comment in such a situation might be:

You're treating our whole group like a nigger when you blast off at us that way without even trying to get to know us.

People who can express themselves openly do become indispensable assets to the group when they learn to do it on a personal, intra-group level.

Dealing with Prejudice in the Community

Often the interaction of a meeting centers around the sharing of a particular injustice experienced by a black member because of

his race. Most of the whites in the group listen in shocked sympathy, for the first time feeling the true impact of being black in a white society. For the blacks, this discussion provides catharsis and sometimes stimulates practical advice for coping with the situation. For the group as a whole, the discussion tends to promote group cohesiveness against the hatred and prejudice in the outside world. If such a discussion goes on too long or if it fades off into an intellectual discourse on discrimination, however, it poses a technical problem for the group leader because it diverts attention away from the feelings that group members are actually experiencing toward one another.

If the problem under discussion seems real but hopeless, the leader can sympathize with the harshness of the situation and point out that, although the members cannot resolve such problems in the group, they can do something about the way they feel about one another. If the discussion does not seem to involve the group emotionally at all, the leader can focus attention on the resistance by indicating, in a personally involved way, that members are concentrating exclusively on a problem outside the group.

At one meeting, Joe spoke enviously of the higher pay received by the white bosses at his plant, implying that, if he weren't black, he would have a higher-paying position. Manny, a white manager at the same plant, listened with paternalistic sympathy. The group leader sensed the covert rage between the two and pointed out that their mutual politeness had an insincere quality. After they were finally able to express some open anger to one another, Manny could see that he was playing the good father to the blacks to cover his feelings of guilt and anger. Joe could see how his hatred of whites was giving him a bad reputation at a plant that was actually actively trying to upgrade the status of its black employees. Joe also learned that, as long as his energies were consumed by hatred of the white establishment, he didn't have to face his fear of his own inadequacy, as he might have to do if he took advantage of the opportunities for advancement that actually existed.

Using Personality Differences

Differences in personality produce both an attractive and a repellent force between individuals in the group. The resultant personality encounters are often so fundamentally meaningful that they make encounters on a racial level between the group members assume secondary significance. The following description shows how using differences in personality may bridge the gap between races while providing an opportunity for mutual support and growth of self-esteem.

The group was meeting for the first time as part of a one-day institute established for the express purpose of promoting dialogue between blacks and whites. None of the members of the group knew one another except for the co-leaders, a white male psychiatrist and a black female social worker who had themselves been participants in an earlier interracial group. There were six blacks and four whites in the group, all middle-class, ranging in age from 27 to 50.

The group began with the comments of one of the older black men, Mike, about the differences between the warmth of the sun and the coldness of the shadows as he had walked to the meeting room. The white male group leader asked him if he felt cold with the group. Mike said that he did not. The leader described a fantasy he had had at that moment of Mike going to a white restaurant, and he asked Mike whether the coldness in the group reminded him of the coldness Mike must feel as a black man entering a white restaurant. Mike again said that he did not feel the coldness, although he might have had some discomfort. Acknowledging the fact that the fantasy could have been his own projection, the group leader cited a situation in which he had felt very cold and rejected because he had seen a sign saying, "No Jews Allowed." Mike responded to this by saying, in effect,

"I'm much worse off than you because a black man can never hide his identity."

Then Mary, a white girl, said:

"I feel cold in any strange group. I don't know if it's because this group is integrated or not."

Another white girl, Ann, said the same thing and looked frightened as she said it.

Mike went on in an intellectual manner about how blacks are left out. The while leader pointed out that there were two cold, frightened girls right there in the group and that Mike was leaving *them* out. Mike ignored this comment and continued his discourse. The two group leaders finally became angry with Mike and pointed out how intellectual he was about everything.

In response to this, Rachel, an older black woman, said:

"I feel sorry for Mary and Ann. They do look frightened and cold."

Ann asked Rachel to sit next to her so that she wouldn't feel so frightened. Rachel said, "Of course," and came over and clasped Ann's hand. Then she took the hand of the other white girl, who was sitting nearby, and commented on how cold they really were. She crossed both her hands with the white girls' hands in a lovely warm gesture.

Mike continued to intellectualize until the white group leader broke in and asked him how he felt about what had gone on among the three women. Mike said it was okay. The white group leader said that he really didn't understand Mike, that he felt it was one of the most beautiful things he had ever seen. The black co-leader broke in and said that she couldn't stand it unless people could feel things emotionally. Mike replied that he had to feel things his own way.

He was given a lot of understanding and support at this point by Mary, one of the white girls who had been so frightened and who was now feeling less anxious. She said:

"I'm glad I was accepted the way I was. I think I can take Mike the way he is."

Mike replied with a grateful, warm smile. Mary reached out her hand to Mike and clasped it warmly.

Physical Activity in the Group

At times, cultural barriers to verbal communication may make it extremely difficult for one group member to understand another. Nuances of phraseology may be misconstrued. Some members may not have had the experience of expressing their feelings in a verbal manner at all. These difficulties make physical activities especially important. Touching, holding hands, putting an arm around a member's shoulders as appropriate expressions of closeness or warmth do as much as or more than anything else to break through racial barriers.

One sensitivity technique that may be employed successfully after the group has been meeting for several weeks involves having the members form biracial pairs. The leader directs the members of each pair to look directly into each other's eyes—to try to feel the other person as a human being, like himself, who enjoys the warmth of wholehearted acceptance. Each member takes his partner's hands and holds them, examines them in detail, noting their strength or softness and their beauty or blemishes, contrasting their color with the color of his own hands, noting how the contrast brings out the individuality of each color—the black a richer black, the white a whiter white. Then each member feels his partner's arms and shoulders, head and hair, going through the process slowly to really experience the touch of a member of the other race. Afterward, each member may share with the group the thoughts and feelings his contact with his partner evoked. Other sensitivity techniques, described by Schutz, may be equally useful for promoting both a sense of racial identity and a group cohesiveness.

Racial Identity, Black Separatism, and Group Cohesiveness

One of the major fears of blacks entering a group has been that pride in blackness and identification as a separate race will be endangered by closeness with whites. This attitude is based on the belief that hostility toward whites is essential for black pride. It is true that pride in blackness has enabled blacks to express latent hatred for whites, but this pride can actually be enhanced when hatred is reduced and replaced by affection.

In a small group the members and the group leaders can easily sense a feeling of group cohesiveness or group divisiveness. At times, identification with one race or the other may interfere with group cohesiveness and may become an important consideration in the work of the group. But there is a healthy component to this identification, just as there is in other group therapy situations. In the usual therapy situation, an individual member becomes angry at the group for trying to take away his individuality, and the group leader is constantly confronted with the paradox of preserving and enhancing what is good in the individuality of a member without destroying group cohesiveness. This problem is even more pressing and important in interracial groups, where the goal is to enhance the value of each race and preserve what is

constructive in racial identities but at the same time to identify more fundamental human values that can unite the races instead of separating them.

White group members are often threatened by talk of black separatism because of the actual hostility expressed by blacks toward whites as they discuss this goal. The whites' reaction also stems from their prejudiced conception of blacks as a potentially dangerous group of savages with whom one may feel safe only as part of a majority group vis-à-vis a nonthreatening, divided minority. Repeated confrontations and clarifications of communication are necessary before black identity, as a group phenomenon, can be perceived as a positive conception that whites can welcome for its promise of a coexistent culture, as a source of strength rather than as a threat.

The small group is a potent medium in which this flow between separation and togetherness can be observed and experienced at an intense level. The therapist and group members must delineate, by their own perceptiveness, those aspects of racial identity that are conducive to the growth of the individual member in the group and those that are destructive. Generally, those aspects of racial identity that are conducive to the growth of the individual member are also conducive to group cohesiveness.

The following examples show how this small group identity may be used to clarify issues of black separatism.

In one group session, Ada described her strivings to find a sense of belonging, security, and pride in blackness. She talked in an open, inviting way that seemed to ask the group to be with her. The group's natural response was:

Yes, you are black, and we like you, and in some strange way it's even easier to like you because you are black.

This reaction seemed to help her to like herself because she was black. Her plea was an open invitation that brought about group cohesiveness and a closeness between the black and white members. It also emphasized her racial individuality.

In another session, a bright and articulate black man told how he had risen from the slums, had gone to graduate school, and now had returned to the slums to work in an effort to help the children there find themselves and learn pride in themselves. His tale was a moving, inspiring one, and all the group members felt close to him.

At the next meeting, however, he felt more open. He began to talk about black thinking and white thinking. He insisted that whites could not possibly feel the same way he did because they were white and he was black and had different experiences. The whites in the group granted that their different experiences prevented identical thinking, but they felt that it was the anger and bitterness in his voice that actually separated them from him. He said he felt it was necessary for blacks to keep to themselves in order to feel their own value because in a primarily white society they would always feel less than they were or could be.

As he spoke of this black separatism, the group became more and more despondent. He was, in effect, denying and destroying what had occurred between himself and the group the week before. Perhaps he had not adequately perceived the group's closeness with him, or perhaps he was running away from the closeness. As a group the members felt almost paralyzed. All the group leader could do was to point out how the black man's denial and rejection of whites made them feel. The black seemed upset and apologetic as he left.

In later sessions the black learned how his quest for black separateness stemmed from his own uneasiness about being black, his own feelings of insecurity about it, and his own rejection of blackness. And he learned through the group medium that his sense of identity as a black could be achieved among whites as well as with people of his own race.

At the almost opposite pole of this problem is the phenomenon of partial acceptance or pseudoacceptance of the other race, which gives either false or temporary cohesiveness to the group but which avoids true dialogue. This phenomenon occurs most frequently when blacks talk of the injustices committed against them by whites outside the group and the white members commiserate with them, but neither group talks about the real feelings of prejudice operative in the group at that moment.

Other Techniques

Techniques other than those commonly used in psychotherapy groups may be em-

ployed to facilitate more intensive involvement or to bring into active participation members who have remained peripheral to the group. Encounter tapes, film clips, and guest speakers may all be used as stimuli for group interaction, especially in a group's formative stages. As the group begins to develop a vitality of its own, it is preferable that techniques evolve from the particular group situation, with group members contributing to their development. This evolvement assures that the techniques will be dynamically relevant to the group's current needs and avoids the contrived, phony feeling that may result from the programmed use of preplanned techniques.

A black policeman was describing to his group an experience in which he had ticketed a speeding white motorist. The group leader sensed that some important material was emerging, but other members seemed bored by the anecdote. The leader suggested that the incident be dramatized by the group—first as it had actually occurred, then with role reversal. Vivid insights and spirited interaction are often stimulated by this type of psychodrama, particularly when blacks play white roles and whites play black roles.

On another occasion, feelings of mistrust within the group became a topic of discussion. The feelings were accented and clarified by the use of a simple technique. A group member of one race lay on the floor, face up, with a member of the other race standing erect at his side, looking down at him. Each member expressed his feelings about the other. Then the supine member held out his arms toward the standing member, and feelings were again exchanged. Finally, the member lying down called for help until the member standing felt that the request was genuine, one he wanted to answer.

CLINICAL EXAMPLES

Despite the importance of this subject, almost no work was done in the field until very recently. Many communities have lately established interracial groups under the auspices of their police departments, school boards, and human relations committees, but no coverage of problems encountered or goals achieved is as yet available.

School Integration Problems

McArdle and Young describe an inter-racial group organized to prevent difficulties anticipated among high school students who were to be moved to unfamiliar schools. Their report is a good example of what can be learned from such a group and of how such groups can be made relevant to almost any problem, current or anticipated, in the community. The principal themes emerging in this high school group, black separatism vs. white fear and a subsequent desire for greater familiarity with blacks, are strikingly similar to themes frequently expressed in other black-white groups.

A number of school boards throughout the country have conducted institutes under federal sponsorship for the training of teachers in desegregated schools:

In a New Orleans workshop, for example, teachers were paid to attend an institute five days a week for a period of six weeks. School visits, seminars, and lectures focused on problems and techniques connected with desegregation. This institute also included a small-group experience in which ten to 12 teachers, both black and white, came together for a period of an hour and a half daily to discuss these problems on a more intimate, intensive level.

Open interaction among the group members depended on several factors: previous participation in similar groups (the one member who had had some experience in a psychodynamically oriented interracial group acted as a constructive catalyst for more open discussion about personal racial feelings), verbal ability, previous attitudes about race, emotional lability, individual expectations of the institute experience, and the training, orientation, and experience of the group leader. A difficulty this group shared with most professional groups was its members' proclivity for lecturing to one another and intellectualizing rather than expressing themselves on a more meaningful, emotional level. Some members did become more open, to the point of expressing anger freely, and this openness frightened others. Those who were able to express their fear emerged feeling more secure than they had before.

Group members discussed their racial attitudes toward one another, their pupils and their parents, their supervisors, and the community in general, and prejudices were identified. Interaction, facilitated by the group leader, was often intense. Members exchanged discoveries from their own personal and teaching experiences to supplement the didactic material in the field of intergroup relations.

Rapport among group members slowly increased, and feelings reached a highly positive state. By their interaction, members grew to see and then to accept one another as individuals rather than as white or black. They were able to talk about and critically review common prejudices that had been unconsciously accepted as fact. Data on African and Afro-American history were particularly useful in helping both white and black teachers enlarge their perspective.

Encounter Tapes

A program of interpersonal exercises designed to improve communication between blacks and whites through their interaction in a small, self-directed group has been taped and is available commercially. The program consists of five one-and-a-half-hour sessions. Instructions for each session are presented on tape. After listening to the instructions, the group proceeds with the activities suggested. After the last session, participants receive take-home material designed to help them find ways in which they can transfer what they have learned in the group to their everyday experiences.

This program's major advantage is that it may be employed when trained group leaders are unavailable, since it was developed for leaderless groups. On the other hand, the absence of a leader severely limits its scope and flexibility, since groups function best when a sensitive and experienced leader is able to pick up and amplify the principal theme and feeling of a particular moment. Also, five sessions provide too brief an exposure to the group experience for lasting changes to occur.

But many people who have had group experiences using these tapes are enthusiastic about them. Despite serious limitations, the tapes appear to be well-designed. The structured activities into which they lead participants enable them to focus directly on their interactions in ways that improve communication and understanding. The tapes may also be useful in helping relatively inexperienced group leaders to get their groups started in the most effective direction. They help participants concentrate on the immediate here-and-now experience and aid both participants and leaders in being more aware of their positive and negative feelings and in expressing them openly. Intellectualism is discouraged. Participants are made aware of certain bags that blacks and whites tend to get into when they are together. Guidelines are provided to help the group avoid getting caught up in rhetoric, games, or posturing. Most important, perhaps, the tapes increase the group's confidence in learning by means of their own personal experiences rather than by intellectual presentation and discussion of concepts. This experience can free the group for more intensive interchange, exposure, and growth in later sessions, while making minimal demands on the inexperienced leader.

Unfortunately, the tapes lead the group to good feelings but not much further. In this program's attempt to get away from the scorching confrontation of whites that usually characterizes such groups, it probably misses opportunities for deeper forms of confrontation, introspection, and change.

Biracial Groups Not Oriented to Racial Problems

Many groups, either therapeutically oriented or community-oriented, have both black and white members but rarely, if ever, deal with interacial problems. If race is mentioned at all in such groups, it is in a context peripheral to the group experience. Racial differences, biases, and prejudices among the members are ignored or suppressed.

Changes were recently instituted in one biracial group that had been functioning in this manner for six months. Its members tended to talk about their problems rather than to relate openly with one another, although some open interchange did occur. Attendance was spotty.

To better realize the group's potential, its leaders converted references to race into direct interaction. When they began to put this program into effect, the attendance of black members dropped even lower. At one meeting, no blacks were in attendance. The blacks were actively encouraged to return, and when they did, there was open working through of their racial feelings. Openness in racial interchanges developed *pari passu* with increased openness in other areas.

Group leaders and members became more excited about the group when this difficult obstacle to free communication was breached, and attendance remained high.

Some good work undoubtedly does occur in biracial groups without direct focusing on race. Snell describes the successful performance of psychiatric evaluations in small biracial groups in a Southern community in which extreme antagonism between the races was expected. In this and similar situations, prejudices are laid aside as the group works on problems whose resolution are seen to be beneficial to all. A by-product of working together toward a common goal is the diminution of racial prejudices among members of the group, but in the absence of the working through of racial attitudes, these changes are not likely to be carried over to persons outside the group.

Biracial Group to Reduce Interracial Tension

An interracial group met for a period of two years to work on the reduction of prejudice. This group ranged in size from eight to 30 members: an original core of six to eight regular members plus others whose participation varied in duration from one to 16 sessions. Membership was usually fairly evenly divided between men and women, black and white.

Meetings were held once a week for two hours, usually followed by informal socializing over coffee. Occasional picnics and parties varied the meeting routine. Meetings were suspended during the summer months. During the second year, one section of eight members, later to become group leaders themselves, met regularly and with consistent attendance as a closed group.

Formative Stages. Immediately after the assassination of Martin Luther King, unrest surged in the New Orleans black community, and fear of violence increased in the white community. To avert reprisal by black activists, blacks displayed black cloths on the front doors of their homes to announce their bereavement and togetherness. Many whites bought guns to protect their families against an expected black attack.

A small group of psychiatrists, all white, who had experience in group therapy decided to see whether they could use some of their skills to bring blacks and whites closer together. They began by dealing with their own prejudices but soon decided that, for the experience to be meaningful, the group should include blacks among its participants. The white psychiatrists decided to enlist black members by calling those they knew either professionally or socially, but the restriction of their contacts was quickly apparent. Only one member had a black friend, and he was reluctant to use him for this purpose. The white psychiatrists eventually obtained the names of some blacks who had been active in interracial committees but found themselves strangely inhibited when it came to inviting them to the meeting. They were confronted by their own prejudices even before they called. They found it extremely difficult to extend an invitation to an unknown black because they were uncomfortably aware that their only reason for asking him to join them was that he was black. They finally realized that this discomfort stemmed from the fact that thinking of a black man as a black defined him for them as inferior. They felt that their invitation would, therefore, convey the same message to him. Others found themselves confronted with an overwhelming feeling of guilt, as if they were personally responsible for all the injustices perpetrated on the black community. These and similar feelings were explored in the early meetings. As the members became aware of their own prejudices, they became freer of them and freer to invite blacks to join them, both as other human beings and as blacks.

The first meetings were awkward. Invitations had been directed to a number of prominent black leaders in the community, but only two attended the first meeting. Some of the original members were painfully aware that the blacks were outnumbered by seven whites, but they did not express this feeling to the group. One of the blacks, a skilled officer in a major civil rights group, spent much of the time talking about various programs in which he was involved. One of the white members later reported the following reactions:

Walter was a large, portly man. Although he spoke well, I had difficulty listening to him because, each time I looked at his lips and his hair, I thought how strange it was for such fluent speech to be coming from someone who looked like a Pullman porter. I said nothing of this fantasy. We all listened politely. He seemed enthusiastic about our plans for a dialogue between the races, but he never returned to our meetings. I think now that, if I had openly expressed my concern about his being outnumbered and if I had shared my prejudiced picture of him in the surprised, nonhostile way in which I myself perceived it, we could have become more involved with each other, and the chances for his returning would have been better.

The early meetings continued to attract only two or three blacks of the 20 or more who had been invited. The initial assumption that blacks would want to attend was probably based partially on prejudicial thinking. They, the powerless blacks, who had so little, would consider it an honor to be invited to meet with whites. It was a shock to realize, when they did not show up, that it was actually the whites who needed them.

One one occasion no blacks had arrived by the time the meeting began, although, as before, all the whites had arrived on time. Some of the white members had been friends before the meetings began, and all of them felt closer since they had been meeting. They wondered why they were failing. Perhaps the blacks were afraid to come to a white neighborhood. Why should they come at all? What were they being offered? Were the whites just using them to assuage their racial guilt? As they spoke, they felt despair. Their relief was marked and their joy apparent when two black women finally arrived. One was a light-skinned Creole. Some of the whites bristled at her aristocratic manner. In later meetings they learned that this manner was not a sophisticated cover-up for underlying feelings of inadequacy, their own mistaken perception, and they came to admire her for her self-confidence instead of resenting her for pretending to feel comfortable in a difficult situation.

The other black woman who came to the meeting was much darker. She looked and sometimes spoke as if she might be a maid, but there was a forcefulness in her voice that commanded attention and a self-assuredness that invoked respect. The contrast between the redness of her mouth, when she opened it to speak, and the blackness of her skin became intriguing. Soon the white members forgot her appearance and listened to her story. A white member recalls:

Sarah had just come from the home of a friend, a black woman who was being terrorized by an unknown white man in her neighborhood. Her friend was being barraged by obscene letters and phone calls from him, threatening to kill her unless she met him. After the police had failed to help her, she had turned to Sarah in panic. Sarah was late in getting to the meeting because she was so reluctant to leave her friend. She had arranged to spend the night with her and, if necessary, to meet the man with her in a direct confrontation. I was astounded by her bravery and deeply touched by her loyalty. The depth of that feeling was matched by the depth of my shame for having reacted to her first on the basis of color. I felt a strange surge of emotion, a mixture of joy at being able to care for her as a person and sadness at my previous prejudice. I wanted to ask forgiveness from this woman, who was so unselfish and far braver than I could be.

Most of the white group members had similar feelings. They had all been transfixed by her story. It proved to be a turning point for the group. Instead of being members of two separate races confronting each other with intellectual questions, the group members were all fellow humans, joined together by the fear and beauty of Sarah's story, anxious to help her and to be part of her life. They needed her more than she needed them. They needed her sense of loyalty and her bravery, and they wanted to become closer to her in order to share these aspects of her life. This was the first of many times in which the members could feel their prejudice dissolving.

As the group began to take shape and come alive, some of the white members expressed a fear of retaliation by white extremists, who might object to the integrated meetings in white neighborhoods. There was no way of gauging the amount of realism in these fears; the ostracism of white parents who had sent their children to an integrated school was still a vivid memory. Some whites in the group fantasied cross-burnings and bombings if they tried to expand the group publicly. They also expressed concern over the discomfort that blacks might feel, coming to the meetings in a white neighborhood. Some whites feared that holding the meetings in their homes would expose their affluence, of which they felt ashamed, and that blacks would resent them for it. The black participants did fear that they might be stopped and questioned by the police for being in a white neighborhood at night, but they made no offers to open their own homes to the meetings. Such an offer came months later and represented a gesture of genuine caring. Neutral areas available for public use were finally chosen as meeting places, and these areas proved to be more readily acceptable to both blacks and whites.

Leadership of the Group. The early meetings were characterized by their leaderlessness. Although most of the participants had been leaders of therapy groups for many years or had had leadership experience in other areas, no one assumed a role of active leadership. When a member did begin to act as a leader on occasion—to promote interaction between two other members, for example—his efforts had an artificial ring. It seemed possible that the emerging leader was actually denying his own prejudices by acting as the director for those members more willing to expose themselves. It became apparent that all the members had to look at their own prejudices in depth before any one of them could attempt to provide direction for others.

Another factor that inhibited assumption of a leadership role was an exaggerated fear of the concomitant responsibility. Most therapists who do group work probably experience a similar anxiety related to the burden of responsibility for so many persons at one time, the fear that each member of the group will hold the therapist responsible for his continuing problems or will demand that the therapist do something about them. In an interracial group this factor is compounded by generations of distrust between the races, current interracial fears and antagonisms, and realistic socioeconomic injustices, so it is not surprising that the leadership role in such a group should be avoided.

In reality, of course, none of these factors are the group leader's responsibility. As an individual, he is responsible only for whatever he may actually contribute to prejudice or to brotherhood. As a group leader, he must help members to express themselves freely with one another and to take responsibility for their own feelings and actions. It is crucial to the success of the group that the leader remain free to perform these functions. If he burdens himself with the grandiose expectation that he must solve the race problem, the weight of such an impossible responsibility can only crush him into an anxious and depressed hopelessness that will ultimately force him to give up in despair.

Community-Wide Programs

The crippling social and psychological effects of racial isolation cannot be ameliorated by merely exchanging a pattern of racial separation for one of closer physical proximity. In fact, when people have stereotypes of one another, more intensive contact may actually increase fear and distrust.

Interracial tensions may be relieved, however, by combining realistic socioeconomic changes, aimed at correcting inequities in these areas, with the development of opportunities for more effective communication between the races. Only by communicating efficiently on both intellectual and emotional levels can blacks and whites penetrate the barriers of bigotry that separate them and work more effectively together in changing, by peaceful means, the appalling imbalances that exist today.

One possible approach to this problem involves the establishment of interracial sensitivity groups in urban areas, schools, businesses, and governmental agencies. No two groups would be the same, since each group would be working on a particular set of problems endemic to its own area of interest.

Most groups of this nature have been conducted by professional workers in the field of mental health. But the requirement of professional status severely limits the availability of group leaders. There are simply not enough professional personnel to staff a far-reaching project of this nature. And of those who are available, few potential leaders have had any experience with interracial groups.

Fortunately, it appears highly practicable to train nonprofessional personnel in a relatively short time to conduct biracial sensitivity groups with reasonable success. Such leaders can be trained to recognize instances of stereotyping and prejudiced thinking, feeling, and behavior in themselves and in others and to work toward freeing themselves and other group members from those restraining and potentially destructive patterns. They can be given a comprehension of basic elements of group process that hinder or encourage progress and can learn how to deal with them. They can also be trained to recognize in group members the existence of emotional problems that should be skirted in the group or whose treatment requires referral to professional personnel.

A fundamental part of this training for group leadership is active participation as a member of an interracial group. This experience may be acquired in an on-going group during a period of several months. The training process may be accelerated by providing intensive workshop experiences for potential group leaders during weekends or weeks of living and working together. Such experiences afford an excellent opportunity to relate openly and intensively in many different situations and to experience personally many of the techniques they will themselves be using in their own groups.

After these leaders begin to conduct their own groups, it is highly advisable that they meet regularly with a consultant for on-going supervision and peer support in an informal group setting, where each leader is free to bring up both personal and group problems arising from his new experiences. In such a context group dynamics and process can most efficiently be illustrated.

The Human Relations Committee of the City of New Orleans sponsored such a pilot study in 1969–1970. A brief description of the pilot group's experiences and findings nay be of assistance to those who wish to nitiate similar programs.

Selection of Leaders. This project had s a major goal the evaluation of the use f nonprofessional personnel in the leader-hip role. Therefore, people with a minimum f experience in conducting groups were ought as group leaders. The qualifications ncluded: (1) active participation in similar roups the previous year, (2) awareness of wn prejudices, (3) freedom from severe rejudice, (4) secure racial identity, (5) wareness of own feelings and willingness to xpress them, (6) sensitivity to the feelings f others and an ability to express empathy n a nonpossessive manner, and (7) a creative pproach to new experiences.

Eight leaders were selected: three black nen, one black woman, one white man, and hree white women. Their occupations were liverse: a salesman, an actor, a clergyman, wo college instructors, two social workers, nd a college recruiter. All were college raduates, but their socioeconomic and eligious backgrounds varied widely.

Leaders were paired so that each of the project's four groups had one leader of each ex and one of each race. In addition, an ffort was made to balance personality haracteristics in each team of co-therapists. The most successful team of leaders con-isted of a mercurial white woman, who was ble to keep the group on a high level of motional involvement, and a well-orga-ized, more intellectual black man, who ncouraged the group's orderly functioning. This pairing provided members with both he emotional stimulus for their own emo-ional involvement and the security of calm ntellectual control.

Training of Leaders. As a group, the eaders met with a consultant for two hours a week during a period of five weeks before hey met their groups for the first time. Similar meetings were held once a week for the 12 weeks the groups were in session. Two additional meetings followed the termina-tion of the groups. These meetings were devoted to an exploration of the leaders' feelings about their groups and about one another more often than not centered around subtle racial issues; to training-in-group techniques, often by experiencing

them in this situation; and to supervision of group experiences. Additional contact be-tween the supervisor and individual leaders was scheduled as it was needed. There was no formal course work.

Countertransference. These regular meet-ings of the group leaders were the pulsating center of the project. Interaction among the leaders often became intense, shouts and tears alternating with feelings of closeness. Often, interracial material encountered in leading their own groups aroused the lead-ers' unresolved intrapsychic racial problems. These difficulties manifested themselves in the relationships between co-therapists and were carried over into the leaders' group. At times, these feelings were hardly noticed at the conscious level in the groups them-selves, but in the safer, more permissive, and more experienced supervisory group, they broke forth loud and clear. Their ex-pression and the reactions provoked had both cathartic and insightful healing value and enabled the leaders to confront more successfully the material emerging in their groups.

In the group led by Ted, a black man, and Martha, a white woman, an angry black woman who had spent weeks raging against white in-justices spontaneously expressed her joy at having been cheerfully greeted by a white woman in the group when they accidentally ran into one an-other on the street. The black woman contrasted this experience with the crushing rejection she felt as a child, when she was ignored by a white girl she had been trying to befriend. Her reaction was experienced as a moving breakthrough by some group members. Martha was very touched by the woman's story and shared this feeling with the group. But Ted seemed annoyed, and he ignored it, pressing on to something else.

At the next supervisory meeting, Martha told Ted how angry she was at his callousness. "Tough," he responded and told her that he was annoyed that the black woman had made such a big thing of the white member's friendship. Another black male leader supported Ted, adding that he couldn't really give a damn right now about any white. Martha reacted to the rejection with tears. The white supervisor broke in with his own rage, saying angrily that the interchange made him feel hatred toward all blacks. A white male leader who had kept his equanimity asked, "Can't you just hate some blacks?" The super-visor responded, "No, this kind of thing is contagious." But in a minute or two, leaders and supervisor were all laughing at themselves.

Ted told the group that he was beginning to see that he was really experiencing a fear of giving up his own black identity by being in such close contact with whites. He realized that he was projecting this fear onto the blacks in his group and that he had actually been trying to keep them distant from the white members. The black leader who had supported Ted said that it had felt good to have Martha experience the same pain of being left out that he always felt as a foreigner in his own country. Everyone present at this meeting achieved new insights into their own racial feelings or consolidated discoveries made previously. Everyone felt closer and better able to work.

Mutual Support. The process of exploring interracial feelings in groups involves periods during which leaders feel hopelessness and apathy. At those times, supervisory and peer support is essential to tide leaders over until the dynamics of the groups can be understood.

Such a period usually occurs between the third and fifth group meetings. At this point, black members have begun to be open with their hostility about their situation, and white members have either listened in disbelief or have been feeling stunned by their own feelings of guilt, but there has been little direct interchange. The blacks are almost ready to express their anger directly against the whites in the group, but few of the whites are able to mobilize their retaliatory rage against the blacks for attacking them and arousing their guilt. Everyone feels hopeless about the situation in the outside world. Everyone dimly fears the anger emerging within himself and other members.

Unless these processes are understood and the underlying feelings expressed, those members who are most afraid of anger will drop out of the group, temporarily or permanently. Their withdrawal from the group will further demoralize the members who remain. At this point, the group leader must remind himself and the group's members that they are not responsible for the burden of solving the country's racial problems, that they will have accomplished a great deal if they can express their own feelings to one another. A sharing of rage and a subsequent honest acceptance of these feelings

is an effective way of breaking through this impasse. The leaders' supervisory group is of tremendous help at this juncture.

Format of Group Meetings. Meetings took place in classroom space provided by the Urban Studies Center of Tulane University. The academic, institutional atmosphere probably had an inhibiting effect on interaction, especially during the early meetings. It would be advisable to hold such meetings in an area less strongly identified as part of the white Establishment and in a warmer, more welcoming atmosphere. Meetings for all four groups were scheduled for the same hour-and-a-half period, once a week. Group interaction often exceeded the time limit. After the meetings a small group of blacks and whites usually went to a nearby restaurant for beer and conversation.

Group Progress. Of the four groups established for this pilot project, three remained intact throughout the 12-week period and showed consistently gratifying progress. Each group went through an early phase of initial anxiety, during which some members withheld expression of feelings while others expressed their views indirectly, in the form of generalized comments on racial issues. Anger was similarly expressed in an impersonal manner, increasing in amount during the second, third, and fourth sessions. The period from the third to the fifth sessions was generally one of depression and despair. Some resolution of interracial conflict within the group occurred gradually between the fifth and eighth sessions. Members began to really listen to one another and to understand one another as individuals. Identification with the group and feelings of closeness with other members developed and were indicated by regular attendance. For some members, the weekly meeting became a valued opportunity for open expression and mutual support.

In the fourth group, the black male leader's overprotectiveness toward black members and his residual prejudices against whites and the white female leader's passivity were not perceived quickly enough to be worked through in supervisory sessions, and attendance in this group dropped off rapidly. An extra supervisory meeting was inally held with the two leaders, and a promising solution was developed, but this solution came too late for the group membership to be rebuilt to a satisfactory level. The remaining members of this group were assigned to one of the three other groups from the sixth meeting on.

The eighth group meeting coincided with the holiday season. A Christmas party for members of all the groups, plus their spouses, was held in the home of the white consultant. Attendance at the party was high. For most of those present, the party was their first really integrated social experience. The efficacy of the groups became apparent in this situation. Initial awkwardness quickly abated as familiar faces were recognized. Most guests had been invited to bring their own refreshments and records, which seemed to encourage a feeling of active participation and sharing.

At the party, many members felt free enough to dance with partners of the other race as frequently as with partners of their own race. The music alternated between a black sound and a white sound, with black music eventually predominating and with white members enjoying the chance to learn to dance to it.

The party provided a new opportunity to participate. Several members were able to feel more free in the relaxed social setting than in the more formal discussion groups. Their participation in the groups themselves later increased. The evening's experiences also provoked the discussion in later group sessions of new material related to deep-seated prejudices and stereotypes concerning masculinity, feminity, and sex, as they are related to racial differences.

A few weeks later, a black member who had previously been hostile to whites invited all the groups to his apartment for music and beer, and a white member held a similar party. These social occasions solidified the growing closeness among members.

During the final few weeks, more and more members began to bring up personal problems concerning their families, jobs, and emotional problems. The group leaders were advised to relate these problems to racial issues, where possible, and to avoid getting into them too deeply on the personal level, a reversal of the approach advocated for earlier sessions. These personal revelations were a strong indication of mutual trust. They signaled the success of the groups by demonstrating that members were truly relating to one another on an individual basis rather than on the basis of race.

As the final meeting approached, some members expressed anger at having to disband the group. Others were sad at what they experienced as a loss and looked forward to the possibility of participation in similar groups at a future date. Some members refused to deal with termination at all, ignoring the leaders' reminders that the last meeting was at hand. Their plans to continue holding meetings independently in their own homes received neither official approval nor disapproval. These meetings were planned primarily as social gatherings and were successfully held for several months after formal termination of the groups.

Results

Clinical Assessment. Most members who attended the groups for the entire 12-week period achieved a better appreciation of members of the other race as real human beings rather than as unidimensional figures labeled black or white. Most members also moved away from a position of fear or resentment or both and closer to one of friendliness toward members of the other race within the group. For some members, there was a similar change in attitude toward people of the other race outside the group. Group members were also able to help one another develop a beginning awareness of the subtle ways in which prejudices influence perceptions, attitudes, and behavior.

Deep-seated identity problems and racial prejudices were probably resolved to only a slight extent in most participants. Major, lasting internal changes and more pervasive changes in attitude would require much more intensive and extensive group experiences and realistic improvements in socioeconomic conditions.

On the whole, however, the approach appears to have been successful as a means for clearing the way to cooperative interaction among members of the two races.

Psychological Tests. Psychological tests

designed to measure racial attitudes, self-esteem, and familiarity with members of the other race were administered to all participants in this project before the first meetings took place and again after the termination of the groups, with a final follow-up testing planned nine months after the end of the project.

Of the 80 persons who were scheduled to participate in the project, 16 were selected by the use of random sampling techniques to serve as a control group for psychological evaluation of the efficacy of the group experience. The controls were told that the group to which they had been assigned would be unable to begin meeting for several months, but they were requested to complete the battery of psychological tests of racial attitudes identical to those administered to all other participants.

The tests employed were the Rosenberg Self-Esteem Scale, the Steckler Anti-Negro Scale, the Steckler Anti-White Scale, the Ford Negative Personal Contacts with Whites Scale, the Ford Negative Personal Contacts with Negroes Scale, the Rosander Anti-Negro Behavior Scale, and the Kelley Desegregation Scale.

To avoid any influence on test results that might be exerted by contact with the group leader or with other members, the pilot study's administrators sent the testing materials in the mail. The package also included a self-addressed, stamped envelope for the return of the material. Unfortunately, the rate of return of the materials was very low, despite the use of follow-up letters and personal calls requesting cooperation. Of the 50 group members who attended most of their groups' meetings, 36 completed and returned the second (postgroup) set of tests, but only one control returned the tests. Therefore, reliable statistical analysis of the data is not possible. Some members expressed resentment of the nature of the testing material; others were hostile toward the very idea of being tested. A number of members of the control group expressed disappointment and anger at their exclusion from active participation.

An analysis of the data available shows a significant decrease in agreement with anti-white statements and a significant increase in agreement with antiblack statements among black participants, as measured by the Steckler scales. On the same scales, white participants showed a significant decrease in agreement with both antiblack and antiwhite statements. No significant changes between pregroup and postgroup test results were found on the other scales employed.

The absence of data from the control group and from those members who dropped out of the program makes it impossible to draw valid conclusions about attitudinal changes resulting from this project. Other standardized evaluative procedures in this area are needed. And, because of great individual variations in response and sensitivity to the testing situation, evaluations should probably be done in the form of personal interviews performed by trained interviewers who can tailor their techniques to fit the needs of the individual respondents.

REFERENCES

Allport, G. W. *The Nature of Prejudice*. Addison Wesley Publishing, Reading, Mass., 1954.

Alsdort, S., and Grunebaum, H. Group psycho therapy on alien turf. Psychiat. Quart., *43* 156, 1969.

Amir, Y. Contact hypothesis in ethnic relations Psychol. Bull. *71:* 432, 1969.

Ayers, G. E. The white counselor in the black community: strategies for effecting attitude changes. J. Rehab., *36:* 25, 1970.

Beisser, A., and Harris, H. Psychological aspects of the civil rights movement in the Negro professional man. Amer. J. Psychiat., *123:* 72 1966.

Binderhughs, C. A. Understanding black power. Amer. J. Psychiat., *125:* 77, 1969.

Brayboy, T. L., and Marks, M. J. Transference variations evoked by racial differences in co-therapists. Amer. J. Psychother., *22:* 474, 1968.

Brody, B. Cultural exclusion, character and illness. Amer. J. Psychiat., *122:* 94, 1966.

Brody, B., and Derbyshire, R. L. Prejudice in American Negro college students. Arch. Gen. Psychiat., *9:* 619, 1963.

Brown, C. *Manchild in the Promised Land*. New American Library, New York, 1965.

Buber, M. *I and Thou*. Charles Scribner, New York, 1958.

Calnek, M. Racial factors in the countertransference: the black therapist and the black client. Amer. J. Orthopsychiat., *40:* 39, 1970

Campbell, D. T. Stereotypes of the perception of group differences. Amer. Psychol., *22:* 817 1967.

Carkoff, R., and Pierce, R. Differential effects of the therapists' race and social class upon patient, depth of self-exploration in the initial clinical interview. J. Consult. Psychol., *31:* 632, 1967.

Cleaver, E. *Soul on Ice.* Dell, New York, 1968.

Grier, W. L., and Cobbs, P. M. *Black Rage.* Basic Books, New York, 1968.

Heckel, R. V. Effects of Northern and Southern therapists on racially mixed psychotherapy groups. Ment. Hyg., *50:* 304, 1966.

Human Development Institutes. *Encountertapes for Black/White Groups: A Racial Encounter Program.* Bell & Howell, Atlanta, 1969.

Kardiner, A., and Ovesey, L. *The Mark of Oppression.* W. W. Norton, New York, 1951.

Malcolm X. *The Autobiography of Malcolm X.* Grove Press, New York, 1966.

McArdle, C. G., and Young, N. F. Classroom discussion of racial identity, or how can we make it without "acting white"? Amer. J. Orthopsychiat., *40:* 8, 1970.

McLean, H. Psychodynamic factors in racial relations. Ann. Amer. Acad. Polit. Soc. Sci., *244:* 159, 1946.

Myrdal, G. *An American Dilemma.* Harper & Brothers, New York, 1944.

Rosenbaum, M., Santowsky, A., and Hartley, E. Group psychotherapy and the integration of the Negro. Int. J. Group Psychother., *16:* 12, 1966.

Samuels, A. S. Use of group balances as a therapeutic technique. Arch. Gen. Psychiat., *2:* 4111, 1967.

Schutz, W. C. *Joy.* Grove Press, New York, 1967.

Senderrich, J. M. Perceived reference group support: racial attitudes and overt behavior. Amer. Sociol. Rev., *32:* 960, 1967.

Seward, G. *Psychotherapy and Culture Conflict.* Herald Press, New York, 1956.

Snell, J. E. Psychiatric evaluations in open biracial groups. Amer. J. Psychiat., *122:* 45, 1966.

10

Videotape Feedback in the Group Setting

Frederick H. Stoller, Ph.D.

INTRODUCTION

The stance an individual takes toward self-examination is crucially important in the effectiveness of self-confrontation through videotape. A helpful stance for self-examination can be fostered or impeded by the characteristics of the specific culture which develops in the group setting. The group may concentrate on behavior elicited within the group and witnessed by all group members, or it may concentrate upon behavior which occurs outside the group. The extent to which it focuses on either kind of behavior will determine the quality of data around which self-examination can evolve.

A theory relating the relevance of videotape self-confrontation to the group setting postulates that the optimum time for videotape feedback comes at a point of intersection between two major developments: that of the group as a particular kind of reference organization and the preparation of the individual for self-examination. The group becomes an arena in which individuals explore a wide variety of roles; the group members function as a very specific reference group. Group members encourage one another to engage in role taking, a process by which one examines objectively reactions to oneself. The therapeutic group evolves through a number of stages corresponding to the classification of reference groups: the individual comes to the group

from his identification group with his values and role membership already formed though unexamined; initially the group functions as an interaction group in which membership is relatively unimportant but the platform for behavior is meaningful; the group then becomes a valuation group in which its value grows and its standards are set; finally, as an audience group, there is active evaluation and active attending to the evaluation. Meanwhile the individual moves from unexamined role behavior to role-playing "group member" in which he goes through the motions of a group member until he learns the process of reflexive role taking, a self-conscious learning about self.

Hypotheses concerning videotape feedback within the group concern the following areas: (1) the relation between the group leader's attitude and the intrusion of the equipment into the group; (2) the increased learning engendered by the mutual use of videotape between group members; (3) since videotape information is less loaded with transference than personal feedback, it can be attended to more directly; (4) the readiness of the individual to use the information is a function of his development within the group; (5) because of its contiguity to behavior, videotape feedback within the session is most helpful; and (6) short edited segments of videotape are most useful.

The introduction of videotape as a tool for the use of a therapeutic group has put many practitioners in the position of emphasizing one set of factors at the expense of other equally important sets. Without a strategy for its use, videotape equipment can become more of a hindrance than a help. It is the purpose of this chapter to describe a framework of theory within which this equipment can be a valuable aid in group therapy and, because of the numerous complexities involved, to present a number of hypotheses that will facilitate empirical testing.

The theory and the hypotheses have emerged with the accumulation of some years of experience in incorporating "focused feedback" in the group setting. Focused feedback entails the playback to group members of selected segments of taped groups procedures. The videotape recorder forms part of the group circle and the playback invites open reaction to self-confrontation in the presence of others. Thus, even though tapes may also be used for research and training purposes (and such use is always specified to group members), the recorder becomes primarily an instrument for the group's own use.

The strategic system that has been developed is heavily influenced by the notions of Mead and his followers with respect to role taking: a group member puts himself in the place of another reacting to his own behavior. The question is, at what stage or stages in the group's procedures will a group member be ready for self-confrontation and capable of taking such a role? When, in other words, can videotape feedback be a meaningful experience rather than one that is merely interesting or even disruptive?

The answer depends upon the nature of the course followed in the attainment of group goals, upon the data accumulated along that course, and upon the points at which the lines of general group development and specific individual development intersect. In short, the problems involved in the use of videotape feedback in group therapy are wholly interrelated with the problems of group therapy per se and must therefore be considered simultaneously.

A THEORY OF SELF-CONFRONTATION IN GROUPS

Group Goals

Group psychotherapy attempts to deal with the global aspects of the individual's environment, that is, to give each individual a view of himself as he moves in a wide portion of his life and in a reasonably broad pathway through the world. The other group members constitute a sample of the world in which he can test this movement, a sample small enough to permit realistic examination of his perceptions and his impacts.

Group goals are more complex and varied, however, than this simplified statement of purpose suggests. Some are goals to be reached and passed as individual group members progress; others—notably a group milieu in which self-examination is supported and valued—must be first achieved and then maintained; and still others are, in effect, ever-present group functions. Examples of the last type are an increase in the individual's contact with his "self" and the provision of tools with which he can evaluate his own circumstances.

The attainment of group goals—ultimate, successive, and continuing—is a product of many factors among which two are crucial: the data on which attention is focused and the working attitude brought to this material.

In-Group and Out-Group Data

Early in the course of group meetings a social organization takes place, a style of communication develops and, according to which conversational subjects command most attention, the group begins to foster certain cultural emphases. When the material upon which attention is focused consists largely of versions of self, behavior, and fate as described by the individual, the group tends to deal in "out-group behavior," definable as the whole range of behavior experienced outside the group by a group member and made known to other members only through his report. If, on the other hand, material receiving the major portion of attention involves primarily the behavior of individuals to which all other group members are first-hand witnesses, the group tends to deal with "in-group behavior." Although only a hypothetical group would deal exclusively with one or the other category of data, therapeutic groups can be characterized by the extent to which each is emphasized. Experience indicates considerable group-to-group variation in this respect.

Experience also shows that the extent to which emphasis is placed on in-group or out-group data affects how relevant to its operations a group will consider self-confrontation on videotape. When the emphasis is on out-group behavior, group members attempt to become expert in a particular frame of reference as they speculate on the word pictures of any given individual. Always getting trapped by the details he chooses to share or withhold, they nevertheless endeavor to be amateur versions of the leader. The introduction of videotape feedback in these circumstances is often seen as either irrelevant or disruptive. When the emphasis is on in-group behavior, however, the major operation of the group members consists of feedback: the specifying of responses and reactions (by "reactors") to specific instances of behavior (on the part of "actors") within the group. And when the major group operation is feedback, videotape feedback is accepted by group members as a natural extension of what they are trying to do: paint pictures of one another.

Group Career and Group Fate. The advantages of focusing the group's attention on in-group behavior, and therefore feedback, are two-fold: (1) the participant gradually becomes aware of the range of his responses and reactions (to most of which he ordinarily pays little or no attention), of their effect upon his behavior and of their impact on others; (2) the cumulation of an individual's direct responses ultimately provides a very valuable picture

of the ways in which he structures and filters the world.

With this type of data it is possible at any point in a group's history to specify, for each participant, a "group career," a description of how he has moved through this particular social environment. Proper specification makes explicit the reasons for his "group fate," that is, a summation of the determinants of group attitude toward him—the group's reactions, expectations, and perceptions. Although his group career and his group fate may not completely parallel an individual's version of his out-group experience, it is frequently possible to build bridges from the in-group data to the out-group data.

Selective Intervention and Routine Operation. In the course of feedback in group sessions, videotape feedback can be used either for selective intervention to accomplish a specific purpose or used as a routine operation, in which case a replay of each segment of group procedures automatically follows its conclusion. Each method has its advantages. For example, a major opportunity for beneficial intervention with videotape feedback arises whenever a group member seems to demonstrate awarenss of discrepancies between his anticipated reception by others and his actual reception.

On the other hand, a major advantage of the routine use of videotape is that what can be obscured in dialogue feedback is likely to be exposed in videotape feedback. If, for example, the participant is dealing with some discomforting feedback from another group member, he may well manage to maneuver the dialogue in such a way as to cover his discomfort. When the incident is replayed on videotape, however, his handling of the feedback will probably manifest itself as a lack of understanding on his part.

The foregoing example also serves to illustrate that the problem under discussion is a much broader one than that of how to use videotape feedback to reach into the basic ambivalence each group member brings to the learning situation: the real nature of the individual's handling of feedback in dialogue may manifest itself on videotape—but to the group leader, possibly to some of the other group members, and not to the individual himself unless he has developed an appropriate attitude toward self-learning, a frame of mind that almost involves physical evidence of concentration. In the absence of this attitude, this stance, self-confrontation on videotape is at best "an interesting experience" and one without impact.

To summarize, the relevance of group data is an extremely important consideration in the use of videotape feedback, but of little importance if the manner in which group members accept, consider, and process the data is inappropriate. How a group is taught to operate is thus a crucial factor not only in the achievement of group goals but also in the successful utilization of the videotape recorder.

GROUP DEVELOPMENT

Role Playing

Most people have unexamined and unexaminable assumptions that behavior outside certain narrow role descriptions would elicit highly undesirable consequences. The assumptions are unexaminable because "the world" and "society" and "they" are entities too big to permit the testing of expectations. As already noted, members of a therapeutic group constitute a global sample small enough to permit realistic testing. Even in the group setting, however, the individual places narrow limits on the range of roles he will permit himself to play. As a consequence, in the early stages of therapy any direct approach to the continuing group goal of increasing the individual's contact with "self" is likely to result in the creation of an atmosphere in which there is merely polarization either to "an authentic self" or to "a phony"—or, at best, to result in the development of a range of selves or roles so narrow that learning is limited and therefore unrealistic.

Much more constructive is an indirect approach, the presentation of a concept of many selves, a concept of the potential in every individual to play many roles and varied roles. It is essential to the effectiveness of this strategy that opportunities be provided for the playing of an extensive range of roles and, thus, for a broad scope of behaviors. Indeed, the group should periodically re-examine its own standards to make certain that it is promoting an adequate variety of behaviors for appropriate exploration.

Once this group function of role playing is well under way (and it should become an integral part of the group's life), group members will begin specifying the reactions they have been building up toward one another. They will be learning to examine their own reactions and developing a skill in specifying them as carefully and precisely as possible. (In a sense, this process will itself constitute a new role for most people: social custom dictates that social reactions are not overtly acknowledged, certainly not to the individual's face, and life-long restraint may have dulled the ability to interpret these reactions.) Soon they will specify not only what they perceive in one another, but also the kinds of expectations they have of one another within the group setting. Here, too, they will and should move away from generalities and be very specific. In this way the group gives sanction to a range of behavioral exploration and develops a particular stance in each of its members in the examination of the others' behavior.

Role Taking

Placing oneself in the position of another reacting to the self is developed and supported by the group. It is only when group members can respond to their own behavior in the specific circumstances of the group that videotape feedback becomes meaningful. It is very difficult for a group to reach this stage in which self-examination is developed and supported.

Types of Reference Groups

Turner has characterized types of reference groups in the following manner: (1) *identification group:* generally the source of values for the individual and the one in which he takes the role of member, (2) *interaction group:* members in these groups are irrelevant but the individual must take them into account in order to accomplish his ends; (3) *valuation group:* the individual places a value upon a group and compares himself against group behavior standards; (4) *audience group:* the individual's performance is actively evaluated and he actively attends to these evaluations.

Within the terms of the present analysis, the individual comes to the therapeutic group with a value system and a set of expectations determined by his identification group. The therapeutic group initially functions as an interaction group, providing an arena for behavior. Self-learning begins as the group itself becomes important and the members and mutual reactions are explored and tested. At this level the group members are learning the business of giving and receiving reactions. But groups must grow past tentative and cautious feedback to the very deliberate examination of an audience group for significant self-learning to occur. It is only at this stage that the participants will support self-examination and be acutely perceptive of evasiveness among group members when they are presented with information about self. Prior to the development of an audience group, the introduction of videotape feedback is rarely very meaningful.

Self-examination in the presence of others is particularly subject to the atmosphere which prevails. It is only where mutual self-examination predominates that subtle evasions will receive the attention of the others. Only when a group member is prepared to attend openly to his own self-examination will he attempt to closely focus upon the evasions of others.

Against the backdrop of the group's development, it is necessary for the individual to develop an appropriate stance for self-examination. When he enters the group, he engages in role playing with little conscious awareness of what he is doing. He is generally unaware of the expectations he has of others toward himself; nor is he aware of how these expectations are often at variance with the range of roles he exhibits. As the group begins to give him feedback about himself, he will often disregard it and attempt to move around it through explanations and word duels with the other group members. As the group develops into a valuation group, the individual will probably develop a skill in playing the role of "group member." In this phase he will go through all the motions of a group participant, making appropriate comments about himself and others but not really adopting an attitude of examination toward himself. Such role playing will often be revealed through the manner in which he uses the opportunity for videotape feedback; he is incapable of dealing with it from the point of view of the other group members.

Reflexive Role Taking

For the videotape viewing to be truly effective, he must adopt the attitude of reflexive role taking. In Turner's words:

One of the most important distinctions which can be made among the kinds of other-attitudes is between those which are expectations or evaluations or images directed toward the self and those which are not. When the attention of the role-taker is focused upon the way in which he appears to the other, the role-taking is reflexive. . . . When role-taking is reflexive, the individual is led not merely to consider the effects of his action or their compatibility with some standard or code but to picture himself specifically as an object of evaluation by someone else.

Within the group the individual must be self-conscious about his behavior. He must regard the other members of the group as agents from whom he can learn about himself. He can no longer regard them as people to be manipulated into giving him the kind of response he is looking for. When the individual has developed this attitude to some degree, his use of the videotape feedback can be meaningful and effective.

Initial viewing of the videotape can be seen as helping the individual develop the reflexive role-taking attitude. As he is given opportunities to look at himself within the group, he is also given training in how to look at himself. Frequently initial self-viewings do not have profound effects, for group members have not yet attained the capacity to perceive themselves from the point of view of others. As this skill is developed, changes in the way an individual deals with the self-confrontation can be seen. By this time he has developed a group career and a group fate and he is now in a position to put this in context with the role-taking stance that has become more conscious.

It should be apparent that effectve use of videotape feedback takes place after considerable group development and individual movement. A line of group development has been described as well as a course of individual movement. The point at which these two trends intersect is the point at which videotape feedback can be used with the greatest strategic effect. While individual and group movement patterns are not independent of each other, they do not necessarily occur at the same time. Individuals within the group move at different rates of speed. The group development can be defined by the prevalence of a particular group atmosphere; it is not dependent upon all group members reaching a given point at the same time.

HYPOTHESES CONCERNING VIDEOTAPE FEEDBACK WITHIN THE GROUP

1. **Equipment.** *The degree to which the presence of videotape equipment will affect the behavior of the group depends upon the placement of the equipment, the attitude of the group leader toward self-viewing, and the preparation of the group members for attending to videotape feedback data.* The position of videotape equipment in the circle of group participants was mentioned in the introduction and has been a basic assumption throughout this discussion. The general premise is restated here as part of the first hypothesis so that this important factor in the successful use of videotape feedback will not be overlooked.

The mere presence of television cameras might be expected to affect group behavior—and it may well be that the ultimate purpose of their presence affects the covert, if not the overt, attitudes of group members—but television equipment has been used for the sole benefit of remote audiences with little detectable effect upon the behavior of group members. Experience with videotape recorders has not been appreciably different from experience with audiotape recorders: participants quickly adapt themselves to the presence of either type of equipment. This is true, however, only when the videotape equipment is appropriately placed in relation to the group.

Initially used for purposes other than focused feedback (for example, for research and training), it was first placed out of the sight of participants even though they knew of its presence. It was brought into the group circle in order to give group members control over its use. Experience has since demonstrated that, regardless of the purpose of its presence, videotape equipment seems less of a threat, less of an intrusion, when it is placed within the group than when efforts are made to hide it from the group's view.

With the cameras and cameramen openly forming part of the group circle, the group leader becomes the key to how much of a distraction and how much of an intrusion their presence will be. His easy acceptance of it will be communicated to the group, as will any concern at the prospect of his own self-confrontation or any possible feeling of guilt for having betrayed group members by opening up their private circle. The manner in which he introduces the subject of the equipment is thus as important as what he says about it and how he prepares the group for its use.

An essential step in the preparation of a group for meaningful self-confrontation on videotape is also an essential step in the progress of any therapeutic group: participants must learn how to give and take feedback. A considerable amount of modeling on the part of the group leader is necessary in the development of this crucial group function. Ultimately, however, the process can be learned only by experience. Group members must repeatedly go through the process of giving and receiving perceptions in order to convert that process into basic operating procedure.

The element of first-hand experience is equally important in dealing with the special type of feedback involved in videotape viewing. The equipment must be accepted as a group tool for use *by* group members, not *on* them, and frequent opportunities should therefore be provided for actual handling of it. It is helpful, for example, to have all group members take turns as cameramen and learn both how to tape group procedures and how to rerun the tapes for feedback purposes.

In short, not only will the presence of videotape equipment have little effect on group behavior, but the equipment can become a valuable group tool if it is placed in the group circle, if the group leader communicates a positive attitude toward its presence and if group members develop skill in giving and taking feedback plus, if possible, skill in operating the equipment in question.

2. **Increased Learning.** *There is much more to be learned from videotape feedback when group members direct it at one another than when it is directed exclusively by the group leader.* Much of the therapeutic benefit inherent in the group situation lies in the fact that individuals are reaching out to help one another. They are exploring a multiplicity of roles rather than the exclusive patient role and, in the process, they are giving as well as receiving help. As a result, their "learnings" are far richer than they could be in the limited dyadic situation.

Giving is as important a group dimension as receiving. There is as much valuable learning in what an individual says about others as in what he says about himself. The contributions made by all group members in their efforts to help one another, that is, in giving feedback, constitute a large portion of the behavior that enables them to learn about one another. In this context, when one group member suggests videotape feedback for another (requests to look at oneself are relatively rare) and cites specific reasons for the feedback at that particular time, he is making an important contribution to his own growth. The very act of extending help (particularly in the mutuality of the group endeavor) leads to significant learnings about self, and the perceptions necessary to make an appropriate suggestion for self-viewing represent an important development in anyone striving for self-understanding.

The suggestion from one group member that another confront himself on videotape is beneficial to the receiver as well as to the giver. Not only is a special type of learning engendered by a peer, but when suggestions for self-viewing continue to come exclusively from the group leader or coleader, the receiver continues to think of help as coming from a superior individual only. At the same time, if suggestions for self-viewing come exclusively from any one person, superior or peer, the recipient is likely to develop a sense of having been brought to a particular point by a particular person, a feeling of having been manipulated. Ideally then, suggestions for self-viewing come from a number of group members, all of them peers.

3. **Neutral Source.** *The information imparted by videotape feedback emanates from a neutral source and is therefore less weighted by the distortion inherent in individual relationships.* From the moment group members make contact with one another they begin to develop feelings about one another. From a feedback standpoint, such feelings can be seen as having two sources: the behavior of one individual and the transference tendencies of the other. Feedback within the group can therefore

rarely constitute pure information because it is generally distorted by the personality of the person who gives it. In other words, the attitude of the receiver of information toward the giver colors, to a considerable degree, the reception of that information. One might say, in an exaggerated fashion, that the information imparted in feedback is, as a result, less important than the individual relationships involved—and this is likely to be the case unless a consensus of the group on the merit of the feedback can be reached.

With videotape feedback, the source of information is, theoretically, a neutral source. The television equipment, in effect, "tells it the way it is" and, because the receiver of the information has not developed any relationship or transference to the equipment, he is in a position to receive the feedback in purer form than would be possible if it came from another group member. It cannot be completely pure because the person who suggests the self-viewing will affect, to a degree, the attitude of the viewer toward the feedback. Videotape nevertheless enables the individual to give more objective attention to feedback than is possible when he deals with information transmitted exclusively through other individuals.

In consideration of the differences between videotape feedback and the usual group member feedback, it is important to state that the group member feedback has a value that can never be minimized. Ultimately it is the individual relationships, the distorted feelings, and the withholdings that constitute essential features of group learning. Videotape feedback should be used not as a substitute for what group members can give one another but as an extension of group functions. On this course it can become a technique that exposes and eases the group struggle in important ways.

4. **Relevance of Data.** *The effectiveness of any given self-viewing on videotape depends upon the relevance of the data presented to what has transpired between the self-viewer and the other group members.* Feedback within the group is most mean-

ingful and has greatest impact when the individual involved perceives an obvious relationship between the information presented and what has transpired between himself and the other group members up to the point of its presentation. His group career and his group fate, in other words, must be clear and explicit before the feedback can have any significance—before his own behavior can be tied to what happens to him among people.

The same relationship exists with respect to videotape feedback except in terms of degree: because the element of transference is minimized, the relevance of the data to the group career and group fate the individual is experiencing is even more important. Any given self-viewing, as noted earlier, can be an interesting experience at one point and a profound experience at another. It is only when the individual has received a considerable amount of reaction from other group members, and when their relationship to him has been made explicit, that the self-viewing is likely to have a change-inducing effect; it is when he has already been thrown off balance by what has occurred between him and the rest of the group that the maximum impact of a self-viewing will be felt.

Most practitioners who have used videotape equipment in the group setting, including the author, have anticipated short-cutting the process of change. There is evidence that behavioral change can occur before changes in self-concept begin to take place, and it is probable that the initial impetus for experimenting with television equipment in group therapy was the expectation that some of the group struggle could be circumvented, and much of it eliminated, by the impact of self-viewing. Experience has demonstrated, however, that videotape feedback has its greatest meaning for the individual when, *because of* extensive group struggle, he has a clear-cut, emotionally heightened awareness of the consequences of his behavior. To repeat, the videotape presentation must be an extension of the group process rather than a substitute for it.

The consequent burden upon the group

leader and the group members with respect to the timing of these presentations is a substantial one. In order to use the equipment to its full advantage, they must develop an awareness, an alertness, a sensitivity that virtually defy description and that are achieved only by experience. As is the case with most techniques, the employment of videotape equipment often makes the basic task of the group more difficult, rather than more simple, until a high degree of skill is attained.

5. **Immediacy.** *The closer the videotape feedback to the behavior that is relevant, the more helpful it will be.* Videotape is a time-binding instrument in the sense that it captures a sequence of behavior in a specific span of time. The taped sequence can be replayed at any subsequent point and the question at hand is: Should the playback occur immediately after the behavior has occurred and while the individual is caught up in the defensiveness and misunderstanding that so often fill the group atmosphere, or should it occur at some later point by which time the individual has had an opportunity for reflection?

There are arguments for each answer and they do not necessarily conflict, because there are some purposes for which one solution is appropriate and others for which the alternate is appropriate. For example, the author has used the delayed playback to give members training in self-confrontation. This reflective approach is also useful for retraining. A delayed viewing of videotapes, particularly when it occurs outside the group setting, can give the individual an opportunity to reflect upon his behavior and develop new frameworks within which to view what has happened to him and what is likely to happen to him. The advantage of the videotape in this connection is that the therapist and the patient have something concrete with which

they can deal rather than the selective, distorted memory of a deeply affected individual incapable of reporting accurately what happened.

It is the author's prejudice, however, that the *sine qua non* of the group situation is its immediacy and that in the exploration of all possible emotional reactions and the consequences of emotional interplay the group is at its most crackling and most pertinent. When a group begins to talk about what happened, when it begins to explain away something that was very much alive, one can sense the life going out of it and much that is caricaturable taking its place. Within the group framework there is a high degree of relevance in immediacy.

As originally formulated, feedback in the group was, in fact, explicitly described as being most potent when closest to the behavior with which it was concerned, and, as such, it was almost defined in terms of its immediacy. This suggests that the only process at work is based on the concept that the more the individual knows about his behavior, the more he is in a position to do something about it. There are, however, two processes at work in which videotape feedback can play an important part. One is the gradual accumulation of specific behaviorism—a smile, a sigh, a pout—that elicits particular reactions on the part of other people. These are presented in small increments of feedback and such information is useful. The second process, described in some detail in connection with the preceding hypothesis, is integrative in nature and involves a crisis in which (1) a variety of behaviors on the part of an individual and (2) his group career suddenly come together with new meaning. Here, as at many other crucial points, instant replay is most appropriate.

REFERENCES

Benne, K. D., Bradford, L. P., and Lippitt, R. The laboratory method. In *T-Group Theory and Laboratory Method*, L. P. Bradford, J. R. Gibb, and Benne, K. D., editors, pp. 80–135. Wiley, New York, 1964.

Korzybski, A. The role of language in the perceptual process. In *Perception: An Approach to Personality*, R. R. Blake and G. V. Ramsey, editors, pp. 170–205. Ronald Press, New York, 1951.

Mead, G. H. *Mind, Self, and Society*. University of Chicago Press, Chicago, 1934.

Robinson, M. B. Effects of Videotape Feedback versus Discussion Session Feedback on Group Interactions, Self Awareness, and Behavioral Change among Group Psychotherapy Participants. Unpublished doctoral dissertation, University of Southern California, Los Angeles, 1968.

Shostrum, E. L. Witnessed group therapy on commercial television. Amer. Psychol., *23:* 207, 1968.

Stoller, F. H. Focused feedback with videotape: extending the group's function. In *Innovations to Group Psychotherapy*, G. M. Gazda, editor, pp. 207–255. Charles C Thomas, Spring-field, Ill., 1968.

Stoller, F. H. Group psychotherapy on television: an innovation with hospitalized patients. Amer. Psychol., *22:* 158, 1967.

Stoller, F. H. Therapeutic Concepts Reconsidered in the Light of Videotape Experience. Paper delivered at Western Psychological Association meeting, 1967.

Stoller, F. H. Use of videotape (focused feedback) in group counseling and group therapy. J. Res. Develop. Educ., *1:* 30, 1968.

Turner, R. H. Role-taking, role standpoint, and reference-group behavior. In *Role Theory: Concepts and Research*, B. J. Biddle and E. J. Thomas, editors, p. 159. Wiley, New York, 1966.

11

The Use of Videotape in the Integrated Treatment of Individuals, Couples, Families, and Groups in Private Practice

Milton M. Berger, M.D.

INTRODUCTION

As more and more private practitioners realize the almost boundless potential for the constructive use and flexible integration of video into psychotherapeutic practice with individuals, families, and groups, its use will expand rapidly within the next decade. Personal communications and correspondence with colleagues throughout the country have indicated that there is a heartening interest in, but still somewhat limited use of, video in the private practice of psychiatry.

Video enhances the clarity of one's psychic, emotional, behavioral, and body identity. In addition, the practitioner's interest in using this new modality constitutes a communication to the patient that the therapist is actively involved in risk-taking and experimentation toward greater therapeutic effectiveness. The impact of the therapist as a model for his patients, a newer and healthier model than they have heretofore been closely involved with in relationships, has often been documented. As patients can identify with the therapist's capacity for acting with responsible freedom and flexibility, they become potentially enriched as they develop and incorporate the concept of new options for themselves.

Videotape playbacks can be used in psychiatric treatment by a therapist with any theoretical view of personality dynamics that acknowledges: subconscious or hidden motivation for one's behavior or attitudes; the significance of signs and symbols that regulate and arrange relationships; resistance; transference, and the impact of the concomitant communication of emotion, behavior, and thoughts through multiple levels and multiple channels in human relationships. Therapists interested primarily in modifying behavioral states by suggestion, direction, education, or desensitization methods can also utilize video constructively to some degree.

More and more manufacturers have entered upon the production of low-cost videotape recorders, and it is possible to install a useful, mobile system in one's office for a minimum price of two to three thousand dollars. When one considers that general practitioners as well as other medical specialists and dentists spend many thousands of dollars for technical equipment in their professional offices, whereas psychiatrists have to spend little or nothing for the purchase of professional equipment, it becomes then a matter of simple education and alteration of habit pattern for psychiatrists to realize that it is in their interest to add special equipment not only for the welfare of their patients but also for their own heightened satisfaction and fulfillment in the practice of psychiatry. It is also important to remember that the cost of special equipment is tax deductible.

It is not only through self-confrontation with a single immediate or past experience in psychotherapy that patients are constructively affected via videotape. Therapeutic impact is also made in a deeper and more effective manner through repeated opportunities to observe, perceive, and integrate the image or picture of self alone or in interaction with others over a period of time. The component processes in working through toward emotional as well as intellectual insight and change in psychotherapy are not completely known. They go beyond recall, free association, abreaction, catharsis, connecting past and present, transference, reality testing, corrective emotional experiences, identification, universalization, education, and maturation. The aforementioned processes and systems, which are mediated through various communicational media and channels, as well as those processes and systems which are operant but still unknown to us function more effectively in the service of working through when the psychotherapeutic process has incorporated in it the intermittent benefit of closed circuit or television playback.

It is worth repeating what is fast becoming axiomatic, namely that the "hardware" must function in the service of the patient rather than the patient's interests becoming subservient to the equipment. The hardware must not dictate therapeutic strategy nor interfere with the basic relationship of trust between patient and therapist. It is important, too, to remind the private practitioner of psychiatry that the professional, ethical, moral, personal, and legal concerns for his patient's welfare include attention to the issues of privacy and privileged communication. Though written permission is not usually required in a private office for use of a videotape, which the patient is assured by his therapist will be destroyed afterwards or not shown to anyone else, it is considered crucial to obtain a signed statement of permission if the tape is to be used for teaching, research, or demonstration purposes. Although a narcissistic, hysteric, masochistic, or exhibitionistic patient may give signed permission in advance for use of a videotape whose reproduction or replay to others is clearly not in the patient's interest, it may rest on the therapist's judgment and integrity to decide not to share such a tape with others. Such determinations go far beyond simple legal considerations, involving as they do deep humanistic concerns.

INTRODUCING VIDEOTAPE TO PATIENTS

There are various methods of introducing the use of videotape to patients:

1. **Res Ipse Loquitor.** This means "the thing speaks for itself." With videotape cameras, recorder, and microphones fully exposed in the office, it is most unusual for a person coming into the room not to notice them and not to question their purpose within the first few sessions. When the therapist notices the patient looking at the equipment, he may ask, "What reactions are you having to the presence of this equipment?," thus flushing out what may otherwise remain unspoken and preparing the patient for the time, perhaps even in the first encounter, for using this adjunct to psychotherapy.

2. **The Fait Accompli.** The lights, cameras, videotape recorder, and monitors are placed in operation just prior to asking the patient or family or group into the office. As they walk in and notice the equipment is working, the therapist may say (a) "I thought you might enjoy getting a more complete look at yourself today, okay?" or (b) "Do you think you're ready to risk a more open look at yourself? I think you are and it will speed up our work together, okay?"

3. **The Advance Notice.** As a psycho-therapeutic session is coming to an end, the therapist may say, "I'm hoping you'll agree to our using the videotape equipment in our next session. How do you feel about it?" Nearly 100 per cent of the time the response is, "Okay, if you think it will be of any value," or, "Okay, but I want you to know I'm anxious about it." One can usually respond with questions such as, "What are you anxious about? What do you fantasy?" The response to these questions may reveal much that has not been so clearly stated and made available before concerning the patient's self-image, degree of narcissism, and fear of "really" being known or seen by someone else, even the therapist.

4. **The Seduction.** This is brought about over a period of time by the therapist intermittently making suggestive, intriguing remarks in different sessions such as, "It's too bad we don't have the video system in operation today. It would be of real value if I could replay the last few minutes of what's gone on between us." Or, "I sure wish I could play back your facial and hand movements as you said that!" Or, "I've just been using the video with my last patient, would you like for us to use it today?" Or, with a couple or group, the therapist may suggest using the video while remarking, "It'll help us to really see what goes on between you to trigger off the difficulties you're having with each other."

The Patient's Advance Reaction

It is of marked therapeutic value to elicit the patient's reactions or fantasies in anticipating his first audiovisual self-confrontation. Significantly laden though mostly unpredicted free associations are often expressed by patients just prior to self-confrontation via closed-circuit television or videotape playback in response to the question, "What is going on in you now as you are about to experience yourself in this new way?"

The usual advance reaction of adults has been to use the imminent self-confrontation as a social situation calling for self-criticism. The following examples support the conclusions of Bahnson, which differ with the notion formulated by many theoreticians that the self-image is "a kind of homunculus existing within the person, ready for inspection on command—very much like a photograph, which at will can be pulled out of a hip pocket, looked at and then put back." Bahnson emphasizes that "such concepts of self-image as a circumscribed cognitive phenomenon may be comfortable to work with, but they are a far cry from the complex and intricate experiences people have of themselves."

For example:

Clarissa, a 20-year-old, shy, immature, single, bright, attractive art student who is inhibited to the point of being at times frightened when with people responds to my question about her reaction to the possible use of the videotape equipment by saying: "When I walked in I assumed you must be interested in photography—maybe motion pictures. Then I thought maybe it's of use in your professional work. Then I thought it might be to take pictures of me. Then that that was stupid. (long silence) The idea absolutely terrifies me. (What idea?) The idea of being watched. (What about it?) It has to do with hiding. I tend to build up little fronts which aren't really me—and if someone is *really* watching, they're bound to see the *real* me. (silence) I know logically I don't have anything to hide. (So what do you hide?) I hide feelings —negative feelings—hate feelings—tense feelings—anxieties. When my feelings are hurt, a lot of times I don't show that—I can't take criticism—I react like inside I don't want to react and I try to hide that. I act very blasé—when I was younger people used to think I was self-assured but inside I was a nervous wreck and I show it more now. I also don't show love or liking. I'm embarrassed to show I like a boy a lot. Then there is the other thing about hiding my body. I never wear very tight clothes— that's hiding—but there is a little part of me that wants to be found out and hopes I'll still be liked. (Liked is the same as being accepted?) Yes . . . (she said as she continued on about being understood). (I commented, I have a feeling that you're confused about being liked— understood and accepted.) Yes, and I explode once in a while because I'm so angry and confused at being this way. Then I feel guilty and feel terrible but I can't help it. I realize I am that way."

She sits silently, looking dejected, with her eyes getting red and moist, but unable to cry. I point out to her how almost all feelings seem to be forbidden, are negative for her, and that she has little inner permission to cry even in rationally appropriate moments like this. She then cries a little and I ask for her associations —her feeling reactions—to what has emerged. She continues: "As a kid my parents would be pleased if we were well-behaved, which meant being nonreactive- -sitting like little statues. My mother has told me she realizes now how foolish this was and that what she thought was healthy wasn't really so and that she's realized how ridiculous it was to expect us to conform to the world. My father doesn't come into the picture (stated disappointedly). He allowed my mother to raise us—my brother and I. (He just wasn't there for you. You had a father and yet you didn't. What are your feelings now?) I love my father and don't feel it right to be angry with him. I wish my father were more manly. He lets my mother take over. He'll just sit by and watch and say nothing as my brother, mother, and I have a big argument. I realize too that my father is the real puritan in the family. (silence) My father thinks sex is more like the icing on the cake—whereas my mother thinks it's more natural. I think my father is terribly inhibited and my mother is less so." Her train of associations reveals an interconnected mixture of superficial and deep thoughts and feelings involved with her I and her not-I, her self and her family, their attitudes and values and hers in past and present.

Some verbatim responses to the question, "What do you anticipate the effect of video playback will be?" have been as follows:

Michael, a handsome, well-built, 25-year-old, intensely driven, single, American-born male whose Dale Carnegie compulsively helpful approach to psychotherapy stirs up an image of the last of the Wild West cowboys galloping after the last of the Western steers says: "It's gonna be exciting to see ourselves as others see us. It'll be quite an adventure! My immediate thought just now was that I'd try to impose a more attractive audiovisual personality on myself. It's funny, but I'm more excited about it for other members of the group—like Randy, who's been told of her sullen, pouty, removed

posture. This might shock her out of it! I'm excited for myself too. So much of the time I assume a little crouched-off contracted posture and it'll be interesting seeing when I feel it if I do assume it and how much. I think there's so few times when I just feel big—feel all there —like a man. There are times when I'm able to relax into that after I ask myself why am I crouching over. What bothers me most is my passivity, which I feel is feminine. . . ."

Aron, a self-effacing 34-year-old, intellectual, repressed, detached, bachelor accountant raised by a typically dominating, overprotective and guilt-provoking mother and an ineffectual, submissive, undemonstrative father, said: "I feel I'll be experimental and am afraid it'll add something artificial which would interfere especially at the beginning. Positively, I think it'll bring home to the people how they react to people and situations—to see how they sit like turds. I'd like to see how I react to thoughts and communications and to listen to my voice and change in timber. And if I do change in group I think I'll bring these changes into my outside life. At the beginning I think the changes will be artificial; that is, if I see I'm sitting in a slovenly position I'll pull myself up and together. It won't be coming from within but it'll be good for me to change my position. It'll help me in my business, and seeing how I hold and carry myself and how others see me—and I want to change and give me more confidence in myself. Also the fact that I can look at a screen will bring the other group members into a perspective I can't get now. It'll be easier to see everybody else in the group that way."

A 28-year-old attractive, detached, markedly alienated, compartmentalized, and extremely intellectual mother of a sickly child, who is separated from her actor-puppeteer husband and who has sought solutions for her underlying depression and loneliness through LSD and hypnosis, spontaneously remarked on first seeing the newly installed videotape equipment in my office as she came into her group session: "I'm angry about it. I'm afraid it means more mechanization and more depersonalization and distraction. I immediately think of Orwell's *1984.*" She then pulled into herself with a disparaging belittling frown and almost hid her presence in the pillows of the couch as she looked down and away from others in her group, taking occasional peeks at them and me from the corners of her eyes.

Andy, a 33-year-old, alienated, untrusting, suspicious, bachelor psychologist raised by a hostile, paranoid father and an inconsistent, frequently absent mother, reacted to the possibility of our using videotape playback by saying: "To be observed means failure. It means to look stupid, inept and that I'll be the laughingstock as I was as a child—and I truly feel stupid. (Do you though?) Sometimes I don't, but ninety-five per cent of the time I feel I'll be laughed at—held in contempt—ridiculous—idiotic—untrained—a phony—a fool. . . . " Andy functions in therapy like a classical help-rejecting complainer.

Joshua, a 27-year-old psychiatric resident, saw the new audiovisual equipment in my office as he walked in for his group session and said: "I don't see it as being of much potential value. I believe I know and see what I do and how I am with others. I feel I need to know more of what's going on inside me which keeps me as I am. I see it as a spectacular gimmick which doesn't get to what really bothers us." He said all this without actually going through an experience with the equipment and in fact was attempting to discourage me from using it with him.

However, a few days later, Joshua was much taken with the videotape playback during his individual psychotherapy session. Initially he stated he felt overwhelmed with the impact of the awareness of how much of an adolescent child he still is. He noted and commented upon the fact that whether he is angry, smiling, or happy that he is consistently speaking like, looking like, pleading like, cajoling like, and feeling like a child. He could now begin to question with much deeper and healthier motivation his need to send nonverbal cues with his boyish "Please don't hit me, I'm lovable" head tilt and smile, so that he would arrange for others to treat him as a boy and not as a man. He said: "I see myself coming through so subdued and watered down I could vomit! I cover up feelings and dress them up with words. It's sickening how I look so winsome and helpless." In a session months later he remarked, "The videotape has certainly helped me to expand my observing ego!"

IMPACT TO SELF-IMAGE

It is quite common for a patient being self-confronted on the monitor of a closed-circuit television system for the first time to make an immediate attempt to reconstitute his idealized image of himself by sitting up straighter or pulling in his waist or straightening out his hair or tie. He then turns his head in different directions to self-experience how he comes through to others from those vantage points. One can use a two-camera system with four monitors and often move the cameras and monitors into positions to give the patient the most opportunities to simultaneously experience his body and self-image that he has ever had. Following the initial self-critical reaction and the acts of self-image restoration, a patient who is not too overwhelmed with self-hate may begin to note and comment on some favorable aspects of himself. This is a favorable prognostic sign.

Immediate image impact reactions occur when the patient is able to watch himself on one or more television monitors during a psychotherapeutic session. In an office with one mobile camera and a fixed-to-the-wall remote control camera as well as four monitors, the therapist can easily arrange the patient's chair position so that the patient can look at the therapist or himself on the monitor while a camera is recording a full view of him. He can thus observe his face, hand, and body movements and expressions while he is talking. The therapist can ask patients to observe whether or not their facial and body expressions are in harmony with their verbal content and inside feelings and to share with him reactions concerning their disharmony as the session goes on.

A variety of responses to such immediate closed-circuit self-confrontation can occur and one should use this approach cautiously in suicidal patients or those whose self-hate is narcissistically or realistically based on their body image. The use of this equipment is different at times in private practice than in institutional settings.

Profound Reaction

There are different types of reactions to immediate image confrontation the first time it is experienced and when it is experienced on later occasions.

An example of a profound reaction was registered by Mildred, a 35-year-old single teacher whose self-effacement and high standards for herself have caused her much pain and little real self-esteem despite her physical endowments of a good figure and good looks, her high intellectual potential, and her artistic, aesthetic talents in sculpturing and interior decorating. She came to therapy because of her inability to create a sustained relationship with a responsible loving man which might lead to marriage.

During our second individual session, she agreed to the use of the videotape system, as I suggested it would be of marked value for her. She sat silently looking at herself in the monitor, twisted her head from side to side while looking herself over critically and commented: "I don't look as stiff as I usually look. The muscular tensions don't show as much as I feel them. People have often said I looked very calm when I wasn't, when I felt scratchy and tense. So it seems I think I show more about myself than I really do. (How do you feel about this?) It's all right. (Just all right?) It's fine. I feel like I still have a hiding place. (What do you have to hide?) My private room, my privacy, my thoughts I don't want to share and my feelings I don't want to show. It seems I then have more charge of me. More of me is at the disposal of my will. (You feel not as vulnerable, not as frail . . . to what?) To public exposure. (She smiles now.) (You smile like you've got a big secret.) The words sounded so loaded, like I was carrying around a big secret. (What's the secret?) At that moment I was thinking about a man in my office I've got a crush on and that if the office gets hold of this they'll have a lot of fun. (You mean ridicule you?) Yes, it'll get on the wire. Many times in life I felt very self-conscious and thought here I am making a perfect ass of myself and yet maybe others never think of me that way at all.

"When your feelings are known to others you can, that is, I can, be hurt and I often expect to be hurt and I anticipate it. It's not a very vigorous kind of attitude. Other people avert so they're just not hurt. Or if they're hurt, so what? It doesn't destroy them, but I for some reason feel destructible. (Are you?) (She smiles) No, I'm not, literally. I tend to survive. I don't think I'm the kind who'd have a complete nervous collapse unless things were really terrible. (Like what?) Like if everybody I loved died right away and I woke up the next morning without a family, without friends. I don't know why this feeling of being exposed—I always relate it to being humiliated, that's not like nervous collapse—like being destroyed—just humiliated. (What do you recall about being humiliated?) I don't recall. Oh, I'm sure this has to do with my father. The only time I can think of is probably not the crucial time. In adolescence when I started to wear makeup all wrong, at thirteen, he'd suddenly attack me and call me 'liver lips' and accuse me of rolling in the flour barrel because I wore too much makeup. He obviously didn't like it and he was saying in his way 'What an unattractive girl you are' and here in my own way I was groping to be attractive and be pretty. I'd just get up and leave the table in tears. (What are you feeling now?) Sort of sad. Feeling sorry for the girl who fled from her family's dinner table because her father scoffed at her. Mother was there. She agreed with Daddy. I always wondered what on earth they thought they were doing. I put on so much powder because I had so many pimples. I always wondered why they didn't try to help me do it right. Mother's attitude was that one shouldn't call attention to oneself. I got confused about contradictory messages they gave. I saw Mother and Daddy nude until I went away to high school at age sixteen or seventeen. I'd see them nude swimming in Maryland at our island in summer and at home nude in their bedroom and in the bathroom. They were quite casual about it. (Were there sexual feelings between you and your father?) I don't remember having any. (pause) One time when I was sixteen he patted my breasts and I was slightly shocked. Now I'm thinking, 'Well, that nasty, sly old man, poking his daughter to see how she was developing, sort of investigating." (Did it occur to you that perhaps he was doing more than objectively investigating; that he was perhaps doing something for himself?) Oh, no. It surprised me because it was without any precedent. He is an old exhibitionist even now at seventy. One time he came to New York City to visit me—I had a roommate. My father was sitting around in his shorts with his penis hanging out—serving drinks. I was shocked and after a while said: 'Is that all you are going to put on?' and he said he'd put more on if I wanted him to."

The basis for Mildred's coming through to me as perplexed and not trusting was amply defined. The background for her confusion and denial about her sexual and other feelings became increasingly clear to me as being grounded in parental double-binding, oedipal ambivalence, and conflict as well as guilt and anger which had to be denied or repressed. It has been difficult to help Mildred to gain insight leading toward a healthier self-image as well as to move toward greater self-assertiveness and self-esteem because of the tenacity of her defensive systems.

WORKING THROUGH

Videotape playback of a portion of an individual psychotherapy session can be profoundly helpful in working through. In the following example, the playback helped to expose underlying dynamics which had impeded constructive growth in the patient for a long time. Her seeming passivity and guardedness with me in psychotherapy sessions was the transferential expression of a security stratagem which literally and figuratively was life-preservative for her.

Dorothea, 33-year-old single, American-born, self-effacing, quiet, unobtrusively dressed, passively sitting social worker whose voice was usually flat, controlled, drab, and colorless, was transfixed as she watched herself during the first playback in an individual session. For fifteen minutes we watched the monitor revealing the stillness of her body as she sat rigid, fixed, almost as if paralyzed except for some movements of her hands, face, and neck. This brought her to quiet tears and almost expressed anger, and she remembered and talked about having been raised in twelve different homes of relatives from age 2 to 7. Her father had died when she was two. She recalled hearing her mother say to her over and over again, thousands of times: "Be good! Be obedient! Mind! Don't give anyone any trouble. I worry if I were to die, and it could happen maybe tomorrow or the next day or next year, then who would take care of you? If they had trouble raising you, you'd go to an orphans' home."

Up to this point, I, as therapist, had been encouraging her to move toward greater mobility in her personal and interpersonal living, not knowing that, unconsciously, greater mobility for Dorothea meant the threat of abandonment. We had both been stimulated to react to the degree of her physical immobility when I presented the playback without sound at both regular and fast-forward speeds.

Herb, a 32-year-old aggressive, alienated, argumentative university instructor had come for psychotherapy one year previously during a hypomanic agitated state. His cynicism and distrust had diminished enough to allow him to participate in a playback of his individual session without insisting it would be "just a waste of time." He stated in a subdued and poignant manner, "I didn't realize I'm in such agony. I'm really suffering! I didn't know I could be so serious. I'm not as bad looking as I thought I was. I see I'm alert and as fast as I thought I was. I respond to you. And, (laughingly) I don't have as bad a Brooklyn accent as I thought I had. I see the way I'm closed-minded, opinionated, and manipulate things 'cause I'm in such pain. I see how I have no tolerance for you; I'm so queasy and restless. I'm also heavy, I didn't realize I was that heavy. Have to do something about that.

"This has given me a lot of confidence in myself. I didn't realize I express myself as well as I did. Though I'd like to have alertness and sparkle in my eyes—not so much pain. I didn't realize I grimaced so much, though people have told me. I thought I'd show more disdain and found I didn't.

"And did you notice? (gleefully) I don't chew my glasses as much. In fact, I didn't chew them once today and I used to chew them all the time."

Another patient, John, observed himself intensely and then stated quietly with marked control.

"I don't recognize that guy as myself. I pity the poor soul. I saw him as cold—like a Mediterranean punk, with sort of a conceit and complacency—even a blandness to him." (John, the third child in a wealthy, alienated family, raised mostly by governesses, gave up early, ruled out love and emotion in his life.) "I felt I'd climb on top of the world, so they'd have to respect me. I lumped together my mother, father, sisters, and others—'friends' who had rejected me. I went for intellect. I feel this terrible hatred for my parents (said real coolly). I really feel guilty about this. I have the school kids' admiration for the Bogarts—the cool—the strong—the unfeeling—the tough—and it's how I used to fancy myself too. A few years ago I'd have admired that punk. Now I saw the agony in his soul. Now I'm in a state of changing values about feeling. Before it was intellect—intellect—intellect! Now it's being a mensch and feeling."

Henry, a 25-year-old furniture designer struggling with homosexual conflicts, responds to his first videotape playback by remarking, "My voice is deeper and perhaps more masculine than I thought. It's interesting—I do not get any pleasure from it—it's interesting. (How do you feel about how you look?) I don't like the way I look—my forehead—my eyes—I never realized how slanty and slit they are—they're ugly. I don't like them—I feel nothing more than describing—like I am editorializing. I do smile a lot. (How do you feel about that?) I think it's strange—I don't know why I'm doing it—it's strange.

"I don't like some of the motions I make with my eyes—movements—motions (What are they?) the closings, the openings—just that they seem so effeminate. I don't like the motions—there is just too much fluttering. The whole face is too—it—uh—is it overreacts—too much—so many inflections to every sentence—to every word—it's overreacting in my face—the eyebrows keep moving—there's so much expression—it's an overexpression. I talk phony too—I drag with a drawl. I think it's amusing to sit here and see myself.

"I move around a lot like a player piano according to one of my friends. My life is like that—I'm at the wrong speed—like I go so fast. I saw this on the television—I saw all these fast movements—the hands, the mouth, the eyes. (I cringe as I listen to you contrive to disown yourself.) I never realized how fast and jerky these movements are—the way I live must be like that too. I'm just so anxious to get on to the next thing—the next event—I never spend a quiet moment. . . ."

Another patient, Harold, a bright, "eager-beaver," 31-year-old single up-and-coming executive in an advertising agency, had come into therapy primarily because of homosexuality. His often absentee, self-effacing, and ineffectual father had not served as an adequate male model while his guilt-provoking aggressive mother had raised him as her bedmate until he was fourteen, and her confidante until he went off to college. Following his first videotape playback he sat stunned, astonished, and silent while tears welled in his big sad eyes. Suddenly he shouted exultantly: "I look like a man! I sound like a man! I'm not really a fag at all." A common immediate reaction to the playback is to be pleased or displeased with the evidence of one's masculinity or femininity.

An example of video's long-term impact in working through is seen with Sandy, a 24-year-old, intellectual, alienated, single college graduate who saw herself on videotape replay in her group after not having seen herself on video for three months. She commented: "I saw how much I operate as a therapist, trying to analyze what goes on in others rather than feeling or reacting to or in myself in a personal way. Although I still saw more facial glumness than I'd like to see and my hair looked raggedy, I had a stronger feeling of liking myself than ever before. I remember initially how I had cringed as I watched the playback, not believing it was me. Though I still felt disconnected with the me on the screen I was fascinated with what I saw. Instead of being overwhelmed as before with the discrepancy between the me I saw and the me I envisioned myself as, I now saw and felt the me in the playback was a real, alive person with whom I could identify. I saw myself as intelligent, sometimes attractive, gesturing a lot when I talked, sometimes whining yet sometimes with a sense of humor, holding back quite a bit of frustration and anger which I saw coming out in movement—a physical boundness I remembered feeling at times during the part of the session played back, which was the way I felt a lot in my childhood. But mainly I was glad to be meeting again with myself, a person I now was feeling I liked a great deal."

Insight

Insight which is more than intellectual may be promoted and integrated through repeated playbacks. For example, a real "Ah-ha!" experience can occur when a patient can see and hear how his repeated help-rejecting complaining leads his peer group members to wind up irritated and frustrated with him, finally refusing to focus on him any longer during a specific group meeting as he dismisses, puts down, or otherwise wipes out their suggestions, advice, reactions, or interpretations. Alger and Hogan emphasize the "second-chance" phenomenon through the use of videotape playback, which allows patients to become aware that the feelings experienced at the time of the original interactional situation were actually not clearly conveyed to others. As an individual becomes aware of this during replay and realizes the discrepancy between what seems to be shown by his behavior on the screen and what he actually remembers feeling, he can clarify through a second communication the feelings he had inadequately expressed before with a resultant improvement of the relationship between those involved. Alger and Hogan, who are also markedly impressed with the value of videotape in the private practice of psychiatry, have noted that the emotional insights enhanced through videotape playback, when added to the more common intellectual insights achieved in psychotherapy, are more likely to bring about significant behavioral changes in patients.

Geertsma (1969) has pointed out that those of us involved in work with videotape, whether it be referred to as "self-image experience," "focused feedback," "self-confrontation," or "self-observation," are operating "on the assumption that externally mediated self-cognition is potentially a powerful technique in psychotherapy and behavior modification." To the degree that video provides for greater depths of observation, perception, and cognition which are interrelated processes basic to psychotherapeutic progress, it is indeed a powerful technique.

The process of bringing about awareness in the service of working through and furthering motivation toward change, following emotional as well as intellectual insight, is enhanced when a patient is given the opportunity for intermittent self-confrontation via videotape playback.

Focused Feedback Confrontation

An example of the impact of focused feedback confrontation with videotape is revealed in reviewing the progress of Aron, the previously mentioned 34-year-old successful accountant suffering with emotional illiteracy, who has severe relationship problems with men as well as women because of his distrust and fear of intimacy. He came to therapy in a panic at the prospect of consummating marriage with Rhonda, whom he felt had guilt-provoked him into giving her an engagement ring after they had been dating and having an affair for six months.

Three months after beginning combined individual and group psychotherapy we agreed to look at closeup films of his face

taken by me during his group psychotherapy session the evening before. His interest in the playback was intense because of his desperation to learn what keeps him running compulsively to and from unsatisfactory, clutching relationships with women. During the playback he made the following remarks and observations:

"I see my father's face, my father's eyes, and I get sad and get the same feeling he had—that life is bad—don't trust people—don't have any friends unless they can do something for you. I'm still holding on now to what I had in childhood—the same impassivity in my face—and the ways of controlling my mother and father to get what I wanted by getting sick.

"There I look like my father sitting by the window—looking out at the world—apart from it—isolated. He had the same pursed look of his eyebrows and his eyes were sometimes expressionless and sometimes yearning. He didn't know how to smile. One of his eyes seemed to face outward and one inward, and yet they seemed to merge.

"I learned to use words to get what I wanted —like my mother. She was very voluble, very quick witted, very adaptable to any circumstance.

"As I keep looking at the picture of myself, I'm reminded of a time when I was twenty and went to the wedding of a friend as best man. I remember talking to his mother a few days before and that I asked his mother, 'Why does he want to get married instead of going to college?' She went to his closet and pointed to a wooden tie rack and said to me, 'That's you—a schtick holz' (in Yiddish). When she pointed to the wood, I knew what she meant and I was very, very silent. As time has elapsed since then I've realized that that was my father too—a piece of wood. Once at home we were drinking—toasting to the New Year and I toasted to 'love' and my father responded, 'I don't know what this is— what love is—or even if it exists.' Everybody laughed including myself and I said inwardly to myself 'Fool! That's how you are—you have no understanding of life—and that's the reason no one understands you and you understand no one.' Feeling the tremendous gulf between us I was thinking 'You'd be better off dead.' The gulf between us was always felt but never expressed.

"Years later, after his second heart attack, he said to me, 'Take a vacation—enjoy life' and I had the feeling that he realized then the type of life he'd led and was telling me in his way not to live the way he did.

"I was thinking now of the positive things I did get from my mother and suddenly began to see her in a different perspective. Yes, she was smothering, domineering, and directing, but my father had no capacity to enjoy life and my mother did. She had a capacity to enjoy life, to live . . . and she blamed my father for denying her that. Last week I realized my sister married a man just like my father and my sister is doing to him and to her kids and herself what my mother did to her and to me. She is absolutely controlling him and still trying to control me . . . and I resent it."

One month after his first playback experience with videotape, Aron remarked during an individual session, "I got angry inside when I saw during the playback my stillness and passivity and nonfeeling when I was in group the other night. I see now how come people tell me I'm such a nice guy, but don't react very much to me. Jesus—look at the lack of expression in me. And yet, with all the inside thoughts and feelings that were going on in me, I sat there with a masked face and still body and finally I moved my lips into a pout!"

One week later he talked of how upset he was to have such a wooden or stone face and added, "My eyes lack luster. They're just not active. I close off and rarely come alive."

Three months later Aron asked me to turn on the videotape equipment so that he could observe himself concomitantly through the closed-circuit television monitors. He free associated aloud as he watched himself during this individual session: "I still remember the first time I saw myself on the playback. I was flattened, masklike. I think I used the word 'stone-faced' as if there was no movement. Now I notice a little more mobility and a more relaxed and a more expressive face. My face before was formless and now there is form. My face before was closed and now it's beginning to be a little more open." There was a minute of silence as he observed himself. . . . "My eyes are a little more open, more expression-filled. I'd still like more mobility, more expressiveness in *the* eyes, and a more relaxed look on my face. I still have the overall impression as I look at *the* face . . . tense . . . (As if what?) . . . as if I am expecting an attack, wary. . . . (Anything else?) . . . noncommittal, very noncommittal." (Note the pattern of shifting from *my* face to *the* face as an expression of Aron's pattern of alienation as well as a statement of increasing anxiety as he confronts that which he sees in his eyes and face with antipathy.) (Anything else going on in you?) "No, I have been busy watching the camera. (The camera?) The picture. (The picture?) Myself. I have always felt the ocular vision was a truer vision than the camera vision. I'm not interested in photography or in seeing pictures of myself unless someone says, 'Gee, he's handsome.' But if they say nothing like that, I'm not interested in looking at a picture of myself. I feel more uncomfortable in the group when we have the camera on than when we don't, particularly as we're talking and watching the screen at the same time. I feel I'm missing the full impact of the vocal and visual imagery. I feel I miss some of the vocal while I'm catching the image on the monitor. I feel the best aspect of the videotape is the playback, when we can watch how we look and sound without interruption.

"I see a change, especially around *the* eyes. (*The* eyes?) My eyes are beginning to open up. I hope they stay that way. My lips are more relaxed and not drawn and tight. My forehead is more relaxed. I think I'm noticing my strides in therapy in recognizing some of my old and present traits and hangups in others . . . more forcefully . . . noticing feelings in others or their relations to others which I never noticed before."

Aron's repeated self-confrontations with the aid of videotape playback have helped him to accept and partially work through many facets of his alienation from self and his distancing or self-isolating maneuvers which are expressions of the distrust of others which his parents, through nonverbal as well as verbal channels, had so thoroughly inculcated in him.

With Aron we found that utilizing video closed circuit and playback over time increased his motivation to work cooperatively in therapy toward change. In addition to increasing perception of his reaction patterns and his impact on others, it also facilitated his verbal communication to his therapist—all this more rapidly than might otherwise have been likely.

CLARIFICATION OF FAMILY ARRANGEMENTS

The use of videotape playback in private practice to demonstrate the patterns and systems of unconscious arrangements, as well as the reponses of family members to each other, can expedite insight, understanding and motivation to change better than any previously used modality.

Revealing Patterns

Typical repetitive, regulating patterns which may be revealed and played in a focused feedback are:

1. *Placate.* "You're right" or, "Yes, I'm wrong about that."

2. *Blame or Provoke Guilt.* "But you made me do it that way" or, "It's your fault because. . . ."

3. *Preach.* "When I was a child . . ." or, "I can't understand how a child who's been given everything like you have can sit there and say that. . . ."

4. *Change the Subject to Something Irrelevant.* "I'll get back to that but I want to point out that the other day. . . ."

5. *Withdrawal of One or More Family Member(s) into Silence, Resignation, and a* "What's the use? It won't make any difference anyway" attitude.

6. *Denial.* "It may have looked that way, but you just don't understand."

7. *Psychosomatic Response.* "Since I've been sitting here my heart is pounding like it's going to break" or, "I'm getting a splitting headache now—you get me upset when you say those things."

8. *Discounting.* A family member used a dismissing type of head nod to the side and down or hand movement with palm down to indicate that what was being expressed by another family member is being "put down" or "discounted."

9. *Being Realistic.* The family is open, truthful, and conscientiously attempts to recognize, accept, and resolve realistic conflicts of interest or problems while being congruent in communicating or relating.

Identifying and Empathizing

Some additional values of video usage with families are: More families who come for help believing their problems are unique can be helped when together they watch a playback of another family with similar difficulties. The experiential process in the here-and-now encounter of a family interview allows the family's reality problems and its distortions and neurotic interactions to be more truthfully perceived in a much shorter time. The family sickness can be approached therapeutically with more directness and effectiveness and with less chance of the therapist's remarks and intent being distorted by one individual family member. The capacity of the therapist to identify with and empathize with each family member as well as with the family as a whole can educate, stimulate, and help the individual family members to identify and empathize with one another. The members of a family may be taught to look at their problem from one another's point of view. They may more readily face up to the paradoxes and contradictions and incongruities of life in general and family life in particular, and learn that these paradoxes and contradictions and incongruities exist for all of us.

Communications

Video can aid in the clarification of the ways in which family members use communications to conceal as well as to reveal truth to one another. For example, some may speak with so many words or so rapidly that the listener cannot really understand what is really going on in the speaker. Or, the nonverbal smile that accompanies the words may reveal the opposite of the actual words spoken. Frequently the tone of voice is so much more important in family communications than the content. Mary, furious at the way her husband Jack had spoken to her, said, "His tone was sheer martyrdom and accusation and indicated a very deep dislike for me, and when he asks questions I feel he's asking not for information but to accuse me." Repeated playbacks were required before Jack could acknowledge the validity of his wife's observations and the impact of his tone on their relationship. A wife may complain of her husband retreating into silence, and say, "I get so annoyed when he just won't say anything to me for a long time." She is denying that his silence is in fact saying a great deal. His silence may communicate that if he opens up he will have to become explosive, violent, and abusive, and would rather not. On replay, video revealed the tremendous angry pressure in the husband's use of his finger to tamp down the tobacco in his pipe while his face and clenched fingers around his pipe revealed his squelched inner fury. His silences may indicate his feelings of futility —that he feels at such a time there is just no sense in talking, as he is aware that she does not want to have a conversation but to convince him of her point of view or to justify her position or her actions.

hectic, anxiety-laden interaction of a family, couple, or group session.

The use of video may help to clarify the tendency to project or externalize onto one's spouse or children or others that which is really in oneself. Such projection may have to do with responsibility or a thought or a feeling or anything else. Blind spots can be exposed. The author has found in his work with groups of married couples that there are many deep similarities in the character of the partners. The partners, however, being blind to this, may be quite hostile to their spouses for possessing traits that exist in themselves. It is easier to see distasteful aspects of ourselves in others than it is to see them in ourselves, but video playback forces us to remove our blinders.

CLARIFICATION OF NEUROTIC CLAIMS

Clarification of the neurotic claims that people make on one another can be accomplished. A neurotic claim exists when we expect what we only have a right to hope for. (See T. S. Eliot's *The Cocktail Party* for a statement of the human condition which requires giving up excessive expectations.) The lack of knowledge of this seemingly simple but oh-so-profound fact has caused untold human misery and despair. When our excessive expectations, which we had no right to have in the first place because we only had a right to hope, are not fulfilled, we tend to feel abused and angry, sometimes even furious. Certainly we feel much more than the kind of disappointment that ensues when a hope is not fulfilled. Many of our abused reactions can be quickly mollified and dissipated if we will ask ourselves, "Am I expecting what I only had a right to hope for?" Neurotic claims, silent as well as verbalized, particularly when they are subtle as they so often are, can be acknowledged in the more objective silent participation of self with others during a playback than in the more

DIAGNOSIS AS PROCESS

Diagnosis is too often conceived of in static frames of reference—whether this diagnosis be made in a social service or psychiatric setting. To conceive of "the diagnosis" as a static fixed entity is analogous to thinking and conceiving of "the unconscious" as a fixed entity or geographical location. Each is to be equally and vigorously attacked and denounced. *Diagnosis*, just as the contents of one's unconscious, whether one be a patient or a psychotherapist, *is a process*. It is in movement. It changes as inexorably as the days of our lives, as the tides and atmospheres. The changing battleground of inner and outer conflict is a person, a human being with soul included, in relationship to his whole self and to the selves of others. At any one moment healthy constructive forces may be in ascendance, and at another moment these forces may be eclipsed by the forces of destructive neurosis or psychosis.

The changing diagnoses of the family members and of the family as a unit when it is together present a challenging kaleidoscope of myriad interaction patterns which reflect intrapsychic and interpersonal health and sickness in varying degrees. These patterns will present themselves differently and in different order, intensity, and variation with different therapists. These diagnostic patterns will frequently be more evidenced by nonverbalized communications than by what is said. These nonverbalized communications will often contradict the verbalized content of the family. When such contradictions occur with consistent inconsistency in the majority of the communications in a family which is unable to truly be with one another, where the child exists primarily to extend the parents' infantile and unfulfilled self-images, then we have a fertile family background for the development of schizophrenia or other serious personality disorders.

When videotape playbacks reveal such contradictions between verbal and nonverbal communications to be only occasional in a family, they may serve to reflect or express the multiple paradoxes of life itself or of the double-standards which exist in many of our ways of life. They reflect the general pathology of our culture. To function within the framework of this general pathology is in fact to appear healthy. We must be careful to distinguish between the kind of strategic duplicity necessary for living within the general psychopathology of our culture and the kind of compulsive duplicity or pathology which is an indication of deep inner character neurosis.

In experiencing the family unit in a therapeutic session, collusion between parents or between children or between the mother and daughter against the father can be sensed and interpreted or otherwise used by the therapist as it is expressed. He may decide not to focus on it until it has been revealed in playback. The use of this collusion to undermine family unity and maintain isolation and conflict can be explored and worked through. Which mother has not silently given a look to her daughter or son and a little head nod or partial benevolently patient smile as she quietly waits out her husband's tirade against the child's behavior? Does this collusion serve to cas-

trate the father in the child's eyes so that Mama is experienced as the real power behind the family throne?

ROLES

Through the playback of an individual, family, or group session patients with massive blind spots or other denial techniques can be confronted repeatedly with the self-defeating, self-isolating, or otherwise self-negating arrangements or "games" they establish and maintain with others. They can be helped more rapidly to recognize and to come to grips with the values of their unconscious compulsive need to enact such roles as:

Jester	Virtuously Honest
Referee-Umpire	Sadist
Catalyst	Overprotective Mama
Don Juan	The Judge
Cockteaser	Kill Joy
The Idiot	Egghead
Injustice Collector	The Baiter
The Abused Type	The Doctor's Assistant
Missionary	Martyr
Crisis Creator	Ombudsman-Guardian
Story Teller	Negativistic Clique
Clock-Watcher	Creator
Whiner	Help-Rejecting
Leader of Opposition	Complainer
Nit Picker	Runt of the Litter
Planner	Sophisticate
Self-righteous Critic	Cockroach
Expert	Troublemaker
Provocateur	Magician
Fragile Baby	Monopolizer
General	Charmer
Intellectual	Iconoclast
Flirt	Victim
Frail Tyrant	Vindicator
Teacher's Pet	Prima Donna
Prosecutor	Strong Silent Type
Seducer	Compulsive Helper
Guardhouse Lawyer	Can't Say No
The Scapegoat	Manipulator
Rejection Collector	Competitor
Saint	Ostrich
Fashion Plate	Fair One
Innocent	Pollyanna
Advice Seeker	Castrator
Guilt Provoker	

CLARIFYING TRANSFERENCE IN MARRIAGE

Following the first ten minutes of a session with a young couple whose marriage was threatened by dissolution, a videotape confrontation was provided. Prior to this session the wife, Stella, had been seen twice in individual sessions and the husband, Melvin, had been seen once. Stella, now 28, has been working as a researcher for a market research corporation since their marriage two years ago. Melvin is a 27-year-old graduate student working for his degree in business administration. I chose to replay on videotape moments of this couple's interaction in which he seemed to wear a particularly significant, serious, and anxiety-provoking facial demeanor. We learned that behind this demeanor is a judgmental person, somewhat detached in the service of intellectual objectivity and noninvolvement, who presents a facade which can be at least anxiety provoking to his wife if not downright frightening. The net result is to produce a feeling of being ill at ease in people who are with him. Asked if she is familiar with this "face" and how it complicates her life with him and is a source of difficulty, Stella immediately responded in a knowing manner with, "Yes! That is what gives us so much trouble! When he looks that way I don't know where I am with him then. When he looks that way I feel very insecure, very anxious."

Talking to her husband directly during the session, Stella said, "Melvin, I don't know where I stand with you at such times and it drives me to ask you for approval, attention, or reassurance, particularly reassurance which I seem to then want and need—reassurance that everything is okay between us. Somehow I try to involve you at such times with food, questions, stories, or sex even though I know it seems to annoy you. It's like I've got to get something from you to know where I am with you and where I am with myself."

Melvin, when asked what goes on in him at times when he is expressing this demeanor, said: "I am weighing what whoever I am with is saying. I am kind of asking, 'Does it make any sense?' 'Does it have any basis?' If it does not make any sense to me, I then have a feeling that the person talking is stupid." Melvin was then informed by me that this particular demeanor has a distancing quality which serves to separate as well as to provoke anxiety. It expresses aloofness and bears a judgmental quality.

As Melvin was able to gradually acknowledge, understand, and free associate to this "look," he stated that he had learned this look from his father. At the dinner table in his childhood home there were often many silences as it was not *de rigueur* to talk unless you had something very worthwhile to say—something intelligent. He recalled that he had to learn to watch what he was saying at the table because he was constantly being put down —"taking grief." He continued with, "I constantly felt I was on trial with everything I said or did when I grew up." Melvin was able to understand that he had incorporated this very look of his father's which had in fact given him so much trouble. Asked by me whether or not he was aware he "wore" that particular face, his wife interrupted and answered for him, saying, "He wears it more with women than with men because he thinks women are more irrational—like his mother. He has told me so many times. He also finds it much easier to be animated and to have fun and let go with men than with women."

During the remainder of the session, Melvin, Stella, and I reviewed the additional dimensions of his "look." We concluded that his "look" is a statement of being in abeyance and yet not of being in neutral abeyance as much as being in malignant abeyance. It is a look of being noncommittal at the moment because he had not learned it is all right to have multiple feelings about or between himself and others at any one moment. So he keeps the mixture of feelings, attitudes, and judgments going on in his inner world private, while he edits and sifts out one feeling or one judgment which he may then feel safe enough finally to state or act upon. When Melvin realized increasingly that this "look" of his was and can be a powerful tool to turn other people off or to make them squirm, he smiled with great pleasure. For despite his veneer of aloof self-sufficiency, he felt inadequate and insecure underneath and was delighted to learn the strength and impact of this weapon which he had been using for years without awareness.

This illustration clearly validates the reports of Mendell and Fisher on the passage of neurotic values and behaviors through multiple generations in the same family.

VIDEO DURING GROUP THERAPY

Some examples of the use of videotape playback during group therapy sessions are:

Fritzi, a 32-year-old, smilingly ingratiating mother of two children, who separated recently from her husband, a biochemist provoked by her to great rages, remarked quietly, after experiencing a playback of herself during a group session: "I could see how I come through phony, as if I'm reciting, which is what I do when I'm talking to Jack. I also picked up that I come through as not telling the whole story. I'm so used to hiding my true feelings I'm afraid to be open. But I didn't think it showed."

Sam, one of her peer group members, who is angered by her manipulating tactics with himself and others, says, "You come through as if you are trapped and afraid to express your anger or any other feeling straight."

Another member of the same group, Mike, said sadly with surprised recognition, "What I see is that what I hate so much in my brother and nephews is in me too. And I finally can acknowledge the bitterness you've told me I come through with."

Jimmy, a hard-core passive-aggressive character neurotic, still plagued with deep anger toward himself and others, commented, "I see I need to go to another therapist . . . to take

elocution lessons. I could hear my Brooklyn accent. But at least I did sound sincere, direct, and warm and felt I came through more with the group. I'm feeling more part of the group these days and I'm feeling more involved with my family at home too. . . . I had a fantasy, Milt, that you're gonna get electrocuted 'cause I feel you're inept with electronics." This last statement was a clear-cut projection of his own self-hate for feeling he was an inept bungler at physical tasks including his sexual impotency with his wife whom he hated but did not have the courage to leave.

Another group member, Mark, insisted that his outer physical appearance is not important. He insisted that the fact that he is unshaved, unkempt, wearing sloppy, dirty, unpressed clothes should not affect his relationships and that only what he is underneath should count. He was helped to understand the tremendous neurotic claim he was making on others, "Love me, love my smell!"

First and Subsequent Playbacks

The first playback experience in group therapy is one in which individuals focus interest primarily on themselves. Though narcissism and neurotic egocentricity are a common basis for this initial focus on self-image, there may also be aspects of healthy curiosity and real self-interest in operation. In later playbacks there is less self-image preoccupation and a greater interest in pathological interactions as well as in characteristic styles of being and relating to one another. In these playbacks there is often a different quality of non-verbal communication amongst the members than in the usual interaction. In the intimacy of the playback there may be seemingly insignificant but very important expressions of caring amongst members. Sometimes patients who have difficulty in letting go their tears during regular group interaction can cry during the playback in a manner similar to those people who can only cry while in a theater watching a movie or play. The lessening of pressure to relate to and with others through words allows for a different kind of involvement to develop which is more in the direction of communion and communing.

INSTANT REPLAY

During a psychotherapeutic session in which a videotape recording is being made it is *sine qua non* to inform all participants that each has the right to request an instant replay at any time during the session. This availability of videotape replay is one of its most unique assets and distinguishes it thoroughly from the use of sound movies of a psychotherapy session. It is easier to arrange to use instant replay in private practice than in an institution where sessions being taped are often used for teaching and research purposes. The reactions of each participant to a second chance to re-experience and examine what has just transpired may bring out evidence of multilevel contradictions, compartmentalizations, and blind spots and offer individuals an opportunity to study, explore, and more clearly understand what one person does which triggers off a reaction in another person. Instant replay can also be employed to make especially difficult or sensitive confrontations without the therapist verbalizing the implication of the full interpretation. There is a reliance here on the concept of *res ipse loquitor*. This helps to assess the patient's capacity for awareness of the implications of his functioning and fosters self-reliance.

Resistance

Resistance to the use of video or audio equipment should be listened to and respected while an attempt is made to understand and undermine the basis for the resistance. As pointed out earlier, the elicitation of fantasies as to what its use may reveal is of significance, as is the flushing out of subtle paranoid trends or needs to maintain secrecy around one major area of concern or another. If a patient is too upset to watch an instant replay, it may be best to postpone the replay while working through the basis for the upset or fear of replay. There is such a state as a patient

being just too raw and vulnerable inside to risk a further confrontation at certain moments, and in the spirit of helping him the therapist should not force him to face what he is not ready to face. This is an individual, delicate matter which depends so much on the skill and art of the therapist to bring to successful fruition. Such self-encapsulating behaviors by patients need to be responded to with empathy and deep understanding of the dynamics in operation in order to work through such blockages.

Indications and Contraindications

In psychotherapy groups, cohesiveness, intimacy, and esprit are heightened during a playback which all members are interested in experiencing. However, when the timing of the playback is not in tune with where the group as a whole is and where the individual members are at a particular moment, the playback is reacted to with disinterest, boredom, impatience, and irritation at the therapist.

During a playback individuals or members of a group may be more open to experiencing compassion for themselves or others than during the regular session. The playback allows for a reflective, feeling experience untarnished by the usual defensive interactional patterns of patients with their therapist or group.

Patients with a paranoid coloring, who through their suspiciousness and projection of malevolent intent to others manage to repeatedly ruin the potential for successful relationship while maintaining their isolation and detachment, are easier to reach with reality through repeated playbacks of a taped segment of interaction revealing their compulsive distortions and projections. In the context of the therapist's consistent, sincere interest and willingness to replay a segment of tape over and over again in order to work through his patient's pathology, the patient may receive enough transferential and/or realistic gratification to motivate him toward giving up his neurotic trend(s).

VIDEOTAPE PLAYBACK AND
THE THERAPIST

The development of trust in the therapist is a cornerstone for the evolution of intimacy and mutuality in a successful psychotherapeutic relationship. Videotape playbacks allow individual or group patients to perceive through many sensory inputs who and how the therapist is for them. They are quietly able during playback to more clearly perceive and integrate the therapist's capacity for empathy, rapport, support, and whether and to what degree he really understands and is with them. They are able to perceive his literal, figurative, or metaphoric communication of "I support you, I hold you in my arms, I cherish you, I nourish you. I care about you. What happens to you is important to me. I have an investment, a personal investment in what becomes of you; I am myself emotionally involved in your fate. . . . I keep you within bounds; I do not allow you free indulgence of impulse, of love or hate. You must respect my position of authority on these grounds. I am strong enough to stand out against your pressures and importunities, your temptations and briberies."

The video recorder captures for repeated replay and understanding that characteristic, nonverbal, behavioral, or physical stance of a person which tells others his mode of being in this world. The author has found that in watching the replay he has at times been able to spot and comprehend an individual's life stance as expressed in this fashion either for the first time or more clearly than ever before. For example, some patients have a way of sitting forward with head crunching into neck and shoulders in a modified turtle fashion, their head partially drooping forward in a helpless fashion while they are pleading to be loved. This plea is in harmony with a repeated nonverbalized statement being made with hands held forward with open-fingered palm held upwards in a "love me, give me—because I have suffered so" fashion. This stance paraphrases

at times the underneath attitude of "the world owes me a living and a loving because I've suffered so!"

The use of video both compels the therapist to see more of what goes on nonverbally than he had previously realized and demands of him an increasing alertness to the nonverbal signs and communications which are ever present so that he can more adequately use focused feedback as a therapeutic intervention. To just play back a long segment of videotape is sometimes experienced with boredom by an individual or group who considers it a therapeutic interference to here-and-now interaction, experiencing, associations, or awareness. The frequent use of the video heightens the therapist's sensitivity to cues having major or minor implications which other therapists are not able to discern as well.

The increasing interest in perceiving, understanding, and utilizing nonverbal behavioral activities in both the understanding of what psychotherapy is as well as in expediting therapy has received a profound impetus since the introduction of videotape into psychiatric training and treatment.

THE PATIENT AS CAMERAMAN

The person who moves the camera to zoom in on or focus on a person or interpersonal interaction sees more of what is going on nonverbally than the other observers and participants present. In watching the monitors, vision becomes focused on the central person or bodily action in the observer's field of vision without the usual degree of distraction by what is seen through peripheral vision. In private practice, patients who are encouraged to use the camera to take pictures of others develop a heightened awareness of what is communicated by hand and other bodily movements.

Sandy reacted with feelings of childlike delight and excitement to the opportunity to be able to "play with a complex adult technological toy." The following day she informed me, "As the other group members came into the office my predominant feelings were of playful fun and a sense of being special as cameraman. I was also feeling an immediate sense of incompetency, saying to myself, 'I can't handle these controls,' although I really wanted to do so. When Sharon mentioned that she too had wanted to use the camera in response to your invitation but had been afraid to speak up, I was so glad that I didn't hesitate despite my conflict.

"Then an increasing sense of responsibility took over and I started to focus less for fun and more on what seemed important, what was really happening. My attention, and therefore the camera lens too, was focused primarily on hand, leg, and body movements. I noticed how often hand, leg, and foot movements were not parallel with verbal expressions. I have a sense that although I was not consciously concentrating on what was verbalized, I still was somehow receiving and responding to what was said. Although later in the session I was able to better hear what was said as well as see what was going on, I feel a more total emotional remembrance and impact from the early portion of the group meeting.

"Although it's now a day later, I retain a clear visual image of what people looked like—what I was picking up on the camera. . . . Mary's pained, holding-back face showing strong emotions inside which she was not expressing and how long she sat this way so very controlled but looking as if she might explode like dynamite at times and not knowing or able to control the continual slight movement of her foot. I recall, too, feeling how Sharon needed support as she kept looking at you or the floor, was so self-conscious and could never seem to get comfortable. I remember how she'd make small facial movements like turning down the corners of her mouth like she wanted to cry and giving off such an air of self-deprecation.

"I had the same feeling of somehow not participating fully with the group that I usually have with any group of people . . . of being quiet . . . of not saying anything yet very aware of everything going on.

"Then I remember feeling a sense of isolation at the camera and a feeling that I must be trying your patience because I was probably focusing on things you wouldn't and not focusing on what you'd want me to as you'd want them on the tape. It was when these self-critical feelings became strong that I stopped using the camera.

"The strongest impression I'm left with is how much significance I've placed up to now on what people were verbalizing and yet how small a component of their total expression that is."

This illustration reveals Sandy's difficulty in remaining joyously involved in a creative new experience. From freedom to participate in a childlike fashion, she gradually moved not only to a mature sense of responsibility but a few minutes later to an exaggerated superego-driven sense of responsibility. In this condition she externalized her own self-critical operations until her anxiety and discomfort became so great she stopped what she was doing. In addition she was able to become aware of how unaware she had previously been of the importance of nonverbalized nuances in relationships, as she had overemphasized the importance of the spoken and written word.

IMPACT OF NONVERBAL COMMUNICATIONS ON PATIENTS AND THERAPIST

Darwin, in *The Expression of the Emotions in Man and Animals,* noted that movements or behaviors which are serviceable in gratifying some desire or in relieving some sensation, if often repeated, become so habitual that they are performed, whether or not still of any service, whenever the same desire or sensation is felt, even to a very weak degree. In understanding nonverbal attitudes and gestures it is necessary to keep in mind that such behaviors usually occur involuntarily and unconsciously and may therefore communicate to an observer what in the expression may still be subliminal or in another level of unawareness.

Appearance and Expressions

It is important that therapists keep in mind not only that movements and gestures are subservient to long-range values in each culture but that values and attitudes may be expressed differently in varying cultures nonverbally. J. Reusch and W. Kees amplified this in 1956 in their book on *Nonverbal Communication*. They point out how amongst Americans gesture is largely oriented toward activities such as keeping occupied, being enterprising, striving for achievement, and being entertained. Amongst Italians, gestures tend to be emphatic, redundant, and flamboyant, serving the purposes of illustration and display for people living in a climate of passionate emotional expression, where there is a desire to express bodily and emotional needs in elaborate and somewhat outspoken terms while simultaneously maintaining warm interpersonal contact; amongst Jews, gesture serves as a device for purposes of emphasis and for interpunctuation, being predominantly discursive and with a jerky tempo. Contactual movements such as grasping, poking, pulling, and shaking are frequently employed.

Most patients are more or less unclear about their own facial and bodily appearance and expressions as well as about the impact these have on others. There are some patients whose facial expression arranges for a profound interpersonal barrier, somewhat like a thick plexiglass shield, to be set up between themselves and others. They are usually unaware of this and unaware of how this barrier serves to perpetuate their isolation and inability to satisfy their social hunger. They know only too well that poignant, internally voiced, frequent self-question: "What's the matter with me? How am I different from others? How come people shun me despite my conformity to the usual customs?"

There are multiple ways in which such patients ward off other people: by wearing their face as if it were a wax mask as in Madame Tussaud's museum; by wearing a menacing facial expression and body manner which says, "On guard! Be careful what you say to me. If you sound like you're stupid I'm gonna really cut you into ribbons"; by wearing such a judgmental, haughty, and omnipotent face that only someone with a fairly healthy ego

would risk offering an opinion in their towering presence (see earlier example of Melvin and Stella); by wearing a facial smile which keeps pleading "gimme more—gimme more—gimme," while it is obvious to others that the demand for "supplies" is insatiable; or by wearing a facial expression or facsimile of a smile which is more "an arrangement of the face rather than an expression of the heart," as Jean Stafford, the short-story writer, has stated.

Parenthetically, many attempts by individuals to obtain psychotherapy have failed due to the nonverbal impact of the therapist's nonempathetic masked "professional face" offered to frightened, anxiety-ridden, self-hating, and self-rejecting patients at a time when they most needed human warmth, contact communication, or a supportive interpretation.

Patient-Therapist Relationships

In a playback session patients not only have an opportunity to observe with an expanded ego their distorted transference reactions toward the therapist but also to quietly observe and assess who he really is as a person. They can assess the degree of his capacity for continuity, constancy, and caring or the lack of it. They can observe and assess the degree of his interest, sincerity, involvement, and integrity or the lack of it. One therapist who watched himself on playback for the first time was shocked as he realized how his patients had been experiencing him. He stated, "I didn't realize how aloof, detached, and intellectual my manner was. I seem to have a superior attitude. I had no idea of the way I had been acting until after seeing it on the screen and hearing the tape." Just as it is with acknowledged patients, therapists often have difficulty in believing or accepting what is said about them by patients, colleagues, or supervisors. It is not easy to maintain such denial tendencies when confronted with oneself audiovisually. In the therapist's ongoing search for his own identity and his own struggle for authenticity, the impact of videotape self-image in interaction is a meaningful and enriching experience which enhances his personal and professional growth.

Who and how the therapist is for his patients is reflected in his seeming lack of haste as he empathetically enters into, remains in, and departs from the patient's presence; in his sensitive countenance and outstretched hand as he greets his patient. The therapist's capacity to apply "tincture of tact" with all of his verbal and nonverbal communications enables the patient to retain his personal dignity while he undergoes the process of disillusionment which is inherent in psychotherapy.

There are many nonverbal communications registering with each patient which serve to inform him whether he is being experienced as an object or thing or case rather than as an individual patient-person or person-patient. I have found that he will react to treatment accordingly. Rosenbaum has repeatedly expressed concern that the practice of individual psychotherapy often makes the procedure barren and reinforces the therapist in his feelings of omniscience, resulting in an I-It rather than an I-Thou relationship.

We must not forget that evidence has accumulated through various studies proving that what is communicated through a doctor's attitude, tone, and nonverbalized personality makeup when he is prescribing a medication has a greater effect on the results of the medication offered than the medication itself. It is the same in psychotherapy.

The Therapist's Reactions

Just as doctors with different personality makeups will bring forth different results in the same patient, so too will different personality makeups of patients stir up reactions in a therapist which may interfere with the curative process. The patient's nonverbalized attitudes, emotions, and transference distortions may stir up countertransferential and other reactions in a therapist which he is unaware of until he experiences a video playback.

Nonverbalized aspects of character structure which may affect the therapist are: (1) the patient who is demanding, pushing, controlling, and irritable; (2) the patient who is scared, shy, bunnylike, or withdrawn; (3) the patient who is clinging, helpless, complaining, dependent, and childlike; (4) the patient who is independent, standoffish, and pain-denying; (5) the patient who is a coy, seductive, narcissistic charmer flinging sexuality about openly and provocatively; (6) the patient whose abused attitude of being an injustice collector is used to make claims for special attention from the therapist via an unstated implication that life and the therapist owe him or her a living and a loving because he or she has suffered so much; (7) the patient who is obsessive-compulsive and perfectionistic; or (8) the patient who is aristocratic, arrogant, and just above-it-all. Video repeatedly demonstrates for us that nonverbal communication, alone and in conjunction with lexical languages, serves not only as a medium for expression, communication, and imparting information, but also to establish, maintain, or regulate relationships.

REPLAY TECHNIQUES

Replay during Session

When a replay of part of a psychotherapy session is used during the actual encounter it represents, it is worth repeating here that most therapists experienced with videotape find it advisable to play no more than 10 to 20 minutes of the tape. Because of the tremendous amount of data communicated in the playback, to go beyond this time usually results in a self-protective loss of interest or in a decreasing emotional involvement or in confusion. If it is possible to tape the patient's spontaneous reactions to the playback, at least on audiotape if not with videotape, both therapist and patient will find the free associations at this time an important aid to the therapeutic process. While it is more common to have a second video recorder in institutional settings than in private practice, the cost for this purpose is very much worth it, as the results are so valuable. Another method is to ask the patient to withhold his remarks until the playback is concluded and then to subsequently record him audiovisually on the same tape as the machine is now available again for recording. Such a record for five to ten minutes after self-confrontation may be reviewed more than once and used for working through.

Picture without Sound

Another method of utilizing either instant or later replay is to play back the picture without the sound so the patient can more objectively experience the impact on others of his nonverbal behaviors and posturings as he sees himself for the first time from others' point of view. He can perceive and begin to understand how his nonverbals influence and help bring about the reaction of others to him.

Stopping the Playback

Stopping the playback at times when a characteristic facial, hand, or body movement or position of a patient is presented may allow the patient and therapist to focus in on this behavior which has had impact on the therapist or on others and which the patient has been either unaware of or aware of only to some marginal degree.

Repeated Replays

At other times it is important for therapeutic progress to stop, and to examine or replay a second or third time a portion of the tape which reveals something about the patient's functioning which is a surprise to both the patient and therapist. Such moments are found to be common with videotape. It encourages humility in the thera-

pist to realize how much really is transpiring that he is not conscious of, yet which is significant. Such experiences serve to prove that how we react to one another is profoundly influenced by subliminally perceived expressions and communications. It is, of course, significant from a psychodynamic viewpoint that a particular statement or behavior was not remembered by either therapist or patient. Exploration of such a transaction may reveal significant transferential and countertransferential implications or may represent denial or a blind spot, because what is being expressed represents a source of anxiety and/or conflict being avoided by patient and therapist.

While watching a playback one frequently observes the presentation of a patient's typical neurotic values, attitudes, mannerisms, or hangups. The appearance on playback of such hangups which the therapist has heretofore been unable to successfully motivate the patient to acknowledge offers an excellent opportunity for the therapist to achieve his therapeutic aim. The representative segment of tape can be played over and over in focused feedback style until the patient finally grasps the impact of its meaning. Such a working through requires the utmost artistic as well as scientific skill on the part of the therapist so that emotional as well as intellectual insight can occur. One of the great values of videotapes is that the playing back of such a segment of tape can be accomplished in a matter of seconds and the repetition does not affect the life, stability, or reproductive qualities of the tape itself.

Sound without Picture

At times during playback it is of value to turn off the video picture in order to accentuate for the patient in the context of what comes before, and what comes after, the impact on others of such vocal variables as tone, inflection, pitch, speed, juncture points, enunciation, accent, volume, rhythm, and degree of articulateness. This is of value in helping a patient comprehend how it is that others react to him the rejecting way they actually do when he believes he is speaking and functioning in a warm, benevolent, kind, or friendly fashion. This technique is of particular value in working with patients who are arrogant, accusatory, pompous, dogmatic, tyrannical, and who demand from, demean, and belittle or discount others. Many patients have blind spots and other resistances to acknowledging these aspects of their personality despite the evidence of it in their disturbed relationships with spouses, children, and others. Video confrontation sometimes forces patients to accept the truth or to insist that the therapist, the group, and the videotape are distorting and do not really understand or see them as they really are and so they terminate therapy with this therapist.

Technique for Latent Paranoid Process

An interesting technique to flush out latent or borderline paranoid processes in a patient who is a member of a therapy group is to ask a patient who comes late to a group meeting which is being videotaped to share his fantasy of what he believes the group said about him prior to his arrival. If a person airs his belief that his peer group members either ignored his absence or talked against him for one reason or another, it may have a salutary effect for him to hear in the playback of the early portion of the group the expressions of concern and caring that were in truth expressed. Such an experience may lead him to give up some of his distrust of others. If there were in fact negativistic, rejecting remarks made, it might be more an expression of psychotherapeutic skill and judgment to neither ask the patient for his fantasy nor to play back the first portion of the meeting, as these would only serve to whet his paranoid systems. At other times such a playback offers an opportunity for the latecomer to catch up on what was going on earlier in the group meeting as well as to offer more objective reactions or interpretations of individual or group process than the other, more subjectively, involved participants.

GROUP-SESSION PLAYBACK IN INDIVIDUAL SESSION

A valuable use of playback is to review a patient's participation in a former group or family meeting during his individual psychotherapy session. This allows for maximum use and benefit from the technique of focused feedback. Analysis and working through of resistance patterns can be accomplished more expeditiously this way than through regular individual sessions, and the patient can be encouraged to risk being different in his next group or family encounter.

A successful 28-year-old television scriptwriter who was singularly ineffectual with interpersonal relationships reviewed the tape of her last group experience during her next individual session. She said through quiet tears, "What bothered me was this smug attitude I have on my face—like I know it all—and I really don't . . . also this very affected speech I seem to have. I noticed a few sibilant s's that were creeping through and it bothered me. I associate it with being theatrical. If a man did it, it would be the mark of a homosexual. The not moving around is more natural for me. The other attitudes are more studied and affected—the smugness, the speech.

"I wasn't participating that much. (Where were you? Did you see what you do with people?) I was just watching what was going on. (Yes, you have been doing that for months.) This isn't new. I sit and watch a situation and figure out my part in it and then I may go into it. I may take six minutes, six months, six years —maybe never. (How do you feel about that?) Frankly I don't feel this is as important as other things that have happened since I was last here. I keep going back to the psychological evaluation and the statement that I am still tied to home. I thought, 'I'll show them'—I just won't go home for months.

"I feel nothing I have to say is important so I have to soup it up by saying it with my mouth and mind but not with anything else. (Certainly not with real feelings.) It seems to be the way I've learned to get attention with this unusual tone—inflection and changes in my voice—I use them to make what I say important and what it does is to make it unimportant as if it were not to be believed. (That's what your group members have told you, isn't it?)"

The replay of a psychotherapy session of a patient meeting with her mother who had come to visit her for a short time was seen by the patient one week later. A week after this playback she came into her session remarking, "I've been grumpy all week realizing how much I hate my mother. Last week and the week before I just didn't feel it. I wasn't really aware of how much I kowtowed to her presence . . . that that's what I've been doing my whole life. I've become progressively more annoyed that she wasn't truthful and that I was confused. At first I was fascinated by what I saw in the playback—having a schizophrenic-like reaction in which I was confused and detached and didn't feel it. But all the past week I realized how I hated her for the way she is whereas in recent years I had felt guilty for not being able to communicate and relate to her. They had convinced me it was my fault—that I was the catalyst for any antagonism between us. (Just what did you come to now that's different?)

"I was in a blue funk because I wasn't expressing my hatred or anger and was depressed 'cause I hadn't expressed it—not to her alone—hadn't even expressed it to you. It's still hard to see how I could express it to her or even if it's desirable to do so. I was tearful because I know I couldn't say anything to her without crying and afraid that if I did start to cry I wouldn't be able to stop. And that's exactly what I went through in childhood. And then I felt terrible 'cause I couldn't stop crying. . . ."

INDIVIDUAL-SESSION PLAYBACK IN GROUP SESSION

Just as we have experienced definite value in bringing a tape of a group, couple, or family encounter into a patient's individual session, it is of value at times, *with the permission of those on the tape,* to bring the tape of a couple or family session into a patient's group meeting. It can bring more reality concerning key relationships to the group than a patient ordinarily brings with his verbal statement of what transpires in his life outside group.

The following verbatim statement was made by a 33-year-old, self-effacing, married college graduate who had been raised in a puritanical righteous-minded family in which she was constantly led to believe

she was to feel guilty, wrong, or insignificant. In her marriage she had tried constantly to appease her husband through compliance and self-abnegation in the expectation of being loved and appreciated. To her husband Herb however, her compliancy and inability to risk differing or being disagreeable stamped her as a passive nonentity which served as an irritant to his grandiose image of himself and his wife, who should be his social and intellectual partner. Although she was in fact still the intellectually bright person he had been attracted to initially, in marriage he now reacted to her self-effacing qualities as a mark of "weakness." This compulsive paradoxical reaction occurred despite the fact that Nellie offered him the kind of unquestioning warm-breasted giving which he had not had earlier from his mother and which he was so desperate to receive. The prospect of a divorce brought her for psychotherapeutic assistance. She was seen in individual sessions twice weekly, one double session with her husband once weekly, and in one group session weekly. After three months' participation in a group, during which time she had functioned mostly as a silent, passive-dependent, other-directed person, she agreed it could be beneficial to allow her peer group members to watch a videotape playback of herself and her husband made during their first couple session three months earlier so that they could gain some more-or-less firsthand understanding of her marital "arrangements" and relationship. Her husband had previously given his permission for this film to be shown to her group. The following comments were made by Nellie in the individual session which immediately followed the group session in which the playback was shown.

"I realized that a lot has happened in these three months. In the beginning of that tape we were sitting silently hating each other in that awful atmosphere of picking on each other. Since then we have learned a lot about what makes for our hostility—anger—tension. As the tape progressed I had feelings—as if the group was—as if I was being revealed to the group. I felt scary. They were seeing me in a different light than they had seen me in the group. It may make it easier for me to be more myself in the group—less guarded. The fear had no form at first as to what they would think. It was the very basic fear of being revealed to somebody and the expectation they would not approve. They'd disapprove of some of the things I said. When I realized what was coming next on the tape, that I'd lose my temper and was really involved with what was going on with Herb, I was sure that they'd disapprove of me.

"There were parts of the replay that were very touching in watching this struggle going on between us. It was sad in a way. Yet encouraging that we are growing more aware, learning things. At the time of that session I was so angry and tense, but watching it now it was different. I could see now how he really didn't know then, and also now lots of the time, what he's feeling and I thought he did! I had seen him as absolute with his pronouncements. Now I could see his confusion and his not knowing was like mine—my not knowing!

"At first when I came here I felt Herb was fairly sure of what he was doing and that he was hurting me. I didn't see we were hurting each other. He was just as mixed up. When you asked what he feels when he sits aloof and detached, if he felt pleasure and power—he didn't know! When we first came I thought he did. I hadn't seen the amount of conflict and unsureness in him or his pain which was so clear on the tape and it wasn't clear to him that he had pain which his face showed—and he didn't know it—how his face looked and showed it.

"I guess that I felt the group's response would be that I'd be wrong when I said something—that I had to always be right. But they didn't respond that way and that was relieving. (That's one of the things that's been holding you back in group, isn't it?) Yes. I hear Herb say things—tossing things into the room and I feel it's just so risky for me if I were to come out with something that was obviously hostile and someone would jack me up on it. That's scary to me and yet that's how I'd learn something."

A properly timed videotape playback can serve many purposes. In this illustration we see that a relatively silent, dependent group member who was extremely fearful of the possibility of criticism because of her active transference to the group of her fears of criticism from her primary family was able to share a replication of her marital dialogue. In the sup-

porting atmosphere of the group she was finally able to risk exposure of her private life. During the playback she could more objectively assess and accept some of her projections to her husband and the consequences of these distortions. She could also realize through reality-testing that the group and others do not automatically react to her with disapproval and criticism as she expects or anticipates all too often to her own detriment.

VIDEOTAPE REVIEW AND SIMULTANEOUS PICTURE PRESENTATION

In order to assess movement or nonmovement of a patient in psychotherapy it is of profound value to review a tape taken weeks, months, or years earlier. With some patients the author has taped five minutes of one of their individual sessions every month for one year in order to have a record of, as well as to review, change during psychotherapy. The replay of the tape of a group session taken six months or more earlier evokes much nostalgic warmth and interest as each group member spots the persistent neurotic foibles of other members more readily than his own.

Another method of using video equipment involves the presence of one or more monitors which present immediate, simultaneously produced camera-eye pictures of what is going on through the closed-circuit system. While some patients initially complain that this is distracting to them, it is noted that gradually patients gain a good deal from this additional approach to self-awareness and self-appraisal at the moment of involvement in interaction with others. It was an experience referred to as serendipity when the author learned that by focusing one or both cameras on a silent member of a group so that he could see himself on two or three monitors simultaneously, he could be stimulated or catalyzed into verbalizing 95 per cent of the time.

On two occasions it was possible to prevent patients from consummating their plan to undergo plastic facial surgery by the use of repeated television closeups of their nose, chin, eyes, and face. They were helped to accept that they had displaced their general self-hate onto some physiological feature of themselves to externalize and simplify their more complex conflicts about their self-image and their difficult relationships with others. It was helpful for them to experience closed-circuit self-image confrontations while with peer group members who could validate or invalidate their impression of the grotesqueness of their hated facial feature.

While some therapists using video believe in hiding or disguising cameras, monitors, microphones, videotape recorders, and similar special equipment, it has been the author's practice to keep everything out in the open. I concur with Wilmer's use of the camera as a participant-observer, and I believe that an open use of such equipment further undermines the focus on secrecy mixed with privacy which is commonly part of the underlying attitudinal system in psychotherapy. The emphasis on openness and the statement of truth undermines not only paranoid potential but self-defeating notions of unhealthy personal uniqueness.

DYNAMIC IMPLICATIONS OF NONVERBAL BEHAVIOR

The study of the dynamic implications as well as the regulatory functions of nonverbal behaviors is made more easily and immediately available to psychotherapists and patients with videotape than with conventional sound films so often utilized by researchers such as Scheflen. In psychotherapy, through the development of skills over time, a therapist can correctly interpret for a patient that the manner in which he reaches for a package of cigarettes, extracts or pours it, tamps it, lights it, blows out his light, and inhales or exhales his first lungful of smoke has become a duplicitous pseudo substitute or facsimile for the poise the patient does not feel. He can help his patient see through repeated videotape playback of such a sequence how his cigarette ritual is used as a time and space filler while the patient fumbles for a reply which will appear to be replete with wisdom or knowledge or at least will sound correct. The patient can learn how he uses automatic or compulsive smoking not only to relive anxiety but also to serve as a small procrastination in the face of a difficult or distasteful task. Scheflen (1969) attempts in his research to discover and identify and interpret units of regulatory behavior in relationships by grouping elements in the communication systems of a culture along a time and space dimension. This is done while relating such units to the multiple behind-the-scenes contexts within which such events take place. An example is reported of repeated context analysis of a sound film in which "the therapist turned out to be taking out a cigarette . . . bringing it and a pack of matches to her lap . . . waiting until the patient finished a story . . . putting the cigarette in her mouth . . . watching until the patient looked away . . . lighting up . . . discarding the match." A simple test used by Scheflen to prove that each element belonged in a structural unit was accomplished by sweeping back and forth through the film and noting: if each element in a proposed unit appears each time every other element appears and does not appear when the others are absent, then all elements are interdependent and represent an entity. In the aforementioned illustration Scheflen interpreted the unit referred to as one "structuring therapist-patient reciprocals." In this situation this patient and this therapist shift the dyadic context from free-ranging conversation to the typical relationship entailing free association and interpretation. The shift into this context may begin during a conversational lull when the therapist lights up and begins smoking and then proceeds to other unitary behaviors.

Through videotape the private practitioner can also research and refine and more clearly define for himself and his patients the nature and kinds of verbal and nonverbal mutual or reciprocal regulating patterns which occur between them, and the influence these patterns or systems have in the life of the patient. Therapists are able to also learn more about their own regulating patterns while making such process observations.

REPETITIVE SELF-OBSERVATION IS BENEFICIAL

To alleviate anxiety amongst private practitioners concerning the possible harmful effects of repetitive self-observation by videotape playback, consider the reports of: (1) Cornelison and Arsenian, who noted that psychotic patients who were confronted with an instantly developed Polaroid photograph of themselves a short time after they were admitted to a mental hospital, seemed considerably more amenable to subsequent therapeutic intervention and acceptance of reality than patients who did not have this opportunity. Their study has stimulated many toward the use of videotape in psychiatric treatment. (2) Geertsma and Reivich (1965, 1968), who researched 64 psychiatric inpatients to elicit its impact on them. Although 77 per cent experienced initial anxiety, 68 per cent responded favorably to the experience. While a smaller number of patients, who were more upset by the experience, tended to dislike it, there was in no patient evidence of sustained negative effect.

In experience with outpatients in private practice as well as with inpatients on a community mental health service (Berger, Sherman, Spalding, and Westlake), the impact of playback confrontation has generally been positive, even with severely ill patients. For example, Sally, a 27-year-old schizophrenic female who has avoided close relationships with males remarked immediately afterwards, "I didn't know how scared and quiet I looked. I just sat there. I looked much sicker. It was a surprise. I knew I was tense but not that bad. And yet I looked like I could be a woman and not just a little girl." Her last remark was a hopeful sign prognostically reflecting as it did a recouping and regrouping of her constructive inner forces to go beyond her level and way of functioning to date.

Another patient, Susan, a 29-year-old woman who is divorced and works as an editorial assistant, suffers with frigidity and multiple psychosomatic symptoms. After experiencing a playback with her psychotherapy group she said, "I didn't really talk. I just talked about things. Not that they weren't really true, but I avoided the really big questions and feelings going on inside me." With the directive support, encouragement, and interest of her therapist and group, Susan could now be helped to open up and explore those intimate matters she had previously resisted sharing and looking into because of difficulties in trusting others.

Marion, an extremely attractive and well-structured 38-year-old college graduate with an M.A. in art history who had been thrice engaged but never married, was a bit startled, and commented after a playback, "When I saw myself on videotape playback with our Tuesday group, I was fascinated by the fact that I could feel such clearcut feelings inside myself and yet would project a watered-down bland version of myself which had no piercing quality! When I see myself on your television I see the blandest kind of Cream of Wheat type person—just a terribly nice person—as if my personality had no cutting edge at all. It sickens me. As if I wasn't in focus—was not a clear-cut personality—as if I had no well-defined edges —like Sara who had been in our group had and could project without saying a word—just with a look!"

It required many months of repeated self-viewing for Marion to give up some of her fear of unexpected hostility from her peer group members and to risk direct expression of her own irritation and hostility with them and the therapist. Working through her transferential fear of her irrationally double-binding, seductively incestuous, and unexpectedly angry father was necessary to help her emerge as a more clear-cut personality with her own identity. Over time, clarity emerged concerning Marion's deep sinister fear of marriage and the degree of and way she was unconsciously driven to sabotage or avoid the possibility of a really loving, nonexploitive relationship with an eligible man which could actually lead to marriage. This working through occurred during her concurrent participation in one individual psychotherapy session per week plus once-a-week participation in two different psychotherapy groups. One group was composed of patients who were more on a sibling level with her. The second group had in its composition a 65-year-old male who could remind her of her father and a woman who reminded her of her detached, onlooking mother.

This other woman, Fay, also had major problems in being closely involved, and her detachment was also in the service of avoiding anger. Through her childhood Fay had repeatedly heard the family myths concerning the legendary angers of her maternal grandfather. What she remembered was how viciously he had teased her older brother while she managed to fade into the woodwork. Fay remembered that her mother's angers were completely inconsistent and irrational and would be expressed with high-pitched screaming. Such outbursts would go on and on and on and on until they would suddenly stop as her mother settled into a period of punitive silence toward her which could last from two hours to a week. In reacting to the playback images of how quietly removed and bland both Marion and she sat in group, Fay remarked, "By the time I was nine I no longer heard her anger. I would dismiss it knowing it was irrational. From my mother I learned how futile anger was

as I saw how little it accomplished with me. I never had a model of realistic anger which was expressed realistically to accomplish something successfully. And you know what happened with my father. He'd sit quiet or depressed when he was angry. And finally he got so angry he committed suicide when I was a teenager. In the past I've panicked at the idea that I might get so angry I might do what my father did and then I'd be abandoning everyone—especially my kids. So I've just not felt my anger even at times when I knew with my head it was appropriate.''

The use of videotape playbacks with this group enhanced the processes of identification, sibling support, and peer encouragement to risk change as well as the working through of transferential hangups. Patients whose observing ego is enhanced and who become more cooperatively and enthusiastically involved in the psychotherapeutic process experience in a deeper fashion and function more holistically.

CONCLUSION

The use of video renews our sense of humility and decreases our omniscience as we learn how much more has been going on in the therapeutic relationship than we heretofore realized. To learn more of the subtleties of what is involved in establishing, maintaining, and regulating relationships is an aid to the ongoing growth of the therapist as well as to his patients.

This chapter has presented some of the richness and variety of manners in which the revolutionary new tool of video can be utilized in the private practice of psychiatry. A practitioner who flexibly integrates its use in working with individuals, couples, families, and groups according to appropriate timing and context can enhance and expedite a more holistic and successful psychotherapy for all who come to him for help.

REFERENCES

Bahnson, C. B. Body and self-images associated with audio-visual self-confrontation. J. Nerv. Ment. Dis., *148:* 262, 1969.

Berger, M. M., and Rosenbaum, M. Notes on help-rejecting complainers. Int. J. Group Psychother., *17:* 357, 1967.

Berger, M. M., Sherman, B., Spalding, J., and Westlake, R. The use of videotape with psychotherapy groups in a community mental health service program. Int. J. Group Psychother., *18:* 504, 1968.

Cole, J. Evaluation of drug treatment in psychiatry. Paper presented at the annual meeting of the American Psychopathological Association, New York City, Feb. 23–24, 1962.

Coleman, J. V. Aims and conduct of psychotherapy. Arch. Gen. Psychiat., *18:* 1, 1968.

Cornelison, F. S., and Arsenian, J. A study of the response of psychotic patients to photographing self-image experience. Psychiat. Quart., *34:* 1, 1960.

Darwin, C. The Expression of the Emotions in Man and Animals. University of Chicago Press, 1965.

Geertsma, R. H. Studies in self-cognition. J. Nerv. Ment. Dis., *148:* 193, 1969.

Geertsma, R. H., and Reivich, R. S. Repetitive self-observation by videotape playback, J. Nerv. Ment. Dis., *141:* 29, 1965.

Hogan, P., and Alger, I. Impact of videotape recording on insight in group therapy. Int. J. Group Psychother., *19:* 158, 1969.

Horney, K. Neurosis and Human Growth, W. W. Norton, New York, 1950.

Mendell D., and Fisher, S. An approach to neurotic behavior in terms of a three-generation family model. J. Nerv. Ment. Dis., *123:* 171, 1956.

Reivich, R. S., and Geertsma, R. H. Experience with videotape self-observation by psychiatric in-patients. J. Kansas Med. Soc., *49:* 39, 1968.

Reusch, J., and Kees, W. *Nonverbal Communication: Notes on the Visual Perception of Human Relations.* University of California Press, Berkeley, 1956.

Scheflen, A. Communication and regulation in psychotherapy. Psychiatry, *26:* 126, 1963.

Scheflen, A. The sound camera breakthrough in research, training, therapy. Roche Report: Frontiers of Hospital Psychiatry, *6:* 11, June 1, 1969.

Wilmer, H. A. Television as participant recorder. Amer. J. Psychiat., *124:* 1157, 1968.

Glossary*

Aberration, mental. Pathological deviation from normal thinking. Mental aberration is not related to a person's intelligence. *See also* Mental illness.

Abreaction. A process by which repressed material, particularly a painful experience or a conflict, is brought back to consciousness. In the process of abreacting, the person not only recalls but relives the repressed material, which is accompanied by the appropriate affective response. *See also* Catharsis.

Accelerated interaction. An alternate term for marathon group session that was introduced by one of its co-developers, Frederick Stoller. *See also* Group marathon.

Accountability. The responsibility a member has for his actions within a group and the need to explain to other members the motivations for his behavior.

Acid. Slang for lysergic acid diethylamide (LSD).

Acrophobia. Fear of high places.

Acting out. An action rather than a verbal response to an unconscious instinctual drive or impulse that brings about temporary partial relief of inner tension. Relief is attained by reacting to a present situation as if it were the situation that originally gave rise to the drive or impulse. *See also* Therapeutic crisis.

Actional-deep approach. Group procedure in which communication is effected through various forms of nonverbal behavior as well as or in place of language to produce character change. It is a technique used in psychodrama. *See also* Actional-superficial approach, Activity group therapy, Verbal-deep approach, Verbal-superficial approach.

Actional-superficial approach. Group procedure in which specific activities and verbal communication are used for limited goals. Verbal interchange and patient-to-patient interaction are of relatively minor therapeutic significance, and the groups are usually large. *See also* Actional-deep approach, Verbal-deep approach, Verbal-superficial approach.

Action group (A-group). Group whose purpose is to discuss a problem—community, industrial, or organizational—and to formulate a program of action. Emphasis is put on problem-solving rather than on developing awareness of self and group process. *See also* T-group.

Active therapist. Type of therapist who makes no effort to remain anonymous but is forceful and expresses his personality definitively in the therapy setting. *See also* Passive therapist.

Activity group therapy. A type of group therapy introduced and developed by S. R. Slavson and designed for children and young adolescents, with emphasis on emotional and active interaction in a permissive, nonthreatening atmosphere. The therapist stresses reality-testing, ego-strengthening, and action interpretation. *See also* Actional-deep approach; Activity-interview method; Bender, Lauretta; Play therapy.

Activity-interview method. Screening and diagnostic technique used with children. *See also* Activity group therapy.

Actualization. Process of mobilizing one's potentialities or making them concrete. *See also* Individuation.

* Edited by Ernesto A. Amaranto, M.D.

I

Adaptational approach. An approach used in analytic group therapy. Consonant with Sandor Rado's formulations on adaptational psychodynamics, the group focuses on the maladaptive patterns used by patients in the treatment sessions, on how these patterns developed, and on what the patients must do to overcome them and stabilize their functioning at self-reliant, adult levels. New methods of adaptation are practiced by the group members in the therapeutic sessions and later in their regular interpersonal relationships. *See also* Social adaptation.

Adapted Child. In transactional analysis, the primitive ego state that is under the parental influence. The adapted Child is dependent, unexpressive, and constrained. *See also* Natural Child.

Adler, Alfred (1870–1937). Viennese psychiatrist and one of Freud's original followers. Adler broke off from Freud and introduced and developed the concepts of individual psychology, inferiority complex, and overcompensation. A pioneer in group psychotherapy, he believed that the sharing of problems takes precedence over confidentiality. He also made contributions in the understanding of group process. *See also* Individual psychology, Masculine protest.

Adolescence. Period of growth from puberty to maturity. The beginning of adolescence is marked by the appearance of secondary sexual characteristics, usually at about age 12, and the termination is marked by the achievement of sexual maturity at about age 20. *See also* Psychosexual development.

Adult. In transactional analysis, an ego state oriented toward objective, autonomous data-processing and estimating. It is essentially a computer, devoid of feeling. It is also known as neopsychic function.

Affect. Emotional feeling tone attached to an object, idea, or thought. The term includes inner feelings and their external manifestations. *See also* Inappropriate affect, Mood.

Affect, blunted. A disturbance of affect manifested by dullness of externalized feeling tone. Observed in schizophrenia, it is one of that disorder's fundamental symptoms, according to Eugen Bleuler.

Affection phase. Last stage of group treatment. In this phase the members experience reasonable equality with the therapist and dwell on affectionate contact with each other in a give-and-take atmosphere rather than dwelling on dependency or aggression. *See also* Inclusion phase, Power phase.

Affective interaction. Interpersonal experience and exchange that are emotionally charged.

Affectualizing. In transactional analysis, the expression of emotions or feelings in group or individual treatment as part of a pasttime or game. It is distinguished from the expression of authentic feelings, which are characteristic of intimacy.

Afro-American. American Negro of African ancestry. This term has significance for blacks who seek a deeper and more positive sense of identity with their African heritage. *See also* Black separatism.

After-session. Group meeting of patients without the therapist. It is held immediately after a regular therapist-led session. *See also* Alternate session, Premeeting.

Agency. The striving and need to achieve in a person. Agency manifests itself in self-protection, the urge to master, self-expansion, and repression of thought, feeling, and impulse. *See also* Communion.

Aggression. Forceful, goal-directed behavior that may be verbal or physical. It is the motor counterpart of the affects of rage, anger, and hostility.

Aggressive drive. Destructive impulse directed at oneself or another. It is also known as the death instinct. According to contemporary psychoanalytic psychology, it is one of the two basic drives; sexual drive is the other one. Sexual drive operates on the pleasure-pain principle, whereas aggressive drive operates on the repetition-compulsion principle. *See also* Aggression, Libido theory.

Agitation. State of anxiety associated with severe motor restlessness.

Agnosia. Disturbance of perception characterized by inability to recognize a stimulus and interpret the significance of its memory impressions. It is observed in patients with organic brain disease and in certain schizophrenics, hysterics, and depressed patients.

Agoraphobia. Fear of open places. *See also* Claustrophobia.

Agranulocytosis. A rare, serious side effect, occurring with some of the psychotropic drugs. The condition is characterized by sore throat, fever, a sudden sharp decrease in white blood cell count, and a marked reduction in number of granulocytes.

A-group. *See* Action group.

Alcoholics Anonymous (A.A.) An organization of alcoholics formed in 1935. It uses certain group methods, such as inspirational-supportive techniques, to help rehabilitate chronic alcoholics.

Algophobia. Fear of pain.

Allergic jaundice. *See* Jaundice, allergic.

Alliance. *See* Therapeutic alliance, Working alliance.

Allport's group relations theory. Gordon W. Allport's theory that a person's behavior is influenced by his personality and his need to conform to social forces. It illustrates the interrelationship between group therapy and social psychology. For example, dealing with bigotry in a therapy group enhances the opportunity for therapeutic experiences because it challenges the individual patient's need to conform to earlier social determinants or to hold on to familiar but restrictive aspects of his personality.

Alternate session. Scheduled group meeting held without the therapist. Such meetings are held on a regular basis in between therapist-led sessions. Use of this technique was originated by Alexander Wolf. *See also* After-session, Premeeting.

Alternating role. Pattern characterized by periodic switching from one type of behavior to another. For example, in a group, alternating role is observed among members who switch from the role of the recipient of help to the giver of help.

Alternating scrutiny. *See* Shifting attention.

Altruism. Regard for and dedication to the welfare of others. The term was originated by Auguste Comte (1798–1857), a French philosopher. In psychiatry the term is closely linked with ethics and morals. Freud recognized altruism as the only basis for the development of community interest; Bleuler equated it with morality.

Ambivalence. Presence of strong and often overwhelming simultaneous contrasting attitudes, ideas, feelings, and drives toward an object, person, or goal. The term was coined by Eugen Bleuler, who differentiated three types: affective, intellectual, and ambivalence of the will.

Amnesia. Disturbance in memory manifested by partial or total inability to recall past experiences.

Amphetamine. A central nervous system stimulant. Its chemical structure and action are closely related to ephedrine and other sympathomimetic amines. *See also* Sympathomimetic drug.

Anal erotism. *See* Anal phase.

Anal phase. The second stage in psychosexual development. It occurs when the child is between the ages of one and three. During this period the infant's activities, interests, and concerns are centered around his anal zone, and the pleasurable experience felt around this area is called anal erotism. *See also* Genital phase, Infantile sexuality, Latency phase, Oral phase, Phallic phase.

Analysis. *See* Psychoanalysis.

Analysis in depth. *See* Psychoanalysis.

Analysis of transference. *See* Psychoanalysis.

Analytic psychodrama. Psychotherapy method in which a hypothesis is tested on a stage to verify its validity. The analyst sits in the audience and observes. Analysis of the material is made immediately after the scene is presented.

Anchor. Point at which the patient settles down to the analytic work involved in the therapeutic experience.

Antianxiety drug. Drug used to reduce pathological anxiety and its related symptoms without influencing cognitive or perceptual disturbance. It is also known as a minor tranquilizer and a psycholeptic drug. Meprobamate derivatives and diazepoxides are typical antianxiety drugs.

Anticholinergic effect. Effect due to a blockade of the cholinergic (parasympathetic and somatic) nerves. It is often seen as a side effect of phenothiazine therapy. Anticholinergic effects include dry mouth and blurred vision. *See also* Paralytic ileus.

Antidepressant drug. Drug used in the treatment of pathological depression. It is also known as a thymoleptic drug and a psychic energizer. The two main classes of antidepressant drugs are the tricyclic drugs and the monoamine oxidase inhibitors. *See also* Hypertensive crisis, Monoamine oxidase inhibitor, Tinnitus, Tricyclic drug.

Antimanic drug. Drug, such as lithium, used to alleviate the symptoms of mania. Lithium is particularly effective in preventing relapses in manic-depressive illness. Other drugs with antimanic effects are haloperidol and chlorpromazine.

Antiparkinsonism drug. Drug used to relieve the symptoms of parkinsonism and the extrapyramidal side effects often induced by antipsychotic drugs. The antiparkinsonism drug acts by diminishing muscle tone and involuntary movements. Antiparkinsonism agents include benztropine, procyclidine, biperiden, and trihexphenidyl. *See also* Cycloplegia, Mydriasis.

Antipsychotic drug. Drug used to treat psychosis, particularly schizophrenia. It is also known as a major tranquilizer and a neuroleptic drug. Phenothiazine derivatives, thioxanthene derivatives, and butyrophenone derivatives are typical antipsychotic drugs. *See also* Autonomic side effect, Dyskinesia, Extrapyramidal effect, Major tranquilizer, Parkinsonismlike effect, Reserpine, Tardive oral dyskinesia.

Antirepression device. Technique used in encounter groups and therapeutic groups to break through the defense of repression. In encounter groups, such techniques are frequently nonverbal and involve physical contact between group members. In therapeutic groups, dream analysis, free association, and role-playing are some antirepression techniques.

Anxiety. Unpleasurable affect consisting of psychophysiological changes in response to an intrapsychic conflict. In contrast to fear, the danger or threat in anxiety is unreal. Physiological changes consist of increased heart rate, disturbed breathing, trembling, sweating, and vasomotor changes. Psychological changes consist of an uncomfortable feeling of impending danger accompanied by overwhelming awareness of being powerless, inability to perceive the unreality of the threat, prolonged feeling of tension, and exhaustive readiness for the expected danger. *See also* Basic anxiety, Fear.

Apathetic withdrawal. *See* Withdrawal.

Apathy. Want of feeling or affect; lack of interest and emotional involvement in one's surroundings. It is observed in certain types of schizophrenia and depression.

Apgar scores. Measurements taken one minute and five minutes after birth to determine physical normality in the neonate. The scores are based on color, respiratory rate, heart beat, reflex action, and muscle tone. Used routinely, they are particularly useful in detecting the effects on the infant of drugs taken by the pregnant mother.

Aphasia. Disturbance in speech due to organic brain disorder. It is characterized by inability to express thoughts verbally. There are several types of aphasia: (1) motor aphasia—inability to speak, although understanding remains; (2) sensory aphasia—inability to comprehend the meaning of words or use of objects; (3) nominal aphasia—difficulty in finding the right name for an object; (4) syntactical aphasia—inability to arrange words in proper sequence.

Apperception. Awareness of the meaning and significance of a particular sensory stimulus as modified by one's own experiences, knowledge, thoughts, and emotions. *See also* Perception.

Archeopsychic function. *See* Child.

Arteriosclerotic cardiovascular disease. A metabolic disturbance characterized by degenerative changes involving the blood vessels of the heart and other arteries, mainly the arterioles. Fatty plaques, deposited within the blood vessels, gradually obstruct the flow of blood. Organic brain syndrome may develop when cerebral arteries are involved in the degenerative process.

Ataractic drug. *See* Major tranquilizer.

Ataxia. Lack of coordination, either physical or mental. In neurology it refers to loss of muscular coordination. In psychiatry the term intrapsychic ataxia refers to lack of coordination between feelings and thoughts; the disturbance is found in schizophrenia.

Atmosphere. *See* Therapeutic atmosphere.

Attention. Concentration; the aspect of consciousness that relates to the amount of effort exerted in focusing on certain aspects of an experience.

Attitude. Preparatory mental posture with which one receives stimuli and reacts to them. Group therapy often involves itself in defining for the group members their attitudes that have unconsciously dominated their reactions.

Auditory hallucination. False auditory sensory perception.

Authenticity. Quality of being authentic, real, and valid. In psychological functioning and personality, it applies to the conscious feelings, perceptions, and thoughts that a person expresses and communicates. It does not apply to the deeper, unconscious layers of the personality. *See also* Honesty.

Authority figure. A real or projected person in a position of power; transferentially, a projected parent.

Authority principle. The idea that each member of an organizational hierarchy tries to comply with the presumed or fantasied wishes of those above him while those below him try to comply with his wishes. *See also* Hierarchical vector, Political therapist, Procedural therapist.

Autism. *See* Autistic thinking.

Autistic thinking. A form of thinking in which the thoughts are largely narcissistic and egocentric, with emphasis on subjectivity rather than objectivity and without regard for reality. The term is used interchangeably with autism and dereism. *See also* Narcissism.

Autoerotism. Sexual arousal of self without the participation of another person. The term, introduced by Havelock Ellis, is at present used interchangeably with masturbation. In psychoanalysis, autoerotism is considered a primitive phase in object-relationship development, preceding the narcissistic stage. In narcissism there is a love object, but there is no love object in autoerotism.

Autonomic side effect. Disturbance of the autonomic nervous system, both central and peripheral. It may be a result of the use of anti-psychotic drugs, particularly the phenothiazine derivatives. The autonomic side effects include hypotension, hypertension, blurred vision, nasal congestion, and dryness of the mouth. *See also* Mydriasis.

Auxiliary ego. In psychodrama, a person, usually a member of the staff, trained to act out different roles during a psychodramatic session to intensify the therapeutic situation. The trained auxiliary ego may represent an important figure in the patient's life. He may express the patient's unconscious wishes and attitudes or portray his unacceptable self. He may represent a delusion, hallucination, symbol, ideal, animal, or object that makes the patient's psychodramatic world real, concrete, and tangible. *See also* Ego model Hallucinatory psychodrama, Mirror, Multiple double.

Auxiliary therapist. Co-therapist. *See also* Co-therapy.

Back-home group. Collection of persons that a patient usually lives with, works with, and socializes with. It does not include the members of his therapy group. *See also* Expanded group.

Bag. Slang for area of classification, interest, or skill. Bringing together members of a group with different bags makes it initially difficult to achieve a feeling of group cohesiveness but later provides the potential for more productive interchange and deeper cohesiveness.

Basic anxiety. As conceptualized by Karen Horney, the mainspring from which neurotic trends get their intensity and pervasiveness. Basic anxiety is characterized by vague feelings of loneliness, helplessness, and fear of a potentially hostile world. *See also* Anxiety, Fear.

Basic skills training. The teaching of leadership functions, communication skills, the use of group processes, and other interpersonal skills. National Training Laboratories' groups include this training as part of the T-group process. *See also* East-Coast-style T-group.

Behavioral group psychotherapy. A type of group therapy that focuses on overt and objectively observable behavior rather than on thoughts and feelings. It aims at symptomatic improvement and the elimination of suffering and maladaptive habits. Various conditioning and anxiety-eliminating techniques derived from learning theory are combined with didactic discussions and techniques adapted from other systems of treatment.

Behind-the-back technique. An encounter group procedure in which a patient talks about himself and then turns his back and listens while the other participants discuss him as if he were physically absent. Later he "returns" to the group to participate in further discussions of his problems.

Bender, Lauretta (1897–). American psychiatrist who has done extensive work in the fields of child psychiatry, neurology, and psychology. She employed group therapy, particularly activity group therapy, with inpatient children in the early 1940's.

Berne, Eric (1910–1970). American psychiatrist. He was the founder of transactional analysis, which is used in both individual and group therapy. *See also* Transactional group psychotherapy.

Bestiality. Sexual deviation in which a person engages in sexual relations with an animal.

Bieber, Irving (1908–). American psychiatrist and psychoanalyst who has done extensive work in the field of homosexuality. He originated the first major scientific study of male homosexuality published as *Homosexuality; A Psychoanalytic Study*.

Bio-energetic group psychotherapy. A type of group therapy developed by Alexander Lowen that directly involves the body and mobilizes energy processes to facilitate the expression of feeling. Verbal interchange and a variety of exercises are designed to improve and coordinate physical functioning with mental functioning.

Bion, Walter R. British psychoanalyst of the Kleinian school. He introduced concepts dealing largely with the group as a whole. He was one of the European workers who demonstrated the use of open wards in mental hospitals and who developed the concept of therapeutic milieu. *See also* Leaderless therapeutic group, Pairing, Therapeutic community.

Bisexuality. Existence of the qualities of both sexes in the same person. Freud postulated that both biologically and psychologically the sexes differentiated from a common core, that differentiation between the two sexes was relative rather than absolute, and that regression to the common core occurs to varying degrees in both normal and abnormal conditions. An adult person who engages in bisexual behavior is one who is sexually attracted to and has contact with members of both sexes. He is also known in lay terms as an AC-DC person. *See also* Heterosexuality, Homosexuality, Latent homosexuality, Overt homosexuality.

Black separatism. Philosophy that blacks, in order to develop a positive identity, must establish cultural, socioeconomic, and political systems that are distinctively black and separate from white systems. *See also* Afro-American.

Blank screen. Neutral backdrop on which the patient projects a gamut of transferential irrationalities. The passivity of the analyst allows him to act as a blank screen.

Blind self. The behavior, feelings, and motivations of a person known to others but not to himself. The blind self is one quadrant of the Johari Window, a diagrammatic concept of human behavior. *See also* Hidden self, Public self, Undeveloped potential.

Blind spot. Area of someone's personality that he is totally unaware of. These unperceived areas are often hidden by repression so that he can avoid painful emotions. In both group and individual therapy, such blind spots often appear obliquely as projected ideas, intentions, and emotions.

Blind walk. A technique used in encounter groups to help a member experience and develop trust. As a group exercise, each member picks a partner; one partner closes his eyes, and the other leads him around, keeping him out of dangerous places. The partners then reverse roles. Later, the group members discuss their reactions to the blind walk.

Blocking. Involuntary cessation of thought processes or speech because of unconscious emotional factors. It is also known as thought deprivation.

Blunted affect. *See* Affect, blunted.

Body-contact-exploration maneuver. Any physical touching of another person for the purpose of becoming more aware of the sensations and emotions aroused by the experience. The technique is used mainly in encounter groups.

Boundary. Physical or psychological factor that separates relevant regions in the group structure. An external boundary separates the group from the external environment. A major internal boundary distinguishes the group leader from the members. A minor internal boundary separates individual members or subgroups from one another.

Brainwashing. Any technique designed to manipulate human thought or action against the desire, will, or knowledge of the person involved. It usually refers to systematic efforts to indoctrinate nonbelievers. *See also* Dog-eat-dog period, Give-up-itis.

Breuer, Josef (1842–1925). Viennese physician with wide scientific and cultural interests. His collaboration with Freud in studies of cathartic therapy were reported in *Studies on Hysteria* (1895). He withdrew as Freud proceeded to introduce psychoanalysis, but he left important imprints on that discipline, such as the concepts of the primary and secondary process.

Brill, A. A. (1874–1948). First American analyst (1908). Freud gave him permission to translate several of his most important works. He was active in the formation of the New York Psychoanalytic Society (1911) and remained in the forefront of propagators of psychoanalysis as a lecturer and writer throughout his life.

Brooding compulsion. *See* Intellectualization.

Bull session. Informal group meeting at which members discuss their opinions, philosophies, and personal feelings about situations and people. Such groups are leaderless, and no attempt is made to perceive group process, but the cathartic value is often great. It is also known as a rap session.

Burned-out anergic schizophrenic. A chronic schizophrenic who is apathetic and withdrawn, with minimal florid psychotic symptoms but with persistent and often severe schizophrenic thought processes.

Burrow, Trigant L. (1875–1951). American student of Freud and Jung who coined the term group analysis and later developed a method called phyloanalysis. Much of Burrow's work was based on his social views and his opinion that individual psychotherapy places the therapist in too authoritarian a role to be therapeutic. He formed groups of patients, students, and colleagues who, living together in a camp, analyzed their interactions.

Catalepsy. *See* Cerea flexibilitas.

Cataphasia. *See* Verbigeration.

Cataplexy. Temporary loss of muscle tone, causing weakness and immobilization. It can be precipitated by a variety of emotional states.

Catecholamine. Monoamine containing a catechol group that has a sympathomimetic property. Norepinephrine, epinephrine, and dopamine are common catecholamines.

Category method. Technique used in structured interactional group psychotherapy. Members are asked to verbally rate one another along a variety of parameters—such as appearance, intelligence, and relatedness.

Catharsis. Release of ideas, thoughts, and repressed materials from the unconscious, accompanied by an affective emotional response and release of tension. Commonly observed in the course of treatment, both individual and group, it can also occur outside therapy. *See also* Abreaction, Bull session, Conversational catharsis.

Cathexis. In psychoanalysis, a conscious or unconscious investment of the psychic energy of a drive in an idea, a concept, or an object.

Cerea flexibilitas. Condition in which a person maintains the body position he is placed into. It is a pathological symptom observed in severe cases of catatonic schizophrenia. It is also known as waxy flexibility or catalepsy.

Chain-reaction phenomenon. Group therapy situation in which information is passed from one group to another, resulting in a loss of confidentiality. This phenomenon is common when members of different groups socialize together.

Chemotherapy. *See* Drug therapy.

Child. In transactional analysis, an ego state that is an archaic relic from an early period of the person's life. It is also known as archeopsychic function. *See also* Adapted Child, Natural Child.

Chlorpromazine. A phenothiazine derivative used primarily as an antipsychotic agent and in the treatment of nausea and vomiting. The drug was synthesized in 1950 and was used in psychiatry for the first time in 1952. At present, chlorpromazine is one of the most widely used drugs in medical practice.

Circumstantiality. Disturbance in the associative thought processes in which the patient digresses into unnecessary details and inappropriate thoughts before communicating the central idea. It is observed in schizophrenia, obsessional disturbances, and certain cases of epileptic dementia. *See also* Tangentiality, Thought process disorder.

Clarification. In transactional analysis, the attainment of Adult control by a patient who understands what he is doing, knows what parts of his personality are involved in what he is doing, and is able to control and decide whether or not to continue his games. Clarification contributes to stability by assuring the patient that his hidden Parent and Child ego states can be monitored by his Adult ego state. *See also* Decontamination, Interpretation.

Class method. Group therapy method that is lecture-centered and designed to enlighten patients as to their condition and provide them with motivations. Joseph Pratt, a Boston physician, first used this method at the turn of the century to help groups of tuberculous patients understand their illness. *See also* Didactic technique, Group bibliotherapy, Mechanical group therapy.

Claustrophobia. Fear of closed places. *See also* Agoraphobia.

Client-centered psychotherapy. A form of psychotherapy, formulated by Carl Rogers, in which the patient or client is believed to possess the ability to improve. The therapist merely helps him clarify his own thinking and feeling. The client-centered approach in both group and individual therapy is democratic, unlike the psychotherapist-centered treatment methods. *See also* Group-centered psychotherapy, Nondirective approach.

Closed group. Treatment group into which no new members are permitted once it has begun the treatment process. *See also* Open group.

Clouding of consciousness. Disturbance of consciousness characterized by unclear sensory perceptions.

Coexistent culture. Alternative system of values, perceptions, and patterns for behavior. The group experience leads to an awareness of other systems as legitimate alternatives to one's own system.

Cognition. Mental process of knowing and becoming aware. One of the ego functions, it is closely associated with judgment. Groups that study their own processes and dynamics use more cognition than do encounter groups, which emphasize emotions. It is also known as thinking.

Cohesion. *See* Group cohesion.

Cold turkey. Abrupt withdrawal from opiates without the benefit of methadone or other drugs. The term was originated by drug addicts to describe their chills and consequent goose flesh. This type of detoxification is generally used by abstinence-oriented therapeutic communities.

Collaborative therapy. A type of marital therapy in which treatment is conducted by two therapists, each of whom sees one spouse. They may confer occasionally or at regular intervals. This form of treatment affords each analyst a double view of his patient—the way in which one patient reports to his analyst and the way in which the patient's mate sees the situation as reported to the analyst's colleague. *See also* Combined therapy, Concurrent therapy, Conjoint therapy, Family therapy, Group marital therapy, Marriage therapy, Quadrangular therapy, Square interview.

Collective experience. The common emotional experiences of a group of people. Identification, mutual support, reduction of ego defenses, sibling transferences, and empathy help integrate the individual member into the group and accelerate the therapeutic process. S. R. Slavson, who coined the phrase, warned against letting the collective experience submerge the individuality of the members or give them an opportunity to escape from their own autonomy and responsibility.

Collective family transference neurosis. A phenomenon observed in a group when a member projects irrational feelings and thoughts onto other members as a result of transferring the family psychopathology from early childhood into the therapeutic group situation. The interpretation and analysis of this phenomenon is one of the cornerstones of psychoanalytic group therapy. *See also* Lateral transference, Multiple transference.

Collective unconscious. Psychic contents outside the realm of awareness that are common to mankind in general, not to one person in particular. Jung, who introduced the term, believed that the collective unconscious is inherited and derived from the collective experience of the species. It transcends cultural differences and explains the analogy between ancient mythological ideas and the primitive archaic projections observed in some patients who have never been exposed to these ideas.

Coma. A profound degree of unconsciousness with minimal or no detectable responsiveness to stimuli. It is seen in conditions involving the brain—such as head injury, cerebral hemorrhage, thrombosis and embolism, and cerebral infection—in such systemic conditions as diabetes, and in drug and alcohol intoxication. In psychiatry, comas may be seen in severe catatonic states.

Coma vigil. A profound degree of unconsciousness in which the patient's eyes remain open but there is minimal or no detectable evidence of responsiveness to stimuli. It is seen in acute brain syndromes secondary to cerebral infection.

Combined therapy. A type of psychotherapy in which the patient is in both individual and group treatment with the same or two different therapists. In marriage therapy, it is the combination of married couples group therapy with either individual sessions with one spouse or conjoint sessions with the marital pair. *See also* Collaborative therapy, Concurrent therapy, Conjoint therapy, Co-therapy, Family therapy, Group marital therapy, Marriage therapy, Quadrangular therapy, Square interview.

Coming on. A colloquial term used in transactional analysis groups to label an emerging ego state. For example, when a patient points his finger and says "should," he is coming on Parent.

Command automation. Condition closely associated with catalepsy in which suggestions are followed automatically.

Command negativism. *See* Negativism.

Common group tension. Common denominator of tension arising out of the dominant unconscious fantasies of all the members in a group.

Each member projects his unconscious fantasy onto the other members and tries to manipulate them accordingly. Interpretation by the group therapist plays a prominent role in bringing about change.

Communion. The union of one living thing with another or the participation of a person in an organization. It is a necessary ingredient in individual and group psychotherapy and in sensitivity training. Both the leader-therapist and the patient-trainee must experience communion for a successful learning experience to occur. *See also* Agency.

Communion-oriented group psychotherapy. A type of group therapy that focuses on developing a spirit of unity and cohesiveness rather than on performing a task.

Community. *See* Therapeutic community.

Community psychiatry. Psychiatry focusing on the detection, prevention, and early treatment of emotional disorders and social deviance as they develop in the community rather than as they are perceived and encountered at large, centralized psychiatric facilities. Particular emphasis is placed on the environmental factors that contribute to mental illness.

Compensation. Conscious or, usually, unconscious defense mechanism by which a person tries to make up for an imagined or real deficiency, physical or psychological or both.

Competition. Struggle for the possession or use of limited goods, concrete or abstract. Gratification for one person largely precludes gratification for another.

Complementarity of interaction. A concept of bipersonal and multipersonal psychology in which behavior is viewed as a response to stimulation and interaction replaces the concept of reaction. Each person in an interactive situation plays both a provocative role and a responsive role.

Complex. A group of inter-related ideas, mainly unconscious, that have a common affective tone. A complex strongly influences the person's attitudes and behavior. *See also* God complex, Inferiority complex, Mother Superior complex, Oedipus complex.

Composition. Make-up of a group according to

sex, age, race, cultural and ethnic background, and psychopathology.

Compulsion. Uncontrollable impulse to perform an act repetitively. It is used as a way to avoid unacceptable ideas and desires. Failure to perform the act leads to anxiety. *See also* Obsession.

Conation. That part of a person's mental life concerned with his strivings, instincts, drives, and wishes as expressed through his behavior.

Concretization of living. As used in psychodrama, the actualization of life in a therapeutic setting, integrating time, space, reality, and cosmos.

Concurrent therapy. A type of family therapy in which one therapist handles two or more members of the same family but sees each member separately. *See also* Collaborative therapy, Combined therapy, Conjoint therapy, Family therapy, Group marital therapy, Marriage therapy, Quadrangular therapy, Square interview.

Conditioning. Procedure designed to alter behavioral potential. There are two main types of conditioning—classical and operant. Classical or Pavlovian conditioning pairs two stimuli—one adequate, such as offering food to a dog to produce salivation, and the other inadequate, such as ringing a bell, which by itself does not have an effect on salivation. After the two stimuli have been paired several times, the dog responds to the inadequate stimulus (ringing of bell) by itself. In operant conditioning, a desired activity is reinforced by giving the subject a reward every time he performs the act. As a result, the activity becomes automatic without the need for further reinforcement.

Confabulation. Unconscious filling of gaps in memory by imagining experiences that have no basis in fact. It is common in organic brain syndromes. *See also* Paramnesia.

Confidentiality. Aspect of medical ethics in which the physician is bound to hold secret all information given him by the patient. Legally, certain states do not recognize confidentiality and can require the physician to divulge such information if needed in a legal proceeding. In group psychotherapy this ethic is adhered to by the members as well as by the therapist.

Confirmation. In transactional analysis, a re-

confrontation that may be undertaken by the patient himself. *See also* Confrontation.

Conflict. Clash of two opposing emotional forces. In a group, the term refers to a clash between group members or between the group members and the leader, a clash that frequently reflects the inner psychic problems of individual members. *See also* Extrapsychic conflict, Intrapsychic conflict.

Conflict-free area. Part of one's personality or ego that is well-integrated and does not cause any conflicts, symptoms, or displeasure. Conflict-free areas are usually not analyzed in individual analysis, but they become obvious in the interaction of an analytic group, where they can then be analyzed.

Confrontation. Act of letting a person know where one stands in relationship to him, what one is experiencing, and how one perceives him. Used in a spirit of deep involvement, this technique is a powerful tool for changing relationships; used as an attempt to destroy another person, it can be harmful. In group and individual therapy, the value of confrontation is likely to be determined by the therapist. *See also* Encounter group, Existential group psychotherapy.

Confusion. Disturbance of consciousness manifested by a disordered orientation in relation to time, place, or person.

Conjoint therapy. A type of marriage therapy in which a therapist sees the partners together in joint sessions. This situation is also called triadic or triangular, since two patients and one therapist work together. *See also* Collaborative therapy, Combined therapy, Concurrent therapy, Family therapy, Group marital therapy, Marriage therapy, Quadrangular therapy, Square interview.

Conscious. One division of Freud's topographical theory of the mind. The content of the conscious is within the realm of awareness at all times. The term is also used to describe a function of organic consciousness. *See also* Preconscious, Unconscious.

Consciousness. *See* Sensorium.

Consensual validation. The continuous comparison of the thoughts and feelings of group members toward one another that tend to modify and correct interpersonal distortions. The term was introduced by Harry Stack Sullivan. Previously, Trigant Burrow referred to consensual observation to describe this process, which results in effective reality-testing.

Contact situation. Encounter between individual persons or groups in which the interaction patterns that develop represent the dynamic interplay of psychological, cultural, and socioeconomic factors.

Contagion. Force that operates in large groups or masses. When the level of psychological functioning has been lowered, some sudden upsurge of anxiety can spread through the group, speeded by a high degree of suggestibility. The anxiety gradually mounts to panic, and the whole group may be simultaneously affected by a primitive emotional upheaval.

Contamination. In transactional analysis, a state in which attitudes, prejudices, and standards that originate in a Parent or Child ego state become part of the Adult ego state's information and are treated as accepted facts. *See also* Clarification, Decontamination.

Contemporaneity. Here-and-now.

Contract. Explicit, bilateral commitment to a well-defined course of action. In group or individual therapy, the therapist-patient contract is to attain the treatment goal.

Conversational catharsis. Release of repressed or suppressed thoughts and feelings in group and individual psychotherapy as a result of verbal interchange.

Conversion. An unconscious defense mechanism by which the anxiety that stems from an intrapsychic conflict is converted and expressed in a symbolic somatic symptom. Seen in a variety of mental disorders, it is particularly common in hysterical neurosis.

Cooperative therapy. *See* Co-therapy.

Co-patients. Members of a treatment group exclusive of the therapist and the recorder or observer. Co-patients are also known as patient peers.

Coprolalia. The use of vulgar, obscene, or dirty words. It is observed in some cases of schizophrenia. The word is derived from the Greek words *kopros* (excrement) and *lalia* (talking). *See also* Gilles de la Tourette's disease.

Corrective emotional experience. Re-exposure, under favorable circumstances, to an emotional situation that the patient could not handle in the past. As advocated by Franz Alexander, the therapist temporarily assumes a particular role to generate the experience and facilitate reality-testing.

Co-therapy. A form of psychotherapy in which more than one therapist treat the individual patient or the group. It is also known as combined therapy, cooperative therapy, dual leadership, multiple therapy, and three-cornered therapy. *See also* Role-divided therapy, Splitting situation.

Counterdependent person. *See* Nontruster.

Countertransference. Conscious or unconscious emotional response of the therapist to the patient. It is determined by the therapist's inner needs rather than by the patient's needs, and it may reinforce the patient's earlier traumatic history if not checked by the therapist.

Co-worker. Professional or paraprofessional who works in the same clinical or institutional setting.

Creativity. Ability to produce something new. Silvano Arieti describes creativity as the tertiary process, a balanced combination of primary and secondary processes, whereby materials from the id are used in the service of the ego.

Crisis-intervention group psychotherapy. Group therapy aimed at decreasing or eliminating an emotional or situational crisis.

Crisis, therapeutic. *See* Therapeutic crisis.

Crystallization. In transactional analysis, a statement of the patient's position from the Adult of the therapist to the Adult of the patient. *See also* Ego state.

Cultural conserve. The finished product of the creative process; anything that preserves the values of a particular culture. Without this repository of the past, man would be forced to create the same forms to meet the same situations day after day. The cultural conserve also entices new creativity.

Cultural deprivation. Restricted participation in the culture of the larger society.

Current material. Data from present interpersonal experiences. *See also* Genetic material.

Cyclazocine. A narcotic antagonist that blocks the effects of heroin but does not relieve heroin craving. It has been used experimentally with a limited number of drug addicts in research programs.

Cycloplegia. Paralysis of the muscles of accommodation in the eye. It is observed at times as an autonomic side effect of phenothiazine and antiparkinsonism drugs.

Dance therapy. Nonverbal communication through rhythmic body movements, used to rehabilitate people with emotional or physical disorders. Pioneered by Marian Chase in 1940, this method is used in both individual and group therapy.

Data. *See* Current material, Genetic material.

Death instinct. *See* Aggressive drive.

Decision. In transactional analysis, a childhood commitment to a certain existential position and life style. *See also* Script analysis.

Decompensation. In medical science, the failure of normal functioning of an organ, as in cardiac decompensation; in psychiatry, the breakdown of the psychological defense mechanisms that maintain the person's optimal psychic functioning. *See also* Depersonalization.

Decontamination. In transactional analysis, a process whereby a person is freed of Parent or Child contaminations. *See also* Clarification.

Defense mechanism. Unconscious intrapsychic process. Protective in nature, it is used to relieve the anxiety and conflict arising from one's impulses and drives. *See also* Compensation, Conversion, Denial, Displacement, Dissociation, Idealization, Identification, Incorporation, Intellectualization, Introjection, Projection, Rationalization, Reaction formation, Regression, Repression, Sublimation, Substitution, Symbolization, Undoing.

Defensive emotion. Strong feeling that serves as a screen for a less acceptable feeling, one that would cause a person to experience anxiety if it appeared. For example, expressing the emotion of anger is often more acceptable to a group member than expressing the fear that his anger covers up. In this instance, anger is defensive.

Déjà entendu. Illusion of auditory recognition. *See also* Paramnesia.

Déjà vu. Illusion of visual recognition in which a new situation is incorrectly regarded as a repetition of a previous experience. *See also* Paramnesia.

Delirium. A disturbance in the state of consciousness that stems from an acute organic reaction characterized by restlessness, confusion, disorientation, bewilderment, agitation, and affective lability. It is associated with fear, hallucinations, and illusions.

Delusion. A false fixed belief not in accord with one's intelligence and cultural background. Types of delusion include:
Delusion of control. False belief that one is being manipulated by others.
Delusion of grandeur. Exaggerated concept of one's importance.
Delusion of infidelity. False belief that one's lover is unfaithful; it is derived from pathological jealousy.
Delusion of persecution. False belief that one is being harrassed.
Delusion of reference. False belief that the behavior of others refers to oneself; a derivation from ideas of reference in which the patient falsely feels that he is being talked about by others.
Delusion of self-accusation. False feeling of remorse.
Paranoid delusion. Oversuspiciousness leading to false persecutory ideas or beliefs.

Dementia. Organic loss of mental functioning.

Denial. An unconscious defense mechanism in which an aspect of external reality is rejected. At times it is replaced by a more satisfying fantasy or piece of behavior. The term can also refer to the blocking of awareness of internal reality. It is one of the primitive or infantile defenses.

Dependence on therapy. Patient's pathological need for therapy, created out of the belief that he cannot survive without it.

Dependency. A state of reliance on another

for psychological support. It reflects needs for security, love, protection, and mothering.

Dependency phase. *See* Inclusion phase.

Depersonalization. Sensation of unreality concerning oneself, parts of oneself, or one's environment. It is seen in schizophrenics, particularly during the early stages of decompensation. *See also* Decompensation.

Depression. In psychiatry, a morbid state characterized by mood alterations, such as sadness and loneliness; by low self-esteem associated with self-reproach; by psychomotor retardation and, at times, agitation; by withdrawal from interpersonal contact and, at times, a desire to die; and by such vegetative symptoms as insomnia and anorexia. *See also* Grief.

Derailment. *See* Tangentiality.

Derealization. Sensation of distorted spatial relationships. It is seen in certain types of schizophrenia.

Dereism. Mental activity not concordant with logic or experience. This type of thinking is commonly observed in schizophrenic states.

Detoxification. Removal of the toxic effects of a drug. It is also known as detoxication. *See also* Cold turkey, Methadone.

Diagnostic and Statistical Manual of Mental Disorders. A handbook for the classification of mental illnesses. Formulated by the American Psychiatric Association, it was first issued in 1952 (DSM-I). The second edition (DSM-II), issued in 1968, correlates closely with the World Health Organization's *International Classification of Diseases*.

Dialogue. Verbal communication between two or more persons.

Didactic psychodrama. Psychodrama used as a teaching method. It is used with persons involved in the care of psychiatric patients to teach them how to handle typical conflicts.

Didactic technique. Group therapeutic method given prominence by J. M. Klapman that emphasizes the tutorial approach. The group therapist makes use of outlines, texts, and visual aids to teach the group about themselves and

their functioning. *See also* Class method, Group bibliotherapy, Mechanical group therapy.

Differentiation. *See* Individuation.

Dilution of transference. Partial projection of irrational feelings and reactions onto various group members and away from the leader. Some therapists do not believe that dilution of transference occurs. *See also* Multiple transference, Transference.

Dipsomania. Morbid, irrepressible compulsion to drink alcoholic beverages.

Directive-didactic approach. Group therapy approach characterized by guided discussions and active direction by the therapist. Various teaching methods and printed materials are used, and autobiographical material may be presented. Such an approach is common with regressed patients in mental institutions.

Discussion model of group psychotherapy. A type of group therapy in which issues, problems, and facts are deliberated, with the major emphasis on rational understanding.

Disinhibition. Withdrawal of inhibition. Chemical substances such as alcohol can remove inhibitions by interfering with functions of the cerebral cortex. In psychiatry, disinhibition leads to the freedom to act on one's own needs rather than to submit to the demands of others.

Displacement. An unconscious defense mechanism by which the affective component of an unacceptable idea or object is transferred to an acceptable one.

Disposition. Sum total of a person's inclinations as determined by his mood.

Dissociation. An unconscious defense mechanism by which an idea is separated from its accompanying affect, as seen in hysterical dissociative states; an unconscious process by which a group of mental processes are split off from the rest of a person's thinking, resulting in an independent functioning of this group of processes and thus a loss of the usual inter-relationships.

Distortion. Misrepresentation of reality. It is based on historically determined motives.

Distractability. Inability to focus one's attention.

Diversified reality. A condition in a treatment situation that provides various real stimuli with which the patient may interact. In a group, the term refers to the variety of personalities of the co-members, in contrast with the one personality of the analyst in the dyadic relationship.

Doctor-patient relationship. Human interchange that exists between the person who is sick and the person who is selected because of training and experience to heal.

Dog-eat-dog period. Early stage of Communist brainwashing of American prisoners during the Korean War. During this period, as described by former Army psychiatrist William Mayer, the Communists encouraged each prisoner to be selfish and to do only what was best for himself. *See also* Give-up-itis.

Dominant member. The patient in a group who tends to monopolize certain group sessions or situations.

Double. *See* Mirror.

Double-bind. Two conflicting communications from another person. One message is usually nonverbal and the other verbal. For example, parents may tell a child that arguments are to be settled peacefully and yet battle with each other constantly. The concept was formulated by Gregory Bateson.

Double-blind study. A study in which one or more drugs and a placebo are compared in such a way that neither the patient nor the persons directly or indirectly involved in the study know which is being given to the patient. The drugs being investigated and the placebo are coded for identification.

Dream. Mental activity during sleep that is experienced as though it were real. A dream has both a psychological and a biological purpose. It provides an outlet for the release of instinctual impulses and wish fulfillment of archaic needs and fantasies unacceptable in the real world. It permits the partial resolution of conflicts and the healing of traumata too overwhelming to be dealt with in the waking state. And it is the guardian of sleep, which is indispensable for the proper functioning of mind and body during the waking state. *See also* Hypnagogic hallucination, Hypnopompic hallucination, Paramnesia.

Dreamy state. Altered state of consciousness likened to a dream situation. It is accompanied by hallucinations—visual, auditory, and olfactory—and is believed to be associated with temporal lobe lesions. *See also* Marijuana.

Drive. A mental constituent, believed to be genetically determined, that produces a state of tension when it is in operation. This tension or state of psychic excitation motivates the person into action to alleviate the tension. Contemporary psychoanalysts prefer to use the term drive rather than Freud's term, instinct. *See also* Aggressive drive, Instinct, Sexual drive.

Drop-out. Patient who leaves group therapy against the therapist's advice.

Drug therapy. The use of chemical substances in the treatment of illness. It is also known as chemotherapy. *See also* Maintenance drug therapy.

DSM. *See Diagnostic and Statistical Manual of Mental Disorders.*

Dual leadership. *See* Co-therapy.

Dual therapy. *See* Co-therapy.

Dyad. A pair of persons in an interactional situation—such as husband and wife, mother and father, co-therapists, or patient and therapist.

Dyadic session. Psychotherapeutic session involving only two persons, the therapist and the patient.

Dynamic reasoning. Forming all the clinical evidence gained from free-associative anamnesis into a psychological reconstruction of the patient's development. It is a term used by Franz Alexander.

Dyskinesia. Involuntary, stereotyped, rhythmic muscular activity, such as a tic or a spasm. It is sometimes observed as an extrapyramidal side effect of antipsychotic drugs, particularly the phenothiazine derivatives. *See also* Tardive oral dyskinesia.

Dystonia. Extrapyramidal motor disturbance consisting of uncoordinated and spasmodic movements of the body and limbs, such as arching of the back and twisting of the body and neck. It is observed as a side effect of phenothiazine drugs and other major tranquilizers. *See also* Tardive oral dyskinesia.

East-Coast-style T-group. Group that follows the traditional National Training Laboratories orientation by developing awareness of group process. The first T-groups were held in Bethel, Maine. *See also* Basic skills training, West-Coast-style T-group.

Echolalia. Repetition of another person's words or phrases. It is a psychopathological symptom observed in certain cases of schizophrenia, particularly the catatonic types. Some authors consider this behavior to be an attempt by the patient to maintain a continuity of thought processes. *See also* Gilles de la Tourette's disease.

Echopraxia. Imitation of another person's movements. It is a psychopathological symptom observed in some cases of catatonic schizophrenia.

Ecstasy. Affect of intense rapture.

Ego. One of the three components of the psychic apparatus in the Freudian structural framework. The other two components are the id and the superego. Although the ego has some conscious components, many of its operations are automatic. It occupies a position between the primal instincts and the demands of the outer world, and it therefore serves to mediate between the person and external reality. In so doing, it performs the important functions of perceiving the needs of the self, both physical and psychological, and the qualities and attitudes of the environment. It evaluates, coordinates, and integrates these perceptions so that internal demands can be adjusted to external requirements. It is also responsible for certain defensive functions to protect the person against the demands of the id and the superego. It has a host of functions, but adaptation to reality is perhaps the most important one. *See also* Reality-testing.

Ego-coping skill. Adaptive method or capacity developed by a person to deal with or overcome a psychological or social problem.

Ego defense. *See* Defense mechanism.

Ego ideal. Part of the ego during its development that eventually fuses with the superego. It is a social as well as a psychological concept, reflecting the mutual esteem as well as the disillusionment in child-parent and subsequent relationships.

Egomania. Pathological self-preoccupation or self-centeredness. *See also* Narcissism.

Ego model. A person on whom another person patterns his ego. In a group, the therapist or a healthier member acts as an ego model for members with less healthy egos. In psychodrama, the auxiliary ego may act as the ego model.

Ego state. In Eric Berne's structural analysis, a state of mind and its related set of coherent behavior patterns. It includes a system of feelings directly related to a given subject. There are three ego states—Parent, Adult, and Child.

Eitingon, Max (1881–1943). Austrian psychoanalyst. An emissary of the Zurich school, he gained fame as the first person to be analyzed by Freud—in a few sessions in 1907. Later he became the first chief of the Berlin Psychoanalytic Clinic, a founder of the Berlin Psychoanalytic Institute, and a founder of the Palestine Psychoanalytic Society.

Elation. Affect characterized by euphoria, confidence, and enjoyment. It is associated with increased motor activity.

Electrocardiographic effect. Change seen in recordings of the electrical activity of the heart. It is observed as a side effect of phenothiazine derivatives, particularly thioridazine.

Electroconvulsive treatment. *See* Shock treatment.

Emotion. *See* Affect.

Emotional deprivation. Lack of adequate and appropriate interpersonal or environmental experiences or both, usually in the early developmental years. Emotional deprivation is caused by poor mothering or by separation from the mother.

Emotional insight. *See* Insight.

Emotional support. Encouragement, hope, and inspiration given to one person by another. Members of a treatment group often empathize with a patient who needs such support in order to try a new mode of behavior or to face the truth.

Empathy. Ability to put oneself in another person's place, get into his frame of reference, and understand his feelings and behavior objectively. It is one of the major qualities in a successful therapist, facilitator, or helpful group member. *See also* Sympathy.

Encounter group. A form of sensitivity training that emphasizes the experiencing of individual relationships within the group and minimizes intellectual and didactic input. It is a group that focuses on the present rather than concerning itself with the past or outside problems of its members. J. L. Moreno introduced and developed the idea of the encounter group in 1914. *See also* Here-and-now approach, Intervention laboratory, Nonverbal interaction, Task-oriented group.

Encountertapes. Tape recordings designed to provide a group with guidelines for progressive interaction in the absence of a leader. They are copyrighted by the Bell & Howell Company and are available commercially from their Human Development Institute in Atlanta, Georgia.

Epileptic dementia. A form of epilepsy that is accompanied by progressive mental and intellectual impairment. Some believe that the circulatory disturbances during epileptic attacks cause nerve cell degeneration and lead to dementia.

Epinephrine. A sympathomimetic agent. It is the chief hormone secreted by the adrenal medulla. In a state of fear or anxiety, the physiological changes stem from the release of epinephrine. Also known as adrenaline, it is related to norepinephrine, a substance presently linked with mood disturbances in depression.

Eros. *See* Sexual drive.

Erotomania. Pathological preoccupation with sexual activities or fantasies.

Esalen massage. A particular type of massage taught and practiced at the Esalen Institute, a growth center at Big Sur, California. The massage lasts between one and a half and three hours and is intended to be an intimate, loving communion between the participants. A variation is the massage of one person by a group. The massage is given without words.

Ethnocentrism. Conviction that one's own group is superior to other groups. It impairs one's ability to evaluate members of another group realistically or to communicate with them on an open, equal, and person-to-person basis.

Euphoria. An altered state of consciousness characterized by an exaggerated feeling of well-being that is inappropriate to apparent events. It is often associated with opiate, amphetamine, or alcohol abuse.

Evasion. Act of not facing up to or of strategically eluding something. It consists of suppressing an idea that is next in a thought series and replacing it with another idea closely related to it. Evasion is also known as paralogia and perverted logic.

Exaltation. Affect consisting of intense elation and feelings of grandeur.

Exhibitionism. A form of sexual deviation characterized by a compulsive need to expose one's body, particularly the genitals.

Existential group psychotherapy. A type of group therapy that puts the emphasis on confrontation, primarily in the here-and-now interaction, and on feeling experiences rather than on rational thinking. Less attention is put on patient resistances. The therapist is involved on the same level and to the same degree as the patients. *See also* Encounter group.

Expanded group. The friends, immediate family, and interested relatives of a group therapy patient. They are the people with whom he has to relate outside the formal therapy group. *See also* Back-home group.

Experiencing. Feeling emotions and sensations as opposed to thinking; being involved in what is happening rather than standing back at a distance and theorizing. Encounter groups attempt to bring about this personal involvement.

Experiential group. *See* Encounter group.

Experiential stimulator. Anything that stimulates an emotional or sensory response. Several techniques, many of them nonverbal, have been developed for encounter groups to accomplish this stimulation. *See also* Behind-the-back technique, Blind walk.

Extended family therapy. A type of family therapy that involves family members, beyond the nuclear family, who are closely associated with it and affect it. *See also* Network, Social network therapy, Visitor.

Exteropsychic function. *See* Parent.

Extrapsychic conflict. Conflict that arises between the person and his environment. *See also* Intrapsychic conflict.

Extrapyramidal effect. Bizarre, involuntary motor movement. It is a central nervous system side effect sometimes produced by antipsychotic drugs. *See also* Dyskinesia.

Extratherapeutic contact. Contact between group members outside of a regularly scheduled group session.

Facilitator. Group leader. He may be the therapist or a patient who emerges during the course of an encounter and who channels group interaction. He is also known as the session leader.

Fag hag. Slang, derogatory expression often used by homosexuals to describe a woman who has become part of a homosexual social circle and has assumed a central role as a mother figure.

Family neurosis. Emotional maladaptation in which a person's psychopathology is unconsciously inter-related with that of the other members of his family.

Family therapy. Treatment of a family in conflict. The whole family meets as a group with the therapist and explores its relationships and process. The focus is on the resolution of current reactions to one another rather than on individual members. *See also* Collaborative therapy, Combined therapy, Concurrent therapy, Conjoint therapy, Extended family therapy, Group marital therapy, Marriage therapy, Quadrangular therapy, Square interview.

Fantasy. Day dream; fabricated mental picture or chain of events. A form of thinking dominated by unconscious material and primary processes, it seeks wish-fulfillment and immediate solutions to conflicts. Fantasy may serve as the matrix for creativity or for neurotic distortions of reality.

Father surrogate. Father substitute. In psychoanalysis, the patient projects his father image onto another person and responds to that person unconsciously in an inappropriate and unrealistic manner with the feelings and attitudes he had toward the original father.

Fausse reconnaissance. False recognition. *See also* Paramnesia.

Fear. Unpleasurable affect consisting of psychophysiological changes in response to a realistic threat or danger to one's existence. *See also* Anxiety.

Federn, Paul (1871–1950). Austrian psychoanalyst, one of Freud's earliest followers, and the last survivor of the original Wednesday Evening Society. He made important original contributions to psychoanalysis—such as the concepts of flying dreams and ego feeling—and was instrumental in saving the minutes of the Vienna Psychoanalytic Society for subsequent publication.

Feedback. Expressed response by one person or a group to another person's behavior. *See also* Sociometric feedback, Transaction.

Feeling-driven group. A group in which little or no attention is paid to rational processes, thinking, or cognition and where the expression of all kinds of emotion is rewarded. *See also* Affectualizing, Encounter group, Existential group psychotherapy.

Ferenczi, Sandor (1873–1933). Hungarian psychoanalyst, one of Freud's early followers, and a brilliant contributor to all aspects of psychoanalysis. His temperament was more romantic than Freud's, and he came to favor more active and personal techniques, to the point that his adherence to psychoanalysis during his last years was questioned.

Field theory. Concept postulated by Kurt Lewin that a person is a complex energy field in which all behavior can be conceived of as a change in some state of the field during a given unit of time. Lewin also postulated the presence within the field of psychological tensions—states of readiness or preparation for action. The field theory is concerned essentially with the present field, the here-and-now. The theory has been applied by various group psychotherapists.

Fliess, Wilhelm (1858–1928). Berlin nose and throat specialist. He shared an early interest with Freud in the physiology of sex and entered into a prolonged correspondence that figures importantly in the records of Freud's self-analysis. Freud was influenced by Fliess's concept of bisexuality and his theory of the periodicity of the sex functions.

Focal-conflict theory. Theory elaborated by Thomas French in 1952 that explains the current behavior of a person as an expression of his method of solving currently experienced personality conflicts that originated very early in his life. He constantly resonates to these early-life conflicts.

Focused exercise. Technique used particularly in encounter groups to help participants break through their defensive behavior and express such specific emotional reactions as anger, affection, and joy. A psychodrama, for instance, may focus on a specific problem that a group member is having with his wife. In playing out both his part and her part, he becomes aware of the emotion he has been blocking.

Folie à deux. Emotional illness shared by two persons. If it involves three persons, it is referred to as *folie à trois*, etc.

Forced interaction. Relationship that occurs in a group when the therapist or other members demand that a particular patient respond, react, and be active. *See also* Structured interactional group psychotherapy.

Ford negative personal contacts with Negroes scale. A scale that measures whites' negative social contacts with blacks. *See also* Kelley desegregation scale, Rosander anti-Negro behavior scale, Steckler anti-Negro scale, Steckler anti-white scale.

Ford negative personal contacts with whites scale. A scale that measures blacks' negative personal contacts with whites. It helps assess the extent to which negative social contacts influence prejudiced attitudes, thus contributing to the theoretical basis for the employment of interracial group experiences to reduce prejudice. *See also* Kelley desegregation scale, Rosander anti-Negro behavior scale, Steckler anti-Negro scale, Steckler anti-white scale.

Formal operations. Jean Piaget's label for the complete development of a person's logical thinking capacities.

Foulkes, S. H. (1923–). English psychiatrist and one of the organizers of the group therapy movement in Great Britain. His work combines Moreno's ideas—the here-and-now, the socio-

genesis, the social atom, the psychological network—with psypchoanalytic views. He stresses the importance of group-as-a-whole phenomena. *See also* Group analytic psychotherapy, Network.

Free association. Investigative psychoanalytic technique devised by Freud in which the patient seeks to verbalize, without reservation or censor, the passing contents of his mind. The conflicts that emerge while fulfilling this task constitute resistances that are the basis of the analyst's interpretations. *See also* Antirepression device, Conflict.

Free-floating anxiety. Pervasive, unrealistic fear that is not attached to any idea or alleviated by symptom substitution. It is observed particularly in anxiety neurosis, although it may be seen in some cases of latent schizophrenia.

Freud, Sigmund (1856–1939). Austrian psychiatrist and the founder of psychoanalysis. With Josef Breuer, he explored the potentialities of cathartic therapy, then went on to develop the analytic technique and such fundamental concepts of mental phenomena as the unconscious, infantile sexuality, repression, sublimation, superego, ego, and id formation and their applications throughout all spheres of human behavior.

Fulfillment. Satisfaction of needs that may be either real or illusory.

Future projection. Psychodrama technique wherein the patient shows in action how he thinks his future will shape itself. He, sometimes with the assistance of the director, picks the point in time, the place, and the people, if any, he expects to be involved with at that time.

Galactorrhea. Excessive or spontaneous flow of milk from the breast. It may be a result of the endocrine influence of phenothiazine drugs.

Gallows transaction. A transaction in which a person with a self-destructive script smiles while narrating or engaging in a self-destructive act. His smile evokes a smile in the listener, which is in essence an encouragement for self-destruction. *See also* Hamartic script.

Game. Technique that resembles a traditional game in being physical or mental competition conducted according to rules but that is used in the group situation as an experiential learning device. The emphasis is on the process of the game rather than on the objective of the game. A game in Eric Berne's transactional analysis refers to an orderly sequence of social maneuvers with an ulterior motive and resulting in a psychological payoff for the players. *See also* Hit-and-run game, Million-dollar game, Pastime, Survival, Transactional group psychotherapy.

Game analysis. In transactional analysis, the analysis of a person's social interactions that are not honest and straightforward but are contaminated with pretenses for personal gain. *See also* Script analysis, Structural analysis.

Genetic material. Data out of the personal history of the patient that are useful in developing an understanding of the psychodynamics of his present adaptation. *See also* Current material.

Genital phase. The final stage of psychosexual development. It occurs during puberty. In this stage the person's psychosexual development is so organized that he can achieve sexual gratification from genital-to-genital contact and has the capacity for a mature, affectionate relationship with someone of the opposite sex. *See also* Anal phase, Infantile sexuality, Latency phase, Oral phase, Phallic phase.

Gestalt therapy. Type of psychotherapy that emphasizes the treatment of the person as a whole—his biological component parts and their organic functioning, his perceptual configuration, and his inter-relationships with the outside world. Gestalt therapy, developed by Frederic S. Perls, can be used in either an individual or a group therapy setting. It focuses on the sensory awareness of the person's here-and-now experiences rather than on past recollections or future expectations. Gestalt therapy employs role-playing and other techniques to promote the patient's growth process and to develop his full potential. *See also* Nonverbal interaction.

Gilles de la Tourette's disease. A rare illness that has its onset in childhood. The illness, first described by a Paris physician, Gilles de la Tourette, is characterized by involuntary muscular movements and motor incoordination accompanied by echolalia and coprolalia. It is considered by some to be a schizophrenic condition.

Give-up-itis. Syndrome characterized by a giving up of the desire to live. The alienation, isolation, withdrawal, and eventual death associated with this disease syndrome were experienced by many American prisoners during the Korean War, particularly in the early stages of Communist brainwashing. *See also* Dog-eat-dog period.

Go-around. Technique used in group therapy, particularly in structured interactional group psychotherapy, in which the therapist requires that each member of the group respond to another member, a theme, an association, etc. This procedure encourages participation of all members in the group.

God complex. A belief, sometimes seen in therapists, that one can accomplish more than is humanly possible or that one's word should not be doubted. The God complex of the aging psychoanalyst was first discussed by Ernest Jones, Freud's biographer. *See also* Mother Superior complex.

Gould Academy. Private preparatory school in Bethel, Maine, that has been used during summers as the site of the human relations laboratories run by the National Educational Association.

Grief. Alteration in mood and affect consisting of sadness appropriate to a real loss. *See also* Depression.

Group. *See* Therapeutic group.

Group action technique. Technique used in group work to help the participants achieve skills in interpersonal relations and improve their capacity to perform certain tasks better on the job or at home; technique, often involving physical interaction, aimed at enhancing involvement or communion within a new group.

Group analysand. A person in treatment in a psychoanalytically oriented group.

Group analytic psychotherapy. A type of group therapy in which the group is used as the principal therapeutic agent and all communications and relationships are viewed as part of a total field of interaction. Interventions deal primarily with group forces rather than with individual forces. S. H. Foulkes applied the term to his treatment procedure in 1948. It is also known as therapeutic group analysis. *See also* Phyloanalysis, Psychoanalytic group psychotherapy.

Group apparatus. Those people who preserve order and ensure the survival of a group. The internal apparatus deals with members' proclivities in order to maintain the structure of the group and strengthen cohesion. The therapist usually serves as his own apparatus in a small therapy group; in a courtroom, a bailiff ensures internal order. The external apparatus deals with the environment in order to minimize the threat of external pressure. The therapist usually acts as his own external apparatus by setting the time and place for the meetings and making sure that outsiders do not interfere; in a war, combat forces act as the external apparatus.

Group bibliotherapy. A form of group therapy that focuses on the use of selected readings as stimulus material. Outside readings and oral presentations of printed matter by therapist and patients are designed to encourage verbal interchange in the sessions and to hold the attention of severely regressed patients. This approach is used in the treatment of large groups of institutionalized patients. *See also* Class method, Didactic technique, Mechanical group therapy.

Group-centered psychotherapy. A short-term, nonclinical form of group therapy developed by followers of Carl Rogers and based on his client-centered method of individual treatment. The therapist maintains a nonjudgmental attitude, clarifies the feelings expressed in the sessions, and communicates empathic understanding and respect. The participants are not diagnosed, and uncovering techniques are not employed.

Group climate. Atmosphere and emotional tone of a group therapy session.

Group cohesion. Effect of the mutual bonds between members of a group as a result of their concerted effort for a common interest and purpose. Until cohesiveness is achieved, the group cannot concentrate its full energy on a common task. *See also* Group growth.

Group dynamics. Phenomena that occur in groups; the movement of a group from its inception to its termination. Interactions and interrelations among members and between the members and the therapist create tension, which maintains a constantly changing group equilibrium. The interactions and the tension they create are highly influenced by individual members' psychological make-up, unconscious instinctual drives, motives, wishes, and fantasies. The understanding and effective use of group dynamics is essential in group treatment. It is also known as group process. *See also* Group mobility, Psychodynamics.

Group grope. Belittling reference to procedures used in certain encounter groups. The procedures are aimed at providing emotional release through physical contact.

Group growth. Gradual development of trust and cohesiveness in a group. It leads to awareness of self and of other group process and to more effective coping with conflict and intimacy problems. *See also* Group cohesion.

Group history. Chronology of the experiences of a group, including group rituals, group traditions, and group themes.

Group inhibition. *See* Group resistance.

Group marathon. Group meeting that usually lasts from eight to 72 hours, although some sessions last for a week. The session is interrupted only for eating and sleeping. The leader works for the development of intimacy and the open expression of feelings. The time-extended group experience culminates in intense feelings of excitement and elation. Group marathon was developed by George Bach and Frederick Stoller. *See also* Accelerated interaction, Nude marathon, Too-tired-to-be-polite phenomenon.

Group marital therapy. A type of marriage therapy that makes use of a group. There are two basic techniques: (1) Inviting the marital partner of a group member to a group session. The other group members are confronted with the neurotic marriage pattern, which gives them new insights and awareness. (2) Placing a husband and wife together in a traditional group of patients. This method seems indicated if the spouses are unable to achieve meaningful intimacy because they fear the loss of their individual identity at an early phase of the marriage, before a neurotic equilibrium is established. *See also* Collaborative therapy, Combined therapy, Concurrent therapy, Conjoint therapy, Family therapy, Quadrangular therapy, Square interview.

Group mind. Autonomous and unified mental life in an assemblage of people bound together by mutual interests. It is a concept used by group therapists who focus on the group as a unit rather than on the individual members.

Group mobility. Spontaneity and movement in

the group brought about by changes in the functions and roles of individual members, relative to their progress. *See also* Group dynamics.

Group-on-group technique. Device used in T-groups wherein one group watches another group in action and then gives feedback to the observed group. Frequently, one group breaks into two sections, each taking turns in observing the other. The technique is intended to sharpen the participants' observation of individual behavior and group process.

Group phenomenon. *See* Group dynamics.

Group pressure. Demand by group members that individual members submit and conform to group standards, values, and behavior.

Group process. *See* Group dynamics.

Group psychotherapy. A type of psychiatric treatment that involves two or more patients participating together in the presence of one or more psychotherapists, who facilitate both emotional and rational cognitive interaction to effect changes in the maladaptive behavior of the members. *See also* Behavioral group psychotherapy, Bio-energetic group psychotherapy, Client-centered psychotherapy, Communion-oriented group psychotherapy, Crisis-intervention group psychotherapy, Existential group psychotherapy, Group analytic psychotherapy, Group bibliotherapy, Group-centered psychotherapy, Individual therapy, Inspirational-supportive group psychotherapy, Psychoanalytic group psychotherapy, Repressive-inspirational group psychotherapy, Social network therapy, Structured interactional group psychotherapy, Traditional group therapy, Transactional group psychotherapy.

Group resistance. Collective natural aversion of the group members toward dealing with unconscious material, emotions, or old patterns of defense.

Group ritual. Tradition or activity that any group establishes to mechanize some of its activities.

Group stimulus. Effect of several group members' communicating together. Each member has a stimulating effect on every other member, and the total stimulation is studied for therapeutic purposes. *See also* Transactions.

Group therapy. *See* Group psychotherapy.

Group tradition. Activity or value established historically by a group. It determines in part the group's manifest behavior.

Group value. Relative worth or standard developed by and agreed on by the members of a group.

Guilt. Affect associated with self-reproach and need for punishment. In psychoanalysis, guilt refers to a neurotic feeling of culpability that stems from a conflict between the ego and the superego. It begins developmentally with parental disapproval and becomes internalized as conscience in the course of superego formation. Guilt has normal psychological and social functions, but special intensity or absence of guilt characterizes many mental disorders, such as depression and antisocial personality. Some psychiatrists distinguish shame as a less internalized form of guilt.

Gustatory hallucination. False sense of taste.

Hallucination. A false sensory perception without a concrete external stimulus. It can be induced by emotional and by organic factors, such as drugs and alcohol. Common hallucinations involve sights or sounds, although any of the senses may be involved. *See also* Auditory hallucination, Gustatory hallucination, Hypnagogic hallucination, Hypnopompic hallucination, Kinesthetic hallucination, Lilliputian hallucination, Tactile hallucination, Visual hallucination.

Hallucinatory psychodrama. A type of psychodrama wherein the patient portrays the voices he hears and the visions he sees. Auxiliary egos are often called on to enact the various phenomena expressed by the patient and to involve him in interaction with them, so as to put them to a reality test. The intended effect on the patient is called psychodramatic shock.

Hallucinogenic drug. *See* Psychotomimetic drug.

Hamartic script. In transactional analysis, a life script that is self-destructive and tragic in character. *See also* Gallows transaction, Script, Script antithesis, Script matrix.

Healthy identification. Modeling of oneself, consciously or unconsciously, on another person who has sound psychic make-up. The identification has constructive purposes. *See also* Imitation.

Herd instinct. Desire to belong to a group and to participate in social activities. Wilfred Trotter used the term to indicate the presence of a hypothetical social instinct in man. In psychoanalysis, herd instinct is viewed as a social phenomenon rather than as an instinct. *See also* Aggressive drive, Sexual drive.

Here-and-now. Contemporaneity. *See also* There-and-then.

Here-and-now approach. A technique that focuses on understanding the interpersonal and intrapersonal responses and reactions as they occur in the on-going treatment session. Little or no emphasis is put on past history and experiences. *See also* Encounter group, Existential group psychotherapy.

Heterogeneous group. A group that consists of patients from both sexes, a wide age range, differing psychopathologies, and divergent socioeconomic, racial, ethnic, and cultural backgrounds. *See also* Homogeneous group.

Heterosexuality. Sexual attraction or contact between opposite-sex persons. The capacity for heterosexual arousal is probably innate, biologically programmed, and triggered in very early life, perhaps by olfactory modalities, as seen in lower animals. *See also* Bisexuality, Homosexuality.

Hidden self. The behavior, feelings, and motivations of a person known to himself but not to others. It is a quadrant of the Johari Window, a diagrammatic concept of human behavior. *See also* Blind self, Public self, Undeveloped potential.

Hierarchical vector. Thrust of relating to the other members of a group or to the therapist in a supraordinate or subordinate way. It is the opposite of relating as peers. It is also known as vertical vector. *See also* Authority principle, Horizontal vector, Political therapist.

Hit-and-run game. Hostile or nonconstructive aggressive activity indiscriminately and irresponsibly carried out against others. *See also* Game, Million dollar game, Survival.

Homogeneous group. A group that consists of patients of the same sex, with similarities in their psychopathology, and from the same age range and socioeconomic, racial, ethnic, and cultural background. *See also* Heterogeneous group.

Homosexuality. Sexual attraction or contact between same-sex persons. Some authors distinguish two types: overt homosexuality and latent homosexuality. *See also* Bisexuality, Heterosexuality, Inversion, Lesbianism.

Homosexual panic. Sudden, acute onset of severe anxiety, precipitated by the unconscious fear or conflict that one may be a homosexual or act out homosexual impulses. *See also* Homosexuality.

Honesty. Forthrightness of conduct and uprightness of character; truthfulness. In therapy, honesty is a value manifested by the ability to communicate one's immediate experience, including inconsistent, conflicting, or ambivalent feelings and perceptions. *See also* Authenticity.

Hook. In transactional analysis, to switch one's transactions to a new ego state. For example, a patient's Adult ego state is hooked when he goes to the blackboard and draws a diagram.

Horizontal vector. Thrust of relating to the therapist or other members of the group as equals. It is also known as peer vector. *See also* Authority principle, Hierarchical vector, Political therapist.

House encounter. Group meeting of all the persons in a treatment facility. Such a meeting is designed to deal with specific problems within the therapeutic community that affect its functioning, such as poor morale and poor job performances.

Hydrotherapy. External or internal use of water in the treatment of disease. In psychiatry, the use of wet packs to calm an agitated psychotic patient was formerly a popular treatment modality.

Hyperactivity. Increased muscular activity. The term is commonly used to describe a disturbance found in children that is manifested by constant restlessness and movements executed at a rapid rate. The disturbance is believed to be due to brain damage, mental retardation, emotional disturbance, or physiological disturbance. It is also known as hyperkinesis.

Hyperkinesis. *See* Hyperactivity.

Hypermnesia. Exaggerated degree of retention and recall. It is observed in schizophrenia, the manic phase of manic-depressive illness, organic brain syndrome, drug intoxication induced by amphetamines and hallucinogens, hypnosis, and febrile conditions. *See also* Memory.

Hypertensive crisis. Severe rise in blood pressure that can lead to intracranial hemorrhage. It is occasionally seen as a side effect of certain antidepressant drugs.

Hypnagogic hallucination. False sensory perception that occurs just before falling asleep. *See also* Hypnopompic hallucination.

Hypnodrama. Psychodrama under hypnotic trance. The patient is first put into a hypnotic trance. During the trance he is encouraged to act out the various experiences that torment him.

Hypnopompic hallucination. False sensory perception that occurs just before full wakefulness. *See also* Hypnagogic hallucination.

Hypnosis. Artificially induced alteration of consciousness of one person by another. The subject responds with a high degree of suggestibility, both mental and physical, during the trancelike state.

Hypochondriasis. Exaggerated concern with one's physical health. The concern is not based on real organic pathology.

Hypotension, orthostatic. *See* Orthostatic hypotension.

Hysterical anesthesia. Disturbance in sensory perception characterized by absence of sense of feeling in certain areas of the body. It is observed in certain cases of hysterical neurosis, particularly the conversion type, and it is believed to be a defense mechanism.

Id. Part of Freud's concept of the psychic apparatus. According to his structural theory of mental functioning, the id harbors the energy that stems from the instinctual drives and desires of a person. The id is completely in the unconscious realm, unorganized and under the influence of the primary processes. *See also* Conscious, Ego, Preconscious, Primary process, Superego, Unconscious.

Idealization. A defense mechanism in which a person consciously or, usually, unconsciously overestimates an attribute or an aspect of another person.

Ideas of reference. Misinterpretation of incidents and events in the outside world as having a direct personal reference to oneself. Occasionally observed in normal persons, ideas of reference are frequently seen in paranoid patients. *See also* Projection.

Ideational shield. An intellectual, rational defense against the anxiety a person would feel if he became vulnerable to the criticisms and rejection of others. As a result of his fear of being rejected, he may feel threatened if he criticizes another person—an act that is unacceptable to him. In both group and individual therapy, conditions are set up that allow the participants to lower this ideational shield.

Identification. An unconscious defense mechanism in which a person incorporates into himself the mental picture of an object and then patterns himself after this object; seeing oneself as like the person used as a pattern. It is distinguished from imitation, a conscious process. *See also* Healthy identification, Imitation, Role.

Identification with the aggressor. An unconscious process by which a person incorporates within himself the mental image of a person who represents a source of frustration from the outside world. A primitive defense, it operates in the interest and service of the developing ego. The classical example of this defense occurs toward the end of the oedipal stage, when the male child, whose main source of love and gratification is the mother, identifies with his father. The father represents the source of frustration, being the powerful rival for the mother; the child cannot master or run away from his father, so he is obliged to identify with him. *See also* Psychosexual development.

Idiot. *See* Mental retardation.

I-It. Philosopher Martin Buber's description of damaging interpersonal relationships. If a person treats himself or another person exclusively as an object, he prevents mutuality, trust, and growth. When pervasive in a group, I-It relationships prevent human warmth, destroy cohesiveness, and retard group process. *See also* I-Thou.

Ileus, paralytic. *See* Paralytic ileus.

Illusion. False perception and misinterpretation of an actual sensory stimulus.

Illustration. In transactional analysis, an anecdote, simile, or comparison that reinforces a confrontation or softens its potentially undesirable effects. The illustration may be immediate or remote in time and may refer to the external environment or to the internal situation in the group.

Imbecile. *See* Mental retardation.

Imitation. In psychiatry, a conscious act of mimicking another person's behavior pattern. *See also* Healthy identification, Identification.

Impasse. *See* Therapeutic impasse.

Improvement scale. In transactional analysis, a quantitative specification of a patient's position in terms of improvement in the course of therapy.

Improvisation. In psychodrama, the acting out of problems without prior preparation.

Impulse. Unexpected, instinctive urge motivated by conscious and unconscious feelings over which the person has little or no control. *See also* Drive, Instinct.

Inappropriate affect. Emotional tone that is out of harmony with the idea, object, or thought accompanying it.

Inclusion phase. Early stage of group treatment. In this phase, each group member's concern focuses primarily on belonging and being accepted and recognized, particularly by the therapist. It is also known as the dependency stage. *See also* Affection phase, Power phase.

Incorporation. An unconscious defense mechanism in which an object representation is assimilated into oneself through symbolic oral ingestion. One of the primitive defenses, incorporation is a special form of introjection and is the primary mechanism in identification.

Individual psychology. Holistic theory of personality developed by Alfred Adler. Personality development is explained in terms of adaptation to the social milieu (life style), strivings toward perfection motivated by feelings of inferiority, and the interpersonal nature of the person's problems. Individual psychology is applied in

group psychotherapy and counseling by Adlerian practitioners.

Individual therapy. A type of psychotherapy in which a professionally trained psychotherapist treats one patient who either wants relief from disturbing symptoms or improvement in his ability to cope with his problems. This one therapist-one patient relationship, the traditional dyadic therapeutic technique, is opposed to other techniques that deal with more than one patient *See also* Group psychotherapy, Psychotherapy

Individuation. Differentiation; the process of molding and developing the individual personality so that it is different from the rest of the group. *See also* Actualization.

Infantile dynamics. Psychodynamic integrations, such as the Oedipus complex, that are organized during childhood and continue to exert unconsciously experienced influences on adult personality.

Infantile sexuality. Freudian concept regarding the erotic life of infants and children. Freud observed that, from birth, infants are capable of erotic activities. Infantile sexuality encompasses the overlapping phases of psychosexual development during the first five years of life and includes the oral phase (birth to 18 months), when erotic activity centers around the mouth; the anal phase (ages one to three), when erotic activity centers around the rectum; and the phallic phase (ages two to six), when erotic activity centers around the genital region. *See also* Psychosexual development.

Inferiority complex. Concept, originated by Alfred Adler, that everyone is born with inferiority or a feeling of inferiority secondary to real or fantasied organic or psychological inadequacies. How this inferiority or feeling of inferiority is handled determines a person's behavior in life. *See also* Masculine protest.

Infra reality. Reduced actuality that is observed in certain therapeutic settings. For example, according to J. L. Moreno, who coined the term, the contact between doctor and patient is not a genuine dialogue but is an interview, research situation, or projective test.

Injunction. In transactional analysis, the instructions given by one ego state to another, usually the Parent ego state to the Child ego state, that become the basis of the person's life script decisions. *See also* Permission, Program, Role, Script analysis.

Inner-directed person. A person who is self-motivated and autonomous and is not easily guided or influenced by the opinions and values of other people. *See also* Other-directed person.

Insight. Conscious awareness and understanding of one's own psychodynamics and symptoms of maladaptive behavior. It is highly important in effecting changes in the personality and behavior of a person. Most therapists distinguish two types: (1) intellectual insight—knowledge and awareness without any change of maladaptive behavior; (2) emotional or visceral insight—awareness, knowledge, and understanding of one's own maladaptive behavior, leading to positive changes in personality and behavior.

Inspirational-supportive group psychotherapy. A type of group therapy that focuses on the positive potential of members and stresses reinforcement for accomplishments or achievements. *See also* Alcoholics Anonymous.

Instinct. A biological, species-specific, genetically determined drive to respond in an automatic, complex, but organized way to a particular stimulus. *See also* Drive, Impulse.

Institute of Industrial Relations. A department of the Graduate School of Business Administration at the University of California at Los Angeles. It has conducted sensitivity training laboratories for business and professional people for nearly 20 years.

Insulin coma therapy. A form of psychiatric treatment originated by Manfred Sakel in which insulin is administered to the patient to produce coma. It is used in certain types of schizophrenia. *See also* Shock treatment.

Intellectual insight. *See* Insight.

Intellectualization. An unconscious defense mechanism in which reasoning or logic is used in an attempt to avoid confrontation with an objectionable impulse or affect. It is also known as brooding or thinking compulsion.

Intelligence. Capacity for understanding, recalling, mobilizing, and integrating constructively what one has learned and for using it to meet new situations.

Intensive group process. Group process designed to evoke a high degree of personal interaction and involvement, often accompanied by the expression of strong or deep feelings.

Interaction. *See* Transaction.

Interpersonal conflict. *See* Extrapsychic conflict.

Interpersonal psychiatry. Dynamic-cultural system of psychoanalytic therapy based on Harry Stack Sullivan's interpersonal theory. Sullivan's formulations were couched in terms of a person's interactions with other people. In group psychotherapy conducted by practitioners of this school, the focus is on the patients' transactions with one another.

Interpersonal skill. Ability of a person in relationship with others to express his feelings appropriately, to be socially responsible, to change and influence, and to work and create. *See also* Socialization.

Interpretation. A psychotherapeutic technique used in psychoanalysis, both individual and group. The therapist conveys to the patient the significance and meaning of his behavior, constructing into a more meaningful form the patient's resistances, defenses, transferences, and symbols (dreams). *See also* Clarification.

Interpretation of Dreams, The. Title of a book by Freud. Published in 1899, this work was a major presentation not only of Freud's discoveries about the meaning of dreams—hitherto regarded as outside scientific interest—but also of his concept of a mental apparatus that is topographically divided into unconscious, preconscious, and conscious areas.

Interracial group. *See* Heterogeneous group.

Intervention laboratory. Human relations laboratory, such as an encounter group or training group, especially designed to intervene and resolve some group conflict or crisis.

Intrapersonal conflict. *See* Intrapsychic conflict.

Intrapsychic ataxia. *See* Ataxia.

Intrapsychic conflict. Conflict that arises from the clash of two opposing forces within oneself.

It is also known as intrapersonal conflict. *See also* Extrapsychic conflict.

Introjection. An unconscious defense mechanism in which a psychic representation of a loved or hated object is taken into one's ego system. In depression, for example, the emotional feelings related to the loss of a loved one are directed toward the introjected mental representation of the loved one. *See also* Identification, Incorporation.

Inversion. Synonym for homosexuality. Inversion was the term used by Freud and his predecessors. There are three types: absolute, amphigenous, and occasional. *See also* Homosexuality, Latent homosexuality, Overt homosexuality.

I-Thou. Philosopher Martin Buber's conception that man's identity develops from true sharing by persons. Basic trust can occur in a living partnership in which each member identifies the particular real personality of the other in his wholeness, unity, and uniqueness. In groups, I-Thou relationships promote warmth, cohesiveness, and constructive group process. *See also* I-It.

Jamais vu. False feeling of unfamiliarity with a real situation one has experienced. *See also* Paramnesia.

Jaundice, allergic. Yellowish staining of the skin and deeper tissues accompanied by bile in the urine secondary to a hypersensitivity reaction. An obstructive type of jaundice, it is occasionally detected during the second to fourth week of phenothiazine therapy.

Johari Window. A schematic diagram used to conceptualize human behavior. It was developed by Joseph (Jo) Luft and Harry (Hari) Ingham at the University of California at Los Angeles in 1955. The diagram is composed of quadrants, each representing some aspect of a person's behavior, feelings, and motivations. *See also* Blind self, Hidden self, Public self, Undeveloped potential.

Jones, Ernest (1879–1958). Welsh psychoanalyst and one of Freud's early followers. He was an organizer of the American Psychoanalytic Association in 1911 and the British Psychoanalytical Society in 1919 and a founder and long-time editor of the journal of the International Psychoanalytical Association. He was the author of many valuable works, the most important of which is his three-volume biography of Freud.

Judgment. Mental act of comparing or evaluating choices within the framework of a given set of values for the purpose of electing a course of action. Judgment is said to be intact if the course of action chosen is consistent with reality; judgment is said to be impaired if the chosen course of action is not consistent with reality.

Jung, Carl Gustav (1875–1961). Swiss psychiatrist and psychoanalyst. He founded the school of analytic psychology. *See also* Collective unconscious.

Karate-chop experience. A technique used in encounter groups to elicit aggression in timid or inhibited participants in a humorous way. The timid one stands facing a more aggressive member. Both make violent pseudokarate motions at each other, without making physical contact but yelling "Hai!" as loudly as possible at each stroke. After this exercise, the group members discuss the experience.

Kelley desegregation scale. A scale designed to measure the attitudes of whites toward blacks in the area of school integration. The scale provides a rough measure of racial prejudice and may be of help in ascertaining the effects on prejudice of participation in an interracial group. *See also* Ford negative personal contacts with Negroes scale, Ford negative personal contacts with whites scale, Rosander anti-Negro behavior scale, Steckler anti-Negro scale, Steckler anti-white scale.

Kinesthetic hallucination. False perception of muscular movement. An amputee may feel movement in his missing limb; this phenomenon is also known as phantom limb.

Kinesthetic sense. Sensation in the muscles as differentiated from the senses that receive stimulation from outside the body.

Kleptomania. Pathological compulsion to steal. In psychoanalytic theory, it originates in the infantile stage of psychosexual development.

Latency phase. Stage of psychosexual development extending from age five to the beginning of adolescence at age 12. Freud's work on ego psychology showed that the apparent cessation of sexual preoccupation during this period stems from a strong, aggressive blockade of libidinal and sexual impulses in an effort to avoid the dangers of the oedipal relationships. During the latency period, boys and girls are inclined to choose friends and join groups of their own sex. *See also* Identification with the aggressor, Psychosexual development.

Latent homosexuality. Unexpressed conscious or unconscious homoerotic wishes that are held in check. Freud's theory of bisexuality postulated the existence of a constitutionally determined, though experientially influenced, instinctual masculine-feminine duality. Normally, the opposite-sex component is dormant, but a breakdown in the defenses of repression and sublimation may activate latent instincts and result in overt homoeroticism. Many writers have questioned the validity of a universal latent homoeroticism. *See also* Bisexuality, Homosexuality, Overt homosexuality.

Lateral transference. Projection of long-range attitudes, values, and emotions onto the other members of the treatment group rather than onto the therapist. The patient sees other members of the group, co-patients, and peers in terms of his experiences in his original family. *See also* Collective family transference neurosis, Multiple transference.

Leaderless therapeutic group. An extreme form of nondirective group, conducted primarily for research purposes, such as the investigations of intragroup tensions by Walter R. Bion. On occasion, the therapist interacts verbally in a nonauthoritarian manner, but he generally functions as a silent observer—withholding explanations, directions, and support.

Leadership function. *See* Leadership role.

Leadership role. Stance adopted by the therapist in conducting a group. There are three main leadership roles: authoritarian, democratic, and laissez-faire. Any group—social, therapeutic, training, or task-oriented—is primarily influenced by the role practiced by the leader.

Leadership style. *See* Leadership role.

Lesbianism. Female homosexuality. About 600 B.C. on the island of Lesbos in the Aegean Sea, the poetess Sappho encouraged young women to engage in mutual sex practices. Lesbianism is also known as Sapphism. *See also* Bisexuality, Homosexuality, Latent homosexuality, Overt homosexuality.

Lewin, Kurt (1890–1946). German psychologist who emigrated to the United States in 1933. His work on the field theory has been useful in the experimental study of human behavior in a social situation. He was one of the early workers who helped develop the National Training Laboratories.

Libido theory. Freudian theory of sexual instinct, its complex process of development, and its accompanying physical and mental manifestations. Before Freud's introduction and completion of the dual-instinct theory (sexual and aggressive) in 1920, all instinctual manifestations were related to the sexual instinct, making for some confusion at that time. Current psychoanalytic practice assumes the existence of two instincts: sexual (libido) and aggressive (death). *See also* Aggressive drive, Sexual drive.

Life instinct. *See* Sexual drive.

Life lie. A contrary-to-fact conviction around which a person structures his life philosophy and attitudes.

Life line. A group technique in which each member is asked to draw a line representing his life, beginning with birth and ending with death. Comparison and discussion usually reveal that the shape and slope of the lines are based on a variety of personally meaningful parameters, such as maturity and academic achievement.

Lifwynn Foundation. Organization established by Trigant Burrow in 1927 as a social community in which the participants examined their interactions in the daily activities in which they were engaged. Lifwynn is currently under the direction of Hans Syz, M.D., in Westport, Conn.

Lilliputian hallucination. False perception that persons are reduced in size. *See also* Micropsia.

Lobotomy. Neurosurgical procedure in which one or more nerve tracts in a lobe of the cerebrum are severed. Prefrontal lobotomy is the ablation of one or more nerve tracts in the prefrontal area of the brain. It is used in the treatment of certain severe mental disorders that do not respond to other treatments.

Locus. Place of origin.

Logorrhea. Copious, pressured, coherent speech. It is observed in manic-depressive illness, manic type. Logorrhea is also known as tachylogia, verbomania, and volubility.

LSD (lysergic acid diethylamide). A potent psychotogenic drug discovered in 1942. LSD produces psychoticlike symptoms and behavior changes—including hallucinations, delusions, and time-space distortions.

Lysergic acid diethylamide. *See* LSD.

Macropsia. False perception that objects are larger than they really are. *See also* Micropsia.

Maintenance drug therapy. A stage in the course of chemotherapy. After the drug has reached its maximal efficacy, the dosage is reduced and sustained at the minimal therapeutic level that will prevent a relapse or exacerbation.

Major tranquilizer. Drug that has antipsychotic properties. The phenothiazines, thioxanthenes, butyrophenones, and reserpine derivatives are typical major tranquilizers, which are also known as ataractics, neuroleptics, and antipsychotics. *See also* Dystonia, Minor tranquilizer.

Maladaptive way. Poorly adjusted or pathological behavior pattern.

Mannerism. Stereotyped involuntary activity that is peculiar to a person.

MAO inhibitor. *See* Monoamine oxidase inhibitor.

Marathon. *See* Group marathon.

Marijuana. Dried leaves and flowers of *Cannabis sativa* (Indian hemp). It induces somatic and psychic changes in man when smoked or ingested in sufficient quantity. The somatic changes include increased heart rate, rise in blood pressure, dryness of the mouth, increased appetite, and occasional nausea, vomiting, and diarrhea. The psychic changes include dreamy-state level of consciousness, disruptive chain of ideas, perceptual disturbances of time and space, and alterations of mood. In strong doses, marijuana can produce hallucinations and, at times, paranoid ideas and suspiciousness. It is also known as pot, grass, weed, tea, and Mary Jane.

Marital counseling. Process whereby a trained counselor helps married couples resolve problems that arise and trouble them in their relationship. The theory and techniques of this approach were first developed in social agencies as part of family casework. Husband and wife are seen by the same worker in separate and joint counseling sessions, which focus on immediate family problems.

Marital therapy. *See* Marriage therapy.

Marriage therapy. A type of family therapy that involves the husband and the wife and focuses on the marital relationship, which affects the individual psychopathology of the partners. The rationale for this method is the assumption that psychopathological processes within the family structure and in the social matrix of the marriage perpetuate individual pathological personality structures, which find expression in the disturbed marriage and are aggravated by the feedback between partners. *See also* Collaborative therapy, Combined therapy, Concurrent therapy, Conjoint therapy, Family therapy, Group marital therapy, Marital counseling, Quadrangular therapy, Square interview.

Masculine identity. Well-developed sense of gender affiliation with males.

Masculine protest. Adlerian doctrine that depicts a universal human tendency to move from a passive and feminine role to a masculine and active role. This doctrine is an extension of his ideas about organic inferiority. It became the prime motivational force in normal and neurotic behavior in the Adlerian system. *See also* Adler, Alfred; Inferiority complex.

Masculinity-femininity scale. Any scale on a psychological test that assesses the relative masculinity or femininity of the testee. Scales vary and may focus, for example, on basic identification with either sex or preference for a particular sex role.

Masochism. A sexual deviation in which sexual gratification is derived from being maltreated by the partner or oneself. It was first described by an Austrian novelist, Leopold von Sacher-Masoch (1836–1895). *See also* Sadism, Sadomasochistic relationship.

Masturbation. *See* Autoerotism.

Mattress-pounding. A technique used in encounter groups to mobilize repressed or suppressed anger. A group member vents his resentments by beating the mattress with his fists and yelling. Frequently, the mattress becomes in fantasy a hated parent, sibling, or spouse. After this exercise, the group members discuss their reactions. *See also* Pillow-beating.

Maximal expression. Utmost communication. In psychodrama, it is the outcome of an involved sharing by the group of the three portions of the session: the warm-up, the action, and the post-action. During the action period the patient is encouraged to express all action and verbal communication to the limit. To this end, delusions, hallucinations, soliloquies, thoughts, and fantasies are allowed to be part of the production.

Mechanical group therapy. A form of group therapy that makes use of mechanical devices. As applied in the early 1950's, it required neither a group nor a therapist. An example of this form of therapy is the playing of brief recorded messages over the loudspeaker system of a mental hospital; the same statement, bearing on some elementary principle of mental health, is frequently repeated to secure general acceptance. *See also* Class method, Didactic technique, Group bibliotherapy.

Megalomania. Morbid preoccupation with expansive delusions of power and wealth.

Melancholia. Old term for depression that is rarely used at the present time. As used in the term involutional melancholia, it refers to a morbid state of depression and not to a symptom.

Memory. Ability to revive past sensory impressions, experiences, and learned ideas. Memory includes three basic mental processes: registration—the ability to perceive, recognize, and establish information in the central nervous system; retention—the ability to retain registered information; and recall—the ability to retrieve stored information at will. *See also* Amnesia, Hypermnesia, Paramnesia.

Mental aberration. *See* Aberration, mental.

Mental illness. Psychiatric disease included in the list of mental disorders in the *Diagnostic and Statistical Manual of Mental Disorders* published by the American Psychiatric Association and in the *Standard Nomenclature of Diseases*

and Operations approved by the American Medical Association.

Mental retardation. Subnormal general intellectual functioning, which may be evident at birth or may develop during childhood. Learning, social adjustment, and maturation are impaired, and emotional disturbance is often present. The degree of retardation is commonly measured in terms of I.Q.: borderline (68–85), mild (52–67), moderate (36–51), severe (20–35), and profound (under 20). Obsolescent terms that are still used occasionally are idiot (mental age of less than three years), imbecile (mental age of three to seven years), and moron (mental age of eight years).

Methadone. Methadone hydrochloride, a long-acting synthetic narcotic developed in Germany as a substitute for morphine. It is used as an analgesic and in detoxification and maintenance treatment of opiate addicts.

Methadone maintenance treatment. Long-term use of methadone on a daily basis to relieve narcotic craving and avert the effects of narcotic drugs.

Micropsia. False perception that objects are smaller than they really are. *See also* Lilliputian hallucination, Macropsia.

Milieu therapy. Treatment that emphasizes appropriate socioenvironmental manipulation for the benefit of the patient. The setting for milieu therapy is usually the psychiatric hospital.

Million-dollar game. Group game designed to explore the psychological meaning of money and to encourage free, creative thinking. The group is told that it has a million dollars, which is to be used productively in any way, as long as the endeavor actively involves all members of the group. *See also* Game, Hit-and-run game, Survival.

Minnesota Multiphasic Personality Inventory. Questionnaire type of psychological test for ages 16 and over with 550 true-false statements that are coded in 14 scales, ranging from a social scale to a schizophrenia scale. Group and individual forms are available.

Minor tranquilizer. Drug that diminishes tension, restlessness, and pathological anxiety without any antipsychotic effect. Meprobamate and diazepoxides are typical minor tranquilizers, which are also known as psycholeptics. *See also* Major tranquilizer.

Minutes of the Vienna Psychoanalytic Society. Diary of Freud's Wednesday Evening Society (after 1910, the Vienna Psychoanalytic Society) as recorded by Otto Rank, the paid secretary between 1906 and 1915.

Mirror. In psychodrama, the person who represents the patient, copying his behavior and trying to express his feelings in word and movement, showing the patient as if in a mirror how other people experience him. The mirror may exaggerate, employing techniques of deliberate distortion in order to arouse the patient to come forth and change from a passive spectator into an active participant. The mirror is also known as the double. *See also* Auxiliary ego.

Mirroring. A group process by which a person sees himself in the group by the reflections that come back to him in response to the way he presents himself. The image may be true or distorted, depending on the level of truth at which the group is functioning at the time. Mirroring has been used as an exercise in encounter group therapy and as a laboratory procedure in the warming-up period of the psychodrama approach.

Mixed-gender group. *See* Heterogeneous group.

MMPI. *See* Minnesota Multiphasic Personality Inventory.

Mobility. *See* Group mobility.

Monoamine oxidase inhibitor. Agent that inhibits the enzyme monoamine oxidase (MAO), which oxidizes such monoamines as norepinephrine and serotonin. Some of the MAO inhibitors are highly effective as antidepressants. *See also* Tricyclic drug.

Monomania. Morbid mental state characterized by preoccupation with one subject. It is also known as partial insanity.

Mood. Feeling tone that is experienced by a person internally. Mood does not include the external expression of the internal feeling tone. *See also* Affect.

Mood swing. Oscillation of a person's emotional feeling tone between periods of euphoria and depression.

Moron. *See* Mental retardation.

Moses and Monotheism. Title of a book by Freud published in 1939. In this book, Freud undertook a historical but frankly speculative reconstruction of the personality of Moses and examined the concept of monotheism and the abiding effect of the patriarch on the character of the Jews. One of Freud's last works, it bears the imprint of his latter-day outlook and problems.

Mother Superior complex. Tendency of a therapist to play the role of the mother in his relations with his patients. The complex often leads to interference with the therapeutic process. *See also* God complex.

Mother surrogate. Mother substitute. In psychoanalysis, the patient projects his mother image onto another person and responds to that person unconsciously in an inappropriate and unrealistic manner with the feelings and attitudes he had toward the original mother.

Motivation. Force that pushes a person to act to satisfy a need. It implies an incentive or desire that influences the will and causes the person to act.

Mourning. *See* Grief.

Multibody situation. Group situation. The term was originally used in the description of the evolution of social interaction in human beings from narcissism through the dyadic relationship to the three-body constellation of the Oedipus complex to the multibody situation prevailing in groups.

Multiple double. Several representations of the patient, each portraying a part of him—one as he is now, another as he was (for instance, five years ago), another at a crucial moment in his life (for example, when his mother died), a fourth how he may be 20 years hence. The multiple representations of the patient are presented in sequence, each continuing where the last left off. *See also* Auxiliary ego.

Multiple ego states. Many psychological stages, relating to different periods of one's life or to different depths of experience. These states may be of varying degrees of organization and complexity, and they may or may not be capable of being called to awareness consecutively or simultaneously.

Multiple interaction. Group behavior in which many members participate in the transactions, both verbal and nonverbal, at any one moment in the session.

Multiple intragroup transference. *See* Multiple transference.

Multiple reactivity. A phenomenon in which many group members respond in a variety of ways to the provocative role or stimulation afforded by one patient's behavior.

Multiple therapy. *See* Co-therapy.

Multiple transferences. Feelings and attitudes originally held toward members of one's family that become irrationally attached to the therapist and various group members simultaneously. *See also* Collective family transference neurosis, Lateral transference.

Mutism. *See* Stupor.

Mutual support. Expressions of sympathy, understanding, and affection that group members give to one another. *See also* Pairing.

Mydriasis. Dilatation of the pupil. The condition sometimes occurs as an autonomic side effect of phenothiazine and antiparkinsonism drugs.

Nalline test. The use of Nalline, a narcotic antagonist, to determine abstinence from opiates. An injection of Nalline precipitates withdrawal symptoms if opiates have been used recently. The most important use for Nalline, however, is as an antidote in the treatment of opiate overdose.

Narcissism. Self-love. It is linked to autoerotism but is devoid of genitality. The word is derived from Narcissus, a Greek mythology figure who fell in love with his own reflected image. In psychoanalytic theory, it is divided into primary narcissism and secondary narcissism. Primary narcissism refers to the early infantile phase of object relationship development, when the child has not differentiated himself from the outside world. All sources of pleasure are unrealistically recognized as coming from within himself, giving him a false sense of omnipotence.

Secondary narcissism is the type of narcissism that results when the libido once attached to external love objects is redirected back to the self. *See also* Autistic thinking, Autoerotism.

Narcotic hunger. A physiological craving for a drug. It appears in abstinent narcotic addicts.

National Training Laboratories. Organization started in 1947 at Bethel, Maine, to train professionals who work with groups. Interest in personal development eventually led to sensitivity training and encounter groups. The organization is now called the NTL Institute for Applied Behavioral Science. *See also* Basic skills training, East Coast style T-group.

Natural Child. In transactional analysis, the autonomous, expressive, archaic Child ego state that is free from parental influence. *Se also* Adapted Child.

Natural group. Group that tends to evolve spontaneously in human civilization, such as a kinship, tribal, or religious group. In contrast are various contrived groups or aggregates of people who meet for a relatively brief time to achieve some goal.

Negativism. Verbal or nonverbal opposition to outside suggestions and advice. It is also known as command negativism.

Neologism. New word or condensation of several words formed by patient in an effort to express a highly complex idea. It is often seen in schizophrenia.

Neopsychic function. *See* Adult.

Network. The persons in the patient's environment with whom he is most intimately connected. It frequently includes the nuclear family, the extended family, the orbit of relatives and friends, and work and recreational contacts. S. H. Foulkes believes that this dynamically interacting network has a fundamental significance in the production of illness in the patient. *See also* Extended family therapy, Social network therapy, Visitor.

Neuroleptic. *See* Antipsychotic drug, Major tranquilizer.

Neurosis. Mental disorder characterized by anxiety. The anxiety may be experienced and expressed directly, or, through an unconscious psychic process, it may be converted, displaced, or somatized. Although neuroses do not manifest depersonalization or overt distortion of reality, they can be severe enough to impair a person's functioning. The neuroses, also known as psychoneuroses, include the following types: anxiety neurosis, hysterical neurosis, phobic neurosis, obsessive-compulsive neurosis, depressive neurosis, neurasthenic neurosis, depersonalization neurosis, and hypochondriacal neurosis.

Nondirective approach. Technique in which the therapist follows the lead of the patient in the interview rather than introducing his own theories and directing the course of the interview. This method is applied in both individual and group therapy, such as Carl Rogers' client-centered and group-centered therapy. *See also* Passive therapist.

Nontruster. A person who has a strong unfilled need to be nurtured but whose early experience was one of rejection or overprotection. As a defense against repetition of this experience, he develops an overly strong show of independence. Sometimes this independence is manifested in group therapy by a member's constant rejection of support and of attempts by other members to get close to him. *See also* Outsider.

Nonverbal interaction. Technique used without the aid of words in encounter groups to promote communication and intimacy and to bypass verbal defenses. Many exercises of this sort are carried out in complete silence; in others, the participants emit grunts, groans, yells, cries, or sighs. Gestalt therapy pays particular attention to nonverbal expression.

Norepinephrine. A catecholamine that functions as a neurohumoral mediator liberated by postganglionic adrenergic nerves. It is also present in the adrenal medulla and in many areas in the brain, with the highest concentration in the hypothalamus. A disturbance in the metabolism of norepinephrine is considered to be an important factor in the etiology of depression. *See also* Serotonin.

Nuclear family. Immediate members of a family, including the parents and the children. *See also* Extended family therapy, Network, Social network therapy, Visitor.

Nuclear group member. *See* Therapist surrogate.

Nude marathon. Encounter group in which members assemble for an emotional experience of prolonged duration (from a minimum of eight hours to a couple of days), with the added factor of physical nakedness as members go about their activities. The theory is that clothes are themselves defenses against openness, that they connote limiting roles and result in stereotyped responses from others, and that they allow participants to avoid facing conflicts about their own bodies. *See also* Group marathon, Sensory-experiential group.

Nymphomania. Morbid, insatiable need in women for sexual intercourse. *See also* Satyriasis.

Observer. Person who is included but is generally not an active participant in therapy sessions. His observations are later discussed in posttherapy meetings with the staff or supervisor. *See also* Recorder.

Observer therapist. *See* Passive therapist.

Obsession. Persistent idea, thought, or impulse that cannot be eliminated from consciousness by logical effort. *See also* Compulsion.

Oedipus complex. A distinct group of associated ideas, aims, instinctual drives, and fears that are generally observed in children when they are from three to six years of age. During this period, which coincides with the peak of the phallic phase of psychosexual development, the child's sexual interest is attached chiefly to the parent of the opposite sex and is accompanied by aggressive feelings and wishes for the parent of the same sex. One of Freud's most important concepts, the Oedipus complex was discovered in 1897 as a result of his self-analysis. *See also* Totem and Taboo.

Ogre. In structural analysis, the Child ego state in the father that supersedes the nurturing Parent and becomes a pseudo-Parent.

One-gender group. *See* Homogeneous group.

Open group. Treatment group in which new members are continuously added as other members leave. *See also* Closed group.

Oral dyskinesia, tardive. *See* Tardive oral dyskinesia.

Oral phase. The earliest stage in psychosexual development. It lasts through the first 18 months of life. During this period, the oral zone is the center of the infant's needs, expression, and pleasurable erotic experiences. It has a strong influence on the organization and development of the child's psyche. *See also* Anal phase, Genital phase, Infantile sexuality, Latency phase, Phallic phase.

Orientation. State of awareness of one's relationships and surroundings in terms of time, place, and person.

Orthostatic hypotension. Reduction in blood pressure brought about by a shift from a recumbent to an upright position. It is observed as a side effect of several psychotropic drugs.

Other-directed person. A person who is readily influenced and guided by the attitudes and values of other people. *See also* Inner-directed person.

Outsider. In group therapy, a member who feels alienated and isolated from the group. Such a person has usually experienced repetitive rejection in his early life and is wary of trusting people in the present. Often much effort is required by the group and the therapist before the outsider trusts someone. *See also* Nontruster.

Overt homosexuality. Behaviorally expressed homoeroticism as distinct from unconsciously held homosexual wishes or conscious wishes that are held in check. *See also* Homosexuality, Latent homosexuality.

Pairing. Term coined by Walter R. Bion to denote mutual support between two or more group members who wish to avoid the solution of their problems. The term is often used more loosely to denote an attraction between two group members.

Panic. An acute, intense attack of anxiety associated with personality disorganization. Some writers use the term exclusively for psychotic episodes of overwhelming anxiety. *See also* Homosexual panic.

Pantomime. Gesticulation; psychodrama without the use of words.

Paralogia. *See* Evasion.

Paralytic ileus. Intestinal obstruction of the nonmechanical type, secondary to paralysis of the bowel wall, that may lead to fecal retention.

It is a rare anticholinergic side effect of phenothiazine therapy.

Paramnesia. Disturbance of memory in which reality and fantasy are confused. It is observed in dreams and in certain types of schizophrenia and organic brain syndromes. *See also* Confabulation, Déjà entendu, Déjà vu, Fausse reconnaissance, Jamais vu, Retrospective falsification.

Paranoid delusion. *See* Delusion.

Parent. In transactional analysis, an ego state borrowed from a parental figure. It is also known as exteropsychic function.

Parental rejection. Denial of affection and attention to a child by one or both parents. The child in turn develops great affect hunger and hostility, which is directed either outwardly in the form of tantrums, etc., or inwardly toward himself in the form of allergies, etc.

Parkinsonism. Syndrome characterized by rhythmical muscular tremors known as pill rolling accompanied by spasticity and rigidity of movement, propulsive gait, droopy posture, and masklike facies. It is usually seen in later life as a result of arteriosclerotic changes in the basal ganglia.

Parkinsonismlike effect. Symptom that is a frequent side effect of antipsychotic drugs. Typical symptoms are motor retardation, muscular rigidity, alterations of posture, tremor, and autonomic nervous system disturbances. *See also* Phenothiazine derivative.

Partial insanity. *See* Monomania.

Passive therapist. Type of therapist who remains inactive but whose presence serves as a stimulus for the patient in the group or individual treatment setting. *See also* Active therapist, Leaderless therapeutic group, Nondirective approach.

Pastime. In transactional analysis, semistereotyped set of transactions dealing with a certain topic. Unlike Berne's term game, a pastime has no ulterior motive and no psychological payoff.

Patient peers. *See* Co-patients.

Patty-cake exercise. An encounter group technique that involves the palm-to-palm contact made by children in the game of patty-cake. This type of contact is familiar and does not usually arouse much anxiety in participants, yet it allows people to bypass verbal defenses in getting to know each other. After this exercise, the group members discuss their reactions. Also called Hand-dance.

Pecking order. Sequence of hierarchy or authority in an organization or social group. *See also* Hierarchical vector.

Peer co-therapist. Therapist who is equal in status to the other therapist treating a group and who relates to him on an equal level.

Peer-group phenomenon. Interaction or reaction of a person with a group of equals. These phenomena include activities he does within the group that he would probably not do individually outside the group.

Peer identification. Unconscious process that occurs in a group when one member incorporates within himself the qualities and attributes of another member. It usually occurs in members with low self-esteem who would like to feel at one with members who have improved.

Peer vector. *See* Horizontal vector.

Perception. Mental process by which data—intellectual, sensory, and emotional—are organized meaningfully. Through perception, a person makes sense out of the many stimuli that bombard him. It is one of the many ego functions. Therapy groups and T-groups aim to expand and alter perception in ways conducive to the development of the potential of each participant. *See also* Agnosia, Apperception, Clouding of consciousness, Ego, Hallucination, Hysterical anesthesia, Memory.

Perceptual expansion. Development of one's ability to recognize and interpret the meaning of sensory stimuli through associations with past experiences with similar stimuli. Perceptual expansion through the relaxation of defenses is one of the goals in both individual and group therapy.

Permission. In transactional analysis, a therapeutic transaction designed to permanently neutralize the parental injunctions.

Personal growth laboratory. A sensitivity training laboratory in which the primary emphasis is on each participant's potentialities for creativity, empathy, and leadership. In such a laboratory the facilitator encourages most modalities of experience and expression—such as art, sensory stimulation, and intellectual, emotional, written, oral, verbal, and nonverbal expression. *See also* National Training Laboratories.

Personality. Habitual configuration of behavior of a person, reflecting his physical and mental activities, attitudes, and interests and corresponding to the sum total of his adjustment to life.

Personality disorder. Mental disorder characterized by maladaptive patterns of adjustment to life. There is no subjective anxiety, as seen in neurosis, and no disturbance in the capacity to recognize reality, as seen in psychosis. The types of personality disorders include passive-aggressive, antisocial, schizoid, hysterical, paranoid, cyclothymic, explosive, obsessive-compulsive, asthenic, and inadequate.

Perversion. Deviation from the expected norm. In psychiatry it commonly signifies sexual perversion. *See also* Sexual deviation.

Perverted logic. *See* Evasion.

Peter Principle. Theory that man tends to advance to his level of incompetence. The idea was popularized in a book of the same name by Laurence J. Peter and Raymond Hull.

Phallic overbearance. Domination of another person by aggressive means. It is generally associated with masculinity in its negative aspects.

Phallic phase. The third stage in psychosexual development. It occurs when the child is from two to six years of age. During this period, the child's interest, curiosity, and pleasurable experiences are centered around the penis in boys and the clitoris in girls. *See also* Anal phase, Genital phase, Infantile sexuality, Latency phase, Oral phase.

Phantasy. *See* Fantasy.

Phantom limb. *See* Kinesthetic hallucination.

Phenothiazine derivative. Compound derived from phenothiazine. It is particularly known for its antipsychotic property. As a class, the phenothiazine derivatives are among the most widely used drugs in medical practice, particularly in psychiatry. Chlorpromazine, triflupromazine, fluphenazine, perphenazine, and thioridazine are some examples of phenothiazine derivatives. *See also* Anticholinergic effect, Autonomic side effect, Electrocardiographic effect, Mydriasis, Paralytic ileus, Parkinsonismlike effect.

Phobia. Pathological fear associated with some specific type of stimulus or situation. *See also* Acrophobia, Agoraphobia, Algophobia, Claustrophobia, Xenophobia, Zoophobia.

Phyloanalysis. A means of investigating disorders of human behavior, both individual and collective, resulting from impaired tensional processes that affected the organism's internal reaction as a whole. Trigant Burrow adopted the word to replace his earlier term, group analysis, which he first used in 1927 to describe the social participation of many persons in their common analysis. Because group analysis was confused with group psychotherapy of the analytic type, Burrow changed his nomenclature to phyloanalysis.

Pillow-beating. A technique used in encounter groups to elicit pent-up rage in a group member who needs to release it in a physical way. The member beats the pillow and yells angry words until he gets tired. The acceptance of his anger by the group is considered therapeutic. After this exercise, the group members discuss their reactions. *See also* Mattress-pounding.

Placebo. Inert substance prepared to resemble the active drug being tested in experimental research. It is sometimes used in clinical practice for a psychotherapeutic effect. The response to the placebo may represent the response due to the psychological effect of taking a pill and not to any pharmacological property.

Play therapy. Type of therapy used with children, usually of preschool and early latency ages. The patient reveals his problems on a fantasy level with dolls, clay, and other toys. The therapist intervenes opportunely with helpful explanations about the patient's responses and behavior in language geared to the child's comprehension. *See also* Activity group therapy.

Political therapist. A therapist who gives strong weight to the personalities of those above him as far as they impinge on his professional activities. He pays particular attention to the personal and historical aspects of authority. *See also* Authority principle, Hierarchical vector, Procedural therapist.

Popular mind. The primitive, fickle, suggestible, impulsive, uncritical type of mind that Le Bon felt was characteristic of the mass. He was referring to the unorganized crowds who lack leadership.

Postsession. *See* After-session.

Power phase. Second stage in group treatment. In this phase members start expressing anger and hostility—usually directed at the leader, sometimes directed at other members—in an attempt to achieve individuation and autonomy. *See also* Affection phase, Inclusion phase.

Pratt, Joseph H. Boston physician born in 1842 generally considered to be the first pioneer in group psychotherapy in America. He is known for his work with tuberculous patients (1900–1906). He formed discussion groups to deal with the physical aspects of tuberculosis. Later, these groups began discussing the emotional problems that stemmed from the illness. *See also* Class method.

Preconscious. In psychoanalysis, one of the three divisions of the psyche according to Freud's topographical psychology. The preconscious includes all ideas, thoughts, past experiences, and other memory impressions that can be consciously recalled with effort. *See also* Conscious, Unconscious.

Prefrontal lobotomy. *See* Lobotomy

Prejudice. Adverse judgment or opinion formed without factual knowledge. Elements of irrational suspicion or hatred are often involved, as in racial prejudice.

Premeeting. Group meeting of patients without the therapist. It is held immediately before the regular therapist-led session and is also referred to as warming-up session and presession. *See also* After-session, Alternate session.

Preoccupation of thought. *See* Trend of thought.

Pressure cooker. Slang phrase to describe the high degree of group involvement and emotional pitch sought by certain intensive groups, such as marathon groups.

Primal father. Hypothetical head of the tribe. He is depicted by Freud in *Totem and Taboo* as slain by his sons, who subsequently devour him in a cannibalistic rite. Later, he is promoted to a god. The son who murders him is the prototype of the tragic hero, and the memory of the crime is perpetuated in the conscience of the individual and of the culture.

Primal scene. In psychoanalysis, the real or fantasied observation by a child of sexual intercourse, particularly between his parents.

Primary process. In psychoanalysis, the mental process directly related to the functions of the id and characteristic of unconscious mental activity. The primary process is marked by unorganized, illogical thinking and by the tendency to seek immediate discharge and gratification of instinctual demands. *See also* Secondary process.

Probe. An encounter technique designed for a specific purpose—for instance, to determine motivation for admission to treatment. The technique is commonly used in such drug rehabilitation centers as Odyssey House.

Procedural therapist. A therapist who places the most weight on the written word, on formal rules and regulations, and on the hierarchical system. *See also* Authority principle, Political therapist.

Process-centered group. Group whose main purpose is to study the dynamics of the group itself—how it operates and through what stages it progresses. Such groups often ask the question, "What's going on here?" rather than the encounter group question, "What are you experiencing or feeling?" *See also* Group analytic psychotherapy, Group-centered psychotherapy.

Program. In transactional analysis, the teaching by one of the parents of how best to comply with the script injunction.

Projection. Unconscious defense mechanism in which a person attributes to another the ideas, thoughts, feelings, and impulses that are part of his inner perceptions but that are unacceptable to him. Projection protects the person from anxiety arising from an inner conflict. By externalizing whatever is unacceptable, the person deals with it as a situation apart from himself. *See also* Blind spot, Future projection.

Projective method. Group treatment proce-

dure that uses the spontaneous creative work of the patients. For example, group members make and analyze drawings, which are often expressions of their underlying emotional problems.

Protagonist. In psychodrama, the patient who is the focal point of a psychodramatic session. He is asked to be himself, to portray his own private world on the stage.

Pseudoauthenticity. False or copied expression of thoughts and feelings.

Pseudocollusion. Sense of closeness, relationship, or cooperation that is not real but is based on transference.

Psychic determinism. Freudian adaptation of the concept of causality. It states that all phenomena or events have antecedent causes that operate on an unconscious level, beyond the control of the person involved.

Psychoactive drug. Drug that alters thoughts, feelings, or perceptions. Such a drug may help a person in either individual or group therapy overcome depression, anxiety, or rigidity of thought and behavior while he learns new methods of perceiving and responding.

Psychoanalysis. Freud's method of psychic investigation and form of psychotherapy. As a technique for exploring the mental processes, psychoanalysis includes the use of free association and the analysis and interpretation of dreams, resistances, and transferences. As a form of psychotherapy, it uses the investigative technique, guided by Freud's libido and instinct theories and by ego psychology, to gain insight into a person's unconscious motivations, conflicts, and symbols and thus to effect a change in his maladaptive behavior. Several schools of thought are loosely referred to as psychoanalytic at present. Psychoanalysis is also known as analysis in depth.

Psychoanalytically oriented group psychotherapy. *See* Psychoanalytic group psychotherapy.

Psychoanalytic group psychotherapy. A major method of group psychotherapy, pioneered by Alexander Wolf and based on the operational principles of individual psychoanalytic therapy. Analysis and interpretation of a patient's transferences, resistances, and defenses are modified to take place in a group setting. Although strictly designating treatment structured to produce significant character change, the term encompasses the same approach in groups conducted at more superficial levels for lesser goals. *See also* Collective family transference neurosis, Discussion model of group psychotherapy, Verbal-deep approach.

Psychoanalytic treatment. *See* Psychoanalysis.

Psychodrama. Psychotherapy method originated by J. L. Moreno in which personality make-up, interpersonal relationships, conflicts, and emotional problems are explored by means of dramatic methods. The therapeutic dramatization of emotional problems includes: (1) protagonist or patient, the person who presents and acts out his emotional problems with the help of (2) auxiliary egos, persons trained to act and dramatize the different aspects of the patient that are called for in a particular scene in order to help him express his feelings, and (3) director, leader, or therapist, the person who guides those involved in the drama for a fruitful and therapeutic session. *See also* Actional-deep approach, Analytic psychodrama, Concretization of living, Didactic psychodrama, Hallucinatory psychodrama, Hypnodrama, Improvisation, Maximal expression, Mirror, Re-enactment, Regressive-reconstructive approach, Role-playing, Role reversal, Self-realization.

Psychodramatic director. Leader of a psychodrama session. The director has three functions: producer, therapist, and analyst. As producer, he turns every clue the patient offers into dramatic action. As therapist, he attacks and shocks the patient at times, laughs and jokes with him at times, and becomes indirect and passive at times. As analyst, he interprets and elicits responses from the audience.

Psychodramatic shock. *See* Hallucinatory psychodrama.

Psychodynamics. Science of the mind, its mental processes, and affective components that influence human behavior and motivations. *See also* Group dynamics, Infantile dynamics.

Psychological defense system. *See* Defense mechanism.

Psychological procedure. Any technique intended to alter a person's attitude toward and perception of himself and others. *See also* Group psychotherapy, Psychoanalysis, Psychotherapy.

Psychomotor stimulant. Drug that arouses the patient through its central excitatory and analeptic properties. Amphetamine and methylphenidate are drugs in this class.

Psychopathology. Branch of science that deals with morbidity of the mind.

Psychophysiological disorder. Mental disorder characterized by physical symptoms of psychic origin. It usually involves a single organ system innervated by the autonomic nervous system. The physiological and organic changes stem from a sustained emotional disturbance.

Psychosexual development. Maturation and development of the psychic phase of sexuality from birth to adult life. Its phases are oral, anal, phallic, latency, and genital. *See also* Identification with the aggressor, Infantile sexuality.

Psychosis. Mental disorder in which a person's mental capacity, affective response, and capacity to recognize reality, communicate, and relate to others are impaired enough to interfere with his capacity to deal with the ordinary demands of life. The psychoses are subdivided into two major classifications according to their origin—psychoses associated with organic brain syndromes and functional psychoses.

Psychosomatic illness. *See* Psychophysiological disorder.

Psychosurgery. *See* Lobotomy.

Psychotherapy. Form of treatment for mental illness and behavioral disturbances in which a trained person establishes a professional contract with the patient and through definite therapeutic communication, both verbal and nonverbal, attempts to alleviate the emotional disturbance, reverse or change maladaptive patterns of behavior, and encourage personality growth and development. Psychotherapy is distinguished from such other forms of psychiatric treatment as the use of drugs, surgery, electric shock treatment, and insulin coma treatment. *See also* Growth psychotherapy, Individual therapy, Psychoanalysis.

Psychotomimetic drug. Drug that produces psychic and behavioral changes that resemble psychosis. Unlike other drugs that can produce organic psychosis as a reaction, a psychotomimetic drug does not produce overt memory impairment. It is also known as a hallucinogenic drug. Lysergic acid diethylamide (LSD), tetrahydrocannabinol, and mescaline are examples of psychotomimetic drugs.

Psychotropic drug. Drug that affects psychic function and behavior. Also known as a phrenotropic drug, it may be classified as an antipsychotic drug, antidepressant drug, antimanic drug, antianxiety drug, or hallucinogenic drug. *See also* Agranulocytosis, Orthostatic hypotension.

Public self. The behavior, feelings, and motivations of a person known both to himself and to others. It is a quadrant of the Johari Window, a diagrammatic concept of human behavior. *See also* Blind self, Hidden self, Undeveloped potential.

Quadrangular therapy. A type of marital therapy that involves four people: the married pair and each spouse's therapist. *See also* Collaborative therapy, Combined therapy, Concurrent therapy, Conjoint therapy, Family therapy, Group marital therapy, Marriage therapy, Square interview.

Rank, Otto (1884–1939). Austrian psychoanalyst. He was one of Freud's earliest followers and the long-time secretary and recorder of the minutes of the Vienna Psychoanalytic Society He wrote such fundamental works as *The Myth of the Birth of the Hero*. He split with Freud on the significance of the birth trauma, which he used as a basis of brief psychotherapy.

Rapport. Conscious, harmonious accord that usually reflects a good relationship between two persons. In a group, rapport is the presence of mutual responsiveness, as evidenced by spontaneous and sympathetic reaction to each other's needs, sentiments, and attitudes. *See also* Countertransference, Transference.

Rap session. *See* Bull session.

Rationalization. An unconscious defense mechanism in which an irrational behavior, motive, or feeling is made to appear reasonable. Ernest Jones introduced the term.

Reaction formation. An unconscious defense mechanism in which a person develops a socialized attitude or interest that is the direct antithesis of some infantile wish or impulse in the

unconscious. One of the earliest and most unstable defense mechanisms, it is closely related to repression; both are defenses against impulses or urges that are unacceptable to the ego.

Reality. The totality of objective things and factual events. Reality includes everything that is perceived by a person's special senses and is validated by other people.

Reality-testing. Fundamental ego function that consists of the objective evaluation and judgment of the world outside the self. By interacting with his animate and inanimate environment, a person tests its real nature as well as his own relation to it. How the person evaluates reality and his attitudes toward it are determined by early experiences with the significant persons in his life. *See also* Ego.

Recall. Process of remembering thoughts, words, and actions of a past event in an attempt to recapture what actually happened. It is part of a complex mental function known as memory. *See also* Amnesia, Hypermnesia.

Recathexis. In transactional analysis, the experiencing of different ego states.

Recognition. *See* Memory.

Reconstructive psychotherapy. A form of therapy that seeks not only to alleviate symptoms but to produce alterations in maladaptive character structures and to expedite new adaptive potentials. This aim is achieved by bringing into consciousness an awareness of and insight into conflicts, fears, inhibitions, and their derivatives. *See also* Psychoanalysis.

Recorder. Person who takes notes during the group or individual therapy session. Also referred to as the recorder-observer, he generally does not participate in therapy. *See also* Observer.

Re-enactment. In psychodrama, the acting out of a past experience as if it were happening in the present so that a person can feel, perceive, and act as he did the first time.

Registration. *See* Memory.

Regression. Unconscious defense mechanism in which a person undergoes a partial or total return to earlier patterns of adaptation. Regression is observed in many psychiatric conditions, particularly schizophrenia.

Regressive-reconstructive approach. A psychotherapeutic procedure in which regression is made an integral element of the treatment process. The original traumatic situation is reproduced to gain new insight and to effect significant personality change and emotional maturation. *See also* Psychoanalysis, Reconstructive psychotherapy.

Reik, Theodor (1888–1969). Psychoanalyst and early follower of Freud, who considered him one of his most brilliant pupils. Freud's book, *The Question of Lay Analysis* was written to defend Reik's ability to practice psychoanalysis without medical training. Reik made many valuable contributions to psychoanalysis on the subjects of religion, masochism, and technique. *See also* Third ear.

Relatedness. Sense of sympathy and empathy with regard to others; sense of oneness with others. It is the opposite of isolation and alienation.

Reparenting. A technique evolved in transactional analysis for the treatment of schizophrenia. The patient is first regressed to a Child ego state, and then missing Parent transactions are supplied and contaminations corrected.

Repeater. Group member who has had experience in another group.

Repetitive pattern. Continual attitude or mode of behavior characteristic of a person and performed mechanically or unconsciously.

Repression. An unconscious defense mechanism in which a person removes from consciousness those ideas, impulses, and affects that are unacceptable to him. A term introduced by Freud, it is important in both normal psychological development and in neurotic and psychotic symptom formation. Freud recognized two kinds of repression: (1) repression proper—the repressed material was once in the conscious domain; (2) primal repression—the repressed material was never in the conscious realm. *See also* Suppression.

Repressive-inspirational group psychotherapy. A type of group therapy in which discussion is intended to bolster patients' morale and help them avoid undesired feelings. It is used

primarily with large groups of seriously regressed patients in institutional settings.

Reserpine. An alkaloid extracted from the root of the *Rauwolfia serpentina* plant. It is used primarily as an antihypertensive agent. It was formerly used as an antipsychotic agent because of its sedative effect.

Residential treatment facility. A center where the patient lives and receives treatment appropriate for his particular needs. A children's residential treatment facility ideally furnishes both educational and therapeutic experiences for the emotionally disturbed child.

Resistance. A conscious or unconscious opposition to the uncovering of the unconscious. Resistance is linked to underlying psychological defense mechanisms against impulses from the id that are threatening to the ego. *See also* Group resistance.

Resonance. Unconscious response determined by early life experiences. In a group, a member may respond by fantasizing at a particular level of psychosexual development when another member functions regressively at that level. The unconscious sounding board is constructed in the first five years of life. *See also* Focal-conflict theory.

Retardation. Slowness of development or progress. In psychiatry there are two types, mental retardation and psychomotor retardation. Mental retardation refers to slowness or arrest of intellectual maturation. Psychomotor retardation refers to slowness or slackened psychic activity or motor activity or both; it is observed in pathological depression.

Retention. *See* Memory.

Retrospective falsification. Recollection of false memory. *See also* Paramnesia.

Review session. Meeting in which each member reviews with the group his goals and progress in treatment. It is a technique used in structured interactional group psychotherapy.

Ritual. Automatic activity of psychogenic or cultural origin. *See also* Group ritual.

Role. Pattern of behavior that a person takes. It has its roots in childhood and is influenced by significant people with whom the person had primary relationships. When the behavior pattern conforms with the expectations and demands of other people, it is said to be a complementary role. If it does not conform with the demands and expectation of others, it is known as noncomplementary role. *See also* Identification, Injunction, Therapeutic role.

Role-divided therapy. Therapeutic arrangement in a co-therapy situation when each therapist takes on a specific function in treatment. For example, one therapist may take the role of a provocateur, while the other takes the role of a passive observer and interpreter. *See also* Splitting situation.

Role limit. Boundary placed on the therapist or the patient by virtue of his conscious position in the therapy group. The patient plays the patient, and the therapist plays the therapist; there is no reversal of roles.

Role model. In a therapeutic community or methadone program, an ex-addict who, because of his successful adjustment and similarity of experience with the patient population, becomes a source of positive identification and a tangible proof of success. *See also* Ego model.

Role-playing. Psychodrama technique in which a person is trained to function more effectively in his reality roles—such as employer, employee, student, and instructor. In the therapeutic setting of psychodrama, the protagonist is free to try and to fail in his role, for he is given the opportunity to try again until he finally learns new approaches to the situation he fears, approaches that he can then apply outside. *See also* Antirepression device.

Role reversal. Technique used in psychodrama whereby an auxiliary ego plays the role of the patient, and the patient plays the role of the other person. Distortions of interpersonal perception are thereby brought to the surface, explored, and corrected.

Role-training. *See* Role-playing.

Roll and rock. An encounter group technique that is used to develop trust in a participant. A person stands, with eyes closed, in a tight circle of group members and is passed around (rolled) from member to member. Then he is placed on his back on the floor, gently lifted by the group members, and rocked back and forth. He is then put back on the floor. After this exercise, the group members discuss their reactions.

Rosander anti-Negro behavior scale. A scale that measures white attitudes toward blacks by asking respondents what their behavior would be in various hypothetical situations involving black participants. The scale can be of aid in determining the degree of prejudice held by whites toward blacks and the influence of a group experience on such prejudices. *See also* Ford negative personal contacts with Negroes scale, Ford negative personal contacts with whites scale, Kelley desegregation scale, Steckler anti-Negro scale, Steckler anti-white scale.

Rosenberg self-esteem scale. A scale designed to measure a person's opinion of himself. Use of this scale gives the therapist a means of evaluating the effect a group experience has on a member's self-esteem.

Saboteur. One who obstructs progress within a group, either deliberately or unconsciously.

Sadism. A sexual deviation in which sexual gratification is achieved by inflicting pain and humiliation on the partner. Donatien Alphonse François de Sade (1740–1814), a French writer, was the first person to describe this condition. *See also* Masochism, Sadomasochistic relationship.

Sadomasochistic relationship. Relationship in which the enjoyment of suffering by one person and the enjoyment of inflicting pain by the other person are important and complementary attractions in their on-going relationship. *See also* Masochism, Sadism.

Satyriasis. Morbid, insatiable sexual needs or desires in men. It may be caused by organic or psychiatric factors. *See also* Nymphomania.

Schilder, Paul (1886–1940). American neuropsychiatrist. He started the use of group psychotherapy at New York's Bellevue Hospital, combining social and psychoanalytic principles.

Schizophrenia. Mental disorder of psychotic level characterized by disturbances in thinking, mood, and behavior. The thinking disturbance is manifested by a distortion of reality, especially by delusions and hallucinations, accompanied by fragmentation of associations that results in incoherent speech. The mood disturbance is manifested by inappropriate affective responses. The behavior disturbance is manifested by ambivalence, apathetic withdrawal, and bizarre activity. Formerly known as dementia praecox, schizophrenia as a term was introduced by Eugen Bleuler. The causes of schizophrenia remain unknown. The types of schizophrenia include simple type, hebephrenic type, catatonic type, paranoid type, schizo-affective type, childhood type, residual type, latent type, acute schizophrenic episode, and chronic undifferentiated type.

Schreber case. One of Freud's cases. It involved the analysis in 1911 of Daniel Paul Shreber's autobiographical account, *Memoirs of a Neurotic,* published in 1903. Analysis of these memoirs permitted Freud to decipher the fundamental meaning of paranoid processes and ideas, especially the relationship between repressed homosexuality and projective defenses.

Screening. Initial patient evaluation that includes medical and psychiatric history, mental status evaluation, and diagnostic formulation to determine the patient's suitability for a particular treatment modality.

Script. In transactional analysis, a complex set of transactions that are adaptations of infantile responses and experiences. The script is recurrent and operates on an unconscious level. It is the mold on which a person's life adaptation is based. *See also* Hamartic script.

Script analysis. The analysis of a person's life adaption—that is, his injunctions, decisions, and life scripts—and the therapeutic process that helps reverse the maladaptive behavior. It is the last phase in transactional analysis. *See also* Game analysis, Structural analysis.

Script antithesis. In transactional analysis, a therapeutic transaction designed to avert temporarily a tragic event in a script. *See also* Script, Script matrix.

Script matrix. Diagram used in transactional analysis to represent two parents and an offspring. It is useful in representing the genesis of life scripts. *See also* Script, Script antithesis.

Secondary process. In psychoanalysis, the mental process directly related to the functions of the ego and characteristic of conscious and preconscious mental activities. The secondary process is marked by logical thinking and by the tendency to delay gratification by regulation of discharge of instinctual demands. *See also* Primary process.

Sedative. Drug that produces a calming or relaxing effect through central nervous system depression. Some drugs with sedative properties are barbiturates, chloral hydrate, paraldehyde, and bromide.

Selective inattention. An aspect of attentiveness in which a person blocks out those areas that generate anxiety.

Self-analysis. Investigation of one's own psychic components. It plays a part in all analysis, although to a limited extent, since few are capable of sustaining independent and detached attitudes for it to be therapeutic.

Self-awareness. Sense of knowing what one is experiencing. For example, realizing that one has just responded with anger to another group member as a substitute for the anxiety felt when he attacked a vital part of one's self concept. Self-awareness is a major goal of all therapy, individual and group.

Self-discovery. In psychoanalysis, the freeing of the repressed ego in a person who has been brought up to submit to the wishes of the significant others around him.

Self-presentation. Psychodrama technique in which the patient plays the role of himself and of related persons (father, mother, brother, etc.) as he perceives them in a completely subjective manner.

Self-realization. Psychodrama technique in which the protagonist enacts, with the aid of a few auxiliary egos, the plan of his life, no matter how remote it may be from his present situation. For instance, an accountant who has been taking singing lessons, hoping to try out for a musical comedy part in summer stock, and planning to make the theatre his life's work can explore the effects of success in this venture and of possible failure and return to his old livelihood.

Sensation. Feeling or impression when the sensory nerve endings of any of the six senses—taste, touch, smell, sight, kinesthesia, and sound—are stimulated.

Sensitivity training group. Group in which members seek to develop self-awareness and an understanding of group processes rather than gain relief from an emotional disturbance. *See also* Encounter group, Personal growth laboratory, T-group.

Sensorium. Theoretical sensory center located in the brain that is involved with a person's awareness about his surroundings. In psychiatry, it is often referred to as consciousness.

Sensory-experiential group. An encounter group that is primarily concerned with the emotional and physical interaction of the participants. The experience itself, not the examination of the group process, is considered the *raison d'être* for the group.

Serotonin. A monoamine that is believed to be a neurohumoral transmitter. It is found in the serum and, in high concentrations, in the hypothalamus of the brain. Recent pharmacological investigations link depression to disorders in the metabolism of serotonin and other biogenic amines, such as norepinephrine.

Session leader. *See* Facilitator.

Sexual deviation. Mental disorder characterized by sexual interests and behavior other than what is culturally accepted. Sexual deviation includes sexual interest in objects other than a person of the opposite sex, such as homosexuality or bestiality; bizarre sexual practices, such as necrophilia; and other sexual activities that are not accompanied by copulation. *See also* Bestiality, Exhibitionism, Homosexuality, Masochism, Sadism.

Sexual drive. One of the two primal instincts (the other is the aggressive drive) according to Freud's dual-instinct theory of 1920. It is also known as eros and life instinct. Its main goal is to preserve and maintain life. It operates under the influence of the pleasure-unpleasure principle. *See also* Aggressive drive, Libido theory.

Shifting attention. A characteristic of group therapy in which the focus changes from one patient to another so that no one patient remains continuously in the spotlight. It is also known as alternating scrutiny. *See also* Structured interactional group psychotherapy.

Shock treatment. A form of psychiatric treatment with a chemical substance (ingested, inhaled, or injected) or sufficient electric current to produce a convulsive seizure and unconsciousness. It is used in certain types of schizophrenia

and mood disorders. Shock treatment's mechanism of action is still unknown.

Sibling rivalry. Competition among children for the attention, affection, and esteem of their parents. The children's jealousy is accompanied by hatred and death wishes toward each other. The rivalry need not be limited to actual siblings; it is a factor in both normal and abnormal competitiveness throughout life.

Slavson, S. R. (1890–). American theoretician who pioneered in group psychotherapy based on psychoanalytic principles. In his work with children, from which he derived most of his concepts, he introduced and developed activity group therapy. *See also* Collective experience.

Sleep. A temporary physiological state of unconsciousness characterized by a reversible cessation of the person's waking sensorimotor activity. A biological need, sleep recurs periodically to rest the whole body and to regenerate neuromuscular tissue. *See also* Dream.

Social adaptation. Adjustment to the whole complex of interpersonal relationships; the ability to live and express oneself in accordance with society's restrictions and cultural demands. *See also* Adaptational approach.

Social configuration. Arrangement of interpersonal interactions. *See also* Hierarchical vector, Horizontal vector.

Social instinct. *See* Herd instinct.

Socialization. Process of learning interpersonal and interactional skills according to and in conformity with one's society. In a group therapy setting, it includes a member's way of participating both mentally and physically in the group. *See also* Interpersonal skill.

Social network therapy. A type of group therapy in which the therapist assembles all the persons—relatives, friends, social relations, work relations—who have emotional or functional significance in the patient's life. Some or all of the social network may be assembled at any given time. *See also* Extended family therapy, Visitor.

Social psychiatry. Branch of psychiatry interested in ecological, sociological, and cultural variables that engender, intensify, or complicate maladaptive patterns of behavior and their treatment.

Social therapy. A rehabilitative form of therapy with psychiatric patients. The aim is to improve social functioning. Occupational therapy, therapeutic community, recreational therapy, milieu therapy, and attitude therapy are forms of social therapy.

Sociogram. Diagrammatic portrayal of choices, rejections, and indifferences of a number of persons involved in a life situation.

Sociometric distance. The measurable degree of perception one person has for another. It can be hypothesized that the greater the sociometric distance between persons, the more inaccurate will be their social evaluation of their relationship.

Sociometric feedback. Information that people give each other about how much closeness or distance they desire between them. It is a measure of how social one would like to be with another. An example of sociometric feedback would be the answer by a group member to the question, "With what three members of this group would you prefer to spend six months on a desert island?"

Sociometrist. Social investigator engaged in measuring the interpersonal relations and social structures in a community.

Soliloquy. *See* Therapeutic soliloquy.

Somnambulism. Sleepwalking; motor activity during sleep. It is commonly seen in children. In adults, it is observed in persons with schizoid personality disorders and certain types of schizophrenia.

Splitting situation. Condition in a co-therapy group. A patient is often unable to express opposite feelings toward one therapist. The splitting situation allows him to express contrasting feelings—positive-love feeling and negative-hostile feeling—by directing one feeling at one co-therapist and the opposite feeling at the other co-therapist. *See also* Role-divided therapy.

Splitting transference. Breaking of an irrational feeling or attitude into its component parts, which are then assigned to different persons. For example, ambivalence toward a mother may be expressed in a group by reacting to one member as to a good mother and reacting to another member as to a bad mother.

Square interview. Occasional session in marriage therapy in which both spouses and each spouse's therapist are present. The therapists and sometimes the patients are able to observe, experience, and respond to the transactional dynamics among the four of them, thus encouraging a common viewpoint by all four people involved in marital therapy. *See also* Collaborative therapy, Combined therapy, Concurrent therapy, Conjoint therapy, Group marital therapy, Marriage therapy, Quadrangular therapy.

Square situation. *See* Quadrangular therapy, Square interview.

Squeaky wheel. Person who is continually calling attention to himself. Because of his style of interacting, he is likely to get more than his share of a group's effort and energy.

Status value. Worth of a person in terms of such criteria as income, social prestige, intelligence, and education. It is considered an important parameter of one's position in the society.

Steckler anti-Negro scale. A scale designed to measure the attitude of Negroes toward Negroes. It can be of use in ascertaining the degree of prejudice blacks have against their own race and in evaluating the corrective efficacy of group experience. *See also* Ford negative personal contacts with Negroes scale, Ford negative personal contacts with whites scale, Kelley desegregation scale, Rosander anti-Negro behavior scale.

Steckler anti-white scale. A scale designed to measure the attitudes of Negroes toward whites. It can be used to ascertain the amount of prejudice blacks have against whites and to evaluate the influence of a group experience. *See also* Ford negative personal contacts with Negroes scale, Ford negative personal contacts with whites scale, Kelley desegregation scale.

Stegreiftheater. *See* Theatre of Spontaneity.

Stekel, Wilhelm (1868–1940). Viennese psychoanalyst. He suggested the formation of the first Freudian group, the Wednesday Evening Society, which later became the Vienna Psychoanalytic Society. A man given to intuition rather than to systematic research, his insight into dreams proved stimulating and added to the knowledge of symbols. Nevertheless, his superficial wild analysis proved incompatible with the Freudian school. He introduced the word thanatos to signify death wish.

Stereotypy. Continuous repetition of speech or physical activities. It is observed in cases of catatonic schizophrenia.

Stimulant. Drug that affects one or more organ systems to produce an exciting or arousing effect, increase physical activity and vivacity, and promote a sense of well-being. There are, for example, central nervous system stimulants, cardiac stimulants, respiratory stimulants, and psychomotor stimulants.

Stress immunity. Failure to react to emotional stress.

Stroke. In transactional analysis, a unit of human recognition. Early in life, strokes must involve physical contact; later in life, strokes can be symbolic—such as, "Glad to see you!"

Structural analysis. Analysis of the personality into its constituent ego states. The goal of structural analysis is to establish and maintain the predominance of reality-testing ego states, free from contamination. It is considered the first phase of transactional analysis. *See also* Contamination, Ego state, Game analysis, Ogre, Script analysis, Transactional analysis.

Structured interactional group psychotherapy. A type of group psychotherapy, developed by Harold Kaplan and Benjamin Sadock, in which the therapist provides a structural matrix for the group's interactions. The important part of the structure is that a different member of the group is the focus of the interaction in each session. *See also* Forced interaction, Go-around, Up.

Studies on Hysteria. Title of a book by Josef Breuer and Sigmund Freud. Published in 1895, it described the cathartic method of treatment and the beginnings of psychoanalysis. It demonstrated the psychological origins of hysterical symptoms and the possibility of effecting a cure through psychotherapy.

Stupor. Disturbance of consciousness in which the patient is nonreactive to and unaware of his surroundings. Organically, it is synonymous with unconsciousness. In psychiatry, it is referred to as mutism and is commonly found in catatonia and psychotic depression.

Subjectivity. Qualitative appraisal and interpretation of an object or experience as influenced by one's own feelings and thinking.

Subject session. Group technique, used particularly in structured interactional group psychotherapy, in which a topic is introduced by the therapist or a group member and is then explored by the whole group.

Sublimation. An unconscious defense mechanism in which unacceptable instinctual drives are diverted into personally and socially acceptable channels. Unlike other defense mechanisms, sublimation offers some minimal gratification of the instinctual drive or impulse.

Substituting. Providing a nonverbal alternate for something a patient missed in his early life. Crossing the room to sit beside a group member who needs support is an example of substituting.

Substitution. An unconscious defense mechanism in which a person replaces an unacceptable wish, drive, emotion, or goal with one that is more acceptable.

Suggestibility. State of compliant responsiveness to an idea or influence. It is commonly observed among persons with hysterical traits.

Sullivan, Harry Stack (1892–1949). American psychiatrist. He is best known for his interpersonal theory of psychiatry. *See also* Consensual validation.

Summer session. In structured interactional group psychotherapy, regularly scheduled group session during the therapist's vacation.

Superego. One of the three component parts of the psychic apparatus. The other two are the ego and the id. Freud created the theoretical concept of the superego to describe the psychic functions that are expressed in moral attitudes, conscience, and a sense of guilt. The superego results from the internalization of the ethical standards of the society in which the person lives, and it develops by identification with the attitudes of his parents. It is mainly unconscious and is believed to develop as a reaction to the Oedipus complex. It has a protective and rewarding function, referred to as the ego ideal, and a critical and punishing function, which evokes the sense of guilt.

Support. *See* Mutual support.

Suppression. Conscious act of controlling and inhibiting an unacceptable impulse, emotion, or idea. Suppression is differentiated from repression in that the latter is an unconscious process.

Surplus reality. The intangible, invisible dimensions of intrapsychic and extrapsychic life. The term was coined by J. L. Moreno.

Survival. Game used in a professionally homogeneous group. It is designed to create awareness of one another's talents. An imaginary situation is created in which the members are no longer permitted to continue in their particular professions and must, as a group, find some other activity in which to work together meaningfully and profitably. *See also* Game, Hit-and-run game, Million-dollar game.

Symbolization. An unconscious defense mechanism whereby one idea or object comes to stand for another because of some common aspect or quality in both. Symbolization is based on similarity and association. The symbols formed protect the person from the anxiety that may be attached to the original idea or object. *See also* Defense mechanism.

Sympathomimetic drug. Drug that mimics the actions of the sympathetic nervous system. Examples of these drugs are amphetamine and epinephrine.

Sympathy. Sharing of another person's feelings, ideas, and experiences. As opposed to empathy, sympathy is not objective. *See also* Identification, Imitation.

Symptom formation. *See* Symptom substitution.

Symptom substitution. Unconscious psychic process in which a repressed impulse is indirectly released and manifested through a symptom. Such symptoms as obsession, compulsion, phobia, dissociation, anxiety, depression, hallucination, and delusion are examples of symptom substitution. It is also known as symptom formation.

Tachylogia. *See* Logorrhea.

Tactile hallucination. False sense of touch.

Tangentiality. Disturbance in the associative thought processes in which the patient is unable to express his idea. In contrast to circumstantiality, the digression in tangentiality is such that the central idea is not communicated. It is observed in schizophrenia and certain types of organic brain disorders. Tangentiality is also known as derailment. *See also* Circumstantiality.

Tardive oral dyskinesia. A syndrome characterized by involuntary movements of the lips and jaw and by other bizarre involuntary dystonic movements. It is an extrapyramidal effect occurring late in the course of antipsychotic drug therapy.

Target patient. Group member who is perceptively analyzed by another member. It is a term used in the process of going around in psychoanalytically oriented groups.

Task-oriented group. Group whose main energy is devoted to reaching a goal, finding a solution to a problem, or building a product. Distinguished from this type of group is the experiential group, which is mainly concerned with sharing whatever happens. *See also* Action group.

Tele. In psychodrama, an objective social process that strengthens association and promotes cohesiveness in groups. It is believed to function on the basis of transference and empathy.

Tension. An unpleasurable alteration of affect characterized by a strenuous increase in mental and physical activity.

Termination. Orderly conclusion of a group member's therapy or of the whole group's treatment as contrasted with a drop-out that is not advised by the therapist.

T-group (training group). A type of group that emphasizes training in self-awareness and group dynamics. *See also* Action group, Intervention laboratory, National Training Laboratories, Sensitivity training.

Thanatos. Death wish. *See also* Stekel, Wilhelm.

Theatre of Spontaneity (Stegreiftheater). Theatre in Vienna which improvised group processes and which was developed by J. L. Moreno, M.D.

Theoretical orientation. Alignment with a hypothetical point of view already espoused by a person or group.

Therapeutic agent. Anything—people and/or drugs—that causes healing in a maladaptive person. In group therapy, it refers mainly to people who help others.

Therapeutic alliance. Conscious relationship between therapist and patient in which each implicitly agrees that they need to work together by means of insight and control to help the patient with his conflicts. It involves a therapeutic splitting of the patient's ego into observing and experiencing parts. A good therapeutic alliance is especially necessary during phases of strong negative transference in order to keep the treatment going. It is as important in group as in dyadic psychotherapy. *See also* Working alliance.

Therapeutic atmosphere. All therapeutic, maturational, and growth-supporting agents—cultural, social, and medical.

Therapeutic community. Ward or hospital treatment setting that provides an effective environment for behavioral changes in patients through resocialization and rehabilitation.

Therapeutic crisis. Turning point in the treatment process. An example is acting out, which, depending on how it is dealt with, may or may not lead to a therapeutic change in the patient's behavior. *See also* Therapeutic impasse.

Therapeutic group. Group of patients joined together under the leadership of a therapist for the purpose of working together for psychotherapeutic ends—specifically, for the treatment of each patient's emotional disorders.

Therapeutic group analysis. *See* Group analytic psychotherapy.

Therapeutic impasse. Deadlock in the treatment process. Therapy is in a state of imminent failure when there is no further insight or awareness and sessions are reduced to routine meetings of patient and therapist. Unresolved resistances and transference and countertransference conflicts are among the common causes of this phenomenon. *See also* Therapeutic crisis.

Therapeutic role. Position in which one aims to treat, bring about an improvement, or provide alleviation of a distressing condition or state.

Therapeutic soliloquy. Psychodrama technique that involves a patient's portrayal—by side dialogues and side actions—of his hidden

thoughts and feelings that parallel his overt thoughts and actions.

Therapeutic transaction. Interplay between therapist and patient or among group members that is intended to improve the patient.

Therapist surrogate. Group member who—by virtue of experience, intuition, or training—is able to be an effective group leader in the absence of or in concert with the group therapist. He is also known as a nuclear group member. *See also* Leaderless therapeutic group.

There-and-then. Past experience rather than immediate experience. *See also* Here-and-now.

Thinking. *See* Cognition.

Thinking compulsion. *See* Intellectualization.

Thinking through. The mental process that occurs in an attempt to understand one's own behavior and gain insight from it.

Third ear. Ability to make use of intuition, sensitivity, and awareness of subliminal cues to interpret clinical observations of individual and group patients. First introduced by the German philosopher Frederic Nietzsche, it was later used in analytic psychotherapy by Theodor Reik.

Thought deprivation. *See* Blocking.

Thought process disorder. A symptom of schizophrenia that involves the intellectual functions. It is manifested by irrelevance and incoherence of the patient's verbal productions. It ranges from simple blocking and mild circumstantiality to total loosening of associations, as in word salad.

Three-cornered therapy. *See* Co-therapy.

Three Essays on the Theory of Sexuality. Title of a book by Freud. Published in 1905, it applied the libido theory to the successive phases of sex instinct maturation in the infant, child, and adolescent. It made possible the integration of a vast diversity of clinical observations and promoted the direct observation of child development.

Tic. Involuntary, spasmodic, repetitive motor movement of a small segment of the body. Mainly psychogenic, it may be seen in certain cases of chronic encephalitis.

Timidity. Inability to assert oneself for fear of some fancied reprisal, even though there is no objective evidence of potential harm. In a therapy group, the timid person may make others fear the destructiveness of their normal aggression.

Tinnitus. Noises in one or both ears, such as ringing and whistling. It is an occasional side effect of some of the antidepressant drugs.

Tolerance. In group therapy, the willingness to put up with disordered behavior by co-patients in the group.

Too-tired-to-be-polite phenomenon. Phenomenon in a marathon group that stems from fatigue and results in the relaxation of the social facades of politeness. Some proponents of marathon groups have stressed the helpfulness of fatigue in breaking through the social games that participants play in the early stages of the group. *See also* Group marathon.

Totem and Taboo. Title of a book by Freud. Published in 1913, it applied his concepts to the data of anthropology. He was able to afford much insight into the meaning of tribal organizations and customs, especially by invoking the Oedipus complex and the characteristics of magical thought as he had discovered them from studies of the unconscious. *See also* Oedipus complex, Primal father.

Toucher. Someone who enjoys touching another person. When the touching is not of the clinging type, such a person in an encounter group usually helps inhibited people lose their anxiety about physical contact and closeness.

Traditional group therapy. Group therapy of a conventional type in which the role of the therapist is clearly delineated and the other participants are understood to be clients or patients who are attending the group meetings to overcome or resolve some definite emotional problems. *See also* Encounter group, Group psychotherapy, Sensitivity training.

Trainer. Professional leader or facilitator of a sensitivity training or T-group; teacher or supervisor of a person learning the science and practice of group therapy.

Training group. *See* T-group.

Tranquilizer. Psychotropic drug that induces tranquility by calming, soothing, quieting, or pacifying without clouding the conscious. The major tranquilizers are antipsychotic drugs, and the minor tranquilizers are antianxiety drugs.

Transaction. Interaction that arises when two or more persons have an encounter. In transactional analysis, it is considered the unit of social interaction. It involves a stimulus and a response. *See also* Complementarity of interaction, Forced interaction, Group stimulus, Structured interactional group psychotherapy, Therapeutic transaction.

Transactional analysis. A system introduced by Eric Berne that centers on the study of interactions going on in the treatment sessions. The system includes four components: (1) structural analysis of intrapsychic phenomena; (2) transactional analysis proper, the determination of the currently dominant ego state (Parent, Child, or Adult) of each participant; (3) game analysis, identification of the games played in their interactions and of the gratifications provided; and (4) script analysis, uncovering of the causes of the patient's emotional problems.

Transactional group psychotherapy. A system of therapy founded by Eric Berne. It is based on the analysis of interactions and on the understanding of patterns of transactions as they occur during treatment sessions. Social control is the main goal of therapy.

Transference. Unconscious phenomenon in which the feelings, attitudes, and wishes originally linked with important figures in one's early life are projected onto others who have come to represent them in current life. *See also* Countertransference, Lateral transference, Multiple transference, Rapport, Transference neurosis.

Transference neurosis. A phenomenon occurring in psychoanalysis in which the patient develops a strong emotional attachment to the therapist as a symbolized nuclear familial figure. The repetition and depth of this misperception or symbolization characterize it as a transference neurosis. In transference analysis, a major therapeutic technique in both individual and group therapy, the therapist uses transference to help the patient understand and gain insight into his behavior. *See also* Collective family transference neurosis, Dilution of transference.

Trend of thought. Thinking that centers on a particular idea associated with an affective tone.

Triad. Father, mother, and child relationship projectively experienced in group therapy. *See also* Nuclear family.

Trichotillomania. Morbid compulsion to pull out one's hair.

Tricyclic drug. Antidepressant drug believed by some to be more effective than monoamine oxidase inhibitors. The tricyclic drugs (imipramine and amitriptyline) are presently the most popular drugs in the treatment of pathological depression.

Tyramine. A sympathomimetic amine that is believed to influence the release of stored norepinephrine. Its degradation is inhibited by monoamine oxidase. The use of monoamine oxidase inhibitors in the treatment of depression prevents the degradation of tyramine. The ingestion of food containing tyramine, such as cheese, may cause a sympathomimetic effect, such as an increase in blood pressure, that could be fatal.

Unconscious. 1. (Noun) Structural division of the mind in which the psychic material—primitive drives, repressed desires, and memories—is not directly accessible to awareness. 2. (Adjective) In a state of insensibility, with absence of orientation and perception. *See also* Conscious, Preconscious.

Underachievement. Failure to reach a biopsychological, age-adequate level.

Underachiever. Person who manifestly does not function up to his capacity. The term usually refers to a bright child whose school test grades fall below expected levels.

Undeveloped potential. The behavior, feelings, and motivations of a person known neither to himself nor to others. It is the unknown quadrant of the Johari Window, a diagrammatic concept of human behavior. *See also* Blind self, Hidden self, Public self.

Undoing. An unconscious defense mechanism by which a person symbolically acts out in reverse something unacceptable that has already been done. A primitive defense mechanism, undoing is a form of magical expiatory action. Repetitive in nature, it is commonly observed in obsessive-compulsive neurosis.

Unisexual group. *See* Homogeneous group.

Universality. Total effect produced when all group members share specific symptoms or problems.

Up. The member who is the focus of discussion in group therapy, particularly in structured interactional group psychotherapy.

Up-tight. Slang term that describes defensive, rigid behavior on the part of a person whose values are threatened or who is afraid of becoming vulnerable and of experiencing painful emotions. Such a person frequently becomes a target for pressure in a therapy group.

Urine-testing. Thin-layer chromatography-testing for the presence of opiates, quinine, barbiturates, and amphetamines. Addict treatment programs use such testing to verify abstinence from illicit drug use.

Vector. An engineering term used to imply a pointed force being felt by the group. *See also* Hierarchical vector, Horizontal vector.

Verbal-deep approach. Procedure used in small groups in which communication is conducted exclusively through verbal means and is oriented to major goals. It is a technique used in analytical group therapy. *See also* Actional-deep approach, Actional-superficial approach, Verbal-superficial approach.

Verbal-superficial approach. Group therapy procedure in which language is the sole medium of communication and the therapeutic process is structured to attain limited objectives. It is a technique traditionally used in the treatment of large groups. *See also* Actional-deep approach, Actional-superficial approach, Verbal-deep approach.

Verbal technique. Any method of group or individual therapy in which words are used. The major part of most psychotherapy is verbal.

Verbigeration. Meaningless repetition of words or phrases. Also known as cataphasia, it is a morbid symptom seen in schizophrenia.

Verbomania. *See* Logorrhea.

Vertical vector. *See* Hierarchical vector.

Vienna Psychoanalytic Society. An outgrowth of the Wednesday Evening Society, an informal group of Freud's earliest followers. The new name was acquired and a reorganization took place in 1910, when the Society became a component of the newly formed International Psychoanalytical Society. Alfred Adler was president from 1910 to 1911, and Freud was president from 1911 until it was disbanded by the Nazis in 1938.

Visceral insight. *See* Insight.

Visitor. Guest who participates in discussions with patients in group therapy. In family therapy, members outside the nuclear family who are invited to the session are considered visitors. *See also* Extended family therapy, Social network therapy.

Visual hallucination. False visual perception.

Volubility. *See* Logorrhea.

Warming-up session. *See* Premeeting.

Waxy flexibility. *See* Cerea flexibilitas.

Wednesday Evening Society. A small group of Freud's followers who in 1902 started meeting with him informally on Wednesday evenings to receive instruction in psychoanalysis. As the society grew in numbers and importance, it evolved in 1910 into the Vienna Psychoanalytic Society.

West-Coast-style T-group. Sensitivity training or encounter group that is oriented toward the experience of union, intimacy, and personal awareness, with relative disregard for the study of group process. It is a style popular in California. *See also* East-Coast-style T-group.

Wild therapy. Group therapy conducted by a leader whose background may not be professional or whose theoretical formulations include widely deviant procedures when compared with conventional techniques.

Withdrawal. Act of retreating or going away from. Observed in schizophrenia and depression, it is characterized by a pathological retreat from interpersonal contact and social involvement, leading to self-preoccupation. In a group setting, this disorder creates a barrier for therapeutic progress.

Wittels, Fritz (1880–1950). Austrian psychoanalyst. One of Freud's early followers, he wrote a biography of him in 1924, during a period of estrangement, when he was under the influence of Wilhelm Stekel. Later, a reconciliation took place, and Freud conceded that some of Wittels' interpretations were probably correct.

Wolf-pack phenomenon. Group process in which a member or the therapist is the scapegoat.

Word salad. An incoherent mixture of words and phrases. This type of speech results from a disturbance in thinking. It is commonly observed in far-advanced states of schizophrenia.

Working alliance. Collaboration between the group as a whole and each patient who is willing to strive for health, growth, and maturation with the help of the therapist. *See also* Therapeutic alliance.

Working out. Stage in the treatment process in which the personal history and psychodynamics of a patient are discovered.

Working through. Process of obtaining more and more insight and personality changes through repeated and varied examination of a conflict or problem. The interactions between free association, resistance, interpretation, and working through constitute the fundamental facets of the analytic process.

Xenophobia. Fear of strangers.

Zoophobia. Fear of animals.

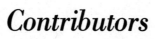

Contributors

Contributors

Milton Berger, M.D.
Assistant Clinical Professor of Psychiatry, Columbia University College of Physicians and Surgeons, New York, New York

Toby B. Bieber, Ph.D
Clinical Instructor in Psychiatry, New York Medical College; Lecturer in Psychology, New York University and Cooper Union, New York, New York

Robert S. Davidson, Ph.D.
Associate Clinical Professor of Medical Psychology, Department of Psychiatry and Human Behavior, University of California

John M. Dusay, M.D.
Clinical Instructor in Psychiatry, University of California School of Medicine and The Langley Porter Neuropsychiatric Institute, San Francisco, California; Vice-President, International Transactional Analysis Institute, Los Angeles, California

Alan Goldstein, Ph.D.
Assistant Professor of Psychiatry, Temple University School of Medicine and Easton Pennsylvania Psychiatric Institute, Philadelphia, Pennsylvania.

Louis A. Gottschalk, M.D.
Professor of Psychiatry and Chairman of the Department of Psychiatry and Human Behavior, University of California, Irvine California College of Medicine, Irvine, California; Program Director of Residency Training, Orange County Medical Center, Orange, California; Chief Consultant in Psychiatry, Veterans Administration Hospital, Long Beach, California

Martin Grotjahn, M.D.
Clinical Professor Emeritus of Psychiatry; University of Southern California School of Medicine, Los Angeles, California; Training Psychoanalyst, Southern California Institute for Psychoanalysis, Beverly Hills, California

Herbert Holt, M.D., Ph.D.
Herbert Holt Institute for Psychoanalysis and Psychotherapy, Yonkers, New York; Past President, New York Ontoanalytic Society, New York, New York

Harold I. Kaplan, M.D.
Professor of Psychiatry and Director of Psychiatric Education and Training, New York Medical College; Attending Psychiatrist, Flower and Fifth Avenue Hospitals; Visiting Psychiatrist, Metropolitan Hospital and Bird S. Coler Memorial Hospital and Home, New York, New York

Benjamin J. Sadock, M.D.
Associate Professor of Psychiatry and Director, Division of Group Process, New York Medical College; Associate Attending Psychiatrist, Flower and Fifth Avenue Hospitals; Associate Visiting Psychiatrist, Metropolitan Hospital; Assistant Attending Psychiatrist, New York State Psychiatric Institute, New York, New York

Arthur S. Samuels, M.D.
Training Psychoanalyst and Senior Supervisor in Psychoanalytic Medicine and Group Psychotherapy, Tulane University School of Medicine; Senior Associate in Psychiatry and Consultant in Group Psychotherapy, Touro Infirmary, New Orleans, Louisiana

Hyman Spotnitz, M.D., Med. Sc.D.
Author: The Couch and the Circle: A Story of Group Psychotherapy (Alfred A. Knopf, 1961); Modern Psychoanalysis of the Schizophrenia Patient (Gruen and Stratton, 1969), New York, New York

Claude Steiner, Ph.D., D.Sc.
Clinical Psychologist, Center for Special Problems, San Francisco, California

Frederick H. Stoller, Ph.D.
Senior Psychologist, Camarillo State Hospital, Camarillo, California

Joseph Wolpe, M.D.
Professor of Psychiatry, Temple University School of Medicine; Research Psychiatrist, Eastern Pennsylvania Psychiatric Institute, Philadelphia, Pennsylvania